EGYPT
GUIDE

BE A TRAVELER - NOT A TOURIST!

OPEN ROAD TRAVEL GUIDES SHOW YOU
HOW TO BE A TRAVELER – NOT A TOURIST!

*Whether you're going abroad or planning a trip in the United States, take Open Road along on your journey. Our books have been praised by **Travel & Leisure, The Los Angeles Times, Newsday, Booklist, US News & World Report, Endless Vacation, American Bookseller, Coast to Coast**, and many other magazines and newspapers!*

Don't just see the world – experience it with Open Road!

ABOUT THE AUTHOR

John J. Bentley IV lived in Egypt off and on while growing up. A graduate of Harvard College, John was a contributor to *Let's Go: Israel & Egypt*. This is his first solo effort. After living in Cairo for a few years, John currently lives in South Royalton, Vermont.

BE A TRAVELER, NOT A TOURIST - WITH OPEN ROAD TRAVEL GUIDES!

Open Road Publishing has guide books to exciting, fun destinations on four continents. As veteran travelers, our goal is to bring you the best travel guides available anywhere!

No small task, but here's what we offer:

• All Open Road travel guides are written by authors with a distinct, opinionated point of view – not some sterile committee or team of writers. Our authors are experts in the areas covered and are polished writers.

• Our guides are geared to people who want to make their own travel choices. We'll show you how to discover the real destination – not just see some place from a tour bus window.

• We're strong on the basics, but we also provide terrific choices for those looking to get off the beaten path and experience the country or city – not just see it or pass through it.

• We give you the best, but we also tell you about the worst and what to avoid. Nobody should waste their time and money on their hard-earned vacation because of bad or inadequate travel advice.

• Our guides assume nothing. We tell you everything you need to know to have the trip of a lifetime – presented in a fun, literate, no-nonsense style.

• And, above all, we welcome your input, ideas, and suggestions to help us put out the best travel guides possible.

EGYPT

GUIDE

BE A TRAVELER - NOT A TOURIST!

John J. Bentley IV

OPEN ROAD PUBLISHING

1st Edition

Photo credits: Front cover – Martin Sutton, EarthWater (Virginia Beach, Virginia). Back cover – Chris Crumley (both images) EarthWater.

Maps by James Ramage.

TABLE OF CONTENTS

15. THE GREAT OASES OF THE WESTERN DESERT 391

16. ALEXANDRIA, THE DELTA, & THE NORTH COAST 425

MAPS

SIDEBARS

SIDEBARS

ACKNOWLEDGMENTS

There are countless folks between South Royalton and Cairo to whom I am indebted. To begin with I want to thank Jon Stein for giving me the opportunity to write this book and for his limitless patience. In New York, thanks to EgyptAir, and Mr. Abdel Moneim Riyad and Ms. El Husseini at the ETA for their assistance. Also a big thank you to Randy Jackson, Leslie Gerheart, Faris Farrag and Sabra Dalby for their hospitality in New York.

In Cairo, a big "Ishta Aleik" to my pals Ayman Samir, Nader "Nigerian Nate" Hassan, Max Kalhammer, Meredith Brody, Colin Sullivan, Laura Piquado, Sherief El Katsha, and Khaled El Sayed. Also thanks to Elizabeth Arragoni, Con O'Donnell, and Mohammed Kamel. I am grateful for the friendship and companionship of Kathryn Jones and Janet Skopic who traveled with me to North Sinai and Luxor respectively. Also thanks to the El Sayed family for their hospitality in Hurghada, Hans Harverhals in Sharm, Wael and Simba at Orascom, and my good friend Ahmed Farghali and his family for opening their home in El Qussia to me.

I am particularly grateful to two families for opening their homes to me on an extended basis. First Chuck and Jason Vokral shared their home (and fridge) with me during what I know was a hard year and for that I am eternally grateful. Second, my affection and gratitude to the El Samahy family is limitless for their hospitality and support. Thanks to Ahmed " the Doctoor" and Kay for sharing everything from their television and dinner table to their son's time. Also thanks to Nora for her room, Om Sayed, and "Dada" (AKA Om Saabet, Om Zakayia) for doing my laundry, getting me to like melokhiya, and whose indomitable spirit and good humor was a source of inspiration and many good laughs as well. Finally, a million shukrans to Rami for countless rides downtown and sharing his space, not to mention a cassette or two and a lifetime of friendship & brotherhood.

Last but not least, I want to thank my family: Pat, Dave, Jane and their families, and especially Helen and Howard Greenlee for sharing their home and resources with me as well as giving me countless rides, wisdom, and other gifts - you're the best. Also my parents for their love and support and showing me the world. In this case I am particularly grateful for the Egyptian childhood. Finally thanks to Scott for his support, good humor and companionship over the years.

1. INTRODUCTION

It may be cliche to say Egypt is a land of contrasts, but there are few countries where old and new, East and West, rich and poor, are so deeply intertwined. It all begins with the Nile, which amidst the vast deserts of North Africa gave birth to an ancient civilization. The civilization of the pharaohs is of course legendary, and so ancient that by the time Herodotus visited Egypt 2,500 years ago, the Pyramids of Giza were already a mind-boggling 2,000 years old, and the Temple of Karnak had been the world's largest shrine for more than ten centuries.

Today these testaments to man's desire for immortality are punctuated by the juxtaposition of modern cities like Cairo, themselves studies in contrast where medieval mosques rub shoulders with glass office buildings; and modern highways crisscross narrow thoroughfares festooned with open souks and choked with rickety donkey carts competing for space with boat-size Mercedes.

In addition to the classic attractions of the Nile Valley, visitors can explore Egypt's wilderness from the starkly beautiful mountains and lush aquatic jungles of the Red Sea coasts to the verdant palm groves and vast dunes of the Western Desert Oases. Egypt is best known for its history and culture, but its natural beauty is equally compelling.

There are almost as many ways to approach a trip to Egypt as there are tombs in the Valley of the Kings or salesmen offering a "special price" in the Khan El Khalili. You can float down the Nile in a luxurious cruise ship and indulge in the sumptuous accommodations of world renowned hotels like the Winter Palace and Old Cataract, or you can wing it on $20 a day and still enjoy Egypt's historical, natural, and cultural offerings. Follow my lead and you'll find your way, but also take the plunge and follow your own instincts, because Egypt is best revealed to those who undertake random exploration. And don't be afraid to engage in personal contact, from the give and take of the bazaars to sharing the communal meal in a Bedouin camp. With this guide as your companion, you can discover Egypt in all its majesty and mystery!

2. EXCITING EGYPT! - OVERVIEW

CAIRO: MOTHER OF THE WORLD

Dubbed by its natives, "Om El Dunya," (Mother of the World) for its unmatched historical legacy, Cairo is a massive city with plenty of massive problems, but is nonetheless a fascinating blend of East and West, and past and present. It's main draw is of course the **Pyramids**, the granddaddies of tourist attractions which were already 2,500 years old by the time Christ was put on the cross. Just down the road, **Memphis** was founded as the first imperial capital in the world in 3,100 BC, and though little of it remains, its necropolis at **Saqqara** features miles of tombs, temples, and monuments, including the **Step Pyramid**, Egypt's first pyramid and the world's first stone building.

Those with more time can make their way even further south to explore the dozens of minor pyramids dating to the Old and Middle Kingdoms. Rounding out pharaonic attractions is the **Egyptian Antiquities Museum** in downtown Cairo, home to the world's largest collection of pharaonic relics with thousands of mummies, statues, and jewels, including the treasures of King Tutankhamun.

Overshadowed by the pharaonic attractions are Cairo's Islamic treasures – diamonds in the rough, mostly lost in the narrow alleys of its medieval quarters, now swamped by the modern city. Islam came to Egypt in the 7th century, and ever since Cairo has vied with Baghdad and Damascus for political, economic, and cultural supremacy within the Arab World; however, unlike those great cities, Cairo was spared the ransacking they suffered at the hands of the Mongols. As a result, Cairo's architectural legacy is intact and its older streets are laden with hundreds of architectural gems including the **mosques of Ibn Tulun and Sultan Hassan**, and **Salah El Din's Citadel**, some the finest pieces of medieval architecture anywhere in the world. Most travelers make first contact with Islamic Cairo at the 15th century **Khan El Khalili**, one the world's oldest,

largest, and most famous bazaars. Though littered with tourist traps, it still affords one the classic give and take experience of shopping in the Middle East and makes an ideal point for exploring the authentically untouristic entrails of Cairo's medieval quarters.

Though Egypt today is a decidedly Islamic society, it became the world's first majority Christian nation in the 2nd century, and Cairo is home to a number of beautiful ancient **churches**. Concentrated in "Old Cairo," these modest temples were originally built in the 4th and 5th centuries and remain active houses of worship. Most were built on sites believed to be used by the Holy Family as places of refuge during their flight from Herod when Jesus was a child.

THE NILE VALLEY

No trip to Egypt is complete without a journey up the Nile Valley. A timeless land where peasants farm their picturesque fields as they have for a millennia, the Valley is strewn with ancient monuments unmatched in size and number anywhere in the world. Most famous are the great tombs and temples of **Thebes** (now **Luxor**) where New Kingdom pharaohs ruled Egypt during its imperial heyday 3,500 years ago. Flush with wealth, rulers like Ramses the Great and Seti I erected massive temples like that dedicated to Amun at **Karnak**. Still the largest house of worship ever built, it covers more than 100 acres and its hypostyle hall alone could contain both Saint Peter's Cathedral in Rome and Saint Paul's Cathedral in London.

On the Nile's west bank across from Thebes, the pharaohs indulged in lavish tombs, with the hope of ensuring their immortality. Though robbed and vandalized in antiquity, royal crypts in the **Valley of the Kings** still contain vivid representations of animal-headed deities, pharaohs, and life in ancient Egypt. To commemorate their own divinity, pharaohs also constructed monumental mortuary temples, the most famous of which is the multi-layered **Temple of Hatshepsut**, constructed by Egypt's only female pharaoh.

From Luxor, most travelers move on to Aswan stopping en route in the valley towns **Esna**, **Edfu**, and **Kom Ombo** to visit their exquisite temples. Built by Greeks and Romans but dedicated to pharaonic deities and built in the pharaonic tradition around the time of Christ, they are among the best preserved monuments in all of Egypt. Should you have time, consider making this journey on the Nile itself. Those looking for a comfortable and leisurely trip may indulge in a **Nile cruise**, while those on tighter budgets or who may enjoy a more rustic and authentically Egyptian experience, can rough it on a *felucca* (sail boat).

A frontier town and crossroads for caravans since the Old Kingdom, Egypt's southernmost city of **Aswan** is it's gateway to Africa and straddles its border with Nubia. Never a national capital, it does not boast monuments equal to those in Luxor, but it does offer travelers a myriad of natural, historic, and modern attractions, beginning with the Nile itself. Aswan overlooks the stunning First Cataract which the ancients believed to be the end of the world and the source of the Nile.

On the island of Elephantine, they built great temples to deities of the Nile and the floods, Hapi and Khnum. Later, when Egypt assumed control over Nubia, Egyptians and Greek Ptolemies built no less than two dozen monumental temples, the most famous of which is the magnificent temple of Isis at **Philae** south of Aswan. Aswan always had a more African flavor than other Egyptian cities, but with the uprooting of a quarter million **Nubians** by the creation of Lake Nasser, it is now thoroughly a Nubian city. Known for their kindness and good humor, the Nubians have a unique historical and cultural legacy that can only be explored in Aswan.

Aswan is also a jumping off point for excursions to the monuments and natural bounties of **Lake Nasser**, the largest man-made lake in the world. The most popular attractions are the temples of Ramses II at **Abu Simbel** best known for the four sitting colossi each standing more than 17 meters tall and weighing more than 1,200 tons. Another popular destination is the relatively infantile Aswan High Dam, the largest in the world upon its completion in 1970, and an impressive piece of engineering that also affords superb views of both the Nile and the Lake. Finally Lake Nasser itself is brimming with wildlife from crocodiles and fish to geese and ducks, and is becoming increasingly popular with bird watchers, hunters, and fishermen attracted by the Nile perch that can tip the scales at more than 65 kilos.

ALEXANDRIA

One of the great cities of antiquity, **Alexandria** is now Egypt's second city and largest port. During a 1,000 year hibernation during which it went into deep decline, "Alex" as it is popularly known, was stripped of the great landmarks that symbolized its status in antiquity. The Great Library and Pharos Lighthouse are now gone, but modern Alexandria is a vibrant city, famous for its beaches, cosmopolitan culture, and fish restaurants. Its humming boulevards and decrepit colonial-era buildings are ideal for random exploration.

Egypt's north coast is lined with resorts popular amongst Egyptians who prefer its temperate climate and accessibility from Cairo. For foreign travelers the resorts do not offer the same variety of water sports and natural beauty as the Red Sea, but you may be tempted to explore the battlefields at **El Alamein**, 100 kilometers west of Alexandria, where more than 12,000 men died in an epic month long struggle that saved the Suez Canal and possibly the British Empire from Axis domination in World War II.

THE SINAI & RED SEA

Though armies, caravans, and prophets made the Red Sea and Sinai the major link between Asia and Africa as long as time can remember, Egypt's east coast and the barren peninsula were always uninhabited lands steeped in myth and mystery. Until the 20th century, nobody except for the hardened Bedouin Tribes who migrated from Arabia centuries ago, saw much point in spending any time here, but since it opened to tourism in recent decades visitors have increasingly discovered the natural and historic attractions of Egypt's Red Sea coasts. Closed to travel and development until 1980 because of Egypt's ongoing wars with Israel, the aquatic jungles and mountain oases of Egypt's eastern coasts now attract upwards of a million tourists a year.

The primary attractions are actually underwater. The coral reefs off **Hurghada** on the mainland and in **Sinai** between **Ras Mohammed**, **Sharm El Sheikh** and the Israeli border at **Taba** are among the best in the world, rivaling the Great Barrier Reef itself for top billing. Many visitors simply tack on a trip to the beach to their larger Egyptian odyssey while others come specifically to explore the wonders of the sea through diving tours. If diving does not suit your fancy or your budget, the year around good weather, sandy beaches, and pristine waters of the Red Sea are ideal for other water sports from wind surfing to water skiing. In fact, thousands of Europeans fly directly into Sharm El Sheikh and Hurghada just to frolic on the beach for a week or two, entirely bypassing the monument-laden chaos of the Nile Valley.

Increasingly, Sinai's interior is also becoming an attraction. The oldest continuously used monastic house in the world, **Saint Katherine's Monastery**, and **Mount Sinai**, where Moses received the Ten Command-ments, have attracted pilgrims for centuries, but visitors are increasingly discovering Sinai's impressive natural bounties. The **mountains** with their exotic and colorful rock formations, canyons, and wadis are a hiker's paradise. Their peaks offer stunning panoramic views that stretch as far as the Gulf of Suez to the west and Saudi Arabia to the east, and campers sleep under the stars, and bathe in the springs of the lush oases which litter the barren landscape.

Most travelers out of Sharm El Sheikh, Dahab, or Nuweiba rent the four wheel drive vehicles necessary to access the rough terrain, while others go at it the old fashion way, on camels. The local Bedouin who have lived here for millennia are famous for their hospitality and are more than willing to guide visitors through the striking Sinai highlands. For those just looking to get their feet wet, excursions as short as an hour or two are possible. On the other hand those off-the-beaten-track types looking for more substantial adventure can arrange safaris lasting as long as two or three weeks.

THE DESERT OASES

Off the beaten tracks of the Nile Valley and the coasts, Egypt's vast **Western Desert** has only opened to travel during the last 20 years. Though the hostile environment of most of the desert has deterred humankind since time can remember, patches of lush oases have enabled human beings to thrive for centuries. Some communities, like those of Siwa, Egypt's most spectacular oasis, have remained defiantly indepen-dent and isolated until the 20th century. Others such as Kharga have long served as way stations on the great caravan routes from Africa and the Sahara. Though all of the oases feature stunning natural beauty, Kharga, Dakhla, Siwa, and the Faiyoum boast fascinating pharaonic, Greek,

Coptic, and Islamic monuments as well. The early Christian necropolis of Begawat in Kharga, for example, is the largest of its kind in Egypt.

Most travelers only have time to visit one, or maybe two of the oases. The most famous and popular, **Siwa**, lies deep in the northern deserts by the Libyan border and boasts beautiful lakes, date groves, and historic monuments. Travelers can visit the famous Oracle of Amun that attracted the likes of Alexander the Great who wanted to be buried in Siwa. Equally intriguing are Siwa's indigenous Bedouin whose unique way of life was virtually untouched by the rest of the world until the 20th century.

Closer to Cairo, **Faiyoum** was always an integral part of Nile Valley, and was even a national capital during the Middle Kingdom. The modern city of El Faiyoum is an eyesore, but the oasis itself offers travelers a unique assortment of natural and historical attractions from Middle Kingdom pyramids to ancient Greek villages. Because the sites are spread over more than 400 square miles, you may be inclined to take a break at the serene and picturesque Lake Karun or even stay at the L'Auberge du Lac hotel, formerly a hunting lodge used by King Farouk. Though not actually in Faiyoum, the Birqash camel market, the largest in Egypt, is a humming affair where Bedouin, fellaheen (farmers), and Sudanese shepherds congregate to trade and barter cows, horses, donkeys and camel.

At the other extreme, **Farafra**, deep in the Western Desert, is undeveloped, and known for its peaceful isolation, brilliant starlit nights and the amazing fungus-like dunes of the **White Desert**, an ideal setting for camping. Further to the south **Dakhla** and **Kharga**, are large oases that were once crossroads for the great caravan routes from Sudan. The caravan routes are now obsolete, but both Kharga and Dakhla present travelers the opportunity to enjoy their beautiful palm groves, hot springs, and fascinating pharaonic and medieval monuments. Dakhla is especially known for its medieval Islamic villages like El Kasr, where Bedouin live a timeless way of life that apart from the use of pick-ups and some other modern appliances hasn't changed in a thousand years. Though its settlements are less picturesque than Dakhla's, Kharga boasts impressive monuments, including the large Persian-built pharaonic temple of **Hibis** and the magnificent Christian necropolis of **Begawat** where Copts were interred as early as the 3rd century.

3. SUGGESTED ITINERARIES

ITINERARY 1

Cairo, Luxor, Aswan, Cairo
Number of days: 10
Transportation: bus, train, and/or plane

Day 1
Should you arrive in Cairo by plane from Europe or the States, you'll probably get in sometime in the afternoon, in which case you should check into your hotel, shower, powder your nose, and decide if and what you want to eat-try to get out of the hotel. If you're downtown, an establishment like Felfela's would be appropriate.

Day 2
Hire a taxi (off the street), and head to the Giza Pyramids as early as possible. Spend several hours taking them in, visiting the Solar Boat and if you so please, crawl inside. Wind down and cool off with a drink at the spectacular Mena House Hotel. If you feel like spending a lot of money, eat lunch there too; otherwise, head back to town for lunch and possibly a siesta. At mid-afternoon, hop in a taxi and make your way to Islamic Cairo. Shoppers should take the plunge into the bazaars of the Khan El Khalili to begin sizing up potential loot. Non-shoppers can stroll about the area soaking in the medieval vibes, slurping on *sheesha* or Turkish coffee at a coffeehouse, or possibly slipping into a nearby mosque such as Al Azhar, El Hakim, or Qalawun. Eat in Islamic Cairo, or head back downtown. Late-nighters can hit the town to explore Cairo's nightlife.

Day 3
Wake up by nine (or ten if you had a late night). Spend the morning at the Cairo Museum feasting your eyes on King Tut's treasures and other attractions. Eat lunch, and head back to Islamic Cairo to visit any or all of Sultan Hassan Mosque, Ibn Tulun Mosque, and the Citadel. Get back to town in time to wash up a bit and eat before getting on a plane or train to Luxor.

Day 4

Arrive in Luxor, settle in to your hotel, and get comfortable. If you took the night train, you'll just be getting in and will probably need to rest for a couple hours. By 1pm you should eat and hit the sites. If it's hot, begin with the Luxor Museum and the Mummification Museum before taking in the Luxor Temple when it gets cooler in the late afternoon. If you want a guided tour of the west bank the next day, begin shopping for guides and tours with travel agencies downtown and on the Corniche. Shower up and eat; or better yet, take a sunset felucca, and then eat. If you're so inclined, "Sound & Light" at Karnak Temple is another option. Stock up on water and other necessities for the next day's trip to the west bank.

Day 5

Wake up as early as possible and spend five or six hours visiting the Valley of the Kings, Deir El Bahri, Tombs of the Nobles, and other west bank attractions. Get back to east bank by early afternoon to lunch, take a dip, and rest up. Spend the later afternoon and early evening shopping or visiting the Luxor Museum, the Mummification Museum, or the Luxor Temple, depending on what you missed the day before. In the evening, take a felucca, shop, or just hang out and eat dinner.

Day 6

Visit Karnak in the morning and try to make an afternoon train, plane, or bus to Aswan. Check into a hotel in Aswan and hit the Corniche for dinner.

Day 7

See the sights of Aswan like the Aswan High Dam, Elephantine Island, the Unfinished Obelisk, and most certainly Philae Temple. The local bazaar is also worth a visit. Head back to the hotel by mid-afternoon to cool down and shower up. Have a drink at the Old Cataract before enjoying a sunset felucca and dinner.

Day 8

Abu Simbel and back. Get on the next plane to Cairo if possible. Otherwise take the train. If you take the plane, check into your hotel and hit the town for dinner. If you're on the train, sleep the best you can.

Day 9

In the morning visit the Christian monuments in Old Cairo. In the afternoon, visit sights in Islamic Cairo like Ibn Tulun, the Citadel, Sultan

Hassan, if you haven't already, or shop at the Khan El Khalili. Another good option is the Islamic Museum.

Day 10

Last day. If you're up to it, by all means visit the Old Kingdom necropolis and the Step Pyramid at Saqqara. In the afternoon, complete any last minute shopping and visit any attractions you might have missed or wish to revisit. If you're toured out, take this day to engage in more recreational activity: a sunrise or sunset, horseback at the Pyramids, a felucca, or a late night belly dance show. Pack and set your alarm, chances are your flight departs early the next morning.

ITINERARY II

Cairo, Luxor, Red Sea Coast, Cairo
Number of Days: 10
Transportation: plane, train, and/or bus

Days 1-5

Same as Itinerary I.

Day 6

Visit Karnak in the morning as in Itinerary I, but in the evening or afternoon if possible, catch the bus to Hurghada instead of Aswan.

Days 7-8

Veg out on the beach in Hurghada or El Gouna. Dive, snorkel, eat fish, or do nothing. In evening of Day 8 or morning of Day 9 catch bus to Cairo.

Days 9-10

Same as Itinerary I.

ITINERARY III

Coming from Israel: Sinai, Cairo, Luxor, Cairo, (Sinai)
Number of Days: 7
Transportation: bus, train, and perhaps plane

Days 1-3

Arrive from Israel and settle into Nuweiba, Dahab, or Sharm El Sheikh for 3 days of R&R before taking on Cairo. Enjoy diving, sunbathing, and other beach activities. If you're interested, take a day to visit Saint Katherine's Monastery and Mount Sinai or make a desert safari. In the afternoon or evening of Day 3 catch a bus or plane to Cairo.

Day 4

If you got in on the night bus from Sinai, check into a hotel and rest up. Then hit the Giza Pyramids. If you have time and energy, make your way to the Khan El Khalili and Islamic Cairo for shopping, mosques (Sultan Hassan and Ibn Tulun are best), and people watching. Eat dinner in Islamic Cairo or downtown. Should you be so inclined take in a folkloric show at El Ghuri near the Khan, relax on a felucca, or truck out to the Giza Pyramids for the "Sound & Light" show.

Day 5

Visit Tut and the gang at the Egyptian Antiquities Museum in the morning. Eat lunch and prepare for a trip to Luxor. If you have time and energy, zip down to Old Cairo to check out 4th and 5th century Coptic churches and the Coptic Museum. Eat dinner and catch the night train to Luxor. If you can afford to fly, by all means do.

Day 6

Check into your hotel, get settled, and rest up. Eat lunch and then in the afternoon visit the Luxor Museum, the Mummification Museum, and the Luxor Temple. If it's not too hot, you can visit Karnak Temple and save the Luxor Temple and the museums for the next day. After sightseeing, tidy up and relax on a felucca, or simply stroll up and down the Corniche before eating and hitting the sack. Shoppers can hit the bazaars, and the "Sound & Light" show is another option.

Day 7

Get up as early as possible and head straight for the west bank. Hire a taxi and spend five or six hours checking out the Valley of the Kings, Deir El Bahri, the Tombs of the Nobles, and other attractions. Arrive back on the east bank in early afternoon and take a dip, eat lunch, and recover from the morning's expedition. In the afternoon, visit the Karnak Temple or the Luxor Temple, the Luxor Museum, and the Mummification Museum, which ever you didn't see the day before. In the evening, eat dinner and hop on a plane or train back to Cairo.

Day 8

Arrive back in Cairo and settle into your hotel. Rest up and recover from the train ride. Eat lunch and then begin visiting sights which you missed in the first two days. The Citadel of Salah El Din, the Manial Palace, and any number of mosques and churches would be manageable after the long trip. If you flew in the morning or the night before, this is a good day to trek out to Saqqara to see the extensive necropolis and the Step Pyramid of Zoser-a sight which should not be missed. Shoppers can hit the

Khan El Khalili in the evening. At night, chill out on a felucca, hit a disco, or take in a show, perhaps the whirling dervishes at El Ghuri or a belly dance at hotel nightclub.

Day 9
Catch up on the sights you missed. Saqqara should be a priority. The Islamic Museum, the Coptic Museum, or any of the aforementioned sites would also be well worth the effort. Shopping, of course is always an option, as is just wandering about the colorful and lively streets of Cairo's older neighborhoods. If you're Cairoed out, hop on a train or minibus and zip to Alex for the day and return in the evening or early the next morning.

Day 10
Last day in Egypt, so do as you please. If you have even a drop of equestrian in your blood, make way to one of the stables by the Giza Pyramids for a sunrise or sunset horse ride. A visit to the textile centers at Wissa Wassef or Kerdessa will give you a glimpse into rural life in addition to the opportunity to visit with Egypt's finest weavers. A fine meal in a rural setting can be had at one of the Egyptian restaurants on the Maryotia Canal.

Day 11
Catch morning plane to next destination or bus to Israel.

ITINERARY IV
Cairo, Luxor, Aswan & Abu Simbel, Red Sea Coast or Sinai, Cairo
Number of days: 14
Transportation: bus, train, and/or plane

Day 1
Arrive in Cairo and settle down. If you have time, take an hour or two to walk around the neighborhood before eating dinner. Get a good night's rest.

Day 2
First things first-catch a cab and head to the Pyramids as early as possible. Spend several hours wandering around, looking at the Solar Boat, and paying the Sphinx a visit. Cool down and enjoy the atmospherics and the view from the spectacular Mena House Hotel. If you have the dough, it's good place to eat lunch. Otherwise, head back downtown to eat and catch your breath. In the late afternoon, walk up Mouski Street

from Ataba Square or take a cab to Islamic Cairo. If you're into shopping, go the Khan El Khalili at Hussein Square. Should you prefer to sample historical buildings, dip into El Azhar or one of the superb mosques on Muizz li Din Street. Eat dinner at Hussein Square and if you're not totally run down, take in the whirling dervishes at El Ghuri.

Day 3
  Wake up as early as possible and hire a taxi or join a tour to Saqqara. Eat lunch at an Egyptian restaurant such as El Dar on El Harraniya Road or along the Maryotia Canal. Head back to the hotel or another appropriate location and relax a bit. In the afternoon complete visiting Islamic Cairo, including the Islamic Museum, or visit 4th and 5th century Coptic Churches and the Coptic Museum in Old Cairo. After taking a breather, eat dinner. Nocturnal types can hit the town to explore Cairo's nightlife.

Day 4
  Make your way to Tahrir Square and the Antiquities Museum to visit Tut's treasures and other attractions. Have lunch in a local eatery, or if you're looking for some peace and quiet, have drink at the Am Ali Cafe at the Nile Hilton. In the afternoon, visit the Manial Palace, or just wander through the city's medieval Islamic quarters. In the evening, eat well and board the train or the plane for Luxor.

Day 5
  Wake up in Luxor and get settled. Rest up, eat, and start exploring the east bank attractions like Karnak, or combine the Luxor Temple, the Mummification Museum, and the Luxor Museum. Try to get in a sunset felucca before eating dinner. Crash early to rest for the next day.

Day 6
  Wake up as early as possible and go straight to the west bank. Hire a taxi or join a tour and spend 5-6 hours exploring the Valley of the Kings, Deir El Bahri, the Tombs of the Nobles and other attractions. Head back to the east bank and spend the afternoon cooling down and resting up. In the evening, enjoy the sunset from a felucca before eating or seeing the "Sound & Light" at Karnak.

Day 7
  Wake up, breakfast, and visit Karnak or the combination of the Luxor Temple, the Luxor Museum, and the Mummification Museum-whichever you missed on Day 5. In the afternoon or evening, catch a bus, train, or plane to Aswan.

Day 8

Spend the day visiting the sights of Aswan; Philae Temple should be a priority. Other attractions include Kalabsha Temple, the Fatimid Cemeteries, the High Dam, Elephantine Island, the new Nubian Museum, and the local souk. In the evening, wash up and enjoy the sunset sipping a cocktail on the terrace at the Old Cataract Hotel or on a felucca. The "Sound & Light" at Philae Temple is another good option.

Day 9

Spend most of the day and all of your energy visiting Abu Simbel. If you can afford to fly, you'll save time and effort. When you get back, see whatever you can of Aswan that you missed the day before.

Day 10

Hop on a bus or plane for Sharm El Sheikh or Hurghada to spend a few days on the Red Sea coast scuba diving or chilling on the beach. If you can afford to fly, it will save you a good ten hours of dealing with the bus. In fact the Aswan-Sharm route is a monster bus ride.

Day 11

Enjoy the beach and the Red Sea. Take it easy. If you're so inclined arrange a desert safari through a local travel agent or your hotel-if you're in Sharm, consider a visit to Mount Sinai and Saint Katherine's Monastery.

Day 12

Another day at the beach. If you want two more days in Cairo, catch the night bus or plane. If you're in no rush, take it the next morning.

Day 13

Get into Cairo and settle down. If there's time, take in some of the sights you missed the first time around.

Day 14

Last day in Egypt. Visit or revisit historical sites. Also, it's your last chance to shop at Khan El Khalili.

Alternatives for Itinerary IV

*You may prefer to visit the Mediterranean coast instead of the Red Sea so as to visit **Alexandria**. Go from Cairo at the beginning or end of the two weeks and adjust Luxor and Aswan accordingly. Spend two or three days in Alex visiting regional attractions like El Alamein.

*If you're not especially interested in either coast or are especially keen on pharaonic monuments, spend a couple extra days in Luxor and make day trips to nearby attractions like the Temple of Osiris at Abydos, the Temple of Hathor at Dendera, and the Temple of Horus at Edfu.

*If you insist on going to Sinai, do it from Cairo instead of Upper Egypt and adjust your schedule accordingly.

Those looking to float down the Nile can use the Luxor/Aswan days to join a 3-4 cruise with stops at temples and other attractions en route. Reservations should be made in advance if possible.

ITINERARY V
Cairo, Luxor, Aswan & Abu Simbel, Red Sea coast or Sinai, Cairo
Number of days: 28
Transportation: Train, bus, and possibly plane

Days 1-5
Settle into Cairo and hit the big sights: the Pyramids, Saqqara, the Cairo Museum, the Khan El Khalili, the Citadel, Islamic Cairo, and Coptic Cairo. Other good ideas: horseback riding by the Pyramids, riding a felucca, a belly dancing show. In the evening of Day 5 board a night train or plane for Luxor.

Days 6-9
Get to work quickly visiting Luxor's endless pharaonic attractions. Spend half days visiting Karnak, the west bank (Valley of the Kings, Deir El Bahri, Tombs of the Nobles et al), and the Luxor Temple, the Luxor Museum, and the Mummification Museum. Hard-core temple enthusiasts can take a day to visit the Temple of Osiris at Abydos. Sunset feluccas, "Sound & Light" at Karnak, and the Tuesday camel market are other attractions worth exploring.

Days 9-12
Float down to Aswan on a cruise. Relax, enjoy the countryside and the temples along the way. If you can't afford to cruise, or just don't want to, spend an extra day in Luxor and visit the Temple of Horus at Edfu or the Temple of Hathor at Dendera. An cheaper, more rugged alternative to a cruise is a felucca journey. This three day trip is better done from Aswan so adjust your schedule accordingly.

Days 13-15
Aswan. Take two or three days to visit the regional sight; Abu Simbel should be a priority. Other attractions worth visiting: Philae Temple,

Kalabsha Temple, the Aswan High Dam, Elephantine Island, the local souk, and the weekly camel market at Daraw. If you want to make the three day felucca cruise to Luxor make arrangements in Aswan.

Day 14-15
Make your way back to Cairo. Flying saves a 15 hour train trip. Catch your breath and take in a few sights. Catch a plane or night bus to Sharm El Sheikh.

Days 15-20
Enjoy the riches of Sinai. Attractions include world class diving, snorkeling and other water sports, Mount Sinai and Saint Katherine's Monastery (at least a day trip), and desert safaris in Sinai mountains and deserts. Those looking for a more low-key, wallet friendly setting can bolt continue on to Nuweiba or Dahab.

Day 21
Back to Cairo. Rest for a day, take in a sight or two.

Days 22-25
Head to Alexandria, Egypt's second city. Spend a day or two visiting the city's attractions: the Greco-Roman Museum, the Harbor, the Fort of Qait Bey, and Pompey's Pillar. Also, Alex offers the best seafood in Egypt and is famous for cafes and patisseries. Historically minded folks should definitely take a day to visit the World War II battlefield at El Alamein.

Days 26-28
Return to Cairo and wrap up last minute shopping and sightseeing.

Alternatives for Itinerary V
*The Oases - Those interested in more rustic, off the beaten track traveling, should consider taking a week or two visiting a combination of oases in the Western Desert. The most attractive, Siwa, is the furthest and is best visited from Alexandria. Kharga and Dakhla should be visited from Assiut in the Nile Valley on the way to or back from Upper Egypt. Farafra can be done from Cairo or combined on a longer journey with Kharga and Dakhla, and Baharia is nearest to Cairo. Should you decide to take on the Western Desert, consider substituting Hurghada or El Gouna for Sinai shave a few days off the Nile Valley.

*Pharaonic buffs should consider exploring the oft-neglected sights of Middle Egypt.

ITINERARY VI

Cairo, Luxor, Luxor-Aswan cruise, Aswan & Abu Simbel, Cairo, Sinai, Cairo, Alexandria & El Alamein, Cairo
Number of Days: 36
Transportation: train, bus, and plane

Days 1-5

Arrive in Cairo and take in the sights: the Pyramids of Giza, the Egyptian Antiquities Museum, Salah El Din's Citadel, the Sultan Hassan and Ibn Tulun Mosques, the Islamic Museum, the early Coptic churches and the Coptic Museum in Old Cairo, and the Manial Palace. Take plenty of time to pound the pavement, especially in the city's medieval Islamic quarters. For recreation, consider a sunset, sunrise, or moonlight horseback ride in the deserts surrounding the Pyramids, a sunset felucca cruise, and a belly dancing show.

Days 6-8

Take a train to Minya. Spend a day or two visiting Beni Hassan, Tuna El Gebel, Tehna El Gebel, and Tel El Amarna.

Days 9-11

Take the train to Luxor and get ready for some the world's most fantastic archaeological sites. In half day chunks visit the Theban Necropolis on the west bank, Karnak Temple, the Luxor Temple, the Luxor Museum, and the Mummification Museum. Don't push yourself too hard. Other attractions include the Tuesday camel market , the "Sound and Light" show at Karnak, and the city's bazaars. Diehard temple types should consider a day trip to Abydos.

Days 12-15

Nile Cruise to Aswan. Relax and watch the Egyptian countryside go by and visit major temples en route. If you can't afford a cruise, consider the felucca alternative. This is better done Aswan-Luxor so adjust your schedule accordingly.

Days 16-18

Aswan. By all means take a day to visit Abu Simbel. Other attractions include Philae Temple, Kalabsha Temple, the Unfinished Obelisk, Elephantine Island, Fatimid Cemeteries, Aswan's souk, and a camel market at Daraw, a nearby town.

Day 19
Fly or take the (monster 17 hour) train to Cairo. Rest up and take in a sight.

Days 20-23
Take the bus or fly to Sharm El Sheikh to rest and relax in Sinai. Enjoy its beauty both on land and underwater-the diving is amongst the best in the world. If you're so inclined, take a day or two to visit Mount Sinai and Saint Katherine's Monastery or undertake a desert safari and camping trip.

Day 24
Back to Cairo and up to Alexandria.

Days 25-27
Visit the attractions of Alexandria and eat seafood and pastries. The grounds of Montazah, the Greco-Roman Museum, Pompey's Pillar and the Fort of Qait Bey are all worthwhile as is a day trip to the World War II battlefield of El Alamein.

Days 28-33
Make the long trip to Siwa Oasis, possibly stopping in Marsa Matrouh for a night. Spend 4-5 days exploring Siwa.

Days 34-36
Make your way back to Cairo by Day 34. Make any last minute shopping or sightseeing expeditions and prepare for departure.

Alternatives for Itinerary VI
*If Siwa seems a bit far, but you'd still like to visit an oasis, consider spending several days in Kharga, Dakhla, Farafra, or any combination thereof. Bahariya and Faiyoum are even closer to Cairo and can be visited in a day or two.

4. LAND & PEOPLE

THE NILE

Described by Herodotus 2,500 years ago as "the Gift of the Nile," Egypt still clings to the mighty river for dear life. More than 90% of Egypt's 65 million people live along the banks of the Nile on less than 5% of the nation's total land area. The longest river in the world, the Nile stretches the length of the country from the Sudanese border to the Delta and Mediterranean Sea. It differs from the world's other long rivers in that it flows against the wind from south to north, rather than north to south-crucial factor in Egypt's economic and political development because it enabled sailing both up and down the river.

Revered by the ancient Egyptians who likened it to a lotus plant with the Delta as a budding flower, the Nile defined the ancient Egyptian way of life. Annual floods fed by the great Ethiopian monsoons at the Nile's headwaters washed up rich silt providing an ideal topsoil for the grains and other crops farmed by the ancient Egyptians who commemorated the floods with lavish celebrations like the annual Opet festival held in Luxor.

The floods continued well into the 20th century when Egypt's rulers sought to control them with the construction of dams, beginning with the Aswan Dam in 1902 and culminating with the **Aswan High Dam** in 1970. The Dam created Lake Nasser – the world's largest man-made reservoir – flooded the Nubian homelands forever, and ended the cycle of flooding. This enabled Egyptian farmers to harvest more than one crop annually and increased the nation's electricity production by more than 30%,. However it also created a number of environmental problems ranging from soil erosion on the Mediterranean Coast to a dearth of nutrients in top soils throughout the Nile Valley.

DESERTS & OASES

More than 90 percent of Egypt is arid, uninhabitable desert. West of the Nile lies the vast **Western Desert**, also known as the **Libyan Desert**.

Often mistaken for the Sahara, it is a separate geological entity separated by mountains stretching from western Sudan through eastern Libya. An extremely hot and arid desert, it covers nearly 3 million square kilometers making it one of the largest deserts in the world. Stretching east of the Nile Valley to the Red Sea is the smaller but equally harsh, **Eastern Desert**.

SINAI

The only land link between Asia and Africa, **Sinai** is part of the Syrian-African Rift where continental plates have pulled Africa and Asia apart over the past million years. The plates are still active and produced the famous earthquake of 1992 that killed more than a thousand people in Cairo. Covered with rugged mountains in the south, and rolling dunes in the north, Sinai's harsh conditions have deterred all but a handful of Bedouin tribes from living there until the 20th century. The waters surrounding Sinai boast some of the most diverse marine eco-systems in the world. This results form a unique combination of strong currents, deep shelves, and warm waters.

CLIMATE

Egypt's climate is hot and dry in the summer, moderate and dry during winters. The Mediterranean Coast is more humid and prone to rain; it tends to be quite cool in the winters and not as searing hot as the rest of the country in the summer. In Upper Egypt, summers are brutal as typical daytime temperatures in locations like Aswan, soar above 100 degrees Fahrenheit. Winters remain pleasantly warm during the day (75-80 degrees Fahrenheit) and cool at night (in the 60's). On the Sinai and Red Sea coasts, the weather resembles that of the rest of the country but suffers from higher wind levels and more cold during the winter. During March and April *khamseen* ("50 days") winds, blow from the south, causing sporadic sandstorms in the Nile Valley and Western Desert.

PEOPLE

Islam

Islam is a monotheistic religion based on the Quran as revealed to the **Prophet Mohammed** by the arch-angel Jabril (Gabriel) over 22 years in the 7th century. Considered the literal Word of God, the Quran is the primary source and ultimate authority for Islamic law and theology. It is organized into 114 chapters called *suras* in order of length from the second sura (the first called *El Fatiha* is a short introduction), which is more than 20 pages long to the last sura which is one line. Besides Mohammed, the Quran names 28 prophets selected by God to deliver His message and shares many characters and stories with the Christian and Jewish traditions. Adam, Abraham, David, and Moses play roles of varying degrees and Mary the mother of Jesus is the most important female figure in the entire Quran. Jesus himself was considered a prophet, though not with divine status as in Christianity. He did perform miracles and was placed on the cross though according to Islamic tradition he was not killed on it.

The central theme of the Quran is the supremacy, omniscience, and compassion of **Allah**. Public calls to prayer, prayers themselves, and every sura, with the exception of the ninth, begin with *basmala* – the invocation of God that starts, "In the Name of Allah, the all-merciful, the all-compassionate." The Quran dictates that each Muslim must fulfill what are known as the **Five Pillars** of Islam, five testaments of faith in Islam and Allah. First, each Muslim must declare the **shahada**-a testament that there is no god but Allah and that Mohammed is his prophet. Second, Muslims must fast and refrain from sexual activity between sunrise and sundown during the Islamic month of **Ramadan**. Third, all Muslims physically and economically able, must make **Haj** pilgrimage to Mecca, at least once during their lifetime. Fourth, they must give **alms** to the poor. Finally, the fifth pillar requires that Muslims **pray** five times daily. Except for the Friday congregational prayers, this need not be done in a mosque.

Beyond the five pillars, Islamic law and tradition dictates other rituals and regulations for all aspects of life in addition to matters of religion; everything from personal hygiene to commerce and economic activity are encompassed in Islamic law.

Apart from the Quran, the second most important source of Islamic law is the example of the life of the Prophet Mohammed himself-known as the **sunna**. As a human being so perfect so as to deliver the literal word of God to humanity he is considered the ideal role model and his examples are to be followed in every aspect of life from the manner in which he cleans his teeth and eats, to his relations with his wife and children, and of course his performing of religious duties.

There is a widely held misconception in the West that there is a monolithic "Islamic Law" proscribed to by especially fundamentalist Muslims. In fact, there have always been differences between sects, the various schools of law, and regions as to questions of law. Unlike Christianity which emerged from a highly codified Roman society, Islamic Arabia had very little in legal tradition to draw on, and rapid expansion of the Islamic soveriegnty focused the efforts of political leaders and theologians on the need to develop a legal system. The major sources of law were the Koran itself, the sunna, and deductions made by a consensus of scholars drawn from the major sources. By the 11th century Islam four major legal schools of thought had been established (Maliki, Hanbali, Hanafi, and Shafi'i). Essentially compatible, they reflect the different priorities of their founder. For example, the Maliki madhab

(Islamic legal school), prevalent in Upper Egypt, draws heavily on the suras revealed during Mohammed's exile in Medina, while the Shafi'i madhab, favored in northern Egypt and Malaysia among other places, places heavy emphasis on hadith (sunna) scholarship and the need for consensus. Shiites, who split with the mainstream Sunni Islam over the issue of caliphal succession after Mohammed's death, have their own legal codes. Egypt's Muslims are 99% Sunni.

Islam in Egypt

Islam was introduced to Egypt ten years after Mohammed's death in 642 with the invasion of Arab armies led by **Amr Ibn El As**. Weary of Roman occupation, Egypt's predominantly Christian population accepted passively Islamic rule while their new Islamic masters respected the autonomy and integrity of the Christian and Jewish populations as they were considered "People of the Book." As Islam is not a proselytizing religion, and Christians were not forced to convert, Christianity remained Egypt's majority religion until the 12th century.

Except for 200 years of Fatimid Shiite rule between the 10th and 12th centuries, Egypt has always been Sunni, and even though the Fatimid Shiites had not converted many Egyptians during their stint in power, their Sunni successors, the Ayyubids, reasserted Sunni dominance with a vengeance, primarily through the introduction of the **madrasah**. The madrasah was a Sunni legal college that educated the *ulema* – the religious elite who, even though political power was concentrated in the hands of amirs (generals), assumed positions in the judiciary and civil administration. Also, Islamic law was the guiding force in Egyptian society until the 19th century and madrasahs were the primarily institutions of higher learning in Egypt until the 19th century and contributed to its status as a center of Islamic and Arabic letters. Though most madrasahs are now redundant, El Azhar University in Cairo remains the world's premier center of Sunni Islamic scholarship – a testament to Cairo's preeminent position in the Islamic world.

The Middle Ages also saw the emergence **Sufis**, Islamic mystics and shaman-like holy men. While their primary goal was to achieve union with God and become better Muslims generally, Sufis played a major role in converting Egyptians to Islam by their acts of public good works on the one hand, and by the alleged performing of miracles by sheikhs, or sufi holy men, on the other. Though Islam does not encourage or recognize the concept of sainthood, many Sufis through the Islamic era in Egypt have achieved a quasi-divine status tantamount to sainthood. These saints (referred to by the title, 'Sayedna') are remembered on their birth or festival days, known as moulids, when sufis and other Muslims congregate at their mausoleum for prayers and celebrations. During the Ottoman era

(16th-19th centuries), sufism was discouraged and the major orders went underground, however in the 20th century, Sufiism has emerged and an estimated 5-6 million Egyptian men belong to a Sufi order.

Islam & Egypt in the 20th century

By the time she achieved independence in 1952, Egypt and the Islamic world generally had been under European domination for 200 years. Many attributed this trend to Islam itself, and the Nasser regime which aspired to modernity above all else, was wholly secular. Yet Islam has played a major role in Egyptian politics throughout the 20th century. In 1922, **Hassan El Banna** founded the **Muslim Brotherhood** with the aim of ridding Egypt of British domination and establishing an Islamic state. The Brotherhood quickly built widespread grassroots support and its violent campaign of agitation and political assassination was critical in paving the way for the July 1952 Revolution.

After a failed attempt on Nasser's life, the Brotherhood was forced underground, but President Sadat welcomed it back from the political wilderness in the 1970's to offset what he perceived to be threats from the left. At the same time, 20 years of failed socialist economics and lost wars with Israel was leading many Egyptians to rediscover their Islamic identity-a trend that has continued into the '90s. For his part, Sadat cracked down hard on Islamicists who turned against him after his peace with Israel, and on October 6, 1981, a young fundamentalist low level officer, Khaled Islambouli, assassinated Sadat during a military parade.

In the '80s and '90s, the Brotherhood has once again become a potent political and social force, in no small part because of its extensive network of social services. With the modest liberalization of the political system in Egypt, the Brotherhood is able to articulate its views through the newspaper *El Shaab*, while its members have come dominate social and professional organizations like unions and bar associations. However, while the Brotherhood has renounced violence, more radical splinter groups like the Gamaat Islamiya have taken up arms against the Mubarak regime and government security forces, and in the early '90s armed confrontations primarily in Middle and Upper Egypt claimed hundreds of casualties on both sides. While a weak economy has the Mubarak regime struggling to retain its legitimacy, the radical Islamicists have lost a good deal of public support by hitting the lucrative tourist industry which employs millions of Egyptians, and by attacking respected political figures like Naguib Mahfouz.

The Coptic Church

The **Coptic Orthodox Church of Alexandria** is one of the oldest and most orthodox Christian sects whose contributions to Christianity include monasticism, and such important figures as Athanasius and Clement of Alexandria. Despite constant persecution since its founding nearly 2000 years ago the Coptic Church has always remained independent and resistant to the domination of others whether they be Romans, Arab or Turkish Muslims, or the secular regimes of today. Though Christianity was the majority religion in Egypt for a thousand years until the 11th century, the country has never been ruled by Egyptian Copts.

According to Coptic tradition, **Saint Mark** founded the Coptic Church in Alexandria after making his first convert, a Jewish cobbler, in 62 AD. Considered the first Coptic patriarch, Mark was martyred on Easter Sunday in 68 AD at the hands of Egyptians marking celebrations of the pagan Serapis cult, and Christians in Egypt continued to face persecution throughout Roman occupation until the 7th century. The worst of this oppression, when thousands of Copts were martyred, occurred during the reigns of **Roman Emperors Decius and Diocletian** (284-305 AD) to whose reign the Coptic Church dates the beginning of its calendar and the **Era of Martyrs**. In the face of persecution, many Christians took to the deserts, oases, and other isolated locations to adapt an ascetic and mystic way of life that is considered the earliest forms of Christian **monasticism**, and a community established in the Eastern Desert by **Saint Antony** is cited as Christendom's first monastery.

Despite persecution, Christianity became well established throughout Egypt by the end of the second century and Alexandria emerged as one of early Christendom's most important theological centers. Building on the traditions of the Great Library, which produced the Septuagint Greek translation of the Old Testament, the **Christian School of Alexandria**, known as the **Didascalium** produced such early Christian giants as Saint Clement, Athanasius, Pantaenus, and Origen as well as all of the early Coptic Patriarchs. However, the school was closed by Roman authorities during the reign of Justinian after the Council of Chalcedon in 451 led to the severance of the Coptic Church from the rest of Roman Christendom.

After conquering Egypt in 642, Muslims on average respected the rights of Copts to practice their faith and to maintain their communities. As **Ahl El Kitab** (People of the Book), the Copts were granted **dhimmi** status under Islamic law which provided them with protection in return for payment of the **jizya** tax. Though there were pockets of history when the Copts suffered great persecution at the hands of their Muslim rulers (most famously during the reign of Fatimid Caliph El Hakim), they have by and large always been able to at least practice their faith without fear of retribution, and have traditionally played prominent roles in commerce and civil society.

Today Copts comprise between five and fifteen percent of the Egyptian population depending on who you talk to. Though many thrive as merchants, academicians, and in other professional capacities, relations with their Muslim countrymen are not always smooth. This is especially the case in poorer parts of rural Middle and Upper Egypt where sectarian violence is common. Copts feel they are the scapegoats for social and economic problems while Muslims claim that the Copts undermine national unity by putting their faith ahead of their country. To this, Copts retort that they have been nationalistic Egyptians from the 1st century, 500 years before Islam even appeared in Egypt.

The Egyptian People

Except for black Nubians and Sudanese, Egyptians appear ethnically homogenous "Arabs" to most western foreigners. Compared to the United States, India, or Indonesia, this might be the case, but Egypt's ethnic makeup is far more complex.

Most Muslim Egyptians consider themselves **Arab** with a strain of native **Egyptian ancestry** that links them to the pharaohs and the Semitic people of **Ham**. In most cases, especially in the north, it's usually more complex than that. Waves of foreign invaders and colonizers from the Greeks, Roman, Persians, Turks and other central Asians, to the Mamlukes and Ottomans with ancestry from the Balkans, the Caucasus and places like Azerbaijan have been assimilated into the Egyptian bloodstream.

The majority of Egyptians who still work the land along the banks of the Nile are known as the **fellaheen**, or peasants. They are the backbone of Egyptian society and are closely associated with the land and the river that has shaped their way of life for thousands of years. The fellaheen are purer in their native Egyptian stock than urban folks who over the years have intermixed, married, and assimilated with invaders and expatriates. Those in Middle and Upper Egypt are called **Sayeedis**, (Upper Egypt is known as the "Sayeed") and are stereotypically known for their hot blood, family loyalty, and stubbornness. Like the Irish in England or southerners in the American northeast, they suffer bad jokes at the hands of urban northern Egyptians who consider them thick and simple-minded.

The **Copts** consider themselves homogenous Egyptians not tainted by Islamic, Arab, or Turkish blood. They trace their ancestry to the ancient Egyptians who converted to Christianity during the first two or three hundred years after the death of Christ. Copts are found throughout Egypt but are highly concentrated in Middle Egypt-towns like Minya, Assiut, and Sohag- and in Alexandria. Other Christian ethnic groups include the **Armenians** and the **Greek Orthodox** both of which were thriving communities in Alexandria and Cairo prior to mass emigration to Europe, the United States, and Canada in the 1950s.

Perhaps those of the purest ethnic stock are the nomadic **Bedouin** clans of the deserts on either side of the Nile and in Sinai. Living in the isolation of the deserts and the oases, they have rarely intermarried outside of their own clans. Clans in Sinai and the Eastern Desert trace their genealogies to the tribes of Arabia, while those in the Western Desert are more often than not ethnic Berbers. As the Sinai and the deserts become increasingly developed and populated with non-Bedouin, it is believed that pure Bedouin bloodlines will soon disappear.

Finally, there are the **Nubians**. A very dark and handsome people known for their intelligence and kind disposition, the Nubians were forced to abandon their homeland after it was submerged under Lake Nasser following the construction of the Aswan High Dam in the 1960's. Today a large portion of them live in Aswan and make their living in the tourism industry. Others have moved to Cairo where they work as laborers and doormen.

Language

Arabic is the national language of Egypt and is spoken by all Egyptians. Egypt is the largest Arabic speaking country in the world and its dialect is widely understood throughout the Arab world because of Egypt's domination of Arabic popular culture through mediums like television, film, and music. While every Egyptian has a right to free primary, secondary, and university education, more than 40% of Egyptians and 65% of females are illiterate.

Copts still use the **Coptic** language in liturgy. Derived from the language of the ancient Egyptians, Coptic resembles ancient Greek. Unfortunately it is now a dead language and is in serious danger of disappearing completely.

Many Egyptians, particularly from higher economic classes and those working in the tourism industry, know at least some English, French or some other western language. English is taught in schools and widely heard on television and in movies. In the early 20th century, French was considered the language of culture and was preferred by Egypt's elite who sent their children to French schools. Boutrous Boutrous Ghali, former Secretary-General of the United Nations for example, comes from a very prominent Coptic family and is a committed Francophone.

5. A SHORT HISTORY

PHARAONIC EGYPT

The history of pharaonic Egypt spanned more than 3,000 years from 3,100 BC until roughly the time of Christ, though some cults continued to function as late as the 5th century. Historians divide the history of Egypt into three major periods: the **Old Kingdom** (preceded by the Early Dynastic Period of the first 2 dynasties), the **Middle Kingdom**, and the **New Kingdom**. Interspersed between these epochs were pockets of disunity, foreign occupation or even anarchy, called "Intermediate periods." The royal families that ruled Egypt, some of them foreign, are categorized into 30 **dynasties**.

THE EARLY DYNASTIC PERIOD

(3,100-2,686 BC)

Pharaonic history began 5,100 years ago in the **Early Dynastic Period**, a formative but mysterious time in Egyptian history. Its central figure was **Menes** (AKA **Narmer**), a noble from Abydos who united Egypt around 3,100 BC and became the first pharaoh. He also founded the world's first imperial capital, **Memphis**, at the base of the Delta 30 kilometers south of present day Cairo. Few detail are known about the reign of Menes and he left behind little in the way of historical evidence except for the **Palette of Narmer** now on display in the Egyptian Museum in Cairo.

After Menes, the Early Dynastic Period was an era of development and transition, but instability as well. Despite the efforts of Upper Egyptian pharaohs to enhance their legitimacy in Lower Egypt (the Delta) by constructing monuments to Lower Egyptian deities, and building tombs and palaces in Lower Egypt as well as Upper Egypt, the two societies remained distant and functionally independent. Yet despite the slow unification process, progress in culture and technology made during the Early Dynastic Period laid the groundwork for the prosperity and power enjoyed during later periods. **Hieroglyphics** were developed from a pictorial system of symbols into a comprehensive written language that remained in use for the next 3,000 years, and Egyptian engineers developed new construction techniques that enabled the construction of monuments like mud brick **mastaba** (bench-shaped) tombs, that later evolved into multi-layered pyramids.

THE OLD KINGDOM

2,686-2,181 BC

During the **Old Kingdom** (3rd-6th Dynasties) Egypt blossomed into one of the world's great civilizations. The emergence of a strong central government and an efficient bureaucracy combined with improved technology and infrastructure enabled the achievement of unprecedented heights economically, politically, and artistically. Memphis and other cities flourished and pharaohs constructed monumental temples and tombs for their gods and themselves. The Old Kingdom also saw the emergence of religious cults like those of **Atum** at Heliopolis and **Ptah** in Memphis as major political and social forces.

During the 3rd Dynasty, two figures, the Pharaoh **Zoser** and his architect and confidante **Imhotep**, were especially important. In his efforts to cement the fragile unification of Egypt, Zoser promoted himself as a deity in addition to claiming the title of Pharaoh. This ideal of a **God-King** became central to Egyptian religion and political ideology; it raised the status of pharaoh from that of mere despot or noble to a divine king, whose rule, at least in theory, was beyond reproach. Imhotep, "the world's first architect" was an ingenious builder who designed Zoser's monumental funerary complex at Saqqara, including the Step Pyramid, the world's first stone building, and one of the oldest man-made structures still standing.

By the 4th Dynasty Egypt's centralized, imperial system of government had matured, and pharaohs were able to efficiently mobilize resources according to their wants and needs. As a divine king, the pharaoh enjoyed widespread legitimacy and near absolute power. After the pharaoh, power was concentrated in the position of **vizier** (chief minister), who was responsible for the treasury and the collection of taxes through **gnomarchs** (provincial governors). Trade was greatly enhanced by the construction of elaborate canal systems and the development of huge boats (as long as 50 meters) large enough to ferry tons of cargo at a time between Aswan and Memphis, and expeditions were launched to Nubia where Egyptians traded for gold, turquoise, and other minerals. The extent of 4th Dynasty power, wealth, and technical prowess is most clearly manifested in the construction of the **Great Pyramids of Giza**, tombs built for the pharaohs Khufu, Khafre, and Menkhare, that until the 19th century were the world's largest buildings.

After the glory of the 4th Dynasty, the 5th Dynasty was a period of slow decline as central authority waned in the face of provincial uprisings, and weak leadership became vulnerable to the narrow interests of rival cults. By the 6th Dynasty, gnomarchs were all but independent and national unity disintegrated.

THE FIRST INTERMEDIATE PERIOD
2,181-2,050 BC

After the death of Pepi II, last pharaoh of the 6th Dynasty, Egypt plunged into a period of disunity that lasted 130 years as central authority gave way to petty dynasties and city-states, none of which succeeded in unifying the Nile Valley. Eventually an 11th Dynasty Theban Lord, **Mentuhotep II**, conquered Upper and Lower Egypt in 2,050 BC and established the Middle Kingdom.

THE MIDDLE KINGDOM
2,050-1,786 BC

The Middle Kingdom was a 300 year period of political stability and economic prosperity. Trade and expansion again became priorities and expeditions were sent to Nubia, Sinai, Libya, and the Land of Punt on the Somali coast. Also beginning with Mentuhotep, who built a grand mortuary temple at Deir El Bahri, pharaohs again enjoyed the wealth to indulge in monumental building. Though the founder of the 12th Dynasty, **Amemenhet**, returned the capital to Memphis and it was later moved to Faiyoum, the Middle Kingdom is significant for the rise of Thebes and its patron sun deity, Amun, whose temple at Karnak was founded by Amemenhet's successor, **Senusert**, and later developed into the world's largest house of worship.

Senusert also moved the capital to the **Faiyoum Oasis** in the Western Desert where he embarked on massive irrigation and land reclamation projects to boost agricultural production. Egypt's population boomed and his successors, **Amemenhet III** and **Senusert III** (builders of the last pyramids) further restricted the powers of the provincial nobility, but despite these efforts, a series of bad harvests led to political uprisings and a collapse of royal authority and the Second Intermediate Period.

THE SECOND INTERMEDIATE PERIOD
1,786-1,567 BC

Though relative stability facilitated an economic rebound during the 13th Dynasty, the Second Intermediate Period was a time of disunity and

foreign invasion. The nomadic tribes of the **Hyksos** established hege-
mony in the Delta while in Upper Egypt, rival pretenders battled over the
throne. Though the Hyksos were of West Asian origin, they styled
themselves as Egyptian pharaohs and honored Egyptian deities. Egyptian
records refer to the Hyksos as barbarians and anarchists, though evidence
recovered by archaeologists indicates they were cultured and traded with
nations as far away as Persia.

The Hyksos also built a new capital at **Avaris** where Cretan style
frescoes indicate close ties with the Minoans. In 1567 BC after 100 years
of civil war, **Ahmose**, brother of the last 17th Dynasty Pharaoh, **Kamose**,
successfully expelled the Hyksos and chased them to Palestine. Thus
began the 18th Dynasty and the New Kingdom, a golden age in Egyptian
history.

THE NEW KINGDOM
1,567-1,085 BC

The New Kingdom was a 500 year period of unprecedented prosperity, stability, and expansion. It began with the 18th Dynasty **Thutmosid**
pharaohs who conquered Nubia, Palestine, and Syria, and built Thebes
into the world's richest and most developed city. **Thutmosis I** (1525-1512
BC) began the tradition of elaborate tomb building in the Valley of the
Kings and his daughter, **Hatshepsut** (1503-1482 BC) constructed the first
of many monumental New Kingdom mortuary temples at Deir El Bahri.
The first and only Egyptian female pharaoh (Cleopatra was Greek),
Hatshepsut assumed the trappings of traditional pharaohdom, including
a male identity yet faced stiff opposition from Thutmosis III, her step-son
whose place in the line of succession she usurped by grabbing power upon
the death of Thutmosis II. Hatshepsut was able to fend off his challenges,
but upon her death, he ordered that every vestige of her rule be expunged
and during his reign, her monuments were defaced and her cartouches
and likenesses chiseled away.

Thutmosis III (1,482-1,459 BC) may have been a man of jealousy, but
he was Egypt's greatest military leader and a tireless builder who made
important contributions to the temples at Luxor and Karnak. His successors, **Amenhophis II** and **Thutmosis IV** built on his success and consoli-
dated Egypt's position as the regional superpower. This paved the way for
the reign of **Amenhophis III**, when New Kingdom Egypt reached its
zenith economically and culturally.

Amenhophis III's heir, **Amenhophis IV** (1379-1362 BC) intensely
revered a minor embodiment of the sun-god known as **Aten**, and soon
after assuming the throne, outlawed worship of any deity except Aten,
estranging the powerful priesthood of Amun, and founding what some
consider the world's first monotheistic religion. He changed his name to

Akhenaten, and moved the capital from Thebes to a new city at **Tel El Amarna** in Middle Egypt which he named **Akhetaten**, the "Horizon of the Aten." Uninterested in maintaining Egypt's empire in West Asia, he adopted a pacifist foreign policy, much to the dismay of his generals.

Akhenaten's confidante and successor, **Smenkhkare** died mysteriously within a year of assuming the throne and was succeeded by **Tutankhaten** (1361-1352 BC). Just a boy, he fell under the sway of a powerful general, **Haremheb**, who persuaded him to revoke support for the Cult of Aten and to return the Cult of Amun to its previous status-it is no accident that the young king changed his name from Tutankh*aten* to **Tutankhamun**. Though his reign was short-lived and dominated by special interests, Tutankhamun is among Egypt's best known pharaohs because his tomb was the only royal tomb in the Valley of the Kings found intact when discovered by Howard Carter in 1922.

The counter-revolution against Cult of Aten continued under Tutakhamun's successors **Aye** and **Haremheb** (1348-1320 BC) who returned the Cult of Amun and the city of Thebes to their preeminent positions in Egyptian society, and undertook a campaign to erase any remnants of the heretical Cult of Aten. Tel El Amarna was entirely torn down and Haremheb, Seti I, and Ramses II used the stones in building their own monuments.

Though Haremheb's vizier and successor, Ramses I, only ruled for two years, his 19th Dynasty successors are among Egypt's most venerated figures. **Seti I** (1318-1304) reconquered lands lost by Akhenaten and extended Egyptian rule into Asia Minor for the first time. He also built a splendid temple at Abydos as well as the northern Hypostyle Hall at Karnak. His son **Ramses II** ruled for 80 years, expanded Egyptian authority in Asia Minor, and constructed a string of colossal temples stretching from Nubia to the Delta including the Ramesseum at Thebes and the temples of Abu Simbel in Nubia. Ramses II's son and successor **Merneptah** (1236-1217 BC) repulsed invasions from the "Sea Peoples" (perhaps Greeks or Sicilians) and the Libyans, but is known as the **"Pharaoh of the Exodus,"** referring to Moses' flight from Egypt, though no evidence of a Jewish presence in pharaonic Egypt has ever been found.

The New Kingdom began a gradual 200 year decline with the onset of the **20th Dynasty** in 1,200 BC. Except for **Ramses III** (1,198-1,166 BC), leadership was poor and Egypt's once vast Asiatic empires withered away. Ramses III rebuffed three invasions by the Libyans and the mysterious "Sea People," and constructed a beautiful palace and mortuary complex at Medinet Habu in Thebes, but the next eight kings, all Ramses', presided over the piecemeal dismantling of the nation's empire and wealth. With economic prosperity went central authority and when Ramses XI moved his capital to the Delta, control of Upper Egypt was usurped by **Herihor**, priest in the Cult of Amun. Soon royal authority was also superseded in the Delta where a vizier, **Smendes** established a capital at Tanis, and founded the 21st Dynasty, but Egypt was divided for the first time in more than 500 years.

THE LATE PERIOD
1,085-322 BC

Though relations between the Priests in Upper Egypt and Smendes were amicable at first, the division left Egypt vulnerable to foreign invasion and in 945 BC, the **Libyans**, who tried to invade Egypt for centuries, finally succeeded in conquering the Delta. The first king of the Libyan dynasty, **Shoshenq**, was the **Biblical Sheshak** who plundered Jerusalem after the death of Solomon and a brilliant general. But after their initial success Libyan control was limited to the western Delta, while the east was divided amongst city states in Bubastis, Tanis, and Sais. This left the Delta vulnerable and in later half of the 8th century BC, Nubians from the south conquered Lower Egypt and reunited the Nile Valley.

Like the Libyans, the **Nubian Kushites** who founded the 25th Dynasty (747-656 BC), had long been dominated, sometimes ruthlessly, by the Egyptians. But in the course of Egyptian occupation, they adopted Egyptian culture and religion, and during their rule in Egypt, made a deliberate effort to continue Egyptian traditions. The cults of Amun, Osiris, and Isis thrived, and there was an artistic renaissance as temples were erected throughout the Nile Valley.

In 667 BC **Assyrians** invading from the east occupied Memphis and sacked Thebes. They quickly withdrew from Egypt to address internal problems, but their support enabled lords from **Sais** in the Delta to unite Upper and Lower Egypt. Founded by **Psammetichus I**, the 26th Dynasty of the Saites (664-525 BC), presided over the last great age of native rule in Egypt, as once again, Egyptian armies went on the march in Nubia, Syria, and Palestine where **Necho II** (610-595 BC) trounced Josiah, the King of Judah, before falling to the Babylonians. Culturally, there was a renaissance in arts and architecture, and a substantial influx of foreign settlers including Greeks, Syrians, and Jews reinvigorated the economy. A canal between the Red Sea and the Nile – and hence the Mediterranean – was dug and though the Saites Dynasty fell before it became functional, the canal became a crucial node in world trade.

In 525 BC, Egypt was conquered by the **Persians**, beginning a 2,500 period of foreign occupation that lasted until the 1952 Revolution. Like other foreigner occupiers, the Achaemenid Persians (525-404 BC), attempted to bolster their legitimacy by constructing temples to traditional Egyptian deities, but a ruthless military occupation and high taxation rates spawned great hatred amongst the Egyptian population and rebellions were common. They did however make constructive contributions to Egyptian history by completing the Red Sea-Nile canal and in founding a fortified city called **Babylon** across the river from Memphis, sowed the seed that later blossomed into the city that is now Cairo. Though Egyptian revolts forced a Persian withdrawal in 404 BC, a succession of unstable dynasties failed to fend off Persian intrusions and in 343, the Persian Emperor Artaxerxes III decisively defeated the last native born pharaoh, Nektanebo II. The Persians however, only managed to control Egypt for a decade before falling to their arch nemesis, Alexander the Great.

ALEXANDER & THE PTOLEMIES: THE GREEKS TAKE OVER

Alexander the Great was master of Egypt at age 25 and wasted no time in making off to Siwa to consult the Oracle at the temple of Amun which "revealed" that Alexander was "son of Amun" and hence the rightful king of Egypt. On his way to Siwa, Alexander chose a site on the Mediterranean coast to build his new Egyptian capital, **Alexandria**. Tradition maintains that his body was returned from Mesopotamia for interment though his tomb has never been located.

Upon Alexander's death Egypt became the domain of an able Greek general, **Ptolemy Sotor**, who founded the **Ptolemy Dynasty**. For 300 years the Ptolemies presided over the wealthiest and most scientifically advanced state in the world. During this golden age, Alexandria was a resplendent city whose economic and scientific preeminence was symbolized the legendary **Pharos Lighthouse**, which towered more than 400 feet, and the **Great Library** intellectual nerve center of the Hellenistic world. Said to contain more than 400,000 volumes, it attracted scholars from all over the Western World including Euclid, the "father of geometry" and the great astronomer Erasthenes who promoted the notion of a round earth.

As Greek rulers of Egypt, the Ptolemies assumed dual identities. In Alexandria, they were masters of the Hellenistic world, spoke Greek, worshipped Greek deities, and conducted trade with the peoples of the Mediterranean. On the other hand, the Ptolemies held Egyptian culture and tradition in high regard and assumed the trappings of traditional Egyptian pharaohdom. This was partly out of their respect for Egyptian culture and partly to enhance their legitimacy in the eyes of the native population.

Despite their respect for Egyptian culture, the Ptolemies were far from loved by their native subjects. Taxes were high and the fruits of increased trade and agricultural production were enjoyed exclusively by the Greek elite. Also, the Ptolemies extensively interfered in the affairs of the hitherto independent religious cults and the priesthoods of Memphis, Heliopolis, and Thebes who enjoyed widespread grass roots support saw their prestige greatly reduced.

CLEOPATRA & THE PTOLEMEIC DEMISE

The Ptolemeic Dynasty had been in decline for almost a century, when the legendary **Cleopatra VI** became the primary political figure in Egypt. After seizing power from her brother and husband, **Ptolemy XIV** she went into cahoots with **Julius Caesar**, who invaded Egypt in 54 BC. After Ptolemy XIV died fighting Caesar at the Battle of the Nile, Cleopatra took full control of Egypt under the eye of Caesar with whom she was intimate and to whom she bore a son.

In 44 BC, Caesar triumphantly brought her to Rome as a trophy but soon thereafter, Caesar was assassinated in the Roman Senate and Cleopatra returned to Alexandria. There she fell in love with **Mark Antony**, arch enemy of the mighty Roman Emperor **Octavian** (Augustus Caesar) who defeated Antony at the **Battle of Actium** in 30 BC. Marc Antony and Cleopatra returned to Alexandria where they committed suicide in the face of sure Roman occupation of Egypt.

ROMAN OCCUPATION & THE ARRIVAL OF CHRISTIANITY

With the onset of Roman domination, Egypt was relegated to the status of a backwater province and Alexandria lost its prestige as an imperial capital. To the Romans Egypt was a bread basket for its huge armies and it was the only Roman province to become the private domain of the emperor himself. Also Egypt's strategic location made it an important junction on Rome's trans-African and African-Asian trade routes and Alexandria remained an important port. The Romans significantly enhanced Egypt's infrastructure by building roads and canals, but did not share the fruits of these labors with the native population and ruled the country with an iron fist. Culturally, the Romans constructed pharaonic style temples like other occupiers of Egypt, but made little cultural impact on Egypt which remained a predominantly Hellenistic society.

In 61 AD a new chapter in Egyptian history began when according to Coptic tradition, **Saint Mark** made his first convert in Alexandria and founded the Coptic Church. Over the next two centuries, a majority of native Egyptians converted to Christianity despite, or even in response to, Roman oppression. The reasons for the rapid conversions are not entirely clear, but most scholars attribute it to the spiritual vacuum left after the passing of pharaonic traditions. Also, the large Jewish population, particularly in Alexandria, made an excellent source for converts because of Christianity's Judaic roots. Christianity became an integral part of the national identity and a rallying point for nationalists in the face of Roman oppression. Egypt was the world's first majority Christian country and remained primarily Christian until the 11th century-500 years into the Islamic Era.

THE ARAB CONQUESTS

In 641 AD, 700 years of Roman dominance in Egypt ended when the Roman garrison at Babylon fell after a short siege to an Arab army led by **Amr Ibn El As**. Though Arabization and Islamization were gradual processes (Christians remained the majority for another 500 years), Egypt was on the path to assuming a new position in the world and a new identity to which it still clings. After centuries of economic oppression and religious persecution under the Romans, the Egyptian people welcomed their new rulers, even though the Romans were Christian like them, and the Arabs were Muslims. Like their Roman predecessors, the Arabs saw Egypt as an agricultural gold mine with which they could feed their armies and new subjects, both of which were expanding exponentially. But unlike the Romans, the Arabs treated their Egyptian subjects with respect.

During the first two centuries of Islamic rule, Amr's garrison settlement of **El Fustat**, "the Camp," developed into a city of more than 200,000 and superseded Alexandria as Egypt's political and economic capital. Built from wealth derived from Egypt's great agricultural production and its position as a prosperous market place at the crossroads of trans-African and African-Asian caravan routes, Fustat became the wealthiest and most developed city west of China. While the Tulunids and the Fatimids built new palace cities of El Qata'i and El Qahira, Fustat remained Egypt's commercial hub until it burned down in the 12th century.

In 868, a central Asian slave, **Ibn Tulun**, was appointed Abbassid governor of Egypt, but usurped the tribute intended for Samara and proclaimed independence. He founded a new royal city called **El Qata'i** northeast of Fustat on the site of ancient Jewish and Christian cemeteries, which he razed. It was commonplace in Islamic history for new dynasties to establish royal cities apart from the main urban centers over which they governed. The centerpiece of El Qata'i was the great **Mosque of Ibn Tulun**, still one of the largest and most beautiful mosques in Cairo, and the only surviving structure from El Qata'i. The rest of the city was ravaged in 905 when the Abbassids reasserted their control over Egypt and wiped out the short-lived dynasty founded by Ibn Tulun, the **Tulunids**.

THE FATIMIDS

Abbassid control was brief and in 969, a fanatical band of Shiites swept into Egypt from Tunisia. Calling themselves **Fatimids** because they claimed descent from the Prophet Mohammed's daughter Fatima, they founded a caliphate that conquered all of North Africa and much of the Near East. For a capital, they constructed a magnificent walled city north of Fustat called **El Qahira**, "The Victorious." A glittering city of monumental palaces and mosques, El Qahira co-existed side by side with Fustat until the latter was destroyed in 1168. El Qahira is still the formal name of the city we know as "Cairo."

The early Fatimid caliphs **El Muizz** (969-975) and **El Aziz** (975-996) were tolerant and beneficent rulers who used their good relations with Copts, Jews, and Sunni Muslims to build a highly efficient and prosperous economy. During the 11th century, mosques and palaces of unprecedented grandeur were erected in El Qahira and the theological university of **El Azhar** became a prestigious institution of higher learning and Islamic jurisprudence. Now the world's oldest university, El Azhar is the preeminent institution for Islamic learning in the world, only today it is Sunni.

Fatimid decline began with the rule of the third caliph, **El Hakim** (996-1021), an insane and cruel despot who brutally persecuted Jews and Christians and destroyed the Church of the Holy Sepulcher in Jerusalem providing the impetus for the First Crusade. After El Hakim, a series of governors and viziers, most notably **Badr El Gamali** successfully protected Egypt from the Crusaders, but in the 1160's Sunni Seljuks became outraged with the Fatimids for making a separate peace with the Franks and invaded. The Sultan's general Shirkoh, occupied Egypt, but his deputy **Salah El Din El Ayyubi**, a slave soldier of Kurdish origin, usurped his command and established a new Sunni dynasty, the Ayyubids.

SALAH EL DIN & THE AYYUBIDS

Upon assuming control of Egypt Salah El Din extended his control to Syria, Palestine, and Arabia, and expelled Crusaders from Jerusalem. Following tradition, he established his own royal fortress, the **Citadel** which remained the seat of government in Egypt for 700 years. To restore Sunni Islam in Egypt after two centuries of Shiite Fatimid dominance, Salah El Din introduced religious colleges known as **madrasahs** which became the primary institutions of higher learning in Egypt and were largely responsible for making El Qahira a capital of Arabic letters. After his death in Damascus in 1193, Salah El Din's empire crumbled and Egypt remained under control of his descendants known as the **Ayyubids**. Apart from **El Kamel** (1218-38), the Ayyubids were weak and after only 70 years of rule, were overthrown by their own slave soldiers, the Mamlukes.

THE MAMLUKES

The **Bahri Mamluke** who ruled from 1250-1383 were Qipchak slaves imported by the Ayyubids from the steppes of the Caspian Sea and were so named because their primary barracks were on the island of Rhoda in the Nile-*bahr* means 'river' in Arabic. The Bahri's came to power under their commander, **Beybars El Bundaqdari**, "Beybars the Crossbow Wielder." A brilliant military mind, Beybars defeated the Mongols in Palestine, saving Egypt from the devastation and plundering suffered by Damascus and Baghdad. However, he was unable to establish a dynasty as his *amir* (general), **Qalawun** killed off his heirs and took the sultan's throne for himself. This established a pattern of fratricide and bloody transition that would plague both the Bahri's and their successors, the Burghi Mamlukes.

Both Qalawun and his son **El Nasir Mohammed** (1294-1340) were great patrons of the arts and constructed numerous mosques and palaces in Cairo and El Nasir Mohammed rebuilt the Citadel. They also maintained an empire in Palestine and Syria and made treaties with the Mongols. After El Nasir Mohammed, infighting between rival Bahri factions made the central state weak and in 1382, it fell to **Barquq**, a Circassian Mamluke. Thus began 130 years of **Burghi Mamluke** rule (1382-1517). *Burg* means 'tower' in Arabic and they derived their name from the tower where they were garrisoned at the Citadel.

Like the Bahris, the Burghis were patrons of the arts and built magnificent mosques. **Sultan Qait Bey** (1468-1496), the greatest of the Burghis extended the Mamluke Empire deeper into the Near East and Arabia and built monuments in Cairo, Palestine, Alexandria, and Mecca. But the Burghi Mamlukes were prone to infighting and fratricide that led to political instability and economic decline. The poor state of the economy was brought on by mismanagement and over taxation to fund wars in the Near East and the building of lavish monuments. It was dealt a crippling blow during the rule of **Qansuh El Ghuri** (1501-1516) when customs revenues plummeted after Vasco de Gamma rounded the Cape of Good Hope, making caravan routes through Egypt redundant. Meanwhile, the Ottoman state was emerging as a regional superpower and in 1517, Mamluki Egypt succumbed to the Ottomans when their aptly named general, **Selim the Grim**, conquered Cairo, and hung the last Mamluke ruler, Sultan Tumanbey from the Bab Zuweila.

THE OTTOMAN TURKS

With Ottoman occupation, Egypt was returned to the provincial backwater status it suffered under the Romans, and Cairo lost its status as an imperial capital and economic hub. During the 17th and 18th centuries, Egypt was governed by Ottoman appointed viceroys, known as

pashas who exercised their authority through Mamluke regiments that survived the Ottoman takeover. As long as they received tributes, the Sultans in Istanbul were content to let the pashas and their Mamluke proxies to do as they liked in Egypt, and they implemented a feudal system that put vast tracts of land and great wealth into the hands of a small Turkish elite.

By the 17th century, control of the pashas began to wane and the country plunged into a period of mutinies and disorder. As the old overland trade routes that made Egypt rich during Fatimid and Mamluke times became redundant with the opening of new shipping lanes, Egypt sank into economic decline and by the time Napoleon invaded in 1798, Egypt's population had declined from eight million at the Islamic takeover in 642, to less than two million.

NAPOLEON'S OCCUPATION

In 1798, Egypt returned to the world stage when **Napoleon** invaded it to cut off Britain from her Asian empire. With their modern military technology, Napoleon's troops easily overwhelmed Cairo's Mamluke defenders who were still using muskets akin to those brought by the Ottomans 300 years earlier. But despite his easy victory, Napoleon was unable to hold the country as **Lord Nelson's fleet** soundly defeated him at Abu Kir east of Alexandria and Napoleon fled back to France after only two years. Control of Egypt reverted back to the Ottomans and in 1805, the very capable and ambitious **Mohammed Ali Pasha** was named viceroy.

As part of the treaty signed with Britain and the Ottomans, the remnants of Napoleon's army were forced to hand over the archaeological treasures collected by French scholars. This explains why the Rosette Stone, so inextricably linked to Frenchman Champollion, is now in the British Museum in London.

THE DYNASTY OF MOHAMMED ALI

Though nominally an Ottoman viceroy, **Mohammed Ali** (1805-1849) quickly established Egypt as his personal domain. To remove any threat from remaining Mamluke elements, he invited them to a lavish party at the Citadel where he ambushed and murdered all of them except for one who according to legend escaped to Upper Egypt. Economically, Mohammed Ali's goal was to modernize Egypt and he hired thousands of European technical experts, military advisers and entrepreneurs. He placed virtually all land under his personal control and introduced **cotton** as a cash crop to raise revenues to build a modern infrastructure of roads, bridges, and canals, and he revived Alexandria as Egypt's preeminent port.

However, much of the wealth generated from his economic programs was squandered when his son **Ibrahim Pasha** led a costly expedition to Anatolia that almost toppled the Ottomans but was severely defeated by the British who intervened of Turkey's behalf.

When Mohammed Ali died in 1849, his dreams of an advanced, independent Egypt were unrealized, but great strides had been made and efforts to promote modernization were continued under his successors **Khedive Abbas** (1848-1854) and **Khedive Said Pasha** (1854-1863) who granted a concession to the French engineer, **Ferdinand de Lesseps** to build the **Suez Canal**. The project was completed in 1869 during the reign of **Khedive Ismail Pasha** (1863-79) and made Egypt one of the world's most important strategic locations, a status that hampered later attempts to win independence. Like Mohammed Ali, Ismail was an ambitious industrialist and poured millions of pounds into Egypt's infrastructure and building Cairo and Alexandria into modern European style cities. However, he overspent on these projects and lavish celebrations to commemorate the inauguration of the Suez Canal, and in 1879 he was deposed by his son **Tewfiq** (1879-1892) and Egypt was essentially into British receivership.

With his own fiscal control hampered by British and French financiers to whom Egypt was hopelessly indebted, Tewfiq became a target for Egyptian nationalist army officers, and in 1882 generals succeeded in forcing him to name an avid nationalist, **Ahmed Orabi**, Minister of War. When Orabi took measures to free Egypt of British and French influence, the British responded with a military occupation that led to a series of bloody riots and skirmishes between Egyptian and British troops that left Alexandria in shambles.

BRITISH OCCUPATION & THE RISE OF NATIONALISM

When British forces landed at Ismailia and Alexandria in 1882 their stated aim was to restore peace and set Egypt's finances in order but they used these factors as a pretext to use Egypt in pursuing its own interests in Africa and Asia, most notably the Suez Canal. Nominally, Egypt retained its sovereignty, but Tewfiq and his successors were in fact British puppets through whom a series of British Consul-Generals ruled the country. The most famous of these officials was **Lord Cromer**, who effectively ruled Egypt from 1883 to 1907.

A racist and dedicated imperialist, Cromer was also an able administrator who successfully restored Egypt's solvency and improved her infrastructure. Despite these improvements, wealth and political control remained the domain of the British and the landed Turkish gentry, much to the discontent of Egyptian nationalists who began to agitate under the leadership of a young lawyer, **Mostafa Kamil** (not Ataturk).

During World War I, Egyptian nationalists, like their Arab brethren throughout the Middle East, sided with their fellow Muslims, the Ottomans, against the British. When the war ended in 1919, prominent nationalist **Saad Zaghloul** petitioned for a seat at the Versailles peace talks and demanded Egyptian autonomy. The British responded by exiling him to a Malta, a move that triggered riots. Zaghloul was allowed to return and in 1922 a treaty ended Britain's protectorate status, and Khedive Fouad was crowned King. A parliament was established, and Zaghloul's nationalist party, the **Wafd** swept elections.

Though Egypt was nominally independent, the 1922 agreement left the British in control of defense, communications, and the Suez Canal, and the period between 1922 and World War II saw great struggle between the nationalist dominated parliament and the British who continued to use military and economic pressure to manipulate the king and cabinet. In 1935, **Farouk**, succeeded Fouad and a year later signed the **Anglo-Egyptian Treaty**, ending a decade of demonstrations, assassinations, and agitation. The Treaty ended occupation but allowed British forces to remain in the Suez Canal Zone, leaving Egypt short of true independence.

With World War II, tensions again mounted between Egyptians and the British as elements of the Egyptian army and populace supported the Germans who promised them liberation. The Wafd tacitly agreed to support Britain, with the understanding that total independence would be granted following the war. In the autumn of 1942, Egypt's north coast became a focal point as Rommel's Afrika Corps mounted an offensive at **El Alamein** 65 kilometers west of Alexandria. The battle ended in defeat for the Germans and saved the Suez Canal from falling into Axis hands. It was very much a turning point as Churchill noted, "Before El Alamein we never won a major battle; after El Alamein, we never lost one."

THE JULY REVOLUTION OF 1952

Following World War II, Egyptians again focused their efforts on achieving independence. The Anglo-Egyptian Treaty of 1936 officially ended British occupation except in the Canal Zone, but for Egyptian nationalists this was still considered unacceptable, and from leftists to the **Muslim Brotherhood**, frustration mounted with an incompetent king, a complacent aristocracy, and the continued precedence of British interests over those of "the nation." Even the Wafd was considered to have been corrupted by power sharing agreements with British, and lost its credibility as the primary exponent for national aspirations, and the late '40's witnessed a string of political assassinations, by the Muslim Brotherhood, against an entrenched political leadership as tension throughout the country mounted.

Things came to a head in early 1952, when a newly appointed Wafdist Prime Minister, **Nahas Pasha**, sought to abrogate the 1936 Treaty but was dismissed by King Farouk. Fifty Egyptian police officers in Port Said then mutinied only to be massacred by British troops. The next day, January 26, 1952, Cairo exploded in protest as thousands rioted and pillaged virtually every major foreign interest in the city. From that point, there was no question of whether a revolution was going to happen, but rather who would carry it out.

In the early hours of July 23, 1952, a dozen mid-ranged army officers, calling themselves the **Free Officers**, surrounded Abdin Palace demanding the abdication of King Farouk. By daylight, the peaceful transfer of power was announced to the Egyptian people in a radio address by an unknown **Anwar El Sadat** and three days later, King Farouk sailed into exile on his royal yacht to the accompaniment of a 21 gun salute. When asked why Farouk was not tried and hanged for his negligence and crimes against the Egyptian people, **Gamal Abdel Nasser**, the true leader of the July Revolution responded, "History will render the appropriate verdict." In parting, the King warned the Officers' figurehead, General Naguib, "Your task will be difficult. It isn't easy you know, governing Egypt." He died ten years later in a Rome nightclub.

THE EMERGENCE OF NASSER

Publicly the July Revolution was led by General Mohammed Naguib, a well regarded political moderate, but real power lay with the younger officers, specifically **Col. Gamal Abdel Nasser** who, in 1954, publicly assumed the reigns of power. An *Iskanderani* (Alexandrian) of Upper Egyptian stock, the charismatic Nasser quickly gained the respect and love of millions across the Arab World; for the next 20 years, he dominated the Arab agenda and made Egypt an important player in world affairs.

DOMESTIC POLICY

Wet behind the ears, the Free Officers came to power with little in the way of political baggage or ideology. Their primary goals were to rid the country of foreign domination, modernize the economy, and redress the social injustices propagated under the old regime. During the 1950's, they concentrated on **land reform**, sequestering the huge estates of the landed aristocracy and limiting private land ownership to 200 feddans, and later 100. After the 1956 **nationalization of the Suez Canal**, large businesses and those owned by foreigners were also brought under state control, often with little or no compensation. Public health, education, and jobs programs were all drastically expanded, but for the Egyptian consumer, the Nasser years were very lean. Nationalization and a state (often army) managed economy led to a growth in industry but basic commodities were often in short supply. The Nasser regime banned all political parties, including the Wafd, except for the Arab Socialist Union, and with censorship and much heavier handed tactics like torture, choked any semblance of political opposition or debate.

THE 1956 SUEZ CRISIS

In 1956, the United States withdrew support for the Aswan High Dam project in protest of Nasser's arms purchases from communist Czechoslovakia. Nasser then stunned the world by announcing the **nationalization of the Suez Canal** and the intention to use its revenue to fund the Dam. This in turn led Britain, France, and Israel to implement a plan whereby Israel would invade Egypt, and Britain and France would retake the Canal under the pretext of separating the two sides. The plan worked militarily and Egypt's undertrained and underequipped army was soundly defeated and Port Said was heavily damaged; however, international pressure forced the British, French, and Israelis to withdraw.

The Suez Crisis vaulted Nasser into the pantheon of Arab and third world heroes. It also led him to nationalize all foreign assets in Egypt and to expel virtually all foreigners, including many Greeks, Jews, and Italians who had lived in Egypt for generations, and were Egyptian in virtually every respect. The move turned out to be short-sighted by Nasser as they took with them extensive capital and know-how.

JUNE 1967: THE SIX DAY WAR

On the morning of June 5, 1967, Israeli jets simultaneously attacked 17 Egyptian airfields, wiping out within hours a totally unprepared Egyptian air force, paving the way for spectacular ground offenses against Egypt, Syria, and Jordan. Within days, Israeli forces occupied Sinai, the West Bank, and the Golan Heights, creating more than 500,000 Palestinian refugees and leaving another 1.5 million under an Israeli occupation that to this day remains one of the primary obstacles to achieving a lasting peace between Israel and her Arab neighbors.

For Nasser in particular, with whom responsibility for the defeat must lie, the blow was especially painful and the stress of trying to recover almost surely contributed to his early death at age 52, three years later. After the extent of the disaster became apparent, a tearful Nasser appeared on Egyptian television to accept responsibility and to tender his resignation. In a moving show of support, hundreds of thousands of Egyptians packed downtown Cairo, chanting his name and begging him not to step down while the People's Assembly vowed to not leave its hall until the resignation was withdrawn. Nasser did so and spent the next three years rebuilding Egypt's military, efforts that paid off after his death when Egyptian forces successfully crossed the Suez Canal in 1973.

THE WAR OF ATTRITION AND THE ROGERS PLAN

Despite the '67 defeat Nasser remained defiant in the face of Israeli occupation and demands for a separate peace. The Six Day War was never officially ended and military conflict between Egypt and Israel continued in the form of the **War of Attrition**. To extract Egyptian concessions, Israeli forces continuously bombed Egyptian military and "industrial" targets, while Egypt responded by firing artillery, often with success, at Israeli forces on the Suez Canal's east bank. More often than not, the "industrial" targets were the heavily populated cities of the Canal Zone, that suffered thousands of civilian casualties and in 1970 were totally evacuated.

It was in this context that American Secretary of State, **William Rogers**, ushered in an era of American dominated diplomacy that eventually led to Kissinger's "shuttle diplomacy," the Camp David Accords, and finally the Egypt-Israel Peace Treaty of 1979. The initial **Rogers Plan** provided a framework for a cessation of hostilities and an Israeli withdrawal (that never got off the ground), but a second **Rogers Initiative** led to a series of cease-fires beginning in the summer of 1970 and hostilities subsided until the October War of 1973.

SADAT: WAR & PEACE

When the towering Gamal Abdel Nasser passed away at age 52 in 1970, nobody in Egypt or the world imagined that **Anwar El Sadat** would succeed as his permanent replacement, let alone change the course of history. Several years earlier Nasser had named him vice-president, which constitutionally made him the legitimate successor to the president, but Sadat was never more than a bit player and political hack for Nasser, and nobody expected him to survive.

Mired in the War of Attrition with a stagnant economy and knowing he was considered a political lightweight, Sadat urgently needed to secure his position. The obvious way would have been to score a major success against Israel, but Egypt did not possess the military might to initiate an offensive, and her Soviet backers were wary of sparking a confrontation with the Americans, and in any case lacked the quality military hardware that might enable Egypt to challenge the Jewish state. Sadat desired a settlement but given Egypt's weakness, correctly figured that Kissinger and Nixon, who he claimed "held 99% of the cards" would hardly give him the time of day, let alone pressure Israel to the table.

Soon after taking power, Sadat established a reputation for taking bold, and very risky political steps. First, in May '71 only 8 months after assuming power, Sadat purged the Arab Socialist Union of Nasser's main constituency, the leftist old guard who he perceived as a threat to his presidency. Second, in July 1972, Sadat announced that all Russian military personnel – all 15,000 of them – had 10 days to leave Egypt. Just like that he kicked out those who for nearly 20 years had supplied Egypt with the bulk of her military and economic aid, including critical assistance in building the Aswan High Dam.

In addition to stunning the Soviets, the Americans and everybody else, Sadat left unanswered the question as to where Egypt was to receive the weapons and the support needed to force Israel's hand, or even to ensure his political survival. This was designed to please the Nixon administration, which it did, but it did not induce them to pressure the Israelis to come to the negotiating table, let alone return occupied land.

THE OCTOBER WAR & SHUTTLE DIPLOMACY

Yet Sadat continued to take bold risks, and on October 6, 1973, Egypt and Syria stunned the world by overrunning Israeli defenses in Sinai and the Golan Heights. Within 90 minutes of their 2 o'clock assault the Egyptians had established bridgeheads on the east bank of the Suez Canal, breaking the supposedly impregnable Israeli defenses known as the **Bar Lev Line**. Israeli and American intelligence had detected Egyptian troop buildups well in advance of the offensive, but failed to believe that the Arabs had the confidence or the ability to launch an attack; after all, for three years Sadat threatened action but always failed to deliver. When the Soviets, who knew of the impending attack in advance, evacuated their diplomatic corps several days before the offensive, the Americans assumed little more than a fallout between the two countries – no surprise given Sadat's unpredictable behavior.

The spectacular success of the first days of the war vaulted Sadat into the pantheon of Arab heroes and gained him the respect and legitimacy he craved. But hesitation on the part of the Egyptian high command, including Sadat, led to a halt in the offensive and Arab forces failed to exploit their breakthroughs to retake all occupied land in Sinai and the Golan Heights. The Israelis quickly regrouped and with extensive assistance from the United States, launched massive counterattacks first in Sinai, and then Golan. On October 16, after the largest tank battles in history in which Israeli TOW anti-tank missiles proved decisive, forces led by Israeli General Ariel Sharon established bridgeheads on the west bank of Suez, cutting off Egypt's Third Army and effectively winning the war for the Israelis.

Militarily, the October War ended in Arab defeat, but psychologically it was considered a victory. Israeli confidence and the myth of their invincibility had been shot, and the Arabs proved their willingness and ability to take action. Most importantly from Sadat's perspective, Kissinger, (who once dubbed Sadat a "buffoon") accepted him as a legitimate if not equal partner, and by 1975, extensive bargaining and "shuttle diplomacy" yielded two disengagement agreements.

JERUSALEM, CAMP DAVID & SADAT'S ASSASSINATION

Sadat made the biggest gamble of his career in November 1977, and stunned the world by going to Jerusalem. The trip produced no break-throughs, but President Carter succeeded in bringing Sadat and Israeli Prime Minister Begin together at Camp David in September 1978, where after extensive arm twisting by Carter they made an agreement of principles. In exchange for peace and a normalization of relations with Egypt, Israel was to return all occupied Egyptian land. Talks would then begin concerning Palestinian issues with the goal being a gradual move towards Palestinian autonomy and final status negotiations. (The frame-work for addressing the Palestinian question was almost identical to that agreed to 15 years later at Oslo, but the Begin government never intended to implement it.) Many details remained unresolved, but the **Camp David Accords** laid the foundation for the signing of the **Israeli-Egyptian Peace Treaty** in March 1979. To guarantee the peace, the Americans agreed to huge economic aid packages for both countries. Many felt this economic assistance was Sadat's goal from the get go given the anemic state of the Egyptian economy.

On October 6, 1981, while reviewing a military parade in commemo-ration of the October War, Sadat was assassinated in spectacular fashion by troops taking part in the parade itself. Though he was the darling of the world media and American public opinion, Sadat's peace with Israel and his brash style of leadership angered many Egyptians, particularly dedi-cated Islamicists.

A month prior to his shooting, Sadat ordered the arrest of hundreds of intellectuals, journalists, and political opponents including Nasserists and Islamic fundamentalists. Twenty years after the Muslim Brotherhood was forced underground by Nasser (they made an assassination attempt on him in '56), Sadat had allowed its reemergence to counteract leftist elements that he considered the most serious threat to his regime. This coincided with a genuine rise in the number of Egyptians rediscovering their Islamic identity and increased public frustration with economic stagnation that led to "the bread riots" in 1977. Egypt's social fabric was frayed by two decades of failed socialist economic policies, war with Israel, and the failure of Sadat to successfully implement a new economic model. The "Open Door" policies of the late 1970's brought some foreign investments to the country, but money only seemed to find its way into the pockets of a few, namely Sadat's cronies. It was in this context that **Khaled Islambouli**, a low level officer and militant Islamicist, carried out one of the most spectacular political assassinations in history.

MUBARAK: SLOW REFORM

Even more than Sadat before him, **Mohammed Hosni Mubarak** came to power an unknown. A career military officer who made his name as Chief of the Air Force in the '73 war, he was named Vice President in 1976, but maintained a low profile and a reputation as a loyal foot soldier. While continuing Sadat's policy of peace with Israel and good relations with America, Mubarak made it a priority for Egypt to reestablish its position as the "natural leader of the Arab world." This meant building bridges to diverse elements throughout the Arab world from Libya, Syria, and Iraq to Saudi Arabia and Jordan. Egypt was a primary backer of Iraq during its war with Iran and courted other Arab states by using its unique relations with the Americans and the Israelis to put forth the Palestinian cause while acting as a go between. By the time Iraq sparked the Gulf Crisis in August 1990, Egypt not only had been readmitted to the Arab League from which it was expelled after Sadat's Jerusalem trip in 1977, but the headquarters was returned to Cairo, and an Egyptian, Esmat Abdel Meguid, was made Secretary-General.

Economically, reforms initiated by Sadat continued, but at a glacial pace and economic growth during the 1980's was anemic at best. Bureaucratic red tape, over-regulation, and corruption all remained obstacles while what little economic growth did occur was primarily sucked up by the upper echelons of Egyptian society who, after the austerity of the Nasser era, were keen to enjoy prosperity. The slump of oil prices in 1984 curtailed drastically the remittances from the two million Egyptians working in the Gulf. Tourism, another primary source of hard currency, was boosted when Sinai was returned in 1982, but the ups and downs of the Middle East during the 1980's from the civil war in Lebanon to the Intifada hampered Egypt's efforts to attract tourists.

Political liberalization has also been slow, and true power remains in the hands of Mubarak, the National Democratic Party, and the military. While opposition parties are allowed to put forward candidates in elections and publish newspapers and manifestos, the government continues to rig elections and harass, even torture, political opponents, particularly Islamic militants who themselves have used violent means to oppose the regime. Meanwhile, to marginalize the militants, the government has implemented more "Islamic" policies of its own, including censorship of books, films, and other media expression of ideals that do not conform to Islam as dictated by the Grand Mufti of El Azhar.

6. PLANNING YOUR TRIP

BEFORE YOU GO

The **Egyptian Tourist Authority**, *Tel. 1-212-246-6960 in Egypt,* can provide a list of travel agents in your region who organize trips to Egypt and toll free phone numbers for major deluxe hotel chains (Sheraton, Hilton, etc.) operating in Egypt. The Authority operates regional offices listed at the end of the following chapter "Basic Information." Also be sure that your **passport** will be valid.

Besides planning logistics, you may wish to familiarize yourself with Egyptian culture and history. At the end of the following chapter, "Basic Information," I've included a sidebar on important Egyptian literature.

WHEN TO GO

Weatherwise the months between November and February are the most pleasant for visiting Egypt; days are moderate and evenings cool. Unfortunately the nicest weather coincides with the high season for the Egyptian tourist industry when vacancies are harder to find and prices highest, especially during the Christmas and Easter holidays. The autumn and spring are warm, but certainly bearable. In March and April, **khamseen** winds blow from the south causing unpleasant sandstorms.

Summer days are brutal as temperatures regularly soar past one hundred degrees Fahrenheit, but evenings are simply gorgeous, especially when there's a slight breeze. Many travelers devise a schedule whereby they sightsee during the morning and evening hours when the sun and temperatures dip to comfortable levels. There are some advantages to traveling in the summer. Hotel rates are considerably lower-as much as 50%-and crowds are much thinner.

HOLIDAYS & THE RELIGIOUS CALENDAR

The Egyptian calendar is peppered with a variety of secular national holidays and Islamic religious holidays. Because the Islamic calendar is lunar, its religious days move eleven days earlier every year.

EGYPTIAN NATIONAL HOLIDAYS

January 1 - New Years Day
April 25 - Sinai Liberation Day
May 1 - May Day (Labor Day)
July 23 - Revolution Day (1952 Free Officers overthrow of monarchy)
October 6 - National Day (commemorates 1973 invasion of Sinai)

Islamic Holidays	1998	1999	2000
Ramadan	12/21-1/20	12/12-1/09	12/01-12/29
Eid El Fitr	1/21	1/10	12/30
Eid El Adha	4/8	3/28	3/17
Ras El Sinna	4/28	4/17	4/06
(New Year)			
Moulid El Nebi	7/7	6/26	6/15
(Prophet Mohammed's Birthday)			

Coptic Holidays
January 7 - Christmas
January 19 - Epiphany
March 23 - Annunciation
Easter - Spring

WHAT TO PACK

When you travel will decide the extent to which you pack warm clothing. Generally you should wear cool, loose fitting clothing covering the arms and legs. Covering arms and legs is important not only to protect you from the powerful Egyptian sun, but to maintain your modesty when visiting religious sites, and in public places generally. This is especially the case for women and cannot be overemphasized-running about in public in shorts and a halter top for example, simply invites unwanted attention. Do bring shorts and a swimsuit for a cool dip after sightseeing or if you plan to hit the beach. Should you travel during the late fall or winter, packing some medium to heavy clothing jacket is advised, especially you plan to go camping.

Protection from the **sun** will be a priority no matter when you visit Egypt. Pack a hat, sunglasses, and sun screen, especially if you are susceptible to sunburn or plan to go to the beach.

Toiletries and items for personal hygiene are generally available in Egypt but it's most convenient to come well prepared. Mid to upscale hotels provide towels, but otherwise pack your own. Also, put together a small first aid kit that includes aspirin or some other pain reliever, moleskin for blisters, Band-Aids, and cough drops. Even if you think you have an iron stomach, bring something for heartburn, diarrhea, and other potential stomach ailments. Insect repellent is also a good idea, but as Harriet Martineau wrote in her "Hints to Ladies" in 1848, bugs may be a problem, "but not worse than at bad French and Italian inns."

You'll definitely want to bring your **camera**. Standard varieties of Fuji and Kodak **film** as well as video cassettes are available in Egypt, but it is cheaper to buy in bulk in the United States. Also quality control is a problem and much of the film sold at tourist attractions may be expired or damaged by over exposure to heat and sunlight. For black and white photography or other specialized photography, you'll definitely want to bring everything from home. A **flashlight** is handy for climbing in and out of dark tombs or up an down minaret towers. Reliefs inside tombs and pyramids are often poorly lit and power outages, while not as regular as in the past, are not infrequent. A pair of **binoculars** is useful during hikes and boating excursions.

If you're planning to **dive** and wear glasses, investing in a **proscription mask** or goggles can make all of the difference. Otherwise all equipment can be rented.

While English language books are available in Egypt, choice is limited and prices high so bring reading from home.

Finally, nothing can provide inertia for disaster like missing or invalid **documents**. Be sure that tickets, driver's licenses, passports, insurance cards, and credit cards are in order and that you bring them. Make photocopies of these documents and keep them separate from the actual documents in case they are lost or stolen.

MAKING RESERVATIONS

Plane reservations should be made well in advance- three or four months or more if you're planning to travel during Christmas or Easter. Your local travel agent can assist you or you can deal with the airlines directly. EgyptAir, Northwest/KLM, Swissair, TWA, British Air, and Air France are some of the major airlines flying to Cairo. If you do not have a travel agent and would feel more comfortable using one, the Egyptian Tourist Authority provides a list of travel agents in your region that organize trips to Egypt.

Reservations are recommended for moderate and upscale **accommodation**, especially when traveling during the winter. Again, travel agents can assist you or you can make reservations yourself by fax or phone. Hotel rates are significantly lower when reservations are made through a travel agent. Individual listings are provided throughout this book in the destination chapters. Cheaper hotels, pensions, and hostels do not require reservations, but contact them in advance just to make sure.

Nile cruises, a popular way to enjoy Upper Egypt for upscale travelers, generally require prior reservation. Travel agents in the United States, Europe, and throughout Egypt can assist you or you can reserve a directly through the major hotel chains which operate cruise boats. Sheraton, Hilton, and Oberoi are the chains which operate luxury cruises. During the slower months of summer some travelers have been known to approach the captains of half filled liners the day before casting off and negotiating rates as low as $35 a day. This requires good bargaining skills and a bit of luck.

Feluccas offer the budget traveler an alternative to the fancy liners for river travel. Make arrangements with local felucca drivers on the spot in Luxor or Aswan.

PACKAGE TOURS & TRAVEL AGENTS

Travel agents are generally excellent sources of information about prices, accommodations, and transportation and can help you organize your trip. Most can also provide you with information and make reservations for **package tours**. Most such tours last at least a week and the flat fee includes all major expenses including transportation, airfares, accommodation, guides, meals, entertainment etc. Most include Cairo, Luxor, and Aswan and many include a Nile Cruise, though some tours also include Sinai, Alexandria, and even the Western Desert oases. Basically, these tours start at about $900 for 10 days. Talk to your travel agent and national companies like Thomas Cook and American Express. Council Travel, Garber, and Liberty are some of the national discount travel agents that organize package tours.

The **Egyptian Tourist Authority** (*Tel. 1-212-246-6960*) will send you brochures and lists of travel agents in your region who operate tours to Egypt. Newspapers and the internet are also good sources of information about tours and trips to Egypt.

VISAS, CUSTOMS, & ENTRY REQUIREMENTS

A visa and a passport, valid for at least six months is needed to enter Egypt. Tourist visas can be obtained from Egyptian consulates by calling or mailing for the proper application. For Americans and western

Europeans, it is cheaper and more convenient to buy a one month tourist visa for LE18 ($5) at the airport upon arrival. A tourist visa prohibits the visitor from working in Egypt.

Business travelers should obtain a **business visa** that requires various statements of sponsorship and financial guarantees. Call the Egyptian Consulate for applications. **Residence visas** and **work permits** are only eligible to expatriates living and working in Egypt who have jumped through all sorts of hoops and met various standards and requirements. Foreign students at Egyptian universities need to obtain a **student visa** good for one year and requiring proof of registration in a valid university or institution. Universities typically take care of this paperwork. Those wishing to stay for an extended period and do not wish to go through the process of obtaining or do not qualify for a **residence visa** can apply at the Mogamma in Tahrir Square, downtown Cairo for an extended **tourist visa**, good for six months and costing a mere LE18 ($4.75). Six month tourist visas are easily extended without leaving the country.

Vaccines are not required to enter Egypt except for those coming from certain nations in sub-Saharan Africa and Asia. Contact one of the consulates listed below with any questions.

Listed below are addresses and telephone numbers for **Egyptian consulates** in the United States:
• *2310 Decatur Place NW, Washington DC (Tel. 202/232-5400)*
• *1110 Second Ave., New York, NY 10022 (Tel. 212/759-7120)*
• *3001 Pacific Ave., San Francisco CA 94115 (Tel. 415/346-9700)*
• *300 S. Michigan Ave., 7th Floor, Chicago, IL 60603 (Tel. 312/443-1190)*
• *2000 West Loop South #1950, Houston, TX 77027 (Tel. 713/961-4915)*

GETTING TO EGYPT

BY AIR

Cairo International Airport is the most common point of arrival and departure for travelers visiting Egypt and dozens of North American, European, Asian, and Middle Eastern airlines fly to Cairo from all over the world. Check with your local travel agent or the Egyptian Tourist Authority about airlines serving your region. If you're with a package tour, transportation to and from the Cairo airport will be provided. Check with you hotel about shuttles. Otherwise, a taxi or chauffeured "limousine" is best for individual travelers.

Fees to and from the airport are flat, non-negotiable, and usually enforced. Public bus No. 900 also runs a route between the airport and

Tahrir Square downtown, but is difficult to negotiate, especially with suitcases.

There are also flights, mostly charters, from Europe and the Gulf states to **Luxor, Alexandria, Hurghada**, and **Sharm El Sheikh**. Check with your travel agent, airlines, and the Egyptian Tourist Authority for details.

Whenever flying, make reservations as far in advance as possible and **reconfirm** your flight at least 72 hours in advance. Also arrive at the airport at least two hours prior to departure and expect the kitchen sink to be thrown at you when it comes to security.

BY SEA

There are daily ferries ($40-60) between **Aqaba, Jordan**, and **Nuweiba**. There are also ferries between **Jeddah**, **Saudi Arabia** and Suez and Port Safaga. In **Suez** contact Misr Travel in Port Tewfiq at *062/223-949*. Tickets for the 36 hour journey range from LE150-400 depending on the comfort. From **Safaga** there are two or three ferries a week and tickets cost between LE175 and LE300. Be sure that you have a visa for Saudi Arabia before getting on the boat. Getting a berth during the Haj Pilgrimage season is virtually impossible.

It's also possible to ship in from Italy, Greece, and Israel to Alexandria, but it takes days, customs are difficult, and it's no cheaper than flying. Basically it's only recommended only if transporting a car.

BY LAND

After the Sinai was returned to Egypt and peace made with **Israel** in 1979, overland travel has become increasing popular and easy, especially for Americans and Israelis. There are two major border crossings. If you're going between Cairo and Israel, you will pass through the Rafah border and if you're coming or going from South Sinai, you will cross at Taba. Expect massive security coming and going in either direction at either point.

Americans going to Israel from Egypt will be issued a visa at the border. Coming into Egypt, Americans need no visa to enter Sinai as far as Sharm El Sheikh but must attain a visa from the Egyptian Consulate in Tel Aviv or Eilat to visit the rest of Egypt. The same goes for traveling from Arab countries such as Jordan. Going to Arab countries, you must inquire through their consulates well in advance about visa details. Needless to say, driving over the Sudanese and Libyan borders is near impossible and not recommended.

BY BUS

From **Israel**, there are buses to Cairo and to Sinai. Those going to Cairo cross the border at Rafah, those going to Sinai cross at Taba (Eilat on the Israeli side). From Eilat, there are regular buses to the border (NIS4) and on the Egyptian side, taxis and buses will take you to Cairo and Sinai destinations (see Taba section in "Sinai" chapter). **Egged Tours** (*Tel. 03/371-101, 59 Ben Yehuda, Tel Aviv,* operate daily buses to Cairo for about $30. They also run buses from Jerusalem, *Tel. 02/235-7777, 224 Jaffa Road.*

There are also buses to **Libya** from Cairo and Alexandria. In Cairo a one-way ticket to Benghazi costs LE110. Buy the ticket and depart from Qulali Bus Terminal off Gala'a Street near Ramses Square. There are also buses from the Abdel Moneim Riyad Bus Terminal next to the Ramses Hilton. Buses to **Jordan**, **Saudi Arabia**, and **Kuwait** (a whopping 48 hours) also depart from these terminals. Check with travel agents or at the terminals themselves for specifics as they change all the time. Also, be sure that you have the proper visas in order.

From Alexandria's Sidi Gabr Bus Terminal, buses depart for Tripoli and Benghazi in Libya, and also to Amman, Jordan; Riyahd, Saudi Arabia; and even Bahrain.

BY CAR

Private vehicles brought into Egypt require a valid *carnet de passage en douane* from the appropriate automobile club in the country of origin; otherwise you may be subject to paying a customs duty worth twice the value of your vehicle. **Emergency triptyques** are available at the port of entry from the **Automobile and Touring Club of Egypt** and will validate your car for three months. Extensions are available from the Club's branch in Cairo, *10 Kasr El Nil Street, Tel. 02/574-3355.* Drivers must possess a valid international driver's license, available at automobile clubs, and needless to say, insurance, registration, and visas must be in order. Americans, Britons, and Canadians may drive on their domestic license for six months. Talk to the Egyptian embassy or consulate in your country for specifics.

Taxis and **"service"** (pronounced *servees*) **minibuses** link Sinai towns and resorts with the Israeli border. Check destination chapters for specifics.

GETTING AROUND

BY AIR

Egypt is big enough that flying is a handy time saver for those trying to cover the country in a hurry. For example, flying Cairo-Aswan takes barely an hour, while the train takes 16 hours. However, flying is not cheap and does not afford the opportunities to canvass the Egyptian hinterlands or rub shoulders with the locals the way that riding a bus or a train does.

The national carrier, **EgyptAir**, with its subsidiary Air Sinai has a monopoly over domestic routes and fares are comparable to what you might expect to pay for similar routes in other countries. Package tours or tours arranged through travel agents usually include airfares. If traveling independently, make reservations well in advance, especially when traveling during the winter high seasons. Below is a basic table with routes, frequencies and fares as of summer 1997. No flights last longer than two hours. Fares are based on one-way routes.

Route	Frequency	Fare
Cairo-Alex/ Alex-Cairo	5 times weekly	$75 (LE250)
Cairo-Luxor/ Luxor-Cairo	6 flights daily (hi season) 3 daily - low season	$150 (LE500)
Cairo-Aswan/ Aswan Cairo	6 flights daily (hi season) 3 daily - low season	$175 (LE575)
Cairo-Abu Simbel/ Abu Simbel-Cairo	3 daily - high season 1 daily - low season	$180 (LE590)
Cairo-Hurghada/ Hurghada-Cairo	2-4 daily	$150 (LE500)
Cairo-El Arish/ El Arish-Cairo	twice weekly (summer)	$125 (LE450)
Cairo-Marsa Matrouh/ Marsa Matrouh-Cairo	3 weekly (summer)	$125 (LE450)
Cairo-Sharm El Sheikh/ Sharm El Sheikh-Cairo	2-5 daily	$150 (LE500)
Cairo-El Kharga/ El Kharga-Cairo	2-3 weekly	$150 (LE500)
Luxor-Aswan/ Aswan-Luxor	3-6 daily	$75 (LE250)
Aswan-Hurghada/ Hurghada-Aswan	weekly	$100 (LE340)

Aswan-Abu Simbel/	4-9 daily	$75 (LE250)
Abu Simbel-Aswan		
Luxor-Sharm El Sheikh/	3 weekly	$150 (LE500)
Sharm El Sheikh-Luxor		
Alexandria-Hurghada/	twice weekly	$150 (LE500)
Hurghada-Alexandria		
Alexandria-Sharm El Sheikh	twice weekly	$150 (LE500)
Cairo-Taba/	weekly	$150 (LE500)
Taba-Cairo		

EgyptAir offices in the United States
Head Office: *720 Fifth Avenue, Suite 505, New York, NY 10019. Tel. 212/581-5600, 956-6039, Fax 212/586-6599*
• *630 Fifth Avenue, New York, NY 10011. Tel. 212/247-4880/1/5*
• *9841 Airport Boulevard, Los Angeles, CA 90045. Tel. 213/215-3900/40/41/43, Fax 213/215-9547*
• *1255 Post Street, Suite 927, San Francisco, CA. Tel. 415/928-1700/826/852*

BY CAR
You can bring your own car into Egypt easily enough and there are plenty of car rentals throughout Egypt, but keep in mind, driving in Egypt is not like driving anywhere else. Avis, Hertz and other international car rental firms operate throughout Egypt. Prices are reasonable: $30-50 a day for an economy sedan plus 100 kilometers; $60-80 for a fancier sedan; and $100 plus for all terrain and four wheel drive vehicles. Rates drop if you rent for a week or more. Basically, the only place you'd consider renting a car is in Sinai.

To drive in Egypt, you must possess a valid international driver's license (consult your local automobile club or DMV), an Egyptian license, or if you are American, British, or Canadian, you should be able to use your native license for six months. If bringing our own vehicle from overseas, check the "By Car" section above ("Arrivals and Departures") for registration and customs requirements. If renting, be sure the registration is valid and that you keep it in the car at all times. Officers at check points frequently ask to see the car registration and your personal license and will make your life miserable if such documents are not in order. Also, whenever driving, always keep your passport with you. It, and not your driver's license, is the only acceptable form of official identification and your license is not valid without it. There are police and/or military check points on all major roads and you may be asked to provide any or all relevant documents.

Though it's hard to believe, there are fines for speeding (LE80-120). The roads to Faiyoum and the Suez Road to the Ahmed Helmy Tunnel at the Suez Canal are most famous for zapping unsuspecting speeders (virtually everybody). Should you be caught speeding, the police will confiscate your license and issue a receipt. You are a valid driver for a week and in the meantime, you must embark on a journey through Egyptian red tape by going to a designated traffic police station to pay your fine and collect your license. If it is not clear where to go, ask the officer.

A combination of poor maintenance, poor road conditions, and hot weather makes the typical Egyptian road a graveyard for **tires**. Always bring a spare and a jack. Tires can be repaired or replaced at service stations throughout Egypt, but it can often be a time consuming process. When filling with gas, always as an attendant to check the tire pressure tip him and don't forget to tip him (50pt).

Gasoline (*benzene*) is widely available in 80 (*tamaneen*) and 90 (*tisaeen*) octane's and costs about LE1 per liter. Gas station attendants should be tipped at least 50pt. There is no self service in Egypt.

DRIVING WARNING!

When driving in Egypt, make no assumptions about what other drivers will do in certain situations. Due to a lack of proper driving education, zero enforcement of traffic regulations, and a fatalistic sense of overconfidence, many Egyptians drive with dangerous and reckless abandon and typically speed, tailgate, and disobey traffic rules, police, and common sense. They also pass at blind curves and in the mistaken belief that it will save their battery, drive without lights at night!? Instead, they drive blind and to warn oncoming traffic, flash the brights and honk the horn-also a common substitute for turn signals. So, always give yourself plenty of space, avoid driving at night, and pray like hell.

BY BUS

Buses in Egypt are cheap, frequent, and serve virtually every destination. However, even 'deluxe' coaches tend to be crowded, noisy, and somewhat uncomfortable. Hence they are handy for short distances, but longer journies are serious character builders.

There are several regional bus companies in Egypt, all of which make Cairo their hub. The **Upper Egyptian Bus Co.** operates in Upper Egypt and the Western Desert. The **West Delta Bus Co.** covers northern Egypt, including Alexandria, Marsa Matrouh and the Siwa Oasis. The **East Delta Co.** services the Suez Canal destinations (Suez, Ismailia, Port Said), the Red Sea (Hurghada, Safaga) and Sinai (Sharm El Sheikh, Dahab, Nuweiba,

Taba). A national bus company, **SuperJet**, operates fancier coaches throughout the country.

In Cairo and Alexandria there are several major bus stations while in most other cities and towns, there is just one. In **Cairo**, buses for Sinai (LE30-LE50) and Jordan leave from the **Sinai Bus Terminal** in Abbassia. Several buses daily go to Sharm El Sheikh, Taba, Nuweiba, and Dahab. Downtown, the terminals at **Qulali** near Ramses Station service the Upper Egyptian Bus Co. and the East Delta Bus Co. buses to the Canal destinations, El Arish, Hurghada, Upper Egypt, Alexandria and the Delta. Fancier buses to the same destinations depart from **Abdel Moneim Riyad Bus Terminal** north of Tahrir Square next to the Ramses Hilton. In Heliopolis, **El Mazah Bus Terminal** is a hub for buses to all national destinations.

Alexandria features two major bus depots. **Sidi Gabr** is the hub for the SuperJet and West Delta Bus Co. where buses depart for Marsa Matrouh, Siwa, Cairo, and the Suez. Many buses also stop at **El Misr** station in downtown Alexandria which is also the hub for local buses to Delta destinations.

Tickets, particularly for longer journeys (Luxor-Cairo or Cairo-Sharm El Sheikh) are usually purchased in advance at the station from which the bus in question departs. For shorter routes, tickets are typically purchased on the bus itself. Fares vary according the quality of bus and the distance. A one-way fare to Sinai aboard a 'deluxe' coach may cost between LE30-50 while short provincial routes (Suez-Ismailia or Edfu-Aswan) won't be more than LE5. Buses from the Nile Valley to Western Desert Oases (Alex-Siwa or Assiut-Kharga) run LE10-20. The Aswan-Sharm El Sheikh route tops the bill at LE110.

The condition and quality of buses vary. 'Deluxe' coaches commonly used by tourists to reach such destinations as Sharm El Sheikh, Hurghada, and Siwa, are air-conditioned and relatively comfortable, though the seats are a bit narrow. Also, conductors can get carried away with the air-conditioning so bring at least a sweatshirt – even in July. Finally, as you'll find out, Egyptians love noise, and bus passengers (and drivers) are no exception. Besides the usual nonstop chatter, crying babies, and obligatory horn honking, buses inevitably feature blaring radios (typically Egyptopop or the Koran), or worse, a video playing a shoot 'em up Arabic or Hindi movie at full blast.

For some reason, videos are especially prevalent on overnight buses making sleeping all but impossible. Local buses mercifully lack the video and radio, but suffer from overcrowding, terrible suspensions, and a general state of disrepair. Invariably used well beyond their intended life expectancy, local buses tend to be vulnerable to regular break downs. A broken down buses leaves you the option of hitching with a passing minibus, or waiting for the next bus to pass which may or may not have room.

Always hang on to your ticket until disembarking because the *comsari* (inspector) will check and recheck tickets throughout the journey. Also, always keep your passport handy for police check points. Food and drink are sold at exorbitant prices on coaches so bring your own. During longer routes, buses often stop at rest stops where you can buy snacks or even full meals for reasonable prices, though sanitation may be suspect. If in doubt, settle for a tea and sheesha (waterpipe) and wait to reach your destination for a substantial meal.

BY TRAIN

Egypt's first railroad in the quarries of Moqattam in the 1830's was the first in Africa and the Middle East, and by the early decades of the twentieth century, rail replaced boats as the preferred method of moving up and down the Nile Valley. Today, there are almost 6,000 kilometers of track stretching from Alexandria to Aswan and from Marsa Matrouh through the Delta to the Suez Canal in the north. Though the present day Eastern European built system is badly in need of an upgrade, trains are the most efficient (aside from planes) and picturesque method of traveling long distances in the Nile Valley.

Purchase tickets at least a day, if not two, in advance. This is especially true if traveling to Alexandria in the summer or to Luxor or Aswan. In most stations, certain windows or booths sell tickets for a certain class to a certain destination. In Luxor and Aswan, they are relatively well marked and easy for foreigners to figure out. Negotiating **Cairo's Ramses Station** or **Alexandria's Misr Station** can be much more difficult. In Ramses, tickets for Alexandria and destinations north are bought from windows in the main hall. Just ask to make sure you're in the right line. For Luxor, Aswan, and other destinations south, make your way through the main hall, take the pedestrian underpass under tracks 8-11 and go to the ticket offices room to the left. Booths on the right sell first and second class tickets. In Alexandria's Misr Station, first and second class tickets are sold in a room next to the Tourist Office and main cafeteria, not from the booths in the main entrance.

Unless you're up for little bit of red tape, buying tickets in Cairo and Alex can be a taxing and time consuming process. You may consider asking your hotel, or a travel agent to assist you for a 5-10% commission. Seats are always assigned and designated in Arabic; do not hesitate to ask an attendant or inspector for assistance. An attendant who assists you with luggage will expect-and should get-a small tip (50pt).

Passengers have a wide variety of choices when it comes to comfort and price. **First class** cars are spacious and feature wide seats and considerable leg room. They also recline and are quite comfortable for sleeping during long night trains. Like buses they tend to be over air-conditioned so bring a pullover and though food and drink are sold on board, it is expensive and of poor quality. The only real drawbacks are the less than spotless bathrooms and the televisions blasting Arabic movies and music videos late into the night. Though prices have practically doubled in recent years, traveling first class is still amazingly cheap. A one-way fare from Cairo to Luxor (11 hours), for example, costs LE82 (LE50 for students).

Second class is very similar to first class only the seats are not quite as spacious and the clientele more middle class. It is also about 30% cheaper. **Third class** seating comprises of simple wooden benches and fellow passengers are just as likely to be goat or chicken as a human being. Incredibly cheap (you can go anywhere for just a few pounds), third class is not available on direct trains between major destinations and is limited to "local" trains that move at a glacial pace and stop in every excuse for a village.

Carlson WagonLits sleepers making the Cairo-Luxor-Aswan route once daily are the most comfortable and expensive way to travel by train. There are only sleeping compartments, not seats, and trains also feature lounge and dining cars. Reservations must be made in advance through your travel agent at home or in Cairo. Otherwise, make reservations directly through the Wagon-Lits office at Ramses Station in Cairo (9am-3pm daily) just outside the main station building (*Tel. 02/574-9474, Fax 02/574-9074*). In Luxor, reservations can be made in the train station at a special window from 9am-2pm and from 5pm-8pm. A one-way fare is roughly LE400.

BY PUBLIC TAXI

One of the most popular means of intercity travel is the beloved **service** (pronpunced *ser-vees*), or public taxi. Usually a Peugeot seven-seater station wagon, Japanese minivan, or canvas covered pick-up, the service is faster than buses and cheaper than trains. However, they can be less comfortable and inefficient when not making a direct route as they constantly stop to let people on or off. Service depots are usually next to the bus and/or train stations, where drivers will be hollering their destinations, e.g. *Iskandaria!* (Alexandria) or *Misr!* (Cairo). Find one going to your destination and when it fills up, you'll be off.

As for payment, there are no tickets or set prices, so you'll have to feel your way. Egyptians simply pay when getting on or off, often without even discussing prices with the driver. For short rides of less than an hour 25-50pt is the norm; for an hour LE1; for two hours, LE2. For a longer jaunt, say between Cairo and Hurghada (5-6 hours), expect to pay LE5-10 and expect to be charged LE1-2 for each piece of luggage. As a foreigner, they may ask you for more. Paying a pound or two more than the locals is appropriate, but do not hesitate to bargain or resist paying an obviously outrageous fee.

BY PRIVATE TAXI

Taxis offer the flexibility of having your own car, without having to personally negotiate Egyptian traffic, and are handy for reaching sites not easily accessed by public transportation. They are considerably more expensive than public transport, but can still be very reasonable, especially if you can split the cost amongst a group. Hiring a taxi for day trip to Alexandria from Cairo for example, the driver may ask for LE300 and after bargaining you may get him down to LE200. Divided four ways, it comes to LE50 ($15) per piece which is incredibly cheap by American standards.

BY BOAT

Between the Nile and the two coasts, Egypt is often best explored by boat, and ferries are also a practical means of getting around. For example, there is a daily **ferry** service between Siqalla Port at Hurghada and Sharm El Sheikh Port. Tickets cost LE110 and can be bought from hotels, travel agencies, or at the ports themselves. The ride lasts from six to eight hours and can be rough, and especially unpleasant for those prone to seasickness.

One of the classic Egyptian experiences is the three-day **felucca** voyage from **Aswan to Luxor**. Interspersed with stops at the magnificent temples of Kom Ombo, Edfu, and Esna, the slow and easy journey is a superb opportunity to soak up the magic of the rural Nile Valley in Upper Egypt. They are easily arranged directly through felucca captains in Aswan or through local hotels. Rates are usually about LE50 ($15) per person per day. See the sidebar on page 360 for details.

Those with a bit more budgetary flexibility may opt instead to join a **Nile Cruise** to leisurely enjoy the sights of Upper Egypt. Cruises last 3-7 days and cost between $50-$200 a day depending on the luxury standard of the boat and the season. Summer rates are decidedly lower, and prices include food, accommodation, monument entrance fees, and guides. Boats depart from Luxor and Aswan and stop at the magnificent temples of Kom Ombo, Edfu, and Esna. While you're not sightseeing the boat leisurely makes its way up or down the Nile affording you the opportunity to enjoy the timeless beauty of the Nile and the surrounding countryside.

There are more than two hundred liners making the Luxor-Aswan/ Aswan-Luxor cruise and most travel agents in the United States who operate tours have contracts with specific boats. The Sheraton *(Tel. 1-800-325-3535),* Hilton *(Tel. 1-800-HILTONS),* and Oberoi *(1-800-5OBEROI)* hotel chains control nearly thirty percent of the market and offer mostly upscale cruises that cost between $60-$150 a day, but if you make arrangements through a travel agent, rates may be lower. For a comprehensive list of cruise lines and agents contact the Egyptian Tourist Authority *(Tel. 1-212-246-6960).*

In Egypt, cruises can be arranged through any major travel agency and when tourism is slow, as during the summer, you can even negotiate cutthroat deals by directly approaching the boats themselves-sometimes rates dip as low as $35 a day, everything included.

HOTELS & ACCOMMODATIONS

Accommodations in Egypt span a wide spectrum from lavish palaces managed by international chains to fleabag piles and charming pensions. In between are establishments of all degrees of quality and price and you should be able to find something in your budget range. Because of over-expansion in the hotel industry in recent years, finding a room is never a problem, but popular and well-known hotels are often booked during the high seasons so it's wise to make reservations. Hotel rates are almost always cheaper when booked through an agent.

The Egyptian Ministry of Tourism has classified most hotels and rated them between one and five stars. **Five star** hotels are deluxe affairs, often managed by international chains with rooms invariably equipped with modern amenities and comforts including air-conditioning, phones, satellite television, and clean, private baths. They are almost always large and have several restaurants, a swimming pool, a bank, shops, and a nightclub. Rates almost never dip below $80 unless you book through an agent or join a tour.

Four star hotels are less stately but the rooms are also equipped with modern amenities. They also may be lacking a certain qualification for a five star rating such as a nightclub. Pricewise, they are often a tad lower than the deluxe hotels, but don't expect to pay less than $60 a night.

Three star establishments are moderately priced and considerably less luxurious than five and four star hotels. Most are new and located in charmless concrete blocks. Amenities usually include air-conditioning, private bath, and a phone, but the appliances tend to be less reliable and the service can sometimes be a bit casual. They usually have restaurants and possibly a bar or nightclub, and a modest, usually rooftop pool. Prices range from LE50 ($15) to $75 and during the low season or anytime business is slow, you may be able to bargain as much as a 50% discount from listed prices. These hotels may or may not accept credit cards.

One and two star hotels are invariably cheap (LE10-50) and services and amenities vary widely. Some of these establishments may have air-conditioning, others not even fans. Hygienic standards are not as well regulated but that doesn't mean every one star is a health hazard either. Often one or two star hotels are homely and charming pensions.

There are some **youth hostels** but they are often crowded or reserved for Egyptians only. Furthermore since you can always find hotels equally cheap with better accommodation, they generally aren't worth it.

Bedouin aside, **camping** has not really caught on. The only places where it's really possible or appropriate are in the deserts and oases of Sinai and the Western Desert. Since it's illegal and dangerous to camp off main roads without a guide or permission, most people arrange camping trips or safaris on the spot in the oases or in Sinai. It is possible to camp on beaches in the Red Sea and Sinai but accessing sites is difficult without private transportation. Also, because the Red Sea and Sinai beaches were heavily mined by both Egyptians and Israelis during the Arab-Israeli wars, it's dangerous to camp off or far away from established sites.

HOTEL CHAINS IN EGYPT

Hilton International (Tel. 800/HILTONS). Operates two landmark hotels in Cairo, six luxurious resorts on Red Sea and Sinai coasts, and an assortment of Nile cruise ships.

InterContinental (Tel. 800/327-0200). Modern, megahotels in Sharm El Sheikh, Hurghada, and Cairo.

Marriott (Tel. 800/228-9290). Two luxurious resorts in Sharm El Sheikh and Hurghada. The Cairo Marriott is a hammed up Arabesque masterpiece.

Movenpick (Tel. 800/44UTELL). Expansive "villages" in Luxor, Cairo, Sharm and Hurghada; Cairo hotel by the Pyramids.

Sonesta Hotels (Tel. 800/SONESTA). Specializes in Red Sea resorts.

Accor Coralia (Tel. 800/233-9208). With Mercure, Novotel, and Sofitel, Accor operates more hotels (21) in Egypt than any other chain including such legends as the Cecil (Alexandria), Old Winter Palace (Luxor), and Old Cataract (Aswan).

Renaissance International (Tel. 800/228-9898). Modern hotels in Sinai, Cairo, and Alexandria.

Oberoi Hotels (Tel. 800/5OBEROI). Mena House Hotel at the foot of the Pyramids and the cruise ships are among the finest in Egypt.

Sheraton Hotels (Tel. 800/325-3535). Three luxury hotels in Cairo and a half dozen Nile cruise boats.

7. BASIC INFORMATION

BUSINESS HOURS

Stores generally open from 9 or 10am-7pm six days a week, and take Friday or Sunday off. Many close during the middle of the day from 1-3pm or 2-4pm, but those catering to tourists, like **bazaars** at the Khan El Khalili tend to remain open. They close on Sunday and major Islamic holidays.

Public sector institutions like **post offices**, **ministries**, and public sector operated businesses close on Fridays and major national and Islamic holidays. Their hours for public business tend to be short as they open at 9am and close at 1 or 2pm. **Banks** generally follow the same hours, but **money changing** outlets may reopen at 5 or 6pm and close again in at 8 or 9pm. Some banks in major hotels (i.e. Nile Hilton) open 24 hours, seven days a week.

During the Islamic month of **Ramadan**, when Muslims fast from sunrise to sundown, business hours throughout Egypt adjust accordingly. Stores and medical clinics reduce their daytime hours and everything shuts down by 3 or 4pm depending on when the sun sets. Most reopen at 8pm and don't shut down until midnight or later. Banks and public sector establishments maintain their normal short day hours, and restaurants, except those catering to tourists, close entirely during the day, but are open throughout the night.

COST OF LIVING & TRAVEL

For those with the resources, Egypt is one of the most splendid and extravagant vacation settings in the world with quality lodging, service, and dining to match. The rest of us can take advantage of Egypt's bargain prices to enjoy the country for costs below what we would pay in our own countries.

Public transportation is an excellent bargain. Intra-city commuting on public buses or metro rarely costs more than 50 piasters (15 cents) a ride while taxis are also cheap by western standards. **Intercity** buses and trains are also extremely reasonable by American and West European standards. For example: a one way, first class fare from Cairo to Luxor costs LE81-the equivalent of $25. Rates for car rentals and airfares are comparable to those in the West. Package tours include most transportation.

Eating a full meal for less than a dollar is possible on the street if you avoid meat. Sit-down restaurants, including many which cater primarily to tourists will generally feed you a hearty meal for LE30 or less while fancy hotel and European style restaurants can charge European style prices-LE40 at least for a meal and LE3 for Coke which at the kiosk outside costs 30 piasters. Food purchased at the retail level, like fresh produce from the local market or bread sold at the local bakery, is extremely cheap as it is subsidized to be affordable for those living on the very lean average Egyptian salary.

Accommodation prices also run the gamut from world class international hotels charging $80 a night and up to bare-boned budget establishments renting rooms for as little as LE10 ($3.50) or less. Keep in mind that quoted prices, especially in mid and upscale hotels do not include a hefty 17% in taxes that will be added. The high and low seasons vary according to region. In Alexandria, hotel rates soar during the summer when Cairenes invade the place for summer vacation, while in Upper Egypt (Luxor and Aswan), hotels are ripe for discounts during summer and charge higher rates during the Christmas and Easter holidays.

Other expenses include entrance fees for tombs, temples, and other attractions, ranging between LE3 ($1) and LE30 ($10); and baksheesh, which includes tips for waiters, drivers, tour guides, and anybody else who may assist you during your trip. Film, toiletries, and other necessities you may need to purchase in Egypt are generally slightly cheaper than in the West.

DISABILITIES

Travelers with disabilities will find Egypt less equipped to deal with their needs than most developed countries. However, most upscale tourist facilities, including hotels, can accommodate you, and historic monuments, with some exceptions like tombs deep in the ground, are accessible. Be sure to discuss any concerns with your travel agent, tour operators, and hotels when making arrangements.

ELECTRICITY

Egypt uses the **220 volt current** compatible with European appliances but will quickly burn right through those designed to handle the 110 volts coming through American outlets. If you are bringing a laptop computer or some other appliance such as a traveling iron, make sure you have an adapter that makes the necessary adjustments or get one from an electronics store. Some deluxe hotels are equipped with adapters to accommodate electric shavers and hairdryers.

Common varieties of **batteries** are available in Egypt but if you require specialized batteries for something like a hearing aid or camera, bring extras from home.

HEALTH CONCERNS

Egypt is the type of place where a bit of misfortune can go a long in making the trip of a lifetime miserable; an hour too long in the sun could mean sunburns and/or heat stroke (absolute misery) while a sip of bad water could lead to diarrhea or worse. Having scared you with that, the point is that common sense and a few cautionary measures should ensure a safe and healthy journey.

Drinking & Water

It is said that he who drinks from the Nile will return to Egypt. Upon his arrival in the 1830's Robert Curzon knelt by the river to drink only to remark that he, "was disappointed in finding it by no means so good as I had always been told it was." Needless to say, you too will be disappointed too if you try to drink from the Nile. However, drinking plenty of **water** will be necessary to avoid dehydration and heat stroke, but stick to bottled mineral water (which purportedly come from springs in oases). Even during the cooler months when the Egyptian sun is deceptively effective at sapping energy, it's important to get plenty of fluids.

Drinking water is especially recommended when suffering diarrhea problems. Tap water may upset an unfamiliar digestive system, lead to diarrhea or worse, and ruin a trip in which you've invested time and money, so stick to bottled water and avoid ice. *Baraka* and *Siwa* are the most popular brands and can be purchased just about anywhere, but are several times more expensive at tourist sites and major hotels than in local convenience stores and kiosks.

Medical care

Egyptian doctors are on average well trained and competent, but medical infrastructure and staff support (nursing) can be less than adequate. Hospitals are listed in destination chapters, and the emergency number for **ambulance** – the Egyptian 911 if you will-is 123. Many upscale **hotels** have infirmaries and trained medical staff on the premises and can refer you to a doctor or hospital as needed. **Pharmacies** are a dime a dozen in every Egyptian town and village and medicine is incredibly cheap by American standards. In Cairo, you can also call the medical officer at the **American Embassy** *(Tel. 02/355-7371)* with any concerns.

Insurance

Check with your insurance company about whether your current health insurance policy will cover any expenses incurred in Egypt and overseas generally. If it does not, you may consider getting some overseas coverage.

MONEY & BANKING

The **Egyptian pound**, designated by "**LE**," contains one hundred **piasters** and is worth about 30 cents. Piasters, designated by "pt" or "p", comprise millemes which for all practical purposes are obsolete. In the past, evading artificially high official exchange rates and searching out the best rate in the black market was standard procedure for those looking to exchange dollars. In the early 1990's the pound was devalued, pegged to the US dollar and settled, more or less, at it's current rate of LE3.40 to $1.

Bank notes come in denominations of 25pt, 50pt, LE1, LE5, LE10, LE20, LE50, and LE100. Coins come in 1pt, 5pt, 10pt, 20pt, and 25pt. Always keep plenty of small change on hand to use for public telephones, bus fares, and other small transactions. Taxi drivers and the like are often unwilling or unable to make change so it's important to be able to make exact change whenever possible. It's also handy for baksheesh (tips).

Traveler's cheques are a safe way to carry currency and you should not have a problem finding banks in major cities and towns willing to accept American Express, Visa, or Thomas Cook cheques; many banks or money-changers charge a commission of one or two percent. Cash is always handy and not a problem to exchange, especially if you present the new high-tech one hundred dollar bills.

Major **credit cards** (Visa, MasterCard, and American Express) are accepted by most mid and upscale hotels and restaurants, as well as car rental firms and merchants. You can also use credit cards to take out a cash advance at most banks though it may cost a small fee-LE1-2. **Automatic teller machines** are becoming more common though some glitches need to be worked out and they often run out of cash, so don't count on them. Check the "Practical Information" sections of individual destination chapters for specific listings of banks and other institutions that exchange currency.

POST OFFICE & MAIL

Post offices are located throughout major cities, towns, and even villages. Major offices open daily except Friday from 8:30am-7pm while smaller branches close at 3pm. Letters and postcards sent to Europe or the United States can take anywhere from a few days to several weeks when sent by normal mail and packages take longer. For faster delivery, use the **Express Mail Service** (EMS), the Egyptian variety of priority mail, which for a higher price (LE30 for letters) will have your parcel in Europe or the States within 48 hours. **Federal Express** and **DHL** also operate in major cities throughout Egypt. Check "Practical Information" sections of destination chapters for specific listings.

Hotels will usually mail letters and postcards for you and some will receive mail on your behalf and hold it. Post offices have **Poste Restante** but items may get lost or misfiled as most postal workers are not familiar with English. American Express offices hold mail for clients and tends to be more dependable. Packages sent overseas will have to be examined by customs officials at the post office so don't wrap them first.

MEDIA & NEWS

Cairo is the media capital of the Arab world but until a few years ago, news in English was limited to *The Egyptian Gazette*, its equivalent on local television, and if you were fortunate to have a short wave radio, the BBC World Service. In recent years deregulation has led to a media explosion, both in print and electronic media. Many will claim that the BBC World Service is still the best source for international news and information (especially for cricket scores) but a satellite and cable boom (just take a peak at the Cairo skyline) means that CNN, CNBC, ESPN, and dozens of European and Arab channels are now available for those endowed with a satellite, including most major hotels.

A good deal of news and information is also available in print. *Time*, *Newsweek*, *The Economist*, and numerous style and special interest magazines (mainly sports and computers) are available at major newsstands and bookstores in cities frequented by foreigners. For newspapers, *USA Today* and *The International Herald Tribune* are available, usually a day or two after publication, as are European and British periodicals.

Should you take an interest in local affairs, a number of home grown English language publications have emerged to complement the old standby government mouthpiece, *The Egyptian Gazette*. Worthy for its historic significance – it was founded in 1874 and launched the careers of such great Egyptian journalists as Mohammed Heikal – the *Gazette* is often mocked for its shameless government propping, and its chief editor Samir Ragab is indeed a classic government hack, whose editorials should be sampled if only for a good laugh. Whatever Mubarak does, whether its cutting the ribbon for a new factory in Zagazig or meeting Bill Clinton on the White House lawn, he's the lead story. On the practical side, the paper does feature information like film and television listings.

Other English language newspapers and magazines may be less entertaining but are far superior journalistically. *Al Ahram Weekly*, an English language weekly newspaper published by Egypt's top daily, *Al*

Ahram, provides excellent insight into major political issues in Egypt and the Middle East-which usually means the Arab-Israeli question. The five to ten weekly articles bashing Israel certainly gets tiring, even for those supporting the Arab point of view, but the *Weekly* prints excellent articles about Egyptian culture and history, and translated editorials by the Arab World's top journalists. *The Middle East Times* is more objective than the *Gazette* and the *Weekly* and covers a broader spectrum of issues, and the biweekly *Cairo Times* is even more colorful, daring, and witty.

For magazines, the major English monthly, *Egypt Today*, prints well written and interesting articles about Egyptian society and culture as well as helpful information about goings on and a directory of services throughout Egypt. The newer *Pose* magazine has expanded beyond its initial style and fashion focus to include articles about arts, culture, and society. The light reading *Life Nite Egypt* emphasizes night time entertainment and may be the most entertaining and humorous magazine in Egypt.

SHOPPING

For many visitors a trip to the medieval bazaars of the Khan El Khalili, the give and take of bargaining, and the sense of relief and reward after consummating a deal is a highlight during their travels to Egypt. To others, the relentless hawkers that seem to materialize at every turn and the sense that every Egyptian they meet is trying to rip them off, ruins the magic of what could be the trip of a lifetime. To be sure, finding the right goods for the right price can be a trying experience and requires patience and even toughness, but if you take the time to sift through the cheap and the tacky, Egypt offers much in the way of treasures for you to take home. Items sold by hawkers at the Pyramids, Valley of the Kings, and other major tourist sites are undoubtedly several times over priced, of very poor quality, and you must bargain to avoid getting scammed. Should you be interested in purchasing souvenirs, your best bet is the **Khan El Khalili Bazaar** in Cairo where the most extensive choice is available and price competition the greatest.

From intricate inlaid gaming tables and impeccably crafted gold jewelry to the tackiest alabaster sphinx lit with an orange light bulb inside, the variety of the goods sold in Egypt is astounding. Some of the more popular items include inlaid boxes and backgammon boards, papyrus, engraved brass and copper, ceramics and glass, jewelry of all sorts, and clothing. Prices and quality vary widely so whatever catches your fancy, take the time to shop around and compare prices. Ask shopkeepers to show you a variety so that you can get an idea of what's available in terms of price and quality. When it comes to **inlaid work**, the glossier items probably contain plastic rather than mother of pearl. **Gold** and **silver** should be stamped to indicate authenticity, and items you intend to use, whether it be a waterpipe, a cassette tape, or anything else, should be tested. Keep in mind that you may be limited by how much you can physically carry back home and that fragile goods like glass and ceramics need to be carefully packed to avoid damage.

One of the great challenges confronting nearly all tourists in Egypt is to avoid falling prey to **scam artists**. If, after being approached by a charming man in the street, the next thing you know you're sipping tea in his papyrus or perfume shop, listening to stories about his brother who lives in Chicago - or wherever it is you just told him you're from- you're in trouble. Some merchants will go to any lengths to lure foreigners into their shops and those naive enough to take the bait are most susceptible to their next scam - the actual sale of goods. Never go into a shop unless it is by your own accord. Do not believe offers which are too good to be true or do not sound right. If you have any doubts about the authenticity of the product you're interested in purchasing don't buy it. If purchasing from somebody in the street, do not give money until the goods are in your possession.

Antiques cannot be taken out of the country without the permission of the Department of Antiquities and most advertised as such are probably fakes anyway. You should also be aware that since the worldwide **ivory ban** was implemented you can be prosecuted for taking even the smallest amounts out of Egypt or into your own country. Formerly used in many handicrafts, it has been widely replaced by camel bone and other substitutes.

For listings of shopping possibilities and markets, look under the "Shopping" sections of destination chapters. For bargaining tips see the "Bargaining" sidebar under the "Khan El Khalili" heading in "Seeing the Sights" in the Cairo chapter (13).

STAYING OUT OF TROUBLE

You should have a trouble free visit to Egypt if you follow some basic guidelines and use common sense.

• Make a copy of your passport and other important documents like tickets, and insurance cards in case of theft or loss.

• Check with your travel agent and the State Department about potential travel advisories. If traveling to Upper Egypt, ask about it specifically as it has been the part of Egypt most susceptible to political violence and instability.

• Whatever you do, do not get caught with hashish or any other type of illicit **drugs**. Egyptian drug laws are extremely harsh and you cannot expect special treatment from the Egyptians because you are a foreigner, nor should you expect any special assistance from your embassy. Egyptian prisons are hell.

• Women especially should take care to dress modestly whenever going into public and particularly when visiting religious monuments. That means covering arms to the elbows and legs past the knees.

• On the Red Sea coast or anywhere in Sinai, do not wander, hike, or drive off major highways or beaches because of **mines**. Though Egypt has not been at war for 25 years, it remains one of the five most heavily mined countries in the world.

• Do not wander or drive off major roads in the desert without permission from the Ministry of Interior, extra gas and water, and sufficient navigational tools.

• Though Egypt enjoys one of the lowest violent **crime** rates in the world, especially compared to the United States, or even Europe, you must always beware of pickpockets and petty thieves-especially in crowded places like public buses. Always lock your hotel room and deposit valuables in a safety deposit box if possible. Some travelers, usually those staying in cheaper hotels, like to bring their own padlock just in case those on hotel doors are less than sufficient.

TELEGRAMS, TELEXES & FAXES

Telegram, telexes, and faxes can be sent from offices in or next to post offices and telephone exchanges as well as from business centers and major hotels. Check the "Practical Information" sections of destination chapters for listings.

TELEPHONES

Public telephones are located in telephone offices called **centrales**, and major public sector buildings like post offices and train stations, and on the street. Centrales usually contain specific booths for local calls, domestic calls, and international calls. Some are coin operated (for local calls), others, especially those for international calls, are operated with **calling cards** purchased at a booth inside the centrale for values of LE30 or LE40. Long distance calls, both foreign and domestic, can usually be paid for in cash in which case the clerk takes the number and dials it for you. Except for credit card calls through AT&T or Sprint, phoning long distance is cheapest from a centrale, but lines are often long and clerks less than friendly.

Most hotels can place long distance and local calls, but add a hefty surcharge of 100-200% meaning international calls may cost upwards of LE10 per minute with the first three minutes costing as much as LE35.

The cheapest way to call the United States is through AT&T at 510-0200 in Cairo or 02-510-0200 from outside Cairo if you have an AT&T

phone card. Sprint and MCI also offer services in Egypt. Check with your hotel or the *Yellow Pages* for their numbers.

If you need a phone number not listed in this book, there is a Cairo *Yellow Pages* with fairly comprehensive listings. Otherwise, hotel personnel can often help, and newspapers and magazines like *Egypt Today* and *Al Ahram Weekly* list phone numbers for restaurants, theaters, and other public establishments.

INTERNATIONAL & DOMESTIC PHONE CODES

The international code for Egypt is '02'. For example, if you need to reach Egypt from the United States, dial 011-20-city code & number. To reach other countries from Egypt, you must dial '00' before the appropriate country code.

Country Codes for major countries

United States/Canada	1	Germany	49
United Kingdom	44	Israel	972
Australia	61	France	33
Greece	30	Italy	39
India	91	Jordan	962
Mexico	52	Netherlands	31
Saudi Arabia	966	Kuwait	965
South Africa	27	Switzerland	41

Egyptian City Codes

(when dialing from out of Egypt, drop the initial '0')

Cairo	02	Alexandria	03
Luxor	095	Aswan	097
Assiut	088	Dahab	062
Dakhla	092	Farafra	010+1405
Hurghada	065	Ismailia	064
Kharga	092	Kom Ombo	097
Marsa Matrouh	03	Nuweiba	062
Port Said	066	Qena	096
Sharm El Sheikh	062	Safaga	065
Siwa	03+934026	Sohag	093
Suez	062	Taba	062

TIME

Egypt is two hours ahead of Greenwich Mean Time (GMT) and seven hours ahead of Eastern Standard Time in the United States. Egypt does go on daylight savings time but the scheduling may differ from the United States and Europe, especially when Ramadan is a factor.

TIPPING & BAKSHEESH

Five-ten percent is appropriate in most restaurants including local food stands. Many establishments add a service charge to the bill, but you can be sure that it fails to find its way to the staff. Doormen, porters, guards at monuments, and other service personnel (except in offices) will expect, and should get, and small tip of 50pt to a pound for whatever it is that they do. A little extra effort or going beyond the call of duty, will deserve a bit extra. When in doubt, err on the high side keeping in mind that most service personnel earn obscenely paltry salaries of less than the equivalent of $40 a month. A few extra piasters out of your pockets makes far more difference to them than to you.

Baksheesh, extends beyond the normal western concept of "tipping." In his classic 1929 guidebook, Karl Baedeker wrote, "The average Oriental regards the European traveler as a Croesus, therefore as fair game, and feels justified in pressing upon him with a perpetual demand for bakshish" – and still today you will indeed find yourself fighting off such demands, sometimes constantly. It will be expected any time bureaucratic or legal corners are cut on your behalf. For example, should a guard let you climb a pyramid, which is officially forbidden, he will expect at least a few pounds. Baksheesh may also be necessary to carry out legitimate bureaucratic procedures like procuring certain permits.

The term also refers to the giving of alms to the poor-an important Islamic tradition. Giving a few piasters to an obviously needy person is appropriate, especially during special times of the year like Ramadan, but you should be wary of beggars in the street. Many of them are scam artists who know they can effectively pull at the heart strings of naive foreigners. Be particularly cautious of those who materialize at tourist attractions.

WHERE TO FIND OUT MORE ABOUT EGYPT

For basic information about traveling to Egypt, including the names of travel agents which organize trips to Egypt, contact the **Egyptian Tourist Authority** at the following locations:

In the US
• *630 Fifth Avenue, Suite 1706, New York, NY 10111. Tel. 212/332-2570, Fax 212/956-6439*

- *Wilshire San Vicente Plaza, 8383 Wilshire BLVD, Suite 215, Beverly Hills, CA 90211. Tel. 213/653-8815, Fax 213/653-8961*
- *645 North Michigan Avenue, Suite 829, Chicago, IL 60611. Tel. 312/ 280-4666, Fax 312/280-4788*

Inside Canada
- **Office De Tourisme Du Gouvernement Egyptien,** *1253 McGill College Avenue, Suite 250 H3B 2y5, Montreal Quebec. Tel. 514/861-4420, Fax 514/ 861-8071*

Inside the UK
- **Egyptian State Tourist Office,** *3rd Floor West Egyptian House, 170 Piccadilly, London Wiv 9DD, England, UK. Tel. (171) 493-5282/3, Fax (171) 408-0295*

Also contact your travel agent and major airlines for further information about flights, or cruises.

Websites
- *www.discover.egypt.com*
- *www.idsc.gov.eg*
- *www.egypt.com*
- *www.pharos.bu.edu*
- *www.sas.upenn.edu*
- *www.arab.net/egypt*

MODERN EGYPTIAN LITERATURE

Naguib Mahfouz, winner of the 1988 Nobel Prize for Literature, is Egypt's most famous writer of fiction and is known for his brilliant story telling and his ability to capture the flavor of life in Egypt during the 20th century, a period of great change and transition. "The Cairo Trilogy," comprising "Palace Walk," "Palace of Desire," and "Sugar Street," spans the first half of the twentieth century and tells the story of a family that lives on Bayn El Qasrayn Street in Cairo and how it faces the challenges of everyday life during a period of great change in Egyptian society. "Midaq Alley," about life in an alley in Islamic Cairo, is in a similar vein.

Other important works by Mahfouz include "The Children of Gebalawi"; "Miramar", a short novel about post-Revolution Alexandria; "The Thief and the Dog"; "Respected Sir"; "Autumn Quail"; "The Beginning and the End"; "The Wedding Son"; and "The Beggar." All books are published in Egypt by the American University in Cairo Press and are widely available in Egypt. In the United States, they are published by Doubleday and can be found in most major bookstores and libraries.

Other well regarded Egyptian authors include Mahfouz's mentor **Taha Hussein**; *playwright* **Tewfiq El Hakim**; *short story specialist* **Yusuf Idris** *("The Cheapest Nights");* **Gamal El Ghitani** *(social criticism and political satire, "Incidents in Zafraani Alley," "Zayni Barakat"); and the Greek Alexandrian* **Constantine Cavafy** *("Collected Poems").*

"Khul-Khaal: Five Egyptian Women Tell Their Stories" by **Nayra Atiya** *is perhaps the best first insight into the lives and concerns of women in Egypt. Published by Syracuse University Press and the American University Press; available in the United States and Egypt.*

"Haram Years: Memoirs of an Egyptian Feminist 1879-1924" by **Hoda Shaarawi** *is the famous autobiography of Egypt's first leading feminist.*

"The Hidden Face of Eve" by one of Egypt's most prominent women of letters, **Nawal El Saadawi**, *addresses a number of controversial issues concerning women in Egypt including family relations, sexuality, and female circumcision. Published by Beacon. She has also written several powerful novels about women in modern Egypt. The most famous, "Woman at Point Zero" (Humanties Press), is a gripping tale about a prostitute who is sentenced to death for murdering her pimp. "My Grandmother's Cactus: Stories by Egyptian Women" is a collection of short stories by Egyptian writers. Translated by Marylin Booth and published by Quartet.*

"Women in Egyptian Public Life" by one of the American University in Cairo's most respected scholars, **Earl A. Sullivan**, *focuses on the increasingly visible role played by women in Egyptian public life. Published by the American University in Cairo Press and widely available in Egypt.*

8. SPORTS & RECREATION

Egypt is known for its ancient temples and vibrant cities, not its golf courses and ski slopes. In fact, until Sinai and the Red Sea were opened to divers in the 1980's Egypt had virtually nothing to offer those looking for athletic recreation. That has changed drastically in the past decade and today the Sinai and Red Sea Coasts are quickly becoming world renowned resort destinations while Egypt's cities are enjoying an unprecedented proliferation of sporting and recreational facilities from golf courses to health spas.

THE SINAI

Since opening to tourism in the early 1980's, **Sinai** has established a reputation as one of the world's most premier scuba diving destinations. Strong currents, warm waters, and deep shelves combine to spawn an aquatic jungle teeming with a variety of marine wildlife not rivaled anywhere else in the world save possibly the Great Barrier Reef in Australia. Dozens of dive centers offer all levels of courses and in addition to day and half day expeditions, most dive centers can arrange dive safaris on live-aboard boats for up to a week or more. Equipment and lessons can always be arranged on the ground in Sinai itself, but those particularly serious about diving may want to inquire with their travel agent or specialized adventure travel agencies about specific dive tours to Sinai. Also, when making plans and arrangements for diving, always make sure that the center you sign up with is properly accredited by a respected international diving federation such as PADI.

If plunging yourself twenty meters below the sea's surface is not your idea of recreation, Sinai offers a myriad of other **water sports.** Healthy winds and low waves make it a particularly ideal location for **wind surfing** though whizzing about on a banana boat, coasting in a catamaran, or simply bathing in the sun like a beached whale are all viable options. Those interested in exploring underwater wildlife, but not in putting out the effort or the dollars needed for diving, can do so by snorkeling or taking a ride in a glass bottom boat which offers you a glimpse into the marine world without even getting wet. Many of the hotels, even at the lower end of the budget scale, also feature pools which are more conducive to the limits of children or swimmers who simply have a strong distaste for getting salt water up their noses. Though not popular, **fishing** is also possible and if you fork up the money for renting good equipment and a boat with a captain who knows the art of trawling, Sinai's waters contain such prized species as tuna, kingfish, dolphin fish, and even sailfish.

Though diving and watersports have been Sinai's main draw, visitors are increasingly discovering the joys of exploring Sinai's interior. Unlike the coast, which has largely gone up in concrete, the interior is still wild and except for the monks at Saint Katherine's Monastery and Bedouin, uninhabited. The main attractions are the beautiful desert mountains and the oases nestled amongst them which are fantastic settings for camping and hiking. In addition to beautiful open space and stunning views, there are opportunities to view fowl and wildlife, and to explore fascinating geological formations in canyons and caves. Because most of the interior is off piste, getting around usually requires a combination of four wheel drive vehicles, hiking, and camel safari. Overnight trips entail camping "Bedouin style" under the magnificent Arabian starlit sky either in the desert or in the oases.

Hiking trips, **camel safaris**, and **jeep safaris** can all be arranged on the spot through hotels and travel agencies in Sharm El Sheikh, Dahab, Nuweiba, and Taba or you can make arrangements in Cairo or even through your travel agent at home. You can also negotiate with the native Bedouins who run their own trips. Known for their honesty and hospitality in addition to the toughness needed to survive in the desert, these native tribesmen native to the desert make the best guides. See destination chapters for specifics.

CAIRO & THE CITIES

Cairo would hardly be considered a sportsman's paradise, but there are plenty of ways to get some exercise apart from dodging traffic in Tahrir Square. Upscale hotels have swimming pools, and usually gyms, spas and tennis courts as well. Those who are not guests can usually use facilities for a fee.

Among the most popular outdoors activities among visitors to Cairo is **horseback riding** in the deserts surrounding the Pyramids at Giza. One can rent horses at the Pyramids themselves or even better, hire a guide and horse from one of the stables near the Pyramids where the famous Arabian steeds are bred. The views, whether by sunrise, sunset, or moonlight, are invariably magnificent.

Once a popular sport with the large pre-Revolutionary expatriate communities in Cairo and Alexandria, **golf** fell out of favor in Egypt after 1952 and until the early 1990's there were only three functioning courses in the whole country. In recent years however, golf has begun a major comeback as investors realize the sport's potential in attracting uppercrust tourists. By the end of the century the number of golf courses in Egypt will have multiplied five fold with many more on the way in Luxor, El Gouna, Sharm El Sheikh, and Hurghada.

Given that Egypt boasts two major coasts and a large chunk of the world's longest river, you would think **boating** might be a major pastime. Sailing and yachting have been major growth industries along the Red Sea coasts, but except for a few boats operated by private sporting clubs, there are few opportunities on the Nile apart from hiring a felucca. If you're in Cairo during October, consider checking out, or participating in, the annual Nile raft races organized by the Cairo Rugby Club-it's a large social (i.e., drinking) event, popular with Cairo's expatriates.

IN THE DESERT

The vast **Western Desert** stretching from the Nile to the Libyan border offers visitors some of Egypt's most spectacular natural attractions such as the **White Desert** and the **Great Sand Sea**, but aside from camping and possibly some camel riding, little that qualifies as sports or recreation. The harsh and hostile environment makes survival, let alone having a good time, nearly impossible for all but the most hardened of human beings. Having said that, those looking for hard-core outdoor adventuring can enjoy the trip of a lifetime. It requires substantial planning and lots of fancy equipment, beginning with a heavy duty all terrain vehicle, but a desert safari offers you the chance to explore beautiful country well off the beaten track by any standards. Siwa, Kharga, and Dakhla all feature beautiful sites for camping and while camel safaris can be organized in Dakhla and Faiyoum.

To organize or join a major desert safari, contact adventure travel agencies at home or explore options with travel agencies in Cairo. Short safaris of several days can usually be organized on the spot in Farafra and Dakhla, while camping in Siwa, Dakhla, Kharga, and Faiyoum just requires that you show up and register with the nearest police.

THE MEDITERRANEAN COAST

The white sandy beaches of the Mediterranean coast have long been the favorite holiday playgrounds for the Egyptians themselves. Resorts such as Alexandria, Agami, and Marsa Matrouh are famous for their temperate climates and white beaches but unfortunately, overuse and poor maintenance have left Egypt's north coast beaches in sorry shape. Also, the Mediterranean coast lacks the recreational facilities available at Red Sea resorts, and because of uncleared mines left from World War II, virgin beaches are off limits to campers. This is unfortunate given this region's fantastic climate and the beauty of its beaches.

9. TAKING THE KIDS

With its monumental ancient temples and exotic looking people who wear flowing robes and turbans while riding camels and donkeys, Egypt is fantasy come true for most kids, and they love it. Furthermore, Egyptians are family oriented as well as charming and affable and they relate to children well. Having said that, there are factors worth considering if you plan to travel in Egypt with children.

One point you will definitely need to keep in mind is that some accommodations are more child-friendly both in terms of comfort and diversions. Given the warm weather conditions, particularly during the scorching summers, a child will be more comfortable in an air-conditioned hotel. Also, since pools are generally popular with children and the weather is almost always accommodating, you may consider staying in a hotel with a pool-most moderate and upscale establishments do in fact have them. On the coasts, many hotels also feature supervised recreational and sporting activities for kids, enabling you to scuba dive or sunbathe in peace.

You'll also want to pace yourself when traveling with kids. Children are almost always fascinated and stimulated by the sights in Egypt, but given their short attention spans, it's wise not to cram as much sightseeing in each day as you otherwise might. Also, when planning your itinerary, try to avoid long overland travel. For example, spare yourselves the 14 hour bus trip from Aswan to Sharm El Sheikh and keep in mind that buses can be especially hard on kids. They tend to be cramped, the air-conditioning is often overwhelming or non-existent, bathroom breaks can be few and far between, and the inevitable blasting music and/or video makes sleeping impossible. Trains are generally more comfortable, but again, longer trips are difficult.

Finding food that kids like is generally not a problem. While some native foods can be exotic or different, most of it is similar to food in the west and not terribly hot or spicy. Roast meats, french fries, rice, and sweets are almost always available and if they really need a hamburger or even a Big Mac specifically, McDonald's, KFC, and Pizza Hut, is available in most cities and resorts. As you will notice, Egyptians almost always include their families in major social occasions, including meals, and in virtually no restaurants are children unwelcome. In fact, it is not uncommon to walk into a nightclub or restaurant past midnight and find hordes of kids running about while the adults enjoy food, a floor show, or some other entertainment. Some eateries, including several branches of the famous Felfela's chain, feature mini-amusement parks with trampolines, bumper cars, and arcades on the premises.

When it comes to attractions specifically designed for children, nothing in Egypt will ever compete with Disney World or Magic Mountain, but there are some viable options. In Cairo there are two amusement parks called Sinbad's, and a new one called CairoLand-all three of which feature rides and games. There is also a circus in Agouza, and the Cairo Zoo is a favorite with local kids though the poor conditions in which the animals must live will probably leave your kids, and you, sad and angry rather than enlightened. The Pharaonic Village in Cairo features people acting as though they are ancient Egyptians; it's cheesy as heck but kids love it. Finally, there are movie theaters in Cairo and Alexandria which almost always play blockbuster pictures from the States. These are especially child and parents friendly, because government censors take care of sex and excessive violence.

Most other potential needs relating to children can be met in Egypt though you can avoid surprise by packing and planning carefully. Diapers, baby formula, and other pharmaceutical type items, including medicines can be readily found in Egypt, though it's probably best that you bring them from home. There are also many highly trained pediatrics and world class medical facilities. Check with your insurance company about whether your children's medical insurance covers them while overseas. In Cairo, professional baby-sitters can be arranged through the Community Services Association, though in a foreign country, you may not trust any stranger taking care of your kids.

If you are considering a long term stay in Egypt, and are interested in schooling, there are dozens of English language pre-schools, kindergartens, as well as primary and secondary schools. Cairo American College in Maadi and the British International School in Zamalek both offer better than average primary and secondary educations.

10. ECOTOURISM & TRAVEL ALTERNATIVES

DIVING

One important consequence of Egypt's 1979 peace with Israel has been the return of the Sinai and the opening of the Red Sea to divers. As the Red Sea boasts some of the world's most spectacular coral reefs and a variety of marine wildlife not found anywhere in the world, this has been tantamount to opening a long lost treasure chest to diving enthusiasts.

Would-be divers can easily join courses and arrange diving excursions and safaris on the spot in the Red Sea or from Cairo by contacting dive centers listed in the Red Sea and Sinai destination chapters. A typical PADI five day introductory dive course including equipment and instruction costs about $300. Such a course will provide you with the instruction and internationally recognized certification needed to dive anywhere in the world. One day introductory courses and guided dives usually cost about $60 but do not lead to certification. Shorter specific skill courses for more experienced divers also cost about $60 a day.

Experienced divers can also join or organize diving expeditions lasting from a half day to a week or more on a live-aboard boat, but should make reservations at least a week in advance for longer excursions. Including food, boat, equipment, and other expenses, they can run as high as $1200 for a ten day safari. Such excursions can also be arranged or joined through stateside travel agents specializing in diving tours, which often combine diving excursions (4 days to a week) with sightseeing in the Nile Valley and even a Nile Cruise. Rates range from $1500 for a week of diving to $4000 for a week or ten days of diving plus a week or ten days of sightseeing in Cairo and the Nile Valley. Listed below are some companies specializing in diving tours:

• **Tropical Adventures Travel**, *111 Second North, Seattle WA, 98109. Tel. 800/247-3483, 206/441-3483. Fax 206/441-5431.*

Caribbean Adventures, World Dive Adventures, *10400 Griffin Road, Suite 109, Ft. Lauderdale FL, 33328. Tel. 800/433-DIVE, 954/433-DIVE, Fax 954/434-4282*

Hundreds of diving centers operating in Hurghada, Sharm El Sheikh, Dahab, and Taba serve hundreds of thousands of clients every year. Many of these centers are accredited and recognized by international federations such as PAID and CAMS. Others are fly by night operations at best. Given the dangers that diving can entail, it's best that you stick to established, internationally recognized dive centers.

CAMPING

There are limited camping opportunities in Egypt, mostly in the Western Desert and along the Red Sea and Sinai coasts. As most tourists do not bring camping equipment with them to Egypt they must join an expedition or organize their own through local agents.

Sinai and the **Red Sea coasts** feature fantastic settings for camping and hiking. On both sides it is quite easy to organize expeditions or safaris by camel, four wheel drive, or hiking through local agents. Sinai in particular offers a stunning array of mountains, canyons, oases, springs, and dunes, all of which are virtually undeveloped and untouched by humans except for Bedouins. In Sinai, most hotels can assist in organizing **treks**, **camel safaris**, and **hikes**, usually lasting a day or two. For more serious trekking, camping, camel and jeep safaris, the agents below can provide assistance.

Sinai

• **Abanoub Travel**, *Nuweiba. Tel. 062/520-201. Fax 062/520-206. Dr. Rabia Barty, Director. In Cairo, call 02/418-2671. Fax 02/418-2332*
• **Explore Sinai**, *Nuweiba New Commercial Center in Nuweiba. Tel. 062/500-140*
• **C.I.T.**, *in Nuweiba, Tel. 062/520-264; Taba, Tel. 062/530-264; Saint Katherine's, Tel. 062/771-004*
• Sheikh Mohammed is a Bedouin guide who organizes hikes and camel safaris lasting from one hour to two weeks. However you must get to his house to make arrangements. He is located south of the Saint Katherine's-Nuweiba Road at the junction of the Wadi Marra Road 38 kilometers from Saint Katherine's.
• Sheikh Musa organizes camel treks in the Saint Katherine's region. He operates out of El Milga Village, *Tel. 062/771-004/457*
• Sheikh Hamid at the junction of Wadi Ghazala and the Saint Katherine's-Nuweiba Road 7 kilometers west of the road to Dahab. Camping is

available and camel safaris, guides, and other treks can be arranged on the spot. For longer journeys up to two weeks call *062/520-201* to make arrangements.

In **Israel**, the Society for the Protection of Nature in Israel organizes hikes, treks, and other nature-oriented tours through **Sinai Tours**, *3 Hashfelah Street, Tel Aviv, Tel. 03/639-0644/537-4425. Fax 03/383-940.*

In **Hurghada**, most hotels and dive centers organize camping trips to the islands off the Red Sea Coast. They also organize overnight camping treks in the Eastern Desert and the surrounding mountains. For longer, more rugged tours, contact **Trackers**, *Tel. 065/442-532 in Hurghada.*

OTHER SPECIALIZED TOURS

Listed below are just some travel agencies and tour operators in the United States that offer specialized and adventure tours. For a comprehensive list of specialized travel agencies and tour operators (not only for Egypt) in the United States consult the **Specialty Travel Index**. To order a copy, call *Tel. 415/455-1643* or consult their website at: *http://www.SPECTRAV.com.*

ENCOUNTER, *Adventure Center, 1311 63rd Street, Suite 200, Emeryville CA, 94608. Tel. 800/227-8747, 510/645-1879. Fax 510/654-4200. E-mail adventctr@aol.com.*

Encounter includes Egypt on trans-African treks through south and east Africa that last from nine to 27 weeks. The Egypt portions feature sailing down the Nile on feluccas and visits to the historic monuments of the Nile Valley. Egypt is also on the itineraries of treks through the Eastern Mediterranean and the Levant.

GUERBA ADVENTURE CENTER, *Adventure Center, 1311 63rd Street, Suite 200, Emeryville CA, 94608. Tel. 800/227-8747, 510/645-1879. Fax 510/654-4200. E-mail adventctr@aol.com.*

An array of tours include itineraries that combine desert safaris and camping in Sinai with sightseeing in the Nile Valley. Options include felucca cruises on the Nile, camel trekking in Sinai and the Eastern Desert, and tours combining Egypt with Jordan, or Tanzania and Kenya in East Africa.

EQUATOR, *PO Box 807, Dubious Wyoming, 82513. Tel. 800/545-0019 for info. and reservations. Fax 307/455-2354. E-mail equitour@wyoming.com.*

Ten day "Pharaoh Ride" for riding enthusiasts includes camping, a visit to a stud farm, and riding through the Western Desert to Faiyoum and the pyramids at Maidum and Dahshur. Prices start from $1,915.

OVERSEAS ADVENTURE TRAVEL, *625 Mt. Auburn Street, Cambridge MA, 02138. Tel. 800/221-0814 for info and reservations.*

Name doesn't suggest it, but specializes in comprehensive upscale tours for people over 50. Fourteen day Egypt trips start at $2990.

TOURS & DIMENSIONS, *400 W. 43rd Street, Suite 22-S, New York NY, 10036-6310. Tel. 212/268-9691. Fax 212/268-9697.*

Runs dozens of mid- to upscale package tours with various combinations of Upper Egypt, Sinai, and Cairo, including specialty tours emphasizing Coptic Egypt and desert safaris in the Western Desert, including major oases.

THE IMAGINATIVE TRAVELER (branch of Himalayan Travel), *Himalayan Travel, 110 Prospect Street, Stamford CT, 06901. Tel. 800/225-2380. Fax 203/359-3669.*

Over 18 mid-range tours to Egypt lasting 3-22 days. In addition to standard tourist fare and combination tours (e.g. diving and Upper Egypt), they offer unique options like water safari in Lake Nasser, overnight felucca cruises, and desert safaris in Sinai.

AEGEAN VISIONS (division of Travelvisions), *Ridgeway Center, 26 Sixth Street, Suite 506, Stamford CT, 06905. Tel. 203/973-0111, 800/550-0091. Fax 203/969-0799.*

Specializes in tours to Greece and the Aegean but offers several tours in Egypt including some which feature cruises on Lake Nasser. They also specialize in tours for honeymoons, and alternative lifestyles.

11. FOOD & DRINK

Egyptian cuisine is a tasty blend of foreign food introduced by conquering peoples over the centuries from the English to the Turks, and indigenous fare enjoyed by Egyptians since pharaonic times. Those familiar with Middle Eastern and Eastern Mediterranean cooking will be in familiar territory when pouring over menus, as flat breads, grilled meats, stuffed vegetables, and a wonderful array of dips and appetizers known as *mezze* are just some of the delicious fare cooked up in Egyptian kitchens; and should you crave continental, Asian, or even, God forbid, McDonald's, you won't have a problem satisfying your urges in most of Egypt.

DAILY BREAD: THE BASICS

The cornerstone of the Egyptian diet is the flat **bread** ("pita" in American) known as **'aish** meaning 'life' in Arabic. At only a few piasters a loaf, the most common type in local bakeries is the whole-wheat variety known as **'aish biladi** while the white flour variety known as **'aish shami** has become more prevalent in restaurants. Baked primarily with flour donated by the United State's government and sold to the people at highly subsidized prices, fresh 'aish cannot be beaten for taste and nutrition and is ideal for making sandwiches, scooping up dips, or even eating plain. Various European-style rolls, buns, and loaves ('aish franga) are also widely available.

After 'aish, the most important daily staple is **fuul medames** (fava beans). Eaten for breakfast, lunch, and dinner, these highly nutritious beans are usually eaten with white cheese, known as **gibna beida**, bread, eggs, and/or tomatoes and onions. While fuul can be terribly bland if plain, spicing it with lemon juice, garlic, and cumin renders a delicious dish. Available for take out or sit-down in food stalls on any major street, fuul sandwiches shouldn't set you back more than 50pt or LE1.

Other dishes enjoyed by the common Egyptian include **ta'amiya**, the Egyptian version of felafel, and **kushari**, a mixture of rice, lentils, and pasta topped with a tasty tomato sauce. Unlike the felafel popular in other Middle Eastern countries made with chickpeas, Egyptian ta'amiya are deep-fried balls of fava beans mixed with spices. Again, a sufficient portion bought in a local diner or food stand shouldn't cost more than LE1-2.

MEZZE: APPETIZERS, DIPS, & SALADS

Throughout the Middle East, a favorite part of any sit-down meal is the wide array of appetizers and finger foods served in the beginning known as **mezze**. Salads, dips, and miniature meat dishes might easily tempt you into eating away your appetite before the main course even arrives. A simple mezze consists of 'aish, tehina, and a green salad while more elaborate mezzes will force you to confront a wider choice. Mezze is usually taken as the first course for a major meal, or it may be enjoyed with drinks or refreshments the way an American might nibble on peanuts while drinking a beer.

Tehina, is the basic dip and garnish used throughout Egyptian cuisine. Derived from a chickpea paste called *tehini*, tehina is often spiced up with cumin, ground coriander, salt pepper, and lemon. **Baba ghanugh**, which has become popular in the West over the past 15 years, combines a tehina base with roasted eggplant and cumin, pepper, and lots of garlic. **Hommus bi tehini**, often referred to as "hommus" ("chickpeas" in Arabic), combines – you guessed it – tehina with mashed chickpeas. A concept imported from Lebanon, **labna** is a fantastic cream cheese made from yoghurt often garnished by mint.

Most salads, **salata** in Arabic, are dressed with oil, garlic, parsley, and vinegar. Greens, tomatoes, and onions are the most popular ingredients, though eggplant, beets, lentils, beans, and potatoes are also common, both in combination or individually. In fancier Arab and Lebanese restaurants, the famous **tablouli** consists of onions, mint, cilantro, and cracked wheat or bulghar. **Fatoush**, another salad imported from the Levant combines greens, onions, and tomatoes with dried 'aish shami bread. Egyptians, and Arabs in general, love **yoghurt** and hence raw vegetables, such as cucumbers, dressed in yoghurt are regular features of the mezze.

Reflecting the Balkan influence in Egyptian cooking, stuffed vine leaves, known as *dolma* in Greece and **wara 'einab** in Arabic, are taken either as part of the mezze or a main course in combination with other stuffed vegetables called **mahshi**. Usually made with ground beef or lamb, it sometimes comes in vegetarian form. Also of Balkan influence are the small savory pastries filled with vegetables and cheese or minced meat called **sambousak**.

Finally there are the meat-based fingergoods. **Kobeiba**, often referred to by its Lebanese name *'kibbeh,'* is a ball of ground lamb meat seasoned with spices like cinnamon and baked in a casing of bulghar and pine nuts. **Kibda** (liver) from the calf and chicken is popular fried, grilled, and in salads, and **mokh** (brain) from the calf is worth trying if you can stand the gelatin-like texture.

SOUPS

'Shorba' in Arabic, soups are usually taken as an appetizer though along with fresh 'aish, they can make a delicious, hearty meal. Common appetizer soups are usually made with a light broth, rice or vermicelli, and chunks of chicken, beef, and vegetable. Lemon, cumin, and garlic are favorite spices. The tasty and very nutritious lentil soup, **shorbat 'adds** is a favorite throughout Egypt, and with a bit of lemon juice and pepper is a truly fantastic dish.

Perhaps **melokhia** comes closest to claiming the title of Egypt's "national dish." Supposedly eaten since pharaonic times, this rich and slimy green soup is made with the indigenous melokhia (Jew's marrow) plant, and usually eaten with chicken or rabbit and accompanied by bread and rice.

MEAT & POULTRY

Most Egyptians would eat red meat (**"lahma"** in Arabic) everyday if they could, but the average salary cannot support such a luxury so **lamb** and **beef** are usually reserved for special occasions. **Chicken** (**"ferakh"** in Arabic) and other poultry like **duck**, **pigeon**, and **quail** are less expensive, well liked and widely available. As **pork** is forbidden by Islamic dietary laws, it's hard to find outside of Chinese restaurants.

The most popular, and one of the tastiest means of cooking meat is to grill it (*mashwi* designates "grilled" in Arabic). **Shish kebab** grilled on a stick is common, as is **kofta** – minced meat mixed with spices, onions, and garlic, also cooked on a stick. The chicken version of shish kebab is **shish tawook**. When not grilled, chicken is usually roasted on spit. Rotisserie chickens are sold on the street through the country and cost LE7-LE10.

Meats and poultry are also prepared with sauces or in stews. **Kebab hala** is a lamb stew and **dawood pasha** is a meatball and onion stew. Also common are European style chicken or veal cutlets with béchamel (white) or tomato sauce.

If you enjoy poultry, try **grilled pigeon** or **quail**, especially if it's stuffed (**"mahshi"**). Egyptians make a tasty stuffing consisting of rice or cracked wheat, chopped liver or meat, and vegetables like onions and carrots.

FISH & SEAFOOD

As you pass through millennia's worth of pharaonic tomb and temple carvings, you will inevitably come across colorful images of ancient Egyptians fishing in a bountiful Nile brimming with fish *(samak)*. Unfortunately, damming, overuse, and pollution have depleted the Nile's fish stocks to virtually nothing except in the deep south and Lake Nasser where the famous **Nile perch** still thrives. On the Red Sea and Mediterranean coasts, however, fresh fish is widely available and of high quality. Mullet, seabass, grouper, **shrimp** *(gambari)* and **squid** *(calamari)* are just some of the seafood Egyptians love and specialize in preparing.

Fish and shrimp are usually fried *(maa'lee)* or grilled *(mashwi)* with lemon and garlic flavoring. Sometimes, whole fish are baked with tomatoes and onions in tasty spices such as paprika, garlic, and pepper. Should you get the chance, **sayyadiah**, an Arab fisherman's dish of rice and fish with onion and spices like cumin and allspice, is well worth a try. Squid is usually fried as *calamari*.

During the spring holiday of Sham El Nassim, Egyptians typically break out a salted rotten fish called **fasikh** – definitely an acquired taste.

VEGETABLES

While Egypt imports the vast majority of the wheat needed for the beloved 'aish bread, most of the fantastic vegetable produce is grown locally and prepared fresh. Egypt is famous for its tomatoes, beans, onions, and carrots all of which are commonly used in sauces, salads, or casseroles. Okra (**bammia**) is especially fancied and is popular in stews.

A favorite way to prepare vegetables is to stuff them. Known as **mahshi** (which means "stuffed" in Arabic), vegetables like peppers, tomatoes, eggplants, grape leaves, and cabbage leaves are stuffed with rice, ground meat, onions, and spices and then stewed in a tomato sauce. Sometimes mahshi is prepared without the meat.

Vegetarians shouldn't have too much of a difficult time in Egypt as kushari, fuul, and other meatless dishes are readily available. However, should you be the invited guest of Egyptians, you may find it difficult to convincingly explain why you won't accept their offerings of meat. Most Egyptians consider meat a luxury and the most prized of foods and hence may be disappointed that you won't eat it. Also, be aware that meat or chicken stock is used in many dishes which otherwise appear to be vegetarian.

SWEETS & DESSERTS

Egyptians have a bigtime sweet tooth and the puddings, pastries, and candies should easily satisfy your own cravings. Sweets are usually taken at the end of meals, are sometimes eaten as a snack with coffee or tea. During special occasions, especially religious holidays, they are even more available than usual and are given as gifts to family, friends, and business associates. To get a good look at the variety, head to a **helwani**, a sweetshop, which can be found on virtually any major commercial street in Egypt.

A simple rice pudding *(roz bi laban)* is the most common of a number of milk based desserts and is available both at fast-food establishments, such as kushari stalls, as well as in upper scale sit-down restaurants. Less common on the street, but regarded by many of the king of Egyptian desserts is **Om Ali** ("the mother of Ali"), a casserole made of filo dough stewed in milk and topped with raisins, nuts, and coconut. Another milk-based delicacy, **mahallabia**, is a jazzed up version of rice pudding with more bells and whistles, often flavored with rose water and best taken in a Lebanese restaurant.

Aside from milky puddings, the most popular desserts are fingerlicking pastries, most of which westerners will identify simply as "baqlava." Pronounced **ba'lawa** in Egypt, the flaky filo pastry dripping with honey and topped by nuts is just one of dozens of such desserts. Other desserts worth trying are **kunafa**, a shredded wheat pastry stuffed with nuts and honey, or *ishta* (thick cream), and **basbousa**, semolina cakes soaked in honey and also topped with nuts. **'Attayyef**, small pancakes or doughballs, coated with honey, must also be tried – bet you can't eat just one.

BEVERAGES

In addition to nourishment, beverages provide a context and an excuse for social interaction. Meeting friends for tea or coffee and discussing sports, politics, and general gossip is an Egyptian pastime as you will find out. Whether in the context of a family gathering or business meeting the sharing of drinks is an indelible social ritual across the society.

Tea (**shai***)* is the favorite drink of Egyptians - hands down. Made popular when the British brought it from India during the 19th century, it's usually taken with sugar and mint, it is often more easily had than simple water, especially if you're trying to protect your stomach.

Originally imported from Yemen during the Ottoman era nearly 500 years ago, **coffee** (**qahwa** or **ahwah**)became an important economic commodity and gave rise to that all important social institution the cafe- known in Arabic, surprisingly enough as the **"awhah."** Today, western variations (*nescafe)* are common as is the thick, muddy, and powerful Turkish coffee traditionally enjoyed by Egyptians. Usually, it's a cheap instant version of Nescafe, but in fancier hotels and restaurants, higher quality brewed coffees, often dubbed "American coffee" on menus, as well as cappuccino and expresso are also available.

Common **soft drinks** are Coke, Pepsi, 7 Up, Sprite, and a variety of Canada Dry and Sweppes products. On the street they cost between 30pt-LE1 while in fancier hotels and restaurants they run as high as LE3-4.

When it comes to refreshment and nutrition, it's hard to beat the **fresh fruit juices** available at **juice bars**. Located throughout cities and towns, they feature juice squeezed fresh on the spot and can be identified by the bags of fruit hanging outside. For LE1.50 you can enjoy thick nourishing orange juice in the winter or mango juice in summer. Strawberry, apricot, sugarcane, and apple are also common. If concerned for your stomach, keep in mind that freshly squeezed juices from peeled fruits are generally okay, but be wary of ice.

Two other popular drinks, often sold on the streets by men in medieval costumes with brass jugs on their backs, are **tammarhindi**, a sweet, cool drink derived from tammarind pulp, and **karkade**, hibiscus tea served hot in the winter and cool in the summer.

ALCOHOLIC DRINKS

Though Islamic dietary laws prohibit the consumption of alcohol, which is banned outright in countries like Saudi Arabia, it is produced and available in most of Egypt. Ancient Egyptian production of beer and wine is well documented on walls of tombs and temples throughout the country, and was undoubtedly an important part of the ancients' diet.

Beer

In 1997, the advent of what Egyptian beer drinkers will tell you is a long overdue revolution in the national beer industry occurred. For decades drinkers were restricted in choice to the local beer, **Stella Local**, a light lager served in green 16 ounce (they used to be 20 ounce) bottles and its more expensive, skunkier and supposedly higher grade cousin **Stella Export**. Notorious for its inconsistency, Stella's quality ranged from drinkable to downright poisonous, but was loved nonetheless by local beer drinkers, while visiting tourists lacking the acquired taste could only grin and bear it. In recent years, the quality of Stella improved significantly and with the privatization of the company in 1997, it is expected to get even better. With technical assistance from the brewers of Carlsberg, Stella's new owners have introduced a new variety, **Stella Premium**, a darker, stronger lager which comes in American style 12 ounce brown bottles and a slick Tut-adorned label imported from Lebanon.

On the way in '98 is Egyptian-produced Lowenbrau to be brewed at the Red Sea resort, El Gouna, and possibly other international name brands. In fancier bars and restaurants, the beer revolution manifests itself in the form of imported draft beers including Fosters, Guinness, and different varieties of McEwans.

Wine & Spirits

While Stella retains the affectionate loyalty of its drinkers despite its many ups and downs, the same cannot be said for local wines, and deservedly so. Tolerable at best, the local red, "Omar Khayyam," and white, "Ginnacles" perform with difficulty their function as a suitable companion to fine dining. Ginnacles is definitely the better of the two and may be acceptable if well chilled. Formerly unbelievable rumors of a rehaul in the wine industry similar to that occurring in the beer industry keep resurfacing, and if Stella can be privatized and Lowenbrau brewed in Egypt, then anything is possible.

When it comes to **liquours** and **spirits**, you're better off sticking to standard western brand names. Bars almost always offer imported liquor, though it can be expensive, up to LE20 or more for single Johnny Walker Red, for example. If you're especially keen on boozing in Egypt, buy up your allotted four bottles at the **duty free** on the way in.

If you insist on sampling local spirits, your best choice is **arak**, an Arab version of ouzo. Brandy, rum, gin, and whisky (all equally foul and dangerous) are also produced locally and sold for cutthroat prices. Be aware that some who have dared to imbibe these poisons have suffered a variety of health problems, including temporary blindness. The industry is under-regulated and rumors of the use of unrefined alcohol are common. Also, do not be fooled by labels in local grocers which shamelessly imitate those of international name brands. For example, take a closer look and you'll find that what you thought was "Black Label" is in fact "Black Table." There are no "liquor stores" in Egypt as such, so buying imported liquor is almost impossible except at duty free shops.

FOOD LEXICON (ARABIC-ENGLISH)

General
bread – *'aish*
butter – *zibda*
cheese – *gibna*
chicken – *firakh*
white cheese – *giba beida*
yellow cheese – *gibna rumi*
eggs – *beid*
meat – *lahma*
fruit – *fawahkeh*
pepper – *felfel*
fish – *samak*
soup – *shorba*
salt – *melh*

vegetables – *khudar*
sugar – *sukkar*

Meals
breakfast – *fitar*
lunch – *ghada*
dinner – *asha*
Ramadan Breakfast – *Iftar*
Ramadan, last meal before sunrise – *Sohour*

Breakfast – Fitar
egg (s) – *beid*
fava beans – *fuul*
honey – *assl*
white cheese – *gibna beida*
jam – *murrabba*

Soups
chicken soup – *shorbat firakh*
vegetable soup – *shorbat khudar*
lentil soup – *shorbat 'adds*
tomato soup – *shorbat tomatem*
melokhia – Jew's marrow soup

Vegetables (Khudar) & Salads (Salatat)
beans – *fusulia*
carrots – *gazar*
eggplant – *bitingan*
cucumber – *kheeyar*
onion (s) – *basl*
okra (usually in stewy tomato sauce) – *bammia*
peas – *bisilla*
pepper (s) – *felfel*
potatoes – *batatas*
tomato (s) – *tomatem* or *oota*
zuchini – *kossa*
wara' aynab – stuffed vine leaves
salad (s) – *salata(t)*
tomato salad – *salatet tomatem*
mixed/green salad – *salatet khudra*
cucumber salad – *salatet kheeyar*
mahshi – means "stuffed" referring to stuffed vegetables

Side Dishes, Dips & Garnishes
tehina – sesame paste dip with oil, lemon, cumin and other spices
babaghanoush – *tehina* paste with roasted eggplant and spice
labna – yoghurt – derived cream cheese
hummos – mashed chickpeas with *tehina*
rice – *ruz*
French fries – *batatas* or *pommes frites*
picked vegetables – *torshi*
hot sauce/hot pepper – *shatta*

Meat Dishes
chicken – *firakh*
meat – *lahma*
duck – *batt*
lamb meat – *lahma dani*
pigeon – *hammam*
stuffed pigeon – *hammam mahshi*
brains – *mokh*
grilled pigeon – *hammam mashwi*
pork – *khanzir*

kebab – meat grilled on a stick
kofta – grilled mincemeat on a stick, usually lightly spiced
kebab halla – stewed lamb
dawood pasha – Egyptian meatballs in tomato sauce
fatta – meat, usually lamb, served on bed of rice and bread soaked in broth
    and topped with garlic and yoghurt

Fish – Samak
grilled fish – *samak mashwi*
shrimp – *gambari*
fried fish – *samal ma'lee*
squid – *calamari*

Sandwiches & Street Food
sandwich (es) – *sandaweetch (at)*
fuul – stewed fava beans, often served in a sandwich
ta'ammiya – Egyptian felafel, deep fried balls of mashed beans and spices
kushari – lentil, rice, and pasta concoction topped with tomato sauce and
    fried onions
shwarma – layered lamb, beef, or chicken meat off of a spit, usually served
    in a sandwich

fateer – Egyptian pizza – like pastry made with filo dough and filled with
  sweet or savory stuffing
kiba – liver, often served on the streets in a sandwich
macarona – baked macaroni casserole with béchamel sauce often available
  ready made on the street

Drinks
water – *mayya*
mineral water – *mayya madannia*
bottle of water – *azzazet mayya*
hot water – *mayya sukhna*
milk – *laban*
soft drink (s) – *haga sa'aa*
ice – *talg*

hot drinks
coffee (usually meaning Turkish coffee) – *qahwah* or *'ahwah*
Turkish coffee – *ahwah toorki*
Instant coffee/Nescafe – *nescafe*
tea – *shai*
tea with mint – *shai bi na' na'*
tea with milk – *shai bi laban*
sahlab – a thick, sweet milk based beverage flavored with coconut,
  cinnamon, nuts, and other spices – served at coffeeshops
karkaday sukhn – hot habiscus drink

Juices
juice – *asseer*
lemon juice – *asseer limoon*
mango juice – *asseer manga*
orange juice – *bortoo'an* or *bortooqal*
sugarcane juice – *'asab*
strawberry juice – *asseer farawla*

Alcoholic Drinks
khamra – denotes alcoholic drinks generally
beer – *beera*
wine – *nibeet*
white wine – *nibeet abeeyad*
red whine – *nibeet ahmar*
ouzo – *'arak*

Fruits
apple – *toofah*
apricot (s) – *mishmish*
banana (s) – mouzh
dates – *balah*
figs – *teen*
limon – *limoon*
mango – *manga*
melon – *shammam*
strawberry (ies) – *farawla*
watermelon – *bateekh*

Desserts – Helwayat
Om Ali – Filo dough or corn flakes baked in sweet milk and topped with
 coconut, nuts, and raisins.
roz bi laban – milk based rice pudding
mahallabia – A jazzed up rice and milk pudding

Pastries
ba'lawa – known in the west as "baqlava" a crispy, flaky, baked filo – based
 pastry usually filled with nuts and dripping with honey.
kunafa – shredded wheat pastry usually filled with nuts and honey or *ishta*
 (cream).
basboosa – semolina pastry with nuts and honey.

Generic Desserts
cake – *caka* or *gateau*
ice cream – *"ice cream" with an Egyptian accent*

Useful words and phrases
menu – *lista* or *menu*
napkin – *foota*
the bill – *il heesab*
lauw samaht – "If you please," used to get attention of waiter or to politely
 make a request e.g. *"Il heesab lauw samaht"* means, "The bill, please."
min gheer or *bidoon* – "without"
ana ayz/ihna ayzeen – "I want/we want"
mish ayz (een) – "I (we) do not want . . ."
sukhn – hot
sa'a – cold
taza – fresh
harr – hot as in "spicy"

12. EGYPT'S BEST PLACES TO STAY

THE SALAMLEK HOTEL

In the Montazah Gardens 15 kilometers east of downtown Alexandria. Tel. 03/547-3585, 547-33244. Fax 03/546-4408. Rates: $175-$1000 per night. Credit Cards: Visa, Mastercard, & American Express.

Nearly fifty years after King Farouk sailed to exile from these very grounds in 1952, the Salamlek palace has reopened in all its original splendor and glory. Originally built in 1892 by Khedive Abbas Helmy II in the magnificent royal gardens of Montazah overlooking the Mediterranean, the palace was designed to resemble an Austrian chalet in order, or so it was said, to please his Austrian mistress. The palace was then handed down to King Fouad I and King Farouk who indulged in some of his most famous escapades here before being forced into exile in 1952.

Walk through the revolving doors from the blazing Egyptian heat and you wouldn't know that royal indulgence ever went out of style. French and Italian upholstered furniture graces the lobby and original royal portraits hang from the walls. The San Giovanni Group that assumed management of the hotel in 1987 spent 10 years and nearly $10 million meticulously restoring the palace's original look, using photographs and consulting experts and former employees of the royal family. Most of the pictures and portraits are authentic as is some of the furniture.

The two-story hotel features 20 suites, each individually designed; some have regal Victorian decor, others more ornate Greek, Arab, or Art Nouveau. Though retaining in every manner the authentic charm and elegance of the place's royal past, all rooms are equipped with modern amenities including air-conditioning, safes, international phones, and fax lines. The most expensive room, the Mawlana has five rooms and a large terrace.

The reception rooms have retained their furnishings and fittings as well but have been converted into a coffee shop, a restaurant, and the King Fouad Bar which contains various relics of the royal decadent past, including tables that King Farouk used to play cards on and store his cigarettes and cigars.

The Salamlek is set in the lush gardens of Montazah. Also founded by Khedive Abbas II in the 1890's, the sprawling gardens contain the larger Montazah Palace, to which the Salamlek was originally an adjunct, which is now used by President Mubarak for state visits by Madeline Albright amongst others. During World War I Montazah was converted into a Red Cross Hospital where E.M. Forster worked.

THE MENA HOUSE HOTEL

At the end of Pyramids Road at the foot of the Pyramids. Tel. 02/383-3222, 383-3444. Fax 02/383-7777. In the United States call 1-800-5OBEROI. Rates: $130-194 single, $160-250 double, $425-1375 suites. Credit cards: All major credit cards are accepted.

Set at the foot of the Pyramid of Khufu, the Mena House Hotel might just enjoy the finest views of any hotel in the world, and that's not the half of it. Built in the 1870's as a hunting lodge for members of the Egyptian royal family, it was converted into a luxury hotel in the 1890's and its elegant grounds have played host to the likes of Franklin Roosevelt and Winston Churchill who initialed D-Day plans here in '44; and Jimmy Carter and Menachm Begin who formally signed the Egypt-Israel Peace Treaty in the main dining hall. Even Jerry Garcia called the Mena House home when the Dead played the Pyramids in 1978.

Now managed by the Oberoi chain, the Mena House offers a variety of rooms, the most elegant of which are in the original 19th century portion of the hotel and feature a classy mixture of fine old fashion European style furnishings and Arabesque decor to go with the postcard views of the Pyramids. All rooms are equipped with modern amenities including phone and fax lines, satellite television, and a fridge.

Recreationwise, guests can cool down in the House's spacious swimming pool, play golf at the foot of the Pyramids, or hop on an Arabian horse for a "wind through your hair," cruise through the dunes that even if just for a minute allows you to realize that cheesy Omar Sherif-Lawrence in Arabia fantasy you've always had. The hotel can also arrange spectacular champagne sunset camel rides by special request.

In the hotel itself, guests can wind down with a cocktail in the deliciously ornate lobby lounge overlooking the Pyramids; or perhaps the Mamluke Bar with its opulent oriental decor of finely carved mashrabia and engraved brass lamps.

For dining, guests can feast on oriental fare such as succulent lamb kebabs and rice with raisins and pine nuts, in the Haroun El Rashid restaurant. Just up the hall the Moghul Room, with its plush carpets and engraved brass tables is appointed for royalty, and serves a wide variety of Indian cuisine from fiery vindaloos to creamy kurmas and piping hot naan flat bread. Many believe the Moghul Room to be the finest restaurant in Cairo.

THE CAIRO MARRIOTT HOTEL & CASINO

Saraya El Gezira Street, Zamalek. Tel. 02/340-8888. Fax 02/340-6667. Rates: $120-160 singles, $125-195 doubles, $485-1500 suites. Credit Cards: all major credit cards are accepted.

With its abundance of elegance and opulent oriental decor, the Marriott in Zamalek combines Arabesque atmospherics and old style luxury with modern amenities and an ideal location in the center of town overlooking the Nile and the sprawling city of Cairo. Set in four acres of botanical gardens, it was originally built by Khedive Ismail as a guest house for Empress Eugenie and other VIP's attending the opening of the Suez Canal in 1869, and has recently been restored to all its glory from the finely carved mashrabia and polished marble floors to the oversized engraved brass lamps and gilded columns.

The palace itself is flanked by two huge towers where most of the rooms enjoy Nile views and modern amenities. Equipped with international phone and fax lines, satellite television, spotless baths, and spacious balconies from whence you can put your feet up and watch the timeless Nile float by, the rooms are essentially modern but touches of oriental decor hint at the hotel's regal 19th century roots.

When this palace was originally constructed in the 1860's the entire island of Zamalek comprised the personal botanical gardens of the Khedive and the Royal Family. Today, the Marriott claims the four acres that are left, now dotted with neo-classical statues that boast no artistic merit, but lend a regal aura to the place nonetheless. Given the hotel's location in the middle of Cairo, the gardens are an especially lovely setting for the hotel swimming pool and the three cafes where you can enjoy a beer or a coffee and a snack. Smokers may wish to partake in an apple sheesha (waterpipe) the sweet aroma of which lends the gardens a distinctively Middle Eastern flavor.

For dining, guests have a wide array of choices ranging from the elegantly formal Gezira Grille and the sumptuously ornate Empress Eugenie dining room to the casual Garden Promenade, a terrace in the botanical gardens with a barbecue and cafe. Later on the Omar Khayyam Casino, with its opulent turn-of-the-century decor, is the most sophisticated gambling establishment in Cairo, while down the hall, the Empress Show Lounge begins six hours of dinner and live oriental cabaret and belly dancing entertainment at 11pm.

Recreationwise, most guests are consumed with the endless splendors of Cairo such as the Pyramids and the bustling Khan EL Khalili bazaars; but the hotel itself has tennis courts, a swimming pool, a health spa and club, and even its own shopping mall where high grade Egyptian handicrafts are sold.

Some complain that the Marriott is ornate and over decorated to the point of cheesiness, but Ismail was not a man of restrained taste, and the opulent, even decadent, aura of oriental splendor is truly worth experiencing.

THE OLD WINTER PALACE

Corniche El Nil Street south of the Luxor Temple. Tel. 095/380-422. Fax 095/374-085. In the United States call 1-800-471-9090. Rates: $150-160 singles, $170-180 doubles, $257-575 suites. Credit cards: all major credit cards are accepted.

Dubbed a "sham" that would be "the end of Luxor" by French Academy member Pierre Loti upon its construction 100 years ago, the Winter Palace is now a historic landmark in itself, to many an indelible destination on their itinerary to the monument laden village of Luxor. Built at the end of the last century in the lush and luxuriant tropical gardens on the banks of the Nile, the Winter Palace has preserved its authentic *fin de siecle* ambiance and elegance while catering to the demands of modern travelers.

A true Victorian gem, the Winter Palace has an elegant and subdued charm with a formal, almost regal, yet intimate aura about it. Unlike other period piece hotels in Egypt, the Winter Palace does not indulge in the garish styles favored in the orient, but rather concedes to European preferences for fine woods, elegant materials and restrained colors.

The true glory of the hotel is in its setting overlooking the Nile dotted with the graceful sails of feluccas, and beyond to the rugged Theban Hills where pharaohs laid themselves to rest more than three thousand years ago. The hotel itself is set amidst meticulously landscaped feriel gardens where guests may wind down with a stroll amidst its leafy promenades, or take tea on the terrace. There is also a swimming pool where one may cool down with a quick dip or catch some rays, cocktail in hand.

The rooms are restrained, but elegant in their decor. Most feature antique wooden desks and upholstered chairs with drapes and bed linen in pastel tones or white. The tiled bathrooms are spacious and the balconies afford guests the opportunity to enjoy the splendid views of the Nile with its timeless beauty, or the lush feriel gardens to the rear.

For dining, the "1886" restaurant is regally appointed to retain its 19th century elegance and formality. The French food is average for

French food, which means that it is excellent, but the food itself is hardly the point. To wind down after a dusty day in the Valley of the Kings, guests can take tea on the Garden Terrace or the River Terrace overlooking the Nile. Indoors, the Royal Bar with fine wood paneling, lavishly upholstered chairs and wonderful teak tables is every bit as ornate and elegant as it was when Theodore Roosevelt drank here 100 years ago.

THE OLD CATARACT

In the Feriel Gardens on Abtal El Tahrir Street, Aswan. Tel. 097/316-0160-8. Fax 097/316-011. In the United States call 1-800-471-9090 for information. Rates: $110-150 singles, doubles $300-700. All major credit cards are accepted.

Built on a steep slope overlooking the Nile in Aswan, the hotel takes its name from the collision of water against the granite gates which form the First Cataract. One of the finest of all Egyptian hotels, the Old Cataract combines elements of Victorian elegance like hardwood floors and a beveled glass elevator, with the Moorish grace of finely carved mashrabia and engraved brass lamps.

The spacious rooms, with fine paneling and elegant antique finishing entices you to ponder the faces of yesteryear who enjoyed these same accommodations: Agatha Christia, Winston Churchill, and Aga Khan III, who spent his honeymoon here. For a breath of fresh air, guests may retreat to the large balconies that afford fantastic views of the enchanting pageantry of the timeless Nile.

Even those who cannot stay either because there are no openings or because it is too expensive, should take the opportunity to watch the sunset over Elephantine Island from *La Terrase Bar* which just begs a khaki outfit and a pith helmet. For dining the "1902" dining hall with its graceful Moorish arches, high ceilings, and live Nubian orchestra recalls the splendor of the Shepheards and colonial comfort that many of us still fondly wish to experience even if it isn't exactly politically correct.

The Cataract was built to accommodate the most discerning of elite travelers and it has maintained to this day, high levels of service and quality worthy of its spectacular setting.

BASATA

43 kilometers south of Taba on the east coast of Sinai. Turn east on the dirt road at Ras Burqa, Tel. 062/500-481 (02/350-1829 in Cairo). A night in the bamboo cabins costs LE18 per person, sleeping on the beach, LE10 per person; and day use of the beach, LE5. Meals cost LE15-20.

In Arabic *basata* means "simplicity," the defining character of this no-frills beach community 45 kilometers south of the Israeli border on Sinai's east coast. Set on beach that was probably imported from heaven itself,

Basata has attained legendary status as an alternative to the mass industrialized tourism that is spreading throughout the rest of Sinai. Founded in 1986 by the charismatic Sherif El Ghamrawy, the camp is an exercise in community living based on the ideals of harmony with nature, and Bedouin traditions of hospitality and mutual respect. All waste is recycled (mostly by the neighborhood goats), water use minimized, loud music is prohibited, and even the reefs are off limits to scuba diving (snorkeling is allowed).

For accommodation, guests can either stay in simple, but clean and comfortable bamboo cabins or on the beach, also known as the "million star hotel." Showers and toilets are shared.

There is a self-service kitchen available for preparing vegetarian or fish meals and bread is baked fresh on the premises. The billing system is based on trust, you write what you take and pay later. Alcohol is forbidden as is excessive noise. Be sure to make reservations well in advance; they're already booked well into 1998 but if you call, you may be lucky enough to snatch up an unexpected opening.

13. CAIRO

Cairo is a heaping, tottering megalopolis that sprawls along the banks of the Nile where the great river divides to form its fertile delta. This strategic location astride the Nile at the crossroads of caravans linking Africa and Asia has been the site of thriving communities and capitals since 3100 BC, when the first Pharaoh Menes conquered the Delta and founded the world's first nation-state. With its capital at Memphis, the state thrived as one of the world's great cities for three millennia before Egypt was subjugated to Persian domination in 525 BC, beginning a 2,500 year period when every ruler of Egypt was of foreign stock. Indeed Cairo was founded and transformed by foreigners, first the Arabs; later a Kurd named Salah El Din; and later Turks, British, and French.

In the Middle Ages, Cairo was the capital of empires that stretched from North Africa to Palestine and while Europe was muddled in the dark Middle Ages, Cairo thrived as the richest and most populous city in the world inspiring one Italian traveler to note in the 14th century that, "If it were possible to place Rome, Milan, Padua and Florence together with any four other great cities, they would not contain the wealth and population of the half of Cairo." After traveling the world from Morocco to Indonesia, 13th century traveler Ibn Batuta dubbed Cairo, *Om El Dunya*–"Mother of the world," or "Mother of all cities." It is a term that Cairenes still employ to reflect their pride in their city's rich historical legacy.

It is that legacy which brings most travelers today. Topping the list are the **Great Pyramids**, the granddaddy of tourist attractions that actually predate Cairo by 30 centuries, followed by the **Antiquities Museum** and the priceless treasures of **King Tutankhamun**. Then they move on to the humming bazaars of the **Khan El Khalili** where spices, textiles, and other goods have been traded and bartered in the heart of Islamic Cairo since the 13th century. Cairo was spared the devastation and plunder that Baghdad, Damascus, and other great medieval cities suffered at the hands of the Mongols and hence her architectural legacy is intact; Islamic Cairo is littered with hundreds of monuments including masterpieces like El

Azhar, the world's oldest university, and the Madrasah of Sultan Hassan considered one of the architectural masterpieces of the Islamic World.

But the historic landmarks are only half the story and many visitors are just as captivated by the colorful streetlife and watching the fusion of east and west and old and new go on before their eyes. For some, taking the plunge is not an easy experience. Cairo is a dense, polluted city and for many travelers, despite the undeniable hospitality of most Egyptians, culture shock is a terrible reality, sped on by subjugation to the hounding of touts and avaricious merchants. The best you can do is grin and bear it, turning your cheek the other way, and coping with the abuse that such a city subjects by even its own citizens. If you can move beyond the initial shock and take the plunge, Cairo's most fascinating aspect, its diverse population, affords endless streams of opportunities for personal and cultural interaction. This is especially the case if you meet and interact with people not associated with the tourism industry itself.

ARRIVALS & DEPARTURES
By Airplane
Cairo International Airport is almost 30 kilometers from downtown Cairo on the northeastern outskirts of Heliopolis. Domestic flights, as well as EgyptAir's international routes and African airlines leave from the old **Terminal 1** while major international airlines, operate out of the newer **Terminal 2**. Getting in and out of customs and immigration is usually quite efficient provided documents are in order and customs officials are in a reasonably good mood (i.e. not during Ramadan).

International passengers must possess or obtain a **visa** before proceeding to immigration, luggage pick-up, and customs. If you have not procured a visa from the Egyptian Consulate in your country, proceed to one of the bank windows (Banque Misr, Thomas Cook, Bank of Alexandria etc.) upon exiting the plane. Any one of them will change money and sell you a visa for $15. Actually it's far more convenient than going through the hassle of dealing with a consulate, as it saves time and costs less. Once you have a visa, proceed to immigration – signs will designate lines for "Egyptians," "Arabs," and "Foreigners."

After getting in the correct line and having your passport processed and stamped, pick up your luggage. Big sturdy luggage carts are available for LE2. You will probably be approached by a number of people offering to hook you up will hotels, to carry your luggage or some other service. Unless you want to shell out baksheesh from the start, politely but firmly decline their offers – they can be persistent. Expect more of the same once you exit customs.

Getting to Town from the Airport

Unless you have prearranged transportation from the airport to your hotel, there are several options for getting into town. For about you can hire a private "**limousine**" (chauffeured Mercedes) from one of the "Limousine" companies located in the arrival hall. They will take you anywhere in town for a flat and slightly expensive fee (LE60-80). Alternatively you can try your luck with the **taxis** outside the hall. Upon emerging from customs you will be hounded by drivers-some legit, some not-begging for your business. A legitimate taxi should cost you about LE40 after bargaining.

Finally, it's not recommended for your first taste of Egypt, but public **buses** #422, #400, and #949 go to Tahrir Square, downtown for 50pt. Buses are slow and tedious, and there may not be room for both you and your luggage. Also, you'll have to get a taxi from Tahrir to reach your hotel.

By Bus

Buses link Cairo and nearly all potential destinations throughout Egypt. Far cheaper than flying, riding the bus is sometimes the only option when it comes to destinations not linked by rail. Always call in advance or check with a travel agency about schedules, fares, and the need to make reservations in advance-especially during holidays.

Super Jet (*Tel. 02/772-663*) deluxe coaches serve major destinations, including the Suez Canal cities, the Red Sea, Sinai, Alexandria and the Nile Valley. Stations are located at El Mazah in Heliopolis, Ramses Street, Giza, and Cairo International Airport. Buses leave for **Alexandria** every half hour from 5:30am to 10pm from Tahrir Square, Giza, the airport and El Mazah station in Heliopolis. Standard one-way ticket costs LE19 for departure is prior to 9pm and LE21 thereafter. VIP bus leaving from El Mazah at 7:15am with phone access costs LE28 if departing from El Mazah and LE32 if taking the VIP bus from the airport. Buses go to Port Said every half hour from El Mazah, and from Ramses Street at 6am, 8am, 9am, 10am, 3pm, and 4:30pm. Tickets cost LE15 one way. If going to Marsa Matrouh, catch the 7am bus which leaves from El Mazah with a stop in Tahrir Square.

Buses for **Hurghada** depart at 8am and 2pm from Abdel Moneim Riyad and stop at El Mazah. Return buses leave Hurghada at noon and 5pm. Tickets are LE45 one-way going in either direction. Daily service **to Sharm El Sheikh** departs at 11pm from Tahrir and stops at El Mazah. A daily bus going the other way leaves Sharm at 11pm. One-way tickets cost LE50 each way.

The **East Delta Bus Company** (*Tel. 02/482-4753*) also services **Sinai** and the **Canal Zone** for slightly cheaper prices and less comfortable buses.

The hub for routes to Sinai is the **El Mahhatat Sina** (Sinai Station) in Abbassia while buses going to Canal destinations depart from Qulali off Ramses Square downtown, with stops at El Mazah and Tagnid Square in Heliopolis. Buses depart for **Ismailia, Suez,** and **Port Said** every 45 minutes beginning at 6:30am with the last bus leaving at 6pm from Qulali and El Mazah. Tickets cost LE6 one way.

To **El Arish** buses depart at 8am and 4pm from Qulali before stopping in El Mazah. One way on the "deluxe" costs LE30 while the merely "air-conditioned" one (which spares you the loud Arabic video) costs LE25. Going to **Sharm El Sheikh** costs LE50 if departing in the morning and LE65 for evening departures. Buses leave every forty-five minutes from 7am-6:30pm from Abbassia before stopping at El Mazah. Daily service to Nuweiba and Taba in a deluxe coach also leaves from Abbassia and then El Mazah at 8am, costing LE50 one-way.

West Delta Bus Company (*Tel. 02/243-1846*) buses link Cairo with the mainland Red Sea destinations of **Hurghada** (departing at 9am, noon, 3pm, 10:30pm and 11pm, LE30), **Safaga** and **El Quseir** (9am & 3pm, LE 35), as well as **Luxor** (9am, LE35) and **Aswan** (5pm, LE50). Buses arrive and depart from Abdel Moneim Riyad next to the Ramses Hilton, and El Mazah Bus Station in Heliopolis.

Finally, Upper Egyptian Bus Co. buses to the **Western Desert Oases** depart from a depot on El Azhar Street off Ataba Square in downtown Cairo. Two buses depart daily for **Bahariya** (LE15-20, 6 hours) at 8am and noon; the first of which continues on to **Farafra** (LE30, 10-12 hours). To **Kharga** (LE25-35, 9 hours) and **Dakhla** (LE30-40, 13 hours), there are three buses daily (via Assiut) at 7am, 5pm and 7pm.

By Car

When driving in Egypt, you must always keep your passport on hand and have a valid international drivers license, an Egyptian license, or if you're an American, Canadian or Briton, you can use your native license for six months. Always make sure that the car is properly registered and always keep a spare tire, a jack, and a fire extinguisher in your car. Car rentals are listed in the following "Practical Information" section. If you're planning on driving around Egypt, we'd recommend picking up a copy of *On the Road in Egypt: A Motorist's Guide,* written by Mary Megalli. It provides in great detail information about everything you need to know about driving in Egypt from fixing a flat to importing a vehicle through customs. Otherwise road maps are available from English language bookstores and some gas stations.

There are two roads from **Cairo to Alexandria.** The **Desert Road** (*El Saharawi*) is just over 200 kilometers from downtown Cairo to downtown Alexandria and skirts the congestion of the Delta. This road is also used to reach the **Monasteries of Wadi Natrun**. The scenery is negligible, but this is the faster of the two routes. It is well paved and fast, making it the most dangerous road in Egypt, so take care and avoid driving on it in the dark. To get on the Desert Road head towards the Pyramids and hang a right on the Alexandria Road. The second, older road is the **Agricultural Road** which is slow and tedious due to congestion. Gasoline is available on both routes.

The fastest route to **Hurghada and the Red Sea coast** is the **Ain Sukhna Road**, also known as El Qattamia Road. You get on it from the Autostrade, the major north-south road that runs along east Cairo. It meets the coast 25 kilometers north of Zafarana. This road will take you to Zafarana, Ain Sukhna, the Monasteries of Saint Paul and Saint Antony (250 kilometers), and on to El Gouna, Hurghada (500 kilometers), Safaga, and El Quseir. It is a toll road so keep a couple of pounds handy and hold on to your ticket stub.

Ismailia is just over 100 kilometers from Cairo on the **Ismailia Road** from Heliopolis. Port Said is another 80 kilometers north. The toll road (LE2) is well marked so it shouldn't be too hard to find your way. Suez (120 kilometers) is reached by a separate road from the Autostrade.

There are different routes to get to **South Sinai** (Sharm El Sheikh, Dahab, Nuweiba, Taba) and **North Sinai** (El Arish). To reach El Arish you must take the Ismailia Road north from Heliopolis to Ismailia (150 kilometers). Fifteen kilometers north of Ismailia, a ferry crosses the Canal and from there it's a straight shot to El Arish. To reach South Sinai, you take the **Suez Road** from the Autostrade in East Cairo to the **Ahmed Hamdy Tunnel** (130 kilometers). Allow 10-20 minutes to get through the Tunnel (LE5) and be prepared for a security search. You will then bear right (south). For **Saint Katherine's Monastery** (450 kilometers), **Nuweiba** (550 kilometers), **Taba** (600 kilometers) and **Israel**, turn left shortly thereafter and cut across the Peninsula. For **Ras Sidr**, (190) **Sharm El Sheikh** (480 kilometers), and **Ras Mohammed** (460 kilometers) continue south past El Tor (240 kilometers). Gasoline is available on either side of the Tunnel and at El Tor.

Except for Siwa, the major **Western Desert Oases** are linked to Cairo by the **Faiyoum Road** that is accessed from the Pyramids Road just before the Pyramids themselves. Faiyoum itself is just over 80 kilometers from the Pyramids. For Bahariya, turn after just 3 kilometers onto the **Desert Oasis Road** also known as the Bahariya Road. This road makes the circuit to Bahariya (400 kilometers from Cairo), Farafra (582 kilometers), Dakhla (900 kilometers), and El Kharga (1200 kilometers). There is little between each oasis save a few check points, so fill up on gas, water, and food when you have the chance.

To get to **Siwa** from Cairo, get on the Desert Road to Alexandria which connect with the road to Marsa Matrouh (follow the signs). **Marsa Matrouh** is 530 kilometers from Cairo and the battle field of **El Alamein** is at the 250 kilometers mark. From Marsa Matrouh, the new road to Siwa stretches 300 kilometers, making it about 800 kilometers from Cairo.

Finally, the Corniche, which straddles the Nile in Cairo continues south onto Beni Suef (120 kilometers) and the cities and monuments of the **Nile Valley**. Though the road has improved, traffic is still slow and tedious, and the scenery, once picturesque, is now cluttered with ugly concrete and brick buildings. If driving to **Luxor** (just over 800 kilometers), consider breaking up the trip with a night in Sohag (450 kilometers) or Assiut (380 kilometers).

By Service

Cairo's premier service depot is at **Ahmed Helmy** next to Ramses Station, with other hubs on Ramses Street and Midan Giza. Service depart constantly for Alexandria (2.5 hours), Port Said (2.5 hours), Middle Egypt (Minya & Assiut), and other destinations in the Delta and Canal Zone. A ride to any destination in the Delta, Canal Zone, and Middle Egypt should cost LE5-10.

By Train

Ramses Station, *Ramses Square (Metro: Mubarak),* is Cairo's, and hence Egypt's, rail hub. Trains north to Alexandria and Delta towns like Tanta, Damiatta, and Mansoura as well as Port Said and Suez Canal destinations leave from tracks 1-7 in the station's main hall. Tickets for these destinations are also purchased at the ticket window in the main hall. Tourist Police and the Egyptian Tourist Authority (ETA) have offices just to the left of the main entrance if coming in from the street. The ETA can provide information about trains and tourism in general. English is spoken. There is also an information booth in the middle of the hall which on good days can be quite helpful regarding schedules and fares. A telephone center is a couple of doors down from the ETA office and around the corner are coin and card operated phones for local calls.

"Torbini" VIP trains to **Alexandria** depart at 8am (LE32 with meal, LE22 without). Standard trains depart at 9am, 11am, noon, 5 pm, and 7pm (LE22 1st class, LE17 2nd class). "Faransawi" (French) trains depart hourly from 6am to 10:30pm (LE20 1st class, 2nd class LE12). There are two daily trains to **Port Said** (6:20am & 8:45am, LE45 1st class, LE26 2nd class).

Trains to **Minya**, **Luxor**, **Aswan**, and other southern destinations depart from platforms 8,9,10,11 outside the main hall. Tickets are sold from the office on the opposite side of those tracks. Take the underpass by turning left after passing through the main station. Window #1 sells 1st class tickets for trains leaving in the mornings, while Window #2 sells 1st class tickets for trains departing in the evening. Windows #3 and #4 handle 2nd class tickets. Trains are often reserved several days before departure so buy tickets at least two days ahead. Students get discounts of up to 50% so have your student card handy.

"Espani" (Spanish) trains without sleepers depart for **Luxor** (1st class LE82, 2nd class LE50), **Aswan** (LE100 1st class, LE60 2nd class), and other major Upper Egyptian destinations like **Sohag**, **Assiut**, and **Minya** at 7:30am, 6:45pm, 9:45 pm, and 11:30pm. The times are subject to change.

"Faransawi" (French) trains with sleepers leave for Luxor and Aswan at 7:40pm and 9pm. Foreigner tourists pay LE294 to Luxor and LE300 to Aswan, but have recently been prohibited from riding these trains by authorities. They prefer for you to ride the **WagonLits** sleepers, with dining and lounge cars, which cost about $125 one-way to Luxor, and $150 to Aswan. For information call *574-9474*. The office is outside of the main hall at Ramses Station and is open daily from 9am-4pm.

ORIENTATION

Tahrir Square & Downtown

The heart of Cairo is undoubtedly the huge, amorphous "square," **Midan El Tahrir** (Liberation Square). Originally parading grounds for British and Egyptian troops, Tahrir evolved into the hub of Cairo and its primary traffic node after 1952 when Gamal Abdel Nasser and the Free Officers overthrew the monarchy. Situated just off the Nile, it is now home to such landmarks as the Egyptian Antiquities Museum, the Arab League Headquarters, the Mogamma, and the Nile Hilton.

It's appetite for traffic is fed by major north-south arteries, **Kasr El Aini** and the **Corniche** along the Nile; and downtown thoroughfares, Talaat Harb, Kasr El Nil, and El Tahrir. They link Tahrir with the eastern districts of Ezbikeyya and Abdin where the still buzzing hubs of Opera Square and Ataba Square were the centerpieces of 19th century Cairo.

Ramses Square & Ramses Station

Cairo's transportation hub (and Egypt's for that matter), is **Ramses Square**, about two miles northeast of Tahrir Square to which it is linked by the ever-clogged Ramses Street. Trains come and go to destinations throughout Egypt from **Ramses Station** and a huge fleet of service taxis operate out of Ahmed Helmy depot.

Shubra & Bulaq

West of Ramses, the quarter of **Bulaq** was Cairo's maritime center in the Mamluki Era and developed into an industrial center during the reign of Mohammed Ali. It fell into disrepair after the opening of the Suez Canal and became a largely forgotten ghetto. Today, it is making a comeback fed by the erection of huge new office buildings along the Nile such as the spanking new Ministry for Foreign Affairs, and the World Trade Center. To improve Bulaq's image, Cairo Governorate is relocating, sometimes forcefully, the poorer inhabitants of these neighborhoods.

North of Ramses and Bulaq, the once modest middle class neighborhoods of **Shubra**, have mushroomed in the second half of the 20th century into one of the most densely populated areas on earth as its crowded residential communities now burst under the pressure of 2 million inhabitants, most of them working class families and rural migrants.

Islamic Cairo & Environs

Beyond Ataba Square to the east, the modern 19th European style city gives way to the medieval Islamic quarters of **El Hussein**, **Darb El Ahmar**, **Salah El Din's Citadel**, and the famous **Cities of the Dead**. Main attractions include the **Khan El Khalili Bazaar**, the masterpiece of Mamluki architecture, the **Mosque of Sultan Hassan**, and **Salah El Din's Citadel**, the seat of Egyptian government between the 12th and 19th century.

East and south of Islamic Cairo, densely populated and poverty stricken concrete housing projects squeeze between **El Moqattam Hills** and the Autostrade Highway, stretching to Maadi in the south and the airport to the north. Now a fast growing middle class suburb, El Moqattam Hills have been quarried since pharaonic times and afford some very fine views of Cairo.

Coming from Maadi, the Autostrade passes Islamic Cairo on its way to **Abbassia** and **Heliopolis**, now a city unto itself. Once a quiet middle class suburb with villas on tree-lined streets, Abbassia has been swallowed by modern Cairo; travelers only come for buses going to Sinai from the Sinai Bus Terminal. North of Abbassia, the European style districts of Medinet Nasr, Misr El Gadida, and Heliopolis are home primarily to middle and upper class Egyptians, including President Hosni Mubarak. Cairo Stadium, site of the city's biggest sporting events, and Cairo International Airport are also in Heliopolis. There are few tourist attractions except for the modest tomb of Egypt's revolutionary and nationalist leader, Gamal Abdel Nasser, and the more ostentatious tomb of his successor, Anwar El Sadat, at the Tomb of the Unknown Soldier across the street from where Muslim militants gunned him down on October 6, 1981.

Kasr El Aini: Garden City & Bab El Louk

The major thoroughfare of **Kasr El Aini** runs parallel to the Corniche south from Tahrir Square between the Mogamma and the American University in Cairo. Stretching to Malek El Salah and Old Cairo, it is lined with shops, theaters, and small eateries. It is also home to the **Maglis El Shaab**-the People's Assembly, Egypt's parliament-and Kasr El Aini Hospital, the main medical center in downtown Cairo. Kasr El Aini divides two very different neighborhoods.

To the west, **Garden City** was founded at the turn of the century as a quaint expatriate British community. Now primarily middle class Egyptian, its once quiet narrow streets become hopelessly clogged during the day, but return to their old tranquillity at night. On the western side of Kasr El Aini, the more populist districts of **Bab El Louk** and **Mounira** feature one of Cairo's biggest indoor markets, the **Bab El Louk Market**.

Misr Qadima: Coptic Cairo, Fustat & Sayeda Zeinab

About five kilometers south of Tahrir Square beyond Garden City, **Old Cairo** is the site of the Roman era fortress of **Babylon**. Besides being the original settlement of what we now know of Cairo, hence the name **Misr Qadima** meaning "Old Cairo," it is home to a handful of 4th and 5th century church and synagogues. East of Babylon, the first Islamic settlement of **Fustat** developed into one of the medieval world's most cosmopolitan cities with as many as 200,000 inhabitants, but burned down during the Crusades and was never rebuilt. It is now a primitive industrial site where bricks and ceramics are manufactured.

Also incorporated into the general region of Misr Qadima, between Islamic Cairo, Fustat, and downtown, **Sayeda Zeinab** is a densely populated working class district and home to one of the most venerated Islamic shrines in Egypt, the **Mosque of Sayeda Zeinab**. Misr Qadima is easily accessible by Metro. Get off at the **Mar Girgis** stop.

The Islands: Zamalek & Rhoda

There are two major islands in Cairo, Zamalek and Rhoda. The larger of the two, **Zamalek**, is a posh address and home to many foreign embassies, upscale hotels, and the most prestigious sporting club in the country, the Gezira Club, which covers half the island. From Tahrir Square, Zamalek is accessed by Tahrir Bridge (the one guarded by lions) and just to the north, the 6 October Bridge. To the north, the 26th July Bridge links Zamalek with Ramses Square and Abdel Moneim Riyad (by the Ramses Hilton).

The second island, **Rhoda**, has a decidedly more populist flavor with concrete, laundry laden apartment buildings stacked on top of each other. With the magnificently ornate 19th century **Manial Palace** and the ancient **Nilometer**, the oldest intact Islamic structure in Cairo, at least it out does Zamalek in the sightseeing department. It is linked to Cairo by the Malek El Salah Bridge by Old Cairo.

The Nile's West Banks: the Districts of Giza & the Pyramids

Undeveloped farmland only 100 years ago, the districts of **Giza** west of the Nile are now home to more than five million. Linked to Zamalek by the 26th July Bridge, **Mohandiseen** has emerged as one of Cairo's up and coming districts. Lacking the charm of Cairo's older districts it features modern glass and concrete buildings and wide streets like **Gamaat El Dowal El Arabia**, lined with modern consumer stores and fast-food outlets. South of Mohandiseen, the older neighborhoods of **Dokki** are also home to mostly middle and professional classes but don't strut quite the vanguard flair that Mohandiseen does.

The southern major district of Giza is simply known as **Giza**. Northern Giza, across the river from Rhoda, features posh apartments along the Nile, the Cairo Zoo, and Cairo University. Meanwhile its southern neighborhoods are very working class and dense with rural migrants. So is **Imbaba**, the poor and crowded district north of Mohandiseen. Separated from its rich neighbor by little more than a street and the proverbial "tracks" it is one of the poorest districts in Cairo. In the early 1990's it became a war zone and suffered armed clashes between Islamic militants and government security forces who at one point called army tanks into the streets.

The major attraction of Giza is of course the **Pyramids**. Situated 15 kilometers west of the Nile, the Pyramids were separated from urban developments by miles of farmland as little as twenty years ago. Today the fast encroaching city bumps right against the great monuments, threatening their desert habitat. **Pyramids Road**, the Pyramids' link with Cairo was only 40 years ago nothing more than a lonely, unpaved country road. Today its a major league thoroughfare which is constantly clogged. Fifteen kilometers south of the Pyramids, the **Step Pyramid of Zoser** and the **Old Kingdom Necropolis of Saqqara** still enjoy their original rural surroundings.

Maadi & Helwan

Fifteen kilometers south of downtown Cairo, the suburb of **El Maadi** was once an exclusive British neighborhood famous for its quiet leafy boulevards, and expansive Art Deco and Swiss cottage style villas. Many of the villas remain and some of the streets are still quiet and tree-lined, but Maadi has taken on many of the trappings of a full blown city from skyscrapers and shopping malls to huge concrete residential apartments and urban slums. The neighborhood of choice for most expatriate

Americans in Egypt because the American School is there, Maadi holds little appeal to the common traveler.

A poor cousin of Maadi, **Helwan** was also a comfy suburb once, favored primarily by middle class professionals; however in recent decades it has been overrun poor urban migrants, and from its bloated work force and inefficiency to its overbearing physical complex and the horrendous amount of pollution it spews into Cairo's already dirty air, Helwan's signature landmark, the Helwan Cement Factory, is a symbol of all that went wrong with Nasser's socialist economic policies.

GETTING AROUND TOWN

By Boat

Water taxis dock at the Maspero Dock in front of the Television Building north of Tahrir Square and run routes to Giza and Imbaba across the river and on to the barrages two hours north. They also make southern routes to Giza and Rhoda en route to Old Cairo (Coptic Cairo). They depart in either direction about every half an hour and cost about 50p per head. Water taxis are inefficient, but relaxing and offer you an opportunity to mix with local folks while enjoying some rather excellent views of the city and the Nile.

By Bus

If you really want to save money and physically immerse yourself in Cairene life, you get around on Cairo's buses, known affectionately as the "red dinosaurs" (or blue in the case of Giza). Because of their frequent routes, cheap fares (10-50p), and that they go virtually everywhere, these buses are the primary mode of transportation for millions of Cairenes-and it shows. As the proverbial 800 gorillas of Cairo traffic, they obnoxiously barrel through Cairo gridlock much to the irritation of drivers in cars, donkey carts, and most of all motorcycles. Inevitably run down and over worked, these buses designed to hold sixty are commonly stuffed like a goose with upwards of two hundred passengers at one time.

Just thinking about riding a bus let alone actually doing it simply overwhelms most foreigners. For most, the biggest turn off is the intensity of the crowds and the lack of any direction in English as coaches are labeled exclusively in Arabic. Yet if you brave it and take a few minutes to figure out the system it can actually be efficient and even fun in a roller coaster kind of way.

Because buses are numbered in Arabic and the writing is often hard to read because of smearing or the speed of a moving bus makes it impossible to make out the actual numbers, it's best to ask fellow commuters and conductors if and when a bus is headed for your destination. **Tahrir Square** is the major hub and buses leave here for all major Greater Cairo destinations. Because of the metro extensions, and efforts by Cairo's governor to clean up Tahrir, the main depot has been uprooted, making bus catching even more difficult. Generally buses headed to Mohandiseen, Agouza, Ramses Square and Heliopolis pass through Abdel Moneim Riyad Square at the Ramses Hilton and north of the Egyptian Museum.

Buses going west and south to Rhoda, Giza, Zamalek, Old Cairo, and Maadi used to leave from the Mogamma but now squeeze through Tahrir Street next to the Arab League Building. You also catch buses for Islamic Cairo from here. See the table for bus numbers. **Ataba Square**, **Ramses Square**, and **Giza Square** also contain major bus depots. Common bus stops are usually discernible by the metal shelters, crowds, and sometimes by signboards listing bus numbers. Purchase tickets from the *comsari*, a conductor usually seated at the rear of the coach.

One indelible image in the memory of anybody who has been to Cairo is that of Cairenes of various shapes, sizes, and ages, expertly hopping on and off moving buses. This is because buses very often do not come to a complete halt at their stops. Should you decide to participate in this local pastime, keep in mind that you need to hit the ground running to avoid a potentially nasty, and surely embarrassing fall.

Bus Routes

To and From Midan Tahrir/Abdel Moneim Riyad
#400 Heliopolis: Roxy Square & Cairo International Airport, Terminals 1 &2
#300 Abbassia & Ain Shams (Heliopolis)
#913 Sphinx and Pyramids in Giza
#815 Port Said Street, El Hussein Square (Khan El Khalili), El Azhar
#50 Ramses Square and Ramses Station
#16 Agouza
#99 Sudan Street Mohandiseen (west), Ataba Square (east)
#949 Nasr City & Cairo International Airport
#174 Sayeda Zeinab, Ibn Tulun Mosque, and Citadel
#900 Kasr El Aini, Rhoda (Manial), and Pyramids Road to the Pyramids
#904 to Ataba, Northern Cemetery (east), Tahrir, Pyramids (west)
#404 Ataba, Citadel

To and from Ataba and Opera Square
#99 Tahrir Square, Mohandiseen
#904 Northern Cemetery (east), Tahrir Square, Pyramids (west)
#404 Citadel (east), Tahrir Square (west)
951, 57 Citadel

#65 El Hussein Square (Khan El Khalili), El Azahar
#948 Cairo International Airport
#48 Zamalek
#410 Cairo International Airport
#93 Fustat and Mosque of Amr
#81 Southern Cemeteries (Imam Shafi'i)

To and From Pyramids
#804 Rhoda, Tahrir Square, Ramses Square, Citadel
#3 Giza Square
#905 Rhoda, Kasr El Aini Street (Garden City), Tahrir Square, Citadel
#904 Tahrir Square, Ataba Square, El Darasa (Northern Cemetery)

To and from Ramses Square and Ramses Station
#804 Tahrir, Rhoda, Pyramids Road and Pyramids
#65 Ataba, El Hussein (Khan El Khalili), Northern Cemeteries
#174 Citadel

To and From Citadel
#404 Ataba, Tahrir Square
#951 & #57 Ataba
#173 Falaki Square and Bab El Louk
#905 Rhoda, Pyramids Road, Pyramids

Minibuses & Service
     To supplement the over extended bus system, the Cairo Governorate operates a fleet of **minibuses**. White with orange trim, they follow many of the same routes for the same fares as the big buses (25-50p). Listed below are some useful minibus routes.

Minibus Routes
2 Tahrir Square-Ramses Square/Ahmed Helmy bus depot-Shubra
#27 Tahrir Square-Abbassia-Heliopolis-Cairo International Airport
#30 &32 Tahrir Square - Abbassia (Sinai Bus Terminal)
#54 Tahrir Square-Sayeda Zeinab (Ibn Tulun Mosque)-Citadel
#83 Tahrir Square-Giza/Pyramids Road/Pyramids
#77 Tahrir Square-El Hussein Square (Khan El Khalili)
#84 Ataba-Giza Square via Cairo University and the Cairo Zoo
#63 Ramses Square-El Azhar and El Hussein Square (Khan El Khalili)
#54 Tahrir-Citadel

     Not to be confused with the minibuses are the **service**, privately owned twelve seater minivans running regular routes throughout the city.

Unnumbered, their routes are written in Arabic on the sides of vehicle and very often the driver's lieutenant shouts out the destination. They stop when flagged down or at stops designated by a symbol resembling the pharaonic winged sun disc. Fees are 60p and the best way to figure out which one you want is simply to ask. There is also intercity service to destinations throughout Egypt departing from the Ahmed Helmy depot at Ramses Square (See *Arrivals & Departures* section above.)

Car Rentals & Chauffeur-driven Cars

To rent a car in Egypt, you must be 25 years old, carry an international driver's license and be a very skillful and self-confident driver if you wish to live. Should you like a private car without having to drive yourself or to hassle with taxis, it is possible to hire a chauffeur driven car for a fixed price at most upscale hotels. For a list of car rental firms in Cairo, see the "Practical Information" section at the end of this chapter. Listed below are companies that offer chauffeur cars for hire:

• **Bita**, *8 Kasr El Nil Street Tel. 02/774-330*
• **Budget Limousine Service**, *Semiramis InternContinental Hotel, Tahrir Square, downtown. Tel. 02/355-7171 ext. 8991*
• **Europcar Interrent Egypt**, *Max Building on Lebanon Street, in Mohandiseen. Tel. 02/303-5630/125. Fax 02/303-6123/575-9554*
• **Limousine Misr**, *Tel. 02/285-6721. Cairo International Airport. Tel. 02/ 418-9675/6. Fax 02/285-6124. 13th floor, Misr Travel Towers in Abbassia Square, Abbassia*
• **Smart Limo**, *151 Corniche El Street, in Maadi. Tel. 02/365-4321. Fax 02/ 6367231*

By Metro & Tram

The first underground in Africa and the Arab World, the Cairo Metro opened in the mid-1980's and is constantly being extended. Built with assistance from the French, it currently features one line running from Helwan south of Cairo to Heliopolis with branches to Shubra, Ataba and Abdin, but new lines will soon reach Giza, Mohandiseen, Islamic Cairo, and Zamalek.

Though crowded during rush hours, the Metro is, unlike buses, easy to use. Signs are in English throughout stations and trains and the **first car in every train is reserved for women**. One-way fares cost between 20 and 60 piasters and more to outreaching stations. Keep your ticket after passing through the turnstiles going in because you will need it to get out. The Metro operates from 5:30am to midnight daily during winter and 1am during the summer. Trains pick up every 5-10 minutes. Be aware that station names do not necessarily indicate location (see sidebar on next page).

METRO STATION NAMES & THEIR LOCATIONS

Many metro stations have been given names with no relation to the station's location, making it difficult for those unfamiliar with the system to know when to get off. Listed below are some important metro stops and their names:

Sadat Station–*Tahrir Square*
Mubarak Station–*Ramses Square and Ramses Station*
General Mohammed Naguib Station–*Abdin*
Gamal Abdel Nasser Station–*Ramses Street between Ramses Square & Tahrir Square*

The **tram** system in Heliopolis is the last vestige of Cairo's old electric trolley system and not of much use to tourists. Lines run the following routes:

• El Darasa (Islamic Cairo) - Matariya (Heliopolis)
• Abbassia-Ain Shams Club (Heliopolis)
• Abbassia- Midan Triomphe (Heliopolis)
• Medinet Nasr-Roxi Square (Heliopolis)
• Ramses-Medinet Nasr

By Taxi

Taxis can be efficient and cheap or a dreadfully expensive hassle. Taxis parked outside hotels and tourist attractions invariably charge exorbitant rates. You can bargain and most will come down a bit, but they're suckering you into thinking you're getting a good deal. The truth is that they won't go down to the prices you can get on the street because they know that after you take off in disgust, some other foreigner who doesn't know better will accept their prices. Also, some travelers are willing to pay the higher prices because these driver speak better English than local drivers and know the sites well.

To pay fares closer to market value, flag down a black and white on the street by shouting your destination as they pass. A 5-10 minute ride within downtown shouldn't cost more than LE2-3, a fifteen minute ride LE5, and a half hour LE12-15. Late at night or during the early morning expect to shell out 50% more. When giving initial directions, simply name a landmark, major street, or nearby neighborhood instead of the exact street address so as not to confuse him. Meters do not apply, so establish the price before leaving, or if you know what you're doing just pay the driver while getting out and thanking him. If a driver's initial offer seems expensive, don't hesistate to bargain-it's standard procedure. Also, it is possible to flag cabs with passengers in them which is cheaper; just ask if the cab is heading in the direction of your destination.

Hotels will arrange taxis for you should you need to go to the airport at some odd hour of the night; just be sure to arrange it ahead of time.

Some recommended rates:
• Tahrir Square-Khan El Khalili – LE5 one-way
• Tahrir Square-Old Cairo (Coptic Cairo) – LE5 one-way
• Tahrir Square-Pyramids – LE15 one-way
• Tahrir Square-Cairo International Airport – LE30 one-way
• Tahrir Square-Zamalek – LE4 one-way
• Tahrir Square-Rhoda – LE5
• Tahrir Square-Saqqara – LE60 round-trip including the wait

On Foot

Cairo is by far too large a city to cover totally on foot, but its old quarters retain mystique, texture and intimacy that can only be savored by an immersed pedestrian. Maps are handy and can be found in any major bookstore or hotel. *Cairo A-Z* contains the most detailed street maps for Cairo, and is available from major bookstores for about LE20. Lehnert & Landrocke and the Palm Press also publish good maps that are widely available.

WHERE TO STAY

Unless you're working or specifically staying in Giza for a view of the Pyramids, stay downtown. This is most convenient vis a vis the Metro, the train station, and the monuments. Another option is the slightly less chaotic island of Zamalek, 5-10 minutes from downtown, 20-30 minutes from Islamic Cairo and 30-45 minutes from the Giza Pyramids by car.

Downtown – Expensive

CAIRO NILE HILTON, *Corniche El Nil Street at Tahrir Square. Tel. 02/578-0444, 578-0666. Fax 02/578-0475. Capacity: 433 rooms. Call 1-800-HILTONS (445-8667) in USA for info and reservations. Rates: $90-210 single, $120-240 double, $220-$1,190 suite. Metro:Sadat. Credit cards: all major credit cards accepted.*

Located in the heart of Cairo next to the Egyptian Museum in Tahrir Square and overlooking the Nile, this is the mainstay of Cairo's luxury hotels and the mother ship of Hilton's seven Egyptian hotels. All rooms are first-rate and feature air-conditioning, mini-bar, and satellite TV. Facilities include an American Express branch, a business center, swimming pool, tennis & squash courts, and exercise facilities with a sauna and steam bath. Golf and horseback riding are accessible. The rooftop nightclub features oriental floor shows and Jackie's Joint, the disco, rotates in and out of Cairo's ever changing list of hot nightspots. There is also a casino, five restaurants (coffee shop, Italian, fancy grille, Middle Eastern), and three bars. The outdoor Amm Ali (Uncle Ali) Cafe on the back terrace packs one of the tastiest, if priciest, waterpipes in town (LE7). The service is first-rate, and the diverse clientele discerning. President Nasser enjoyed his last hurrah here when he successfully brokered the bloody Black September dispute between Yasser Arafat and King Hussein at an Arab summit just days before his death in 1970.

SEMIRAMIS INTERCONTINENTAL, *Corniche El Nil in Tahrir Square. Tel. 02/355-7171. Fax 02/356-3020. Telex 94259 IHCSM UN. Capacity: 840 rooms and 95 suites. Rates: $95-210 single, $110-240 double, $300-$1900 suite. Metro: Sadat. Credit cards: all major credit cards accepted.*

Built in the 1910, the original Semiramis lingered in the shadow of the world famous Shepheard's, but this new InterContinental edition towers over its old rival literally and figuratively. Regarded by many as the best hotel in Cairo it features first rate service, good location and excellent views overlooking the Nile, but lacks the atmospherics of say, the Mena House or the Marriott. The business center offers secretarial services, fax, DHL courier, meeting rooms, and a local reference library. Dining options include fine Middle Eastern and continental cuisine and the Harun El Rashid nightclub features Middle Eastern floor shows.

CAIRO RAMSES HILTON, *1115 Corniche El Nil. Tel. 02/575-8000. Fax 02/575-7152. Telex 94262 HIRAM UN. Capacity: 838 rooms, 3 Executive Floors, Hilton CLUBROOM, and especially equipped rooms for guests with disabilities. Rates: $80-210 single, $110-210 double, $250-$2500 suite. In USA, call 1-800-HILTONS (845-8667) for info and reservations. Metro: Sadat. Credit cards: all major credit cards accepted.*

This newer cousin of the Nile Hilton is the tallest hotel in Cairo and is a mile north on the Corniche overlooking the Nile. Still within walking distance of the Egyptian Museum and Tahrir Square, it offers more extensive facilities including better access for the disabled. It contains six restaurants including a decent Chinese, and three bars. The Windows on the World on the top floor offers a great view of the Cairo skyline and recreation facilities include a casino, outdoor swimming pool, sundeck, and exercise facilities with jacuzzi and steambath. Clever modern architecture aside, the Ramses gets a C- for atmospherics.

SHEPHEARD'S HOTEL, *Corniche El Nil off Tahrir Square in Garden City. Tel. 02/355-3800. Fax 02/355-7248. Rates: $90-130 single, $100-150 double, $250-600 suite. Metro: Sadat. Credit cards: all major credit cards accepted.*

This reincarnation of the granddaddy of Cairo's luxury hotels now lingers in the shadows the InterContinentals of the world. But with its restrained Arabesque decor, it exudes a subtle sense of class and old world charm not found in, say, the Ramses Hilton. Its good location and lower prices for excellent service and quality make it an excellent choice for those looking to enjoy a more distinctly Cairene experience.

CAIRO KHAN SUITES HOTEL, *12 26th July Street, Cairo. Tel. 02/ 392-201 390-67005. Fax 02/390-6799. Telex 21093 CKHAN UN. Capacity: 96 rooms, 192 beds. Rates: $52.50 single, $65 double, $110-160 suite. Metro: Ataba. Credit cards: Visa.*

Right in the heart of noisy downtown, the Khan is an excellent value. Rooms are modern and comfortable if not charming. You won't get a view of anything more than Mohammed Farid Street, but rooms feature satellite TV, air-conditioning, and clean baths. Suites have kitchen facilities.

CLEOPATRA HOTEL, *2 El Bustan Street on Tahrir Square. Tel. 02/ 575-9900/23, 575-9712. Fax 02/575-9807. Telex 21230 CLTEL UN. Capacity: 84 rooms, 164 beds. Rates: $62 single, $75 double, $140 suite. Metro: Sadat. Credit cards: Visa, Mastercard, American Express.*

Apart from its location and the Korean restaurant on the bottom floor, the Cleopatra is nothing to rave about. In a city full of charming old buildings, there's no reason to subject yourself to staying in this 1970's concrete monstrosity. Also, the service can be less than enthusiastic and the rooms shabby. The views of Tahrir Square are unlike anything you've experienced before and the noise even more so.

Moderate

COSMOPOLITAN HOTEL, *off Kasr El Nil Street on Ibn Talaab Street. Tel. 02/392-3663, 392-3845, 392-7522. Fax 02/393-3531. Telex 21451 COSMA UN. Capacity: 84 rooms, 168 beds. Rates: $40-50 single, $50-60 double, $65 suite. Metro: Tahrir Square. Credit cards: Visa, American Express, and Diners Card.*

A grand hotel, the Cosmopolitan is a beautiful relic from the 1940's. From the old fashioned English bar and the vintage elevators to the upholstered antique furnishings and the tiled bathroom floors, it is a setting worthy of a scene in *The English Patient*. Though some travelers liken the faded grandeur to shabbiness, it's more likely you will agree that it lends a touch of authenticity to its charm. Rooms are air-conditioned with televisions, fridges, and phones. The location is very central; we'd recommend asking for a balcony room even though the views or somewhat less spectacular than at some other hotels.

VICTORIA HOTEL, *66 El Gomhuriya Street. Tel. 02/589-2290/1/2. Fax 02/589-3008. Capacity: 100 rooms. Rates: $35 single, $44 double. Metro: Ataba. Credit cards: Visa, Mastercard.*

A pre-World War II hotel with large air-conditioned rooms furnished in mahogany, the Victoria doesn't quite measure up to the Cosmopolitan in the charm category, but it is pleasant, centrally located, and reasonably priced.

THE WINDSOR HOTEL, *19 Alfi Bey Street. Tel. 02/591-5277, 591-5810. Fax 02/592-1621. Telex 93839 DOSS UN. Capacity: 50 rooms, 103 beds. Rates: $30 single, $35 double. Metro: Ataba. Credit cards: Visa.*

Though it is beginning to show its age, this Edwardian gem is still a classy and charming hotel with history to boot. The rooms each retain some individual character, differing in size and shape, some with private bathrooms, others without, but they all feature a combination of the old and the new: modern air-conditioning, and old school wooden furnishings. The star of the establishment, however is definitely the bar- a classic, if subdued, watering hole that takes you right back to 1940.

Located in a part of town that was once the center of expatriate social life, the Windsor was once the site of a Turkish bath house before becoming a British Officers Club in the 1930's. Its guest list includes among others, Monty Python veteran Michael Palin, who set up shop here while filming *Around the World in 80 Days*.

THE GRAND HOTEL, *17, 26th July Street. Tel. 02/757-700. Fax 02/757-593. Metro: Orabi. Rates: $24-30 single, $30-40 double, $66 suite. Credit cards: Visa.*

An Art Deco style hotel that feels as if it may have been grand back in the days when grand hotels were really called "the Grand Hotel." Art Deco aside, the Grand features vintage 1930's elevators, a bar, a fountain, and a restaurant. Rooms are comfortable and souped up with air-conditioning, television, clean private bathrooms and phone.

Budget

PENSION ROMA, *169 Mohammed Farid Street east of Opera Square. Tel. 02/391-1088. Metro: Ataba. Rates: LE30 single, LE50 double, LE60 suite.*

This well-known establishment consistently gets good reviews from travelers who applaud its cleanliness, good location, and friendly and helpful management. Its reputation is enhanced by the *fin de siècle* atmospherics shaped by hardwood floors, antique furniture, and an ancient grilled elevator. Most rooms do not have private showers, but the common baths are spotless. Rooms are comfortable, well maintained, and feature fans. Breakfast is included, and it's an excellent place to meet and share experiences with other travelers.

GRESHAM HOTEL, *20 Talaat Harb Street. Tel. 02/575-9043. Metro: Sadat. Rates: LE30-35 single, LE40-45 double.*

A relic from the 1940's, the Gresham is well located and charming but is beginning to show its age; the old fashioned furniture and decor are homey but shabby and timeworn. Rooms are spacious, clean, and comfortable. The more expensive are air-conditioned with private showers, but hot water is sporadic. The Gresham one-ups the competition with its recently renovated bar.

ISMAILIA HOTEL, *1 Tahrir Square on the eighth floor. Tel. 02/356-3122. Metro: Sadat. Rates: LE20 single, LE40-50 double.*

One of the most popular budget hotels in Cairo, the Ismailia lacks the charm or atmospherics of the Gresham or the Pension Roma, but gets high marks for its staff, location, and facilities. The rooms are plain but quite clean, comfortable and fanned. The showers work well with plenty of hot water and the lounge features satellite television. If possible, try to get a room with a balcony overlooking Tahrir Square. The view is mind boggling if not aesthetically graceful. If there are no rooms at all, you may be allowed to camp out in the lounge or in the halls for LE10-15.

CARLTON HOTEL, *21, 26th July Street next to the Cinema Rivoli. Tel. 02/575-5022. Fax 02/575-5323. Metro: Orabi. Rates: LE55 single, LE75 double.*

Another downtown establishment in a dingy, but charming old building with marble floors, the Carlton offers rooms with air-conditioning, television, and decently clean bathrooms. However, it's not kept up or as clean as it might be.

THE TULIP HOTEL, *3 Talaat Harb Square on the third floor. Tel. 02/393-9433. Fax 02/361-1995. Metro: Sadat. Rates: LE20-40 singles and doubles.*

The Tulip is popular and well located but does not stand out. Rooms are plain with fans and those without full fledged bathrooms have sinks. Try to get one with a balcony for ventilation and viewing purposes. The management can be moody and uptight.

ANGLO-SWISS HOTEL, *14 Champollion Street on the 6th floor. Tel. 02/575-1497. Rates: LE20-25 single, LE35-45 double.*

The Anglo-Swiss gets mixed reviews from travelers. Those who like it enjoy the spiral staircase, the piano in the lounge, and the homey dining room. Critics cite the pushy touts, the bad paint job, and the shabby condition of the building generally. Pricier rooms are larger; all rooms feature fans, and showers are shared.

HOTEL VIENNOISE, *11 Bassiouni Street. Tel. 02/574-3153. Fax 02/575-3136. Rates: LE25-35 singles and doubles.*

A shabby establishment with large rooms, the more expensive of which have private baths. Better to concentrate on getting a room with one of those fantastically large balconies.

HOTEL DES ROSES, *33 Talaat Harb Street. Tel. 02/393-8022. Metro: Sadat. Rates: LE31-45 single, LE45-65 double.*

It's only worth the money if you get an upper-level room with the super-duper view of the city. Also be sure to examine the furnishings; some renovated rooms feature classy Art Deco furniture while other rooms have not been renovated at all and are poorly furnished. The more expensive rooms contain private baths. Hot water is sporadic generally.

OXFORD PENSION, *32 Talaat Harb Street. Tel. 02/758-173. Metro: Sadat. Rates: LE10-40 dormitories, singles and doubles.*

For a long time, the Oxford was the most popular budget hotel in Cairo and a legend in its own right; despite the buzzing atmosphere, it is drab and sketchy. There are no rooms with private baths, but the Oxford is more accommodating to those looking to stay in Cairo long term.

HOTEL MINERVA, *on an alley between Sherif and Talaat Harb streets where they meet 26th July Street, on the 6th floor. Tel. 02/392-0600. Metro: Sadat. Rates: LE26-30 single, LE28-35 double.*

The recently renovated rooms are spacious, clean, and well maintained generally, but there is no hot water or air-conditioning. The alley location is a bit of a downer.

Ataba & Islamic Cairo

THE NEW RICHE HOTEL, *47 Abdel Aziz Street off Ataba Square Tel. 02/390-0145, 390-5380, 390-6390. Fax 02/390-6390. Capacity: 37 rooms, 74 beds. Rates: LE 40-70 singles and doubles, LE115 triples.*

Rooms feature air-conditioning and private baths but are still overpriced. The Ataba location is ideal for those who enjoy immersing themselves in the thick of things. It is 15 minutes walking from the Khan El Khalili and Islamic Cairo, a half hour walk from downtown. The management can be uptight, but looks after female guests.

EL HUSSEIN HOTEL, *El Hussein Square in the Khan El Khalili off El Mouski Street. Tel. 02/591-8664, 591-8089. Capacity: 56 rooms, 112 beds. Rates: LE30-50 single, LE40-60 double.*

In the heart of Islamic Cairo in the Khan El Khalili, El Hussein overlooks El Hussein Square. If you can get a room with a view of the square and can handle the colorful noises of wedding parties and call to prayers, it's worth ignoring the drab rooms and staying here for a night or two. You will be rewarded with an immersion in Cairo's medieval city not available when staying in other hotels. Best of all, El Fishawi's coffeehouse is but five meters away. Some rooms come with a private bath and all are air-conditioned. The rooftop restaurant is an excellent locale for a kebab dinner and gives you a good shot of witnessing, if not participating in, an Egyptian wedding-a worthwhile dab into local culture.

Ramses

FONTANA HOTEL, *Ramses Square. Tel. 02/922-145, 922-321. Fax 02/922-145. Metro: Mubarak. Rates: LE60 single, LE90 double.*

The Ramses Square location is a mixed bag of accessibility to intra- and inter city transportation and vulnerability to some of the busiest and noisiest traffic anywhere in the world. The hotel itself is a quirky kind of place and modest as it is, features a rooftop pool where you can enjoy overlooking the hubbub while you cool down, and a functioning disco. Besides that, the rooms are comfortable and clean with bathrooms and air-conditioning.

Rhoda

LE MERIDIEN LE CAIRE HOTEL, *on the northern tip of Rhoda Island off the Corniche in Garden City. Tel. 02/362-1717. Fax 02/362-1927. Telex 22325 HOMERUN. Capacity: 274 rooms, 482 beds. Rates: $145-210 single, $125-195 double, $550-1800 suite. Credit cards: all major credit cards accepted.*

This masterpiece in modernism dominates the northern tip of Rhoda island and commands the best views of the Nile of any hotel in Cairo and though its quality and service has dipped in the past, it appears to have reasserted itself as one of Cairo's top hotels. The rooms are modern and well equipped with deluxe amenities: spotless bathrooms, air-conditioning, full stocked minibar, and satellite television. Within the confines there is a swimming pool, several fine restaurants with excellent views of the Nile, and a shopping arcade. The oriental nightclub often features top belly dancing and popular singing stars.

Zamalek

CAIRO MARRIOTT HOTEL & CASINO, *El Gezira Street, Zamalek. Tel. 02/340-8888. Fax 02/340-6667. Telex 93465 MAR UN. In USA, call 1-800-228-9290 for info and reservations. Capacity: 1042 rooms, 108 suites, and 7 Presidential suites. Rates: $120-170 single, $125-$195 double, $485-$1500 suite. Credit cards: all major credit cards accepted.*

No hotel in Cairo boasts the combination of superior quality and facilities, convenient location, and atmospherics of the Marriott. Khedive Ismail built the splendid Arabesque palace at the core of the hotel in 1869 to house visiting VIPs attending the inauguration of the Suez Canal. After taking it over 20 years ago Marriott renovated to the hilt and with its over the top chandeliers, marble floors, fine mashrabia, and lots of brass, its current edition will certainly live up to your orientalist fantasies. Whether you consider it gaudy and ostentatious or the apogee of 19th century elegance is a matter of taste, but it cannot be denied that the Marriott is a work of art.

The four acres of lush gardens complete with fountains and baroque statues is an oasis of tranquility right in the heart of Cairo. Most of the 1,200 rooms are in the two modern towers, and are large and well furnished with modern amenities. Upper rooms feature excellent views of the Nile and the city. Popular with businessmen and diplomats, as well as tourists, it is home to the American Chamber of Commerce, a shopping mall, and business and conference facilities. Recreationally, guests can enjoy the pool, a health club, casino, and tennis courts. Even if you don't stay here, it's worth a walk through.

GOLDEN TULIP FLAMENCO HOTEL, *2 El Gezira El Wosta Street, Zamalek. Tel. 02/340-0815. Fax 02/340-0819. Telex 22025 FLAMN UN. Capacity: 157 rooms, 241 beds. Rates: $55-88 single, $72-107 double, $107-230 suite. Credit cards: Visa, Mastercard.*

Popular with mid-level European tour groups, the Flamenco lacks the cheesy flare of most three star establishments in Cairo, and that, along with the Nile views, sits well with most Americans. The staff is courteous and professional and room amenities include satellite television, air-conditioning and clean baths. The in-house Italian restaurant, Florencia, is more than decent.

THE NEW STAR HOTEL, *34 B Yehia Ibrahim Street, Zamalek. Tel. 02/ 340-1865, 341-1321, 340-0928. Fax 02/341-1321. Capacity: 28 rooms, 56 beds. Rates: $30 single, $40 double, $45 suite. Credit cards: Visa.*

The New Star Hotel features clean and well equipped rooms with air-conditioning, satellite television, decent bathrooms, and kitchenettes.

LONGCHAMPS HOTEL, *21 Ismail Mohammed Street, Zamalek. Tel. 02/340-9644, 340-2311. Capacity: 30 rooms, 60 beds. Rates: $27 single, $35 double.*

Best known for its bar, the Longchamps is a modest three star hotel with a classy sounding French name that offers decent air-conditioned rooms and a relatively quiet location.

MAYFAIR HOTEL, *9 Aziz Osman Street, Zamalek. Tel. 02/340-7315. Rates: LE25-45 single, LE30-60 double, LE50-70 suite.*

In the heart of Zamalek, the Mayfair offers a quiet location with a pleasant shady terrace to hang out on. Hopping cosmopolitan 26th July Street is just a block or so away. Rooms with air-conditioning and private showers are more expensive.

Giza & the Pyramids

THE MENA HOUSE, *at the end of Pyramids Road at the base of the Pyramids entrance. Tel. 02/383-3222, 383-3444. Capacity: 500+ rooms. Rates: $130-200 single, $130-250, double, $400-$1400 suite. In USA, phone 1-800-5-OBEROI for info and reservations. Credit cards: all major credit cards accepted.*

Located at the base of the Great Pyramid of Khufu, the Mena House enjoys the mother of all views with modern facilities and elaborate arabesque atmospherics to match. A historical landmark in its own right, it hosted a summit between Churchill and Roosevelt during World War II and the signing of the Arab-Israeli Peace Treaty in 1979. Other celebrity guests include the Grateful Dead who stayed here when they played the Pyramids in 1978. The only disadvantage is the distance from downtown and Islamic Cairo, but the superb views more than compensate. If up for a splurge by all means try the Moghul Room one of the finest Indian restaurants anywhere (Oberoi is an Indian chain). Recreation facilities include a golf course, casino, and an outdoor swimming pool. Horseback riding at the pyramids is also convenient.

CAIRO MOVENPICK JOLIE VILLE HOTEL, *Alexandria Road several kilometers past the Pyramids. Tel. 02/385-2555, 385-2666. Fax 383-5006. Capacity: 240 rooms. Rates: $115 single, $145 double, $250-350 suite. Credit cards: all major credit cards accepted.*

Apart from the superb breakfast buffet, the Jolie Ville's main attraction is the location up the road from the Giza Pyramids and the magnificent views. A very modern, European establishment, the Jolie Ville offers space and quiet and is a half hour commute from downtown. Facilities include a beautiful pool with views of the Giza Pyramids, several restaurants and bars, tennis courts, and a healthclub. Rooms are well furnished, comfortable, and feature all amenities expected at a five star resort. The Jolie Ville is popular with high priced *veilles dames Francaises* type European package tours.

SOFITEL LE SPHINX, *1 Desert Road to Alex near the Pyramids. Tel. 02/ 383-7444, 383-7555. Fax 02/383-4930. Rates: 277 rooms. Rates: $105-15 single, $120-260 double, $495-750 suite. Credit cards: all major credit cards accepted.*

The Sofitel is a shiny new resort on the Desert Road to Alexandria near the Pyramids in the mold of the Forte Grande and the Jolie Ville. It's a luxurious facility with views of the Pyramids, but also a long commute on Pyramids Road to downtown. The service will pamper you and the rooms are comfortable and well furnished with air-conditioning, satellite TV, and all the rest, but there's lack of Egyptian flavor that is not blatantly manufactured.

FORTE GRANDE PYRAMIDS HOTEL, *on the Desert Road to Alex. Tel. 02/383-0383, 383-0117, 383-0772. Fax 02/383-1739, 383-0023. Capacity: 523 rooms. Rates: $125 single, $160 double, $230- $530 suite. Credit cards: all major credit cards accepted.*

Very similar to the Sofitel in location and style, the Forte Grande is slightly more expensive. The large swimming pool and deck features great views of the Pyramids and doubles as a disco on Thursday nights in the summer.

HOTEL LES 3 PYRAMIDES, *229 Pyramids Road. Tel. 02/582-2223. Fax 02/582-3700. Capacity: 233 rooms. Rates: $65-80 single, $80-95 double, $110-140 triples and suites. Credit cards: all major credit cards accepted.*

This concrete '70s monstrosity on Pyramids Road is popular with middle class French tour groups. Upper level rooms feature views of the Pyramids but otherwise, the location is a drawback; it's noisy, far from downtown, and not as close to the Pyramids as you might be led to believe. Rooms are sufficiently furnished with air-conditioning and private baths, and spruced up with the all too typical hokey papyrus decor.

Dokki & Mohandiseen

CAIRO SHERATON, *Galaa Square in Dokki. Tel. 02/336-4601, 336-9800. Fax 02/336-4602. Capacity: more than 1200 rooms. Rates: $151-193 single, $117-224 double, $278-1000 suite. Credit cards: all major credit cards accepted.*

With more than 600 rooms in each tower, the Cairo Sheraton is the largest hotel in town and it feels that way. Designed so that every room enjoys a view of either the Pyramids or the Nile and perhaps both, it offers every amenity expected in an international luxury hotel and its high standards and good service attract many leading political and business figures. Business centers, health club facilities, a movie theater, and a half dozen restaurants offer plenty of distractions for those needing a break from business or site seeing. On the other hand it lacks any real Egyptian ambiance or style and feels very much like the big international name hotel that it is.

PYRAMISA HOTEL, *60 Giza Street. Tel. 02/336-9000, 336-7000, 336-8000. Fax 02/360-5347. Capacity: 188 rooms. Rates: $80-100 for singles, $90-120 for doubles and $200-300 for suites. Credit cards: all major credit cards accepted.*

Stay in the Pyramisa and you can pretend to stay in the Cairo Sheraton-it's only across the street. Unfortunately, their common border is not El Nil Street, but noisy Giza Street and the Pyramisa is not on the Nile, nonetheless, upper level rooms do offer good views of the city and the Nile to the east, and the Pyramids to the west. Facilities and amenities are modern and comfortable – just what you'd expect in a four or five star hotel, if just a notch lower than the big name establishments. Fine dining, drinking, and pool/health club facilities are located on the premises.

AL NABILA CAIRO HOTEL, *4 Gamaat El Dowal El Arabia Street in Mohandiseen. Tel. 02/303-0302. Fax 02/347-6958. Capacity: 180 rooms: Raes: $80 single, $150 double, $200-340 suite. Credit cards: Visa, Mastercard.*

Gamaat El Dowal Street is better known as the home of McDonald's, not Mohammed Ali. There's little interest to tourists in Mohandiseen and Gamaat El Dowal is one of the noisiest streets in Cairo. Apart from that, El Nabila is a good little hotel offering clean rooms with television, air-conditioning, and medium size baths. Despite the high listed prices, you can try to bargain them down. Guests can relax by the small pool or in the bar.

ATLAS ZAMALEK HOTEL, *20 Gamaat El Dowal El Arabia Street, Mohandiseen (not Zamalek!). Tel. 02/346-5782, 346-7230-, 346-6569. Fax*

02/347-6958. Telex 93281 ATLAS UN. Capacity: 74 rooms. Rates: $70 single, $85 double, $102-178 suite. Credit cards: Visa, Mastercard.

Known for its nightclub, the Atlas is on Gamaat El Dowal Street—Cairo's testament to western consumerism. Apart from the uninteresting and noisy environment, the Atlas is a modest upper mid-scale hotel, with comfortable clean rooms, and professional service. It's popular with middle class Europeans and Gulf Arabs.

CONCORDE HOTEL, *146 El Tahrir Street, Dokki. Tel. 02/336-1194/ 3/8. Fax 02/336-1189. Capacity: 71 rooms. Rates: $33-40 for singles and $44-50 for doubles. Credit cards: Visa.*

Tahrir Street is a traffic nightmare but it offers easy access to Zamalek and downtown. Room rates are very reasonable and the rooms themselves comfortable and modeStreet The Sheraton and all of its various playgrounds are around the corner. The Concorde will be more appealing once the Metro underneath Tahrir Street opens sometime in 1998.

INDIANA HOTEL, *16 Hassan Rostom, Dokki. Tel. 02/335-5403, 335-4422, 349-3775. Fax 02/360-7947. Capacity: 115 rooms. Rates: $41 single, $50 double, $69-75 suite. Credit cards: Visa.*

It's hard to imagine two more different places than Cairo and Indiana, but inexplicable names aside, this modest establishment in residential Dokki offers a small pool, an eatery and a bar. Rooms are air-conditioned and feature televisions and modest baths.

PHARAOHS HOTEL, *12 Lotfi Hassouna Street, Dokki. Tel. 02/361-0871/2/3. Fax 02/361-0874. Telex 933383 FAROS UN. Operates 102 rooms and charges $27-42 for singles, $36-55 for doubles, and $52-61 for triples. Credit Cards: Visa.*

Cheap for a three star hotel with air-conditioned rooms, but the Dokki location is less than ideal for most tourists - at least it's quiet. During low season you'll probably be able to negotiate a discount.

MARWA HOTEL, *11 El Khatib Street, Dokki. Tel. 02/348-8830/25. Fax 02/360-8989. Telex 94058 MPHTL UN. Capacity: 118 rooms. Rates: $37-44 singles, $54 doubles, $120 suites. Credit cards: Visa.*

Another nondescript three star establishment in Dokki with a professional staff and comfy rooms featuring decent baths, air-conditioning, and televisions.

Maadi

SOFITEL MAADI TOWERS HOTEL, *29 on the Corniche in Maai 12 kilometers south of downtown. Tel. 02/350-6022, 385-3005. Fax 02/351-8449. Rates: $110-154 singles, $132-187 doubles, $385-550 suites. Credit cards: all major credit cards accepted.*

The Sofitel is far from downtown and Islamic Cairo in the leafy suburb of Maadi, but it commands excellent views of the Nile and the upper stories have some of the best views of the Pyramids and Saqqara apart from the hotels actually at the Pyramids themselves. The amenities are all five-star and there are several eateries, a bank, and a shopping arcade. The in-house Egyptian restaurant, El Dorna features a superb buffet for LE45, not including drinks.

WHERE TO EAT

Downtown

FELFELA, *15 Hoda Shaarawi Street off Talaat Harb Street about 1/2 mile from Tahrir Square and a block from Talaat Harb Square. Metro: Sadat. Hours: 9am-12:30am daily. Credit cards: not accepted.*

The mothership of Egypt's most popular restaurant chain is known for its extensive menu, super-kitsch decor, and slow service. Not as tasty or cheap as some other places, it's an excellent introduction to Egyptian cuisine. Try any variety of fuul or ta'amiya dishes for a pound or two; or munch on classic Egyptian meat platters like kebab, grilled pigeon, or lamb *fatta* with yoghurt and garlic. The takeaway outlet around the corner on Talaat Harb Street serves up fuul, ta'amiya, and shwarma sandwiches for LE1-2. Local beer and wine is served in the main restaurant.

PAPRIKA, *1129 Corniche El Nil by the Television Building and close to the Ramses Hilton. Metro: Sadat. Tel. 02/749-447. Hours: 12am-12pm. Credit cards: Visa.*

Quality mezze, a long menu of Egyptian and continental dishes, and an almost romantic ambiance forged by dim lighting and tuxeod waiters are the hallmarks of this popular restaurant. If you don't fill up on appetizers tehina, labna, and chicken livers in garlic oil, we'd strongly recommend the whole baked fish for a main course if it's available. Otherwise the grilled meats and fowl are also excellent. A full meal costs about LE35 per person and beer and wine is served.

AL HATY, *at Halim by the Windsor Hotel off 26 July Street by Opera Square. Metro: Ataba. Hours: 12am-2am.*

With its high ceilings, fans, mirrors, and chandeliers Al Haty is a vintage old school Egyptian eatery dating to the 1920's that retains its elegant charm in mint condition and makes a wonderful setting in which to feast on mezze, kebab, vine leaves and other Egyptian favorites. It won't win Michelin stars but it's hearty, authentic, and reasonably priced; expect to pay LE30 a head for a full meal. There is a second branch of this restaurant on the other side of 26 July Street which accepts Visa and is also in a charming pre-War setting.

ALFI BEY, *3 Alfi Street near the Windsor Hotel and Opera Square. Metro: Ataba. Tel. 02/771-888, 774-999. Hours: noon-midnight. Credit cards: not accepted.*

Another pre-Revolutionary relic (founded 1936) serving good oriental food in a vintage setting forged by high ceilings, wood paneling, and old fashion chandeliers. Prices are moderate; soups and appetizers range from LE1-8 while main courses shouldn't set you back more than LE15. Regulars recommend grilled chicken. No alcohol is served

ARABESQUE, *6 Kasr El Nil Street. Hours: 12am-4pm & 7:30pm-midnight. Tel. 02/759-896. Credit cards: Visa.*

Arabesque is a very elegant, classy establishment that looks like a hole in the wall from the outside. It is entered through a modern art gallery which contrasts with the old style arabesque (what else) decor of the restaurant interior. The food is Lebanese/Continental and excellent if not overpriced. Traditional grilled meats and mezze are probably your best bet; expect to pay between LE40-60 for a full meal. Otherwise, check in for a beer at the bar which is dressed to the hilt in mashrabia and engraved brass.

FATARI PIZZA EL TAHRIR, *on Tahrir Street two blocks from Tahrir Square. Tel. 02/355-3596. Hours: open 24 hours.*

Excellent, but over priced fatir (LE6-12) is the specialty of the house. Sweet or savory, the Egyptian style pancakes can make a filling meal, or if split among two or three, a good snack. Unlike most *fataris* (fatir makers), these guys are used to serving foreigners and provide menus in English. Despite its popularity with tourists, the tiled floors, mirrored walls, and plenty of local customers maintain Fatara Pizza El Tahrir's authentic flavor.

GROPPI'S, *Talaat Harb Square. Hours: 7am-10pm.*

Once upon a time, this classic cafe was a focal point in Cairo's buzzing pre-Revolutionary social scene, but lost its charm and status after the original Italian-Egyptian ownership sold out and the colonials went home. Some say that it went downhill after a Muslim bought the place and stopped serving alcohol, others when its service came to resemble that in a state-owned department store (it takes three trips to the register to pick up a simple order). In any case, the sweets are still fantastic, and the dining hall serves poor food and has lousy service but is nice for a cool drink while taking a break from the city.

GREEK CLUB, *above Groppi's on Talaat Harb Square; accessible from Bassiouni Street. Hours: 7:30pm-11pm.*

Located just above Groppi's on Talaat Harb Square, this low key, old timey Greek establishment serves good, solid Egyptian food like kebab, tehina and oriental salads. The terrace is a great locale for drinks in the summer. Nothing flashy.

CAROLL, *12 Kasr El Nil. Tel. 02/574-6434. Hours: 11:30am-3pm &*
7:30pm-11pm.

Another solid mid-scale restaurant popular with big tour groups,
Caroll's features days-gone-by ambiance, good service, and the usual
menu of mezze, grilled meats, and Arabic desserts. Alcohol is served.

ESTORIL, *12 Talaat Harb Street between Talaat Harb Street and Kasr El*
Nil Street. Tel. 02/743-102. Hours: noon-4pm & 7-11pm.

This classy little establishment dates to pre-Revolutionary days, and
despite the recent makeover retains its vintage flavor. Once known the
place for dirt cheap mezze and beer, Estoril has upped its prices, but one
can still enjoy a full oriental meal for LE40 or under and the food, from
the tehina and labna to the kofta and fatta, is excellent. The old bar,
popular with local middle class business types, is a masterpiece. All in all,
an excellent choice for food or just drinks.

Cheap Eats & Street Food Downtown

Virtually every major street in downtown Cairo is lined with stalls,
take-out joints, and cafeterias hawking cheap food like kushari, fuul,
ta'amiya and shwarma. Falaki Square, Ramses Square, Mansur Street (off
Falaki Square), and Kasr El 'Aini are especially thick with such eateries.
Out of the hundreds from which to chose however, some have risen from
anonymity to become household names.

The most famous kushari houses are **El Tahrir** and **Lux**, *both on Tahrir*
Street off Tahrir Square. At both establishments a big bowl of kushari
(noodles, rice, and lentils topped with zesty tomato sauce) cost less than
LE1. There is a second Lux branch on 26th July Street near Sherif Street.

For fuul and ta'amiya, there is always Felfela's (see above), but locals
have traditionally favored **El Tabie El Dumyati** *on Orabi Street by the Orabi*
Metro stop. Though it has been upgraded into a slick American style fast-
food and takeaway joint, it still serves a variety of tasty fuul and ta'amiya
platters and sandwiches, as well as salads and mezzes. Try the *fuul bil salsa*
(*fuul* with tomato sauce) or *fuul damees* (with chopped onion and tomato)
if you're vegetarian. If you're not, consider indulging in *fuul bil bayd bil*
basturma (*fuul* with eggs and pastrami), one of the most fattening foods
ever invented. A la carte dishes go for LE1-5 and for about LE6 a fuul
platter comes with with salad, bread, tehina, and french fries, in addition
to the beans. El Tabie recently opened a second branch *on Gamaat El*
Dowal El Arabia Street in Mohandiseen.

Garden City

Kasr El Aini Street is lined with cheap, local fast food style eateries:
fuul, ta'amiya, roast chicken, and the lot. There are also numerous grocers
on this major thoroughfare.

ABU SHAKRA , *69 Kasr El Aini Street across from Kasr El Aini Hospital. Hours: 1-6pm & 7pm-midnight; but closed on Fridays & during daytime in Ramadan.*

This well known grill isn't fancy, but many Cairenes claim it's the best kofta and kebab joint in town. Not a place for vegetarians or for that matter, alcoholics; this establishment is run by strict Muslims.

Islamic Cairo & the Khan El Khalili

Islamic Cairo is littered with food stalls and local restaurants. In El Hussein Square alone there are no less than a half dozen kebab houses where a full meal including bread, salads, dips, and a quarter kilo (half pound) of mixed grilled meats will set you back about LE30. For vegetarians or those looking for lighter fare, a very local fuul and ta'amiya take away is situated in front of El Fishawi near the cassette shops and sells sandwiches for 50p. Cheap eats, including kebab, roast chicken, shwarma, and sweets can all be had on the alley running along the west side of El Hussein Mosque. El Azhar Street itself is teeming with kushari, ta'amiya, and kebab eateries situated on almost every block between the blue pedestrian bridge and Salah Salem Street up the hill to the east, a kilometer past the Khan and El Hussein Square.

For fatir, that doughy half-pizza, half-pancake concoction, most tourists head to the famous **Egyptian Pancakes** restaurant between El Mouski and El Azhar streets. Though it's expensive (LE8-12 per pancake), the service is friendly, the joint is clean, and it offers seating; shiny tiles and mirrors brighten the ambiance. Sweet (jam, cream, coconut, powdered sugar, nut) or savory (minced meat, tomato, olive, egg) pancakes make a meal for one or a snack for two. For a cheaper fatir in the Khan itself, a friendly stall just north of El Fishawi's coffee shop serves them for LE5 per piece, and a real local cutthroat deal (LE1-2) can be had at the hole in the wall place next to Abu Dahab Mosque across El Azhar Street from El Hussein Square.

Finally, for those in need of a break from the local goings on, the **Naguib Mahfouz Coffeeshop and Restaurant** *in the heart of the Khan El Khalili,* is an ideal, if pricey refuge. In addition to the clean restrooms and cool drinks, its main draw is the air-conditioned oriental appointed dining hall. For those looking to eat, whether it be a kofta sandwich (LE10) or full blown Arabic meal (LE30-50 per head), the food is excellent and the service professional. Major credit cards are accepted.

AHWAS-EGYPTIAN CAFES

Ever since coffee, tea (shai), and tobacco were introduced in the late Middle Ages, the wafting aroma of flavored sheesha smoke and the sound of dominos being slapped on marble table-tops have been hallmarks of the **ahwa**, *the Egyptian coffeehouse which is the focal point of male bonding in virtually every neighborhood. Part cafe, part sports bar (with no alcohol), the typical ahwah is a charmingly shabby establishment with high ceilings and tiled sawdust covered floors where men meet to talk sports and politics, play dominos and tawla (backgammon), or just to read the paper. In the past, smoking hashish and listening to a qasa (story teller) recount epic tales were favorite pastimes, but in recent decades, television and radio have replaced the oral tradition for entertainment and government crackdowns have made hashish toking as thing of past.*

Today, most ahwas serve turkish coffee (ahwa) and tea (shai) for 25-50 pt, and a thick milk based beverage called sahlab which is served warm (50pt-LE1). Smokewise, the ahwah is the place to go for a **sheesha** *– the oriental waterpipe also known as a narghila, hookah, or in pure touristspeak, "hubbly bubbly." Tobacco comes in several flavors the most prevalent of which are ma'asl (molasses) and tufah (apple).*

Finding an ahwa is never a problem – there's one on practically every street – but some are particularly worth a visit. In the Khan El Khalili, **El Fishawi's**, *with its wood paneling and cracked mirrors, is the oldest and most famous in Cairo. In Tahrir Square, the* **Wadi El Nil** *and* **Tahrir** *ahwas feature an especially diverse clientele, and the* **Ali Baba** *(also off Tahrir Square), is a favorite haunt of Naguib Mahfouz. Chess players may consider challenging the local masters at* **El Shataranj** *(which means 'chess') in Sayeda Zeinab Square. Most upscale hotels feature plush and very expensive ahwas, the nicest of which is the Amm Ali at the Nile Hilton. Though a sheesha is LE5 (an excellent) and tea LE2, the quiet, outdoor terrace setting is an ideal setting for relaxing and upscale people-watching.*

Dokki, Mohandiseen & Agouza

These districts are home to a broad spectrum of eateries from Japanese sushi bars in five star hotels to fuul and ta'amiya stalls on the street. Cheap, fast-food is never more than a few blocks away and the bigger streets such as Tahrir Street and Dokki Street are absolutely teeming with kushari, ta'amiya, and rotisserie chicken. For western style fast food, head to Gamaat El Dowal El Arabia Street in Mohandiseen where McDonald's, Baskin Robbins, Chicken Tikka, Subway, Taco Bell, and others are piled on top of each other.

ALADIN, *Cairo Sheraton, Galaa Square Dokki, Giza. Tel. 02/336-9700, 336-9600. Hours: 1-4pm & 8pm-midnight. Credit cards:all credit cards accepted.*

A favorite of Yasser Arafat who frequents the place about once a month Aladin is the best and priciest Lebanese restaurant in town. The menu, which is set, includes a sinful spread of Lebanese appetizers followed by superbly grilled meats accompanied by oriental rice. The service of course is excellent and later in the evenings, live oriental music and dancing, is featured. Expect to pay about LE70 per person.

CHOPSTICKS, *24 Syria Street off Gamaat El Dowal El Arabia Street in Mohandiseen. Tel. 02/304-8667/8/9. Credit Cards: Visa & Mastercard.*

This new Chinese restaurant offers some of the best, most authentic Asian food in town. It serves not only the usual Chinese fare like wontons, spring rolls, fried rice, and crispy duck, but Singaporean, Malay, and other regional specialties including Hong Kong Style dim sum style "Shau Mai" dumplings. Dishes include a very tasty Singaporean chili crab, plenty of spicy Sichuan specialties, and Singaporean curries. It's not Orchard Road, but the excellent service, moderate prices (appetizers run LE5-19; main dishes LE15-40 for the crabs), and clean and quiet atmosphere make this the place if you're dying for Asian cuisine. Takeout and delivery are available by calling the listed number; LE15 minimum for delivery.

FELFELA, *Ahmed Orabi Street, Mohandiseen. Hours: 11am-midnight. No credit cards accepted.*

The Mohandiseen branch of the famous chain is a bit drab, but still serves solid Egyptian cuisine for reasonable prices.

LE CHATEAU, *El Nasr Building on El Nil Street, Giza. Tel. 02/348-5321. Hours: noon-midnight. Credit cards: Visa, Mastercard.*

Once considered the finest French restaurant in Cairo, Le Chateau has fallen a few notches since Swissair stopped managing it several years ago, but the river views and quiet, candle-lit setting still make it a favorite with lovers and business types. Gentlemen should wear coat and tie.

PAPILLON, *26 July Street, Tirsana Commercial Center, Mohandiseen. Tel. 02/347-1672. Hours: noon-1am. Credit cards: Visa.*

Papillon is an excellent casual Lebanese eatery-ideal for lunch. Though not outrageously expensive, it's not dirt cheap either; appetizers, of which you'll be ordering plenty, go from LE2-6 and main dishes can set you back more than LE20, but it's worth it to try fine Arab cuisine.

TAJ MAHAL, *5 Lebanon Street, Mohandiseen. Tel. 02/302-5669. Hours: noon-midnight. Credit cards: Visa.*

This cozy eatery on a quiet street in Mohandiseen serves quality Moghlai (north Indian Muslim) standards and the service is excellent. It's not up to the standards of the Moghul Room, but neither are the prices and while the food may disappoint those looking for super hot and spicy curries, it's tasty and made with fine ingredients.

AL OMDAH, *6 Gaza'ir Street on the same block as Atlas Zamalek Hotel off Gamaat El Dowal El Arabia Street in Mohandiseen. Hours: 11am until late.*

The flagship for a fast growing chain of fast food Egyptian style-a kind of "Gen X" Felfela. Pricier than real street food, the fuul, ta'amiya, and kushari still won't set you back more than a couple of pounds a sandwich and is quite tasty. The atmosphere is definitely slick and plastic, but the happy music, crowds of *shebab* (youth),and sheesha gurgling give it some color.

MY QUEEN, *Gamaat El Dowal El Arabia Street, Mohandiseen. Hours: mid-day until late night (early morning).*

Fast food extrordinaire. My Queen is a favorite with locals and especially late nighters who come from all over Cairo to fill up after a night of drinking and dancing. Favorites include superb shwarma, chicken kiev, and other sandwiches.

West Giza & the Pyramids

MOHGUL ROOM, *Mena House Hotel at the end of Pyramids. Tel. 02/ 384-2222/444. Hours: 12:30am-2:45pm & 7:30pm-midnight. Credit cards: all major credit cards accepted.*

From the fiery vindaloo to the luxurious and sophisticated setting, this fine restaurant consistently ranks among the best in Cairo. Set in an opulent and elegant dining hall complete with antique handicrafts on the walls and live sitar music, it features first rate fine Indian cuisine with service to match. Some food critics claim that aside from Singapore and London, it may be some of the best Indian food anywhere in the world aside from India itself. It is however, quite expensive; expect to fork out anywhere from LE50-100 per person.

CHRISTO'S, *10 Pyramids Road. Tel. 02/383-3582. Hours: 11am-3pm. Credit cards: Visa, Mastercard, American Express.*

They say don't eat fish in Cairo, but fish lovers need not pass up Christo's waiting to go to Alex. As is the custom in Egyptian fish restaurants, the catch is displayed and patrons select their choice which is then weighed and grilled or fried according to order. While the fish is cooked you fill up on baba ghanug, fresh bread, salads, and a host of other highly munchable mezze. Food, however is not the only appeal of eating at Christo's, the views of the Pyramids are first rate. Christo's is very popular with tour groups, but getting a table usually isn't a problem. Diners can sit outside or in; the second floor has better views.

FELFELA VILLAGE, *along Maryotia Canal off Pyramids Road. Tel. 02/ 383-4209. Hours: 10am-7pm. Credit cards: Visa.*

Felfela on steroids? Here, Cairo's favorite chain takes the dining experience to new heights; not only do you enjoy "typical" Egyptian food, but a zoo, acrobats, live music, and even camel rides and dancing horses as well. It may be a bit much, but kids love it as do those who enjoy a good laugh, if not a bit of noise. The food is of course decent, hearty, and best of all authentic. All in all, a very, well, Egyptian experience.

LA ROSE, *No. 58 along Maryotia Canal off Pyramids Road. Tel. 02/383-5712. Hours: 11am-1am. Credit cards: Visa.*

An outdoor Egyptian restaurant serving good mezze, and grilled fowl and meats. Less famous with Egyptians and less prone to invasion by tour groups, it exudes a slightly more authentic, and quiet, atmosphere from say Andrea's, the Farm, and certainly Felfela Village.

ANDREA'S, *No. 60 along Maryotia Canal off Pyramids Road. Tel. 02/385-1133. Credit cards: Visa.*

Andrea's serves excellent grilled fare (chicken is the specialty) and is a favorite with tour groups-meaning the cleanliness is trusted if nothing else. Bread is baked fresh on the premises and guests dine outdoors in a pleasant "rural" setting, but usually in the company of at least a few mosquitoes.

Maadi

PETIT SWISS CHALET, *Road 151 off Midan Horreya in Madi by the Maadi Metro stop. Tel. 02/351-8328. Hours: noon-midnight. Credit cards: Visa.*

This cozy and quiet Italian restaurant is one of the most pleasant eateries in Maadi and from the LE4 tomato soup to the LE30 T-bone steak, the food is more than decent and reasonably priced. The portions are not overwhelming but are certainly sufficient, leaving just enough room for tasty deserts. The cozy and intimate setting makes it popular with Maadi lovebirds and expatriate families living in Maadi. Easily reached from the Maadi metro station.

FELELA EL NIL, *El Corniche Street on the Nile at the main turnoff into Maadi.*

The outdoor setting overlooking the Nile and its verdant west banks south of Cairo should afford diners a relaxing and peaceful change from the freneticism of the city. Unfortunately, this edition of Felfela's also doubles as a shooting club during the summer when skeet shooting contests are held (noisy indeed), and features an amusement park complete with tramopolines, a video arcade, and bumper cars that seems to attract every Maadyite between the ages of five and fourteen. However if you make it at dusk, the sunset views are superb and you should be in and out before the shooting begins. The Egyptian food is quite good and beer and sheesha are available.

BUA KHAO, *Road 152 Maadi. Tel. 02/350-0126. Hours: noon-midnight. Credit cards: Visa.*

Egypt's first Thai restaurant gets high marks from expats jonesing for Asian food who come to feast on pad thai, tom young cang soup, and other tasty Thai specialities. It's a bit of haul from downtown but being only a block away from El Maadi Metro station it's easier than it may seem. They have opened a new branch in the food court at the Nile Hilton Shopping Mall. Alcoholic beverages are served.

SEEING THE SIGHTS

Downtown & Tahrir Square

Known prior to the 1952 Revolution as 'Ismailia', **downtown Cairo** stretches from Opera Square and Ezbekiya in the east to the Nile, and from Ramses and Bulaq to Garden City. Conceived by Khedive Ismail in the 1860's as part of his grand scheme to modernize Egypt, it was built by architects imported from France and Italy who succeessfully aped the *fin de siecle* neo-Neopolitan and neo-baroque styles popular in Europe at the time. Today the grand apartment buildings and villas with their ornate rococo moldings and mansard roofs are crumbling and caked with dirt, and the once spacious and tree-lined avenues are consumed by hordes of pedestrians complicating an already chaotic, exhaust-spewing traffic free for all. Most of the French style cafes and boutiques that catered to Cairo's European elites have given way to airline offices and cheap clothing and shoe stores, and department stores like Sednaoui and Omar Effendi, that once matched in choice and quality the great department stores in Europe, are but shadows of themselves 40 years after their nationalization by the Nasser regime.

The epicenter of Cairo is undoubtedly **Midan El Tahrir** (Liberation Square), a mass of confusion that is home to many of the city's best known landmarks including the Arab League Building and the Egyptian Antiquuities Museum. Chaotic and drab, it is here that city's diverse melange of citizenry cross paths- emerge from the Metro station and you'll meet a vast array of folks from the civil servants working at the Mogamma and Arab League diplomats to the aristocratic youth studying at the American University in Cairo, and rural migrants in their fellahi galabiyas who work as laborers on whatever infrastructure project happens to be in progress. Rounding it out are the ever present taxi drivers, small time hawkers, and bemused, if not lost, tourists.

Originally parade grounds for British and Egyptian troops Tahrir came into its own as Cairo's primary hub after 1952 when the **Mogamma**, the huge dirty gray building flanking the square to the south opened. Designed to house the entire government it is now the ultimate symbol Egypt's bloated bureaucracy and with over 3,000 rooms and 13,000 employees, it is a black hole of red tape where some people literally spend years getting sent from office to office for this stamp or that, trying to get anything from a new passport to a tax refund. Should you have to renew a visa, you will have pleasure experiencing it firsthand.

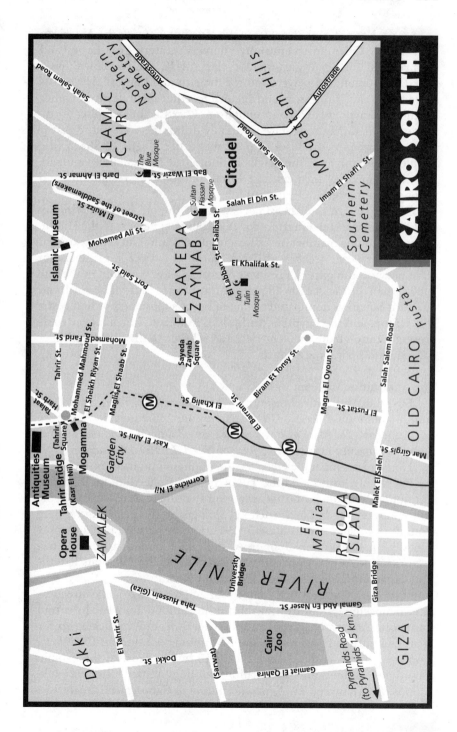

CAIRO SOUTH

Across **Kasr El Aini Street** from the Mogamma stands the **American University in Cairo**, an American style university catering to "the best and the brightest" of Egypt's aristocratic elite, "AUC" as it's known, has a mixed reputation as a playground for the rich and famous, that boasts some world class professors and relative to other institutions of higher learning in Egypt, an excellent reputation. **Kasr El Aini**, running north-south, is a major thoroughfare invariably brimming with traffic that is home to Egypt's two houses of parliament, the **Maglis El Shaab** (the People's Assembly) and the **Maglis El Shura** (the Consultative Council), as well as ministries, theaters, and dozens of foodstalls, restaurants, and shops-a great place for cheap eats.

Off the square's northeast corner stands the old **Foreign Ministry Building** and the **Headquarters for the Arab League** next to the Hilton. Egypt, a founding member of the League after World War II was expelled following its peace treaty with Israel but after a decade of persistent diplomacy on the part of President Mubarak was reinstated in the late 1980's when the League's headquarters returned to Cairo. The north end of Tahrir Square is dominated by one of Egypt's most famous hotels, the Nile Hilton, and the **Egyptian Antiquities Museum**, which moved to its present location from Bulaq in 1902 and is home to the world's premier collection of pharaonic artifacts.

The Antiquities Museum

Egyptian Antiquities Museum, *on the northern end of Tahrir Square next to the Nile Hilton. Tel 02/754-319. Hours: 9am-4pm. Admission: LE20 general, LE10 students. The Mummy Room requires an additional LE60 ticket (LE30 students). Cameras: LE10 without flash or tripod, LE100 video camera.*

Home to an unparalleled collection of pharaonic artifacts, including the Palette of Narmer and the Tutankhamun Collection, the Egyptian Antiquities Museum is one of Cairo's top attractions. A relic in itself, the Museum was founded by French Egyptologist in the 1850's and moved from its original Bulaq location in 1902. Exhibits are arranged chronologically on the bottom floor from the Old Kingdom to the Roman occupation while the upper floor features specialized exhibits like the Tutankhamun Collection and the Mummy Room.

If you don't come with a guided tour and would like some direction, official museum guides are available for hire at LE40 for a two hour tour (too short). Alternatively, you can act as your own guide by picking up one of several museum guides sold in the Museum bookstore. *A Guide to the Egyptian Museum* is the cheapest at LE10 but categorizes the exhibits according to subject and not location; nor does it offer historical explanations. Alternatively, *The Egyptian Museum in Cairo-Official Catalogue* is ten times more expensive at LE100 but provides a more practical catalogue of displays with some historical explanation. For the Mummy Room there is a separate booklet available for LE3. Listed below are some highlights.

The Museum's Ground Floor

Apart from the Atrium, which comprises an assortment of unrelated "highlights," the ground floor exhibits are "organized" chronologically. West (left) of the entrance, they begin with the **Old Kingdom** (Rooms 31, 32, 36, 37, 41, 42, 46 & 47) and moving clockwise from there, visitors will pass through the **Middle Kingdom** (Rooms 11, 12, 16, 17, 21, 22, 26 & 27); the **New Kingdom** (Rooms 1-10, 14, 15, 19 & 20); the **Late Period** (Rooms 24, 25, 29 & 30); **Greco-Roman Egypt** (34, 35, 39 & 40); and the **Nubian exhibits** (44 & 45).

The Atrium & Rotunda

Before hitting the Old Kingdom galleries, most visitors warm up by exploring the **Rotunda** and the **Atrium** along the central axis of the bottom floor. Visitors are greeted with several large statues, including three **colossi of Ramses II** and a large head of the 5th Dynasty (Old Kingdom) Pharaoh Userkaf. Sitting at the entrance to the Atrium past the Rotunda is a limestone statue of **Zoser**, the 3rd Dynasty pharaoh who built the Step Pyramid at Saqqara.

Room 43 contains two 12th Dynasty (1990-1780 BC) **solar barges**, smaller versions of the huge boat at the Pyramids intended to carry the deceased's *ba* (soul) through the afterworlds after death. These particular boats were excavated at Dahshur, south of Saqqara.

Room 38 contains an assortment of sarcophagi. Of particular significance is that of **Aye**, an adviser to Akhenaten who survived the Theban counter-revolutions and succeeded Tutankhamun before being deposed himself by the general Haremheb. **Room 33** also contains sarcophagi, including those of Hatshepsut and Thutmosis I, as well as capstones from pyramids at Dahshur. The most impressive piece is the **sarcophagus of Merneptah**, successor of Ramses II and allegedly the "Pharaoh of the Exodus" who was in power when Moses and Israelites were to have fled Egypt. The sarcophagus itself was usurped by the 21st Dynasty Pharaoh Psusennes and discovered in Tanis in the Delta and not in Thebes where Merneptah was buried.

The Atrium's *piece de resistance* is a **floor from Akhenaten's palace** at Tel El Amarna. Though the palace was destroyed by Akhenaten's successors, this beautifully painted floor depicting a colorful river scene somehow survived. Beyond the Akhenaten's floor in **Room 13** is the **Israel Stele**. Possibly the only pharaonic reference to Israel (there are no others), this stele from Karnak lists among the conquests of the New Kingdom Pharaoh Merneptah, a country some scholars believe might have been Israel. The final exhibit of the Atrium are larger-than-life statues depicting the New Kingdom ruler Amenhophis III and his family.

The Old Kingdom Exhibits

Returning to the **Old Kingdom** exhibits, **Rooms 46 & 47** feature an assortment **funerary statues, sarcophogi, and statuettes** of figures undertaking everyday tasks like planting and baking. At the end of the hall is a piece of the **Sphinx's beard** (the other yard of it is in the British Museum in London) allegedly shot off by Napoleon's troops.

In **Room 41** is a smattering of more funerary ware including tomb reliefs from Maidum and 2nd Dynasty sacrificial tables. Next door, **Room 42** contains some of the most important pieces in the entire Museum including an exquisite **statue of Khafre**, builder of the second Pyramid at Giza, that was excavated from his mortuary temple next to the Sphinx, and the **Palette of Narmer**, one of the oldest examples of hieroglyphic writing and the only depiction of Narmer, the legendary first Pharaoh. Also known as Menes, Narmer unified Upper and Lower Egypt around 3100 BC, founding what some consider the world's first nation state.

The last of the Old Kingdom displays are in Rooms 31 & 32. In **Room 31** are reliefs from a stone temple at Wadi Maraghah in Sinai where the Egyptians mined turquoise. Also in Room 31 are wooden panels from the tomb of Hesyre, a 3rd Dynasty scribe and the first known dentist in world history.

The main feature in **Room 32** is the beautiful and charming statue of Prince Rahotep and his wife, Princess Nefert which, despite its age of 4,500 years old, still retains superb color. Also worth noting is the tableaux of the dwarf Seneb with his wife (embracing him) and naked children.

The Middle Kingdom Exhibits

Moving onto **Room 26**, we leave the Old Kingdom for the **Middle Kingdom** (2050-1786 BC). After the anarchy and civil wars of the First Intermediate Period, the Middle Kingdom saw the reunification of Upper and Lower Egypt and a return to centralized authority. However, the Middle Kingdom did not achieve Old Kingdom levels of wealth and, nor did it leave behind as rich an artistic legacy. In Egyptian history it is significant for the rise of Thebes and the emergence of the Cult of Amun at Karnak as the state cult.

Among the important Middle Kingdom pieces in the Museum are ten **statues of Senusert**, builder of the first major temple to Amun at Karnak, in **Room 22**. Also worth noting is the **double statue of Amemenhet III** in Room 16; the double image commemorates his dual roles as ruler of both

Upper and Lower Egypt. The only relic dating to the chaotic First Intermediate Period is a statue in Room 26 depicting a sober looking Nebhepetre Mentuhotep discovered by Howard Carter at Deir El Bahri in Thebes.

The New Kingdom Exhibits

During the New Kingdom (1567-1200 BC), pharaonic Egypt reached its zenith as an imperial power as pharaohs like Thutmosis III, Seti I, and Ramses II built massive Egyptian empires in Palestine, Syria, and Asia Minor. Egypt also achieved new levels of economic prosperity and in the royal capital Thebes, this new wealth enabled the construction of temples such as Karnak on unprecedented scales, and royalty and nobility indulged in lavish tombs and mortuary temples on the west bank. Most of the treasures buried in the tombs were robbed in antiquity but those that were salvaged and are on display here give a taste of the New Kingdom's great wealth and the expertise of its artisans.

Highlights include an assortment of masterpiece sculptures and other relics from **Deir El Bahri** in **Room 12**. On the Nile's west banks at Thebes Deir El Bahri is the site of Hatshepsut's famous mortuary temple that was later usurped by Thutmosis III, her half-brother and stepson. Jealous because Hatshepsut assumed his spot in the line of succession when he was a child, Thutmosis usurped and defaced nearly all of her monuments; he also became Egypt's greatest empire builder. Among the pieces in Room 12 from Deir El Bahri are reliefs depicting Egyptian excursions to the Land of Punt on the Somali coast. Also from Deir El Bahri is a **shrine dedicated to Hathor**, built by Thutmosis III featuring a brilliant statue of the goddess in her bovine form suckling the infant king.

Entering **Rooms 6 & 7** in the northern wing, you will be greeted by a pair of statues of the lion headed goddess,Sekhmet, followed by a collection of sphinxes all bearing the face of Hatshepsut. **Room 8** contains a **replica of a house** excavated at Akhenaten's capital city of Tel El Amarna in Middle Egypt, while **Room 3** is a gallery dedicated entirely to his reign.

A radical non-conformist, **Akhenaten** (1,380-1,362 BC) broke with pharaonic orthodoxy by banning the Cult of Amun, stripping it of its wealth and prestige, and making the monotheistic Cult of Aten the national religion. He built a new capital at Tel El Amarna in Middle Egypt and presided over a revolution in Egyptian art as artisans were encouraged to abandon the idealistic rigidity favored by previous generations in favor of naturalism and realism. Hence while previous pharaohs invariably had themselves portrayed as superhuman divinities with idealized physiques, Akhenaten is depicted in his natural state – flabby and awkward. Also, he is commonly seen performing such menial tasks as eating, playing with his children, and even vomiting – activities traditionally not engaged in by royalty, particularly on the walls of tombs. In Room 3, the most glaring example of Amarna Art, as it came to be known, are the four colossi of Akhenaten with his long face and bulging belly and thighs. Other fascinating pieces include the steles in Cases F & H and tomb reliefs. Given that Akhenaten's successors did all they could to wipe out any trace of Akhenaten's reign, which they considered heretical, we are fortunate to have recovered these few revealing relics.

Moving on from Akhenaten's gallery, **Rooms 9 & 10** feature more traditional New Kingdom art, primarily in the form of funerary statues and sarcophagi. Off to the side, Room 4 breaks with chronology and features exhibits of Greek and Roman coins. From this corner of the Museum, you can head upstairs to the Tutankhamun Collection, which makes sense chronologically since he was a New Kingdom pharaoh, or you can continue on to the last of the New Kingdom exhibits and those concentrating on later periods in the east wing.

Rooms 15 &14 continue with the New Kingdom and feature a variety of statues and reliefs many of which emphasize the martial prowess of various pharaohs, many of whom never fought a battle.

The East Wing-The Late Period, Greco-Roman Egypt, & Nubia
Beginning around 1,000 BC, the New Kingdom's 500 years of glory came to an end and the country became vulnerable to foreign domination. Beginning with the Libyan 22nd Dynasty that began around 950 BC a series of foreign powers gained control of Egypt, though most of them assumed the trappings of traditional pharaohdom and patronized Egyptian style art. The Nubians, who had been dominated by the Egyptians for millennia and had adopted Egyptian religion and culture, were particularly keen to promote traditional Egyptian art and religion. The works in **Rooms 25,25,29, & 30** date mostly from this Nubian period (750-650 BC) and from the Saite Period (645-525 BC) when a series of city states emerged after a brief Assyrian occupation left Egypt with no central authority. In this section of the Museum, Room 25 with its assortment of various, sometimes strange deities, is particularly interesting.

With Alexander the Great's conquering of Egypt in 332 BC began almost 1,000 years of Greek, and later Roman domination in Egypt. During this period, Alexandria emerged as the political, economic, and artistic center in Egypt, and the Greco-Roman Museum there contains most of the finer works from this period. While Alexandria was a thoroughly Hellenized city, the Ptolemies (the Greek dynasty in Egypt) also adopted the trappings of traditional pharaodom primarily to enhance their legitimacy with the local population, but also because they believed pharaonic religion to be an incarnation of their own. Their art reflects this in interesting, and sometimes comical attempts to fuse Greek artistic and theological traditions with those native to Egypt. That they lacked the artistic expertise to perfectly mimic the beauty of pharonic make their artistic endeavors appear almost clumsy. In Room 49, for example, are some quirky statues and sarcophagi featuring an awkward combination, or perhaps clash, of Egyptian and Greek styles.

Though they don't measure up in any artistic quality to earlier pharaonic artifacts the relics excavated from **Nubian tombs** at Abu Simbel in **Room 44** are quite unique. They include saddlery, weaponry, and a mummified horse skeleton.

The Upper Floor & the Tutankhamun Collection

For many visitors, the highlight of a trip to the Antiquities Museum, or even to all of Egypt, is the immense collection of treasures excavated from the tomb of the New Kingdom Pharaoh **Tutankhamun** (1,361-1,352 BC). Discovered by British archaeologist Howard Carter in 1922, the tomb was the only one in all of Thebes to be intact when excavated. In fact, Tutankhamun was a such a minor pharaoh (he died a teenager) with such a small tomb that it was hidden for more than 3,000 years beneath the much larger crypt of Ramses VI. Given the wealth of treasure exhibited in this collection, one can only wonder what kind of splendors must have been buried in the tombs of the truly great pharaohs like Ramses II and Seti I.

Contained in more than ten rooms in the northern and eastern wings of the Museum's upper floor, the Tutankhamun Collection features almost 2,000 pieces. If this does not wear you out consider a visit to the **Royal Mummy Room** containing 11 pharaonic mummies, and more than 30 overall dating to the New Kingdom. Entrance requires an additional LE60 ticket. Those not interested in forking out the cash just to look at Ramses in the face may consider a visit to Room 53, which is free and contains a fascinating assortment of mummified birds and animals.

The Tutankhamun Collection is best approached through **Rooms 49 & 50**, which feature rotating exhibits of recent discoveries. Standing guard at **Room 45** are two life-size black statues of "Tut" himself, and the main attraction is a **shrine to Anubis**, the jackal protector of the dead, and an ebony and ivory ornamental **board game**. Though Tutankhamun probably never fought a battle in his short life the painted chests (used to store clothing) in this room depict him smiting enemies, once from a chariot, and once in the form of a lion-bodied sphinx. Between **Rooms 30 and 35**, check out the **royal toilet seat** en route to **Room 30** which along with **Rooms 25 and 20** feature a number of ornate thrones and other furniture. Room 30 also contains a musical instrument resembling a horn that somebody actually tried to "play" in 1939 and Room 20 holds immaculately carved alabaster jars and a chalice.

Towards the corner, **Room 15** contains symbolic **sacred barges** for use by the deceased in his travels through the underworld. Naturally, he would also need to sleep, hence the gilded beds in **Rooms 10-15**; the sleeping equipment continues in Room 10 with ivory headrests. The main attraction of **Room 9** is the chest of alabaster **canopic jars** used store the Pharaoh's internal organs after mummification.

Rooms 7 & 8, the main halls of the northern wing, are dominated by four large **gold boxes** that fit one inside the other like Russian Babushka dolls. Tutankhamun's sarcophagus was placed inside the inner box. The corner of the outer box is flanked by Nephthys, a companion of Isis and guardian of the dead often seen on the corners of sarcophagi.

Room 3 boasts the *piece de resistance* of the entire collection, **Tutankhamun's gold funerary mask**. Inlaid with lapis, quartz, and other gems, it is a magnificent piece of craftsmanship and never ceases to amaze even those who have seen it a hundred times. Not too shabby either are the **two inner coffins**, also in this room. The innermost, featuring a likeness of the pharaoh in the classic Osirian pose, is also laden with gobs of gold and other precious stones. The second coffin is "only" sheeted in gold. To put things straight, the mask was placed on the mummy (now in his tomb in Thebes); which was placed in the two coffins in this room; that were then placed in the outer coffin in the sarcophagus; and that inside the four gold boxes in Rooms 7 & 8. The more than 100 amulets, also in Room 3, were placed inside the innermost coffin and the mummy donned the gold sandals, also encased here.

Though Room 3 takes the cake, **Room 4** is not far behind. Known as the **Jewelry Room** for its overwhelming collection of ornate crowns and diadems, its highlights include a Greco-Roman gold crown recently discovered in the Western Desert oasis of Kharga and a 6th Dynasty falcon head from Hieraconpolis (100 kilometers south of Cairo) and the crowns and necklaces of 12th Dynasty Princess Khnumyt.

On the opposite side of Room 3, **Room 2** contains the reconstructed **furniture of the Old Kingdom Queen Hetepheres**, namely a sedan chair and a canopied bed; and various relics discovered in three caches at Tanis in the Delta including jewelry and a coffin.

The Mummy Room and other assorted second floor galleries

Closed for 15 years because President Sadat felt it offensive that Egypt display the corpses of its national leaders for the viewing pleasure of tourists, the **Royal Mummy Room (Room 52)** reopened in 1995. Containing 30 royal mummies including 11 pharaohs, it requires a separate LE60 ticket to enter. The mummies themselves are quite decomposed but given that they are over 3,000 years old (they are all New Kingdom), they really are in quite good shape. Indeed, it's a mindboggling and eerie experience to find yourself staring Ramses the Great right in the eyes. Among the other prominent royal here are Seti I, the Thutmosids I, II, and III, Amenhophis III, and Queen Nefertari. Many of these mummies were found stashed in the tomb of Amenhophis II, having been placed there presumably by priests who felt that because the tomb had already been robbed of its original treasures, it would not be subject to further vandalisation.

Next to the Royal Mummy Room, **Room 52** contains a variety of **mummified animals** and does not require a special entrance ticket. Egyptians often associated their various deities with animals whose traits and form they would then bestow upon the deity. To pay homage to the deities the Egyptians mummified, often thousands at a time, the animals to which they were linked.

The west wing of the upper floor features a pot pourri of pharaonic knick knacks from Middle Kingdom canopic jars to **model soldiers** (Room 37). Highlights include contents from the **tomb of New Kingdom noble Sennejem**, including a fine sarcophagus, in **Room 17**; and the 28th Dynasty funerary wigs and the mummy of a gazelle in **Room 12**.

For a change the **east wing** features a variety of specialized rooms. **Room 14** holds the **Faiyoum Portraits**, mummies dating to the first and second centuries AD featuring Roman type realistic portraits of their owners pasted on the mummy itself. For writing buffs, **Room 24** contains a fascinating collection of **papyri and ostraca** (limestone writing palettes); and Room 29 exhibits writing instruments and painting tools.

Talaat Harb & Other Downtown Thoroughfares

Originally named Suleiman Pasha Street after one of Mohammed Ali's most trusted aides, downtown's main avenue which links Tahrir Square with Talaat Harb Square is **Talaat Harb Street**. Renamed after the 1952 Revolution for a prominent nationalist banker and industrialist, Talaat Harb is now home to such Cairo landmarks as the 1940's eatery, Estoril, and Felfela's, arguably Cairo's most famous, if not best loved restaurant, as well has dozens of small merchants and airline offices. Once a resplendent street lined with suave cafes and boutiques, it is now drab and chaotic; swamped with such dense pedestrian and automobile traffic that it's easy to miss its crumbling elegance.

Talaat Harb Square is still home to **Groppi's**, Cairo's preeminent cafe prior to the Revolution. The burning of its rotunda in the Black Saturday fires of January 1952, the passing of ownership from the Groppi family to various proprietors (including a strict Muslim who banned alcohol), and the general decline in quality and atmosphere makes Groppi's an obvious symbol of bygone Cairo. Other landmarks, such as the Savoy Hotel are long gone though its old building with its classic

THE METRO CINEMA

Cairenes have always been enthusiastic movie-goers and for decades beginning in the 1930's, **Cinema Metro** *on Talaat Harb Street was the city's swankiest theater. A popular rendezvous for Cairo's most cosmopolitan socialites and headquarters for MGM Studios in Egypt, its marquee was dominated by the classic MGM lion logo and the slogan "Pride of the Orient." Inside, this art deco building featured a plush foyer and richly decorated smoking room in addition to the multi-layered theater itself. VIPs sitting in the loge enjoyed upholstered reclining seats and King Farouk maintained a special arm chain, "the throne."*

In many ways the Metro is a metaphor for cinema in Cairo. During the '30's and '40's it flourished as Cairenes packed it nightly not only for classics of Nagwa Fouad, but to relish Casablanca and Gone with the Wind. In the 1947 it suffered a setback when the Muslim Brotherhood exploded a bomb, killing a handful of movie goers, but the theater made a comeback in the 1950's when 3-D and cartoons became the rage. Since nationalization in the '60's the Metro, like so many Cairo landmarks has suffered a gradual and depressing decline though in 1978 it held enough clout to host Princess Alexandra of Kent for a showing of Death on the Nile.

Now decrepit and shabby, the Metro will soon get the renovation its deserves to reemerge from the shadows of newer, nearby rivals, the Odeon and the Radio Cinema.

mansard roof remains. Today, the Square contains the main branch of **Madbuli's**, Cairo's most famous bookstore chain, several banks, and cheap hotels of which the Tulip is the best known. Beyond the Square, Talaat Harb Street houses some of Cairos most famous, but largely dilapidated cinemas.

Other streets crisscrossing old Ismailia also feature the contrast of modern post revolutionary and socialist Egypt against the backdrop of the old facade of the European imperial past and Ismail's aspirations of grandeur. On **Kasr El Nil Street** Greek and Jewish-owned shops have given way to slick juice stalls and modern clothing shops, their windows crammed with gaudy ware designed in tastes favored by the middle class Egyptian consumer. On older buildings, nameplates advertising *bijoux*, *medicins*, and *avocats*, and the chipped molding and dirt covered rococo facades are remnants from the days when Cairo's builders in no way tried to hide their aping of Parisian grandeur.

Tucked into the modern chaos are such gems as **L'Orientaliste** bookstore, specializing in old books, maps and lithographs, and the **Continental Hotel**, located down a side street, two blocks from Tahrir.

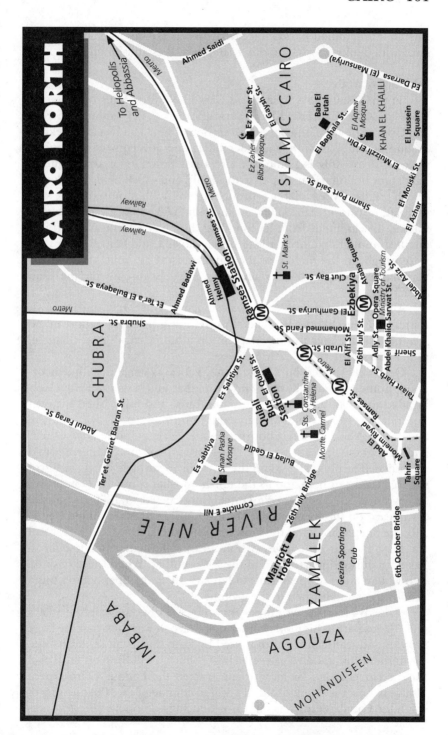

CAIRO NORTH

To Heliopolis
and Abbassia

Metro

Ahmed Saidi

ISLAMIC CAIRO

Ed Darrasa (El Mansuriya)

Bab El
Futah

Ez Zaher St.

El Gaysh St.

El Aqmar
Mosque

Ez Zaher
Bibrs Mosque

El Baghala St.

KHAN EL KHALILI

El Muizzli El Din

El Hussein
Square

Railway

Railway

Ramses St.

Metro

Sharm Port Said St.

El Mouski St.

El Azhar

St. Mark's

Ahmed Badawi

Et Ter'a El Bulaqeya St.

Ahmed
Helmy

Ramses Station

Clut Bay St.

Ezbekiya

Azaba
Square

Abdel Aziz St.

Metro

Shubra St.

Es Sabtiya St.

Metro

El Gamhuriya St.

Mohammed Farid St.

Opera Square

Ministry of Tourism

Abdel Khaliq Sarwat St.

SHUBRA

El Alfi St.

El Urabi St.

26th July St.

Adly St.

Sherif

Talaat Harb St.

Abdul Farag St.

Ter'et Geziret Badran St.

El Qulali St.

Qulali
BUS
Station

Sts. Constantine
& Helena

Ramses St.

Abd El
Moneim Riyad

Es Sabtiya

Sinan Pasha
Mosque

Bulaq El Gedid

Monte Carmel

Tahrir
Square

Corniche E Nil

RIVER NILE

26th July Bridge

Marriott
Hotel

ZAMALEK

Gezira Sporting
Club

6th October Bridge

IMBABA

AGOUZA

MOHANDISEEN

Bustan, **Mohammed Farid**, and **Sherif** streets are other major avenues lined with banks, shops, and other commercial establishments.

Ezbekiya & Ataba

From Talaat Harb Square and Kasr El Nil Street, it's only several blocks on **Adly** and **Abdel Khaliq Sarwat Streets** to **El Gomhuriya Street** and **Opera Square** in the once regal section of Cairo known as **Ezbekiya**. A short street lined with small merchants and government and public sector offices, Adly is home to Cairo's last functioning **synagogue**, a handsome building that is open to the public and which holds services on Jewish holidays when a rabbi is brought from Israel. A substantial Jewish population (more than 50,000 in the '40s) played an integral role in Cairo's development from its founding, however all but a handful of families emmigrated, primarily to Israel, Canada, and Britain, after they were caught in the middle of the Egyptian-Israeli conflict, and Nasser nationalized their businesses (and everybody elses) following the 1956 Suez War.

Abdel Khaliq Sarwat Street is very similar to Adly Street, and is known for its **gold merchants** who generally offer lower prices that those in the Khan El Khalili because they depend on a more frugal local clientele, rather than tourists, for their business.

Originally located on a large pond, Ezbekiya was a posh neighborhood, home to Mamluke and Turkish pashas and beys until Napoleon invaded in 1798, when he drained the canal and established his own headquarters here. When Mohammed Ali took power in 1805, the lake and the neighborhood were both reconstructed, large gardens were built, and throughout the 19th century, Ezbekiya was constantly reinvented and upgraded. Theaters, clubs, and the first European style hotels in Egypt were constructed here and to the north on what is now El Gomhuriya Street stood the **Shepheard's Hotel**. Constructed in 1850 by Samuel Shepheard on the former location of the palace of Mohammed Bey El Alfi, the Shepheard's was the most opulent hotel in the Middle East and the most famous of a series of European style luxury hotels built in Ezbekiya during the later half of the 19th century. When Cairo erupted into violent anti-European riots in January 1952, the Shepheard's was a prime target and burned to the ground.

Ezbekiya was further Europeanized by Khedive Ismail in the 1860's and '70's as part of his modernization of Cairo. It was then that the large squares and traffic circles, connected by wide European style avenues, were established as Cairo's street network which is still the basic road plan for the current city. Ismail also constructed the famous Cairo **Opera House** to host the debut of Verdi's *Aidi* to commemorate the opening of the Suez Canal. Verdi was late in producing the opera (*Rigoletto* was performed instead), but the stucco and cedar Opera House was considered to be one of the finest in the world outside of Europe.

Present-day Ezbekiya is but a shadow of its former self. The once swinging theaters, clubs, and hotels are now gone and Opera Square is surrounded by decrepit old buildings and charmless new ones. The Opera House burned down in the 1970's and a non-descript carpark now stands on the site. The entire south side of the square is a mass of billboards, the traffic is generally horrific, and only the stately statue of Ibrahim Pasha hints at the square's former glory.

Abdin

Several blocks south of Opera Square on El Gumhoriya Street, is **Abdin Palace**. When Khedive Ismail made it the seat of government in 1874, the Palace became the first seat of Egyptian government outside the Citadel since the arrival of Salah El Din in the 12th century. It was also here that the Free Officers made their coup d'etat in 1952. Today the palace has been converted into a "presidential palace" and is used for state functions. It is not open to the public.

The surrounding middle class neighborhood is also called "Abdin" and is home to El Gomhuriya Theater, Cairo's preeminent performing arts hall between the burning of Ismail's Opera House in 1971 and the opening of the new Cairo Opera House in Zamalek in 1989.

Ataba

Passing under **El Azhar Bridge** (which leads to the Khan El Khalili) from Opera, you'll shortly come to **Ataba Square** where Ismail's planned western city begins to give way to the medieval Islamic cities of the Fatimids, Ayyubids, Mamlukes, and Ottomans. A major traffic and commercial hub, Ataba is home to Cairo's central post office (see below), the major fire station, and hundreds of shops selling everything from nuts and bolts and bicycle tires to antiques and household goods. Some turn of the century masterpieces in architecture remain, but their glory barely peeks through the decades of dirt and soot caked onto their exteriors.

From here the colorful **Mouski Street**, packed with vendors and suffocated with traffic, was the center of turn of the century nightlife and was lined clubs, bars, and theaters. Today it has returned to its medieval commercial roots as local merchants and consumers haggle over every consumer product imaginable from women's lingerie to electronics. **Mohammed Ali Street**, also famous in the past for its nightlife and to this day, its musical instrument industry, also begins in Ataba Square and stretches to the Sultan Hassan and Rifa'i mosques at the base of the Citadel. Just north of Ataba, the recently restored **National Theater** is a wonderfully ornate theater decorated to the hilt in the baroque-arabesque style favored by the royal family in the 19th century.

Off Ataba are several **major markets**. The indoor Ataba market contains myriad of fresh produce and meat and is well worth a visit to absorb some local color, but it's not for the squeamish. To the northeast is the paper market.

The **Post Office Museum** *is on the second floor of the Central Post Office in Ataba Square. Hours: 9am-1pm. Admission: LE1.* The modest museum traces the history of Egypt's postal system and contains a variety of post-related exhibits including an interesting stamp collection.

ISLAMIC CAIRO

For a thousand years, the minarets and domes of Cairo's mosques, palaces, and walls towered over the city, dominating it's skyline. Though modern skyscrapers now clutter its horizon, Cairo's 20 square kilometers of medieval quarters are still resplendent with more than a millennia's worth of the world's greatest Islamic monuments. Unlike Baghdad, Damascus and other great Islamic cities to the East, Cairo was spared the wrath of the Mongols, and its monuments saved from sure destruction. Unfortunately, most visitors fail to make more than a cursory visit to this portion of the city.

Introduction to Mosque Architecture

A **mosque** is simply a space or structure designated for prayer, but throughout the Islamic World it often assumes the role as focal point for social, economic, and political activities of communities, nations, and even empires. Throughout Islamic history, mosques have doubled as schools, mausoleums, medical clinics, inns, military garrisons, and even prisons.

A GUIDE TO ISLAMIC CAIRO

Those with a keen interest in the history and architecture of Islamic Cairo should consider picking up a copy of **Islamic Monuments in Cairo, a Practical Guide** *by Caroline Williams (previous editions by Richard Parker& Robin Sabin). A superb practical guide it lists more than 300 monuments and provides clear and easy to understand directions, vivid accounts of the monuments' histories, and interesting explanations of their architectural significance. It should be available in any hotel bookstore or any bookstore selling English language publications and costs about LE60 per copy–a LE60 well spent.*

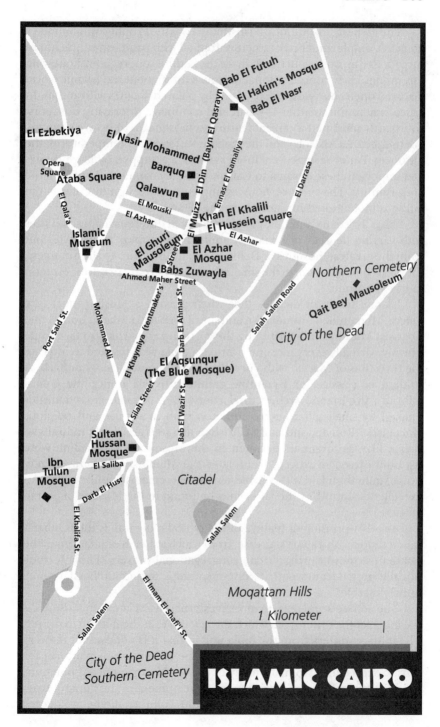

El Ezbekiya

Opera Square
Ataba Square

El Nasir Mohammed

Barquq

Qalawun

Bab El Futuh

El Hakim's Mosque

Bab El Nasr

(Bayn El Qasrayn)

El Din

Ennasr El Gamaliya

El Darrasa

El Mouski

El Azhar

El Muizz

Khan El Khalili

El Hussein Square

El Azhar

Islamic Museum

El Ghuri Mausoleum

El Azhar Mosque

Street

Babs Zuwayla

Ahmed Maher Street

El Qala'a

Port Said St.

Mohammed Ali

El Khaymiya (tentmaker's)

Darb El Ahmar St.

El Silah Street

El Aqsunqur
(The Blue Mosque)

Bab El Wazir St.

Salah Salem Road

Northern Cemetery

Qait Bey Mausoleum

City of the Dead

Sultan Hussan Mosque

El Saliba

Citadel

Ibn Tulun Mosque

Darb El Husr

El Khalifa St.

Salah Salem

Salah Salem

El Imam El Shaf'i St.

Moqattam Hills

1 Kilometer

City of the Dead
Southern Cemetery

ISLAMIC CAIRO

The earliest mosque located in Medina was the Prophet Mohammed's house. A simple mud brick structure topped with palm leaves, the house surrounded an open courtyard where the faithful congregated. Following this model, early congregational mosques throughout the Islamic world featured open courtyards surrounded by pillared arcades with arches. In Cairo, where the weather is warm and conducive to praying outdoors, courtyards remained a central feature to mosque architecture throughout the ages. As Anatolia and the Balkans suffer colder temperatures, the Ottoman Turks designed enclosed sanctuaries, topped by large domes and imported these designs to Cairo when they conquered Egypt in the 16th century. The most obvious example of this design in Cairo is the bulbous Mohammed Ali mosque in the Citadel.

Like Christian churches, mosques come in different shapes and sizes with varying degrees of ornamentation. They employ many styles but from the greatest mosques of Delhi, Istanbul, and Cairo to the humblest, simplest concrete room in the smallest village, there are features common to every mosque.

Islamic tradition dictates that when praying a Muslim must face Mecca, Mohammed's hometown and site of the Kaaba, Islam's holiest site. To assist Muslims in determining the correct way in which to face while praying, virtually every mosque features a **qibla** wall, marked to indicate the direction of Mecca, with curved niche in the wall called **mihrab**. A student of classical or Byzantine architecture will notice the typical mihrab's pre-Islamic architectural roots: shell shaped, curved niches flanked by small pillars, were common both in secular and religious Hellenistic, Roman, and early Christian architecture. Early mihrabs in Cairo, like the original specimen in the Mosque of Ibn Tulun, were typically carved in stucco, while later the Mamlukes introduced very ornate mihrabs inlaid with marble, a style that remains popular today. An execellent example of the latter may be found in the Mosque of Sultan Hassan.

Another prominent feature of the typical qibla wall is the **minbar**-a raised pulpit with a short staircase, from which a sheikh or imam gives the **khutba** (sermon) during Friday congregational prayers. Though traditionally crafted from wood, it's not uncommon to find minbars in stone, usually marble.

The architectural feature most Westerners associate with mosques is the **minaret**-the tower from which the *muezzin* calls the faithful to prayer. The minaret differs from the qibla wall in that it is not present in every mosque, but it is similar in that it became an important platform for artistic expression. Home to many of the world's magnificent minarets, Cairo is an ideal locale for tracing the development of the minaret from the early spiral Mesopotamian style of Ibn Tulun to the pencil shaped design preferred by the Ottomans. Fatimids developed the multi-sectioned minaret that typically rose from a square base and peaked with a rounded, ribbed top. The Mamlukes built on this style to produce the prototypical Cairo minaret with an octagonal base that becomes thinner, more ornate, and spherical at the top. After conquering Egypt in the 16th century, the Turkish Ottomans introduced the simpler straight pencil shape.

Fatimids introduced **domes** to Islamic architecture in Egypt after their 10th century conquest. Traditionally placed above mausoleums, domes were originally rib-shaped and made of plaster. Later the Mamlukes advanced the use of stone in domes and introduced increasingly complex ornamentation-the interlocking geometric and floral patterns on the dome of the Mausoleum of Qait Bey in the Northern Cemetery is typically considered the finest in Cairo. The transition from the square shaped base buildings to the rounded domes was facilitated by the ingenious use of squinches in corners that typically resemble a honeycomb and stalactites. During the Fatimid era these niches, called **muqarnas**, were simple and purely functional but later the Mamlukes developed them into highly ornate and complex art forms. Muqarnas were also incorporated into the monumental doorways preferred by the Mamlukes and found in normal ceilings and on building exteriors and interiors. The earliest examples of muqarnas in Cairo can be found on the exterior corners of the Mosque of El Aqmar on Bayn El Qasrayn Street near the Khan El Khalili.

During the Ayyubid (1171-1250) and Mamluki (1250-1517) periods mosques began to assume functions in addition to the traditional role as house of prayer. To reinforce Sunnism after two hundred years of Fatimid Shiite rule the Ayyubids introduced the **madrasah**, a Sunni legal college attached to a mosque where judges and civil servants, in addition to religious leaders were educated. It became standard practice for Mamluke sultans and generals to endow their mosque with a madrasah and for more than 500 years from the 14th century to the 18th, madrasahs were the premier institutions of higher learning in Egypt.

Imported from Persia, the most common design for the madrasah complex was the cruciform which incorporated a courtyard, known as a **sahn**, typically surrounded by four **liwans** (vaulted arches) each representing one of the four major Sunni legal schools: Hanafi, Shafi'i, Hanbali, and Maliki. Later madrasahs were sometimes enclosed and more compact because of lack of urban space. The apex of the madrasah complex design was reached in the Madrasah of Sultan Hassan, constructed in the 1360's. Its size, grace, and fantastic workmanship place it amongst the most impressive Islamic buildings in the world.

In addition to madrasahs, Ayyubids and Mamlukes typically incorporated their own mausoleums into their mosques, a practice some contemporary Muslims consider to have been too self-edifying and Islamic. They also commonly built into their mosques **khanqahs**, institutions for housing Sufi mystics pursuing an ascetic lifestyle of prayer, fasting, and other pious activities.

Like others, Islamic builders borrowed heavily from other architectural traditions, especially the Hellenistic-Byzantine and Persian. Take a visit to any early mosque in Cairo, such as the Mosque of Amr, and you will find Greek or Roman columns-usually usurped from older monuments. The Mosque of Ibn Tulun located in southern Islamic Cairo provides a brilliant example of how Muslim architects adopted pre-Islamic Mesopotamian designs and technique and incorporated them into the traditional arcaded courtyard of congregational mosques. Domes were introduced to Egypt from North Africa by the Fatimids, and mihrabs typically incorporate Hellenistic style ribbed niches and mini-columns. Mosaic, stone masonry, and the use of arches were other architectural devices adopted by Muslim architects who then made them their own.

Islamic Museum

The Museum is on the corner of Port Said and Mohammed Ali Streets between Ataba Square and the Citadel. Tel. 02/341-8672. Hours: 9am-4pm daily, closes during noon prayers (1pm when daylight savings time is in effect in the summer). Admission: LE16 general, LE8 students.

This museum, often neglected, contains one of the world's premier collections of historic Islamic artifacts. Though many displays are poorly lit and lacking explanation, one only need examine the fine work to understand the stratospheric level of expertise achieved by Islamic artisans. Exhibits are displayed chronologically (Fatimid, Ayyubid, Mamluke etc...) or by a discipline (glass work, wood work, tiles, etc...).

Through the entrance the first exhibits feature some exquisite examples of wood-work including mashrabia, furniture inlaid with semi-precious stones, and inscribed wood panels, usually featuring verses of the Koran. There are also several examples of rare, wooden mihrabs.

Other impressive displays include the hand written and richly embellished Korans in the back rear. In addition to immaculate, flowing Arabic calligraphy, many of them are adorned with gold leaf (on every page) and geometric and flowery designs of such detail, you need a magnifying glass to perceive the extent of it. Along the eastern axis of the museum building, are fine displays of tapestries and carpets (mostly from Turkey and Persia) as well as fine examples of enameled glass lamps and inlaid candlesticks.

Fustat

When **Amr Ibn El As** led Islam's first invaders into Egypt in 642, they took six months to lay siege to the Roman fort of Babylon now in Old

Cairo and built their barracks to the northeast. These earliest settlements of Arab troops became **Fustat**- "The Camp," where Amr built the first mosque in Egypt. Following the fall of Babylon, Fustat quickly evolved from a military camp into one of the largest and most cosmipolitan cities in the world. It also became known as *Misr*, today the official name of Egypt and the popular name for Cairo itself. Later Islamic dynasties would build new capital cities to the north, but Fustat continued to develop into one of the Islamic world's premier urban centers with a population numbering as many as 200,000 during the Fatimid Era.

Famous for its handicrafts, it was major commercial hub with a highly developed infrastructure including roads and aqueducts. A Persian traveler Nasr I-Khusrawi, remarked that there were buildings that towered 14 stories, an immense engineering feat for the early Middle Ages. In 1168, Fustat was supposedly razed by the Fatimids to spare it from the invading Crusaders and never rebuilt. Though rubble remains are evident behind the Mosque of Amr, Fustat has never been rebuilt and is now a center for the manufacture of bricks and ceramics.

The Mosque of Amr, *on Sidi Hassan El Anwar Street several hundred meters north of the Fort of Babylon and Coptic Cairo. Any taxi driver will know it or you take the metro to the Mar Girgis stop and turn left (north); the mosque will be on your right. Entrance: LE6.*

The first Arab Islamic invader of Egypt, Amr Ibn El As, built the original version of this mosque shortly after conquering Babylon in 642 making it the oldest mosque in Egypt. Doubled in size in 827, it was renovated, restored, and partially rebuilt not less than 10 times since and nothing of the original mosque is in evidence-it's like the hammer of which you've replaced the handle and the head, but it's still the same hammer. In the heyday of Fustat, the Mosque of Amr was the city's major congregational mosque and hence the center of social life. After the great fire of 1168, Salah El Din restored the mosque a second time. Later restorers include Murad Bey (1798), Mohammed Ali (1845) and various regimes throughout the 20th century.

Mosque of Ibn Tulun

The Mosque of Ibn Tulun, *off Saliba Street by Sayeda Zeinab can be reached by taking the Metro to Sayeda Zeinab; by foot from Midan Mohammed Ali by the Madrasah of Sultan Hassan under the Citadel; or by taxi (any driver will know it). Hours: 8am-5pm. Admission: LE12 general, LE6 students.*

By many accounts the most splendid mosque in Egypt and one of the finestest Islamic monuments in the World, this grand and graceful house of worship was constructed by **Ibn Tulun** between 876-879. The son of a slave to the Abbassid dynasty in Iraq, Ibn Tulun was dispatched to govern Egypt on behalf of the Abbassids in 868, but garnered enough power by way of tribute to declare himself independent of Baghdad, establishing his own dynasty and city. He constructed the new city, **El Qita'i**, meaning "the wards," on fabled land where legend said Noah's Ark had parked and Moses supposedly confronted Pharaoh's sorcerers. The short-lived city revolved around this great mosque until the Abbassids razed it while reclaiming Egypt in 905; only this magnificent building was left intact. As Amr's mosque was renovated and rebuilt to the extent that nothing of the original structure remains, Ibn Tulun's is the oldest intact original mosque in Cairo though it became obsolete as the major congregational mosque after the destruction of El Qita'i. Except for a period during the 12th century when it served as a *caravanserai* for pilgrims going to Mecca from North Africa, it was neglected until the Mamluke Sultan Lagin made substantial renovations in the late 13th century.

Upon entering you will be struck (unless there are hordes of tourists) by the serenity of this immense building as well as its simplicity and grace. Its large open courtyard once held thousands of worshippers every Friday, and reflects the earliest Arabian traditional style; but for the most part, this mosque is a rare Cairene example of Iraqi and Mesopotamian architecture-thus reflecting the roots of Ibn Tulun himself. The simple but hauntingly human like crenellations lining the tops of the walls, the use of stucco and the carvings within the beautiful arches, and the original base of the minaret all are clear examples of Mesopotamian influence.

The minaret itself probably spiraled all the way to the top (like the great minaret at Sammara) with an outside staircase, but the upper sections of its current edition, reconstructed by Sultan Lagin, are in the early Bahri Mamluki style. Lagin also added the dome atop the ablution fountain in the middle of the courtyard. Along the qibla wall facing Mecca, the original mihrab is an excellent example of the Kufic style Arabic calligraphy favored during the 9th and 10th centuries.

The Gayer-Anderson Museum

Adjoining Ibn Tulun's mosque to the southeast, are two medieval Islamic houses, now combined as the **Gayer-Anderson Museum** or **Bayt El Kritliya** ("house of the Cretan woman"). Gayer-Anderson was a British major who restored and lived in the houses in the 1930's which now contain his eccentric collection of English, Chinese, and Arabic art and furniture. The site for some of the scenes in the 1979 James Bond thriller *The Spy Who Loved Me* (Ibn Tulun was also featured), Gayer-Anderson is an excellent example of medieval domestic architecture and interior design.

The entrance fee is LE20 and the museum opens from 9am-4pm except on Fridays when it closes for the mid-day prayer.

Saliba Street

The Madrasah of Amir Sarghatmish, *on Saliba Street, just west of Ibn Tulun and on the same side of the street. Hours: 9am-5pm. Admission: LE6 general, LE3 student.*

As many as sixty students at a time enrolled in this 14th century Quranic school of the Hanafi *madhab* (legal school). It was endowed by the reputedly handsome Amir Sarghatmish who administered Egypt during the reign of the Mamluke Sultan Hassan (builder of his own world renowned madrasah). Similar to other Mamluki madrasahs it features the cruciform configuration imported from Persia with four liwans (vaulted arches); one on each side of the central courtyard. Surrounding the liwans, cells and rooms were used for student and teacher housing.

The Mausoleum and Madrasah of Amir Seif El Din Salar and his companion Amir 'Alam El Din Sangar El Gawli, *two hundred meters west of Ibn Tulun and the Madrasah of Amir in a bend in Saliba Street (also called El Khudari Street, the "street of the vegetable sellers"). Hours: 9am-5pm. Admission: LE6.*

The mausoleum for the two *amirs* (princes) for whom it is named, as is the custom contains their tombs under the domes. It also functioned as a madrasah and khanqah where traveling merchants and sufis could rent rooms. Amir Sangar enjoyed a prosperous career as a governor in Palestine and Syria, but his pal Amir Salar was less fortunate. A victim of court intrigue, he perished in prison in 1310.

Sultan Hassan & Rifa'i Mosques

These mosques, very popular with visitors, are located just under the Citadel on Midan Mohammed Ali. From Ibn Tulun they are about 3/4 of a kilometer east on Saliba Street. From Ataba Square they can be reached by proceeding along Mohammed Ali Street, (also known as El Qala'a Street) and from the Khan El Khalili on foot by going to Bab Zuweila and cutting left (east) to Darb El Ahmar Street which then turns into Bab El Wazir Street- a good way to explore medieval Islamic Cairo. An alternative is to continue walking straight after Bab Zuweila until you hit the major thoroughfare of Mohammed Ali Street, and then hooking left. Upon reaching the end of Bab El Wazir, the Citadel will be up to your left and Midan Mohammed Ali and the two mosques will be on the right. If ever in doubt, just ask any local willing and able to speak the slightest amount of English any taxi will know these monuments. Hours: 9am-5pm daily, closes for Friday prayers. Admission: LE12 general for each mosque, LE6 students.

Should you visit one mosque in Cairo, let it be the **Madrasah of Sultan Hassan**, the crowning achievement of Bahri Mamluke architecture. Though Ibn Tulun's mosque rivals Sultan Hassan in architectural dexterity and beauty, it is uniquely Mesopotamian while Sultan Hassan is the masterpiece of Mamluki architecture indigenous to Cairo. Ironically the grandeur and workmanship of Sultan Hassan's Mosque is unmatched, but the red-bearded sultan was a weak leader, easily manipulated, and ultimately assassinated in 1361 before his mosque and mausoleum were completed. His mausoleum is perhaps the finest in Cairo, but his body was never recovered and only his two sons are buried here.

The mosque's setting on Midan Mohammed Ali (obviously it was not called that then as Mohammed Ali ruled 350 years later) was in the heart of Mamluki Cairo and the site of the most important religious and military parades and processions. In dominating these quarters of the city, the monument was in effect dominating the urban landscape of Mamluki Cairo, then a power center in the Islamic world. Beside its commanding location, the dimensions and size of the complex were unprecedented. Covering nearly 8,000 square meters, the main facade is 77 meters long and reaches nearly 37 meters high. The minaret towers 68 meters above ground level and four huge arched liwans- one for each of the four major Sunni schools of Islamic law (Hanbali, Hanafi, Maliki, and Shafi'i)- surround the heart of the complex, an open courtyard.

Sultan Hassan, is a typical Mamluki royal complex. The qibla wall and mosque sanctuary facing Mecca, feature a fantastically ornate mihrab inlaid with marble and in the Turko-Persian tradition, a large dome tops the mausoleums in a separate room next to the qibla. The madrasah classrooms, libraries and dormitories are fronted by the four large liwans (vaulted arches) surrounding the open courtyard.

For such a beautiful and graceful building, the Sultan Hassan complex has endured a troubled, if not cursed past. Original plans included two minarets above the entrance in addition to that on the corner of the building. However, during construction in 1360, one collapsed killing more than a hundred laborers and the plans were dropped. Constructed in the 1670's, the present minaret and dome replaced the originals which suffered heavy damage during rebellions against Sultan Barquq in the 1390's, and 1517 when the last Mamluke sultan, Tumanbey bunkered in the complex while resisting the Ottomans. The minaret collapsed in 1659.

Rifa'i Mosque

Across from Sultan Hassan's complex stands the highly ornate **Rifa'i Mosque**. Though commissioned in 1869 by Princess Khushyar (mother of Khedive Ismail and consort of Ibrahim Pasha), it was built in traditional Mamluki style, keeping intact with the architecture of other monuments in the neighborhood. Built on the site of a former *zawiya* (complex housing sufi mystics), it originally contained the remains of Sheikh Ali El Rifa'i; a sufi saint, a companion to the Prophet Mohammed, Sheikh Abdall El Ansari; as well as Princess Khushyar herself and her descendants, including King Fouad (the first Egyptian constitutional monarch),

Khedive Ismail, Sultan Hussein Kamil, and King Farouk who was overthrown by Nasser and the Free Officers in 1952. Also interred here is the
last Shah of Iran who was overthrown during the 1979 revolution led by
Ayatollah Khomeini.

Though it doesn't compare with the magnificence and grace of Sultan
Hassan, El Rifa'i is impressive for its size and elaborate ornamentation.
Upon entrance, you face the tomb of Sheikh El Rifa'i, namesake for the
mosque and still considered by those who come to touch and kiss the
tomb in return for a blessing. Situated to the right is the highly ornate
mosque and sanctuary portion of the complex. The grilles, marble
columns (19 varieties), and the gold imported from Turkey on the ceiling
attest to the extent to which Egypt's last royal family would pay for
ornamentation of their monuments leaving one to ask: but what of their
people?

The Citadel

*The Citadel is off Salah Salem Street, the Autostrade, and Mohammed Ali
Square. By public transportation, the Citadel can reached from Tahrir Square on
Minibus #54, or Buses # 905 (Pyramids Road), #174 (Ramses Square), #404
(Ataba & Tahrir), and #173(Falaki & Bab El Louk squares). Hours:8am-5pm
(winter) & 6pm (summer). Admission: LE20 general, LE10 students.*

Perched on the Moqattam Hills overlooking the city like a sentry on
duty, the Citadel ("El Qala'a" in Arabic) was the seat of Egyptian
government for more than 600 years. Originally constructed by the
legendary **Salah El Din Ibn Ayyub** at the end of the 12th century, it housed
the organs of central government, palaces, and military installations until
the 19th century. Mamlukes, Turks, and Mohammed Ali all made
extensive renovations, extensions, and additions. Today, it still houses a
functioning prison and a police installation besides the numerous mosques,
museums, and palaces open to the public.

A Kurd by blood, **Salah El Din Ibn Ayyub** came to Egypt in 1168 as
lieutenant to Shirkoh to subdue a Fatimid state thought to be in cahoots
with the Crusaders. An extremely capable leader, Salah El Din grabbed
control of Egypt himself, and restored Egypt back to the Sunni fold after
200 years of Shiite domination. It has been Sunni ever since.

Construction on the Citadel itself began in 1176. Like other major
new dynasties, the **Ayyubids** desired a new and improved seat of government for themselves and the hilltops of Moqattam provided an ideal
setting for a new fort. Overlooking the city and highly fortifiable, the site
was long considered for such a project but a weakened Fatimid state could
never muster the resources to actually build. Little remains of Salah El
Din's original citadel except the impressive western walls and towers.
During the early 13th century, Salah El Din's nephew Kamel, who ruled

after Salah El Din and his brother Adel, constructed substantial residential quarters in the southern quarter of the complex. These were destroyed by the Mamluke **Sultan El Nasir Mohammed** (1299-1309, 1310-1341) who made extensive additions himself. Except for his green-domed mosque, nothing remains of El Nasir Mohammed's buildings because they either fell into disrepair themselves or were destroyed in the early 19th century by **Mohammed Ali**. It is very much his Citadel that we visit today.

Though he nearly rebuilt the entire Citadel, Mohammed Ali made his statement with the **Mohammed Ali Mosque**, also known as the **Alabaster Mosque**, which for 150 years has dominated the skyline of Islamic Cairo. Built in the classic imperial Ottoman Turkish tradition, its hallmarks include a huge dome over the main prayer hall and two pencil shaped Ottoman minarets, each standing 82 feet tall. According to Ottoman tradition, only the sultan was to erect more than one minaret on his mosque (sultans' mosques usually have four) so by building two, Mohammed Ali inteded to make a political statement. He backed up his boasts in the 1830's when his armies, led by Ibrahim Pasha (whose statue stands in Opera Square), swept through Syria and were poised to invade Anatolia, when the British intervened.

In any case, the Mohammed Ali Mosque, impressive by Cairene standards for its size, doesn't hold a candle to the magnificent mosques of Istanbul that it aspires to match. In fact, most architectural historians consider it to be a third rate imitation- "a box with domes"- unworthy of dominating the skyline of city so rich in true architectural beauty and splendor.

Decked to the hilt in green and gold the mosque's interior is a first rate example of the baroque-arabesque style favored by Mohammed Ali and must be one of the gaudiest interior design jobs known to man. Likened to everything from a Faberge egg to a bad movie set for *War & Peace*, it must be seen to be believed.

Lost in the shadow of Mohammed Ali's grandiose monstrosity, the **Mosque of El Nasir Mohammed** (constructed in the 1330's) with its superb masonry and ornate minaret bespeak classic Mamluki architecture. The green dome has been rebuilt several times and the marble which originally adorned the courtyard was usurped by Egypt's Ottoman conqeror, Selim the Grim, in the 1500's, but El Nasir Mohammed's mosque is still an elegant reminder of the Citadel's medieval origins.

North of El Nasir's Mosque, **The Military Museum** *(Tel. 02/920-955)*, is by far the largest of the Citadel's museums and a gold mine for military buffs and those interested in Egypt's modern political and military history. Located in Mohammed Ali's former Harem Palace, the museum was founded by King Farouk in the 1930's to commemorate and glorify the exploits of his dynasty, beginning with the reign of Mohammed Ali (1805-1848). Since the Revolution of 1952, the exhibits have been constantly updated to include the 1952 Revolution, the wars with Israel, as well as the political deeds and achievements of Presidents Nasser, Sadat, and Mubarak.

Besides the typical displays of uniforms and weapons, the museum provides interesting insight into Egypt's history with extensive explanations, both in English and Arabic, that very much tell an "official" version of history, but are informative nonetheless. As you might expect, the '73 October (Yom Kippur) War enjoys a good share of attention as does the 1956 Suez Crisis while the small exhibit about the 1967 Six Day June War, was probably not out of coincidence, closed on the 30th anniversary of the war. Perhaps the most interesting exhibits are those concerning the military and political history of Egypt in the 19th and early 20th centuries- a fascinating period of change and transition often overshadowed by pharaohs, sultans, and the modern giants of Nasser and Sadat.

At times the exhibits become tedious and that's when its time to enjoy the building itself. A superb example of the 19th century Ottoman-Egyptian Euro-arabesque, its ornate gilded capitals and baroque tinted romanticized landscape murals in green and gold is a site to behold. On the way in or out take time to examine the artillery and planes on exhibit outside, as well as the statue of Ibrahim Pasha, a replica of the statue in Opera Square.

Far smaller than the Military Museum but intiguing nonetheless is the **National Police Museum**, *situated off the courtyard on the Citadel's west side*. This modest, but interesting collection dedicated to criminology throughout Egyptian history takes but 10 minutes to breeze through, and is certainly worth a peek. One of the more interesting exhibits is that about political assassination in Egypt over the past 100 years, but noticeably absent is any display about the most important assassination- that of President Anwar El Sadat in 1981.

The **El Gawharah Palace Museum** *is south of the Mohammed Ali.* Though *gawharah* means "jewels" in Arabic, this palace never contained a jewel collection. Rather it served as one of Mohammed Ali's reception halls after its completion in 1814. The model royal bedroom and reception hall feature prime examples of the neo-baroque, green lined with gold, gaudy style of interior design fancied by Mohammed Ali and his dynasty and which, unfortunately, remains popular with Egyptians of all classes to this day.

North of the Military Museum, the **Carriage Museum** features a variety of ornate carriages used by Egypt's royal family throughout the 19th and 20 centuries.

Behind the Carriage Museum lurks the rarely visited Ottoman-era **Mosque of Suleiman Pasha**. Built in the early 1500's, its lavish decoration, particularly in the domes, bespeaks the beginning of Turkish building in Egypt. Built before the Ottoman style morphed into the gaudy imitation baroque of Mohammed Ali, Suleyman Pasha's mosque exudes the grace and style usually associated with medieval monuments in Cairo.

Bab El Wazir, El Tabbana & Darb El Ahmar Streets
Between El Azhar/ Khan El Khalili & the Citadel/Sultan Hassan

These streets linking Bab Zuweila with the Citadel and the Sultan Hassan Mosque, make an excellent walk for those wishing to get away from the tourist bazaars and soak up the sites, sounds, and smells of Islamic Cairo's medieval residential neighborhoods. Cluttered with Mamluki and Ottoman Era mosques, madrasahs and other monuments, they are typically neglected by tourists but are littered with gems nonetheless. It is possible to walk in either direction to Bab Zuweila from Mohammed Ali Square (AKA Salah El Din Square), or vice versa, in 20 minutes to a half an hour if you do not stop at any monuments. Otherwise, it's easy to spend countless hours or even days exploring the monument laden entrails of these districts.

If starting at Mohammed Ali Square head west and turn left up the hill on **El Mahgar Street**. The Citadel and its 19th century gate, **Bab El Azab**, should stand to your right. According to legend, lone survivor, Amin Bey, of Mohammed Ali's ambush that wiped out the Mamlukes after a lavish party at the Citadel, escaped by leaping over this gate on his horse before fleeing to Upper Egypt. (In fact Amin Bey never attended the party and quietly fled to Syria.) To the left on the curb jutting slightly into the square is the humble **El Mahmudia Mosque** (entrance is free). Constructed in a modest Mamluki style in 1689 by the bloodthirsty Ottoman governor of Cairo, **Mahmoud Pasha**, its most interesting feature is the wooden ceiling inscribed and painted with beautiful, though not ostentatious, Islamic calligraphy and geometric patterns. If you can spare a bit of time, this modest structure built by a very mean spirited man is worth a quick visit.

Moving up El Mahgar Street, bear left, turning away from the Citadel after reaching a large, seemingly out-of-place modern looking archives building marked with a post office sign. Beyond several hundred yards of neighborhood cafes and shops, El Mahgar Steet becomes Bab El Wazir Street and you will find the **Mosque of Aytmish El Bagasi** on the right and past it up a small alley, the **Mausoleum of Tarabay El Sharifi**. Aytmish, a Mamluke general, constructed his mosque in the 1380's while Tarabay, also a Mamluki officer, built his in 1503. Should you have time, check out Tarabay's domed mausoleum (which is all that really remains anyway), an excellent example of typical Mamluki decoration and design.

The next monuments, the **Mosque of Khayraq** and the **Mosque of Aqsunqur**, several hundred meters on the right, are the most famous monuments on Bab El Wazir Street. Though half the minaret is missing, Khayraq's monument is impressive but his story is even more compelling. An important Mamluki general and viceroy of Aleppo in Syria, he connived with the Ottomans who then defeated Sultan El Ghuri (Khayraq's boss) and took Egypt. Khayraq became the first Ottoman governor of Egypt and built this complex in 1502 incorporating the **Palace of Alin Aq**, next door.

Originally constructed by a Mamluke in 1346, **the Mosque of Aqsunqur** is popularly known as the "**Blue Mosque**" for the blue Ottoman tiles added 300 hundred years later by the Ottoman Ibrahim Agha who is buried in the highly ornate mausoleum next to the minaret. Take time to notice the rare marble minbar and the Mamluki style mihrab. That Ibrahim Agha usurped the building and made extensive additions makes this an interesting hybrid between the classic Mamluki-style mosques found throughout Islamic Cairo, and the later, more ornate Ottoman Turkish tradition. Though not in the same league as the famous Blue Mosque in Istanbul, Aqsunqur's mosque is very much worth visiting.

Just beyond the Blue Mosque stands the large **Waqf of Ibrahim Agha** originally built in 1652, and the **Minaret of Zawiyat El Hunud** (a "zawiya" housed sufis) built in 1260. The oldest Mamluki minaret in Cairo, it reflects the transition in minaret styles from the ribbed mini-dome of the Fatimids to the smaller, spherical design developed by the Mamlukes.

About a hundred yards beyond the Blue Mosque, the double-domed **Madrasah of Om El Sultan Sha'aban** (built in 1368) stands on the left. A typical Mamluki complex, it features a cruciform shaped madrasah with a courtyard, and a mausoleum flanking the mosque sanctuary. In Mamluki mosques, domes traditionally cover mausoleums hence the two separate tomb chambers-one for men, and one for women- create the need for two domes. Though Sultan Ashraf began this monument for his mother (*Om* is 'mother' in Arabic), she claimed its endowment and it is her tomb, shared with her daughter, which is large and ornate while the Sultan, who was assassinated in 1376, is interred in the simpler tomb next door with his son, El Mansur, who was himself briefly sultan.

The **Bayt of Ahmed Katkhuda El Razzaz**, next to the Madrasah of Om Sultan Sha'ban was a modest structure when originally constructed in the 1400's but has mushroomed over the centuries into the massive building that it is now. A classic example of Mamluki domestic architecture, complete with fine mashrabia windows and open courtyards, it is well worth a visit if open.

Beyond Bayt of Ahmed Katkhuda El Razzaz, the street once again changes identities as Bab El Wazir turns into Tabbana Street which stretches until the Mosque of Qajmas El Ishaqi when it bears west (left) and becomes Darb El Ahmar Street. The centerpiece of Tabbana is the **Mosque of Altinbugha El Maridani**, a Mamluke governor of Aleppo in the 1330's. Two hundred meters north, the Mosque of Qajmas El Ishaqi is an example of a fine Circassian madrasah and is well worth a peak if it is open.

To make the walk and experience the monuments described above, but beginning at **Bab Zuweila**, take a hard left after passing through the huge gate on Darb El Ahmar Street instead of heading straight on the Street Tentmakers. On the corner between the two streets stands the **Mosque of Salah Tilai**, a Fatimid wazir who endowed the building of the mosque (the last built by Fatimids) by *waqf* (religious endowment) in 1160. Beautiful for its simplicity, its plan reflects the traditional design of mosques dating to the Prophet when a courtyard surrounded by arcades with columns was typical. Damaged by an earthquake in 1303, which claimed the minaret, immediate restorations included the bronze facings on the main door and the mashrabia screens on the porch. The minbar was also a later addition made in 1300. Notice how low the mosque lies-the original ground level at the time of building – which presents a great challenge to those trying to save the building from modern era water table levels and subterranean infrastructure.

The Street of the Tentmakers & the Street of the Saddlemakers

Just south of Bab Zuweila, the gawking and flapping of live fowl announces that you're entering a small live stock souk, but just beyond it begins the covered **Souk El Khayyamiya**, the **Tentmaker's Market**. It is also known as Qasaba Ridwan Bey, a 17th century mamluke official who originally built it. Here in dozens of small shops, craftsmen stitch together by hand beautiful appliqués and tent coverings traditionally used to cover funerals and weddings. Designs are usually based on classic Islamic geometric patterns but lately pharaonic motifs have also become popular.

The smaller appliqués, often made into pillow or cushion covers shouldn't set you back more than LE15-50 depending on the workmanship and size while the large bedspread size (2-3 meters by 2-3 meters) usually go from LE300-600. Bargaining may get you a slightly better deal than the initial offer but not much more than 15%. Apparently merchants have more or less set prices.

Beyond the textile merchants, the Street of the Tenmakers becomes the **Street of the Saddlemakers** which continues on to Mohammed Ali Street between Ataba Square and the Mosque of Sultan Hassan. Though it isn't littered with monuments to the extent of Bab El Wazir or Muizz li Din, this street is a colorful medieval throroughfare that is still littered with leather shops. There is a cluster of modest Mamluke structures just beyond the textile markets that include the Mosque of Mahmoud El Kurdi, the Madrasah of Inal El Yusufi, and the Maq'ad Ridwan Bey, a 17th century palace that is largely ruined and has been been incorporated into the local souk.

Towards Mohammed Ali Street, there is another bunch of Mamluke and Ottoman structures. The **Mosque and Mausoleum of Ganim El Bahlawan** is a fine example of late (16th century) Mamluki architecture that features a magnificently carved dome and an equally ornate minaret. Across the street, the Gate to the Mosque of Qawsun was once the entrance to one of medieval Cairo's primary landmarks before it was largely destroyed in the construction of Mohammed Ali Street.

Bab Zuweila to El Hussein & the Khan El Khalili

At the northern end of the Tentmakers' Street where it meets Darb El Ahmar, stands the majestic **Bab Zuweila**, the southern gate of the Fatimid city. Distinguished by two fifteenth century minaret towers added later, the gates were originally built by the Armenian Fatimid General **Badr El Gamali** in 1092. In the Middle Ages, the grand *mahmal* procession of pilgrims carrying the black covering for the Kaaba to Mecca passed through these gates as sultans, amirs, and other high officials looked on from up top. In 1516, the last Mamluke Sultan, Tumanbey was hung from these gates by the Ottoman general, Selim the Grim, and in the 19th century, the gate also became known as Bab El Metawali for a local Sufi miracle worker.

The stretch of Muizz li Din Street that links Bab Zuweila to El Azhar is a colorful souk with small merchants hawking everything from cooking appliances to textiles. About two thirds of the way between Bab Zuweila and El Azhar Street is one of only two tarboush makers in Cairo. The tarboush (also known as the 'fez') was the headress of choice before the 1952 Revolution when it was banned. There are also some modestly impressive monuments. Just inside the Bab Zuweila, the **Mosque and Madrasah of El Muayyid** (LE6, LE3 students) was constructed by a 15th century Mamluke who had been so plagued by lice and fleas that he vowed that if he came to power he would convert a prison on this site into a mosque. It is a lavish affair indeed though many architectural historians do not think the workmanship matches the quality found in some other buildings. It is well worth a visit if only to the access to the Bab Zuweila towers with their magnificent views of the medieval city. A block to the north on a bend in the street is the Sabil Kuttab of Tawsun, a classic example of Ottoman decor.

At the end of Muizz li Din where it meets El Azhar Street are two structures associated with the Mamluke **Sultan El Ghuri** (1501-1516). To left, with shops and stalls cluttered around its base, the Madrasah of El

Ghuri, distinguished by its twin-peaked minarets, suffered structural damage during the 1992 earthquake. On the right the Mausoleum of El Ghuri, was a lavish structure that cost El Ghuri more than 100,000 dinars to build, but alas his body was never recovered after he died in battle near Aleppo, Syria and hence was never buried in it. Though the once fine tiled dome is gone (a victim of poor design and earthquakes), the mausoleum is full of finely crafted Mamluki style decor and is well worth a peak inside. It doubles as a cultural center (see sidebar below) where concerts and lectures are given. Admission is free.

WHIRLING DERVISHES IN EL GHURI'S MAUSOLEUM

Every Wednesday and Saturday evening at 8pm, free whirling dervish concerts are held in El Ghuri's Mausoleum on El Azhar Street. The dances are based on rituals performed by the Mowlawiya Sufi Sect from Turkey, that represent the Sufis' discarding of their worldly possessions and desires. The whirling and dancing was also a way to attain a trance-like state and achieve union with God. Real Sufis can also be seen dancing themselves into trances in El Hussein Square during the Prophet's Birthday and the Moulid of Sayedna Hussein.

El Qahira

Founded by Shiite Fatimids who swept into Egypt from Tunisia in 969, **El Qahira** was one of the great medieval cities and still boasts dozens of historic medieval mosques, madrasahs, and other monuments. It also features miles of bazaars, the most famous of which, the **Khan El Khalili**, is a standard stop on most tourists' itinerary. Unfortunately most visitors never make it beyond the confines of the tourist bazaars to explore the miles of alleys and small streets strewn with local markets, or the dozens of Islamic monuments within the Fatimid city.

Delineated by the impressive gates of **Bab Zuweila** to the south and **Bab El Fatuh** and **Bab El Nasr** to north, El Qahira was the seat of government until Salah El Din El Ayyubi constructed the Citadel in the late 12th century, but has remained a vibrant center of commerce and culture to this day. At its heart is the thoroughfare, **El Muizz li Din Allah**, which stretches from Bab Zuweila past the monuments of El Ghuri, El Azhar, and the Khan El Khalili and onto Bab El Fatuh and Bab El Nasr. Littered with Fatimid, Mamluki, and Ottoman relics it is a fantastic walk. Meanwhile, across El Azhar Street from El Hussein Mosque and the Khan El Khalili, **El Azhar Mosque & University** (founded 970) is the world's oldest university and remains the most important center of learning and theology in Sunni Islam. To reach **Bab Zuweila** and the **Tentmakers Street** cross El Azhar Street by the blue pedestrian overpass and continue past the Mosque and Madrasah of El Ghuri and the textile souks on Muizz li Din Street.

El Azhar Mosque & University

Open 9am-7pm except during Friday prayers. Entrance: LE12 general admission; LE6 students.

Across El Azhar Street from El Hussein, **Gamaat El Azhar** is the oldest university in the world and the oldest Fatimid congregational mosque in El Qahira. Founded as a Shiite shrine in the 970 by the Fatimid General Gawhar El Siqilli, El Azhar is today the foremost center for Sunni law and theology and its graduates, recognizable by their red skull caps wrapped in white, make up the vast majority of Egypt's sheikhs and imams. Though the university now operates ten branches throughout Egypt and faculties of medicine, law, and commerce, it is still primarily a religious institution that attracts scholars from Morocco to Malaysia. The Sheikh of El Azhar is the highest religious position in Egypt and is the premier authority for questions of Islamic law and theology throughout the Sunni world and is routinely consulted by the president of Egypt and other Islamic leaders. Its libraries contain nearly 100,000 rare and ancient Islamic volumes and manuscripts and its student body numbers over 100,000.

The El Azhar complex has just undergone a facelift, the latest of many renovations and extensions over the centuries. Throughout Cairo's history, rulers from different epochs have left their mark on this mosque, making it a patchwork of different styles. The presence of a courtyard and the use of stucco hark back to Islamic architecture's roots, while the ornate minarets and marble madrasahs are pure Mamluke. The complex is entered through the double-arched **"Gate of the Barbers"**-so named because students were shaved here-into a Mamluki style marble court. It is flanked to either side by two Mamluki madrasahs, **Aqbughawiya** (1340) and **Taybarsiya** (1309), which contains El Azhars collection of rare manuscripts. The main court is entered through a gate dating to the reign of Sultan Qait Bey in 1475, but itself dates to the Fatimid Era.

It is only at the sanctuary, distinguished by richly carved stucco, that you reach El Azhar's original Fatimid structure; beyond are the Ottoman era extensions of Abd El Rahman Katkhuda (1750) which doubled the size of the complex. To the east of the extensions, the **Tomb and Madrasah of the Eunuch Amir Gawhar Qunqubay**, treasurer under Sultan Barsbey, dates to 1440. The recently restored mausoleums feature typical Mamluki marble work, intricately inlaid wooden doors, and stain glass windows. The dome with brilliant interlacing floral patterns is also a vintage Mamluki piece.

The minarets date to the 15th and 16 centuries. The first was constructed by Sultan Qait Bey, the second was added by Sultan El Ghuri. For a bit of *baksheesh*, the gatekeeper will take you up the minarets' towers which afford fine views of Islamic Cairo.

El Azhar Environs

Tucked behind the mighty El Azhar, are some of Cairo's most colorful markets where merchants, butchers, and grocers hawk everything from live chickens and rabbits to colorful clothing and fly blown meat. It is a photographer's paradise-just be discreet or ask permission if you plan to photograph a particular individual. On Sheikh Mohammed Abduh Street, which you reach from El Azhar through the ornate Bab El Sa'ida Gate, take a few minutes to admire the **Sabil Kuttab and Wikala of Sultan Qait Bey**. Built in 1477 it is one of three wikalas surviving from the Burghi Mamluke period. Once containing forty rooms for travelers, merchants, and other lodgers, it is now in poor shape, but the beauty of its decorative panels and richly ornate portal and windows make it worth a visit. Plans are underway for renovation. The surrounding neighborhood of El Butneya was famous for being a haven for organized crime where hashish was openly sold in the streets until crackdowns in the late 1980s.

Just west of El Azhar, stands the 18th century **Mosque of Abu Dahab**, distinguished by its squat Ottoman style dome. Little of the building remains intact today but it is significant as the last major Mamluke monument built in Cairo – Mohammed Ali wiped them out 25 years later. Abu Dahab grabbed power in the 1770's during a lapse in Ottoman control and attempted to reestablish the Mamluki empire, but was killed in battle in Palestine. His name, "Abu Dahab," meaning "Father of Gold," was given in recognition of his generous distribution of gold on the occasion of his investiture.

Behind Abu Dahab is the **Wikala of El Ghuri**. A classic Mamluki structure featuring protruding windows with wooden mashrabia, it has been converted into an artists' cooperative and the old lodging rooms and stables are used as studios where artisans and craftsmen paint, mold, and weave. This is an excellent example of a medieval commercial hotel and is basically intact. The admission fee is LE5 and it opens from 8:30-3pm when the shops close though you can still wander about until 5pm.

El Hussein Mosque

Standing astride El Hussein Square and the Khan El Khalili, the **El Hussein Mosque** was originally constructed in the 12th century and renovated in the 1870's by Khedive Ismail, who added the Ottoman minarets. While El Azhar is the institutional center of the Sunni establishment, the Mosque of Sayedna El Hussein is the focal point around which

Cairo's popular Islamic culture revolves and the most important congregational mosque in Egypt, where the president and other high officials come to make public displays of their faith. The grandson of the **Prophet Mohammed** and son of the fourth caliph, **Ali**, Hussein became the patron saint of Shiism after his martyrdom at the hands of Sunnis at the Battle of Kerbela in 680, and his head was supposedly brought here from Syria (Syrians maintain it is still in Syria) in the 12th century.

Though Egypt reverted to Sunnism 800 years ago and orthodox Sunnism does not encourage or recognize the sanctity of relics, the shrine remains an important pilgrimage destination because popular beliefs and traditions still hold that as the grandson of the prophet, Hussein's shrine is a source of **baraka** (blessings). This is one of a handful of mosques in Egypt off limits to non-believers, but you can peak through the doors.

EL HUSSEIN & RELIGIOUS FESTIVALS

The epicenter of popular religious culture in Cairo, El Hussein comes to life during major religious festivals like the Moulid El Nabi (Mohammed's Birthday), Eid El Fitr (end of Ramadan), Eid El Adha (Feast of the Sacrifice), Moulid Sayedna Hussein (Hussein's own festival), and for the entire month of Ramadan. For all of these holidays, which attract thousands from Cairo and all over Egypt, the mosque is dressed up in colored lights and neon, as tents and banners are raised and hundreds of merchants set up shop. In the square itself festivities often include drum banging and other music and during the moulids, sufi orders and brotherhoods perform zikrs (trance dances) to achieve more union with god. During Ramadan, hundreds of tables are set up in the square where free iftar (sundown breakfast) is provided to the poor. If you come to the El Hussein during Ramadan after dark, check out the live folk music in the cafe off the northwest corner of the mosque. All of these festivities all well worth checking out, but be prepared for crowds, do not flaunt valuables, and women would be wise to go in male company to ward off would-be gropers.

Khan El Khalili & the Bazaars of Medieval Cairo

The Khan El Khalili is located off El Hussein Square and El Azhar in Islamic Cairo. It is linked to Tahrir Square by bus #815 and minubus #77, Ataba Square by bus #65, and Ramses by bus #65 and minibus #63. You can also take a cab (LE5 from downtown) or if you're up for walk, we'd recommend taking the Metro to Ataba Square and walking up Mouski Street.

Located in the heart of Fatimid Cairo off El Azhar Street and El Hussein Square, the famous Khan El Khalili bazaar is a maze of small alleys where merchants hawk wares and goods from spices and handicrafts to kitchen utensils and women's undergarments. The Khan derives its name from a *khan* (caravanserai) constructured here in 1382 by Sultan Barquq's Master of the Horse, Jarkas El Khalili. During the Ottoman Era (16th-19th centuries) the name came to refer to the souk that grew around the original Khan, which was dominated by merchants from all over the Ottoman world-namely Greeks, Armenians, and Jews. These ethnic groups continued to operate in the market until the 1950's when most emigrated and native Egyptians moved in. In the quarters frequented mostly by tourists, the goods are of the handicraft/souvenir variety, namely inlaid boxes and game tables, perfumes, brass and copper, textiles, antiques, and of course jewelry.

Though a high percentage of goods may be tacky or of poor quality, there are plenty of quality items available in all price ranges, many of which make suitable gifts, souvenirs, or even viable museum pieces. Many of the finest goods, diamonds in the rough, can only be found by sifting through piles of junk and by discovering those shops dealing in quality goods amongst the hordes of merchants hawking low quality, over priced souvenirs. It is often in back rooms and up hidden staircases where the true gems of the Khan El Khalili are uncovered. For a comprehensive guide to the more than 500 shops in the Khan El Khalili pick up a copy of Ola Seif's book, *The Khan El Khalili* (available at AUC and hotel bookstores) which features a map listing *every* shop as well as tips as to where and how to shop for what.

More interesting and colorful than the tourist bazaars are the various **souks** (markets) which surround and overlap the Khan El Khalili. Many of these markets, which cater to the local population, specialize in one

EL FISHAWI'S: THE CAFE OF MIRRORS

Just off El Hussein Square in the heart of the Khan El Khalili through the cassette souk, the sweet smell of apple sheesha smoke beckons the tired traveler to El Fishawi's, Cairo's most venerable and purportedly oldest ahwa (cafe). Part elegance (marble tables and beautiful carved wood paneling), and part kitsch (the stuffed crocodile hanging from the ceiling), El Fishawi's was opened in the late 18th century and has been run by the same family ever since. Nicknamed Cafes des Miriors, "Cafe of Mirrors," for the cracked mirrors that adorn it walls, El Fishawi's is a wonderful place to rest your bones while enjoying a mint tea and sheesha, and the diverse clientele and roaming vendors hawking everything from fake Rolex's to palm-size waterpipes makes great people watching.

particular type of good, whether it be spices, cucumbers, or car parts, while others sell everything under the sun and then some. Some markets, such as the spice market and the gold market have been in the same location for centuries and merchants remain true to the techniques and standards of their medieval predecessors.

Mouski Street

One of the most colorful routes to approach the Khan El Khalili is to make the 15 minute walk up **Mouski Street** from Ataba Square. The main commercial drag of pre-modern Cairo, Mouski still buzzes with commercial activity as vendors hawk everything from women's lingerie and electric appliances to *faseekh*, a rotten fish especially popular for Sham El Nessim (the ancient spring holiday celebrated in late April). Packed at virtually all hours, it's ideal for people watching, but you've also got to watch yourself. Take your eye off the road and next thing you know a Suzuki mini-truck or a donkey cart piled with watermelons will roll right over your feet if not the rest of you. Just when you wonder how much local color you can take, the local market quickly gives way to the plastic inlaid boxes and gaudy T-shirts of the less chaotic and exotic Khan El Khalili.

Where Mouski Street meets the Khan El Khalili, it intersects with **Muizz li Din Allah Street**, Fatimid Cairo's main thoroughfare. If your nose is tickled by the wafting aromas of musk, cumin, and coriander, you know that you're in the right place, for this intersection is in the heart of the **Spice Market** and **El Attarayn**, the perfume souk. You need not feel intimidated by the spice merchants, but the perfume sellers are known for their crafty and devious sales techniques, so think twice before forking out LE80 for a small amount of a concoction like "Cleopatra's Kiss" or "Fumes of the Pharaohs" from a gent who just told you he has a brother in Chicago, or wherever it is that you told him you're from.

North of the spice and perfume markets on El Muizz li Din, is the **gold market** and dozens of shops selling a myriad of crafts and souvenirs for tourists. Like the spice and perfume dealers, the gold merchants have been located on Muizz li Din for centuries. Past the gold souk approaching magnificent Mamluke mosques and mausoleums of Qalawun and Barquq (see below), the tourist bazaars of the Khan El Khalili once again assumes a local flavor as you approach the **copper and brass souk**, lined with shops selling everything from cooking ware to the giant lunar crescents which top the city's minarets.

El Muizz li Din Allah Street (Bayn El Kasrayn)

Once Fatimid Cairo's main avenue, El Muizz li Din Allah Street is home to some of Cairo's most significant Islamic buildings including mosques, madrasahs, and sabil kuttabs (fountains). Stretching from the

BARGAINING

Almost every sale in the Khan El Khalili (jewelry being the exception) necessitates at least some haggling should you wish to pay anything near a reasonable price. This usually lengthy process of engaging salesmen whose employ such shamelessly insidious come-ons as to make a visit to your local used car salesman seem like a trip to Southeby's intimidates Americans especially, who are used to self-service supermarkets and department stores where there is little or no interaction with salesmen. Bargaining in Egypt is a very interactive and social experience. Establishing at least the facade of a personal bond is considered good etiquette at the very least and may enhance your chances for a good deal. Expect to be asked about your personal life (marital status, how many you kids have etc.), and don't hesitate to join a shopkeeper for a glass of tea or a cold drink. Just remember that you're not required to buy anything and never should you let yourself feel that you are being pressured.

Your most valuable assets will be patience and persistence. Give yourself plenty of time to compare prices, play shopkeepers off one another, and for the process itself. Generally offer 20-30% of the asking price to begin with and work yourself up-hesitantly. Good strategies include telling the shopkeeper that you found better deal up the street, or that you'll come back tomorrow. If you do, you should be able to work a better a deal, and storming out in (sometimes feigned) disgust usually leads to shopkeepers dropping their price 20-50% on the spot for fear of losing your business. Expressing a deep desire for an item with an "if only the price was right" attitude often does the same trick. Remember, the shopkeeper will play on your emotions, so do not hesistate to play on his. Finally, and not surprisingly, the more you buy, the bigger the discount, especially if you bargain hard.

northern gate of El Qahira, Bab El Fatuh, to El Azhar Street and on to Bab Zuweila and the Tentmakers' Street it passes through numerous markets and neighborhoods including the Khan El Khalili, the gold markets and, as your nose will tell you, the spice souks. The portion which skirts the Khan El Khalili and features the gold market is also known as "Bayn El Kasrayn" which means "between the two palaces," a reference to the two Fatimid palaces that dominated the street in the 11th and 12th centuries, but were later torn down to make way for Mamluki and Turkish buildings.

"Bayn El Kasrayn" is also the title of the first book in Egyptian novelist Naguib Mahfouz's masterpiece *The Cairo Trilogy*, an epic work about a middle class family living on Bayn El Kasrayn, and the challenges of urban life during the upheavals of the early 20th century.

On the corner of Mouski and El Muizz li Din Allah streets, is the first of dozens of Islamic monuments between the Mouski and Bab El Fatuh, the **Mosque of Sultan El Ashraf Barsbay** (entrance fee LE6, LE 3 students). Not as impressive as some other monuments in the area, this simplistic structure was built in the heart of the spice market in 1425 AD. The Sultan himself is not actually buried here, but his wife and son are. Should you be willing to fork out a few extra pounds, the doorman will show you up the minaret that offers splendid views of the minarets and domes of the medieval city as well as the cluttered and often garbage ridden rooftops of the Khan El Khalili and spice markets. To the north you can admire the domes and minarets of Qalawun, El Nasir Mohammed, and beyond, the Mosque of El Hakim. To the south, the Citadel, Sultan Hassan, and the twin towers of Bab Zuweila are all visible. Going up to the minaret, check out the rundown rooms used to house the students, teachers, and Sufis living at the madrasah (religious college) and khanqah (sufi house).

Across Mouski Street from El Ashraf Barsbay, stands the **Sabil Kuttab** (fountain) and **Mosque of Sheikh Mukhtar**. Abd El Rahman Katkhuda constructed the fountain and Sheikh Mukhtar added the mosque in 1745. Just up the block and to the left on El Maqasis Street, is the still active **Wikala of Gamal El Din El Dahabi** (*Dahab* means "gold" in Arabic). Wikalas were inns for traders-in this case gold merchants-who could store their goods on the ground floor and sleep in chambers upstairs. This particular one was built in the 1630's and is named for a gold trader.

Back on Muizz li Din Allah north on the right, is the **Sabil Kuttab** (fountain) **of Khusraw Pasha** (built in 1535), an Ottoman governor of Egypt, and the adjoining **Mosque and Madrasah of El Salah El Ayyub**. El Salah was the last ruler of the Ayyubid dynasty, founded by Salah El Din, that ruled Egypt between the Fatimids and the Mamlukes. Though most of his mosque and madrasah is now ruined, the complex was one of the state's premier legal courts in Mamluke times, and the minaret is noteworthy as it is one of the only Ayyubid towers left in Cairo. The dome, in accordance with tradition, covers the mausoleum, and also provides an early example of muqaranas, the stalactite squinches used in transition from a square base to a circular dome. To the north of El Salah's complex once stood the **Madrasah of Beybars El Bunduqdari** (the "crossbow wielder"). Also known as Beybars I (1260-1277), he was one of the greatest Mamlukes, having defeated the Mongols in Syria, thus protecting El Qahira and her wealth of monuments from the destruction suffered by Damascus and Baghdad.

Located on the western side of the street across from El Salah El Ayyub's mosque is the huge complex endowed by **El Mansur Qalawun**, another important early Mamluke Sultan, who succeeded Beybars in 1279

AD. Featuring a madrasah, mosque, mausoleum, and a hospital that still functions, Qalawun's complex (LE6, LE3students) was constructed during the 1280's. Unfortunately the mosque is under renovation as of 1997, but the splendid mausoleum is for the most part in good shape- only the mihrab portion of the qibla wall is still damaged from the earthquake of 1992. The hospital, located at the southernmost part of the complex was for centuries one of Cairo's best and still provides clinical services to the local community.

Unlike many Mamluke sultans, Qalawun is due credit for more than just his graceful monument and his ability to fight off Crusaders and would-be usurpers; members of his family dominated Egypt through most of the Bahri Mamluke Era (1250-1382), and provided Egypt with at least a semblance of dynastic stability though there was still plenty of intrigue and backstabbing to be sure. During this period, medieval Islamic Egypt achieved its greatest heights militarily, economically, and artistically.

Just north of Qalawun's complex stands the **Madrasah and Mausoleum of El Nasir Mohammed**. Built in 1296 by one of Islamic Egypt's most prolific builders and one of its stronger leaders, this complex is notable for the fine carvings on the minaret (constructed later) and the fact that it was the first madrasah in Egypt to employ the cruciform design-the use of four liwans surrounding a courtyard. Another interesting feature is the European Gothic style arched doorway at the entrance that was usurped from a Crusader church in Syria by El Nasir Mohammed's predecessor El Ashraf Khalil. Nasir also built major portions of the Citadel, but only his green domed mosque and segments of the wall remain standing-the rest having fallen victim (unfortunately) to Mohammed Ali's proverbial wrecking ball.

Across the street from this complex sits the 19th century **Sabil Kuttab of Ismail Pasha**, built and named for one of Mohammed Ali's sons. On a street dominated by Mamluki and Fatimid masterpieces, this very Ottoman Turkish fountain feels a bit out of place (like a lot of Mohammed Ali's monuments).

Towering astride the complex of El Nasir Mohammed to the north is the magnificent **Madrasah of Sultan Barquq**. Completed in 1386 by the first Burghi Mamluke sultan, Barquq, this impressive structure is located at the heart of Bayn El Kasrayn. Though Barquq was a Circassian Burghi Mamluke, his mosque represents the pinnacle of Bahri Mamluke architecture who ruled Egypt for nearly a century and a half prior to his rise to power. Its madrasah design employs the cruciform featuring four large vaulted arches (one each for the four major schools of Islamic law), surrounding a small courtyard. The use of very ornate muqarnas (stalactite-like niches) in doorways, squinches, and domes is highly developed and the geometric patterns employed throughout the mosque, especially on doorways, is splendid. The emphasis on monumental size follows the precedent of major Bahri works like the mosques and madrasahs of Sultan Hassan and Qalawun. Though not to the extent of next door El Nasir Mohammed, you can detect along the facade, a Gothic influence imported to Egypt by Bahri Mamlukes who successfully expelled European Crusaders from Syria and Palestine. *Admission: LE6 general, LE3 students.*

BARQUQ & THE BURGHI MAMLUKES

Perhaps ironically, the splendor and grace of Barquq's monument does not reflect the career or character of its builder. Barquq usurped the power of the Bahri Mamlukes through marriage, intrigue, and violence, ushering in the bloody era of the Burghi Mamlukes. Referred to as Burghi, because they were stationed in the towers of the Citadel (burg means "tower" in Arabic), these Mamlukes were Circassian slave soldiers imported from the Caucucus-renowned for their fighting ability which more often then not they employed against each other. While the Bahri Mamlukes achieved new heights in terms of economic wealth, military success, and cultural achievement, the period of Burghi Mamluke rule was distinguished by increased fratricidal and patricidal tendencies, a preoccupation with backstabbing, and the squandering of Egypt's wealth – partly on ornate monuments like Barquq's Mosque and Mausoleum.

Across the street from Barquq and a bit to the north, the **Kasr (Palace) of Bashtak** is fine – and rare – example of 14th century domestic architecture. To enter head around the corner to Darb El Qirmiz Street. Bashtak was a wealthy merchant married to the daughter of El Nasir Mohammed.

If you continue up Darb El Qirmiz Street, passing the humble **Tomb of Sheikh Sinan** (built 1585), on the right you will find the **Madrasah of Amir Mithqal** – an interesting building for several reasons. Built in the 1360's by Sabiq El Din Mithqal, the head eunuch for raising and teaching young Mamlukes, its location marks the site of a major Fatimid palace. It is also suspended over the street, and not constructed at ground level, a rarity for medieval Islamic buildings.

Back on El Muizz li Din and heading north, you'll pass the broken down Ayyubid era **Madrasah of El Kamel Ayyub** before coming to a fork in the road at the Ottoman era **Sabil Kuttab** (fountain) **of Katkhuda**. Though the Ottomans ruled Egypt in the 18th century when this fountain was built, Mamluke slave soldiers continued to play major roles in Egyptian military and political life, and Katkhuda himself was a Mamluke *amir* (general) who built dozens of monuments throughout Cairo. This particular fountain is a beautiful expression of the influences that define Ottoman architecture. The Mongol style floral patterns reflect the Ottomans' east and central Asian roots, while the arches flanked by columns are rooted in the pre-Islamic Hellenistic culture of the Ottoman heartlands in Anatolia. On the other hand, the use of inlaid marble, mashrabia, and muqarnas in the exterior transition from the first to the second floor were architectural devices developed in the Arab and Persian Islamic world to which the Turks so well adapted upon their arrival from central Asia in the 11th century.

At the fork in the road at Katkhuda's Sabil, take a left and continue north to the modest **Mosque of El Aqmar**. Though hardly monumental, it broke new ground for Islamic architecture in Cairo. Built in 1125 by Mamun El Batahi, a wazir (minister) to the Fatimid Caliph El Amir, it was the first mosque in Cairo to feature a decorated stone facade and to use a ground plan whose qibla wall is not parallel to the street. This means that the ground plan adjusts to the existing urban street plan. This breakthrough enabled later builders to be increasingly innovative with their floor plans since they didn't necessarily have to design a facade parallel to the qibla wall. Finally, the Mosque of El Aqmar was the first to employ muqarnas, the stalactite-like squinches that became a prominent feature in the transition from square bases to round domes in later monuments. Here the simple muqarnas are found on the exterior walls at the corners.

A block north of El Aqmar up the alley of Darb El Asfar to the left, is the **Bayt El Suhaymi**, currently closed for renovation. One of the few surviving examples of medieval domestic architecture, it was a merchant's house built during the 16th and 17th centuries. Traditionally such houses were divided into the salamlik, public quarters on the bottom floor with open spaces, the domain of men; and the haramlik, the private quarters upstairs where women spent most of their time. Worth noticing in Bayt El Suhaymi are the *tahtabush*, an area where the owner could receive visiting merchants or official visitors, and the *maq'ad* on the second floor where he lounged about with his closer friends. The space in this building is beautifully used and in the midst of the hustle and bustle of cramped Islamic Cairo, it is an oasis of serenity and space. High ceilings, marble, brass lamps, arches, and mashrabia were all typical features in houses similar to this in Cairo throughout the Middle Ages.

Back on Muizz li Din, the **Mosque and Sabil of Suleiman Agha El Silahdar** was built in the 1830's by the official in charge of arsenals during the reign of Mohammed Ali. Though Mamluke in form, the sabil features the very European baroque decoration popular during Mohammed Ali's reign. Inside, the ground floor features a small court with an Ottoman style domed arcade while the mosque is on top.

Down the alley behind Suleiman's Sabil, the **Mosque of Abu Makr Muzher** dates to the reign of Sultan Qait Bey in the late 15th century.

At the end of Muïzz li Din in the midst of the **onion and garlic market** before Bab El Fatuh and the northern border of the Fatimid City is the bulky **Mosque of Hakim** (990-1010. Loosely modeled on the Mosque of Ibn Tulun, its construction was begun by Hakim's father. Like Tulun's, it features a spacious central court and the use of plaster. However the monumental protruding entrance is a Fatimid trademark imported from North Africa. Especially worth noting are the minarets. Restored by

THE MAD CALIPH: EL HAKIM

*No account of Fatimid Egypt is complete without mention of **El Hakim** (990-1013) the eccentric and bigotted third caliph who ruled by an arbitrary and cruel whim. When a tutor scolded him for poor work as a teenager, the young Hakim killed him on the spot, as he later did advisers who even gave the slightest indication of disagreement with him. A dedicated misogynist, El Hakim sought to restrict the movement of women in public, first declaring a ban of them in the streets, and later forbidding cobblers from stitching women's shoes. He also imposed drastic taxes on Christians and Jews and forced them to wear certain burlap clothes and to ride donkeys. While his treatment of women and non-Muslims can at least be attributed to misguided hatred, some of his edicts simply did not make any sense at all. On various arbitrary whims he ordered all the honey in Cairo be pored into the Nile, that all dogs in Cairo be killed, and that all business transactions be conducted at night.*

*A loner and introvert, El Hakim spent much of his time, particularly at night, wandering about the nearby deserts on his donkey, "Qamr" (Moon)–apparently the only being for which he felt any affection. One night, El Hakim failed to return from his evening ride. Most speculate that he was murdered by one or some of the many who were wronged by him, probably members of his family. This appears most plausible, but a small group of Hakim's followers, led by a man named Darazi, believed him to be a divine being who ascended to heaven that night. Chased out of Egypt following Hakim's death, Darazi and his companions, known as **Druze**, fled to Syria and Palestine where the Druze sect continues to be a prominent minority.*

Beybars II after an earthquake in 1303, their massize bases protrude into the streets. Like other monumental mosques, it has suffered periods of disuse and abuse. It was used as a prison for Crusader prisoners of war and as a fortress by Napoleon Bonaparte when he occupied Egypt in 1798. In the mid-20th century it served as a school.

If you have the opportunity, it is worth climbing the northern minaret to examine the fine Fatimid decorations on its exterior. In the 1980's an Indian Shiite sect restored the mosque and added the shiny marble laden mihrab.

The Northern Walls and the Gates of El Fatuh and El Nasr

Along the northern side of El Hakim's mosque run the northern fortifications of the Fatimid City El Qahira. Originally built by Egypt's Fatimid conqueror, El Gawhar, they were expanded in the 1080's by the Armenian Fatimid general, **Badr El Gamali El Guyushy** who imported masons from Armenia. A rare example of pre-Crusader, Islamic military architecture, they were built to protect Cairo from a Crusader invasion that never came.

Next to El Hakim's Mosque **Bab El Fatuh**, "Gate of Conquest," is one of three gates still standing (Bab El Nasr and Bab Zuweila are the others) from the original 60 that once accessed the walled city of El Qahira. It marks the end of Muizz li Din Allah Street which stretches to the Khan El Khalili, Mouski, and El Azhar to Bab Zuweila. Bab El Fatuh is dominated by two rounded towers featuring fine decorative carvings on both the interior and exterior. To get inside, find the custodian (probably at El Hakim's) to open it up. Inside are several rooms for housing troops and storing arms. Vaults figure prominently in both the rooms and the stairs. On your way up the stairs, notice the carved reliefs, including a hippopotamus, an indication the stones were usurped from pharaonic monuments. From the top, the view of the sea of domes and minarets is one of the best in Cairo. Tucked between the two gates, mom and pop stores and street stands cater to the working classes which live here. Around the gate itself, at the **Souk El Fatuh**, fruits and vegetables are sold from dozens of donkey carts – very vibrant and worthwhile if you're looking for local color, especially given the dramatic historical setting.

East of Bab El Fatuh, and still attached by a tunnel in the walls, is the other surviving northern gate, **Bab El Nasr**, the "Gate of Victory." Similar to Bab El Fatuh except the towers are square and not round, it is decorated with various martial symbols and an inscription invokes the name of Badr El Gamali, its Armenian builder. Also, like Bab El Fatuh, its interior gives insight into military architecture of the times and features vaulting and apertures for firing arrows and pouring oil on invading forces.

Bab El Nasr to El Hussein & the Khan El Khalili

Assuming you made your way to the northern gates via Muizz li Din, consider returning to the Khan El Khalili by way of **El Nasr** and **El Gamalia Streets**. Though this route does not feature the grand religious monuments of Muizz li Din, it does offer a glimpse into El Qahira's medieval commercial districts. El Nasr Street, which becomes El Gamalia Street as it approaches the Khan El Khalili was major a node in the spice and textile trades of the 17th and 18th centuries. Goods loaded in Bulaq were brought here where wholesalers sold them to retailers. Among the historic buildings are several wikalas (caravanserais), sabils, and mosques. Most are now ruined and neglected, a testament to both Egypt's oversupply of historic buildings and the dearth of resources to keep them up. Egypt's best known novelist, **Naguib Mahfouz**, was born and raised in this neighborhood.

South of Bab El Nasr and beyond the large, but ruined Mamluke era wikalas of Sultan Qait Bey and Amir Qawsun is the **Khanqah of Sultan Beybars El Gashankir**, also known as Beybars II. After deposing Nasir Mohammed in 1306, and rebuilding the minarets of El Hakim's mosque, Beybars was overthrown himself by Nasir who grabbed back power after capturing and strangling him. In his brief three year stint as sultan, Beybars built this khanqah, a house for Sufi mystics. It is entered through a doorway featuring pharaonic blocks as a floor. It is no coincidence that those who enter are meant to step on the images of pagan deities. The interior is one of the most richly decorated of all khanqahs in Cairo and features a cruciform design. It also contains a mosque and tomb, a first for khanqahs in Cairo.

After several hundred meters of ruined Mamluki sabils, wikalas, and mausoleums, take a left at the Mosque of Marzuq El Ahmadi on Darb El Tablawi to reach the **Musarfikhana Palace**; if you need directions, ask any local. Not as famous as the Bayt El Suhaymi, this may be a more impressive example of medieval domestic architecture. Built primarily in the 18th and 19th centuries, it is nonetheless Mamluki in form and spirit. Extensive mashrabia, inlaid marble, open courts, and magnificent inlaid fountains and ceilings are just some of the beautiful artistic work featured in this mansion. Originally owned by a wealthy merchant, it was bought by the Egyptian royal family in the 19th century. Khedive Ismail, who ruled Egypt from 1863-79, was born here in the small room above the dining chamber. Currently undergoing renovation, the Musarfikhana is being converted into an artistic cooperative like that at the Wikala of El Ghuri.

The Cities of the Dead

Covering a vast area stretching from Abbassia to beyond the Citadel nearly all the way to Maadi, and the Moqattam Hills to Salah, the **Cities**

of the Dead consists of two medieval Islamic cemeteries that are now home to some two million Cairenes. Though orthodox Islam does not sanction a culture of the dead, Egyptians and their rulers inherited one from their pharaonic forefathers and the practice of monumental tomb building has been pursued since the earliest centuries of Islamic rule in Egypt. The greatest monuments in these cemeteries were built during Mamluke times and are among the finest in all of Cairo. The Mausoleum of Qait Bey is considered an especially example of Mamluki architecture. Those of you with more time, should take the opportunity to wander about these cemeteries which contain hundreds of architectural gems in addition to the few masterpieces mentioned here.

The Southern Cemetery

Also known as the **Qarafrah El Kubra**, "the Great Cemetery," and as "**El Khalifa**," for the Abbassid Caliphs buried in these cemeteries, the Southern Cemetery covers a vast area from Ibn Tulun to the west and the Citadel to the north almost as far south as Maadi.

Beginning just east of Ibn Tulun's mosque and moving south, **El Khalifa Street** is lined with a series of important monuments including the **Mausoleum of Shagar El Durr**. Shagar El Durr was not only the only woman sovereign in Egyptian Islamic history, having ruled in name or by proxy from 1249-1257; she was also the bridge between the Ayyubid Dynasty founded by Salah El Din Ibn El Ayyub and the rule of the Bahri Mamlukes. After her first husband, Sultan Salah El Ayyub passed away in 1249, she briefly assumed the throne for herself before marrying the Bahri Mamluke, El Muizz Aybak, and governing from behind his throne. After Shagar El Durr bungled an assassination attempt against Aybak, his other wife had her beaten to death. Her tomb is 200 meters from the beginning of El Khalifa Street which features several other important mausoleums, also dedicated to women, including the **Mausoleum of Sayeda Ruqaya**, a stepsister of Sayeda Zeinab, and the **Mosque of Sayeda Nafisa**, the third holiest shrine in Egypt which is closed to non-believers.

Just east of Sayeda Nafisa's Mosque are the **Tombs of the Abbassid Caliphs**. The name confuses some who are led to believe these are the tombs of the famous Abbassid Caliphs of Baghad, like Haroun El Rashid of *Arabian Nights* fame. But these are in fact the tombs of their successors who were expelled from Baghdad and accepted into exile in Egypt by the Mamluke Sultan, Beybars who later appropriated the domed mausoleum for his own sons. The tombs are modest, and usually closed. The last Abbassid Caliph was put to death in 1517 after the Ottoman conquest of Egypt.

The most important tomb in the Southern Cemetery is the **Mausoleum of Imam El Shafi'i**, a founder of one of Sunni Islam's four major

Islamic schools. It is located off El Shafi'i Street directly south of Sayeda Aisha Square and then off Salah Salem after it breaks west, recognizable by its elegant dome, topped with a weather vane. Originally constructed in 1211 by a nephew of Salah El Din, El Kamel, it has been constantly expanded and restored, and reflects numerous styles including Mamluki, Ayyubid, and Ottoman.

The high point of the building is the dome's interior with its elaborate stalactite muqarnas and the elaborately decorated cenotaph in which believers slip prayers written on paper with the hope that the venerated Sheikh may help them to be realized. Annually, tens of thousands converge on the tomb to commemorate Shafi'i's Moulid during the eighth month of the Islamic year, Sha'aban (August-September in '98 and '99). The exact starting date is not set. *Admission: free (baksheesh expected). Hours: 7am-sunset.*

The Northern Cemetery

Not nearly as expansive as the Southern Cemetery, the **Northern Cemetery** extends from the Citadel to Abbassi. It is easily accessible from the Khan El Khalili by walking up the hill on El Azhar Street and then cross Salah Salem.

The **Mausoleum of Sultan Qait Bey** (check the LE note for a preview) *can be reached from the intersection of Salah Salem and El Azhar Street by following the narrow alleys. It is recognizable by the intricately carved dome which with the minaret resembles a helmeted sentry holding a lance. Admission: LE6 general, LE3 students. Hours: 8am-5pm.*

Sultan Qait Bey ruled Egypt for 28 years beginning in 1468 and presided over the most stable and prosperous period of Burghi Mamluke rule. A prolific builder who constructed monuments in Alexandria, Mecca, and Palestine, Qait Bey is remembered, unlike most Mamlukes, as a fair and righteous leader. His mosque, considered amongst the finest in Cairo, features the cruciform-four liwans (vaulted arches) style typical of Mamluki mosques and madrasahs. The mosque's interior is characterized by finely carved wooden ceilings and walls, an ornate inlaid marble mihrab, and a mashrabia style wooden minbar. The mausoleum, which is next door, is a bit more plain, but the stone-carved qibla wall and mihrab is exquisite. But Qait Bey's *piece de resistance* is undoubtedly the dome. Immaculately carved with interlocking geometric and floral patterns, it represents the highwater mark in Mamluki stone work. To view it, you must ascend to the roof where you can also climb the minaret. You'll need to ask the doorman to open the passage for you, but he'll willingly oblige in return for a bit of baksheesh (LE5 is appropriate). At dusk, the minaret affords superb views of the sun setting over the Northern Cemetery with the Citadel in the background.

Misr El Qadima: Coptic Cairo

Though it's referred to as "Misr El Qadima," meaning "old Cairo," these quarters, boasting some of the world's oldest Christian monuments, predates the Fatimid city of El Qahira (Cairo) by at least 1,000 years. Located just off of the **Mar Girgis** (Saint George) Metro stop 15 minutes from Tahrir Square, this ancient Coptic community was contained inside the walled Roman fortress of **Babylon**. Exactly when Babylon was founded, or how it became known as Babylon, nobody is sure. Some believe it was constructed during Egypt's occupation by the Persians (525-330 BC) who may have imported the "Babylon" concept. The classical Greek scholar, Diodoros Siculus claimed that during the pharaonic Middle Kingdom around 2,000 BC, slaves and prisoners of war were captured from Mesopotamia and brought to Egypt where they built Babylon to protect themselves during a revolt against the pharaonic authorities. Whatever the case, the **Romans**, who occupied Egypt in 30 BC, made Babylon the primary military garrison from which they administered their tax collection in the Nile Valley until the Arab conquest of Egypt in 642.

Christianity arrived in Egypt during the 1st century and by the end of the 2nd century, a majority of native Egyptians had converted, despite – some even claim because of – Roman persecution. As the Egyptian Christian community flourished, churches, monasteries, and convents were established throughout Egypt. Some of the most oldest, and most important of these institutions were built here in Old Cairo. When the Arab Muslims successfully invaded in 641, Babylon was laid to siege, but not destroyed.

The Coptic Christians, weary of overtaxation and religious persecution at the hands of the Romans, willingly accepted their new Islamic masters who for their part were content to let the Coptic Church function in peace as long as it did not resist. Muslims considered Christians to be **Ahl El Kitab**, "people of the Book," and hence allowed them autonomy within their own community and made them immune from persecution. As a result of this protection, the churches and monuments of Old Cairo and Babylon were left intact and have been restored countless times since their original construction.

Upon getting off the Metro or bus, one immediately notices the round **Roman Tower** built during the reign of the Emperor Trajan around 100 AD. It offers little to see, but the adjoining Coptic Museum features a brilliant collection of Coptic artifacts from ancient manuscripts to medieval icons, and several churches, some of which date to the 5th century, are also open to the public. Also located in these quarters is the Ben Ezra Synagogue, a lonely testament to Cairo's once flourishing Jewish community.

Coptic Museum, *Mar Girgis. Tel 02/841-766. Hours:Sunday-Thursday 9am-noon & 1pm-4pm. Admission: LE8 general, LE4 students.*

This excellent museum contains the world's largest collection of Coptic art and artifacts with most of its displays dating to the development of the Coptic religion in its formative period during the Roman occupation. Its collection of icons (on the first floor), ancient manuscripts, and textiles is truly amazing and insightful, particularly into the transition from the traditional pharaonic religions to Christianity. In some early woodwork and icons, you can even find the Christian cross in the shape of an ankh (key of life).

El Kineesa El Moallaka: The Hanging Church

Located off the southwestern corner of the Coptic Museum. Entrance is free and Coptic Services are held (in Coptic) from 8-11am on Friday, and 7-10am on Sundays.

This, the most famous church in Old Cairo, derives its name from the fact that it is suspended over the old watergate to the fortress of Babylon. Though nobody knows for sure when this church was founded, it served as seat of the Bishop of Babylon beginning in the 7th century and in the 11th century was named seat of the Coptic Patriarchate; many believe the site housed a church going as far back as the 4th century.

Having been rebuilt in the 9th century and restored countless times before and since, the church retains something of a patchwork quality, containing relics and structures from various epochs, some of which predate the church itself. With its finely carved lattice screens, colorful 10th century icons, and symbolic pillars, it is in many ways a prototypical Coptic church.

The Monastery & Church of Saint George

Located through the first gateway beyond the Coptic Museum coming from the Hanging Church. The monastery is usually closed and the church opens roughly from 8am-1pm and from 2-3:30 pm daily.

One of Egypt's few round churches, Saint George's was reconstructed in 1904 after the original church fell victim to fire. There is not much to see except for the original stain glass windows which are quite vivid. Unlike its neighbors, Saint George's is an Orthodox, not Coptic, church. On April 23 it is the site of a great festival as Copts and Greeks gather together to celebrate the **Feast of Saint George**.

From the Monastery and Church of Saint George, make your way north up the main road and through the underpass into Babylon proper. Here the narrow winding cobblestone alleys would seem to take you back 1,000 years if it wasn't so sparse and sanitized. It is still a fascinating place to wander and imagine how cozy it must have been when hawkers, livestock, and Byzantine soldiers rubbed shoulders on these intimate streets.

The Convent of Saint George

Shortly after entering the old city, the Convent of Saint George will be past the first gate to your left. Technically it's off limits, but you can still enter the chapel through the hall of a Fatimid mansion.

Though the nunnery is officially closed to visitors, you can still make your way through a hall of what was once a Fatimid residence to a chapel featuring lofty 30 foot high cedar doors. The chapel contains a casket with relics of Saint George and here the nuns perform a fascinating ritual of wrapping chains around themselves to commemorate the persecution of Saint George.

From the Convent, make your way deeper into the old city. When you hit the 'T' you have two choices. To the left (north), but if you have time, the path leads to a cemetery, which makes for an interesting stroll, the Church of the Virgin, and a second Church of Saint George. Known as the **Kasriyyat El Rihan** (Pot of Basil) because of the Greek Church's association with the herb, the Church of the Virgin was granted to the Greek community in the 10th century by the mother of the Sultan El Hakim (a terrible man himself). It is of little significance except that it contains a small collection of icons painted by John the Armenian in the late 18th century. West of the Church of the Virgin is a second **Church of Saint George**-this one Coptic-that originally dates to the 7th century, but was reconstructed in the 19th.

South of the 'T' (right), the alley will lead you to the more impressive and historically significant **Church of Saint Sergius**.

Kineesa Abu Sarga: The Church of Saint Sergius

Dedicated to Roman soldiers who were martyred in Syria and allegedly a site visited by the Holy Family during their flight to Egypt, Abu Sarga is one of the holiest sites in Coptic Egypt. Thought to be founded in the 5th century, it is one of the oldest churches in Egypt. Its main features are a series of Corinthian marble capitals lining the narthex and an impressive collection of 12th century icons. The Holy Family was to have stayed in the now flooded crypt beneath the alter. Their sojourn to Egypt is celebrated annually with special services on June 1.

The Church of Saint Barbara

From the Church of Saint Sergius, the Church of Saint Barbara is east-take the alley to the left when facing Saint Sergius.

Relatively new by Coptic Cairo standards, the Church of Saint Barbara dates to the 11th century and was built on the site of a previous church that was burnt down during the reign of the Fatimid Caliph El Hakim. It is named for a 3rd century martyr who died at the hands of her father whom she tried to convert. Her remains are allegedly buried here as are those of Saint Katherine, the martyr for whom the monastery at Mount Sinai is named. This is problematic since the Greek monks in Sinai maintain that Katherine's remains were found in Sinai on Gebel Katherina, having been transported there by angels. Saint Barbara's is a Coptic church.

The Ben Ezra Synagogue

Located south of Saint Barbara's (left when exiting).

Restored after suffering severe vandalism after the Six Day War in 1967, this lonely reminder of Cairo's once thriving Jewish population boasts a fascinating history. Converted from a church that Copts sold in the 9th century so that they could pay taxes to the then governor of Cairo, Ibn Tulun, it was allegedly the site of an ancient temple of Jeremiah and some even believe that it was here that the pharaoh's daughter (the pharaoh would have been Ramses II) found baby Moses. If it seems unrealistic because there are no reeds, keep in mind that the Nile used to flow further to the east than it does today. The Holy Family is also thought to have sought refuge here.

The Synagogue was restored in partnership between the American Jewish Congress and the Egyptian government with financial support from private donors. Upon entrance you will be meeted by a cheerful old gent who will be more than happy to give you a tour. In many ways, with its mashrabia, inlaid marble and church-like form, it is a hybrid of medieval Christian, Muslim, and Jewish architectural traditions.

Rhoda Island

Though it ranks a notch or two below its northern neighbor, Zamalek, on the pecking order of Cairo's chic neighborhoods, **Rhoda** offers more in the way of historical sights and interesting places to visit. Its major landmark, the **Manial Palace** on the island's north eastern banks, was but the last of numerous palaces and estates built by sultans, caliphs and pashas since the Arab invasion in 642. In the 13th century, Rhoda emerged a political center as the chief barracks for the **Bahri Mamlukes** (who ruled Egypt from 1250-1392) though nothing of their massive fortress remains.

Rhoda's character has been dramatically altered in recent decades as it burgeoned into a high density residential area. In stark contrast to the historic monuments on the southern tip, the northern tip of Rhoda is dominated by the ultra-modern **Meridien Hotel** commanding splendid views of the Nile and downtown Cairo. Rhoda is connected to Cairo's east banks by the Malek El Salah bridge and to Giza by the Kubri El Gama'a, (University Bridge).

The Nilometer and Manastirli Palace, *on the southern tip of Rhoda Island. Hours: 9am-5pm. Admission: LE6 general, LE3 students.*

Built in 861 under orders of the Abbassid Caliph El Mutawakkil and used to measure the river's levels, the Nilometer is the oldest Islamic building in Cairo in that it is the oldest one that retains its original form. Reading the river's levels was a critical function during the flooding season when Cairo's administration used it to determine to what extent the canal from the Red Sea to Cairo (now Port Said Street) was to be dammed. Also an important economic indicator, water levels were used by government officials to predict agricultural production and to set tax rates. It no longer serves as a measuring stick for the Nile's levels and the tunnels and well have been blocked. The conical top was added in the 19th century.

In 1830 Hassan Pasha El Manastirli, built a palace adjoining the Nilometer, but little more than a wall remains. It once contained a great marble fountain that is now in the gardens of the Museum of Islamic Art on Port Said Street. The Palace is slated for major renovations in 1998-99.

Manial Palace Museum, *Rhoda Island. Tel. 02/936-124. Hours: 9pm-5pm. Admission: LE12 general, LE6 students,*

Constructed from 1901-1929, the Manial Palace was the residence for Prince Mohammed Ali (not to be mistaken for **Mohammed Ali Pasha** who ruled Egypt from 1805-1848), a son of Khedive Tawfik and one time heir to Farouk's throne. Upon his death in 1955, he left the estate to the nation to be used as a museum, though a portion of the complex was converted into a hotel. Unfortunately, the one time Club Med committed the criminal act of violating the botanical gardens with modern bungalows.

An excellent example of the lavish living standards enjoyed by Egypt's elite prior to the 1952 Revolution, the palace is entered through lush gardens and a richly decorated arabesque reception. Its prime attraction, the residence, will probably knock your socks off with its overwhelming ornamentation. From the marble floors and rich carpets to the furniture inlaid with mother of pearl and the finely carved arabesque ceilings it bespeaks of the "let them eat cake" approach Egypt's royals took in governing their country. The museum itself contains Mohammed Ali's personal art collection including fine woven textiles, porcelain china, jewelry, photographs, clothing and other personal effects. Finally, the nearby Hunting Museum, features King Farouk's token self-indulgent contribution – an obscene collection of stuffed and mounted game shot by the King.

Zamalek

The northernmost of Cairo's two major islands, **Zamalek**, like much of Cairo east of Ezbekiya was undeveloped until the 1860's when Khedive Ismail covered it with botanical gardens and constructed an ostentatiously luxurious palace on its eastern banks. Built to accommodate foreign dignitaries like Empress Eugenie attending inauguration celebrations for the Suez Canal in 1869, it was converted by the end of the century into a hotel. The current version, the **Cairo Marriott** is one Cairo's most famous landmarks and one of the most splendid hotels in Egypt. The construction of the "Kasr El Nil Bridge" (distinguished by the lions at either end) in 1872, also by Khedive Ismail, established the first permanent link between Cairo and Zamalek and paved the way for the island's development. Around the turn of the century, it became a posh address favored by expatriates, especially the British, and most of the old botanical gardens were converted into the Gezirah Sporting Club, an exclusive country club whose polo grounds and golf club were off limits to Egyptians.

After the 1952 Revolution, the "Club" was nationalized and today its 100,000 strong membership is almost entirely Egyptian, while the grounds still dominate the island's southern half. The northern half is an upscale residential neighborhood favored by Egyptian professionals and expatriates. In 1989, the spanking Cairo Opera House at the end of the Kasr El Nil Bridge was opened. A striking modernist complex with a twist of arabesque, the Opera's construction was largely funded by the Japanese.

Museum of Modern Art, *Cairo Opera House complex at the end of the Tahrir Bridge. Hours: 10am-1pm & 5pm-9pm daily except Mondays. Admission: LE10.*

The Museum has a collection of Egyptian art from before 1908 and regularly features rotating exhibits of contemporary artists.

Mukhtar Museum, *by Gala'a Bridge, Zamalek. Tel. 02/805-198.*

Designed by Ramses Wissa Wassef (founder of the Wissa Wassef Weaving School in Harraniyah), this modest museum is dedicated to the life and works of sculptor **Mahmoud Mukhtar**. Few modern Egyptian artists have better articulated the aspirations of modern Egypt. His most famous work is the **Awakening Egypt** sculpture in Giza in front of Cairo University. This sculpture, portraying a woman taking off a veil flanked by a sphinx, represents a Egyption shaking off centuries of backwardness to meet the challenges of independence in the 20th century. The sphinx represents Egypt glorious past to which she aspires to recreate. His other most prominent works are two statues of the early 20th century Egyptian Nationalist **Saad Zaghloul**; one is down the street in front of the new Cairo Opera in Zamalek, the other stands in Saad Zaghloul Square in Alexandria. Mukhtar's tomb is in the basement of this museum.

Burg El Qahira–The Cairo Tower, *the middle of Zamalek between the Tahrir and October Bridges. Hours: 8am-midnight. Admission: LE10.*

Built in 1967 with money given to Nasser by the CIA in an effort to buy him off in exchange for turning on the Soviets – hence the nickname "Dulles" erection – the odd looking 590 foot tower is something of a commemoration of Nasser's independence from the west. A hollow cylinder enclosed with concrete lattice, it is modeled, though not successfully, on the lotus motif commonly found in ancient Egyptian art. The idea is that the upper section revolves giving viewers a rotating view of the city. More often than not, it does not work, but the view is nonetheless unsurpassable. On a clear day in particular, the views of the Nile, the Pyramids, and even Saqqara in the distance are truly spectacular.

Hadeeqa El Asmak, *Zamalek between Om Kalthum Street and Hassan Sabri, south of 26th of July Street. Hours: 9am-4pm. Entrance fee: 50pt.*

These quirky gardens with outdoor aquariums is a pleasant spot to relax, except on Fridays when the locals really pack it up.

Giza

Barely a hundred years ago the western banks of the Nile opposite Cairo contained but a few rural villages and the mighty Pyramids, built by those villagers' ancestors more than 4,000 years ago. In ancient times, prior even to the building of the Pyramids, the Old Kingdom capital of **Memphis** stood on the west banks, but withered away 1,500 years ago. In 642, Amr Ibn El As established the town of **Giza**, but it remained nothing more than a minor village until the 20th century. While sultans, amirs, and pashas built Cairo into the largest and richest city in the Middle East, the banks across the Nile remained simple farmland similar to that found along the river's banks from the Delta to Nubia. The first full length bridge across the Nile was not completed until 1872 and only when the **Zoological Gardens**, opened to the public in 1891 was any major public institution established here.

The population explosion of the 20th century led to massive development and today more than five million live and work in the fast growing **Governorate of Giza** – a separate municipality from Cairo. Giza's major districts such as **Mohandiseen** and **Dokki** have emerged as major residential and commercial centers, especially for Cairo's professional and upper middle classes while other neighborhoods like Imbaba have become magnets for poor rural migrants. These newer modern urban centers lack the old world charm and quirkiness found in the old quarter on the east bank and there but a few major attractions apart from the Pyramids and the necropolis at Saqqara.

Pyramids Road

The great monuments are located 13 kilometers from the Nile at the end of **Pyramids Road** (*Sharia El Haram*), one of Giza's main thoroughfares. Constructed by Khedive Ismail in 1868 to accommodate VIPs like Empress Eugenie attending the inauguration of the Suez Canal , the road remained unpaved until the 1950s and apart from thegarish nightclubs where many of Egypt's most famous belly dancers and musicians performed in extravagant venues only 25 years ago most of this region was still verdant farmland. Some of the clubs remain, but neglect, Nasser, and the rise of five star hotels mean that only overpriced, seedy second rate entertainment plays today.

Today Pyramids Road is one of the most congested thoroughfares in Cairo and the surrounding areas, known as **El Haram** are piled high with concrete apartment complexes. At the end of Pyramids Road at the base of the Pyramids in the former hunting palaces of the Mohammed Ali Dynasty is the **Mena House**, one of Cairo's premier hotels.

The Pyramids at Giza

The Pyramids are 15 kilometers west of the Nile in Giza at the end of Pyramids Road. They are open from 6am until 6pm and tickets cost LE20, LE10 for students. To enter either of the two larger Pyrmids, it is an additional LE20.

Throughout history, visitors have marveled at these leviathan testaments to power, mass, and man's quest to live forever. Indeed they are so ancient that they were already 2,000 years old by the time Alexander the Great swept into Egypt in 332 BC and had witnessed more than 30 centuries before the Fatimids founded El Qahira. They inevitably evoke a reaction of awe, though some find their self-indulgence repulsive. In 50 AD, Pliny the Elder remarked that they were, "an idle and foolish exhibition of royal wealth," and many historians speculate that the pyramid builders spent the Old Kingdom into decline. This may have been true, but that does not make their having been built at all any less formidable or impressive, for they remain the largest stone buildings in the world and until the 19th century, they were also the world's tallest.

The largest and oldest of the Giza Pyramids is that of the Pharaoh **Khufu** to the north. Also known by his Greek name, "Cheops," Khufu ruled Egypt from 2551-2528 BC and was son of the Pharaoh Sneferu and Queen Hetpeheres. Though previous pharaohs built their pyramids south at Saqqara near Memphis, and at Dahshur (his father is believed to have been buried there), Khufu broke with tradition by establishing his funerary complex north on the Giza Plateau. His father was known as a kind and beneficent ruler, but Khufu is thought to have been militaristic and even cruel. Ironically his pyramid stands as arguably the greatest monument of antiquity, but the only known depiction or representation

THE SOLAR BOAT

*On the southern side of Khufu's pyramid is a small modernist structure, the **Solar Boat Museum**. It holds a 43 meter long wooden boat discovered in one of the long pits near the pyramid's southeastern corner. The boat may or may not have been used to ferry the Khufu's mummy to the pyramid, but its main purpose was to transport the pharaoh's ba (posthumous soul) in the afterlife. After its discovery in 1954, the boat was reconstructed, with the exception of the rope bindings, entirely with original materials and it is indeed an impressive sight. The museum is open from 9am-4pm. Admission: LE10 general, LE5 students. Cameras: LE10 (with no flash), LE100 videos.*

of his is a small statue of about four inches that was discovered hundreds of miles south at the Temple of Osiris at Abydos.

The measurements of Khufu's pyramid tell an unmatched tale of engineering ingenuity, master craftsmanship, and what must have been a mindboggling coordination of labor and raw material. Consisting of over 2,300,000 blocks of granite and limestone averaging 2.5 tons each (some weighed more than nine tons), the Great Pyramid stands 449 feet (137 meters) tall. Today it is 32 feet shorter than its original height of 481 feet (146.5 meters) because of the loss of the outer casing. The original length of each side of the base was 754 feet (230 meters) and is now 745 feet (227 meters). The area of the base covers more than 13 acres (568,500 square feet) or the equivalent of 7 city blocks – an area sufficient to accommodate the cathedrals of Florence, Milan, Saint Peter's in Rome, Saint Paul's in London, and Westminster Abbey put together. The maximum difference in error between any two sides is less than 0.1% – an engineering feat that would make any 20th century contractor proud and is even more impressive considering it was achieved in an age ignorant of the wheel and pulley, not to mention computers.

The second pyramid at Giza belongs to **Khafre**, son of Khufu, also known as Chefren, who was Pharaoh of Egypt from 2520-2494BC. Besides the second largest pyramid at Giza and in Egypt, he built the mighty and mysterious Sphinx and the beautiful granite Valley Temple which flanks it. He also built a mortuary temple and a causeway linking it to the Valley Temple and the Pyramid itself. While his father Khufu has only been found depicted in a four inch statue, several beautifully crafted life-size representations of Khafre have been found and according to archaeologist Mark Lehner, there were emplacements at the Valley Temple for 58 statues, including two 26 foot long sphinxes.

Khafre's pyramid appears to be the biggest of the lot, but actually he built it higher ground than Khufu's and it is in fact smaller. Nonetheless, the measurements are still staggering. Using similar blocks to those used by Khufu, it was originally 471 feet (143.5 meters) tall, and the side of each base is 704 feet long. Because the loss of the outer granite casing, it now stands at 446 feet (136 meters), but its area still covers more than eleven acres. With an incline of slightly more than 53 degrees, its sides are steeper than those on Khufu's pyramid (inclining 51 degrees). Perhaps its most distinguishing characteristic is the remaining layer of casing stone on its upper portion, the only remaining outer layer on any of the Giza Pyramids. The rest was confiscated primarily during the Middle Ages by mamlukes and Ottomans for use in the construciton of their own monuments.

The third and smallest of the Great Pyramids, that of **Menkaure**, seems almost modest compared to those of his forefathers. Also known by his Greek name, Mycerinus, Menkaurae ruled Egypt from 2490-2472 BC. Though dwarfed by the leviathan creations of his immediate predecessors, this third pyramid still stands a more than respectable 203 feet (62 meters), and the length of each base is 344 feet.

The Sphinx

The mysterious colossus with a man's head and lion's body is thought to be a representation of the Pharaoh Khafre, builder of the second Pyramid, but nothing about its identity or its purpose is known for sure. Some speculate that it is a guardian figure rather than the pharaoh

CLIMBING IN & ON THE PYRAMIDS

From Herodotus to Mark Twain, it was practically a rite of passage for visiting tourists to climb the Great Pyramids, usually with several dozen baksheesh craving locals entow. However, in the mid 1980s after several deaths and coming to the conclusion that it probably was not so great for the monuments themselves, authorities forbid climbing on the Pyramids. The lone exception is for those going inside the Pyramids. To be sure, crawling about inside does not offer the views that a trip to the peak does-and it certainly is not comfortable for anybody remotely claustrophobic- but it does afford some perspective (as if you needed more) as to the size and scale of these impressive constructions. To protect them, the authorities close one of the three each year (Khufu in '98) for renovations. Also, for the first time, they have opened one belonging to a queen, Metpheres, which stands next to Khufu's. Like the bigger pharaohs' pyramids its interior does not feature inscriptions. Entering any pyramid costs LE10 (LE5 students).

himself, and others claim that it's not related to Khafre at all, but in fact predates the Pyramids by 2,000 years. The Greeks believed it to be an incarnation of one of their own mythic creatures-called '**Spinx**' – who would ask passers-by certain questions and if they answered falsely, proceeded to slay them. The name stuck with this character even though this structure most surely did not have anything to do with the Greek myth. Perhaps the Arabic name, *Abu Hol* – 'father of terror' or the 'awesome one' – is more appropriate.

Debated with nearly equal vigor is the question of what happened to its beard. This is not entirely clear, but it is believed to have been knocked off sometime in the early 19th century by Napoleonic soldiers taking target practice. A meter long piece is now in the British Museum in London, and the other bit can be seen in the Egyptian Antiquities Museum in Tahrir Square

The Sphinx was largely neglected during later pharaonic times except when Thutmosis IV built a stele there to commemorate a vision he had in which he was told that if he uncovered the Sphinx from the sand which buried it, he would come to power. He did so and unexpectedly assumed the throne. The Ptolemies largely ignored it, but the Romans touched it up for a visit by the emperor Nero. It was again neglected by the Christian and Islamic Egyptians and their rulers who could not be bothered by a relic of the pagan past.

By the time Napoleon arrived in 1798, the Sphinx was covered to its neck in sand and only in the 1840's when French archaeologists excavated the Sphinx was the most famous sculpture in world history fully uncovered for the first time since the 3rd century. Not only was it was unveiled for all to view, but for the first time since antiquity the Sphinx was exposed to the elements, and more recently, to the horrendous pollution and humidity of modern Cairo. Like other monuments in Egypt, most notably the Luxor Temple, the Sphinx suffers from flaking caused when salt crystals form after humidity dries. The crystals then flake off taking with them pieces of the soft limestone. This phenomenon is attributed to climate and water table changes resulting from the creation of Lake Nasser and the increase in pollution.

Kerdessa, Harraniya, and the Road to Saqqara

Kerdessa is a mass textile market located on the Maryotia Canal, and is easily combined with a visit to the Pyramids. Harraniya and the Wissa Wassef Art Center are on the road to Saqqara which begins a kilometer before the Pyramids on Pyramids Road. It is easily to tack onto a tour of Saqqara and Memphis. Both roads feature restaurants serving Egyptian cuisine in picturesque agrarian settings.

HORSEBACK RIDING AT THE PYRAMIDS

One of the great ways to experience the Pyramids is from a distance on the back of a horse. When visiting the Pyramids, you will be accosted by horse touts and camel jockeys begging, practically forcing you to ride their animal, but don't waste your time with those jokers. It is far better to rent horses from the nearby stables off the Saqqara Road by the Sphinx. For twenty pounds per person per hour, you can ride a vintage Arabian steed through the dunes which surround the Pyramids-an exhilirating experience indeed. You can also make the 4 hour journey to Saqqara by horseback, stopping at the Pyramids of Abu Sir en route; and you can also rent camels, which makes a great photo op, but isn't quite as smooth a ride. Sunrise and sunset are the best times to go riding, and when the moon is full, night rides are also well worth while. Stables worth trying are MG, Tel. 02/385-3832, Eurostables, Tel. 02/385-5849, and AA, Tel. 02/385-0531.

Kerdessa, *5 km north of the Pyramids Road along Maryutiya Canal.*

Originally an end point for Western Desert caravans, this small weaving village mushroomed in the past three decades into one of Cairo's preeminent textile centers. Now a major market where wholesalers and retailers sell material and finished products ranging from Bedouin clothing and high quality carpets to galabiyas, head scarves, and other goods used by common Egyptians in everyday life. In the old days, Kerdessa was a great place for bargains. It still is, but it is more difficult now that package tour groups have made it a regular stop en route to the Pyramids. Many of the goods are cheap imitations of quality Bedouin textiles and Wissa Wassef tapestries so be careful of deals that seem too good to be true.

Harraniya & the Wissa Wassef Art School, *Harraniya Village on the Road to Saqqara 3 kilometers south of Pyramids Road. Hours: 9:30am-5pm. Entrance is free.*

Founded fifty years ago by renaissance man Ramses Wissa Wassef (he was primarily an architect), the Wissa Wassef Art School was originally just a weaving school and before the addition of a museum designed by Egypt's most famous architect, Hassan Fathi. In addition to its progressive roots and beautiful setting, the school is known for its high quality tapestries woven here-considered by many to be the finest in Egypt-depicting life in rural Egypt and wildlife. Tapestries vary in size, quality of workmanship, and price. A small wall hanging or hot pad with a simple bird or tree design cost LE10-20 while larger tapestries with complex designs requiring the skill of a master fetch thousands of dollars a piece.

Numerous imitators have sprung up on the same road, but none match the quality or tradition of Wissa Wassef.

Memphis

Located 4 kilometers north of Saqqara at the village of Mit Rahina. Museum hours: 9am-5pm. Admission: LE7 general, LE3.50 students. Cameras: LE10, LE30 video.

The world's first imperial city and first capital of a united Egypt, **Memphis** was among the world's richest and most important cities for the better part of 3,000 years. Situated where Upper and Lower Egypt converge 100 kilometers south of the Delta, Memphis was founded by the legendary first pharaoh, **Menes**, around 3100 BC and remained the nation's capital during the Old and Middle Kingdoms. Though Thebes superseded it in the New Kingdom, Memphis retained importance as the northern capital and an important economic center. For a period, Memphis reclaimed the title of national capital during the reign of Ramses II and again retained it during the Late Period until Alexander the Great's invasion of Egypt in 332 when Alexandria became the nation's capital. Many Ptolemeic statues have been found at Memphis indicating that it remained an important city until the Roman occupation when it went into a gradual decline that led to its final abandonment after the Arab invasion of 642 AD.

After centuries of neglect and flooding, little remains of Egypt's first and possibly greatest city, for unlike their temples and tombs, which they designed to last forever, the ancient Egyptians did not construct permanent buildings for everyday use. Tombs and temples were built of stone and consumed the bulk of expensive materiel and man power, but city buildings and houses, including royal palaces, were built of perishable mud brick. Temples incorporated into the city were built of stone, but

THE CULT OF PTAH

*God of craftsmanship and engineering, **Ptah** was the patron deity of Memphis. During the first four dynasties, his cult was the most powerful and important in Egypt. It controlled vast tracts of agricultural land and held great sway over the early pharaohs, setting a precedent for later cults like that of Amun at Thebes. During the 4th dynasty, the Cult of Ptah began to lose its prestige to that of Atum at Heliopolis. Though it never recovered its status as Egypt's most powerful cult, Ptah remained the patron deity of Memphis and later became a god of the dead under Osiris. Hence he was often depicted in tombs wearing the loin wrappings of a mummy.*

Romans and Arabs plundered the masonry for use in their monuments. In fact little was known about Memphis until the nearby ruins of Saqqara were discovered in the mid-nineteenth century by French archaeologist Auguste Mariette. The grandeur of that necropolis, the largest and most important in ancient Egypt, testifies to the status of the city to which it was attached. Today, there are but a few statues on display at an outdoor museum at Memphis. The main attraction is a colossus of Ramses II and a 90 ton alabaster sphinx.

Saqqara

Saqqara is 32 kilometers south of Cairo on the west bank of the Nile, opposite Helwan. Hours: 8am-5pm. Admission: LE20 general, LE10 for students.

To reach **Saqqara** using public transport there are several options, none of which are very efficient. The first is to catch a public bus to Midan Giza, then a minibus or service to El Badrasheen and then another minibus to Saqqara. Second, take a public bus to the Pyramids Road and get off at the turnoff to Saqqara a kilometer before the Pyramids themselves. Then catch a service for Saqqara. Third, take the metro, minibus, bus, or service to Helwan. From Helwan take a service to the river or Mazniq bridge; cross the bridge or take a ferry to El Badrasheen and then a service to Saqqara. All of these routes can take up to two hours.

Given the energy and time needed to explore Saqqara itself, we'd recommend hiring a private taxi for LE70 for the day from downtown Cairo. This makes it cheaper for a group than for an individual. You can also join tours organized by major tour companies such as Thomas Cook and American Express for about $30 per person. For those with a smaller budget, Salah Abdel Hafez *(Tel. 376-8537; contact him at a day or two before you want to go)* has become a Saqqara guide extraordinaire and organizes trips to Saqqara, Memphis, and the Wissa Wassef Art Center for about LE25 per person. Finally, check the Maadi Messenger or call organizations like the American Research Center and the Egypt Exploration Society which may be offering tours with top flight Egyptologists.

On a plateau at the edge of the Western Desert overlooking verdant palm orchards and alfalfa fields, lies Saqqara, the vast necropolis of Lower Egypt and one of the world's great historical and archaeological sites. Stretching eight kilometers in length and 1.5 kilometers in width, Saqqara was the heart of a much wider area used for burial that extended from the cliffs of Abu Roash north of the Pyramids at Giza to the vast pyramid complexes south of Saqqara itself. Like Thebes and other major archaeological sites in Egypt, Saqqara was almost entirely lost beneath of the sands of the Western Desert until European scholars "discovered" and excavated it in the mid-nineteenth century. Since Auguste Mariette's first discovery of the Serapeum in 1851, Saqqara has revealed itself to be a bottomless pit of historical treasures, where many more important finds undoubtedly lie waiting to be uncovered.

Named for a nearby village which derived its name from **Sokar**, the Memphis god of the dead, Saqqara contains relics from all periods of ancient Egyptian history, but is best known for monuments dating to the Old Kingdom (2686-2181 BC) that include **Zoser's Funerary Complex**. Dating to the 3rd Dynasty, it features the **Step Pyramid**, Egypt's first pyramid and the first building in the world constructed with dressed stone. Other attractions include a half dozen pyramids (mostly ruined) the most famous of which it that of Unas, adorned with the famous Pyramid Texts; dozens of noble and royal tombs called **mastabas**: and the **Serapeum**, a complex network of underground galleries where mummified animals were interred. The painted and carved reliefs in Saqqara's tombs are considered the finest in Egypt.

The monuments at Saqqara are too many and too spread out to cover in one day. If one is all you have, we'd recommend that you make the Funerary Complex of Zoser (including the Step Pyramid), the Mastaba of Ti, the Serapeum, and the Pyramid of Unas priorities.

The Step Pyramid & the Funerary Complex of Zoser

Built for the great 3rd Dynasty Pharaoh **Zoser** by his ingenious architect **Imhotep**, this funerary complex is the largest and most important in Saqqara. Besides the pyramid, it comprises a large open court, a mortuary temple, northern and southern buildings, and a Jubilee Court. Surrounded by a wall containing numerous false doors so that Zoser's *ba* (posthumous soul) could easily access it, and approached through an entrance colonnade, the Funerary Complex covers an area 500 meters by 250 meters. The pyramid itself originally stood more than 60 meters tall with a base 140 by 120 meters. Excavating the complex in 1925, French Egyptologists found graffiti written by pilgrims dating from the 28th Dynasty that described the Complex of Zoser "as though heaven were within it."

It is entered through a door in the southeastern corner into the **colonnaded hall**. Consisting of 40 restored pillars resembling bundles of papyrus and palms, this corridor ends in a wider hypostyle hall leading to the **Great Court**. Here you will be greeted to the right by a frieze of cobras. Egyptians identified the cobra with a fire breathing Delta goddess, **Wadjet**, and made it a symbol of royalty that was commonly featured on crowns. Near the frieze is a deep shaft dropping nearly 30 meters to **Zoser's Southern Tomb**. Believed to be identical to the actual tomb underneath the Step Pyramid it features a depiction of the Pharaoh running between two symbolic altars representing Upper and Lower Egypt. The pharaoh performed this feat to exhibit his strength and fitness to govern at royal celebrations like the **Heb Sed Jubilee** – a commemoration of 30 years of a pharaoh's reign over the "Two Lands."

The unification and duality of the "Two Lands" was of major importance during the Old Kingdom and pharaohs wore separate crowns, worshipped separate deities, and even maintained separate courts for Upper and Lower Egypt. This duality is manifested in the middle of the Great Court where the bases of two altars remain, each served as pedestals for thrones during the Heb Sed Jubilee when the pharaoh re-enacted his coronation, once on each throne to reassert his supremacy over both kingdoms. It is also believed that the second tomb down the shaft was built so that the pharaoh may have tombs representing both Upper and Lower Egypt.

The Step Pyramid itself was by far the largest structure in the world when it was constructed in the 27th century BC. Designed by Zoser's confidante, **Imhotep**, it was also the first structure built with dressed stone and is the world's oldest standing building, considered by many to represent the founding of architecture. It is a clear step in the evolution of royal tombs from the original mud brick mastabas used during the first two dynasties to the great pyramids of the Fourth and Fifth Dynasties. It appears that Imhotep upgraded Zoser's tomb by placing six mastabas on top of one another. Later pharaohs refined this design to produce the smooth sided, true pyramids at Giza.

East of the Step Pyramid stands a structure known as the **South Building** featuring columns modeled on the lotus plant, the symbol of Upper Egypt. To the north, the **Northern Building** contains papyrus columns, representing Lower Egypt. Both buildings contained funerary chapels.

In the northern portion of the Funerary Complex, a stone box known as the **Serdab** contains a replica of a statue of Zoser that represented his ka (spiritual double), since moved to the Egyptian Antiquities Museum in Cairo. Seated, the representation of the pharaoh peers north towards the heavens associated with eternal life. Just west of the Serdab lies the ruins of the mortuary temple. While the ka had a home in the Serdab, the mortuary temple was a special locale where the priests rose the ba (posthumous soul) out of the pharaoh's corpse so it could proceed to the afterworld. The ka remained with the body. If the body and the tomb were not properly intact, the ba could not survive in the next world.

The Pyramid & Causeway of Unas
The Pyramid of Unas is south of Zoser's Funerary Complex.

From the outside, this 5th dynasty pyramid appears to have fallen victim to the wrecking ball of time and is an indication of the decline in pyramid building that followed the construction of the 4th Dynasty pyramids at Giza. Excavated by the French archaeologist Gaston Maspero whose efforts were sponsored by Thomas Cook & Sons in the 1880's, the Pyramid of Unas revealed some of ancient Egypt's most important secrets in the form of the **Pyramid Texts** (see sidebar). It is possible to enter the pyramid and explore these texts.

The second feature of Una's complex worth noting is the kilometer long causeway that extended to the banks of the Nile in the east. The causeway featured a mortuary temple at the other end (near the ticket office) where priests prepared Una's body for burial, a process that entailed cleaning it, removing the vital organs and placing them in canopic jars, and finally embalming the corpse. These procedures were accompanied by the recitation of hymns, prayers, and spells to ensure that the pharaoh's ba would rise upon burial and proceed through the afterworld. A second temple was situated in the pyramid complex itself.

THE PYRAMID TEXTS

*The **Pyramid Texts** are the oldest known inscriptions inside a pyramid and the earliest, least corrupt, and most comprehensive collection of pharaonic funerary. Comprising hundreds of prayers, hymns, and spells, they are one of our most important sources in understanding pharaonic religion, funerary rites, and political ideology. In announcing the pharaoh to the heavens, the texts recount his life and genealogy, military exploits, and his status as a divine king. Hymns and spells also call on the pharaoh's ba to rise upon his death, and provide the ba with directions how to proceed through the afterlife. Others list aspects of his life on earth that he wishes to take with him to the afterlife. Finally, another text recounts the earliest known version of the Osiris Myth.*

Around the Pyramid of Unas

South of the Pyramid of Unas are tombs of **Persian Nobles** (6th century BC) buried deep into the ground. Built for a physician and an admiral, they contain some vivid funerary reliefs. A guard will let you in; this is the type of place where it's handy to have a flashlight, but if you don't he'll light it for you. Further up the hill from the Causeway of Unas is the ruined 5th century **Monastery of Saint Jeremiah**. It doesn't offer much now, having been destroyed in medieval times by fanatical Muslims (sound familiar?), but did yield some spectacular icons and wall paintings that are now in the Coptic Museum.

Also south of the Pyramid of Unas is the **Tomb of Haremheb**, successor to Tutankhamun. Not of royal blood Haremheb (1348-1320 BC) built this tomb while he was still a general, but upon assuming the throne, he built a royal tomb in the Valley of the Kings in Thebes where he was eventually interred. This one is closed, but if you can baksheesh your way in, it features superb carvings and animate reliefs depicting Haremheb smiting terrified prisoners.

If you have time, consider exploring the unfinished **Pyramid of Skhemket** west of the monastery, otherwise head to the **Tomb of Akhtihotep and Ptahhotep** *between the Step Pyramid and the rest house*. This father-son pair were both judges and auditors of the treasury and during the 5th Dynasty reign of Jedkare. They also managed the finances for government departments responsible for the building and maintaining of pyramids. The reliefs in this tomb are colorful and feature vivid scenes of the pair hunting, eating, and pursuing other aristocratic pleasures. The high quality of workmanship of the carvings and their animate qualities are typical of the Old Kingdom.

South Saqqara

Just as the 5th Dynasty pharaohs established their own necropolis at Abu Sir, so the 6th Dynasty established their own royal cemeteries south of the main necropolis and the Step Pyramid. The necropolis begins nearly a kilometer south of the Step Pyramid and covers more than 3 kilometers. Reaching the main pyramids requires extensive walking or hiring a donkey or camel.

The site itself features a series of ruined yramids, two of which are worth noting. That of **Jadkare-Isesi**, due west of Saqqara Village, stands 25 meters tall and when excavated in the 1940's was found to contain the pharaoh's very ruined mummy. The Pyramid can be entered through a passage from the north. The **Pyramid of Pepi II**, whose reign allegedly lasted an astounding 94 years, is to the northwest and is missing its casing stones but otherwise is in relatively good shape. The burial chamber, entered by a tunnel, features extensive texts and painted stars on the roof. The surrounding pyramids were built for his wives and the smaller tombs for various ministers and officials.

North of the Step Pyramid

Beyond the rest house for the judges' tomb is the **Philosophers' Circle**, a Ptolemeic set of statues portraying Plato, Thates, Homer, and other important Greek philosophers. It was once part of an avenue of sphinxes linked to the temple of the apis bulls at the Serapeum.

One of the most fascinating and bizarre monuments at Saqqara is the **Serapeum** *(by the rest house)*, a temple to the apis bulls that features a vast network of underground galleries where mummified bulls were intered. Originally constructed by Ramses II in the 13th century BC, the catacombs were extended by the Ptolemies to 200 meters in length and held

25 mummified bulls in sarcophagi weighing more than 65 tons each. Egyptians believed the bull to be an incarnation of **Ptah**, the patron deity of Memphis. These particular mummified bulls were believed to have been divinely conceived and were raised in the temple before being mummified at death. To experience the full power of the Serapeum's mystique, try to visit the catacombs alone, sans tour group.

Due west of the Serapeum is the **Mastaba of Ti**, an able Old Kingdom official who married into the royal family, and held a variety of important positions during the reigns of three Pharaohs, including that Vizier of the Pyramids, Vizier of Public Works, and Royal Hairdresser(?). His tomb is extremely well preserved and features brilliant scenes of everyday activities in the Old Kingdom including hunts, farming, and ship building. East of Ti's mastaba is a cluster of 3rd Dynasty tombs that scholars believe may contain the hitherto unfound tomb of Imhotep, architect of the Step Pyramid. Still farther to the northeast are the **Ibis and Baboon Galleries** where mummified baboons and ibises sacred to Thoth were interred in an underground series of catacombs similar to those at Tuna El Gebel in Middle Egypt.

The Pyramids of Abu Sir

Six kilometers north of Saqqara in the desert, the **5th Dynasty Pyramids of Abu Sir** must be visited by horse or camel hired from the Pyramids or Saqqara, or by foot. Reaching them by horse requires at least three hours in the saddle and by foot, the trip is even longer. Of the original 14 pyramids at Abu Sir, those built for Neferirkare, Nyuserre, and Sahu Ra are really the only ones worth visiting. They are in varying degrees of disrepair with the most intact being that of Neferirkare which stands nearly 50 meters. The only one open to the public, Sahu Ra, features a modest tomb. Though the pyramids themselves are not spectacular, they afford fantastic views of the desert with the Pyramids of Giza to the north and Saqqara to the south.

Downtown Giza & Dokki

Across the Nile from Rhoda Island is the heart of metropolitan Giza where large. apartments hover over wide, but ever clogged streets, overlooking the Nile to the east and the Giza Pyramids to the west. On Giza Street Khedive Ismail initiated the development of modern Giza by building a palace and **Zoological Gardens** that opened to the public in 1891. Once considered among the finest zoos in the World, the Cairo Zoo is now in sad shape, as neglect and underfunding ensure that animals and facilities are not properly maintained. It only gets sadder when you actually see the poor polar bear trying to weather five months of Cairo's summer. In the 1920's, the Egyptian University moved its major campus to Giza. Its most distinguished landmarks are the low arching dome and the **Mahmoud Mukhtar** sculpture, *Awakening Egypt*. Flanked by a sphinx representing the prosperity of pharaonic Egypt to which a free Egypt is committed to surpassing, the young woman in the sculpture is depicted removing her veil, a symbol of Egypt's past backwardness-ironically as the 21st century approaches more and more female students at the University are putting on, rather than taking off, the veil. Later named Fuad I University, the institution is now **Cairo University**, Egypt's largest western style institution of higher learning.

North of the University begins the district of Dokki, built on the site of an ancient farming village of the same name and now the home to many of Cairo's professional and upper classes. Its major, **Nadi El Seid** (The Shooting Club) is one of Cairo's most exclusive sporting clubs and a focal point for upper class socialites. To its west, the **Ministry of Agriculture**, an assortment of gray, drab Eastern European modernist buildings, is home to the surprisingly impressive Agricultural Museum.

Agricultural Museum, *Ministry of Agriculture, Dokki. Tel. 02/702-366, 702-933. Hours: 9am-2pm daily except Tuesday and Friday. Admission: 10 piasters.*

In 11 hectares of gardens, this historical institution founded in 1938 features half a dozen smaller museums including the **Cotton Museum**, the **Natural History Museum**, the **Museum of Ancient Egyptian Agriculture**, and the **Museum of the Social Life of the Arab nations**. Exhibits include models of Egyptian villages and farms throughout history, stuffed animal specimens, and a variety of agricultural tools. Particularly interesting is the Cotton Museum which tells the tale of modern Egypt's cash crop.

The Cairo Zoo & Hadeeqa El Orman (Orman Park), *Giza Street next to Cairo University, Giza. Zoo hours: 9:30am-6pm. Admission: 10 piasters.*

Built by Khedive Ismail in the 1870's and 80's, the Zoo and Orman Park were the first modern developments west of the Nile. For a period around the turn of the century, the Zoo was considered the finest in world as the British imported many animals that thrived in Egypt's moderate climate. Today the Zoo is usually packed with children, with their families on the weekends or on school field trips during the week. While the gardens make a peaceful refuge from the surrounding city, the zoo is in very sad shape. Neither the funding nor the expertise is sufficient to provide anything near suitable care for the animals.

NIGHTLIFE & ENTERTAINMENT

Though an Islamic capital, Cairo has been cosmopolitan since birth and the indulgences enjoyed after dark have always been a part of its texture. Before the Revolution of 1952, the Long Bar in the Shepheard's Hotel was among the most famous in the world and the neighborhoods of Alfi Bey and Pyramids Road were notorious for their garish and raffish nightclubs. Though some of the clubs on Pyramids Road remain, they are but a shadow of their former selves and the bordellos of Clot Bey and Alfi Bey are long gone as is the Shepheard's. But the 1990's has seen a revival of sorts in Cairo's nightclub and bar scenes, the belly dancing industry is in full swing, and those less interested in vice indulgence can join the majority of Cairenes who prefer to spend their evenings in cafes, restaurants, or even just on the bridges or promenades of the Nile.

Bars and western style nightclubs are concentrated in five star hotels-which have at least one of each-and upscale districts like Zamalek, Mohandiseen, and downtown. Big hotels also contain gambling casinos, and "oriental "nightclubs," upscale venues where big name dancers and pop stars perform. Many mid-scale hotels also feature bars, and throughout town there are also seedy and cheaper bars and nightclubs. *Egypt Today* and *NiteLife* magazines can give you the latest lowdown on what's going down as far as nightlife and entertainment in Cairo. *NiteLife's* "Nite Guide" employs more than 30 colorful symbols and decals to inform you about every aspect, facility, and service in each establishment from minimum charges and dress requirements to sheesha and parking availability.

Bars & Pubs – Downtown

WINDSOR HOTEL'S "BARREL BAR", *Windsor Hotel at 19 Alfi Bey Street, off of 26 July Street, near Opera Square, downtown. Minimum charge: LE7. Dress casual.*

With its wood paneling, mounted antelope antlers, and dim lighting the Barrel Bar is an unpretentious relic of pre-Revolution British *fin de siecle* Cairo. Friendly, casual and usually quiet, it's ideal for winding down after a day of sightseeing and is a perfect local writing a letter or reading a book. Local Stella is only LE7 and local spirits and wine are also available.

CAP D'OR, *Abdel Khaliq Sarwat Street, downtown off Opera Square.*

This classic downtown bar was recently overhauled, but the newly tiled floors and wood-paneled walls still do justice to its reputation as one of Cairo's great old watering holes. Wonderfully pretentious and downright seedy at the same time, it's a period piece whose vitality is maintained by the colorful cast of characters who make up the clientele: the hapless lute player who likes to lecture on the evils of Sadat; the hustlers and con men who seem to be able to charm the money right out of the wallets of unknowing tourists; and the jokers who fancy themselves to be political pundits and would have you believe that everything, right down to the change in the Stella lable is some sort of imperialist conspiracy. It's a wonderful neighborhood bar and Stella is only LE5.50.

HURRIYA BAR, *on Falaki Square east of Tahrir Street or El Bustan Street from Tahrir Square.*

With its tiled sawdust-strewn floors and high ceiling fans, this wonderful old bar which dates to the thirties, has all the shabby charm of a good ahwah. Furthermore, it serves fresh, cold Stella, which is more than you can say for a lot of upscale bars, and they're only LE4.75.

NAPOLEON BAR, *First floor in Shepheard's Hotel on El Corniche Street, off of Tahrir Square Dress: Casual. Minimum charge: LE 15. Credit cards: all major credit cards accepted.*

The Napoleon is a subdued bar characterized by classy wood paneling, brass tables, and plenty of pictures of its namesake. Not in with Cairo's cool crowd, it's generally pretty quiet, relaxing, and mercifully not swamped with testosterone. Billiards and pool in an adjoining room cost LE21 an hour and live casio style music begins at 9:30. Stella Export costs LE13 a pop and three star food is available at five star prices.

ODEON PALACE, *6 Abdel Hamid Said Street off Kasr El Nil between Tahrir Square and Talaat Harb Square. Tel. 02/776-637, 767-971. Hours: open 24 hours.*

On the roof of the hotel, this 24 hour bar and restaurant is popular with young western expatriates, Egyptian artsy types, middle class alcoholics, and a colorful assortment of other characters. Though it features cheap food and a menu a mile long, most folks come here simply to enjoy a few beers, some mezze, and possibly a sheesha. Decor is kind of kitsch and cheap, enhancing the dicey ambiance.

LOS AMIGOS, *InterContinental Hotel on the Corniche by Tahrir Square. No Minimum charge. Credit cards: all major credit cards accepted.*

One of the better and more upscale tex-mex (emphasize 'tex') joints in town. The service is excellent and the complimentary chips and salsa are the most authentic in Egypt. For drinking there is no minimum charge and local Stellas cost about LE10. Margaritas, (this is one of the only places in town that has them) are well done and cost about LE20. For a quiet dinner come at 7pm if not earlier; for a more swinging, drinking scene (especially on weekends) come after ten, when karaoke starts.

Zamalek

DEALS, *on Sayed El Bakry Street, Zamalek. Visa accepted.*

Popular with expats and a colorful assortment of upper class Egyptians, this cozy pub features good food, good music, and an old fashion smoky bar type atmosphere. Unfortunately the ventilation isn't is good as it should be and it also gets crowded – a testament to its popularity.

L'AUBERGINES, *on Sayed El Bakry Street just down the block from Deals.*

The bottom floor is a quaint Italian restaurant that often features "soft" live music (a violin and casio synthesizer). The menu changes daily and the food tends to be excellent and original. On the second floor is the closest thing to a jazz bar in Cairo. Dimly lit, it seems to be the only place in town featuring jazz-and by that I mean the real thing: the Duke, Miles Davis, Ella Fitzgerald et al. A darling with hipper bohemian types and expatriates.

HARRY'S PUB, *in the Cairo Marriott Hotel. Credit cards: all major credit cards accepted.*

The wooden bar, (fake) beer taps, and posters of Kitchener asking you to join the British army all bespeak an English pub, but no matter how much Harry's hams it up, can't seem escape its hotel bar identity. Yet it remains popular with a vast assortment of folks from tourists and upper class Egyptians to US marines and Filipino karaoke singers-Thursday is karaoke night. The menu features good pub food-Egyptian American, and British – but being the Marriott it's of course a bit pricey. Stella costs LE10.

THE CELLAR, *the Presidential Hotel on Taha Hussein Street, Zamalek. Minimum charge: LE25. Credit Cards: Visa, Mastercard, AMEX.*

Low ceilings, stucco, and lots of copper and brass give the Cellar a distinct Mediterranean feel. Popular with middle-age business types, it has happening potential if they were a bit less snobbish at the door and swung a more rocking style of music (or muzak as is now the case). No local Stella is available and the Export goes for LE10. Italian food and mezze is available for those with an appetite. The dim lighting and soft atmosphere give the Cellar date potential as well.

JOHNNY'S, LE PACHA 1901, *1901, El Gezira Street, Zamalek. Tel. 02/ 340-6730. Credit cards: all major credit cards accepted.*

Posh-nosh bar on a boat with great mezze, Johnny's is part of a larger complex that features several bars and restaurants including an excellent Lebanese. The Nile views are great but prices are high and there is LE20 minimum charge.

PUB 28, *28 Shagar El Durr Street, Zamalek. Tel. 02/340-9200.*

Pub 28 is a snug and comfy neighborhood lounge with bar and table seating. It doesn't usually get very rowdy but once and a while, a few of the neighborhood handbags liven things up. The menu features mezze and mediocre continental cuisine.

Mohandiseen & Dokki

LE TABASCO, *8 Amman Square (up the street from the Nadi Seid), Mohandiseen-Dokki. Tel. 02/336-5583. Hours: 7pm-2am. Credit cards: Visa.*

Though it's a viable dining option, this darling of Cairo's yuppies and foreign expats is primarily a drinking venue. The ambiance is definitely uppity but relaxed, and the rock'n'roll makes a nice change from the techno-disco and Egyptopop that seems to permeate the rest of the city.

TOP 5 SUNSETS IN CAIRO

With the Pyramids for a backdrop, Cairo's skyline with the Nile and "a thousand minarets" is a great setting to experience sunsets. Listed below are 5 ideas about where to watch the sun set, not necessarily in any order.

1. **The Pyramids** are an obvious choice, and you can experience views from one of the nearby hotels like the Mena House, or better yet from horseback in the surrounding deserts (see sidebar on page 207).

2. The rooftop piano lounge **Windows on the World**, at Cairo's tallest hotel, the Ramses Hilton, is cheesy as heck but the views of the Nile and the city with the Pyramids beyond is magical.

3. From the minaret of **Qait Bey Mausoleum** in the Northern Cemetery near the Khan El Khalili the dusk view features the sun setting behind domed Medieval cemeteries with Sultan Hassan, the Citadel, and the city in the background; if it's clear, the Pyramids may also be visible. Because the sun sets late in summer, Qait Bey is only a sunset option during winter. See the Northern Cemetery section in "Seeing the Sights" above.

4. The **Salah Salem** roadside just north of the Citadel, affords the classic view of the sun going down behind the domes and minarets of the Sultan Hassan and Rifa'i mosques with cemeteries in the foreground and modern Cairo in the background. From the Khan El Khalili, it's a five minute taxi ride, or a 20 minute walk west on El Azhar Street and south on Salah Salem.

5. Finally, the **Nile** offers endless potential sunset masterpieces, but we'd recommend a sunset felucca (sailboat) ride. The boats can be hired for about LE20 an hour downtown next to the Meridien Hotel, or better yet next to Felfela's in Maadi where the Nile's west banks are lined with verdant palm groves. Felfela El Nil is also an excellent option.

The menu features nouveau Egyptian and continental cuisine including great mezze and pasta, but ventilation is a problem and it gets very smoky-good for the rock'n'roll clubby atmosphere, but bad for the health. Also, by Cairo standards it's expensive (local Stella LE10; main courses LE15-30). If you're going on a Thursday or Friday night and want to sit, or have a big group, call in advance for a table.

ABSOLUTE, *Amman Square (around the corner from Le Tabasco), Mohandiseen-Dokki. Tel. 02/349-7326. Credit cards: Visa.*

Brought to you by the same folks who brought you Le Tabasco, Absolute is a more posh establishment that requires smart dress to enter. It's also expensive-don't expect to pay any less than LE20, even if you don't have more than a couple of beers.

WHISKIES, *Atlas Zamalek Hotel, Gamaat El Dowal El Arabia Street, Mohandiseen. Tel. 02/346-7230, 346-4175. Credit cards: Visa.*

Young and predominantly male, Whiskies is chiefly a way station for dancers on their way to the Roman Tamango disco upstairs, but a lively clientele and billiards table make it a viable option in itself.

Discos & Nightclubs – Downtown

JACKIE'S JOINT, *Nile Hilton Hotel, Tahrir Square. Reservations: Recommended. Credit cards: all major credit cards accepted. Dress: Casual, but not too casual.*

NiteLife magazine's "Nite Guide" labels it "the queen of the scene," and indeed it seems that since bringing in a "disco consultant" (called Jackie) from England to manage renovations and expansion, Jackie's Joint once again claims the title it held in the mid 80's as Cairo's hottest nightspot. With a snack bar, billiards, and even private karaoke booths in addition to the bar and dance floor, Jackie's offers more in the way of distractions, and more importantly space. Be aware that unless you're with a member or are a guest in the hotel, it can be difficult to get in without reservations, especially if you are a dateless male, or even worse a group of dateless males. Also the LE40 entrance charge, which goes towards the tab, is a bit steep as are drink prices (LE14 Stella Export).

UPSTAIRS, *in the World Trade Center. Tel 02/ 580-428. Hours:. Minimum charge: LE40. Credit Cards: all major credit cards accepted. Dress: Smart casual, i.e. no shorts and T-shirts. Reservations required.*

Cairo's most exclusive club, Upstairs is a place to be seen. Every Thursday and Friday night, Cairo's wealthiest yuppies make it in full force, mobile phone and all, bumping and grinding to the not so latest beats and flashing colored lights, and most of all to pursue sexual conquest. But to be honest, it's really not that appealing. It's impossible to get it, it's expensive (LE50 cover charge, LE20 for a beer), and it's so crowded and dark inside, that it's hard to see what all the fuss is about.

THE ROMAN TAMANGO CLUB, *Atlas Zamalek Hotel on Gamaat El Dowal El Arabia Street, in Mohandiseen. Hours: 10pm-4am. Credit Cards: Visa. Dress: Casual.*

The epicenter of Cairo's disco scene in the late '80's/early '90's, "Atlas," as it's popularly known, is now less exclusive and more casual. They play more danceable Arabic music (more fun than the tired not so latest dance tunes from Europe) that are way overplayed everywhere else.

AFRICANA'S, *El Haram Street, (Pyramids Road) about a third of the way towards the Pyramids on the northern side. Minimum charge: LE20. No credit cards accepted.*

Sketch city, no doubt, Africana's is a local joint packed with local guys and women from south of the border up to what can best be described as dubious activity at best. But as long as you keep to yourself and don't step on anybody's toes, you should be respected as a neutral party when the inevitable fight does break out (always a good show). With the DJ spinning reggae and older pop favorites, and the gritty, sweaty, smoky atmosphere Africana's exudes an authentic hole-in-the-wall kind of quality missing at the glossy upscale hotel discos. If you can handle a bit of sleaze, this place just might be a worthwhile "cultural experience."

CASANOVA, *El Borg Hotel, Zamalek. Tel. 02/341-4746. Credit cards: not accepted.*

High heels and handbags are pretty much the name of the game at Casanova. It's seedy to be sure, but the dynamics of local males competing over excessively made-up and overdressed working girls in the cheap discotheque setting is worth the price of admission just for the laugh. The whole scene is harmless, and even when fights do break out, women, children, and foreigners are generally spared.

Belly Dancing

Cairo is the world capital of belly dancing and it was in the garish clubs along Pyramids Road in the 1930's and 1940's that stars such as Nagwa Fuad made what has been viewed as a salubrious activity associated with

CAIRO WEDDINGS

Egyptian weddings are invariably exuberant and noisy affairs, usually held on Thursday and Friday nights when Cairo's main thoroughfares are taken over by waves of cars decked out in streamers, the drivers of which honk their horns with even more enthusiasm than usual. Whether the venue is the Marriott Aida Ballroom or an alley in a biladi district like Butneya, the party itself is a music extravaganza with dancing and live bands going all night. For their soirees, the rich favor employing the country's biggest dance an singing acts, while the normal folks typically hire a small Sayeedi ensemble or synthesizer-tabla combo to which they belly and stick dance.

Weddings begin with a procession, called the "zaffa," in which the bride and groom enter the venue to drum beating, ululation, and a shower of rice or rose petals. It is followed by a reception where the guests line to congratulate the couple and their families, which gives way to an all night dance and foodfest. In rural and some working class weddings, the sexes are segregated while at middle and upper class one, they are typically integrated. Should you have the opportunity to attend a wedding, whether local or upscale, by all means do – it's invariably a good show.

brothels into a respectable mainstream art form. It may seem odd that a national art form in one of the world's biggest Muslim countries features a scantily clad woman shaking her body with frank sexuality, but apart from the most conservative of Muslims, it is widely accepted and performed not only in nightclubs but at weddings as well. Indeed, the most famous belly dancers like Fifi Abdou, Dina, and Lucy enjoy celebrity status equal to that of the country's biggest sport and film stars and command five figure fees for a single performance.

Big name stars perform only at the deluxe nightclubs in five star hotels or at private weddings and parties. Typically entrance fees at fancy dancy hotel venues begin at LE60 but often top LE100, and the party begins around 10pm or midnight with a dinner and several hours of warm-up acts before the marquee attraction rolls out around 1 or 2am and things don't wind down until 3 or 4am. In other words, taking in a first rate belly dancing show requires a substantial investment of money, time, and lost sleep. Listed below are some major "oriental" nightclubs. Keep in mind that smart dress is required.

ALHAMBRA, *Cairo Sheraton, Giza. Tel. 02/336-9700. Credit cards: all major credit cards accepted. Closed on Mondays.*

Home of Dina, Cairo's, and hence the world's, hottest belly dance star. Call for reservations and expect to pay big bucks.

ABU NAWAS, *Mena House Hotel, Pyramids Road, Giza. Tel. 02/383-3444. Credit cards: all major credit cards accepted.*

EMPRESS, *Cairo Marriott Hotel & Casino, Zamalek. Tel. 02/340-8888. Credit cards: all major credit cards accepted.*

HAROUN EL RASHID, *InterContinental Hotel, Corniche El Nil Street, Garden City. Tel. 02/355-7171. Credit cards: all major credit cards accepted.*

LA BELLE EPOQUE, *Meridien Hotel, Corniche El Nile Street, Rhoda Island. Tel. 02/362-1717. Credit cards: all major credit cards accepted.*

The entertainment docket often includes up and coming pop stars in addition to belly dancing.

More raucous and less formal shows can be enjoyed at the sleazier clubs along **Pyramids Road**. During their heyday in the 1930's and 1940's these establishments were the preferred venues for top belly dancing, popular music, and cabaret performers, but since the 1970's, deluxe hotels have largely replaced them.

Now decidedly shabby and tacky, the clubs on Pyramids Road cater primarily to Gulf Arabs who are willing to pay big bucks to enjoy a boys night out and they aren't much cheaper than the upscale clubs downtown. If you are interested, and it can be quite an experience, the **El Parisiana** *(102 Pyramids Road, Tel. 383-3911)*; **El Liel** *(334 Pyramids Road, Tel. 02/850-001)*; and **L'Auberge** *(352 Pyramids Road, Tel. 02/851-713)* are among

POPULAR MUSIC IN EGYPT

The classical Arabic music that has dominated airwaves and concerts halls from Morocco to the Gulf in the 20th century is actually a hybrid combining true classical Arabic music with its rich scales and lyrical melodies, with western-style orchestra, march, and show music. Concerts are typically extravagant affairs lasting for hours which feature vocal soloist, backed by mammoth ensembles that include not only full blown western orchestras with violins, cellos and so on, but also traditional Arabic instruments like the tabla drums, qanun (oriental harp), nay (oriental flute), and an oud (oriental lute). Often full scale male and female choirs are thrown in for good measure. If not patriotic in nature, vocals are invariably passionate and poetic laments about lost love and heartbreaks.

Pioneered at the turn of the century by the legendary **Sayid Darwish**, *and fully developed by the superlegend* **Mohammed Abdel Wahab**, *modern classical Arabic music's brightest star is undoubtedly* **Om Kalthoum**, *who has dominated the airwaves since the 1940's even though she passed away in 1975. Known as the "Voice of Egypt," her weekly performances on radio and television routinely brought the country to a standstill. Close behind Kalthoum is* **Abdel Halim Hafez**, *an Elvis-like heartthrob who spoke for the 1952 Revolution like the Beatles spoke for boomers in the '60s. A soft spoken man who succumbed to bilharzia in his early forties, Abdel Halim exuded an emotional vulnerability uncharacteristic in a society that encourages machismo and this enabled him to touch to the nation's emotional soul in an era of great upheaval and tragedy.*

Other popular music genres include **Sayeedi** *and fellahi music, folksy types that feature epic lyrics about Islamic and national heroes accompanied by small ensembles limited to indigenous instruments. Beginning in the 1970's, traditional rhythms were usurped by urban artists like* **Ahmed Adawia** *who developed a gritty pop style known as "shaabi" that spoke to the frustrations and pressures of Egyptian urban life. The late 1980's and '90s saw the development by megastars like* **Amr Diab** *and* **Mostafa Qamr** *of shaabi into a more polished commercial style favored by middle class youth. Eminently danceable, it is characterized by cheesy synthesizers, shallow lyrics, and catchy melodies that end up all sounding the same.*

Sampling and buying music in Egypt is extremely easy. Cassette shops abound and they will allow you to listen to a tape before buying it. At LE5-8 tapes are also very cheap. If you're interested in sampling classical Arabic music, tunes like Daret El Ayam by Om Kalthoum are an obvious choice, but her music is somewhat laborious to western ears, and Abdel Halim Hafez's famous hits like "Ihwak," "El Tooba," "Mawa'ood," and "Zay El Hawa" are lighter and catchier. Among contemporary popular stars, Amr Diab is the current king and Mohammed Mouni, and Mostafa Qamr are also big names.

the better known clubs. Call in advance to find out what's playing and when. Like the hotel clubs, they often charge a large set fee (LE60-100) that usually includes dinner.

Better and far cheaper for equally titillating entertainment are the clubs on Alfi Street off Opera Square. The **Schehrazade** and the **Arizona** *(both on Alfi Bey Street)*, and the **Palmyra Club** *(16B 26th July Street)*, are all working class establishments where entrance fees don't top LE10-20. The venues are garish, the dancing is second rate, but the harmless seediness of these establishments and the thumping live music makes for an excellent night out.

Gambling & Casinos

Islamic law expressly forbids gambling, but nearly every five star hotel in Cairo contains a casino where you can play roulette, black-jack, poker, slots and punto bacco. The buzzing atmosphere of the grand casinos in Vegas or Macao is certainly lacking, but that doesn't deter the throngs of Gulf Arabs who flock to Cairo in the summer from chasing their luck. Generally rich, and unable to gamble in their own countries because of strict Islamic laws, their money is more than welcome in Egypt. Egyptians, however, are forbidden from even entering casinos. Gaming is conducted in dollars or other hard foreign currency but not in Egyptians pounds. As long as you play, you're usually entitled to free drinks and sometimes food and cigarettes. Listed below are major gaming establishments.

Downtown Casinos

Cairo Ramses Hilton, *Ramses Hilton, Corniche El Nil Street north of Tahrir Square. Tel. 02/574-4400, 575-8000, 768-888. Hours: 3pm-9am.*

Nile Hilton Casino, *Nile Hilton, Tahrir Square. Tel. 02/578-0444, 578-0666. Hours: 1pm-10am.*

Casino Semiramis, *Semiramis InterContinental Hotel, Corniche El Nil Street in Garden City south of Tahrir Square. Tel. 02/355-7171.*

Zamalek Casinos

Le Casino, *El Gezirah Sheraton, Zamalek. Tel. 02/341-1333. Open 24 hours.*

Omar Khayyam Casino, *Marrriott Hotel and Casino, Zamalek. Tel 02/340-8888. Open 24 hours.*

Giza, Dokki & the Pyramids

Cairo Sheraton Casino, *Cairo Sheraton, Giza Street, Dokki. Tel. 336-9700, 336-9800. Open 24 hours.*

Sheherazade Casino, *Mena House Hotel at the end of Pyramids Road (El Haram) in Giza. Tel. 02/383-3222/444. Hours: 8pm-6am.*

Heliopolis Casinos

Movenpick Casino, *Movenpick Cairo-Heliopolis Hotel, Heliopolis. Tel 02/291-9400, 247-0077. Hours: 5:30pm until morning.*

Casino Libnan El Salam, *Swissotel Cairo El Salam Hotel, Heliopolis. Tel. 02/297-4000, 297-6000.*

Movies

Cairo is the movie capital of the Arab world and theaters are found in every district, if not every neighborhood. Many of the older theaters are 40-50 years old and despite showing their age still emanate a faint ambiance reminiscent of film's golden age. Theaters feature mainly Arabic language movies, however many of the major theaters also show blockbusters (often heavily edited especially when it comes to sex) from Hollywood six months to a year after US release dates.

The **Cairo Film Festival** is usually held in November and presents a good variety of new releases from Europe and the US as well as the Arab World. It's the only time the censors don't get to take their scissors to the celluloid and, hence, is very popular with locals. If you're not interested in watered down versions of last year's blockbusters, various national cultural centers, such as the French Cultural Center or the German Goethe Institute, often sponsor film screenings. Listings for English language movies both in public theaters and at cultural institutes centers are printed in *The Egyptian Gazette, The Middle East Times,* and other local English language publications. Below are some major cinemas.

Downtown Cinemas
- **Cosmos I & II**, *12 Emad El Din Street. Tel. 02/ 574-2177*
- **Diana**, *17 Alfi Street. Tel. 02/974-727*
- **Karim**, *15 Emad El Din Street. Tel. 02/591-6095*
- **Kasr El Nil**, *Kasr El Nil Street. Tel. 02/575-0761*
- **Lido**, *23 Emad El Din Street. Tel. 02/934-284*
- **Metro**, *35 Talaat Harb Street. Tel 02/393-7566*
- **Miami**, *38 Talaat Harb. Street. Tel. 02/574-5656*
- **Odeon**, *4 Abdel Hamid Said Street. Tel 02/575-8797*
- **Radio**, *Talaat Harb Street. Tel. 02/575-5053*
- **Ramses Hilton**, *Ramses Hilton Mall annex off Corniche El Nil. Tel. 02/574-7436*
- **Rivoli I & II**, *26th July Street. Tel. 02/ 575-5053*

Giza, Dokki, Mohandiseen & Rhoda Cinemas
- **Al Tahri**, *112 El Tahrir Street, Dokki. Tel. 02/335-4726*
- **Cairo Sheraton**, *Cairo Sheraton Hotel, Giza Street, Dokki. Tel 02/360-6081*
- **Sphinx**, *Sphinx Square, Mohandiseen. Tel. 02/364-4071*

Heliopolis & Maadi Cinemas
• **Al Horreya 1 & 2**, *Al Ahram Street, Korba in Heliopolis. Tel. 02/452-9980*
• **Normandy**, *31 Al Ahram Street, Heliopolis. Tel. 02/258-0254*
• **Roxy**, *Roxy Square, Heliopolis. Tel. 02/ 258-0344*
• **Swissotel Cairo Al Salam Hotel Cinema**, *65 Abdel Hamid Bedawy Street, Heliopolis. Tel. 02/297-4000 or 297-6000*
• **MGM**, *Maadi Grand Mall in Digla by Victoria College. Tel. 02/352-3066*

Performing Arts

It isn't Paris, New York, or Vienna, but there's plenty going on in Cairo for classical music buffs and patrons of high culture. One legacy of European domination was appreciation for western style classical music, opera, and dance. Cairo boasted one the world's most famous opera houses, which hosted the premiere of *Aida*, for which Verdi was commissioned to commemorate the opening of the Suez Canal in 1869. That opera house, located in Opera Square, burned down in 1970, but in 1989, Cairo's performing arts got a shot in the arm with the opening of the state of the art **Cairo Opera House** in Zamalek. Check English language publications such as *Egypt Today*, *The Egyptian Gazette*, *The Middle East Times*, and *Al Ahram Weekly* for listings and information about performances. Also, contact the major venues for tickets and information, keeping in mind that schedules and prices can change without notice.

Cairo Opera House, *in Zamalek by the Kasr El Nil Bridge. Tel. 02/341-2926 or 342-0601.*

Built with Japanese assistance, this new facility opened in 1989, and is now the major forum for performing arts and home to the **Cairo Symphony**, and the **Cairo Opera & Ballet Company**, and the **National Arabic Music Ensemble**, specializing in classical Arabic music. Small groups, solo performances, and jazz concerts are held in the Small Hall. Men must wear coat and tie when attending performances in the Main Hall.

Another major venue, the somewhat run down **El Gumhuriya Theater** *(Tel. 02/374-2864)* in Abdin on El Gomhuriya Street is used mostly classical music performances. In Agouza, on the Giza side of the Nile, the **Balloon Theater** *(02/347-745)* is the place if you want to experience Egyptian folkloric dance and music troupes like the **Folklore Orchestra of Egypt**, while the **Sayid Darwish Concert Hall** *(Tel. 02/560-2473)* is the premier venue for classical Arabic music and groups like the National Arabic Music Ensemble. Listings for all cultural events can be found in the English language *Al Ahram Weekly* newspaper.

SPORTS & RECREATION

Most visitors come as tourists with an itinerary so crammed with the city's endless attractions that they don't have the time or energy to then hit, say, the squash court. Nothing hits the spot after a dusty day of camel jockeying out at the pyramids like a cool dip in the pool or a relaxing felucca ride on the breezy Nile. Almost all four and five star hotels operate swimming pools of good size and sanitation which are often open to nonresidents for a fee. Some also feature gyms and spas. During the period of British occupation in Egypt, a number of very elegant and exclusive country clubs were established and reserved for Brits and Europeans only. The populist President Nasser saw an end to that in the fifties and the clubs are but a shade of their former selves in terms of elegance and luxury, but they are at the heart of the sporting, social, and recreational life for the upper middle classes. Most of them have pools and other sporting facilities open to foreign visitors for a fee.

Amongst the masses, soccer is the number one sport and many a time your taxi or bus will have to slow down to evade a shot gone awry from a nearby pickup game. Cairo's most popular professional teams, El Ahly (National) Club and the Zamalek Sporting Club do battle at Cairo Stadium in Heliopolis attracting hordes of ecstatic fans sometimes numbering over 100,000. Below are some ideas and listings for sporting and recreational options.

Feluccas & Boating on the Nile

From April until October (during the winter it gets a bit chilly at night), no place in Cairo is as peaceful and relaxing as the Nile itself. For as little as LE20 an hour you and as many friends as you like can bring food, beer, or other refreshments and pile into one of the famous **felucca** sail boats and withdraw from the three ring circus times ten that is Cairo. Be aware that toilet facilities are nonexistent so do what you have to do beforehand.

Felucca outlets line the Nile downtown and **Dok Dok** just north of the Meridian sails about between Rhoda and Zamalek is one of the most prominent. About ten kilometers south of the Corniche, just north of Felfela at the main turnoff into **Maadi** is another family run felucca operation. Sailing out Maadi is pleasant because the banks of the Nile, especially to the west, are underdeveloped and decidedly rural whereas downtown you sail among the towering concrete and glass of the city. To avoid the taxi from downtown (LE15-20 one-way), take the Metro to El Maadi Station (20 minutes from Sadat), and cab it from there; it won't take more than 3 minutes and just tell the driver "Felfela El Nil" which is right next door.

Swimming

All of the five star hotels listed have nice pools that non-guests can use for the day, usually for a fee of LE20-40. Those by the Pyramids (the Mena House, Sofitel, Forte Grande, and the Jolie Ville) offer spectacular views of the monuments.

Sporting Clubs

El Ahly Sporting Club, *Tel. 02/340-2112, 340-2113. El Gabalaya Street, Zamalek.*

El Ahly (the National Club) is home to Egypt's greatest football team and houses facilities for tennis, squash, and martial arts. Ironically it is located in Zamalek, the namesake of its arch rival which is actually situated in Mohandiseen.

The Shooting Club/Nadi Seid, *Nadi Seid Street, Dokki. Tel. 02/337-4535.*

Egypt's most uppity sporting club socially is primarily a hunting and shooting club, but has facilities for other sports as well.

Gezirah Sporting Club, *Tel. 02/341-5270, 340-6000/6. Located in Zamalek.*

Historically the largest, most prestigious, and most famous of all Egyptian clubs dating to the British Era, the Gezira Club still covers half of Zamelk and now has more than 100,000 members. In addition to tennis, squash, martial arts, and swimming it has one of the few **golf** courses in Egypt.

Maadi Club, *Tel.02 375-2066, 350-5455. Maadi.*

Maadi Yacht Club, *Tel. 02/350-5169, 350-5455, 350-5693. 8 Palmer Street, Maadi.*

Water sports activities available in addition to usually sporting facilities.

El Nil Sporting Club, *Tel. 02/847-626. At the end of El Abbas Bridge in Giza.*

Nile Country Club, *Tel. 02/374-3334, 347-2211. Corniche El Nile.*

In addition to usual sporting facilities, it offers bowling, water sports, and facilities specifically for children.

Saqqara Sporting Club, *Tel. 018/201-791. Saqqara Road, Giza.*

Located in a beautiful rural setting off the Saqqara Road, the Saqqara Club offers use of their pool and a full lunch buffet for LE60 per person. Horseback riding and raquet sports facilities are also available.

El Shams Sporting Club, *Tel. 02/244-0094, 244-1278, 243-3501. Heliopolis.*

Swimming, martial arts, racquet sports and other general athletic facilities available.

Tawfikieh Tennis Club, *Tel 02/346-1930. Ahmed Orabi Street in Mohandiseen.*

Zamalek Sporting Club, *Tel. 02/263-3001. Mit Oqba in Mohandiseen.*

Golf

Before the 1952 Revolution, golf was one of the popular sports with Egypt's expatriates and all the major sporting clubs featured courses. But with the onset of the Nasser regime and the expulsion of most foreigners only three clubs remained in Egypt at the Alexandria Sporting Club, the Gezirah Sporting Club, and at the Mena House by the Pyramids.

In the 1990's golf is making a comeback and the number of golf courses will quadruple by the end of the century. Contact the **National Golf Federation** (*Tel. 02/340-6000*) for information.

Health Clubs, Gyms, & Spas

There are dozens, if not hundreds, of health clubs, gyms, and spas throughout greater Cairo. Many of the nicer facilities are in upscale hotels and resorts. For specific listings and information concerning your needs, check the listings of *Egypt Today* and *Sports & Fitness* magazines.

SHOPPING

The hustle and bustle of crowded markets, aggressive and devious salesmen, unfamiliarity with price, and the bargaining process make shopping in Cairo a challenge. Most visitors make their only shopping ventures to the medieval Khan El Khalili bazaars in Islamic Cairo, or the souvenir stores in their hotel but all of Cairo is teeming with retail stores, boutiques, antique dealers, and public markets, most which is make for a show even if you're not an interested buyer.

Arts & Crafts

Wood work, jewelry, and glass are just some the crafts for which Egypt has been known for centuries. Many maintain that the standards of quality in Egypt have dropped since Nasser nationalized private businesses and deported thousands of artisans and merchants of non-Egyptian ethnic stock (Armenians for example have always been famous jewelers) in the '50's and '60's. This may be true, but a strong economy and recent government and private initiatives to resuscitate the Egyptian arts and crafts industries have led to a revival.

Listed below are some reputable art galleries and shops. Virtually all accept Visa payment and open 10am-5pm Saturday-Thursday.

Senouhi, *54 Abdel Khaliq Sarwat Street, 5th floor, Downtown. Tel. 02/ 3910955. Hours: Monday-Friday 10am-5pm, Saturday 10am-1pm.*

Small and cramped, Senouhi may be finest shop in Cairo, with its extensive array of goods from Bedouin textiles to vintage prints and books. It's expensive and prices are nonnegotiable, but for quality goods or just browsing, it can't be beat.

Nomad, *14 Saraya El Gezira, Zamalek & Cairo Morriott Hotel, Zamalek.*
Interesting jewwelry, textiles and traditional handicrafts.

Bashayer, *58 Mossadaq Street, Dokki*
Jewelry, art, textiles, and other fancy stuff.

Taraneem, *27 Abdel Moneim Riyad Street, Mohandiseen.*
Arts and handicrafts.

Sahara, *34 Nabil El Wakad Street, Heliopolis.*
Sells Bedouin arts and crafts and offers art classes.

Sheba, *6 Sri Lanka Street, Zamalek.*
Fancy textiles, jewelry, paintings, and other handicrafts.

Khan Misr Touloun, *across from the Ibn Touloun Mosque off Saliba Street in Sayeda Zeinab.*
Specializes in handicrafts from rural Egypt and the oases.

Ethno and The Workshop, *38 Road 6, Maadi.*
Exhibits and deals arts and crafts from contemporary artists and offers art classes and lectures.

Wooden Crafts & Mashrabia

It may seem strange given that Egypt is 95% desert, but as early as pharaonic times, wood has been a favorite artistic medium with Egyptian craftsmen. During the medieval Islamic periods, brilliantly carved wooden screens and windows, called **mashrabia**, became a hallmark of Egypt's cities, and even today should you walk through some neighborhoods in Islamic Cairo like Darb El Ahmar, you will find houses that still feature mashrabia. Today, mashrabia is available throughout the Khan El Khalili and in furniture stores and boutiques throughout Cairo. While a love seat or room divider may be out of your league, very simple and attractive frames and mirrors are easy to carry home and shouldn't set you back more than LE50-150.

Apart from mashrabia, wood is commonly inlaid with mother of pearl (or plastic that looks like mother of pearl) and used in ornate inlaid boxes, game tables, and furniture. The art of inlaying wood with other wood, mother pearl (and recently plastic), and other semi-precious stones was imported from Persia during the Mamluke period and has been a favorite medium ever since. In the Khan El Khalili and other boutiques, inlaid wooden products range from small boxes inlaid with plastic (you can tell because it shines more than real mother of pearl) that cost LE5, to masterfully crafted game tables that convert from cards to backgammon and vice versa, that cost as much as LE50,000.

Bookstores

Most upscale hotels contain some bookshops selling mainly guidebooks, coffee table picture books, and sometimes foreign newspapers and magazines, literature, and postcards. Listed below are major bookstores which sell English language publications, books, and newspapers.

Al Ahram, *branches at 165 Mohammed Farid Street, Nile Hilton Mall, and Semirams InterContinental, Cairo Sheraton. Hours: 8:30am-10pm.*

Operated by the same folks who publish the newspaper *Al Ahram* and other major Arab newspapers and magazines, Al Ahram sells foreign newspapers like the *International Herald Tribune, USA Today, The Wall Street Journal,* and locally published newspapers and magazines as well as numerous tourist and academic books about Egypt.

American University in Cairo Bookstore, *Main AUC Campus, 113 Kasr El Aini Street. Tel. 02/357-5377. Hours: 8:30am-4pm Sunday-Thursday, 10am-3pm on Saturday. Closed on Friday and during the month of August.* **Second Branch:** *16 Mohammed Ibn Thaleb Street, Zamalek. Tel. 02/339-7045. Hours: 9am-4pm Sunday-Thursday & 10am-3pm Saturday.*

Catering to university students, the AUC bookstore has the most extensive offerings of English language books in Cairo.

Anglo-Egyptian Bookshop, *165 Mohammed Farid Street, downtown. Tel. 02/391-4337. Hours: 9am-1:30pm & 4:30pm-8pm. Closed Sunday.*

L'Orientaliste, *15 Kasr El Nil Street downtown. Tel. 02/575-3418. Hours: 10am-7:30pm. Closed Sunday.*

Pricey, but a great place to find old books and maps which make great gifts.

Lehnert & Landrock, *44 Sherif Street, downtown. Tel. 02/393-5324. Hours: 9:30am-2pm & 4pm-7pm. Closed Sunday.*

Lehnert & Landrock features a wide selection of books, fiction and non, in French and German as well as English.

Madbouli, *Talaat Harb Square downtown with second branch at 45 El Battal Ahmed Abdel Azziz Street in Mohandiseen. Hours: 7am-2am daily.*

An Egyptian Barnes & Nobles if you will, Madbouli's carries mainly Arabic language publications and books but also sells a good deal of English language books, magazines, and newspapers. The long hours and central location make it convenient.

Cassettes & Music

Cassettes are sold on virtually every major street for LE5-8 a piece. In the Khan El Khalili, a small alley off El Hussein Square and El Fishawis cafe, features a half dozen cassette shops and is a good place to start.

Gold, Silver & Precious Stones

The historic gold and silver souks have for centuries been located on and around **Muizz li Din Allah Street** in the Khan El Khalili. As you probably notice, Egyptians love jewelry-the more the better. They not only enjoy wearing it, but it is also, despite recent slumps in gold prices, a favorite investment. Prices for both gold and silver are set, so there's little or no bargaining. Check the *Egyptian Gazette* for official prices per grams.

Gold is usually sold in 21 or 18 carats and both gold and silver should be stamped for authenticity. A gold camel stamp indicates gold-plated metals, usually brass. Though Khan El Khalili is the most famous gold market, try **Abdel Khaliq Sarwat Street** and **Sikket El Manakh**, both off Opera Square. These merchants cater to frugal local consumers and prices are usually a tad lower than in the Khan El Khalili.

Buying precious stones can be tricky. Egypt does not produce them, so they are imported and if you know you're stuff you'll immediately notice that merchants are always trying to pass off fakes. One shop that can (probably) be trusted and does a first rate job in setting stones is **Nasser Bros.**, *on the main artery inside the Khan El Khalili (Sikkit El Bedestan)*, but they aren't cheap.

Brass & Copper

Crafted and sold primarily in Islamic Cairo on Muizz li Din Street by the Khan El Khalili in the **brass and copper souk (souk el nahaseen)**, these metals are shaped into all types of products from teapots and banquet trays to fuul pots and minaret crescents.

Textiles

Egypt does not boast the tradition of fine carpet weaving that Iran and Afghanistan do, but from T-shirts made from its world famous cotton to rustic rugs and tapestries woven from camel hair, there are plenty of textile products worth looking into. Some products, like the colorful clothing and tapestries of Bedouins are cheapest in the oases themselves but in Cairo can be found in the Khan El Khalili, Kerdessa, and major souvenir shops. Many believe that Egypt's finest textiles are those woven at the **Wissa Wassef** Center for the Arts on the Saqqara Road in Giza (see the Wissa Wassef entry in the "Seeing the Sights" section above).

Expertly woven by hand, they feature finely detailed depictions of rural life in Egypt and natural scenery. Imitators abound, so remember that the only authorized dealer other than the Wissa Wassef Center itself is Senouhi at 54 Abdel Khaliq Sarwat Street downtown.

Another Cairo textile specialty is the **appliqué** work of the tentmakers at Tentmakers' Street in Islamic Cairo (see "Islamic Cairo" section in "Seeing the Sights" above). There, craftsmen expertly stitch appliqués originally used in the tents put up for weddings and funerals. Originally, the patterns were Islamic and geometric. Now they have adopted pictorial scenes, often of a Pharaonic style, and make pillow cases, wall hangings, and bed spreads. Appliqués range in price from LE15 for a simple pillow case to LE600 or more for giant hangings, bed spreads, and tents. These things can be real winners and make excellent gifts.

Finally, both western and "oriental" style **clothing** like galabiyas (robes worn by men) and caftans are available ready made or tailored in Cairo. In the Khan El Khalili, shops like **Ouf** and **Atlas** on Sikkit El Badestan sell rather handsome and formal garments, which can be pricey (LE50 and up). For cheap galabiyas and melayas (the black gowns worn by women) exit the Khan for Mouski Street and Muizz li Din Allah Street between El Azhar and Bab Zuweila. Kerdessa off the Pyramids Road is another good option, and there are clothing outlets throughout the city. As for western-style clothing, T-shirts with all sorts of Egyptian-related designs (Stella shirts are most popular) are sold in the Khan and on Mouski Street. They should not cost more than LE10-12 a piece and less if you buy in bulk.

Fancier shirts, slacks, and jackets are sold in many upscale boutiques like *Safari, Mobacco,* and *Bennetton* which are mostly located in shopping malls attached to big hotels like the Inter-Continental and the Hiltons.

Leatherwork

Excellent quality wallets, purses, and camel saddles are some of the more popular leather goods made and sold in Cairo. The Khan El Khalili offers the most variety in terms of goods, quality, and styles, and there is also the Street of the Saddlemakers south of the Street of the Tentmakers in Islamic Cairo (see "Islamic Cairo" in "Seeing the Sights" above). Otherwise, leather products are widely available in hotel shopping centers.

Papyrus

Tourist souvenir *extraordinaire,* papyrus is the ancient Egyptian type of paper made from a plant of the same name. Painted with decorations ranging from copies of classic pharaonic scenes, to third rate imitations of the Mona Lisa, papyrus is sold everywhere but one man dominates the market. Almost single-handedly, Dr. Ragab revived the ancient tradition of papyrus making and painting, and he operates the most prominent papyrus shops in Cairo. We'd recommend buying from him simply because so much of the stuff passed on as papyrus in other shops is actually made from banana leaf buying so from him at least you know you're getting the real thing.

Dr. Ragab's Papyrus Institute, *located on boats in from of the Cairo Sheraton in Dokki; open daily 9am-7pm, Tel. 989-476,* not only sells papyrus products ranging from personalized bookmarks (your name in hieroglyphics in a cartouche) for LE10 to monumental paintings worth thousands of pounds, but demonstrates the ancient art of making papyrus. He also operates shops in Luxor, Aswan, and Alexandria as well as the **Pharaonic Village** near the Institute where actors dressed up as ancient Egyptians act out scenes from pharaonic Egypt-very cheesy.

Glass

The Mamlukes and Fatimids specialized in glasswork, often decorating their drinking glasses and glass lamps with intricate geometric designs and beautiful Arabic calligraphy. Mouski glass, a cheap blown glass manufactured off Mouski Street in the Khan El Khalili imitates this tradition. Usually colored blue, green or purple, the glass is shaped into candlesticks, glasses, and vases and sold for less than LE10 per piece. Be aware, they are very delicate and easily shattered. A store worth trying is **Abd El Raouf** in the Khan El Khalili.

Spices

A major node in the great spice routes since the early Middle Ages, Cairo's **Spice Market** off Mouski Street in the Khan El Khalili still tempts visitors with enticing aromas and vivid colors. However, with the globalization of the spice trade, there's really nothing you probably can't get at home.

Hotel Shopping Centers

Five star hotels usually contain shopping centers with upscale boutiques, hair salons, travel agencies, and other assorted consumer. Though pricey by any standards, consistently offer high quality handicrafts, jewelry and fabrics. The **Nile Hilton Mall**, adjoining the courtyard in the back, which is itself lined with travel agencies and boutiques, is three stories and contains boutiques and a food court with Egyptian, Thai, and American food and a bar with a pool table. Decent enough food, but pricey (kebab plate LE30, cola LE3.50).

There is a similar shopping center annexed to the Ramses Hilton and smaller malls within the InterContinental, the Marriott and the Sheratons, all of which contain shops selling handicrafts, jewelry, and souvenirs.

Maadi

Road 9 is Maadi's commercial center. Between the two main bridge passing over the street are numerous fast-food shops, a post office, El Maadi Metro Station, and assorted other shops. Just south of the metro station, the midan and the main bridge is a Thomas Cook branch and several grocery stores catering primarily to expats living in Maadi and selling everything from Purina dog food and Tabasco sauce to Stella. Also operating are several Khan El Khalili style shops, and specialized service shops like framers, electricians, and flower stands.

Just over the Road 153 Bridge and around **Midan El Horreya**, shops, boutiques, and restaurants cater to a more local clientele while the **Maadi Grand Mall** in Digla by Victory College is still short of completion but already hosts dozens of shops, eateries, a bowling alley, and a movie theater.

EXCURSIONS & DAY TRIPS

The Birqash Camel Market

Located 35 kilometers northwest of Cairo in the town of Birqash is Egypt's largest camel and livestock market. Here thousands of *fellaheen* (farmers), Sudanese camel herders, and Bedouin from as faraway as Sinai and Siwa come to barter and trade camels, goats, cattle, and donkeys. It's a fascinating scene redolent of the Middle Ages, but it's not for the squeamish. Herders routinely beat animals and camel are forced stand on three legs (the fourth is tied up) to keep them from running away (which they do anyway). Those with red 'X's on them are due for slaughter. The market operates daily, but is most active on Friday mornings beginning around 6am. For a half day excursion from Cairo, hire a private taxi for about LE70, which isn't too much if split between a group.

Alexandria

Two and half hours by automobile, public bus, or train, Alexandria is a feasible day trip and an easy overnight trip from Cairo. Though it has little to show for its rich history, its Corniche, colonial-era buildings, Greco-Roman Museum, and fantastic seafood make it a worthwhile excursion. Check "Arrivals & Departures" in the "Alexandria" section of Chapter 16 for details.

The Monasteries of Wadi Natrun

Situated off the Desert Road two thirds of the way to Alexandria, these fortified monasteries have been among Egypt's most important since their founding over 1,000 years ago. Tours can be arranged through travel agencies or through the Coptic Patriarchate (*Tel. 02/960-360*). Alternatively you can arrange a private taxi or take a public bus from Abdel Moneim Riyad Terminal behind the Egyptian Antiquities Museum. If you plan to use public transport, you probably cannot visit all four of the monasteries in one day. To arrange spending the night, you must make prior arrangements through the Patriarchate.

Sinai

Making the trek to Sharm El Sheikh and the other major resorts of Sinai's east coast requires more than a day trip, but the beach resorts of Ras El Sidr on Sinai's west coast along the Gulf of Suez do make an easy getaway from Cairo. For accommodation you can choose from an assortment of 'holiday villages' most of which offer an assortment of water sports and other recreational options as well as comfortable, moderately priced accommodation. There are also several springs and other natural attractions and the views of the Red Sea and the surrounding mountains are also quite spectacular. Ras El Sidr is most easily reached by private automobile (2.5-3 hours) or you can have a bus going to Sharm El Sheikh from the Mahatta Sina in Abbassia drop you at your hotel. See Chapter 19 for information about hotels and local attractions.

The Red Sea Coast: Ain Sukhna and the Red Sea Monasteries

Egypt's stunning Red Sea coast also offers an easy beach getaway from Cairo. There are several resorts and hotels along the coast of Ain Sukhna two and a half hours away from Cairo where you can swim, dive, and sunbathe in peace. There are also public beaches that tend to crowd up with picnicking Cairenes on weekends and holidays. It is possible to camp, but to find a suitable spot you need to hire or rent a car. If you plan to camp, always stay on marked public beaches because many areas are still heavily mined.

Also along this stretch of coast are the oldest monasteries in the world, those of **Saint Antony** and **Saint Paul**. Misr Travel agency arranges tours, or contact the Coptic Patriarchate (*Tel. 02/960-360*) if you wish to make arrangements for staying overnight. If you have transportation, it's a feasible day trip from Cairo. For details about hotels and directions, see the *Red Sea Coast* chapter.

Faiyoum Oasis

Located 100 kilometers southwest of Cairo, the picturesque Faiyoum oasis with its waterwheels, water falls, and Middle Kingdom pyramids, makes a pleasant day or overnight trip from Cairo if you have your own transportation. There is plenty of public transport to Faiyoum city, but it's an eyesore with little access to the sites and reaching the attractions by public transport can be more trouble than it's worth.

Among the attractions are the ruins of the ancient Greek city of Karanis, the "Collapsed Pyramid" of Maidum, and the waterfalls of Wadi Riyan. See the "Faiyoum" section of Chapter 15 for details.

PRACTICAL INFORMATION

Airlines

• **Air France**, 2 *Talaat Harb Street, Talaat Harb Square. Tel. 02/574-3300, 574-3465, 574-3479, 574-3516*

• **Air Sinai**, 12 *Kasr El Nil Street. Tel. 02/760-948, 772-2949*

• **Alitalia**, *Nile Hilton Commercial Center, Tahrir Square. Tel. 02/578-5823/ 4/5/6. Fax 02/779-903. Airport Tel. 02/418-8168/9*

• **American Airlines**, 20 *El Gehad Street, Mohandiseen. Tel. 02/299-0222. Fax 02/299-02302*

• **British Airways**, 1 *Abdel Salam Aref Street. Tel. 578-0741/2/3. Fax 578-0739. Airport Tel. 417-5681/2*

• **Delta**, 17 *Ismail Mohamed Street, Zamalek. Tel. 02/342-0861. Fax 02/341-9626*

• **El Al Airlines**, 5 *El Maqrizi Street, Zamalek. Tel. 02/341-620, 3408912, 341-1429*

• **Gulf Air**, 64 *Gamaat El Dowal El Arabia Street. Tel. 02/348-7781/2/3. Fax 02/349-0955*

• **Iberia Airlines**, 15 *Tahrir Square. Tel. 02/578-9955-578-9716. Fax 02/761-988. Airport Tel. 02/761-988*

• **KLM Royal Dutch Airlines**, 11 *Kasr El Nil Street. Tel. 02/574-7004/5/6. Airport Tel. 02/418-2386*

• **Lufthansa Airlines**, 6 *El Sheikh El Marsafly Street, Zamalek. Tel.02/393-3015. Airport Tel. 02/666-975*

• **Royal Jordanian**, 6 *Kasr El Nil Street. Tel. 02/337-5905, 575-0614 Zamalek Club Building, 26 July Street, Mohandiseen. Tel. 02/344-3144, 346-7540*

• **SAS Scandanavian Airlines System**, 2 *Champollion Street. Tel. 02/575-3955/627/546/718*

• **Saudi Arabian Airlines**, 5 *Kasr El Nil Street. Tel. 02/574-1200, 574-7388/ 94. 10 Talaat Harb Street. Tel. 02/574-7575. Zamalek Club Building on Gamaat El Dowal El Arabia Street, Mohandiseen. Tel. 02/ 346-0757*

• **Trans World Airlines (TWA)**, 1 *Kasr El Nil Street. Tel. 02/574-9904/8. Airport Tel. 02/244-1050*

• **United Airlines**, *Bon Voyage offices, 42 Abdel Khalek Tharwat Street. Tel. 02/390-8099, 390-5090. 16 Adly Street. Tel. 02/ 391-1950. Airport Tel. 02/245-5099, 245-2116 ext. 7218*

American Express

American Express exchanges currency and traveler's cheques. As a travel agency it handles airline reservations, car rentals, tour bookings, and other sightseeing arrangements. Half day tours available to Old (Coptic) Cairo; Egyptian Museum; Memphis and Saqqara; and the Pyramids and Sphinx for about $20 each person.

Listed below are American Express offices in Cairo:
- **Giza Headquarters**, *21 Giza Street, Giza. Tel 02/567-2304/5/6/7. Fax 02/ 570-2665*
- **Nile Hilton Hotel**, *Tahrir Square. Tel. 02/578-001/2. Fax 02/578-5003*
- **Downtown Cairo**, *15 Kasr El Nil Street, Tel. 02/574-7991/96. Fax 02/574-7997*
- **Zamalek-Marriott Hotel**, *Tel. 02/340-6542/6855. Fax 02/ 342-0136*
- **Heliopolis**, *72 Omar Ibn Khattab Street. Tel. 02/418-2144/5/6/7. Fax 02/ 290-9157*
- **Mohandiseen**, *4 Syria Street. Tel. 02/337-7908/914. Fax 02/337-7912*

Banks & Currency Exchange

Upon arrival at **Cairo International Airport**, you will come across a slew of bank windows and stalls including Bank of Alexandria, Banque Misr, Thomas Cook, and others. A good place to start, these banks will change at essentially the same rate as anywhere else, so there's no reason not change here. Otherwise major hotels of four stars and up should have currency exchange bureaus. Most will change traveler's cheques with a commission charge of one or two percent and make cash advances on Visa and MasterCard. Keep in mind, buying back dollars can be a hassle and expensive so don't change more money than you will spend.

In downtown Cairo, there are 24 hour exchange facilities and ATM's in the Nile Hilton, Intercontinental, and the Cairo Sheraton.

Car Rentals

Should you be brave, able, and willing enough to drive in Cairo and Egypt, there are no shortage of car s available for rent. Remember that should your country's license be recognized by Egypt, you may drive with it for one month. After that, you may only drive with an international or an Egyptian license. Rental rates generally run from $40-$150 per day, including 100 free kilometers, depending on the type of car. Fiats, Hyundai's, etc., are usually cheapest, while Mercedes and four wheel all terrain vehicles are most expensive.

Listed in the sidebar on the next page are major car rental outlets; for more extensive listings, check the *Yellow Pages*.

CAR RENTAL COMPANIES IN CAIRO

Budget
• *Headquarters, Zamalek. Tel. 02/340-0070, 340-9474, 340-2565. Fax 02/341-3790*
• *Marriott Hotel & Casino in Zamalek. Tel. 02/340-8888*
Cairo International Airport. Tel. 02/265-2395

Hertz
(offers car rentals and chauffeur driven cars)
• *Central Reservations Office, 195, 26th July Street in El Agouza, Giza. Tel. 02/347-4172, 347-2238, 303-4241. Fax 344-6627*
• *Ramses Hilton Hotel on Corniche El Nil Street. Tel. 02/574-4400, 575-8000*
• *Semiramis Intercontinental Hotel on Corniche El Nil Street. Tel. 02/ 354-3239, 357-1847*
• *Cairo International Airport . Tel. 02/265-2430*
• *Forte Grande Hotel, Alexandria Road, Giza. Tel. 02/383-0383, 383-0772, ext. 4089*
• *Sonesta Hotel. Tel. 02/262-8111, 261-7100*

M. Hafez Co.
(offers car rentals, with or without chauffeur)
• *#4A, Haroun Street, Dokki, Giza. Tel. 02/360-0542, 348-6652.Fax 02/348-1105*

Limo 1 Rent a Car
(offers car rentals and chauffeur limousine services)
• *159, 26th July Street, Zamalek. Tel. 02/340-5920, 340-4817*

Thrifty Rent a Car
• *Headquarters at 1, El Entesar Street, behind the Sheraton in Heliopolis. Tel.02/266-3313. Fax, same*
• *Cairo International Airport. Tel. 02/291-4255/66/77; ext. 2620*
• *Novotel at Cairo International Airport. Tel. 02/291-8520/77; ext. 261*
• *Sofitel, Corniche El Nil, Maadi. Tel. 02/350-6092/3; ext. 1656*

Counseling

Alcoholics Anonymous & Al-Anon, *Community Services Association, Road 21 Maadi. Tel. 350-5284, 376-8283. Call for meeting times and locations.*

Couriers

• **Federal Express**, *Cairo hot lines 02/357-1304 & 02/351-6070;* Head Office, *1079 Corniche El Nile in Garden City. Tel. 02/355-1063, 357-0427;* Mohandiseen, *24 Syria Street Tel. 02/349-0986, 360-1276;* Maadi, *31 Golf Street Tel. 02/351-6070;* Heliopolis, *21 Mohamed Ghoneim Street Tel. 02/290-7333, 291-3410*

• **DHL**, Garden City, *2 Gamal El Din Abu El Mahassen Street. Tel. 02/355-7118 or 355-7301;* Mohandiseen, *16 Lebanon Street. Tel. 02/302-9801;* Heliopolis, *35 Ismail Ramzy Street. Tel. 02/246-0324;* Maadi, *43 Road 6. Tel. 375-2363 or 375-8900*

• **I.T.C.**, *17 Mahmoud Bassiouni Street. Tel. 02/575-9102/3.*

• **SOS Sky International**, *45 Shehab Street, Mohandiseen. Tel. 02/346-2503.*

• **TNT Skypak**, *33 Dokki Street, Dokki. Tel. 02/348-8204, 348-7228.*

• **United Parcel Service (UPS)**; Downtown, *19 Adly Street. Tel. 02/390-8099, 390-7669;* Heliopolis, *25 Ibrahim Street Tel. 02/259-1945, 259-1311;* Maadi, *2 Mustafa Kamel Street Tel. 02/350-1160.*

Cultural Centers & Institutes

Cultural centers and institutes are excellent resources for those looking to explore Egypt beyond the usual tourist attractions. They often sponsor lectures, often featuring world class academics, language courses and cultural exhibitions and events such as recitals and films.

American Center for Press and Cultural Affairs, *5 Latin American Street, Garden City. Tel. 02/354-9601. Hours: 8:30am- 4:30pm Sunday-Thursday. Operates a library and sponsors fim screenings and other cultural events.*

American Research Center in Egypt, *2 Midan Simon Bolivar, Garden City. Tel. 354-8239, 355-8683, 356-4681. Hours: 8:30am-3:30pm Sunday-Thursday. Primarily a resource for visiting scholars, ARCE sponsors lectures and fieldtrips led by top scholars. Call or drop by for info.*

Austrian Cultural Section, *5 Wissa Wassef Street, Giza. Tel. 02/570-2975. Sponsors lectures and other cultural exhibitions and events.*

British Council, *192 El Nil Street in Agouza, Giza. Tel. 303-1514, 347-6118, 344-8445. Library hours: 9am-2pm & 3-8pm Monday-Thursday. Call for information about Arabic courses, library usage, and other programs like film screenings.*

Canadian Cultural Center *(Tel. 02/354-3119) is located in the Canadian Embassy at 6 Mahammad Fahmi Al Sayed Street in Garden City.*

Egyptian Center for International Cultural Cooperation, *11 Shagar El Durr Street, Zamalek. Tel. 341-5419. Hours: 9:30am-8pm. Sponsors exhibitions, concerts, excursions, and other cultural events. Call for information.*

Egypt Exploration Society, *Tel. 02/301-0319. Sponsors lectures and expeditions to archaeological sites. Call for information.*

French Cultural Center, *1 Madressat El Haquq El Frinseya Street, Mounira. Tel. 02/354-1012, 354-7679, 354-1057, 355-3725. FCC operates a library, sponsors film screenings, and offers French language courses.*

Embassies & Consulates

Call embassies for information about visas, letters of recommendation, lost passports, or any other questions.

Australia, *World Trade Center, Corniche El Nil Street, Bulaq. Tel 02/575-0444. Fax 02/578-1638.*

Canada, *5 Midan El Sarai Kobra (behind American Embassay), Garden City. Tel. 02/354-3110. Fax 02/356-3548.*

France, *29 Murad Street, Giza. Tel. 02/570-3916-20. Fax 02/571-0276.*

Germany, *8 Hassan Sabri Street, Zamalek. Tel. 02/341-0015. Fax 02/341-0530.*

Great Britain, *7 Ahmed Rageb Street, Garden City. Tel. 02/354-0852-4. Fax 02/354-0859.*

Israel, *6 Ibn Malek Street, Giza. Tel. 02361-0380. Fax 02/361-0414.*

Italy, *15 Abdel Rahman Fahmi Street, Garden City. Tel. 02/354-3194/5. Fax 02/354-0657.*

Palestine, *33 El Nahda Street, Dokki. Tel. 02/360-2997/8. Fax 02/360-2996.*

Saudi Arabia, *2 Ahmed Nessim Street, Giza. Tel. 02/349-0775. Fax 02/349-3495.*

Syria, *18 Abdel Rahman Street. Tel. 02/337-7020. Fax 02/335-8232.*

Tunisia, *26 El Gezira Street, Zamalek. Tel. 02/341-8962. Fax 02/341-2479.*

Turkey, *25 El Falaki Street, Bab El Louk. Tel. 02/356-3318. Fax 02/355-8110.*

United Arab Emirates, *4 Ibn Sina Street, Giza. Tel. 02/360-9722. Fax 02/570-0844.*

United States, *5 America El Latiniya, Garden City. Tel. 02/355-7371. Fax 02/357-2300.*

Emergencies
• Ambulance *Tel. 123*
• Fire, *Tel. 125;* Tahrir Station, Downtown, *Tel. 02/391-0466, 391-0715; ext. 260;* Giza, *Tel. 02/361-0257/8;* Gezirah (Zamalek), *Tel. 02/341-9966, 340-2664;* Heliopolis, *Tel. 02/243-0954;* Maadi, *Tel. 350-0183*

• **Hospitals: El Salam International Hospital**, *on the Corniche to Maadi south of downtown. Tel. 02/363-8050, 363-4196.* One of the most respected private hospitals in Cairo; **Cairo Medical Center**, *Higaz Street off Midan Roxi in Heliopolis. Tel. 02/258-1003.*
• **Police Emergency**, *Tel. 122*

Language Classes

Listed below are some the major institutions running **Arabic language courses**, both colloquial and Modern Standard (reading and writing). For private tutors, check the adds in local English language publications such as *The Middle East Times, Egypt Today, Cairo Times,* and *The Egyptian Gazette.* For courses in other languages, your best bet is to contact with the cultural centers listed above. For example, should you want to take French lessons, get in touch with the French Cultural Center. For Arabic, the British Council has an excellent reputation as does the American University in Cairo. Again, you can also read the ads in the aforementioned publications for other options.

News & Media

In the old days, it was the *Egyptian Gazette*, it's equivalent English news on Egyptian television (Channel 2), or if you were lucky you could use a short-wave radio to pipe in the *BBC's World Service*. Today major newsstands and luxury hotels carry any or all of *The International Herald Tribune, USA Today, TIME, Newsweek, The Economist, US News & World Report*; as well as style magazines-*Vogue* and the like- and an assortment of British, French, and German publications. Locally produced magazines like *Egypt Today, Alive, NiteLife,* cover local issues and goings on.

Four and five star hotels nearly all have satellite television which usually includes CNN, CNBC, a sports channel, and perhaps Turner's Cartoon Network and other movie and entertainment stations.

Passports & Visas

Visas can be extended *on the second floor of the Mogamma in Tahrir Square between 9am and 2pm daily Sunday-Thursday. A six month extension costs LE18 and if you're lucky, not more than half an hour of your time.*

Post Services

Central Post Office, *Ataba Square. Hours: 9am-7pm daily except for Friday when it opens 8am-noon. There are hundreds of other branches throughout the city, but public post offices tend to be crowded and difficult to figure, so you may consider buying stamps from your hotel. If they do not sell, them, try the bookstore in the Hilton.*

Telephone, Fax, & Telex

24 hour telephone centrale, *Ramses Station; Tahrir Square; Salah Eddin Square; Cairo International Airport; Abbassia Square; 26 July Street in Zamalek; 19 Alfi Street downtown; and El Manial Street on Rhoda Island.* When asking directions, ask for telephone 'centrale.' These offices sell calling cards and place domestic and international calls, as well as faxes and telexes.

Hotels of three stars or more should be able to place international calls from your room and many have business centers offering fax, telex, and telegram services.

Thomas Cook

The company and namesake of Egypt's first major tour operator has offices throughout Cairo and Egypt. Currency and traveler's cheques exchange, individual and group package tours for in and out of Egypt, day tours around Cairo, and basic travel agency services are available at Thomas Cook. Below are the complete listings for the Greater Cairo:

• **Downtown Cairo** - *17 Mohammed Bassiouni Street. Tel. 02/ 574-3955. Fax 02/762-750*
• **Cairo International Airport** - *Windows are open 24 hours and located in the arrival and departure halls in the international terminal. Tel. 02/ 291-4255. Fax 02/291-6378*
• **Mohandiseen** - *26th July Street. Tel. 02/346-7187. Fax 02/303-4530*
• **Heliopolis** - *Heliopolis Club on El Mirghani Street. Tel. 02/677-239*

Travel Agencies

American Express, *See "American Express" above.*

Belle Epoque, *17 Tunis Street, New Maadi. Tel. 02/352-24775. Fx. 02/ 353-6114. Operates the only luxury cruises in Lake Nasser-well worth while.*

Blue Sky Travel, *14 Champollion Street. Tel. 02/574-4566. Fax 02/ 7740907. Specializes in Red Sea and Sinai travel including dive trips and desert safaris.*

Bon Voyage Egypt, *16 Adly Street. Tel. 02/390-5090, 390-7669. Fax. 02/ 391-1104.*

Eastmar Travel, *13 Kasr El Nil Street. Tel. 574-5024/34/56. Fax. 02574-3482. Specializes in moderately priced Nile Cruises.*

Gaz Tours, *7 Bustan Street. Tel. 02/575-9711, 575-2782. Fax. 02/578-9825.*

Karnak Travel, *12 Kasr El Nil Street. Tel. 02/575-0600, 575-0868. Fax. 02/762-744. EgyptAir's sister company offers extensive services including tours, Nile cruises, accommodation, and airline reservations.*

Memnon, *18 Hoda Shaarawi Street.. Tel. 02/393-0195. Fax. 02/391-7410. Specializes in Nile Cruises.*

Misr Travel, *1. Talaat Harb Street. Tel. 02/393-0010. Fax. 02/392-4440. Biggest travel agent in Egypt. Services include sightseeing tours in Cairo, Nile cruise arrangements, and package tours.*

Seti First Travel, *16 Ismail Mohamed Street, Zamalek. Tel. 02/341-9820. Fax. 02/340-2419. Megatravel agency specializing in Nile cruises.*

Tourist Information

Egyptian Tourist Authority, *Misr Travel Tower (headquarters), Abbassia Square. Tel. 02/285-4509, 284-1970. Fax 02/285-4363;* **Adly Street,** *off Opera Square downtown. Tel. 02/391-3454;* **Ramses Station,** *Ramses Square. Tel. 02/764-214.*

Travel agencies and hotel personnel are generally good sources of information about anything relating to transportation, tours, accommodations or directions.

14. THE NILE VALLEY

Amidst the vast deserts of North Africa, the **Nile** not only enabled humankind to survive, but gave birth to and shaped one the world's first and most successful civilizations. Indeed, by the time Herodotus termed Egypt, "the gift of the Nile" 2,500 years ago, a civilization had already been thriving on the river's banks for more than 30 centuries. To the ancient Egyptians the river was likened to a lotus plant; the Delta was the flower, and the narrow valley the stem. This stem was, and remains, the heartland of the Egyptian nation, known to the ancients as **Kemet**.

With virtually no rainfall, Egyptians in Kemet depended on the annual floods of the Nile fueled by monsoon rains at the river's headwaters 1,500 miles to the south in Ethiopia. Though the floods killed hundreds, sometimes thousands annually, the Egyptians welcomed, even worshipped them for the life they gave, and every year in August and September the inundation was greeted by great religious festivals like the Opet Feast in Thebes. During winter and spring they planted and harvested their crops and then rested during the heat of the summer, before the cycle started over. This way of life continued through 3,000 years of pharaonic rule, Persian, Greek, Roman and Arab occupations, before the construction of the High Dam in 1969 ended the floods forever.

The Nile enabled Egyptians to develop a settled way of life and the confined geography of its valley enabled their rulers to build the world's first centralized nation state. This pharaonic state survived in some form through nearly 30 dynasties over 3,000 years and enjoyed enough wealth that its rulers were able to build great empires in the Near East, and erect massive temples to honor their gods and lavish tombs to commemorate themselves. These temples and tombs are the main attraction for travelers today, though the scenic beauty of the Nile Valley and the timeless way of life of its inhabitants are equally intriguing.

Travelers have a choice in how to approach travel in the Nile Valley. Most head straight to Luxor to visit the Karnak and Luxor Temples and the royal crypts in the Valley of the Kings. If they have time they may work their way down to Aswan and the colossal temple at Abu Simbel stopping en route to visit the temples at Esna, Edfu, and Kom Ombo. Those with extra time may wish to explore the less beaten paths of Middle Egypt between Cairo and Qena where the provinces of Minya, Assiut, and Sohag contain some of Egypt's most important Coptic sites and some interesting pharaonic attractions as well such as Akhenaten's city at Tel El Amarna.

In recent years Middle Egypt has been increasing passed over because of frequent clashes between Islamic militants and government security forces and sometimes Copts as well.

Traveling in Upper Egypt

Coming from Cairo, there are choices to be made regarding transportation. Flying is quick (1 hour Cairo-Luxor), but expensive ($150 one-way) and doesn't allow you to view the colorful countryside the way the train does. The train is cheap (LE82 Cairo-Luxor) and comfortable, but takes a bit of time (10 hours Cairo-Luxor). Buses are the cheapest way to travel, but are slower and far less comfortable than trains. Once you get down to Upper Egypt, buses become more viable because the trips are rarely more than a few hours (4 hours Luxor-Aswan) while trains are less frequent and efficient. You can also ride the zippy public taxis known as service which are faster and cheaper than buses (4 hours Luxor-Aswan, LE7).

Land travel is practical and even scenic but Upper Egypt offers travelers the best opportunities to explore the Nile itself. Beginning at $60 a day, **Nile cruises** between 3-7 days afford you a leisurely and comfortable setting from which to enjoy the Nile and the picturesque surrounding countryside. Between Luxor and Aswan, these cruises stop daily at attractions en route like the temples at Esna, Edfu, and Kom Ombo. Reservations can be made through travel agents in the US or Europe or from any travel agency in Cairo, Luxor, Aswan, Alexandria, and even Sinai. See "Getting Around Section" in Chapter 6 at the beginning of the book for more details.

A cheaper and more rustic way to travel the Nile is by **felucca**. For about LE30 per person per day you sail down the Nile from Aswan to Kom Ombo, Edfu, Esna, and Luxor taking in the temples while enjoying the serenity of the river and the timeless beauty of its banks. See the Aswan section for details.

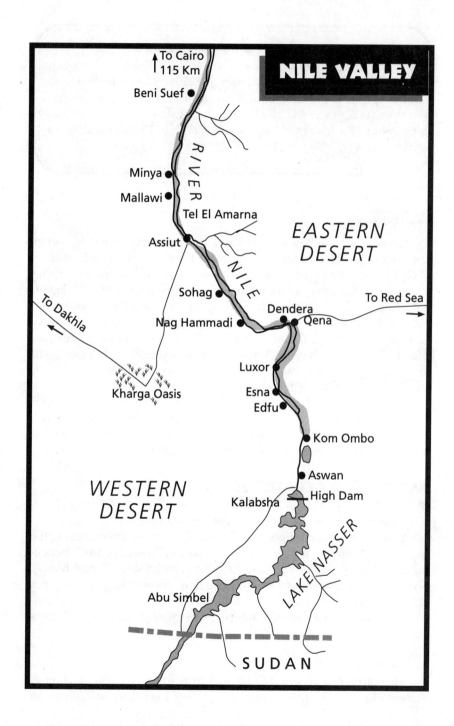

A GUIDE TO UPPER EGYPT

*There are oodles of books and guides for Upper Egypt many of which are excellent, however, we'd recommend, Jill Kamil's **Guide to the Monuments of Upper Egypt**. Published by Longman Press, and widely available throughout Egypt, it is a pocketsize book with concise but detailed and insightful descriptions of the monuments of the Nile Valley from Minya to Abu Simbel.*

MINYA

Known for its well-groomed Corniche, fine views of the Nile, and its easy pace of life, **Minya** makes an agreeable break from the tourist Meccas of Cairo and Upper Egypt. It is also the most convenient base for visiting a myriad of historical monuments spread throughout Middle Egypt, including vividly decorated Middle Kingdom tombs at **Beni Hassan**, the ruins of the short lived capital of Akhenaten at **Tel El Amarna**, the spooky catacombs at **Tuna El Gebel**, and some of the most important Christian sites in all of Egypt. They don't rival the great monuments of Upper Egypt or Cairo in size or scale, but are unique and tell some of the most offbeat, and fascinating, tales of Egyptian history.

The town itself offers little in the way of historical attractions, and is primarily a provincial capital and hub for surrounding villages and farms. However, its beautiful Corniche and the fading glory of its colonial buildings make it bearable, if not outright attractive.

ARRIVALS & DEPARTURES

By Bus

Minya's bus station is two hundred meters south of the train station.

Cheap buses depart hourly to Cairo (LE10-12, 4-5 hours) during the day but the ride is bumpy and the buses spartan. There are also frequent buses to Assiut (LE4, 2-3 hours), Beni Suef, and Sohag (LE6, 4 hours). Sometimes there is a bus to Hurghada and in summer there is a daily bus direct to Alexandria (LE20, 7-8 hours).

From Cairo, buses depart hourly from Qulali Station near Ramses (LE12, 4-5 hours).

By Service

Minibuses from **Cairo** (LE6) depart from the *service* depot at Ramses Station while in Minya, they come and go from a small depot underneath the bridge several hundred meters south of the train station. Most minibuses headed south go as far as **Assiut** (LE4), passing through **Abu Qurqas** and **Malawi** (both LE1). You probably won't have trouble hitching a ride further south and in any case Assiut makes for easy connections to **Sohag**, **Qena**, some times **Luxor**, and the oases of **Kharga** and **Dakhla**.

By Train

Minya's train station is on Saad Zaghloul Street in the center of town.

No less than a dozen trains run between **Cairo** (from Ramses Station and Giza) and Minya daily but the authorities often restrict foreigners to the three daily "Espani". First class costs LE42; second class, LE30. Moving **south** to Assiut, Sohag, Qena, Luxor, and Aswan, the same policy is applied. Inquire at your hotel or at the station for schedule and fare information.

ORIENTATION

Most restaurants, shops, and hotels are within several hundred meters of the train station along **El Gomhuriya Street** which links **Midan Mahatta** (Station Square) with the Nile. About halfway between the station and the river, **Tahrir Square** is a popular hangout spot and sprouting from it are north-south streets as Sultan Hussein which buzz with commercial activity and are lined with small eateries. Along **Corniche El Nil Street**, which believe it or not runs along the Nile, lovers, families, and friends congregate in shaded green lawns, overlooking a serene river and the desert cliffs that rise above the narrow east bank. Also on the Corniche are several banks and government offices including the Minya Governorate headquarters.

Several kilometers south of El Gomhuriya Street's intersection with the Corniche, the **Minya Bridge** links the east and west banks and on summer evenings becomes a favorite meeting spot. Along the train tracks runs **Saad Zaghloul Street** where the post office, telephone centrale, and the bus and minibus stations are located. On the west side of the tracks, the **Ibrahimiya Canal** is the proverbial "tracks" on the other side of which charming colonial Minya gives way to modern concrete working class neighborhoods. Parallel to the tracks and Saad Zaghloul on the other side of the canal, **El Burgaya Street** is Minya's main road link to the south and towns like Malawi, Abu Qurqas and Assiut.

GETTING AROUND TOWN

While visiting most sites requires a half day excursion and a combination of water and motor transport, walking does just fine within town.

Virtually nothing of interest or concern is more than a five or ten minute stroll away and besides, it gives you best opportunity to enjoy Minya's street life and people which even by Egyptian standards are well dispositioned. Furthermore, since Minya is not a tourist trap like Luxor or Aswan, you needn't fear that every person who approaches you has some ulterior motive other than genuine interest or curiosity. The Corniche is especially pleasant for an evening stroll.

Should you need other transportation, to carry luggage for example, **taxis** are readily available and your hotel will assist you in hailing gone. Another viable option is the **kaleche**, the old fashion horse drawn carriage, especially enjoyable for clip clopping up and the down the Corniche. Neither taxis nor a kaleche should cost more than LE2-3 for each 10 minutes. To reach outlying villages, head to the pick-up depot 200 meters south of the bus station, from which trucks and minivans regularly depart. For visiting the sites, check individual listings.

WHERE TO STAY

THE MERCURE GRAND HOTEL, *Corniche El Nile Street 3 kilometers north of El Gomhuriya Street. Tel. 068/341-515/6/7. Fax 068/326-467. Capacity: 96 rooms. Rates: $44-50 single, $54-61 double. Credit Cards: Visa, Mastercard.*

The only establishment approaching international standards, the Mercure overlooks the Corniche, the Nile, and its own well-groomed gardens. The rooms are air conditioned and feature private baths, dish television, a fridge and phone. Other facilities include two restaurants, a tennis court, and a pool. Catering primarily to business types and package tours, it's definitely the finest hotel in Minya but by any other standards it's nothing particularly special.

THE AKHENATON HOTEL, *Corniche El Nil Street several blocks south of El Gomhuriya Street. Tel. 086/325-918. Rates: LE40-79 singles & doubles.*

Though it is clean and the views of the Nile are fine, the Akhenaton lacks flavor and character. Rooms come with nice balconies, a private bath, air-conditioning, and television. The restaurant is overpriced and bland, both in food and atmospherics.

THE LOTUS HOTEL, *Saad Zaghoul Street several blocks north of the train station. Tel. 086/324-500, 324-541, 324-545. Fax 086/324-576. Capacity: 45 rooms. Rates: LE40 single, LE50 double.*

The Lotus is a friendly two star establishment offering simple, but functional rooms with air-conditioning that isn't quite as powerful as it might be. What cheesy and bland decor subtracts from the atmosphere is easily made up for by the friendly service and the colorful crowds which turn up every night at the bar-cafeteria on the roof. Proximity to the railroad translates into lots of noise and a modest hike to reach the Nile. Rooms come with a private bath, air-conditioning, and television.

THE BEACH HOTEL, *El Gomhuriya Street a block from the Corniche. Tel. 086/322-307, 323-117. Capacity: 32 rooms. Rates: LE15-30 single, LE25-40 double.*

A homey pension, the Beach Hotel is for those in need of simple comfort and modest prices. Rooms with or without air-conditioning and private showers are available. Rates include breakfast (cream cheese and bread) in a cafeteria most notable for the Nile view. The staff is friendly but management can be maddening when they try to sell you a single for LE50 or a double LE70.

WHERE TO EAT

Except for the continental offerings at the **Mercure Hotel**, you're limited to the usual Egyptian fare: fuul, ta'amiya, roasted chicken, kebabs and so on. There are no less than a half dozen popular eateries in Mahatta Square by the train station, the most popular of which is **Abu Galal** situated where El Gomhuriya Street begins. El Hussein Street, off Tahrir Square is also littered with popular restaurants and food stalls.

Two blocks south of Tahrir Square, **El Badiya**, recognizable by its red sign and trimmings (the sign is in Arabic), specializes in grilled chicken and kebab. Just across the street a small **fitari** whips ups pizza like pancakes, sweet or savory, for a couple pounds a pie.

SEEING THE SIGHTS

Minya's historical attractions include a smattering of pharaonic, Christian, and Greco-Roman sites, that will not overwhelm you with their size and scope, but are fascinating and unique if not downright weird. The most important, **Tel El Amarna** was the short-lived capital city of Akhenaten, who turned the New Kingdom world on its head by rejecting the traditional polytheistic pantheon of gods and cults in favor of the monotheistic Cult of Aten. The other major pharaonic site, **Beni Hassan**, features more than three dozen tombs (four are open to the public) of Middle Kingdom nobles that contain vivid depictions of everyday life in ancient Egypt while in the strange and spooky catacombs at **Tuna El Gebel**, hundreds of mummified baboons and ibises, manifestations of the scribe god, Thoth, are buried in a maze-like underground necropolis. Nearby, the once grand temple of Hermopolis stood on what ancient Egyptians believed to have been the site of universe's creation. Today, all that remains are two castrated baboon colossi.

North of Minya, the Roman era temple at **Tehna El Gebel** is spectacularly set in cliffs overlooking the Nile Valley and reflects an interesting mix of Roman and pharaonic religious and artistic traditions while **Deir El Adhra** (Monastery of the Virgin) is one of Middle Egypt's most important Coptic sites. It comes to life in early June when tens of thousands of pilgrims flock to the small village and church for the Feast of the Virgin Mary. Closer to the town itself are two minor attractions, the local cemeteries of **Zawiyet El Mayateen** with its thousands of domed mausoleums, and the small **Church of Aba Hur**.

The historical attractions in the vicinity of Minya are spread throughout the countryside to the north and south, making it difficult to cover all of them in one day or even two. This is especially true if you intend to use public transportation which to say the least, is not tourist friendly. It's far more efficient to hire a private taxi or to arrange private transport through a travel agency. Hotels can usually arrange a driver and more times than not will set you up with Joseph, an English speaking free lance travel broker who can arrange a car and driver for about LE100 a day. This is reasonable if you can split the cost amongst a group, but given that both he and the hotel will take a cut, you can negotiate a better deal bargaining directly with local taxis.

In planning your excursions, consider combining the sites south of Minya, Tel El Amarna, Beni Hassan, and possibly Tuna El Gebel and Hermopolis in one day and Tehna El Gebel and Deir El Adhra in another half day. Zawiyet El Mayateen and Church of Aba Hur can easily be tacked onto either journey.

BENI HASSAN

Twenty kilometers south of Minya & halfway to Malawi. Hours: 8am-4pm. Admission: LE12 general, LE6 students. Each person will be charged an additional LE7.50 for the ferry and minibus. The gatekeeper might expect baksheesh-LE1 or 2 is appropriate.

To reach Beni Hassan by public transportation take a bus or service to the town of Abu Qurqas and catch another service 3 kilometers to the Nile ("El Nil" in Arabic). Tickets need to be purchased at the booth before taking the ferry to the east bank where a minibus and a half dozen armed escorts will take you up to the path to the site. The tombs themselves are two hundred meters up a moderately steep hill.

Though hardly spectacular, the 40 tombs at Beni Hassan are fascinating and important. Constructed during the 11th (2133-1991 BC) and 12th dynasties (1991-1786 BC) they represent a transitional stage in tomb architecture between the mastabas and pyramids built on and above the earth's surface during the Old Kingdom and the deep subterranean tombs of the New Kingdom. Built by and for regional governors and nobles, these tombs feature reliefs that differ slightly from those found in royal tombs. While pharaohs' tombs were almost entirely preoccupied with theological themes such as relations between pharaoh and deities and death and the afterlife, these provincial reliefs paint a vivid picture of everyday life in the Middle Kingdom.

Of the four tombs open to the public, the southernmost tomb of **Kheti** (#17), is usually the first shown to visitors. Kheti was an 11th Dynasty *gnomarch* (provincial governor) and son of Baquet III (whose tomb is next door). Immediately to the left upon entrance are animate wall reliefs portraying hunting and papyrus harvesting as well as scenes of weavers, craftsmen, and entertainers. Kheti, always the largest and most prominent figure, and his wife can be seen enjoying a musical recital and receiving offerings and gifts. On the rear wall, the reliefs assume a more violent tone as wrestlers are portrayed in a variety of positions (a Beni Hassan hallmark), while below Kheti invades an enemy stronghold. Moving clockwise from the rear wall to the southern wall, the emphasis of the carvings reverts to domestic themes and reliefs depict agricultural activities like wine making, farming, and cattle herding. Just south of the door, are some interesting images of cargo ships on the Nile.

Just north of Kheti's tomb, is that of his father, **Baquet III** (#15), also a gnomarch. On the northern and southern walls reliefs portray economic and agricultural activity, tax collecting and cattle herding on the southern wall; harvesting and river scenes on the northern. As in Kheti's tomb, the rear wall features hundreds of wrestlers putting a vast assortment of moves on each other.

About 200 meters north of Baquet's crypt is the 12th Dynasty tomb of **Khnum Hotep** (#3). While most of the reliefs feature more of the same (agriculture, tax collecting, citizens brown-nosing the tomb's proprietor) there are two particularly interesting sets of reliefs. Just left of the entrance on the western wall, Khnum Hotep is seen performing the pharaonic equivalent of the Muslim's haj to Mecca – a pilgrimage to the great temple of Osiris at Abydos. Preparations for the voyage to Abydos (a 200 kilometer jaunt), and embarking on the journey itself are shown on the southern wall. Unlike the other three tombs open to the public at Beni Hassan, this one does not feature wrestling on its rear wall but rather impressive murals with lively hunting and fishing scenes.

The northernmost and final tomb (#2) is that of Khnum Hotep's predecessor, **Amemenhet**. Besides engaging in activities typical of a provincial official like tax collection, hunting, and in typical Beni Hassan fashion, wrestling (in its rightful position on the rear wall), Amemenhet is seen making a pilgrimage to Abydos in front of the niche at the tomb's rear. Those who spend a good deal of time in the kitchen will enjoy the tomb's southeastern corner where the murals feature fascinating scenes of bread baking and a fish barbecue.

TEL EL AMARNA

Tel El Amarna is almost 60 kilometers south of Minya, half way to Assiut and 12 kilometers past Malawi. The site is open 8am-5pm. Flash photography is prohibited inside the tombs.

Drivers who work with tourists know the site, but should you need to give directions, you want to turn east off the main road towards the Nile at Kafr El Khozm village. At the Nile 3 kilometers north of the village of Deir El Mawass is a ferry that can accommodate cars to the village of El Til where tickets are purchased tickets (LE12 general admission, LE6 students) for entrance to the northern tombs, and transportation (usually a tractor). To visit ruins other than the northern tombs requires a private vehicle and local drivers will demand a hefty amount of baksheesh because technically everything except the northern tombs are off limits. Given that there isn't much to see anyway because the monuments were almost entirely destroyed in antiquity, only the most gung ho Egyptology buffs will want to make the effort.

History

For a brief 20 years, an unseemly looking pharaoh named **Akhenaten** (1379-1362), with his beautiful wife **Nefertiti** alongside, turned upside down over 2,000 years of Egyptian ideological and theological tradition by discarding the traditional pantheon of deities and cults in favor of a single god, **Aten**. Dubbed by some (notably the Egyptian Ministry of Tourism) "the world's first monotheist," Akhenaten pursued his experiment at Tel El Amarna where he constructed, but did not finish, a royal capital complete with temples, palaces, military barracks and gardens.

Artistically, he abandoned the self-glorification of his predecessors who idealistically portrayed themselves as superhuman deities, and instead encouraged artists to portray him in his natural form with all his physical imperfections, from the sagging pot belly and skinny legs to the thick neck and bulging buttocks. He also allowed himself to be depicted engaging in perfectly normal, but menial human activities like eating and vomiting that were certainly off limits in traditional pharaonic art.

Born **Amenhophis IV**, Akhenaten was something of a chip off the old block. His father, **Amenhophis III**, began defying pharaonic convention when he made as his chief queen, **Tiy**, a Nubian concubine. He then depicted himself in steles and monuments in a realistic fashion, including his rather large belly, breaking with the tradition portraying divine kings as physically supreme. He also began to revere the sun-disc deity, Aten, though he did not make it the sole deity. Upon Amenhophis III's death, the details of the transfer of power remain in doubt. Some believe that Amenhophis IV ruled jointly with his mother, Queen Tiy, while others maintain that he ascended the throne by himself immediately. In any case, the heir was certainly still young, an adolescent at most, and Tiy retained a position of influence well into his reign. After Amenhophis IV came of age and married his stunningly beautiful wife **Nefertiti**, she too became an important partner, assuming an unprecedented Hillary Clinton-like role in the decision making process.

Barely five years into his rule, Amenhophis IV made his conversion, and that of the nation, to **Aten** total, barring worship of traditional gods and destroying their idols. Aten, represented as sun disc from which individual rays extended, was not a novel concept, and that of worshipping the sun goes back to earliest periods of Egyptian history. Indeed, according to tradition, the Pharaoh was considered the 'son of the sun,' and during the Old Kingdom, the cult of the sun god Atum had been dominant while the most important cult during the New Kingdom, that of the Theban deity Amun, was also solar oriented.

Both Amenhophis III and Thutmosis IV (Amenhophis III's father) had paid homage to the newer form of Aten, but without replacing the Theban Triad (Amun, Min, and Khnum) or other traditional gods like Osiris. Amenhophis IV, who at this time changed his name to Akhenaten, meaning 'Splendor of Aten', made Aten the sole god of Egypt, thus ushering in the novel concept of **monotheism**. In completing his break with the Theban establishment he moved his capital to Tel El Amarna three years later.

The conversion to Aten meant a complete change in approach to both religion and government. Worship of traditional deities was banned and no longer were the priests of important cults, most notably the Theban Triad, able to wield the influence and power they previously enjoyed, and the **army** also saw its traditional prestige diminished. For thousands of years pharaohs emphasized their martial achievements, listing with pride on their temples and tombs battles won (both real and imaginary), and peoples conquered. Under Akhenaten, this pursuit of military glory was abandoned in favor of pacifism. He severely reduced military expenditures and excluded generals upper reaches of power. That the empire inherited by Akhenaten was severely weakened during his reign, was not lost on the military establishment which fully backed the Theban counterrevolution and return to the old order that ensued Akhenaten's passing.

One of the most intriguing aspects of Akhenaten's new order was the prominent role played by his wife, **Nefertiti**, or at least until their apparent estrangement during the later years of his reign. Besides the traditional duties of loving wife and mother-which reliefs admirably portray her fulfilling-Nefertiti assumed a public role as Akhenaten's chief adviser and confidante, roles traditionally reserved for viziers and high priests. Her name was engraved in cartouches (usually reserved for pharaohs), and she was depicted participating in state functions alongside her husband.

However, towards the end of Akhenaten's reign it appears that the two had a falling out. They began living apart and Akhenaten named his son-in-law, **Smenkhkare**, as co-regent, a role previously held by Nefertiti. Smenkhkare briefly assumed the throne himself upon the death of Akhenaten, however he died shortly thereafter in mysterious circumstances as did how own successor Aye, who was followed by the legendary boy-king, Tutankhamun.

Though his background remains obscure, Tutankhamun was almost certainly originally named Tutankh*aten* and that he changed his name to revere Amun, is a testament to how quickly the nation returned to the old Amun-based order after Akhenaten's passing. For reasons mentioned above, institutions like the military, the high priesthood, and the government bureaucracy were eager to see Akhenaten's legacy vanish as quickly as possible. Hence when the young Tut became pharaoh, the power behind his throne, General **Haremheb**, was only too happy to begin a process, known as the **Theban counter-revolution** of reinstating the old order. Akhenaten's name was banished from the official annals of pharaonic history, and Tel El Amarna was abandoned and destroyed, its building stones reused in the construction of such monuments as the Temple of Karnak.

As a result, it was not until the early 20th century, when excavations began in earnest at Tel El Amarna, that historians came to realize the extent and importance of Akhenaten's revolutionary and heretical reign.

The Site Itself

As the city, palaces, and temples of Tel El Amarna were so utterly destroyed during the Theban counter-revolution, visitors are usually only shown the **Northern Tombs**, six kilometers northeast of the demolished city center. Built for high officials, they provide fascinating insight into Akhenaten's reign. Unfortunately, visitors are rarely shown the **Southern Tombs** which include Amarna's finest, that of **Aye**, one of Akhenaten's closest advisors, and what is believed to be the **royal crypt** is officially off limits.

That the sites are so spread out and barely navigable even by automobile makes covering all of them extremely difficult. Meanwhile, virtually nothing of the city itself remains except foundations, and even the best preserved reliefs in the tombs have been largely defaced with cartouches and faces chiseled away. As you'll notice when visiting the tombs, virtually none were completed, a testament to the brevity of the Aten and Tel El Amarna experiment.

The Northern Tombs

The Northern Tombs are divided into two major clusters. Tombs #1 and #2 are just under a kilometer west of Tombs #3-6, and are often not shown to visitors. As they are important and fascinating, and since you've made the effort to come this far, we'd recommend that you insist on being taken to them.

Tomb of Huya (#1)

This Tomb of Huya, Chief of the Royal Harem and Chief Steward to the Queen Mother Tiy, reveals the high degree of respect paid to family matriarch. On the southeastern wall, for example, Akhenaten gives her a personal tour of the temple built in her honor while on the southwestern wall she is seen respectfully sipping wine. Akhenaten meanwhile is, very unpharaoh-like, munching like a teenager to his heart's desire. At the rear of the first chamber, Huya can be seen receiving various honorary awards from the pharaoh. The rear niche contains an unfinished statue of Huya and a shaft in the middle chamber originally held his mummy.

Tomb of Mery Re II (#2)

Built in the later stages of Tel El Amarna's development, the tomb of Mery Re II, Chief of the Two Treasuries (one each for Upper and Lower Egypt), is significant for the light it sheds on the murky role of Akhenaten's co-regent and successor, Smenkhkare. On the rear wall, unfinished reliefs show Mery Re II receiving decoration from Smenkhkare and his wife (Akhenaten's daughter), Meritaten. All of Akhenaten's cartouches were rubbed out in favor of Smenkhkare. While it was not uncommon for pharaohs to usurp the cartouches of predecessors, that Smenkhkare did it to his patron and father-in-law begs us to question the nature of their relationship; perhaps Smenkhkare was under pressure as soon as Akhenaten died to turn his back on the Aten experiment.

Tomb of Ahmose (#3)

If it seems the least impressive of the lot, perhaps that is because it belonged to Akhenaten's chief fanner-the most important qualification for which was probably a high security clearance and good connections. It is interesting however because it contains martial scenes, a rarity in Amarna reliefs.

Tomb of Mary Re I (#4)

Given that Mery Re I held the position of high priest of Aten it is of no surprise that his tomb is one of the largest and most impressive of the lot, nor that theological matters dominate the well preserved reliefs. The bulk of the reliefs portray Akhenaten visiting the Great Temple of Aten accompanied by an entourage of family and confidantes. On the north-western wall, Akhenaten, Nefertiti, and their daughters are depicted worshipping the sun-disc in the presence of Mery Re while moving counterclockwise from the entrance, one follows his procession to the temple where the priesthood awaits (rear wall). Like most tombs at Tel El Amarna, this one is incomplete.

Tomb of Pentu (#5)

Little remains of the tomb of Pentu, Chief Physician of Tel El Amarna. The busted statue in the rear niche is supposed to be the doctor himself, but who could tell.

Tomb of Panesi (#6)

Located several hundred meters south of the tomb of Pentu, this tomb of a high priest at the Temple of Aten is interesting for its well-preserved exterior and that Copts later converted it into a Christian chapel. The reliefs to the right of the entrance depict Akhenaten and Co. worshipping above a crowd of servants.

The Royal Tomb

5.5 kilometers east of Tel El Amarna up the Wadi El Maluk. Make arrangements with your driver and officials at the ticket booth. Sometimes this tomb is closed and reaching it can take up to two hours or more if you get stuck in the sand. Baksheesh will of course be expected.

The exact arrangements for the interment of Akhenaten and his kin has never become entirely clear. This tomb, located about 5.5 kilometers east of Tel El Amarna, is believed to be that of Akhenaten himself, and probably the rest of his family. If this was the case, then Akhenaten could once again claim a first in pharaonic history. Never before had the notion of a family crypt been applied by pharaohs in ancient Egypt. However, due to the extensive damage done to the tomb by Akhenaten's successors, and the lack of identifiable mummies, it's difficult to know what the arrangements were. Some believe that members of Akhenaten's family, including his maternal grandparents and sons, were buried in the Valley of the Kings, but evidence to support this claim is also hazy.

The Southern Tombs

15 kilometers southeast of the ticket office. Officially off limits but visitable. The doorman will expect baksheesh.

Though 20 tombs are spread over several small hills, two in particular are appropriate to visit.

The Tomb of Mahu (#25)

Just as security forces are considered a crucial cog in the wheel of government in modern Egypt, so it was in pharaonic times. Mahu, the guest of honor in this particular crypt, was himself a high police official and the major motif of the reliefs in this tomb is a visit by Akhenaten and Nefertiti (in chariot) to police posts. Their guide is no less than Mahu himself. The visit begins on the wall to the right upon entrance, and continues around the room counterclockwise. Mahu can also be seen fulfilling other duties.

The Tomb of Aye (#9)

Perhaps the finest crypt in Tel El Amarna, this tomb was constructed for the multi-titled Aye. A close confidante of Akhenaten he was married to one of Nefertiti's chief ladies in waiting and was also caretaker of the pharaoh's horses. The tomb is important, not only for the quality of the reliefs, which depict Akhenaten, Nefertiti, and family, along with Aye, paying homage to Aten, but also because it contains the most complete version of the famous **Hymn to Aten**. Ironically, while Aye was a such a close and trusted advisor of Akhenaten who enjoyed the privilege of one of Tel El Amarna's most impressive tombs, this tomb was never completed and Aye was in fact buried in Thebes. After the deaths of Akhenaten and Smenkhkare, Aye loyally served Tutankhamun, the young pharaoh who presided over the Theban counter-revolution.

The City & the Great Temple of Aten

Just about a kilometer south of El Till, stood the **Great Temple of Aten**, the spiritual center and architectural highlight of Tel El Amarna. Unfortunately, very little of it remains, but before Akhenaten's successors had the opportunity to destroy it the temple stretched a mile long and contained numerous buildings within its confines. Unlike temples dedicated to traditional gods like Osiris at Abydos and Amun Ra at Karnak where the priests did their thing in extreme secrecy and idols were kept deep inside a well-guarded temple, this temple was open, literally and figuratively. Openness was critical to gain access to the rays of the sun, with which Aten was so strongly identified, and the temple and its shrines were also more open to the populace in general. Today there is little to do but gaze at what remains of the foundation, for this was surely one of the first targets of the Theban counter-revolution. An Islamic cemetery now covers much of it.

The **city** itself was just south of the Great Temple of Aten and again, little remains except for the outlines of foundations. Major buildings and institutions included the **Archives** and the **Palace** at the northern end of the city. On the eastern side of the city's main avenue, now a dusty road, stood a ceremonial palace used for state functions. On the western side, Akhenaten and family had their private residences. South of these palaces stood a smaller temple to Aten, probably for private use by the royal family. Further south, the nobility lived in large mansions or villas which included extensive gardens and pools. The poor lived still further south on the outskirts of town. It was in these residential quarters that the famous bust of Nefertiti, now in the Berlin Museum, was discovered.

About equidistant from El Till to the north, are the outlines of **Northern Palace of Nefertiti**. The best preserved structure apart from the tombs, it was Nefertiti's retreat following her apparent estrangement from Akhenaten in the later years of his reign. The most impressive remains from this palace include floor mosaics, the most impressive of which are in the Egyptian Antiquities Museum in Cairo.

Steles & the Southern Palace

A third royal palace once stood about 17 kilometers south of the city in the vicinity of the present day village, El Hawatah. It was primarily used for relaxation and pleasure by Akhenaten and Nefertiti, but there is nothing left of it today.

Around the boundaries of Tel El Amarna, various steles were carved in the cliffs. Though hard to reach, they portray Akhenaten and Nefertiti in classic poses and have been most informative to archeologists researching tale of Akhenaten and Nefertiti.

TUNA EL GEBEL & HERMOPOLIS

Twenty-five kilometers southwest of Minya and 20 kilometers northwest of Malawi. Hours: Tuna El Gebel is open daily from 9am-5pm. Admission: LE12 general; LE6 students. Cameras: LE10. Hermopolis is an open site and no tickets are required.

If Tuna El Gebel wasn't so captivating in a unique quirky kind of way, visiting these two sites, both associated with the cult of the scribe god, Thoth, would hardly be worth the trouble. However the unique network of catacombs containing hundreds of mummified baboons and ibises, justifies a visit and though nothing but a pair of giant castrated baboons remain from the site's temple, Hermopolis, it is worth a glimpse if only to recall its ancient status as the site of Creation.

THE STATUS OF TUNA EL GEBEL & HERMOPOLIS

These two sites were officially closed in 1997 for "restorations" though word on the street had it that Islamic militant strongholds in surrounding villages was the true reason. Consult the ETA office in Minya to determine its status.

Tuna El Gebel

The burial grounds for Thoth's cult, Tuna El Gebel is home to one the most bizarre sites in all of Egypt. Besides several modest crypts constructed for priests and local notables, its grounds hold miles of subterranean **catacombs** containing thousands of mummified baboons and ibises-the sacred animals of Thoth. Entered from a staircase located to the right upon entering the complex, the mazes of crypts complete with withered baboons' corpses, is downright spooky, especially when you do it alone and in the dark. Unless you're claustrophobic, take your time here and notice the mummy near the steps.

Apart from the catacombs, two tombs on the graveyard's ground level are particularly worth visiting. The **tomb of Petosiris**, a high priest of Thoth's cult early in the Ptolemeic Era (c. 300 BC), is a colorful example of the early integration of Greek and Egyptian mythology. His mummy is in the Egyptian Antiquities Museum in Cairo. Constructed for a "martyr" to the floods, the **tomb of Isadora** still holds her mummy. Continue beyond her tomb to check out the local well and its impressive waterwheel.

Hermopolis

Hermopolis, so named by Greeks because they associated Thoth with their own deity **Hermes**, was an important religious site as early as the Old Kingdom. According to an early Egyptian creation myth, Hermopolis was a primordial mound where the sun hatched from an egg laid by Thoth in his ibis form, setting in motion the cycles of the universe such as day and night, life and death. As a baboon Thoth announced the beginning of creation by shrieking, as baboons do at dawn, during the first sunrise. Two giant, formerly well endowed baboons commemorating the event are all that remains of a large temple on the site, constructed by **Ramses II**. A Ptolemeic shrine and a Coptic Church were later built here. The castratees suffered their fate at the hands of early puritanical Christians.

GEBEL EL TEIR

To reach Gebel El Teir, which is 20 kilometers north of Minya on the east banks of Nile, catch a minibus from Minya to Samalut and take the ferry or hire a taxi in Minya. During the Festival of the Virgin in early June, there is plenty of direct transport from the minibus depot in Minya to Gebel El Teir. Hours: roughly 9am-5pm. Admission: free, but a donation is appreciated.

Except for the first two weeks in June when tens of thousands of Coptic pilgrims flock here for a week of partying and prayer, Gebel El Teir is of little interest to the common tourist. Significant as a place where the Holy Family sought refuge during their flight from Herod, Gebel El Teir was the site of one of Jesus' earliest miracles. According to Coptic tradition, a large stone was collapsing on the Holy Family when the infant Jesus raised his hand to stop it, leaving a print embedded in the stone. Empress Helena, mother of Constantine ordered that a cloister be constructed here in 328 AD.

Unfortunately, the recently renovated small church now located on the site of the original cloister is hardly impressive. The main attractions are several 11th century icons depicting Saint George, the Virgin Mary, and local saints.

FESTIVAL OF THE VIRGIN MARY

Every year in early June (40 days after Coptic Easter), the sleepy town of Gebel El Teir comes to life as tens of thousands of Coptic Pilgrims congregate for a week of celebrations commemorating the Virgin Mary. By every means of transport, from donkey to Toyota pick-up, the celebrants arrive in a jovial mood, banging drums, chanting, all dressed their best clothes. For a week, most of them camp on the outskirts of the usually quiet town that transforms into a giant medieval-like carnival, for when the faithful are not busy kissing icons and baptizing their young, they pass their time enjoying the festival's many distractions. Magic shows, bumper cars, swings, and even Ferris wheels offer plenty of family amusement, and hawkers sell every religious related item from jars of holy water and colorful icons to multi-lingual Bibles and tattoos of Saint George; food and beverage stalls also abound.

Barely publicized, this huge event offers travelers an ideal opportunity to get "off the beaten track" and to experience Coptic culture and a rare public celebration of Egypt's primary minority – a segment of society, who for domestic political reasons is often kept "indoors" and out of sight from the rest of Egypt and the world.

TEHNA EL GEBEL

Tehna El Gebel is on the east bank of the Nile between Minya and Gebel El Teir and is best reached by taxi. Hours: roughly 9am until sundown. Admission: LE6.

Spectacularly built into rocky hills overlooking the verdant Nile Valley, Tehna El Gebel is a fascinating mish-mash of pharaonic Egyptian, Greek, and Roman religious and architectural traditions. After wading up a hill and through the ruins of Greco-Roman-Coptic city, you'll come to a temple dedicated to Amun and Sobek by the Roman Emperor Nero, though the entrance columns commemorate Hathor. Swing up around the cliff to the right and in the caged room, is a moth-eaten crocodile mummy. The other room contains finer reliefs of Roman and Egyptian priests carrying out religious rites. For extra *baksheesh*, the guard will escort you another hundred meters or so to a cache containing several statues, including one of Bastet, the feline-avenger goddess.

ZAWIYET EL MAYATEEN & DEIR ABA HUR

Four kilometers south of Minya on the Nile's east bank near the village of El Sawadah, are the thousands of domed mausoleums that make up Zawiyet El Mayateen, "the Corner of the Dead" – Minya's necropolis. The impressive sea of domes is best viewed from the higher ground of the cliff-side edge of the necropolis which also offers great views of the Nile Valley itself. This also gives you an excuse to explore the mazes of alleys which lend the necropolis the feel of a medieval city. Among the most impressive burial complexes is that of **Hoda Sha'arawi**, widely considered the most important Egyptian feminist of the 20th century.

A kilometer down the road from El Sawadah, dug underground is the **Church of Aba Hur**. Not especially significant, it was named for a young Copt whose strength of faith under torture converted a Roman governor of Pelusiam to Christianity. Take time to notice the finely carved heikal screen and the crypts containing generations of bishops and other local Coptic notables. In early July local Christians gather here for a festival.

NIGHTLIFE & ENTERTAINMENT

When the weather is pleasant and a cool breeze blows off the Nile, locals enjoy spending their evenings strolling along the Corniche or hanging out on the bridge. The streets are active and the coffee shops full, but if you're looking for drinking and dancing, Minya is not really happening. There is something of a bar at the **Mercure** several clicks north of the city center on the Corniche. Otherwise, the rooftop cafeteria in the **Lotus Hotel** *on Saad Zaghloul Street three blocks north of the train station,* is kind of cheap and seedy and serves local Stella, wine, and spirits.

SHOPPING

Given that Minya is not at all a major tourist magnet it comes as no surprise that there is little to buy in the way of souvenirs, local handicrafts and the usual cheap merchandise fed to tourists. **Food stores** and **boutiques** are concentrated on the streets emanating from Tahrir Square and around the railroad station. Kiosks selling bottled water, cigarettes, and other such goods are on every major street.

PRACTICAL INFORMATION

Banks & Currency Exchange

There are two banks on El Corniche Street. The one *on the corner of El Gomhuriya Street, open 8:30am-2pm and 5-8pm (winter) & 6-9pm (summer)* handles Visa cash advances in addition to changing foreign currency and traveler's cheques.

Emergencies

• **Ambulance**: *Tel. 123*
• **Hospitals**: *Tel. 324-098 (public) & 323-077 (private)*
• **Police**: *Tel. 323-122/23*

Post & Courier Services

Post Office & EMS (express mail), *Saad Zaghloul Street by the train station. Hours: 8:30am-3pm Sunday-Thursday. EMS closes at 2pm.*

Telephones, Telex, & Fax

24 hour telephone centrale, *Midan Tahrir, but will move shortly to Saad Zaghloul Street. The centrale can place international and domestic calls, faxes, and telexes. Most hotels can also place phone calls.*

Tourist Information

Egyptian Tourist Authority, *the Corniche two blocks north of the intersection with El Gomhuriya Street. Hours: 8am-2pm & 6-9pm daily. Tel. 086/320-150.*

ETA offers the rare visitor plenty of smiles, broken English, and the usual assortment of useless grainy brochures. They can give directions and provide information about the status of sites which frequently seem to close for renovations or security reasons. They can also assist in making arrangements for visiting regional attractions.

Tourist Police: *Tel. 324-527*

ASSIUT

Conventional wisdom says that of all Nile Valley destinations, **Assiut** is the least worth visiting. Lacking in sites and short on character, Egypt's third city offers foreign travelers little more than a link to the oases of Kharga and Dakhla. Assiut was a provincial capital during the pharaonic and Ptolemeic eras, but apart from inscriptionless tombs dug into the cliffs along the road to Dirunka, there are no monuments of consequence.

The monasteries and convents of **Deir El Muharriq** in El Qussia and **Deir El Adhra** at Dirunka are significant pilgrimage sites for Copts who believe that the Holy Family took refuge in both locations during their flight to Egypt; but aside from the huge summer festivals, which are very much worth attending, they are of little interest to the average tourist. In Islamic and Medieval times, Assiut was the terminus of the Forty Days Road, the famous caravan route from the Sudan, and hence a major node in the slave trade and site of a major souk. The slave trade ended at the end of the nineteenth century, but Assiut has retained its status as a commercial hub.

ASSIUT & CONFLICTS WITH THE ISLAMICISTS

In the early 1990's, Assiut's already dubious reputation was further tarnished as it became a major flash point for violent confrontations between Islamic militants and government security forces. For a period in 1991-1994, hardly a week went by without a shoot out, raid, or ambush, and during the first years of the decade both sides suffered hundreds of casualties. For some reason some militants also felt that targeting civilians and foreign tourists would also serve their cause, but fortunately no such attacks have occurred since '95.

Christian-Muslim relations also suffered as the large Christian community felt scapegoated and that its interests were violated and neglected as both the government and the militants raced to establish Islamic credentials. After nearly half a decade of often brutal crackdowns, Mubarak's regime claimed victory against the militants and the number of incidents have diminished to a handful since 1995. As a foreigner, particularly as an independent traveler, the chances of being targeted are slim to nil and the authorities will go to great, often absurd lengths to assure your safety. Chances are you won't be left in public without an armed escort.

ARRIVALS & DEPARTURES

Fortunately, the train station and the bus and service depots are conveniently within meters of each other. Generally, service taxis are most efficient for traveling within Middle Egypt and as far south as Luxor. For longer journeys, consider the train which is more comfortable and reasonably priced. Buses are cheap and necessary for travel to Kharga, but generally uncomfortable.

By Bus

South of the train station and next to the service depot, the **bus station** services buses to all major points in the Nile Valley as well as Cairo. A dozen buses depart for Cairo daily, most of which are air-conditioned (LE10-20, 6 hours). Six air-conditioned buses leave daily for Luxor (LE8-12, 4-5 hours) and half of them continue on to Aswan (LE15-20, 8-10 hours), but it's not an easy or comfortable ride. To closer destinations like Minya (LE3) and Sohag (LE3), buses depart twice hourly.

There are also daily buses to Alexandria (LE25, 10 hours), Hurghada (LE20, 6 hours), and six daily to Kharga (LE10, 4-5 hours) two of which continue on to Dakhla (LE15, 8 hours). Check with the station for the exact schedule and to make reservations.

By Service

Service taxis come and go from a **depot** next to the bus station and south of the train station. They are handy for reaching destinations within the Nile Valley like Minya, Sohag, and Qena. If going further, you may have to change or consider taking a bus or train. Service also go to Kharga, but departures are sporadic. During Christian feasts and moulids, especially in the last week of June and the first three weeks of August, service depart constantly to Deir El Muharriq and Deir El Adhra.

To Middle Egypt destinations, fares should not top LE5 while if you go on to Cairo or Luxor, expect to pay LE7-10 per person. To the Deir El Muharriq and Deir El Adhra, you should not pay more than LE1-2.

By Train

The train station is on El Geish Street in the city center. Trains come and go between Assiut and Cairo hourly but most are local trains that stop in every excuse for a village and move at a glacial pace. In any case, the authorities usually restrict foreigners to the "Espani" and "Faransawi" trains which run between Cairo and Luxor and Aswan.

To Luxor (LE55 1st class, LE35 2nd class, 5-6 hours) and Aswan (LE65 1st class, LE40 2nd class, 8 hours) trains depart Assiut 3-4 time daily, as well as to Cairo (LE50 1st class, LE30 2nd class, 6 hours). These trains also stop in Minya, Sohag, and Qena. Check with the station for schedules and make reservations in advance. Remember that students pay half price.

ORIENTATION

Most of the city's hustle and bustle revolves around the train station. Fortunately for travelers, most hotels, restaurants, and services (post office, banks, etc.) are located within walking distance of each other and the railroad station. Streets worth knowing include **El Geish Street** which runs along the train tracks to the east; **26th of July** which runs parallel to the tracks two blocks west before turning the corner to run east-west just north of the Akhenaten Hotel; the curvy **Talaat Harb** another block west of 26th of July; and **El Gomhuriya Street** which branches off El Geish Street several hundred meters north of the station and then curves towards the **Nile** which is hugged by **El Nil Street (the Corniche)**. The most direct route from the train station and El Geish Street to the Nile is **Hellaly Street** which begins at the Reem Hotel.

About ten minutes from the city center is the **Nile**, and the streets that run along it are the most pleasant to stroll about. While most of the city is architecturally uninspired (lots of concrete blocks), streets by the Nile are still lined with slowly dilapidating, but charming colonial structures, most of which now house government offices. Another area worth a stroll is the **souk** (public markets) south of the station which buzzes with all sorts of commercial activity.

GETTING AROUND TOWN

As most activity concerning travelers is concentrated within a kilometer of the train station, walking is sufficient for getting around Assiut. Should you have luggage, or need to go further, blue and white taxis are readily available and shouldn't charge you more than a pound or two to go anywhere in town.

Minibuses and buses also run throughout the city, but they really aren't worth the trouble as taxis are cheap, and authorities discourage their use. For getting around the old fashionedway, hail a horse-drawn *kaleche* (carriage). A ten minute jaunt shouldn't cost more than LE2.

WHERE TO STAY

Expensive/Moderate

BADR HOTEL, *El Thallaga Street across from the train tracks. Tel. 088/329-811/2. Fax 088/322-820. Capacity: 44 rooms. Rates: $20 single, $25 double, $40 suite. Credit cards: not accepted.*

Stroll into the red padded and mirrored lobby and you might feel if you've made a wrong turn into a time warp back to the '70's. Though it feels a bit seedy, have no worries, the Badr is safe, clean and well managed. The smallish rooms are comfortable and feature private baths, air-conditioning, and dish television with Lebanese and Italian stations. The restaurant is overpriced but quite decent (no alcohol). The Badr is generally considered the top hotel in Assiut.

ASSIUTEL HOTEL, *146 El Nil Street. Tel. 088/312-121/2/3. Fax 088/ 312-122 Capacity: 31 rooms. Rates: $23-28 single, $26-31 double. Credit cards: not accepted.*

This new establishment located just off the Nile is a bit far from the transportation hubs and the train station. Clean and friendly, its rooms are equipped with private baths, air-conditioning, and color TV.

CASABLANCA HOTEL, *Mohammed Tawfik Khashaba Street. Tel. 088/ 337-662, 336-662. Fax 088/336-662. Capacity: 48 rooms. Rates: $25 single, $32 double, $50 suite. Credit cards: not accepted.*

It's not as sexy as its name might lead you to believe, but the downtown location (ten minute walk to the train station) is convenient and the rooms are sufficiently comfortable and feature air-conditioning, television, and private baths.

HAPPYLAND HOTEL, *El Sawra Street off the Nile. Tel. 088/320-444, 321-944. Fax 088/320-444. Capacity: 52 rooms. Rates: LE60-65 single, LE75 double, LE105-150 suite. Credit cards: not accepted.*

The Happyland has a surreal if silly aura about it. Complete with gaudy fake pharaonic statues, the lobby is a masterpiece in bad taste and the restaurant-bar which is an evening hub for local Sayeedi alcoholics, offers a real cross cultural experience indeed. As for the rooms, they're a bit of a let down but feature semi-functional air-conditioning, private baths, and televisions. Some also have reasonable views of the Corniche and the Nile.

REEM HOTEL, *El Nahda Street just down the block from the Badr near the train station and bus depot. Tel. 088/311-421/2/3. Fax 088/311-424. Capacity: 40 rooms. Rates: LE50 single, LE75 double. Credit cards: not accepted.*

Padded walls and mirrors echo the Badr, but many consider this to be better value. It's cheaper, the rooms are comfy, the air-conditioning works, *and* the satellite features more channels.

AKHENATON HOTEL, *Mohammed Tawfik Khashaba Street. Tel. 088/ 337-723, 331-600, 338-181. Fax 088/331-600. Capacity: 35 rooms. Rates: LE30 single, LE35 double.*

It's little more than a stark concrete block, but with private baths, air-conditioning, and color televisions, the rooms are good value. Planned renovation will mean a different set-up and higher prices in the future.

Budget

YMCA, *El Gomhuriya Street. Tel. 088/323-218. Rates: LE10-20 double.*

Could be the fanciest LE20 you spend on accommodation in Egypt if you can actually get a room. Double rooms with air-conditioning and sometimes television cost just a bit extra with a private bath.

HOTEL EL HARAMEIN, *Hellaly Street between El Nahda and the Nile. Tel. 088/320-426. Rates: LE10 double.*

No frills at all, but at least the rooms have fans.

HOTEL ASSIOUT DE TOURISM, *El Geish Street. Tel. 088/322-615. Rates: LE15.*

The rooms are in better shape than the building's exterior might let on, but are still pretty bare-boned, and proximity to the train station and train tracks ensures plenty of noise. Shared baths and no fans.

ZAM ZAM HOTEL, *Hellaly Street by the overpass. Tel. no phone. Rates: LE15 double.*

Bare and somewhat grimy rooms with fans. Nothing much else to it.

WHERE TO EAT

Upscale hotels feature restaurants but the food is over priced and the ambiance boring; better to venture out (not heeding the advice your police escort who will insist that it's better to eat in) and munch with the locals. Cuisine doesn't stray much from the usual roast chicken, fuul, and ta'amiya et al. Some popular eateries worth trying include **El Hussein Restaurant,** *by El Hussein Hotel across by the service station*; **El Azhar** *on Saad Zaghloul* (good for chicken and baked *macarona*); and **El Rahman** *on 26th of July*. None of these joints will fill you up for much more than LE6-7.

For a bit more, the quiet, air-conditioned **El Haty** offers kebab (LE28 per kilo), grilled chicken, mixed rice, and pasta. A full meal costs little more than LE10, if that. It is *on El Geish Street (west of the tracks) just south of the underpass opposite the large mosque and church.* The spanking new fatir shop, **Ali Baba** *(El Gomhuriya Street)* will fill you up for LE10 or less and makes a good excuse to hit the up and coming El Gomhuriya Street.

SEEING THE SIGHTS

You almost surely have time on your hands if you find yourself sightseeing out of Assiut. The city itself is devoid of any attractions and most of the regional sights are conveniently reached from Minya to the north and Sohag or Luxor from the south. Yet within the vicinity of Assiut are two major Christian sites, **Deir El Adhra (Convent of the Virgin Mary) at Dirunka,** 12 kilometers from the city; and **Deir El Muharriq (the Burnt Monastery)** in the outskirts of **El Qussia,** 45 kilometers north of Assiut. Just beyond Deir El Muharriq, cut into the dunes and rocks off the green edge of the Nile Valley, are the rarely visited, but fascinating **Tombs of Meer,** built by and for Old and Middle Kingdom officials. They feature reliefs that vividly portray the daily life and activities of gnomes (provincial governors) and their underlings.

If you really have time to kill or need an excuse to explore the local countryside, may consider a visit to the village of **Beni Marr**, the ancestral home of **Gamal Abdel Nasser**. He was born and grew up in Alexandria, but took great pride in his Sayeedi roots and did pay the village many visits. A local attendant will open the small museum for you, and others, some claiming to be relatives and friends, will rattle off tales and anecdotes relating to the legendary leader's early years and roots. Sabr at the Badr Hotel may be able arrange a trip (God knows for how much) or you can find a minibus at the service depot by the train station.

Deir El Adhra – The Convent of the Virgin at Dirunka

Deir El Adhra is 12 kilometers north of Assiut and can be reached by service from the main depot by the train station. Otherwise hire a taxi for LE10 each way. The caves are open to the public daily from 9am to 5pm when a procession of the icons is held.

Like many major Coptic pilgrimage destinations, the **Convent of the Virgin** is on a site supposedly used for hiding by the holy family during its flight from Herod. The actual location of the Family's stay at Dirunka are several caves well up in the cliffs overlooking the mostly Coptic village.

Most of the uninspired modern structures were constructed within the past decade to accommodate the huge numbers of pilgrims who make their way to Dirunka from August 7-22 to celebrate the **Festival of the Virgin Mary**. For two weeks the sleepy town metamorphoses into a lively and mystical medieval festival as hundreds of small time entertainers, magicians, and musicians set up shop to entertain adults and children taking a break between baptisms, prayers, and processions. Meanwhile hawkers peddle religious icons and relics and tattoo artists drill thousands of crosses and images of Saint George into the arms of the faithful.

The highlights of each day are the two evening **processions** when dozens of priests and altar boys parade near the caves with the most revered icons which are thought to have miraculous powers. The first procession is held at 5:30 and the larger and more important one takes place at 7pm. Make sure to stake out a position along the route or else you'll have no chance of getting a good look. Expect heavy duty crowds and a big push when the icons pass as the faithful strain to touch and even kiss the icons and their handlers.

Deir El Muharriq

Deir El Muharriq is five kilometers outside of El Qussia, 45 kilometers north of Assiut. Take a minibus from Assiut to El Qussia (LE1, 1 hour), and catch a pickup service going to "Deir El Muharriq." During August or late June (festival seasons) you may be able to find a minibus going straight to Deir El Muharriq from Assiut. Otherwise, hire a private taxi in Assiut and combine Deir El

Muharriq with Dirunka and Meer on the itinerary. As this will entail at least half a day, expect to pay at least LE30-40 round trip. Bargaining will be necessary. There is no entrance fee, but a donation is appropriate. If you can find a monk who speaks English, he may be willing to give a tour.

A huge walled complex, Deir El Muharriq is one of Middle Egypt's most important theological centers and a major destination for pilgrims. In addition to believing that the Holy Family hid in caves here during their flight to Egypt, local Coptic tradition maintains that it was the site of the **first church in Egypt**, constructed shortly after the arrival of Christianity during the second half of the first century. Its significance is further enhanced by the belief that in the caves here, Joseph received a message from the Lord, through an angel in a dream, that Herod had passed away and that it was safe to return to Palestine.

In addition to two major chapels, the complex is home to the **only active monastery in Upper Egypt**; a seminary for training monks; and extensive facilities to accommodate thousands of pilgrims who make their way here throughout the year. The main attraction for pilgrims is the **Church of the Virgin**, situated on caves where the Holy Family allegedly hid, and site of the original Church of the Virgin which some claim to have been Egypt's first Christian chapel. Of particular significance is the alter stone which is said to have served as a door that blocked the caves when the Holy Family was hiding here. It is engraved with a date in 747 AD when the significance of the stone manifested itself to a worker who was removing it under the orders of an abbot. While pulling the stone, the workman found himself face to face with a vision of Christ who ordered him to leave it in place. The current 19th century version of the chapel is not especially spectacular except for the history it represents and the emotions it conjures in the faithful.

A second major chapel, that of **Saint George**, was also built in the 19th century, and is believed to be the site of a church constructed more than 16 centuries earlier by Saint Paul, a founder of monasticism, and Saint Peter (not the Apostle). The monastery itself was founded in the 4th century AD by **Saint Pachom**, who established a dozen monasteries throughout Egypt. His brand of monasticism combined a highly regimented and ascetic lifestyle within, as opposed to isolated from, the larger community. Should you acquire written permission from the Antiquities Department in Cairo, you will be granted access to the monastery's collection of **historic icons and artifacts** stashed away upstairs.

Meer

Several kilometers past Deir El Muharriq to the north, no less than a half dozen Middle Kingdom nobles' tombs are carved into the sloping desert hills. A guard will let you in for LE12 per person or perhaps a smaller amount of *baksheesh*. The tombs feature colorful portrayals of local **gnomarchs** (provincial governors) who during the Middle Kingdom enjoyed increased autonomy from the central authorities of the pharaoh.

NIGHTLIFE & ENTERTAINMENT
The Happy Land, Akhenaten, and El Salam hotels all contain seedy bars, serving local Stella and spirits to a somewhat unsavory clientele. A night out can make for interesting interaction with a colorful Assiuty subculture, but be prepared to deal with a freak or two. Women should take extra care.

For sheesha and tea, there are dozens of coffee shops on all the main streets. For anything more, hop on a minibus and head 400 kilometers south to Luxor.

SHOPPING
Not really much to get excited about, however should you like to stock up on fruit or other munchies for a train ride or say a bus to Kharga, plenty of vendors sell fresh produce in the souks south of the train station. Public sector department stores and mom and pop type shops litter the area around the train station which is the city's major commercial district. Sabr at the Badr Hotel used to run a tourist bazaar and closed since tourism dried up in the early nineties, but he still peddle textiles and souvenirs. If you're interested, bargain hard and don't fall for his stories about his financial predicaments.

EXCURSIONS & DAY TRIPS
Anything worth visiting from Assiut, with the possible exception of **Dirunka**, requires a least a half day trip. **Meer** and **Deir El Muharriq**, combined with Dirunka, will take the better part of day. **Tel El Amarna** will take a day and is better combined with a visit to **Beni Hassan** from Minya. Also accessible are the **Red and White Monasteries**, and the sites of **Akhmim** at **Sohag**, the next major town up the river (see the Sohag section). Catch a train or service to Sohag – they run about every ten minutes – and from there hire a local taxi.

PRACTICAL INFORMATION
Banks & Currency Exchange
Banks are concentrated on **Midan El Banuk** ("Banks Square") where branches of **Bank of Alexandria**, **National Bank of Egypt**, and **Banque Misr** are located. They open from 8:30am-2pm and again from 5-8pm in winter and from 6-9pm in summer. As they close on Fridays and Saturdays, it is wise to cash up before the weekend.

Emergencies
- **Ambulance**: *Tel. 123*
- **University Hospital**, *University Street: Tel. 322-016*
- **El Mabara Hospital**, *Mohafaza Street: Tel. 323-600*
- **Police**, *Main station on the Corniche at end of Hellaly Street: Tel. 122 or 352-562*

Post Services
   Post Office & EMS (express mail), *off El Geish Street by Hotel Assiout De Tourism, two blocks from the train station. Hours: 8am-3pm daily except Friday.*

Telephones, Telex, & Fax
   24 hour telephone centrale, *the train station. Offers telephone, telex, fax, and telegraph services. Some hotels also offer telephone and sometimes fax services.*

Tourist Information
   Assiut's status as a tourist destination is illustrated by the fact that it's the only major city where the Egyptian Tourist Authority does not have an office.

Tourist Police: *Tel. 122 or 322-562*

SOHAG & AKHMIM

   Located just over 100 kilometers south of Assiut, the modest city of **Sohag** rarely sees many foreigners. Known for its large Christian community, an increasingly important university, and the fertile earth of the surrounding countryside, Sohag is home to two important Coptic sites, the **Red Monastery** and the **White Monastery**.
   Nearby, the ancient village of **Akhmim** is famous throughout Egypt for its textiles and was the site of a discovery of a massive statue depicting the New Kingdom princess Merit Amun.

ARRIVALS & DEPARTURES
By Bus
   The bus station is around the corner from the main square at the railroad station. Buses to Assiut to the north and Qena (3 hours) and Balyana (1 hour) to the south leave about every half hour (LE1.50-3). Seven buses make the long 8 hour trip to Cairo (LE20) daily. One bus goes to Luxor (LE8,) and then Aswan (LE18), departing early in the morning around 6am. Your alternative is to get to Qena or Assiut where buses are more regular.

By Service
The service depot on Midan Europa north of the train station is the hub for service going north including Assiut (LE3, 1.5 hours), Minya (LE6, 3-4 hours), and Cairo (LE20, 6-8 hours). The depot for services to the south, namely Qena, is south of the railroad station. For destinations south, you're best off getting to Qena (LE3-5, 2 hours) and making a connection. Sometimes, they continue on to Luxor (LE5, 3 hours).

By Train
The train station is on El Mahatta Street in the city center.
The train is most useful for reaching further destinations like Cairo (LE50 1st class; LE30 2nd class; 6-7 hours) and Aswan (LE50 1st class, LE30 2nd class). Check at the station for departure times and buy tickets in advance.

ORIENTATION
Most visitors concentrate their activities in the center of town near Sohag's primary landmark, the railroad station which is on El Mahatta Street where most cheap hotels and eateries are located. Running along the Nile, El Gomhuriya Street is home to several banks and makes a nice stroll. The German-built Sohag Bridge links the Sohag's city center with the east bank where newer districts and the university are located. Akhmim is also on the east bank and to the south.

GETTING AROUND TOWN
A highlight of any visit to Sohag is ride in one of the vintage Fords and Dodges from the '40's and '50's, that make up most of the taxi corp. The taxis are also the best way to reach local sites like Akhmim and the Monasteries. For getting around downtown, walking should suffice unless you need to cross the river.

WHERE TO STAY
MERIT AMOUN HOTEL, *the east bank. Tel. 088/601-985. Fax 088/603-222. Rates: LE70 single, LE80 double.*
Sohag's finest hotel barely earns its three stars. Rooms feature bathrooms and air-conditioners but are far from luxurious. There is a modest restaurant and some unkempt gardens in the rear.
CASANOVA HOTEL, *just beyond the Merit Amoun on the east bank. Tel. 088/601-185. Rates: LE30-40 single, LE35-45 double.*
Just a notch below the Merit Amoun is the Casanova which offers rooms with and without air-conditioning and private rest rooms. Breakfast is included.

THE ANDALOUS HOTEL, *across the street from the train station. Tel. 088/324-328. Rates: LE10 single, LE15 double.*

The best option in town certainly isn't fancy. It's in the noisiest part of town and it's cramped, perhaps unfit for unaccompanied women. However, compared to the neighboring Ramses and El Salam hotels, it's idyllic.

WHERE TO EAT

There's a great chicken-on-a-spit joint called **El Aman** and several fuul and ta'amiya establishments across from the station. Otherwise, the **Nadi El Shorta** (Police Officers' Club) *north of downtown on the east bank*, may admit foreigners. The location is quite and overlooks the Nile. Expect to pay LE20 for a full kebab meal. The **Merit Amoun** and **Casanova** hotels also feature modest restaurants.

SEEING THE SIGHTS

Except during festivals, when service depart constantly for the monasteries, sites are most easily visited by private taxi. Expect to pay at least LE20 for a round trip to both monasteries and more if you take a lot of time. Akhmim can also be reached by private taxi or by service.

Deir El Abyad (White Monastery)

Twelve kilometers northwest of Sohag. Hours: 8am-8pm daily. Admission: free but donations are appropriate.

So named for the white limestone with which it is built, **Deir El Abyad** (also known as Deir Anba Shenouda) was founded in the 4th century by a follower of **Saint Pachom** (see sidebar below), **Saint Pgol**, and enlarged by **Saint Shenouda**. The main building in the complex, the Church of Street Shenouda, was also constructed in the fourth century and contains three vaulted apses with portraits of Saint Shenouda (center), and Saint George, and the Virgin Mary. Though it once housed several thousand monks, the monastery is no longer in use. Local Christians celebrate **Shenouda's Moulid** in mid-July.

Deir El Ahmar (Red Monastery)

Four kilometers beyond the White Monastery. Hours: 8am-8pm daily. Admission: free but donations are appropriate.

Founded by a student of Saint Shenouda, **Saint Bishoi**, in the 5th century, the Red Monastery resembles the White Monastery in its simplicity, but is a bit smaller. The main church, that of Saint Bishoi features 10th century murals and finely carved niches and apses. The icons over the sanctuary portray Saint Pgol, Saint Shenouda, and Saint

SAINT PACHOM

*In the 4th century AD, shortly after Saint Antony founded monasticism in northern Egypt, a convert Upper Egyptian named **Pachom** founded a new monastic order. Trained by the great Upper Egyptian religious leader Palomen, Pachom based his new community on the principle that a committed spirit required a committed body and a committed lifestyle. Hence life in his community was based on rigid discipline, and strict rules governing all aspects of life were dictated and enforced by Pachom himself. Even the slightest indulgence, like a minor case of over eating or drinking, led to harsh and swift disciplinary action. Pachom's order, originally established near Akhmim, was adopted in more than a dozen monasteries, including the Red and the White Monasteries near Sohag, and its ideals were later spread in Europe through the writings of Saint Jerome.*

Bishoi – three generations of followers of Saint Pachom. In the southeastern corner of the complex, a chapel dedicated to the Virgin Mary is thought to be the oldest part of the monastery which, like the White Monastery is no longer active.

Akhmim

A Coptic community that traces its lineage to pre-Dynastic Egypt, **Akhmim** is best known for the carpets and other textiles which its people have been weaving for generations. For those interested in watching the weavers do their thing, there is a weaving cooperative *across from the post office next to the statue of Merit Amoun*. You can also ask locals where to locate other shops.

Named for the ever phallicly erect god of fertility, **Min**, Akhmim recently enjoyed a burst fame after the 1981 discovery of a **statue of Merit Amoun**. A daughter of Ramses II, she was a priestess at the local temple of Min and later became queen. Though the temple in which she served was destroyed, the huge statue of her, rouge lipstick and all, warrants a visit to Akhmim. The statue was discovered during work on a locale infrastructure project and led to speculation that many more treasures lie underneath the community. Local folks, however, are not so keen to see their community uprooted in the name archaeology.

Finally, Akhmim's weekly livestock market, known as *Setta Aziza* is held on Wednesday mornings at the town's main infrastructure also home to the 8th century **El Amri Mosque**, a handsome but worn down piece of early Islamic architecture.

SHOPPING

In addition to textiles and the Wednesday livestock market in Akhmim, the **Souk El Itneen** is a second weekly animal market on Mondays in Sohag. Both animal markets are colorful, lively affairs, but not for the squeamish or faint of heart.

PRACTICAL INFORMATION

Banks & Currency Exchange

There are two banks on El Gomhuriya Street. One is 200 meters south of the Sohag Bridge while the second is south of the train station. Both open 8am-2pm Sunday-Thursday. Both change currency and travelers' cheques and should be able to make a Visa cash advance.

Emergencies
• **Ambulance**: *Tel. 123*
• **Police**: *Tel. 122*

Post & Courier Services

Post Office & EMS (express mail), *El Gomhuriya Street south of the train station.*

Telephones, Telex, & Fax

24 hour telephone centrale, *the train station.* You can place international and domestic calls as well as send faxes and telexes.

Tourist Police

The Tourist Police are on duty in the train station and in Akhmim.

BALYANA & THE TEMPLE OF ABYDOS

The ultimate goal for ancient Egyptians – the equivalent of Muslims making haj to Mecca – was to visit the shrines of **Abydos**, home to the **Cult of Osiris**, Egypt's most ancient and important deity. The site of Egypt's first great necropolis built on what was considered the "gates to the underworld" in predynastic times (before 3,000 BC), Abydos was perhaps the most sacred place in Egypt until Christianity became the dominant religion in the second century. Hence it retained its divine status more than 3,000 years, longer than any site in Egypt.

Located in the heart of the Nile Valley, Abydos probably derived its sacred status from the fact that it was an early power center from which the legendary first Pharaoh Menes emerged to unify Upper and Lower Egypt around 3,100 BC. As a function of Abydos being the ancestral home of Egypt's first pharaohs, its patron deity, Osiris became Egypt's first and most important national deity. Thought to be based on a legendary early leader who achieved divine status after death, Osiris became the embodiment of the central tenets of Ancient Egyptian theology and ideology, namely the ideals of divine kingship, the cycles of death and resurrection, and an eternal afterlife after death.

Today, Abydos' main draw is a magnificent New Kingdom temple built by Seti I and Ramses II. As the nearby town **Balyana** is little more than an eyesore with virtually no facilities to accommodate travelers, Abydos is usually visited in a day trip from Luxor which is 160 kilometers to the south.

ARRIVALS & DEPARTURES

Most visitors join a guided tour or hire a taxi out of Luxor, though some travelers approach Abydos from Sohag or Qena, which are closer but far less tourist friendly. In town, 10 kilometers from the temples, the train, bus, and service stations are all located one, two, and three blocks east of the canal in the center of town. The temple is easily reached from town by service.

By Bus

Buses depart hourly to Qena (LE4, 1 hour) and Luxor (LE5, 2 hours) to the south, and to Sohag (LE2, 45 minutes) and Assiut (LE5, 2.5 hours) to the north.

By Service

Service taxis leave just as frequently to the same destinations as buses for approximately the same prices. Service to the temple from Balyana cost 50p.

By Train

Trains leave frequently for Qena and Luxor to the south and to Assiut and Sohag to north, but are often not air-conditioned, and stop at every possible village en route, making them very inefficient.

ORIENTATION

Most travelers simply zip right into the temple complex from Luxor on their hired taxis and buses, sparing themselves the trip through the nondescript sugar refinery town of Balyana 10 kilometers away. Should you decide to stay in Balyana, hotels, eateries, and the transport hubs are all located within two or three blocks east of the canal.

GETTING AROUND TOWN

Service minibuses shuttle constantly between the temple and Balyana(50p). Within town itself, transportation hubs, eateries, and hotels are all within walking distance of each other.

WHERE TO STAY

Basically you don't want to stay in Balyana if you can help it; the accommodations here make those in Sohag and Qena look like the Sheraton, which they most surely are not.

ABYDOS HOTEL, *250 meters in front of Abydos Temple. Tel. 096/812-102. Rates: LE30-50.*

With basic rooms with beds, fans, and a bit of dirt thrown in for good measure, the LE30 seem expensive.

OSIRIS PARK RESTAURANT & CAMP, *in front of the temple grounds at Abydos, 10 kilometers from Balyana. Tents with cots LE5 per person; pitch your own tent, LE5.*

Very basic camping facilities featuring cold water showers and basic tents. The location in front of the temple is ideal and the gent who runs the place is as cool as his pharaonic name, "Horus."

WADI MELOUK HOTEL, *Balyana two blocks east of the canal. Tel. 096/801-658. Rates: LE5 single & double.*

A very basic establishment with common showers but no hot water; not especially clean.

WHERE TO EAT

In Balyana itself, you're limited to the cheap eats like fuul, ta'amiya, and roast chicken, while at the temple, you're limited to overpriced fare for tourists. The **Osiris Park** at least offers you a chance to hang with Horus, the proprietor, which makes up for the jacked up prices. Still, you can eat a decent meal for LE10-20. The Park also serves beer and features a view of the temple – a great combination.

SEEING THE SIGHTS
THE TEMPLES OF OSIRIS AT ABYDOS

Ten kilometers west of the town Balyana 160 kilometers north of Luxor. Hours: 7am-5pm daily. Admission: LE24 general, LE12 students.

The temples and necropolis of Abydos were built on a site that ancient Egyptians believed to be the "gates to the underworld" through which they must pass to achieve resurrection after death. An established religious and burial center before the 1st Dynasty (3,100 BC), Abydos remained an area of sanctity until the Roman Period in the 2nd century

AD – a period spanning more than 3,200 years. Dedicated to Egypt's national deity and the central hero of its most famous myth, Osiris, the temple was the most important destination for pilgrimage and during the Early Dynastic Period, the necropolis was the equivalent of a national cemetery. Those who could not make it in life aspired to make it in death and the ritual pilgrimage to Abydos is recounted on the walls of many-a-royal tomb.

The Myth of Osiris

The legend of Osiris is one of the most ancient and most important in pharaonic Egyptian mythology. Featuring all the ingredients of a good story from love and jealousy to revenge and a happy ending, its theme is indeed the concept around which life and religion in ancient Egypt revolved, that of death and resurrection. Retold hundreds of times in many versions, it dates to at least the Old Kingdom when it was recounted in the Pyramid Texts in Saqqara, but a version told by the Greek Plutarch is most familiar.

According to the legend, Osiris was a just and righteous king who ruled over a prosperous and peaceful Egypt, when his jealous brother Seth hatched a plot to get rid of him. After tricking Osiris into climbing into a box under the pretense of measuring his size, Seth slammed the box shut and tossed it into the Nile. Overwhelmed by grief, Osiris' loving wife, **Isis** and her sister Nephthys searched over all of Egypt for the box, and after they eventually found it, they hid the body under a tamarisk tree.

However, Seth found the corpse while hunting and decided to do away with Osiris for good by cutting his body into many pieces and dispersing them throughout Egypt. While Isis again set out to collect Osiris' remains, their son Horus, raised from boyhood secretly in the marsh reeds of the Nile, set out to avenge his father's murder, and defeated Seth at a duel at Edfu before exiling him to the Western Desert.

After searching every corner of Egypt from Nubia to the Delta, Isis recovered the dismembered limbs of her beloved husband and prayed to the gods to breathe life into Osiris. The Heavens answered her prayers and Osiris rose from the dead to become eternal king of the underworld.

This is how Osiris became the primary god of the afterworld and a symbol of reincarnation. It is believed that the tale may have been derived from the story of a true leader who was so revered that upon his death, his status was raised to that of deity. In any case, thus began the tradition of ancestor worship and the belief in life after death in pharaonic Egypt.

The Temple of Seti I

Though Abydos was a major religious center as early as the Early Dynastic Period, the New Kingdom **Temple of Seti I** now dominates the site. Decorated with some of the finest carved bas-reliefs in Egypt, Seti's complex is a multi-purpose temple dedicated to the theme of the afterworld and includes shrines to several deities, including Seti I himself, and of course Osiris. Seti himself built on this site during his reign from 1318-1304 BC and his son, the indefatigable builder Ramses II completed it during his long reign of 67 years. Those reliefs dating to Seti's reign, generally found in the interior, are of considerably higher quality than those carved which date to the rule Ramses.

Seti's temple is approached through a **ruined pylon** and an **open court**. There isn't much to view in the first court, but the western wall features reliefs depicting Ramses II defeating the Hittites at the **Battle of Kadesh** in Syria. A major theme of carvings in all of his monuments, this battle was really a draw from which Ramses was lucky to escape alive.

The second court is also quite plain with serious reliefs beginning at the entrance to the **hypostyle hall**. At the rear of the court, twelve pillars feature portraits of Ramses making offerings to Osiris and commiserating with other deities while texts relate that Ramses found the temple begun by his father unfinished and that he completed it on his behalf. To the right of the doorway are representations of Osiris, his wife Isis, and their son, Horus. In the next set of reliefs, Ptah at Heliopolis records Ramses' name for eternity as Ra Harakhte presents Ramses with a crook and flail, symbols of Osiris and pharaohdom. Meanwhile Thoth, the ibis-headed scribe god, records the event for posterity.

Though Ramses claims to have completed the temple in honor of Seti, most scholars believe that the artists who worked on the **hypostyle hall** during Ramses' reign were less than the best. Indeed, the quality of these reliefs does not compare with those in the inner portions of the temple built by Seti himself.

The hall itself is more than 60 meters wide and contains 24 papyrus-style columns supporting a roof. Originally, it was entered through seven doors to seven shrines for seven deities, but these doors were blocked during Ramses' extensions. On the back of the entrance wall immediately to the right, Ramses is seen facing Seshat, goddess of archives and records. They measure the temple in front of Osiris; Ramses then presents the results to Horus.

On the right wall, Ramses offers a box to Osiris, Isis, and Horus before going to temple with Horus and Wepwawet, the jackal guardian of the dead at the Abydos necropolis. To the left of the door on the rear wall of the entrance facade, Seti is depicted receiving purification from the sun deities, Amun Ra of Thebes, and Atum of Heliopolis, who pore the symbols of eternal life and prosperity over him. Seti is purified again in the left corner, this time by Thoth and Horus. On the left-hand side wall, Seti is suckled by Hathor, goddess of maternity and is presented to Ptah, patron god of Memphis, by the ram-headed Khnum, the creation deity. Finally on the rear walls of the first hypostyle hall, Ramses presents offerings to Amun Ra and Mut on both sides of the doorway, and in the far right corner gives Osiris the title deeds for the temples of Abydos.

Beyond the first hall is a **second hypostyle hall** featuring 36 pillars that dates entirely to the reign of Seti. On the right hand wall, exquisite reliefs portray a very realistic (we know from his mummy) representation of Seti making offerings to Osiris and Horus, and worshipping a shrine with an enthroned Osiris. Osiris is accompanied by a posse of female goddesses including Maat, goddess of Justice; Renoet, goddess of the annual cycles; Isis; Amentet, a goddess of the dead; and Nephthys.

At the rear of the second hypostyle hall are the **Seven Shrines** dedicated to (right to left): Horus, Isis, Osiris, Amun Ra, Ra Harakhte, Ptah, and Seti himself. The niches between the shrines were made available for offerings, and originally each shrine contained a symbolic sacred barge and a false door. The barge was used to parade idols during holy feasts; the false door served as a passage for spirits. Later, Christians vandalized some of the reliefs in these shrines, but most are in very good condition, and even retain their color.

Through the shrine of Osiris (third from the right), is the **Hall of Osiris**, another roofed chapel featuring ten columns and colored reliefs. Like other portions of this temple, parts of this one fell victim to the chisels of early Christians. Chapels to the right upon entrance are dedicated to Isis, Horus, and an Osirian incarnation of Seti. All the reliefs in these small chambers depict deities bestowing eternal life and prosperity upon Seti. In the shrine of Horus, Seti makes offerings while Horus bestows upon him the symbols of "Life, Stability, and Long Reign" and declares that Seti will enjoy "years like those of Ra," meaning eternal life. Meanwhile, Isis is seen supporting an Osirian Seti; she too receives offerings.

After completing the main axis of the temple, visitors move on to the southern wing containing the **Hall of Sokar** and the famous **Corridor of Kings**. The Hall of Sokar was dedicated to two deities, Sokar, and Nertum, associated in Lower Egypt (the Delta) with the cycles of life, rebirth, and resurrection. It once contained statues, and reliefs depict Seti making offerings and receiving purification from these and other deities.

Perhaps the most significant portion of the entire temple, the **Corridor of Kings** features a list of the cartouches of all pharaohs beginning Zoser-except for Akhenaten and Hatshepsut. This list served to prove Seti's royal lineage (in reality he was an officer not of royal blood) and has been of immense use to Egyptologists. The reliefs also feature a portrait of Seti with his son who later became Ramses II.

The Osirion and the Temple of Ramses II

These two structures are ruined, and in the case of the Osirion, underwater. The **Osirion** was built on a site long sacred. A 13th Dynasty stele declared that it was so holy that nobody was to set foot there. Seti I however chose the site for his Osirion, a symbolic tomb and place of refuge for the pharaoh's spirit before it was to meet Osiris at the "gates to the underworld." The waters were also believed to have healing powers.

A quarter of a mile from the Osirion is a pile of rubble that was once the **Temple of Ramses II**. Like other monuments constructed by Ramses II, this one must have been grand and resplendent. Built of limestone, several types of granite, and superior alabaster, it contains what Jill Kamil stated "must undoubtedly have been the most beautiful sanctuary in Egypt." Reliefs that survive include a glorious banquet scene on the right-hand wall of the second court and depictions of Ramses battling the Hittites at Kadesh on the outer walls.

NIGHTLIFE & ENTERTAINMENT

Nocturnal fun is pretty much limited to a cold Stella at the Osiris Park by the temple, or sheesha and shay (tea) in town.

SHOPPING

Overpriced tacky souvenirs not worth bothering about.

PRACTICAL INFORMATION

Banks & Currency Exchange

Change money in Luxor.

Emergencies

Contact the Tourist Police at the Temple of Seti I.

Post Services

There is a post office in Balyana, but a lack of English comprehension on the part of mailmen means it's quicker and safer to mail from Luxor, or even home.

Telephones

The hotels and the train station have phones.

Tourist information

Try Horus, the gent at the Osiris Park.

Tourist Police
Stationed at the Temple of Abydos.

QENA & THE TEMPLE OF DENDERA

A crossroads where north-south Nile Valley traffic intersects with the main artery to the Red Sea Coast, **Qena** is best known for the nearby **Temple of Dendera** and as a flash point in the ongoing conflict between Muslim fundamentalists and government security forces. Don't worry, you needn't spend much time in this drab town as it's just 60 kilometers and an easy day trip from Luxor. Those of you reading up on the place in old travelogues know that Qena was once known for debauchery and prostitution. But don't expect anything of the sort today; Qena is one of the most conservative towns in Egypt.

ARRIVALS & DEPARTURES

By Bus
The bus station is next to the train station 5 kilometers from the temple.

Rickety buses shuttle between Qena and Luxor hourly (LE2, 1 hour) and eleven of them go on to Aswan (LE9). There are two air-conditioned SuperJet buses to Cairo daily (LE30) and nine buses make the three trip route to Hurghada (LE8) on the Red Sea Coast, six of which go on to Suez (LE25-35, 10 hours). The fancier SuperJet to Hurghada (LE20) departs at 4:30 and 8:30pm. There are also two morning buses to El Quseir (LE8) and Safaga (LE10). Buses also leave at least hourly for major Nile Valley towns to the north (Assiut, Minya, Sohag and Balyana) and a ticket shouldn't set you back more than LE10.

By Service
The service depot for northern destinations is about a kilometer west of town. For southern destinations, the depot is beyond the foot bridge on the other side of the canal from the train station.

Minivans depart every 15-30 minutes to destinations like Balyana and Assiut as well as Luxor (LE2, 1.5 hours).

By Train
The train station is downtown next to the canal.

Trains are less efficient than service and buses for closer destinations and express trains to further destinations tend not to pass through Qena.

Cheaper local trains depart frequently to Luxor, but local authorities may be reluctant to sell you a ticket. In any case, a first class ticket to Luxor costs LE10 and an air-conditioning second class fare is LE7.

ORIENTATION

Most of Qena's hotels and restaurants are downtown south of the train and bus stations on El Gomhuriya Street. The **Temple of Dendera** is 5 kilometers east of town in the village of Dendera and is reachable by service or kaleche (horse carriage). El Aqsur Street, parallel to the train tracks off El Gomhuriya, is handy for its restaurants, a bank, and the post office.

GETTING AROUND TOWN

The most enjoyable way to make your way around is hop on a **kaleche** (horse buggy), but this requires fierce bargaining. You shouldn't pay more than LE5 to get between any two destinations in town while a trip from town to the temple shouldn't be more than LE15. Alternatively, you catch a service taxi to the temple from the depot off El Aqsur Street one kilometer west of town for LE1.

WHERE TO STAY

At Dendera Temple itself

HAPPYLAND CAMP, *next to the Temple of Dendera in the village of Dendera five kilometers from Qena. Tel. 096/322-330. Rates: LE35 single, LE45 double.*

Run by a bunch of Laurel and Hardy types, the HappyLand offers mediocre rooms with fans and common bathrooms as well as space for camping (LE10). Dinginess aside, the rural setting is quite beautiful and the location next to the temple entrance affords a unique opportunity to experience the temple in all its glory at sunset, sunrise, and if your lucky, in the moonlight. Should you get chummy with the employees, they may treat you to a local wedding or some other off-the-beaten-track type experience. Also, the cafeteria sells beer which is hard to find in town.

In Qena

There is absolutely no reason to stay in Qena and many reasons not to, beginning with the dearth of satisfactory accommodation.

NEW PALACE HOTEL, *behind the Mobil Station after the first left on El Gomhuriya Street after the Midan, from the train station. Rates: LE10-20 for singles and double.*

Dingy, but the best place in town. Some rooms feature fans and private (but less than spectacular) bathrooms.

WHERE TO EAT

Should you stay at the HappyLand, they run a cafeteria that can hook you up with food from town if the kitchen isn't running. In town, the **Restaurant Hamdi**, and the **El Prince Restaurant** on El Aqsur Street serve typical Egyptian fare like roast chicken, rice, tehina, bread et al. There is also kushari, ta'amiya, and chicken on El Gomhuriya Street and near the station. In no place does a meal cost more than LE10.

SEEING THE SIGHTS

THE TEMPLE OF HATHOR AT DENDERA

Five kilometers west of Qena on the west bank of the Nile in the village of Dendera. Hours: 7am-6pm daily. Admission: LE12 general; LE6 students.

The Ptolemies and Romans erected this magnificent and nearly perfectly preserved temple between 125 BC and 60 AD. Though dedicated to one of Egypt's oldest and most important deities, **Hathor**, this particular temple was among the last to be built in the traditional pharaonic style. According to pharaonic tradition, Hathor was the wet nurse and mate of Horus and it was here at Dendera that she gave birth to their child.

Though built as the sun set on pharaonic Egypt, we know this temple was built on the site of many previous shrines dedicated to Hathor and that a necropolis at the site contains tombs dating to the 6th Dynasty.

HATHOR, GODDESS OF LOVE & MATERNITY

The goddess of love and maternity, Hathor was one of ancient Egypt's oldest and most popular deities. Identified with the cow, whose form she often assumed, Hathor is often seen on walls in temples and tombs suckling infant pharaohs as a royal and divine matriarch. Her association with the cow, an important source of livelihood for Egyptian peasants, and her appeal as a maternal giver of life also made her an important symbol for the masses.

*Her most important festival, during which her sacred idol was brought to Edfu for a conjugal visit with Horus, was even known as the **Festival of Drunkenness** because on no other day during the year did Egyptians indulge as much in wine and beer. During the Greek occupation of Egypt that began with Alexander the Great (332 BC), the Ptolemies identified Hathor with the Greek goddess of love Aphrodite and built this temple in her honor.*

The Pylon & Great Hypostyle Hall

Six of the famous "Hathor columns" dominate the facade of the large pylon through which the temple is entered. Eighteen such columns then comprise the **Great Hypostyle Hall**, the first portion of the temple. Built by Romans, the walls in this portion of the temple depict various Roman emperors such as Augustus, Tiberius and Nero in pharaonic form making offerings to Egyptian deities. On the ceiling, a sky motif features vultures, pharaonic zodiac signs, and Nut, the sky-goddess who gives birth to the sun, and like Hathor is a goddess of maternity.

The Halls of Appearances, Offerings, & the Sanctuary

The Great Hypostyle Hall gives way to a second hypostyle hall, the **Hall of Appearances** featuring six columns. Though highly ornate, the reliefs on these columns are a good example of what scholars maintain is a decline in the quality of workmanship compared to that found in Old and New Kingdom monuments. Those on the wall separating this hall from the first hypostyle hall are quite fascinating as they recount the construction of this temple. The chambers to the sides of the columns were used for storage.

Beyond the Hall of Appearances is an ante chamber known as the **Hall of Offerings** where important sacrifices were made, and wall reliefs portray priests and pharaohs making offerings to Hathor. You can climb a stairwell to the top of the pylon to enjoy superb views of the temple grounds and the Nile Valley. During special festivals, priests carried the statue of Hathor up these stairs to the **roof** where she overlooked the festivities and the surrounding countryside. Two **chapels on the roof** are dedicated to the resurrection of Osiris. In the western room, the goddesses Isis and Nephthys mourn Osiris as he makes his way through the afterworld. The ceiling in the eastern chamber features a copy of a plaster now in the Louvre known as the Dendera Zodiac. Held up by four goddesses, its reliefs depict the night sky inscribed with Zodiac signs imported by the Romans.

Beyond the Hall of Offerings is the heart of the temple, the sanctuary known as the **Hall of the Ennead** which was the permanent home of statues of idols used in Hathor-related celebrations. The wall reliefs contain the texts of hymns used in such festivities, and to the side, small chambers also contained items and clothing used in festivities. The actual **sanctuary** which held the sacred statue of Hathor, is to the right. Once a year this statue made a journey up the Nile on a sacred barge to Edfu where Hathor paid a conjugal visit to her mate, the hawk-headed god, Horus. Walls on either side portray the only people allowed into the sanctuary, the pharaoh and the high priest, performing the annual rituals of opening up the sanctuary and making offerings. The rear wall of the sanctuary portrays the son of Hathor and Horus in his classic pose, playing with a rattle and sistrum.

After visiting the sanctuary, make your way to the **small side chapels** to the west which contain some fantastic ceiling reliefs with astrological motifs featuring Nut, the sky-goddess. Behind the sanctuary several more small chapels and crypts dedicated to the annual New Year Celebrations contain intriguing representations of pharaohs and priests paying homage to Hathor in her various forms.

External Chapels

Behind the main temple is a ruined chapel known as the **Birth House of Isis**. Constructed by the Roman Emperor Augustus, it is one of three birth shrines incorporated into the Dendera complex during the Greco-Roman period. Towards the front of the temple beyond the **Sacred Lake** that was used for ablutions, is a **sanitarium**. An ancient Egyptian spa, it was visited by the lame and sick who believed that it held Hathor's magical healing powers.

The sanitarium is flanked by another birth house built by **Nektanebo**, a 30th Dynasty, pre-Ptolemeic pharaoh. Next to his birth house is a 5th century **Coptic basilica**. The Copts often built on or next to pharaonic temples, in part to supersede their legitimacy. Finally, furthest to the north is the **Roman Birth House**, the newest of the birth houses.

BETWEEN QENA & LUXOR

There is of little to speak of between Qena and Luxor. Twenty-three kilometers south of Qena, the village of **Bellas** is famous for the manufacture of pottery, the type you may see miraculously balanced women's heads. South of El Ballas, the ancient Christian village of **Naqada** is home to a weirdo pigeon house known as **Kasr El Hammam**, the "Palace of Pigeons." Erected by a monk 100 years ago, it provides food and refuge to more than 10,000 migrating birds at one time and is as a constant source of food for its human keepers.

Between Qena and Luxor on the east bank, the town of **Qus** was once Egypt's second city in medieval Islamic times. The only potential attraction now is **El Amri Mosque** which features a fine minbar and mihrab.

NIGHTLIFE & ENTERTAINMENT

If you're staying at the HappyLand, you may be lucky enough to catch a local village wedding. Otherwise, nocturnal fun is restricted to a sunset beer at the HappyLand or *sheesha* and backgammon in one of Qena's many ahwas.

SHOPPING

Qena is famous for **pottery**, manufactured at El Ballas 25 kilometers to the south, and sold at the town's weekly **Thursday market (Souk El Khamees)**—an attraction itself for those who enjoy "local color" and "bustling markets." Otherwise, Qena offers little and even a white earthen pot is rather unexciting and difficult to carry home.

PRACTICAL INFORMATION

Banks & Currency Exchange

Two banks are located on El Aqsur Street west of El Gomhuriya Street. *Hours: 8:30am-2:30pm and 6-9pm (sometimes) Sunday-Thursday.* They exchange currency, travelers' cheques, and should be able to handle Visa cash advances, but don't count on it.

Emergencies
• **Ambulance:** *Tel. 123*
• **Hospital**: best to get to Luxor
• **Police:** *Tel. 325-284 (at the train station)*

Post Services

Post Office, *El Aqsur Street. Hours: 8am-3pm Saturday-Thursday.*

Telephones, Telex, & Fax

24 telephone centrale, *El Gomhuriya Street.*

Tourist information

For transportation info, inquire at the appropriate depot or station; otherwise, hotel personnel, drivers, and the Tourist Police may, or may not, be of assistance.

Tourist Police

They should be on duty at the train station and the Temple of Dendera.

LUXOR

The resplendent capital of pharaonic Egypt during its imperial New Kingdom heyday, the provincial town of **Luxor** reemerged as a premier destination for travelers and scholars in the 19th century after 2,000 years of near total neglect and today survives and (sometimes) thrives on the tourism industry that brings two million visitors annually. The array of monuments and relics that visitors come to see are overwhelming in their age, scale, and historic significance. On the east banks, the graceful temple of Luxor dominates downtown, while upriver, the gargantuan temple of Karnak is unrivaled by any other house of worship in the world in terms of size. In and amongst the valleys of the Theban Hills, pharaohs like Ramses the Great, Hatshepsut, and Tutankhamun indulged in lavish tombs and stupendous mortuary temples.

The town of Luxor is hardly anything to rave about and with tourism being the only game in town, it's near impossible to escape the constant pestering of shopkeepers and touts begging, even demanding that you do everything from riding their hantour to visiting their "factory." The best you can do is grin and bear it, or escape to the rural solitude of the west bank where fellaheen farm sugar and alfalfa fields as their ancestors have for millennia.

History

After the disintegration of central authority in Memphis at the end of the Old Kingdom around 2,200 BC, a Theban lord Mentuhotep emerged to fill the subsequent power vacuum, reunited Egypt, and founded the Middle Kingdom in 2,133 BC with Thebes as its capital. Shortly thereafter the capital moved back north to Faiyoum and the Middle Kingdom went out of business in 1785 BC, but Theban supremacy in Upper Egypt was established and the Cult of Amun at Karnak became a national cult.

Thebes rose to prominence again during the New Kingdom (1567-1080 BC) when Egypt reached new imperial heights. As pharaohs like Thutmosis III, Seti I and Ramses II continued to expand the empire abroad, Thebes and the priesthood for its patron deity Amun became increasingly wealthy and the temples of Karnak and the Luxor Temple were built on a scale hitherto unknown except for the Pyramids. The capital was briefly transferred from Thebes to Tel El Amarna during the heretical reign of Akhenaten, but essentially it was the center of the Egyptian universe for 500 years.

After Egypt and Thebes succumbed to foreign rule, first with the Persians in the 6th century AD, and later to the Ptolemies, Thebes remained a regional hub, but lost its imperial status. By the time of the Arab invasions, the magnificent city of Thebes with its pharaonic cults and temples had faded into oblivion and it was not until the 19th century when Europeans became obsessed with ancient Egypt that it reemerged from obscurity.

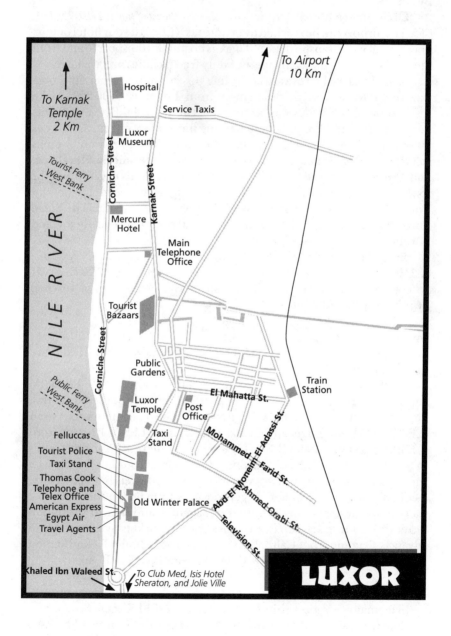

To Airport
10 Km

To Karnak
Temple
2 Km

Hospital

Service Taxis

Luxor
Museum

Corniche Street

Karnak Street

Tourist Ferry
West Bank

NILE RIVER

Mercure
Hotel

Main
Telephone
Office

Tourist
Bazaars

Corniche Street

Public
Gardens

Train
Station

Public Ferry
West Bank

El Mahatta St.

Luxor
Temple

Post
Office

Felluccas

Taxi
Stand

Mohammed El-Farid St.

Tourist Police

Taxi Stand

Thomas Cook

Telephone and
Telex Office

American Express

Old Winter Palace

Abd El Moneim El-Adassi St.

Ahmed Orabi St.

Egypt Air

Travel Agents

Television St.

Khaled Ibn Waleed St.

To Club Med, Isis Hotel
Sheraton, and Jolie Ville

LUXOR

ARRIVALS & DEPARTURES

By Air

Luxor International Airport, *five miles northeast of town, Tel. 095/384-655.* The airport can be reached by private taxi (LE20) if your hotel or tour does not provide transportation. There is no public transport to and from the airport. Currency exchange and duty-free facilities are available.

Schedules and fares vary according to season, but generally a one-way ticket to any Egypt destination from Luxor is $100-200. Make reservations as far in advance as possible There are 4-6 EgyptAir flights between Cairo and Luxor (1 hour) during the low season and as many as 20 during winter. EgyptAir also flies 4-6 times daily to **Aswan**; 3 times weekly to **Sharm El Sheikh**; twice weekly to **Kharga**. **Alexandria, Hurghada**, and **Abu Simbel** can all be reached through connections in Cairo and/or Aswan. Internationally there are weekly flights between Luxor and **Frankfurt, Jeddah, London, Kuwait, Paris Orly**, and **Zurich**. Some European tour operators also fly direct charters between Luxor and European destinations.

EgyptAir, *Old Winter Palace, Corniche El Nil Street. Tel. 095/380-580/ 1/2/3/4. Fax 095/380-585. At the airport: Tel. 095/380-586/7/8. Fax 095/ 380-589.* **Karnak Travel** (EgyptAir's sister travel agency) can be reached by phone at *095/382-360.*

By Bus

The Upper Egypt Bus Co. depot is on Television Street. Tickets are sold from a small kiosk that is open virtually all day.

There are two air-conditioned buses daily to **Cairo** (LE50, 12 hours) and four to **Hurghada** (LE20-40 depending on amenities, 4-5 hours). More frequently buses depart hourly during daylight hours to **Aswan** (LE8-12, 4-5 hours), Qena (LE3-5, 1 hour), Esna (LE3-5, 1 hour), Edfu (LE5, 2 hours) and Assiut (LE10-15, 4-5 hours). There are also daily buses to **Sharm El Sheikh** (LE110, a taxing 12-15 hours). Your hotel or a travel agent should be willing to assist you in purchasing tickets but may charge a commission of 5-15%. For longer journeys to major destinations like Cairo and Hurghada, check with a travel agent, your hotel, or the station ticket office for exact departure times and buy tickets at least a day in advance. Coming from Cairo, buses depart from Ahmed Helmy Station in Ramses Square and possibly Abdel Moneim Riyad and Qulali.

By Service

The main depot is behind Luxor Temple off El Karnak Street.

Service is efficient for reaching **Nile Valley destinations** like Esna (LE3, 45 minutes), Qena (LE2, 45 minutes), Aswan (LE8, 4 hours), and Edfu (LE6, 2 hours).

Should you wish to hire a minibus privately, negotiate directly with drivers at the depot or contact a travel agency. Expect to pay at least LE100 per day; more if you go all the way to Cairo.

By Train

The train station is on Ramses Street on a small midan at the end of the semi-major thoroughfares of El Adassi Street and El Mahatta Street.

Apart from flying traveling by first or second class on the train is the most efficient and comfortable way to travel between Cairo and Luxor.

Unlike Ramses Station in Cairo and other major rail hubs, Luxor's station and its staff are relatively well prepared to deal with English speaking passengers. First class tickets are sold from Window #2, and second class from Window #3. "Direct" trains for **Cairo** via Qena, Sohag, Assiut, and Minya depart 3-4 times daily (LE82 1st class, LE52 2nd class, 10-12 hours), and at least 4 times daily to **Aswan** (LE40 1st class, LE22 2nd class). Remember that students get a 30-50% discount and that you should buy tickets at least one day in advance. "Local" trains also leave frequently for Minya, Assiut, and Sohag to the north; Esna, Edfu, and Kom Ombo to the south, but are extremely slow and inefficient.

Trains from Cairo to Luxor depart from **Cairo's Ramses Station** and stop at Giza Station, 4 times daily.

If you want to travel by sleeper between Cairo and Luxor, the authorities have disallowed foreigners from taking the "regular" sleeper trains which means that you'll to take the **Carlsson Wagons-Lit sleepers** which cost a staggering $130 per person one-way. To make reservations in Cairo, check the Cairo chapter for details. In Luxor, the office is in the station and opens approximately from 9am-noon & 3-6pm.

By Cruise

One of the most popular means of travel between Luxor and Aswan is by cruise ship. Generally reservations for such journeys are made well in advance, but you can probably make arrangements on the spot in Luxor through travel agencies which advertise vacancies in their office windows-check those in the basement of the Old Winter Palace. When business is good, a berth on a moderately luxurious boat costs $60-100 per person per day everything (food, guides, accommodation) included.

When business is slow, you can negotiate even better deals (as low as $35) by approaching the ships themselves. Most cruises take 3-5 days and stop at Esna, Edfu, and Kom Ombo en route.

By Felucca

For those looking to make the famous felucca excursions between Luxor and Aswan, it's better to start in Aswan because leaving from Luxor leaves you at the mercy of the winds. If they die, you find yourself going backwards. In any case, you can find captains in Luxor willing to make the trip. Expect to pay about LE400 for a three day excursion. See the "Arrivals & Departures" section of the Aswan for details.

GETTING AROUND TOWN

By Bicycle

As the insanity of Luxor's traffic is not nearly on the same scale as Cairo's, many travelers take the opportunity to rent bikes from one of the numerous rental outlets throughout town. Biking is cheap (LE10-30 a day) and saves you the travel of having to deal with avaricious taxi and kaleche drivers. Also, should you have the time and the stamina, biking from monument to monument on the west bank can be more agreeable both in pace and style than scooting about in a taxi or tour bus, and it offers you a chance to absorb a bit of local color.

However, should you decide to bike on the west bank be aware that unless you have several days, you will be hard pressed timewise to get in even the most basic highlights in one day. Also, even in cooler weather, the sun can be extremely strong, so pace yourself and drink lot's of water.

By Boat

For crossing the Nile to the west bank, see the "West bank & Theban Necropolis" section under "Seeing the Sights" below.

Besides providing transport to the west bank, **feluccas** (Egyptian sailboats) offer a relaxing way to enjoy the Nile during sunset. They can be hired anywhere on the Corniche where captains congregate and generally cost LE20 for each hour, more if you have a group of more than 10. Bargaining may be necessary.

By Kaleche (Horse Carriage)

The clip-clop of horses' hooves and the cling-clang of carriage bells are an integral thread of Luxor's fabric. Unfortunately, so is the persistent pestering of drivers calling for your business. Once you get past the posturing and arrive at a reasonable price (LE5 and up depending on how far you're going for how long), taking a carriage is one of the more pleasant ways to get around. Simply hail one down if they don't find you first, or approach them at one of their main congregating points such as the Luxor Wena Hotel. To Karnak from Luxor Temple, they ask from LE15-20 for one way and you should probably settle for LE5-10. Shorter distances (any one-way ride within town) shouldn't cost more than LE5 unless there is an agreement for them to wait.

In Arabic a horse carriage is known as a *hantour* or *kaleche*.

By Foot

Downtown Luxor is easily negotiated by foot. Most hotels are within walking distance of either the Luxor Temple, Karnak, or both. Unfortunately, Luxor as a city in and of itself, is primarily a tourist town and there isn't the local flavor to take in by walking as there is in say Cairo or Aswan. Nonetheless, it's hard to beat an evening stroll along the Corniche and the views of the sun setting behind the Theban Hills on the west bank.

By Taxi

Taxis are more expensive in Luxor than in Cairo distance for distance and time for time, but they are ideal for efficient and customized sightseeing on both sides of the Nile. Cabs congregate at major hotels and sights, and at the airport, the train station, and most notably, just outside the Luxor Wena Hotel. Major hotels will arrange cabs for set prices which are just a bit more than reasonable. Otherwise, you have to bargain.

On the west bank, hordes of cab drivers and brokers will approach you upon arrival at the boat docks if not on the ferry itself. For a solid five or six hours of sightseeing whereby the taxi takes you from site to site and waits, you should be able to negotiate a price of LE50. For longer journeys, adjust your price demands accordingly.

WHERE TO STAY

Expensive

SOFITEL WINTER PALACE HOTEL, *Corniche El Nil. Tel. 095/380-422/3/5. Fax 095/374087. Telex 92160 WINTER UN. Capacity: 238 rooms, 434 beds. Rates: $150-160 single, $170-180 doubles; $257-573 suites. Credit cards: all major credit cards accepted.*

Favored by discriminating travelers from Theodore Roosevelt and Agatha Christie, to Jimmy Carter and Sean Connery, this turn of the century Edwardian gem retains its colonial elegance and charm in every respect from the finely upholstered furnishings and extensive wood paneling to the immaculately landscaped gardens. The rooms, beautifully furnished and well decorated in Edwardian style, overlook the Nile to the front, and the colorful Palace gardens to the back. Dining, recreation, and drinking facilities are shared with the New Winter Palace. The Winter Palace is well located just south of the Luxor Temple and the center of town.

MOVENPICK JOLIE VILLE LUXOR HOTEL, *Crocodile Island. Tel. 095/374-8555. Fax 095/374-936. Capacity: 334 rooms, 656 beds. Rates: $80-160 single, $100-205 double, $240-400 suites. Credit cards: all major credit cards accepted.*

Situated south of town on its own lusciously verdant island, the Movenpick combines the comforts and luxuries of a modern tourist resort with an outback, almost tropical setting. As the rooms are clumped in bungalows, most of them don't have views, but the rural setting is tranquil. In addition to several restaurants, bars, a swimming pool, tennis courts and other such facilities, the grounds contain a small zoo that kids love. The main disadvantage is the five kilometer distance from down-town, but the hotel provides automobile and boat shuttles frequently.

LUXOR HILTON HOTEL, *New Karnak by Karnak Temple. Tel. 095/374-933. Fax 095/376-571. Capacity: 261 rooms, 415 beds. Rates: $67.50-140 single, $85.25-168.75 double, $281-1500 suites. Credit cards: all major credit cards accepted.*

A large, new resort hotel offering deluxe amenities, but none of the charm of say, the Winter Palace. Located next to Karnak, it's a bit far from the hustle and bustle of downtown, which is inconvenient for those looking to enjoy Luxor's bazaars, cafes, and other distractions. Facilities include a swimming pool, tennis courts, a casino, a shopping mall, and several restaurants.

ISIS HOTEL LUXOR, *Khaled Ibn Waleed Street. Tel. 095/372-750, 373-366, 370-100. Fax 095/372-923. Capacity: 516 rooms, 1006 beds. Rates: $70-96 single, $80-114 double, $143-385 suites. Credit cards: all major credit cards accepted.*

This gigantic modern complex lives up to its own pretensions of modern luxury, but aside from the hokey "traditional" folk shows and belly dancing doesn't let on that it's in Egypt. It is however very comfort-able and the two pools and well maintained gardens provide a nice setting in which to wind down after a dusty day of sightseeing. For eating and drinking, there are no less than a half dozen restaurants and bars serving Chinese, Egyptian, and Italian cuisines. This place is popular with *veilles dames francaises* type tour groups.

LUXOR SHERATON HOTEL & RESORT, *Khaled Ibn Waleed Street. Tel. 095/374-013, 374-544, 374955. Fax 095/374-941. Capacity: 296 rooms. Rates: $60-155 single, $75-187 double, $248-1250 suites. Credit cards: all major credit cards accepted.*

It's about what you'd expect from Sheraton: modern amenities, good service, little charm, and bundles of package tourists. The Nile views are sensational.

MERCURE LUXOR HOTEL, *Corniche El Nil Street half a kilometer north of the Luxor Temple. Tel. 095/ 380-944, 374-944. Fax 095/374-912. Capacity: 306 rooms. Rates: $35-82 single, $44-99 double, $193-275 suites. Credit cards: all major credit cards accepted.*

Formerly, and still popularly known as the "Etap," the Mercure boasts one of the finest locations in Luxor on the Corniche, halfway between the Luxor Temple and the Luxor Museum. Though it lacks the elegance of the Old Winter Palace or the exotic setting of the Movenpick, the Mercure offers rooms complete with the amenities expected from an international chain hotel including air-conditioning, satellite television, phones, and functional clean baths. External facilities comprise several restaurants and bars, and a nice pool. The Nile views are superb, the rates, extremely reasonable, and the disco and bar are among the most popular in town.

LUXOR WENA HOTEL, *opposite the Luxor Temple. Tel. 095/380-018. Fax 095/380-017. Capacity: 86 rooms, 172 beds. Rates: $52 single, $62 double. Credit cards: all major credit cards accepted.*

An old timey, colonial era hotel, the Luxor Wena doesn't measure up to the Old Winter Palace but does offer ambiance, location, and good value. Situated just across the street from the Luxor Temple in the heart of the city, the Wena grounds contain a large pool (often used for Arab wedding parties), somewhat inconsistently maintained gardens, and several restaurants. Rooms are spacious and all have air-conditioning and reasonably clean bathrooms.

NOVOTEL EVASION LUXOR HOTEL, *Khaled Ibn El Waleed Street. Tel. 095/380-925. Fax 095/380-972. Capacity: 185 rooms, 296 beds. Rates: $53-66 single, $44-99 double. Credit cards: all major credit cards accepted.*

On the banks of the Nile facing the Theban Hills, the Novotel can't be beat for the views, and with the Luxor Temple and downtown just a half kilometer away, the location isn't bad either. Thoroughly modern in style and attitude, the Novotel is comfy and convenient, but lacks charm. The discotheque is one of the most happening in town, particularly on weekend evenings. All rooms are air-conditioned and with minibars, satellite television, and balconies.

Moderate

ARABESQUE HOTEL, *Mohammed Farid Street. Tel. 095/ 372-193, 371-299, 382-820. Fax 095/372-884. Capacity: 36 rooms. Rates: $35 single, $45 double. Credit cards: Visa.*

This one of the better 3 star hotels, especially given its location on Mohammed Farid Street just down the street from the Luxor Temple. Should they be available, streetside rooms on the upper floors look over the Wena Hotel and the Luxor Temple. Amenities include television, private bath, air-conditioning, and telephones. The restaurant and the rooftop pool leave a bit to be desired, but there are always other options. As the establishment is run by Muslims, no alcohol is served.

EMILIO HOTEL, *Youssef Hassan Street. Tel. 095/373-570, 374-884, 386-666; Fax 095/374-884. Capacity: 48 rooms, 96 beds. Rates: $35 single, $45 double Credit cards: Visa.*

This is one of the better managed and better maintained of the mid-ranged hotels and it shows in the prices. The cheerful rooms feature dish television, air-conditioning, private baths, and telephones.

NEW EMILIO HOTEL, *Youssef Hassan Street. Tel. 095/371-601,/2/3. Fax 095/370-000. Capacity: 53 rooms. Rates: $30 single, $35 double. Credit cards: Visa.*

The folks running the original Emilio were so successful, they managed to open this sister hotel just in time for tourist bust after the Deir El Bahri shootings. Let's hope it doesn't squeeze them too much because the New Emilio is every bit as clean, comfortable, and professionally managed as its next door namesake.

KARNAK HOTEL, *Corniche El Nil Street 3 kilometers north of downtown. Tel. 095/374-155. Fax 095/374-155. Capacity: 44 rooms, 88 beds. Rates: $20-39 single, $26-52 double. Credit cards: Visa.*

A new three star hotel near the Karnak Temple, this establishment offers a pool, gardens, and great views of the Nile from the front rooms. Rooms are clean, air-conditioned and feature clean and functioning bathrooms. The location is quiet, somewhat far away (3 kilometers) from the hub of Luxor. During summer, prices are considerably (up to 50%) lower – don't hesitate to bargain.

SHADY HOTEL, *Television Street. Tel. 095/381-262, 381-377, 374-859. Fax 095/374-859. Capacity: 50 rooms, 115 beds. Rates: $30 single, $38 double. Credit cards: Visa with 10% surcharge.*

One of the better and more popular three star establishments- a reputation helped in no small part by the pool. Though not exactly large, and sometimes somewhat green, it becomes a hub for juvenile activity, not only for in house guests but with budget travelers from nearby hotels who pay about LE 10 to use the facilities. The staff is friendly, the rooms are clean, and the food better than average for most such hotels (which isn't saying much). Amenities include private bath, air-conditioning, television, international phones, and a bar and restaurant. Also, don't hesitate to bargain, especially if business looks slow.

FLO-PATER HOTEL, *Khaled Ibn Waleed Street. Tel. 095/374-223, 370-418. Fax 095/370-618. Capacity: 40 rooms, 80 beds. Rates: $20-28 single, $25-35 double, $120 suites. Credit cards: Visa.*

Another new concrete three star hotel with a quirky name the Flo-Pater is clean with good working amenities and a small pool, but a drab location with no views, except from the roof.

MERRY LAND HOTEL, *Nefertiti Street off the Corniche a block south of the Luxor Museum. Tel. 095/381-746, 376-903, 371-746. Capacity: 32 rooms, 64 beds. Rates: $23 single, $30 double. Credit cards: not accepted.*

Merryland Hotel is somewhat plain, but offers excellent location and well furnished rooms; amenities include phones, clean and private showers, television, and air-conditioning. The rates are also excellent.

PHILIPPE HOTEL, *Dr. Labib Habashy Street. Tel. 095/372-284, 376-604. Fax 095/380-060. Capacity: 40 rooms. Rates: $27 single, $34.50 double. Credit cards: Visa.*

It features the typical three star set-up with a bar and pool on the "roof garden" and a nondescript restaurant. The rooms are typically modest with air-conditioning, private baths, and balconies. The Philippe is also cleaner than many other hotels in the same price range.

MINA PALACE HOTEL, *on the Corniche north of the Luxor Temple near the Luxor Museum. Tel. 095/372-074. Rates: LE45-65 single, LE50-88 double.*

Rooms have air-conditioning, a private bath, and views of the Corniche and Nile; corner rooms also look over the Luxor Temple. There is a restaurant and terrace bar on the street. The location is excellent and rates dip during the summer.

NILE HOTEL, *Dr. Labib Habashy Street next to the Philippe. Tel. 095/372-859, 372-334. Fax 095/382-859. Rates: LE40-60 single, LE55-75 double.*

It's a concrete blob with nondescript air-conditioned rooms with private baths, televisions, and balconies, but the prices are better than many comparable hotels. The lower rates apply during summer.

HORUS HOTEL, *Karnak Street north of the Luxor Temple and Mahatta Street intersection. Tel. 095/372-165, 370-465. Fax 095/373-447. Rates: LE30-35 single, LE40-45 double, LE65-70 triple.*

The Horus is right in the thick of things on Karnak Street next to the bazaars and any five star hotel would kill for the views of the Luxor Temple. The trade off is the noise, both from the streets and the Abu El Haggag Mosque. The rooms are a bit musty, but other than that modest and clean with air-conditioning and phones. Guests can use the Windsor Hotel pool for LE7 and there is a pleasant restaurant selling lunch dinner, and beverages, including beer. Breakfast is included.

Budget

There are oodles of cheap hotels and pensions in Luxor catering to backpacker type budget travelers. When getting off the train, you will be accosted by all sorts of characters with all sorts of offers and claims about their hotels; some are true and some aren't. We've tried to include only those hotels with established reputations, but you never know when standards change, so ask around before committing. Most of them feature simple, sometimes musty rooms with and without private showers and air-conditioning. Almost all of them will offer to arrange tours of the west bank. Shop and ask around before committing, because some of these tours end up total flops.

All of the hotels are just about dirt cheap, but you can still haggle down prices, especially during low seasons (summer and spring). None of the following hotels accept credit cards.

SAINT MINA HOTEL, *Cleopatra Street just north of El Mahatta Street by the train station. Tel. 095/386-568. Rates: LE30-35.*

This small hotel offers clean, well maintained rooms with or without private showers and air-conditioning. It gets good reviews from travelers for its friendly and helpful service and for its cleanliness.

GRAND HOTEL, *off Mohammed Farid Street two blocks past the Oasis Hotel. Tel. 095/374-186. Rates: LE5.*

The name is a bit misleading but this modest and well managed hotel consistently gets high marks from guests who enjoy the affable staff and cleanliness. The bathrooms are shared, but fairly clean with hot water, and rooms have fans. There is a rooftop terrace and facilities for washing laundry. An older gent, Ahmed, organizes donkey trips to the west bank for LE40 a head and will show a book of guest comments telling what great experience it is. The inland location in a local residential neighborhood is somewhat far from the main attractions of the Corniche, but it's quiet and makes a nice refuge from hawkers, taxi drivers, and all the rest of the tourism related commotion.

OASIS HOTEL, *Mohammed Farid Street. Tel. 095/381-699. Rates: LE6-10 single, LE12-16 double.*

This hotel overlooking Mohammed Farid Street offers clean rooms some of which have private showers. The common showers are clean and have hot water. The more expensive rates are for rooms with air-conditioners that seem to do little other than push a bit of air around, but at least it's something. The other rooms have fans.

EVEREST HOTEL, *off Television Street. Tel. 095/370-017. Rates: LE10-20.*

The location overlooking a dead end alley leaves something to be desired, but the rooms are quite clean. The more expensive rooms have noise making machines that resemble air-conditioners and the others have fans. All rooms have private showers with hot water.

VENUS HOTEL, *Youssef Hassan Street. Tel. 095/372-625. Rates: LE8-10 single, LE14-20 double.*

The modest rooms come with fans, but no air-conditioning and some have private showers. The location is excellent and there is a restaurant and even a bar that serves cold Stella.

FONTANA HOTEL, *Radwan Street off Television Street. Tel. 095/380-663. Rates: LE10-20.*

There is an assortment of rooms, with and without air-conditioning and private showers. The rooms are generally clean and there is also a rooftop terrace and a washing machine.

ANGLO HOTEL, *south of the square in front of the train station. Tel. 095/381-670. Rates: LE 10-20.*

It's an affable place with singles and doubles featuring fans and shared bathrooms; there are also a few doubles with private showers.

Hostels & Camping

THE YOUTH HOSTEL, *off El Karnak Street 2 kilometers north of downtown Luxor. Tel. 095/372-139. Rates: LE7 with membership; LE8 without membership.*

The hostel features rooms with three beds or more which are clean, but the bathrooms aren't nearly so attractive. The hostel is far enough out of town that you'll spend so much money trying to get there that you won't save any money by staying here; besides, nicer accommodations are available in town for similar prices.

REZEIKY CAMP, *El Karnak Street just south of Karnak Temple. Tel. 095/381-334. Rates: LE10 for camping; LE15-20 simple bungalows; LE30-50 air-conditioned rooms.*

Set in a leafy complex away from the bustle of Luxor's souks and traffic, the Rezeiky allows you to pitch a tent or you can rent a simple no frill room in a bungalow. For a LE30-50 the rooms are cleaner and air-conditioned. The friendly confines feature a rather sad swimming pool, a restaurant, and a nice terrace on which to relax with a beer. The staff is cheerful and helpful.

Staying on the West Bank

The majority of travelers stay on the Nile's east bank in and around the nondescript town of Luxor, unaware that the west bank affords a rare opportunity to sample rural life in Egypt. Though the west bank is known for its historic attractions it also features functioning farms and villages where the fellaheen live an agrarian life very similar to that of their pharaonic ancestors. You don't have the same access to Luxor's bazaars (which gets tedious anyway) or the nightlife (no loss there), but there is the ferry. The only drawback is that accommodations tend to be less than posh and the dining options are rather limited, usually to the particular hotel in which you stay. To get around the west bank, rent bicycles near the local ferry or from one of the hotels, or hire a taxi.

PHARAOHS HOTEL, *up the road from the Antiquities Office in Nag Lohlah village. Tel. 095/310-702. Rates: LE35-60 single, LE45-70 double.*

A cozy hotel with 15 rooms, the Pharaohs' main attraction in addition to its location is its well-tended garden that features an excellent restaurant. Rooms are priced according to season and whether they have fans or air-conditioning.

ABUL KASSEM HOTEL, *Wadi El Maluk Road east of Seti I's mortuary temple. Tel. 095/310-319, 372-502, 581-515. Fax 095/581-590. Rates: LE20-40.*

Abul Kassem is clean, well managed, and offers carpeted rooms with fans, fridges, and private showers with hot water. The views from the roof are superb and there is also a restaurant. You can rent bikes or hire out donkeys for touring the west bank. The only drawback is its distance from the ferries and other sites, but you wouldn't walk from the other hotels either. Prices vary according to season.

MERSAM HOTEL, *across from the Antiquities Offices near the road to the Tombs of the Nobles. Tel. 095/382-403. Rates: LE20-25 single, LE25-30 double.*

You can stay in the simple mud brick rooms of the adjunct or in the more modern main building which is more comfortable. All rooms have fans and the bathrooms are shared but are quite clean and have hot water. There is also a pleasant garden with views of nearby farms. This place was once run by the legendary Sheikh Ali who participated in the excavating of Seti I's tomb; it is now run by his son.

HABU HOTEL, *next to the Mortuary Temple of Ramses in Medinet Habu. Tel. 095/372-477. Rates: LE10-15 single, LE20-25 double.*

With it's fellahi-Nubian architecture, the heat shouldn't roast you the way it can some other places. The spacious rooms come with fans and the roof features magnificent views of Ramses III's temple and is a great place to wind down with a beer. There is also a nice garden and terrace. The place is a bit run down, but renovations should give it a nice upgrade, not to mention a reason to raise prices.

WHERE TO EAT

Luxor doesn't offer the culinary diversity or quality that Cairo or Alexandria does, but there's no shortage of eateries suitable for any budget. Most four and five star hotels contain at least two restaurants on their premises, including at least a large dining room and a coffee shop. Three star establishments also serve food, but it's usually sad attempts to mimic continental food which the cook has probably never tasted himself. Buffets are common in hotels and typically consist of less than stellar continental and "oriental" fare. For those on a tighter budget, there is no shortage of cheap food, often tastier than the pricey stuff of luxury hotel restaurants.

Local eateries serving fuul, ta'amiya, and grilled fare are concentrated along Television Street, Abdel El Moneim El Adasi Street, El Mahatta Street, and Karnak Street. For big bowls of kushari, try Sayeda Zeinab on Television Street or Sayeda Nafisa on Youssef Hassan Street

DAWAR EL OMDAH, *next to the Luxor Wena Hotel across the street from the Luxor Temple. Hours: 11am-midnight.*

Set in a garden next to the Luxor Wena, the Dawar El Omdah offers a smattering of Egyptian dishes in a relaxing outdoor setting. Though more expensive then local budget restaurants, its food is decent and the atmosphere pleasant. On some evenings, live Egyptian music and dance is featured. Main courses run up to LE25 while appetizers range from LE3-8. Stella and sheesha are also available.

ALY BABA CAFE, *Luxor Wena Hotel across from the Luxor Temple. Hours: 9am until late.*

Aly Baba's Egyptian fare rivals Dawar El Omdah's and costs half the price. Perched on a rooftop terrace overlooking the gardens of the Wena Hotel and the Luxor Temple, it's quite popular with budget travelers. Sheesha is served but not alcohol-a good place for a lemonade or a cup of coffee.

CLASS RESTAURANT, *Khaled Ibn Waleed, 400 meters from the Novotel and just north of the Isis Hotel. Credit cards: Visa.*

It's not as classy as the name might suggest and it's quite expensive (LE30-40 for a full meal), but the continental and oriental cuisine is decent.

KING'S HEAD RESTAURANT, *Television Street. Hours: 11am-midnight. Credit cards: Visa.*

Sister to the popular King's Head Pub and the King's Head Restaurant offers a similar menu: a vast array of Egyptian mezze and main courses, continental food, as well as several Indian dishes and appetizers. Though it's not fantastic, the Indian food makes for a tasty change from the usual Egyptian and continental fare, but for those on a tight budget, it may be a bit of a reach. A full meal will set you back at least LE30 after drinks and taxes. Though not oozing with atmosphere, it's a pleasant and clean establishment in which to enjoy a meal.

MISH MISH, *Television Street. Hours: midmorning to midnight.*

Mish Mish is a colorful, cheesy pizzeria type place that offers a variety of cheap salads, sandwiches, soups, and pizzas. It's air-conditioned and comfortable and you can eat for LE10 or less.

SULTANA RESTAURANT, *Television Street. Hours: morning to midnight.*

Little more than a hole in the wall, it should accrue a more intimate and homier feel once its ages a bit (it only opened in 1997). The Egyptian food is cheap, the place clean, and the management friendly.

PINK PANDA, *Isis Hotel on Khaled Ibn Waleed Street. Hours: noon-3pm and 6-11pm. Credit cards: Visa, Mastercard.*

It's only worth it if you're really hard up for Chinese food and even then , it's very pricey and the quality is disappointing. Appetizers and soups are hard to find for less than LE5 and main dishes less than LE20. Somehow nothing about it seems quite authentic, which is really not surprising given that we're in Luxor.

LA TERRAZZA, *Isis Hotel on Khaled Ibn Waleed Street. Hours: noon-3pm and from 6-11pm. Credit cards: Visa, Mastercard.*

Diners enjoy a serene dining atmosphere either outside in a leafy garden setting or in an enclosed terrace. Though the first bite of garlic bread won't take you straight to Bologna, the assortment of pizzas, pastas, and antipasti appetizers is the best Italian fare in Luxor. Though it isn't cheap, you can enjoy a solid meal for LE25 or LE35 with a beer.

GARDEN COFFEE SHOP, *the New Winter Palace Hotel on Corniche El Nil Street. Hours: open 24 hours. Credit cards: all major credit cards accepted.*

The overpriced international menu is about what you'd expect from an upscale hotel coffee shop, but the salad bar certainly deserves a mention. For LE15 you can stuff yourself with fresh salads from tabouli to tuna. You just have to bear paying that LE5 for a coke to go along with it.

SEEING THE SIGHTS

This is what it's all about. For all the pestering cabbies, and *kaleche* drivers, the twelve hour train ride from Cairo, the bus from Hurghada, the towering and exquisite monuments of ancient Thebes make coming to Luxor worth it all a hundred times over.

THE LUXOR MUSEUM

The Luxor Museum is on the Corniche about 500 meters north of the Luxor Temple. Hours: 9am-1pm and 4-9pm (winter), 5-10pm (summer). Admission: LE20 general; LE10 students. Cameras: LE10 without flash or tripod, LE100 video.

In contrast to the Antiquities Museum in Cairo, this classy little museum is well laid out, easy to follow, and easy enough to absorb in just one two hour visit. It doesn't contain massive pieces, but many of the Middle and New Kingdom statuettes and amulets are exquisite indeed. Of particular interest is the Akhenaten exhibit on the second floor that features a depiction of him with wife making offerings to the sun disc, Aten. The reliefs were originally from Tel El Amarna but were usurped by later pharaohs who used them in constructing the ninth pylon at Karnak Temple where archaeologists excavated them. The other must-see exhibit, in a special wing off the ground floor, features 24 life-size New Kingdom statues discovered by accident at the Luxor Temple in 1989.

THE MUMMIFICATION MUSEUM

The Mummification Museum is on the Nile side of the Corniche in the Visitor's Center complex several hundred meters north of the Luxor Temple. Hours: 9am-1pm & 4-9pm (winter), 5-10pm (summer). Admission: LE30 general, LE15 students. Cameras: not allowed.

This spanking new one room exhibition about mummification in ancient Egypt is worth every piaster of the steep LE30 cost of admission. The exhibits take visitors on a short but mesmerizing tour of the mysterious world of mummification in ancient Egypt. There are detailed explanations of the mummification process and its place in Egyptian theology. Exhibits include fantastically well-preserved examples of mummified cats, fish, dogs, baboons, and human beings.

LUXOR TEMPLE

The Luxor Temple is on the Corniche and the end of El Mahatta Street. Hours: 6am-9pm winter; 6am-10pm summer. Admission: LE20 general, LE10 students.

History

While not as overwhelming or massive as Karnak, this magnificent temple in the heart Luxor, is refreshingly manageable and easily digested in one visit. Dedicated to the **Theban Triad** of **Amun Ra**, his consort **Mut**, and son, **Khonsu**, it was initially constructed by Amenhophis III with substantial additions by Ramses II. Tutankhamun, Haremheb, Hatshepsut, Thutmosis III, Seti I, and Seti II, all new Kingdom Theban leaders, also left their marks- in some cases just a cartouche or two. Later Alexander the Great, the Romans, and even Muslims also made their own additions.

In the 2nd century AD, the rise of Christianity and the decline of the Cult of Amun left the temple in disrepair. A local settlement sprouted on the site and the temple was engulfed by sand, debris, and eventually an Arab Islamic village. The **Abu El Haggag Mosque** was built during the Fatimid Era in the 11th century and the village remained atop the forgotten monument until the 19th century. Upon visiting the Temple in 1822, English aristocrat Frederick Henniker noted "this temple swarms with dogs, Arabs, houses, and other filth" and was so covered with debris that the door, which uncovered stands more than 15 meters high, could not "admit a man without stooping." It was only later in the century when Egypt became a fad with European tourists and scholars that the temple was excavated.

Like Karnak, the Luxor Temple testament not only to the strength and prosperity of the New Kingdom (1570-1080 BC) and its capital, Thebes, but the great wealth and prestige enjoyed by the **Cult of Amun** priesthood. During the annual **Opet Festival**, held in the second month of the inundation, sacred idols were brought out of Karnak by the high priests and paraded to Luxor Temple on barges. Great festivities were held, animals sacrificed, and the idols remained at Luxor Temple for 24 days before returning to Karnak. This annual religious highlight in Thebes was the only time the most important priests and idols went before the public.

The Temple

Ramses II constructed the **entrance pylon** the reliefs of which display him battling the Hittites at Kadesh in Syria. At the entrance, he originally placed four statues of himself, two of which still stand, and two granite obelisks, including that now standing in the Place de la Concorde in Paris. Just through the pylons is the **Court of Ramses II**, noteworthy for its papyrus columns and the beautiful statue of Ramses standing at the rear. To the right upon entrance Hatshepsut erected three small **shrines** dedicated to Amun Ra, Mut, and Khonsu. Thutmosis III, Egypt's most successful warrior pharaoh but a jealous rival of Hatshepsut, usurped them, and Ramses II restored them. On the rear wall to the right and behind the Ramses statue is an intriguing relief of Luxor Temple itself during the Opet festivals. Reliefs feature representations of fattened animals waiting for sacrifice and a procession of Ramses II's with his family.

On the left of the entrance to the Court of Ramses II is the **Mosque of Abu Haggag**, built during the Fatimid Era (11th century AD) and named for Luxor's most venerated sufi saint. Though seemingly misplaced, the mosque's presence is interesting for two reasons. First, the ground below the mosque remains unexcavated, a case in point that no matter the significance of any archaeological site, Islam and Islamic monuments and institutions take precedence in Egypt. It would be very unseemly to any red blooded Muslim that a mosque be disturbed in favor of another house of worship; particularly a pagan pharaonic monument. Second, the of a mosque perched on the unexcavated portion of the temple is an excellent example of how societies build directly over the neglected remnants of past civilizations, often unknowingly or without interest. You can literally view different eras of history layered one over the other.

Beyond the Court of Ramses II, the splendid **Colonnade** of 14 papyrus columns was constructed by Luxor Temple's founder Amenhophis III. The flanking walls display scenes of the opulent Opet festival. On western walls (towards the Nile) are images of the commencement of the festival and the procession of idols from Karnak to Luxor. Priests are seen carrying the barge of Amun to the flooding river while masses of people celebrate by clapping and performing athletics and gymnastics. Priests then place the Pharaoh's barge on display and make offerings to the Theban Triad. Following reliefs on the eastern wall heading back north towards the front of the temple we find slaves, soldiers and other officials accompanying the procession back to Karnak where offerings are made.

Beyond the Colonnade is the heart of the temple, the **Court of Amenhophis III**, distinguished by papyrus-budded columns. To the rear you will find the **sanctuary**, home to the temple's most sacred idols. Romans later converted the original entrance into a shrine of their own- notice the faded images of Roman emperors in classical dress plastered over the original pharaonic reliefs.

Through the entrance is a small court, the **Hall of Offerings**. The sanctuary itself is at the center of this small complex of rooms later renovated and rebuilt by Alexander Great. Just east of the Hall of Offerings is a small room, known as the **Birth Room**, which tells the story of Amenhophis III's birth. Not of royal lineage himself, these reliefs tell the tale his miraculous birth and his descent from Amun. Reliefs portray Amun holding the key of life to the nostrils of the queen while Khnum, the ram-headed god of creation, shapes an infant Amenhophis III and his *ka* (spiritual double) from clay on a pottery wheel. This story indicates that Amenhophis III felt the need to legitimize his claim to the throne, not having royal blood himself. Here in 1989, local employees discovered 26 magnificent life-size statues which are now on display at the Luxor Museum.

KARNAK TEMPLE

Karnak is on Corniche El Nil Street 3 kilometers north of the Luxor Temple. Admission fees: Admission: LE20 general; students LE10. Hours: 9am-6pm (winter), 9am-7pm (summer).

The miles and miles of wall reliefs, statues, obelisks and pylons commemorating the achievements, ideals, and aspirations of the New Kingdom Pharaohs who built this magnificent temple are simply mind boggling. The crumbling mud brick remains of later Roman add-ons and adjuncts only seem to emphasize underscore the superior engineering, craftsmanship, and the sheer dedication of the pharaohs and their builders to honor their gods and themselves. More so than any Theban monument Karnak shows the degree to which the **Cult of Amun** and its priesthood not only penetrated the highest reaches of Egyptian society, but became its driving force. At its peak during the 19th Dynasty, the Cult of Amun priesthood owned tens of thousands of slaves, farmed huge tracts of prime agricultural land, raised 300,000 heads of cattle, and operated hundreds of chariots and dozens of ships.

Covering more than one hundred acres and containing dozens of shrines within itself, Karnak temple was constructed over 1,500 years beginning in the 10th Dynasty (2,050 BC) before the founding of the Middle Kingdom. By the height of the New Kingdom in the 18th and 19th Dynasties, it was of importance to each pharaoh that he, or she in the case of Hatshepsut, construct taller pylons and larger statues than his predecessor. As was common in pharaonic Egypt, pharaohs routinely stripped the monuments of their predecessors to build at Karnak. Akhenaten's palaces and temples at Tel El Amarna south of Minya were especially abused in this respect after he abandoned the Cult of Amun and its priesthood in favor of the Cult of Aten.

Like other pharaonic monuments Karnak saw modest additions by Greeks and Romans before falling into disuse after Christianity became Egypt's preeminent religion. For nearly two thousand years history buried Karnak which like the nearby Luxor Temple became the site of a local village. European archaeologists set about excavating it in the 19th century and restoration has continued ever since; in '97 the entire southern axis was closed for repairs.

The Entrance Pylon

Visitors now enter Karnak through an **avenue of ram-headed sphinxes**. The ram was considered the sacred animal of Amun, and in this avenue of sphinxes, each ram bears a small likeness of Ramses II, one of Karnak's major contributors. The sphinxes lead to the huge unfinished **Entrance Pylon**. Believed to have been constructed by the Nubian Kushites during the 25th Dynasty (600 BC), it spans more than 130 meters across, and is the largest pylon in Egypt. Through the pylon, you will enter the **Great Court**, also a late contribution by the Nubians.

To the left stands a sandstone and granite shrine constructed by Seti II in honor of the Theban Triad that was also a way station for sacred barges used in the processions of idols during important festivals. The lotus capital in the center of the court was erected by the Kushite Pharaoh Taharka who originally built ten such columns.

The Temple of Ramses III

To the right upon entrance through the entrance pylon, this classic New Kingdom shrine is the best example of the temple within a temple phenomenon at Karnak. Though not as prolific as his namesake Ramses II, **Ramses III** (20th Dynasty, 1,100 BC) was a very productive builder responsible for such monuments as the impressive mortuary temple at Medinet Habu. With typical pharaonic hubris, the entrance pylon reliefs

SOUND & LIGHT AT KARNAK

*Perhaps the finest **Sound & Light show** in Egypt, the 90 minute presentation affords the stunning sight of Karnak's pylons and halls bathed in blue light against a starlit sky. The commentary, needless to say is as hokey as ever, but does provide historical background. There are three or four shows nightly. The English version begins at 7:30pm in winter (8:30 summer) Wednesday- Sunday; 6:15pm on Monday (7:15 summer); and 8:45pm (9:45 summer) on Tuesdays. The entrance fee is LE35 (no student discounts). In winter, dress warm; the weather can get quite chilly.*

recall Ramses' military victories and depicts him smashing prisoners in front of an approving Amun. This pylon gives way to a small open court surrounded by covered halls and passages. On the walls Ramses assumes the usual poses with deities: giving alms, receiving the key of life, and receiving blessings. As was usually the case in New Kingdom temples, a pillared hypostyle hall leads to the rear of the temple where sanctuaries are located. In this case the shrines are dedicated to the Theban Triad of (from right to left) Amun, Mut, and Khonsu.

Though not spectacular in the context of humungous Karnak, this temple is fun to explore because it's usually quiet and empty, allowing you to ponder the size and age of the place without the distraction of large tour groups.

The Second Pylon & the Great Hypostyle Hall

After dipping into the temple of Ramses III, return to the main court and make way to the **Second Pylon**, constructed during the 19th Dynasty when construction at Karnak was most intense. Not nearly as massive as the entrance pylon, it contains thousands of blocks usurped from Akhenaten's temples of Aten at Tel El Amarna south of Minya. The handsome granite statue of Ramses II, with a much smaller Queen Nefertari standing between his feet, left of the door was discovered underneath this pylon.

Through the second pylon you will enter the majestic **Great Hypostyle Hall**, Karnak's *piece de resistance*. Containing **134 columns** 23 meters tall, and covering some 5,000 square meters it is, according to Jill Kamil, "the largest single chamber of any temple in the world."

Thought to have originally featured 10 or 12 columns, the Hall was augmented by **Seti I** who added the northern wing and **Ramses II**, who built the southern – many subsequent pharaohs also inscribed their cartouches on these great towers. The later columns feature papyrus capitals while calyx capitals top the original columns. On most columns, reliefs depict the pharaohs making offerings to and receiving blessings from, a vast assortment of gods and deities.

More interesting than the column reliefs are those on the walls, both inner and outer. **Seti I** constructed the northern wing (to the left upon entrance) where interior reliefs depict the unveiling of Amun's barge on the western wall and Thoth's recording of Seti's glorious reign and achievements. On the outer walls, his military prowess is graphically depicted as he battles the Canaanites in Syria and Palestine on the eastern walls and thrashes the Libyans on the western end. Notice the register of Lebanese cedars at the top.

Scholars and tour guides love to compare Seti's reliefs with those of **Ramses II** on the southern wing of the Hypostyle Hall. Ramses' sunken cookie cutter depictions of religious rites are considered a testament to his commitment to quantity rather than quality while Seti's more creative and finely carved reliefs are considered amongst the best in Egypt. Interestingly enough, scholars make the same comparison concerning the reliefs of Seti and Ramses at Abydos. On the interior walls Ramses is crowned by Horus and Thoth before Amun. There are also depictions similar to those on Seti's walls including the unveiling of Amun's sacred barge. On the exterior walls, the famous **Battle of Kadesh** against the Hittites, also depicted at the Ramesseum and Abu Simbel, is recreated in some of the temple's most graphic reliefs.

The 3rd, 4th, and 5th Pylons

Like the first two, the **third pylon**, constructed by Amenhophis III (father of Akhenaten) in the 18th Dynasty, contains stone usurped from previous monuments. In recent years, archaeologists have reconstructed what they believe to be a 12th Dynasty Middle Kingdom temple using the original stones usurped by Amenhophis III and used in the construction of this pylon.

Between the third and fourth pylons, Thutmosis I, Thutmosis II, and Thutmosis III (18th Dynasty) erected four obelisks, known as the **Thutmossid Obelisks**. All but one have toppled, but the one standing, built by Thutmosis II stands 23 meters tall and is thought to weigh 145 tons – another testament to the technical superiority and megalomania of pharaonic builders. Beyond the **fourth pylon**, constructed by Thutmosis I, stands the **Obelisk of Hatshepsut**, the most famous of all obelisks. At 27 meters in height, and weighing over 320 tons, this is the largest obelisk still standing in Egypt-its twin stands in Rome. Like all of Hatshepsut's monuments, Thutmosis III, her half brother and chief rival, usurped this obelisk and claimed it for himself.

The **fifth pylon**, built by Thutmosis I (Hatshepsut's father) gives way to a largely destroyed colonnade containing Osiride statues built on the site of Karnak's original Middle Kingdom shrine. The **sixth pylon**, also mostly destroyed, is known for its outer wall, the **Wall of Records**, listing the military triumphs of **Thutmosis III**, one of Egypt's greatest military heroes. Amongst the vanquished are assorted western Asians to the left and Nubian Africans to the right. To the north stand two impressive statues of Amun and the goddess Amentet. In Amun, scholars see the face and features of **Tutankhamun**, and believe he was the builder.

The Sanctuary

Beyond the sixth pylon, you will finally arrive at the sanctuary, the most sacred shrine in the entire temple. It was here that the holiest idols were kept, to be viewed and maintained only by the highest strata of the temple's priesthood. The sanctuary now in place was constructed around 300 BC by **Philip Arrhidaeus**, half-brother of **Alexander the Great**, over existing sanctuaries dating to the 18th Dynasty and the Middle Kingdom. Reliefs depict Philip's coronation by Thoth and the giving of offerings to Amun. He is also portrayed performing ablution and purification rites. The boat is the sacred barge of Amun.

Relics left by numerous pharaohs clutter the area behind the sanctuary, the most important of which date to the 18th Dynasty reign of **Thutmosis III**. To the right two pillars carved into papyrus and lotus plants feature reliefs depicting the pharaoh mingling with Amun and other gods. To the left on the exterior of the sanctuary, Thutmosis III recorded his military accomplishments over reliefs originally commissioned by **Hatshepsut**. Behind the sanctuary an open court was the core of the original 12th Dynasty Middle Kingdom Temple of Amun.

The Temple of Thutmosis III

Behind the second open court stands the Temple of Thutmosis III, nominally dedicated to Amun, but in reality a celebration of Thutmosis himself. The structure includes dozens of rooms and chambers. A main hall was originally supported by dozens of columns and pillars upon which the pharaoh is seen in the presence of various divine dignitaries. Some of the more interesting chambers include, to the southwest, a relic of the Table of Kings which pays homage to previous pharaohs, except of course Hatshepsut. Also to the left, a chamber with four columns, features depictions of various plants and animals captured and imported from Syria and Palestine.

Beyond the Temple of Thutmosis III are a smattering of **shrines dedicated to lesser deities**, also constructed by Thutmosis III, that were used primarily by common folk who did not enjoy access to the major temples. Here Ramses II erected a 30 meter tall obelisk that was confiscated by **Constantine** who relocated it to Rome where it became known as the **Lateran Obelisk**. It is believed to be the sister of the gigantic Unfinished Obelisk in Aswan.

The Sacred Lake

After exploring the length of Karnak's primary axis, make your way back to fourth pylon and cut left to the South. Pass through the Cachette Court and make another left towards the **Sacred Lake**. Here is a shaded cafe where you can enjoy an over priced soft drink, and relax your legs. Priests bathed and performed ablutions and purification rites in the waters of the Sacred Lake. En route to the cafe, you will notice a **gigantic scarab**, connected to the kiosk sized **Osirion of Taharka**, a 25th Dynasty Nubian pharaoh. The scarab represents the rebirth of the sun and new life, hence its connection with Osiris, the God of the Afterlife. On the eastern side of the cafe a nilometer was used to measure the levels of the river, which the priesthood used to set tax and tribute rates.

The North-South Axis

As the primary axis is more than enough for most tourists to handle, especially in one visit, the secondary north-south axis is usually neglected and in 1997 it was closed in any case for restorations. When it finally reopens, it should be well worth the extra time and leg work needed to explore its more than 2 square kilometers of ruins.

It is entered through the **Cachette Court**. Under these grounds the priesthood stashed tens of thousands of statues and statuettes, presumably for safekeeping when faced by the threat of invasion. In 1904, **50,000 bronze relics** alone, some dating to the Old Kingdom, were discovered here. The eastern and northern walls are the backside of **Ramses II's** southern wing of the Hypostyle Hall and portray him primarily in battle. Of particular interest is the replica of a relief on the eastern wall. It list peoples conquered by Merneptah, Ramses II's successor, including one nation some believe to be Israel. This would make it the only reference to Israel found in pharaonic Egyptian chronicles and scholars are still uncertain of whether Israel is in fact the nation in question.

The **seventh and eighth pylons** were constructed during the 18th Dynasty (by Thutmosis III and Hatshepsut, respectively) but dotted with reliefs by a number of 18th and 19th Dynasty rulers. The row of pharaohs in front date to the Middle Kingdom and remnants of statues of Thutmosis III lie on the other side. Beyond the eighth pylon, four more colossi depict an assortment of New Kingdom pharaohs.

Haremheb, successor to King Tut, erected the ninth pylon in the 19th Dynasty (1,340 BC). As was the trend in the immediate post-Akhenaten era, this pylon was built with material stripped from the temples of Aten at Tel El Amarna. East (left) of the huge court beyond the ninth pylon is the **Temple of Amenhophis III**. Like the Temple of Thutmosis III, it was built in the name of Amun but its true agenda was the assertion of the pharaoh's own divinity. This temple contains fine reliefs and paintings still in their original colors, mostly depicting the Pharaoh in traditional poses with Amun and other deities. Finally, at the end of the huge, empty court, the remains of the tenth pylon, also constructed by Haremheb, mark the southern boundaries of the Karnak complex. An avenue of sphinxes stretches beyond towards the Temple of Mut, nearly 300 meters to the south.

Temples within a temple

The vast complex of Karnak, the largest temple in the world, made a perfect base onto which pharaohs could add additional temples and shrines, leaving their own personal imprint on the master temple. The temples of Ramses III, Thutmosis III, and Amenhophis III, already described, are the most obvious examples, but numerous other temples have also been tacked on, some quite out of the way. These temples are generally in poor shape and often off limits to the common tourist. Consult the Antiquities Authority, your tour guide, or the local guard to see what is open. A bit of *baksheesh* has been known to open a few doors.

The Temple of Khonsu, *in the southwestern corner of the Karnak complex, to the left from the main entrance.*

Dedicated to Khonsu, third member of the Theban Triad and child of Amun and Mut, this well preserved but poorly carved temple was originally constructed by Ramses II and enlarged by Ramses IV, Ramses XII, and Hrihor, a high priest who usurped the throne at the end of the 20th Dynasty. The crude carving is a testament to decline in workmanship and prosperity during the later half of the New Kingdom. Most reliefs depict Hrihor as pharaoh cavorting with the usual deities. He was able to usurp power, thus dividing Egypt, after the Ramessids moved their capital to the Delta in the middle of the 20th Dynasty.

Next to the Temple of Khonsu, stands the finely carved **Temple of Optet**. Built during the Ptolemeic Era, it is dedicated to the mother of Osiris often depicted as a hippopotamus. Unfortunately, this temple is often closed to the public.

The Temple of Mont, *outside the Karnak complex to the North 400 meters from the main axis of the main temple, just beyond the Temple of Ptah.*

Erected by Nubians during the 28th and 29th Dynasties, this temple is dedicated to Mont, a falcon-headed deity whose importance dates to the Old Kingdom when he was worshipped as a war-god. Though poorly taken care of, the temple is now being renovated by the French Institute of Archaeology.

The Temple of Ptah, *just south of the Temple of Mont, 380 meters north of the main Karnak axis.*

Ptah was the patron god of Memphis dating to the early dynasties of the Old Kingdom. Unfortunately, little remains of this temple except for a headless statue of Ptah himself. The temple was erected by the most prolific builder at Karnak Thutmosis III, and later expanded by Nubians and Ptolemies.

The Temple of Aten, *100 meters east of the main Karnak complex.*

Built by the heretic pharaoh Akhenaten, this shrine was a precursor to the great temples of Aten at Tel El Amarna, south of Minya. Like those temples, this one suffered destruction at the hands of Akhenaten's successors, Haremheb, Seti I, and Ramses II who stripped it and used the stones for their own monuments.

The Temple of Mut, *300 meters south of the tenth pylon beyond the avenue of sphinxes.*

This temple, which features a sacred lake, is now being renovated. Mut, was the consort of Amun, and the second member of the Theban Triad. Little remains of the temple except for some statues erected by Amenhophis III. Also lying about is a headless colossus thought to depict to Amenhophis III.

THE WEST BANK & THE THEBAN NECROPOLIS

After the Pyramids themselves, no burial grounds have captured the world's imagination like the vast cemeteries that make up the **Theban Necropolis.** Here New Kingdom (18th-20th Dynasties, 1567-1080 BC) pharaohs like Ramses the Great, Thutmosis III, and Tutankhamun indulged in preparations for eternal life in the afterworld by constructing not only highly ornate tombs, but leviathan mortuary temples as well. Ancient Egyptians believed the cycle of death and rebirth mirrored that of the sun, rising in the east and setting in the west and hence were laid to rest on the Nile's west bank. Though time and generations of vandals have stripped monuments of many of their original treasures, there is more than enough to see, and plenty of it is certainly magnificent if not outright magical.

For millennia, these monuments to self-indulgence have attracted scholars and visitors from all over the known world, many of whom did their part to strip the west bank of their treasures. Archaeologists, antique collectors, and scholars for generations plundered the tombs and temples of some of their most valuable artifacts, not without the assistance of locals whose ancestors built, and usually within a generation, robbed the supposedly well concealed tombs. We know that the thousands of artifacts in the glass casings and vast store rooms of the world's museums are but a fraction of the treasures produced and crafted by the ancients.

Seeing the West Bank

As most visitors zip through Luxor in two or three days, they barely have an opportunity to explored but a fraction of what the west bank offers. For many that's just fine, as they find themselves "templed out" after a day or two, weary of hieroglyphics, hard pressed to visit yet another tomb or temple. For others, it means that planning and efficiency is crucial to covering the greatest number of monuments possible. If you have any time at all, it's best to break down your touring of the west bank into several visits. This enables you to enjoy the history and importance of each monument while not succumbing to fatigue that can make trooping about the west bank more of a chore than the enlightening

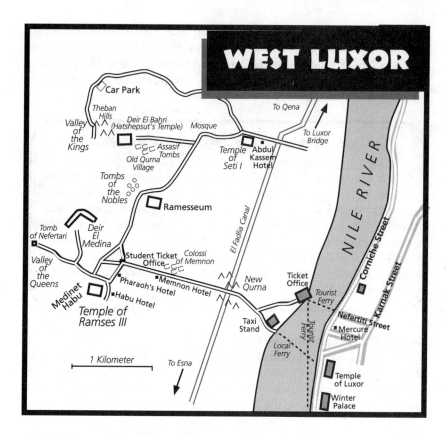

sojourn it should be. This is especially the case in the hot months (April-October) when more than several hours of touring at a time will leave you exhausted if not miserable and downright ill.

In planning your tour of the west bank, it's best to do a bit of homework first – to decide which monuments you'd like to visit, if nothing else. Virtually everybody makes the required pilgrimage to the **Valley of the Kings**, home to the most impressive tombs of the most important pharaohs. As more than a dozen tombs are open to the public at any one time, take a few minutes to peruse their descriptions to determine which you find the most interesting. Most visits take about two hours, more if it's crowded or if you choose to take in more than the three tombs allotted by the basic entry ticket.

After the Valley of the Kings, the other absolute must see, can't miss attraction is **Hatshepsut's Mortuary Temple** at **Deir El Bahri**. After that, visitors are faced with a myriad of choices to round out their itinerary. The **Valley of the Queens** is quite impressive and can be easily seen in an hour or two as can the massively impressive mortuary temples of **Medinet**

Habu and the **Ramesseum** — each of which takes between half an hour to two hours a visit. We'd recommend however, that if you visit anything else on the west bank, that it be so the **Tombs of Nobles** as their vivid portraits of everyday life in ancient Egypt make a refreshing change from the rigid, funerary motifs of the royal tombs.

WHAT TO WEAR, WHAT TO BRING

Given the powerful sun and the need to respect local sensitivities, the trick is to cover up while cooling down-even when it's not scorching in winter, the powerful Egyptian sun burns and dehydrates. Light, loose clothing covering arms and legs, a comfortable pair of sturdy walking shoes, and a hat are most recommended. Sunglasses are also a good idea and those of you who wear glasses, should bring both sunglasses and clear glasses or you won't be able to see a thing inside the tombs. Other items worth bringing: water (which is very expensive at the sites); a camera and extra film; and a flashlight.

Getting There: Crossing the Nile

The spanking new **Luxor Bridge**, crossing the Nile 7 kilometers north of town, makes it easy for motor vehicles to access the monuments of the west bank from Luxor itself. You can now hire a taxi on the east bank and easily cross over avoiding the ferries. Tour buses can also zip right over.

The easiest, cheapest, and most colorful way to cross the Nile remains the rickety old rusty **local ferry** that sets off across the Corniche from the Luxor Temple, and costs foreigners LE1 each way. It runs constantly from 6am until midnight and will give you a good glance of the locals (and their goats and chickens) doing their thing. The **tourist ferry** that puts out north by the Mercure Hotel, is almost as cheap and just as efficient, but just doesn't have the buzz of the local ferry. You can hire motorboats or feluccas anywhere on the Corniche. Depending on the size of your group, expect to pay LE2-5 a head one-way.

Tours & Transportation on the West Bank

Transportation on the west bank ranges from the old fashioned rustic donkey ride to the sleek, air conditioned, high tech "super deluxe" bus coach. How you choose to get around will depend on your taste, your budget, and your schedule. Donkeys and bicycles are slow and cheap, taxis and buses fast and pricey. Using local transport really isn't an option.

If you desire a **guided tour**, you can often arrange it your hotel or one of the dozens of travel agents dotting Luxor's major streets. For LE75 a person, they arrange transport (usually some sort of bus), a guide, and entrance tickets. Unless you insist on organizing a private tour, you may be combined with, or tacked onto a larger group. In this case you may have little say in the itinerary, and forced to visit the monuments at a pace other than your own-i.e.. whizzing through at breakneck speed. It's worth it to check with other travelers from whose experience you may be able to draw on. If you'd rather go at it at your own pace, you're better off picking up one of Jill Kamil's guide books and doing it alone.

The most efficient means of scooting about the west bank for independent travelers, is by **taxi**, which you can hire upon arrival on the west bank, on the ferry (taxi drivers approach you), or in Luxor itself. Naturally you will have to bargain them down from the LE75 or whatever sum they offer to a reasonable rate. LE45, plus a tip at the end, for 5-6 hours touring is fair. If your group numbers six or seven, paying LE10 or LE20 extra is reasonable. Taxis will take you where you want to go and will wait while you sightsee. Invariably the driver will also want to take you to a "factory" where he gets a small commission just for bringing you and a hefty one if you buy anything. If the driver behaves himself and you have an extra minute, granting him the favor of passing through the factory is a nice gesture. Besides, the sheer kitsch of the souvenirs is worth a glimpse and who knows, you may actually find something worth taking home.

For those with more time and energy, **cycling** presents an opportunity to take in the monuments and local color at a leisurely pace. It's easy enough to rent bikes in Luxor on any major street (Mohammed Farid, Television, et al) for LE30-40 a day or on the west bank a hundred meters or so inland from the local ferry. It cannot be emphasized enough that you must drink plenty of fluids and protect yourself from the sun. The ride up to the Valley of the Kings is especially taxing.

If bicycles aren't exotic enough, try **donkeys**, but be aware the advantages are few. This is slowest and least comfortable way to get around. For LE30 per person a day, budget hotels and travel agents will fix you up with an ass. Donkeys are good for getting off the beaten path and exploring the surrounding countryside or making a jaunt to high points in the desert hills inaccessible by bus or car.

Finally, for the ultra sturdy industrial traveler, **walking** is an option. After reaching the west bank and purchasing tickets, hitch a ride to the Colossi of Memnon, Medinet Habu, or the Ramesseum depending what you need to see. From the Ramesseum, it's just a half kilometer north to Qurna Village and the Tombs of the Nobles. It's just another 500 meters onto Hatshepsut's Temple; from there, you can hike over the hill another kilometer to the Valley of the Kings. Should you desire, the Temple of Thutmosis III is but 500 meters northeast of the Ramesseum and can be included on the itinerary just mentioned.

PURCHASING TICKETS
FOR THE THEBAN NECROPOLIS

Tickets for all sites must be purchased from a booth next to the tourist ferry dock about a kilometer north of the local ferry dock, or at the Antiquities Office for those with student cards (students pay half price). Listed below are the prices of tickets for each monument(s). Extra tickets must be purchased if you wish to photograph inside tombs (but not temples): LE10 for each tomb with no flash. Flash photography is not allowed. If you wish to visit the Tomb of Nefertari tell your tour leader in advance or contact the Egyptian Antiquities Authority in Luxor to make prior arrangements because daily admission is restricted to 100-150. Tickets are numbered according to the monument they access.

1. Valley of the Kings (3 tombs)	LE20
2. Tomb of Tutankhamun	LE20
3. Temple of Hatshepsut at Deir El Bahri	LE12
4. Temple of Ramses III at Medinet Habu	LE12
5. Ramesseum	LE12
6. Assasif Tombs	LE12
7. Tombs of the Nobles (Kheruef & Anch-Hor)	LE12
8. Tombs of the Nobles (Rekhmire & Sennofer)	LE12
9. Tombs of the Nobles (Ramose, Khaemhet, & Userhet)	LE12
10. Deir El Medina (tomb & temple)	LE12
11. Valley of the Queens	LE12
12. Tomb of Nefertari	LE100
13. Tomb of Seti I	LE12
14. Assasif Tombs (Tomb of Pabasa)	LE6
15. Tomb of Peshedu	LE6
16. Tomb of Aye	LE6
17. Tombs of the Nobles (NeferRonpet, Dhutmose, & Nefer-Sekheru)	LE10
18. Tombs of the Nobles (Khonsu, Userhet, & Benia)	LE6

The Colossi of Memnon

The Colossi are 3.5 kilometers inland along the main road between the Nile and the monuments. You can't miss 'em. Admission: no ticket necessary.

These two gigantic, but weathered and lonely statues, sit on the site of the once the massive **Temple of Amenhophis III**, father of Akhenaten. Later pharaohs plundered the temple and reduced it to nothing, but the massive statues became the stuff of legend.

Greeks named them Memnon because after an earthquake the second statue was heard to "sing" every day at dawn. Memnon had been killed by Achilles at Troy and was believed to be greeting his mother, Eos, who herself, was the "dawn" in Greek mythology. His father, Tithonus, had been an Egyptian, hence the connection between Memnon and these Egyptian statues. The sound was probably caused by wind passing through small crevices in the slowly dilapidating statue and the legend of the singing Memnon became so great, attracting thousands of visitors, that the Roman Emperor Septimus had it fixed in 199 AD. It hasn't "sung" since.

The Valley of the Kings

Tucked in a valley deep in the Theban Hills, this, the most celebrated cemetery in the world was to be the final resting place the great pharaohs of the New Kingdom. While their Old Kingdom predecessors erected the most ostentatious tombs on the earth, the Pyramids of Giza, the New Kingdom pharaohs were primarily concerned with the security of their graves and the possessions therein which they would need in their forthcoming life. Pharaonic tradition held that for the soul to be content in the afterlife, the body must be preserved (hence mummification) and in peace so that the soul may return to it. Pharaohs realized that to protect their graves and mummies from thieves, they needed a secure locale in which to bury.

This small valley, first used by Thutmosis I (ruled 1525-1515 BC) , high and deep in the hills of the west bank was supposed to be the solution. Builders burrowed deep into the ground, sealed the tombs with plaster, covered them with huge stones, and then camouflaged the entrances. Yet except for the small tomb of the minor pharaoh, Tutankhamun, every tomb was violated and robbed long before the 20th century. Most experts believe that workers who participated in the construction of the tombs were usually the culprits meaning the integrity of the tombs lasted less than a generation.

Tomb Design

Nearly all the tombs in the Valley follow a particular pattern of design. Usually an entrance chamber led to a long shaft stretching deep into the ground. A small chamber, or perhaps several chambers, then preceded the burial chamber itself which contained a sarcophagus; smaller surrounding chambers were often used for storing the pharaoh's belongings. In every tomb, a symbolic door, known as a "**false door**," was built to allow the *ba* (the soul) access to the body and its possessions. This was thought to be a requirement for a healthy afterlife.

WHICH TOMBS TO VISIT?

As you will discover upon buying your entrance ticket for the Valley of the Kings, one ticket entitles you entrance into any three tombs, except Tutankhamun's, which requires a separate LE20 ticket. This may leave you asking, "How do I know which three tombs I want to visit? What is the difference between Ramses IV and Thutmosis IV, or Seti II and Seti I?" The best way to find out is to make multiple visits and see every tomb, but this is usually impossible. Generally, the tombs of Seti I, Haremheb, Amenhophis II, and Ramses IX are considered the finest. The tomb of Ramses VI is colorful but the workmanship is less than stellar and that of Septah is modest but the reliefs are excellent.

Ironically, the greatest pharaohs did not necessarily build the greatest tombs. Thutmosis III's, for example, is unfinished and lacks notable workmanship, and the tomb of Ramses II does not meet the standards set by his vast assortment of other spectacular monuments. The tomb of Seti I, however, is one case where quality of workmanship and the size of the tomb befits his status as a great pharaoh. The temples of Thutmosis IV, Seti II, and Ramses I are considered the weakest tombs.

The Tomb of Ramses IV (#2)

Fifty meters pass the entrance gate on the right.

Not especially spectacular, this tomb has suffered a high degree of deterioration at the hands of tomb robbers, Ptolemeic vandals (who left volumes of graffiti), and time. The depiction of the night-goddess Nut on the ceiling is the best relief in the tomb.

The Tomb of Yuya & Thuya (#46)

Up the path past the Tomb of Ramses IV (#2) to the left and just beyond tomb #3.

There's virtually nothing of interest in this tomb, the owners of which were the parents of Queen Tiy and grandparents of Akhenaten. Their origins are a matter of some controversy as Yuya's mummy was not typical of Egyptian royalty. From a bust found depicting Queen Tiy, it appears that they were of Nubian descent, but Egyptologist Ahmed Osman believes that Yuya may have been the Old Testament Joseph whose belief in one god supposedly influenced Akhenaten who adopted a monotheistic faith in Aten.

There is, however, no hard evidence to support this theory and no indication in any pharaonic relics of a Jewish presence in Egypt.

The Tomb of Ramses IX (#6)

Fifty meters past the Tomb of Ramses IV.

This stretched-out tomb, built during the 20th Dynasty at the end of the New Kingdom, slopes into a row of three main chambers. Along the entrance corridor to the left, the pharaoh makes offerings to a variety of gods while on the right hieroglyphics recite the *Book of the Dead.* Check out the scary looking creatures of the underworld on this side of the wall. Further on the left, reliefs depict various stages of a symbolic funeral. The pharaoh is reincarnated as Osiris and then shown making his way through the next world. Notice the serpents guarding the entrances to different sections of the corridor.

The first chamber features more processes through which the pharaoh must pass on his way to paradise. The second chamber is largely unfinished, but the third, the burial chamber, features a beautiful long and naked Nut, on the ceiling and excellent funerary reliefs on the walls. She is seen swallowing the sunset at dusk and giving it in rebirth in the morning, representing the cycles both of earth and of life.

LIFE AFTER DEATH - THE TOMB & THE AFTERLIFE

*To pharaohs, the tomb was a way station between this world and the eternal afterlife. Everything placed in the tomb and the texts written on the walls were intended for use by the pharaoh in making this transition. Egyptians believed in a dual essence of the human being. The **ka** (symbolized by double arms) a spirit close to the actual body was to remain with the body while the **ba**, or soul, which only came into being after death (denoted by a human-headed bird) made the journey from the tomb into the next world. For the ba to survive, the ka and the body had to remain intact, hence the need for mummification and the preservation of organs in canopic jars. The ba makes journeys between the tomb and the afterworld through the **false door** found in virtually every tomb. The vast amount of goods stored in the tombs were for use by the pharaoh in his afterlife and to ensure the survival of the ka and by extension, the ba.*

The Tomb of Tiy or Smenkhkare (#55)

Next to the main rest house.

This tomb is significant because of the mysterious mummy found in it at the turn of the 20th century. The mummy might be Queen Tiy, the mother of Akhenaten; Smenkhkare, his successor; or, because of the wide pelvis, Akhenaten himself. A stele found inside portraying Tiy with Akhenaten as pharaoh indicates that it dates to the Amarna period but does not provide a definitive answer as to whose tomb this is.

The Tomb of Ramses II (#7)

Opposite the Tomb of Ramses IX.

The tomb of Ramses II (1304-1237 BC), Egypt's longest reigning pharaoh and greatest builder, is disappointingly modest for antiquity's most prolific monumental builder. It is currently closed to the public but his mummy is on display in the Mummy Room at the Egyptian Antiquities Museum in Cairo.

The Tomb of Merneptah (#8)

Up a path to the right just past Ramses II.

Considered by many to be pharaoh of the Biblical Exodus, Merneptah (ruled 1235-1223 BC) was son of Ramses II, and grandson of Seti I. The tomb's steep entrance corridor is decorated with the ancient religious text the *Book of Gates*. The ceilings are covered with vultures and other assorted creatures charged with the impossible task of protecting the tomb from intruders. Designed to thwart unwanted visitors, the first chamber – a dummy burial chamber – contains quality reliefs but undoubtedly failed to fool ancient vandals. In the actual burial chamber, Merneptah is depicted as Osiris in the company of Isis.

The Tomb of Tutankhamun (#62)

Though in the Valley of the Kings, the tomb of "King Tut," requires an additional LE20 ticket that can be purchased at the main ticket office.

The most famous tomb in the Valley, that of Tutankhamun, is in fact one of the smallest and belonged to a minor pharaoh who died before reaching the age of 20. Yet, because it is tucked underneath the much larger tomb of Ramses VI, it was hidden from tomb robbers and intact when Howard Carter opened it in 1922. The treasures found included dozens of statues, jewelry, canopic jars, four coffins, and most famously, a magnificent gold burial mask. The extent of the loot inspired awe throughout the world and left Egyptologists dreaming of what might have been stored in the tombs of the truly great pharaohs like Ramses II and Thutmosis III. Except for the innermost coffin and mummy which are in the tomb, the all artifacts recovered from the tomb are in the Antiquities Museum in Cairo.

Known popularly as "**King Tut**," Tutankhamun (1361-1352 BC) is historically significant as a successor to Akhenaten, whose reign presided over the return of the Cult of Amun as a guiding force in society after Akhenaten abandoned it in favor of the Cult of Aten. Tut himself probably had little role in shaping the policy as he was little more than a child and pawn being played by the Amun priesthood and the army, led by Haremheb who later became pharaoh himself.

The tomb itself is modest but the reliefs are well preserved. On the rear wall behind the coffin, Tut is shown commiserating Osiris and other deities. To the right, his mummy is accompanied by an entourage of priests and generals, including Haremheb. To the left, some rather charming baboons stand for the 12 hours of the day, which in turn represent the cycles of life.

The Tomb of Ramses VI (#9)

Next to Tut's tomb on the right, past the path to Merneptah's tomb.

The primary significance of this tomb is that it shielded Tut's tomb, protecting it from tomb robbers until Howard Carter's excavation in 1922. Originally constructed by Ramses V, the tomb was usurped by Ramses VI (1156-1148 BC). The long entrance corridor is adorned with passages from holy texts such as the *Book of Gates,* and the *Book of Caverns*, giving explanation to the deceased how to proceed through the under-world. The reliefs are of a lower quality than those in earlier tombs, but are colorful and fascinating nonetheless. Particularly worth noting are those on the ceilings of the burial chamber, featuring texts of the *Book of Day* and the *Book of Night* and is canvassed with a night sky that includes Egyptian zodiac signs. Nut is depicted, as she often is in these tombs, giving birth to the sun.

TOMB #5: THE TOMB OF THE SONS OF RAMSES II

In May 1995, after more than seven years of work, Kent Weeks, an American archaeologist at the American University in Cairo announced that he had discovered the largest tomb in the Valley of the Kings. Strangely enough, it was not built for a king, but for the sons of Ramses II. That Ramses was almost as productive a father as he was a builder (he fathered more than 100 children) explains the size, though the exact number of sons originally buried is still unknown.

Though explorers had long known the tomb existed, it was not until Weeks began working on it in the late '80's, after saving it from a proposed parking lot, that its importance was realized. At first it was speculated that because it was a family crypt, it may have dated to Akhenaten's reign, as the tombs at Tel El Amarna are the only known New Kingdom family tombs. In '94 it was discovered to be larger than earlier thought and in the spring of '95, the breakthrough was made when Weeks discovered a corridor and second floor of chambers. News of the discovery sparked an Egyptmania reminiscent of that which followed Carter's discovery in 1922, as Weeks made the covers of Time and Newsweek and other major periodicals. Though few relics have been found, it will take at least a decade for Weeks and his team to clear out debris washed in by the flash floods that rip through the Valley once every two or three hundred years.

The Tomb of Ramses III (#34)

Up a short trail on the left of the path that begins beyond the Tomb of Ramses VI.

This huge tomb was closed to the public in 1997, but the first sections can still be approached. Built for the same pharaoh who erected the great mortuary temple at Medinet Habu, its tone is refreshingly light after the heavy theological themes that dominate other royal tombs. While there are plenty of offerings to be made, the first portions of the tomb feature colorful scenes of fishing, farming, and boats. Just before the first small chamber on the left some ten meters in, is the well-known depiction of two harpists playing for the deities, Shu and Atum. Take time to check out the side chambers used for storage. Unlike most storage rooms, they include reliefs, listing possessions the pharaoh desired to be taken with him into the next life.

The Tomb of Haremheb (#57)

West of Ramses III up the path that branches right after Ramses VI.

Haremheb (ruled 1348-1320 BC), the power behind Tutankhamun's throne, was the first pharaoh not of royal blood to build a tomb in the Valley of the Kings. Though he began his career during the reign of Akhenaten, he used his position as a powerful general to preside over the dismantling of the Cult of Aten and engineered the return of the Cult of Amun—a process he began during Tut's reign and completed during his own. This counter-revolution included the destruction of the city of Tel El Amarna and a campaign to erase Akhenaten's memory forever.

The entrance corridor to Haremheb's crypt, one of the finest in the Valley, is undecorated, but the middle and later sections of the tomb feature some reliefs a very high quality, both in workmanship and preservation. On the walls of the second chamber, Haremheb commiserates with Anubis before the usual assortment of death related deities: Osiris, Isis, and Horus. In the chamber at the end of the second corridor, the pharaoh is again depicted in the presence of Hathor, Osiris, Isis, and Anubis along with other deities. The tomb chamber itself was unfinished, but on the walls you can see the instructions and plans workmen would have used to complete it. The developed reliefs portray the various hours of night representing various stages in the afterworld. Finally, the granite sarcophagus contains some excellent workmanship in the depictions of Isis and Nephthys, both winged, guarding the body.

The Tomb of Amenhophis II (#35)

About 100 meters from Haremheb's Tomb on the path directly to the right.

Unfortunately for those who are claustrophobic, this fine tomb is one of the deepest in Thebes. Though robbed in antiquity, excavations in

1898 revealed more a dozen mummies, including nine royals. Among the pharaohs were Seti II, Amenhophis III, Thutmosis IV, Ramses IV, Ramses, V, Ramses IV, and Amenhophis II, himself. Presumably, members of the priesthood stashed these mummies to protect them from grave robbers. That they stashed them here remains a mystery. Perhaps they felt that because the tomb was already violated, potential grave robbers might leave it alone.

The plain entrance corridors lead to a false burial chamber before turning left to the actual burial chamber. The actual tomb is supported by six pillars decorated with drawings and paintings, not carvings, of the pharaoh with various deities. The ceiling features the night sky often found in royal tombs and the wall is covered primarily with sacred funerary texts. The rooms off to the side of the burial chamber contained the extra mummies.

The Tomb of Septah (#47)

On the left branch of the fork around the corner from Haremheb's tomb.

This recently opened tomb contains some the finest reliefs in the Valley, noteworthy for their color and preservation. Particularly worth noting is the ceiling featuring a sun disc and a very azure sky with vultures.

The Tomb of Tawsert/Sethnakht (#14)

Up the path to the left when you reach the fork coming from Haremheb or Ramses III. It's on the right on the way to the Tomb of Seti II.

Originally built for Queen Tawsert, wife of Seti II (1216-1210 BC), this tomb was usurped by Pharaoh Sethnakht (1200-1198 BC). He abandoned his own tomb, which later became that of Ramses III, and though he usurped this one from Queen Tawsert, somehow neglected to remove her mummy. Perhaps he thought he'd be kind enough to leave it in peace or maybe he had enough of a grudge against Seti II that he'd insult him by spending eternity with his wife. In any case, the reliefs-primarily mortuary texts – are well preserved and of fine quality. The granite sarcophagus in the tomb is Sethnakht's.

The Tomb of Seti II (#15)

Fifty meters past the tomb of Tawsert and Sethnakht.

Out of the way and undeveloped because of Seti II's early death (1216-1210 BC), this tomb is rarely visited. Those reliefs which are completed (located primarily in the entrance) are of fairly good quality, but hardly merit one of your three ticket punches. This tomb was used for storage by Howard Carter while he excavated Tutankhamun's tomb.

The Tomb of Thutmosis III (#34)

150 meters up the right hand path in the second fork from Haremheb, past the turnoff for Tawsert and Seti II.

Though Thutmosis III (1504-1450 BC) built a great empire in Asia and constructed much of Karnak Temple, he is best remembered as the jealous rival of Hatshepsut whose monuments he did his best to destroy out of vengeance.

As you can tell from the location of this tomb, Thutmosis III went to even greater lengths than his counterparts to protect his final resting place. Alas, like those of other pharaohs, except for Tutankhamun, Thutmosis III's attempts, however extensive, failed. After making the steep ascent into the cliffs and passing through the entrance corridor, you must cross the bridged pit before arriving in the first chamber. While the ceiling is decorated with the customary night sky, the walls feature a fascinating register of more than 500 different gods, spirits, and demons.

The burial chamber, shaped like a cartouche, features drawings, not carvings, of mortuary texts that resemble papyrus text. This indicates a job rushed by the need to close the tomb upon the pharaoh's death. Though Thutmosis III was a great pharaoh who presided over a large empire and a strong economy, the size of his tomb and the quality of its reliefs do not measure up to those of many less significant pharaohs.

The Tomb of Ramses I (#16)

The Tomb of Ramses I is the first tomb on the right if you bear left coming from Tutankhamun's Tomb. It is just before the Tomb of Seti I.

Except for founding the 19th Dynasty, Ramses I was an insignificant pharaoh who ruled only for two years (1320-1318 BC)—a fact borne out in the modesty of this tomb. The entrance corridor is very short and plain, leading to the only room in crypt – the burial chamber. Its walls are decorated with representations of the pharaoh commiserating with important deities, funerary scenes, and funerary texts from the *Book of Gates*.

The Tomb of Seti I (#17)

Beyond the Tomb of Ramses I on the right. Bear left after passing King Tut.

Belonging to one of the New Kingdom's most important pharaohs, this tomb is the grandest and finest in the Valley as well the deepest. A successor of Haremheb, Seti I won back the empire lost during the pacifist years of Akhenaten, a task begun by Haremheb. He also constructed the northern wing of the Hypostyle Hall at Karnak and had it not been for the success of his son, Ramses II, Seti I might be considered the New Kingdom's greatest pharaoh. His tomb is one of few cases where the quality of the tomb lives up to the reputation of the pharaoh who built it.

In the entrance corridor, Seti is seen in the presence of various manifestations of the sun-god such as the falcon headed Ra Harakhte. The first stairway after the first section is guarded by the traditional female guardians of the dead, Isis and Nephthys. More representations of the sun deities then appear passing through the underworld in the second corridor. In the first mini-chamber at the end of the second section of corridor the reliefs depict Ra Harakhte overcoming the evil Serpent of Chaos. Beyond the hole, is a pillared room where on the rear wall Seti is presented to Osiris, god of the underworld, by his son, Horus. On the wall to the right, the *Book of the Gates* is recounted; the dead-end chamber (containing two pillars) contains more funerary texts.

Make your way into a second set of corridors. In the first portion is a representation of the Opening of the Mouth ritual, meant to purify the deceased's organs for the afterlife. In the second section of this corridor, Seti makes offerings to deities while recounting more funerary hymns. In the first chamber at the end of this corridor, the gods greet Seti and bless him with eternal life, confirming his divinity. The pillared hall that follows once contained the sarcophagus, which is now in London and features the traditional night sky motif associated with the afterworld on the ceiling. The side rooms of this chamber were used for storage purposes and some feature text and depictions of the goddess Nut.

The Tomb of Thutmosis IV (#43)
Past the Tomb of Seti I on the left-hand branch of the fork.

This huge tomb, only recently open to the public, is largely unfinished. It is worth noting the drawings on the walls portraying the pharaoh with various deities, were outlines for carvings that were never made. Also, check the fine carvings on the large sarcophagus.

HIKING FROM THE VALLEY TO HATSHEPSUT'S TEMPLE

If the heat isn't absolutely scorching and you're moderately fit, consider hiking from the Valley to Hatshepsut's Mortuary Temple at Deir El Bahri. The appeal of the 45 minute jaunt, in addition to the extra exercise are the views of the temples of the Nile Valley as well as the peculiar landscape of the hills. To reach Deir El Bahri from the Valley, head southeast over the hills behind the tombs of Seti I and Ramses I. Be sure that you have sturdy walking shoes and that if you came with a taxi, you've arranged to meet him on the other side. If you have any questions as to where you're going, simply ask a local, "Fein Deir El Bahri?" and he should point you in the right direction.

The Tomb of Monthu-Hir-Khoshef (#19)

To the left of, and under the Tomb of Thutmosis IV, past the Tomb of Seti I.
This insignificant tomb belonged to a son of Ramses IX. The highlight is the entrance corridor with fine reliefs of the deceased making offerings to gods of the afterworld such as Anubis and Horus.

The Mortuary Temple of Ramses III at Medinet Habu

This classic New Kingdom mortuary temple is often overlooked by visitors who concentrate on the Valley of the Kings and Hatshepsut's temple at Deir El Medina. It features some of the best preserved and most interesting reliefs on the west bank and its grandeur is unsurpassed. It is best visited first or last as it is the first monument on the way in from the river or the last on the way out.

One of the last great pharaohs, **Ramses III** (1198-1165BC), a 20th Dynasty king, conducted successful military ventures in Palestine and Nubia during an era when pharaonic Egypt was in a state of general decline. These military campaigns, vividly depicted, are the primary theme of this temple, modeled on the **Ramesseum** constructed by Ramses II. Like other mortuary temples it celebrates the pharaoh's divinity, but it also contained a palace where the pharaoh resided.

Just beyond the entrance-an ancient Assyrian (Syrian) fortress-are two small chapels, one to the right and one to the left, in front of the temple's monumental pylons. To the right (north), built on a site where the ancients believed the **primeval mound** emerged from Chaos at the beginning of creation, stands the larger of the two chapels. Besides commemorating creation, it also encapsulates a mini-version of New Kingdom temple building history. Originally constructed by Hatshepsut, it was usurped by Thutmosis III who in typical fashion decimated her cartouches and claimed it for himself. Akhenaten then converted it to the Cult of Aten and tried to erase all traces of Amunism. His successors, Haremheb and Seti I, then returned the temple, as they did others all over Egypt, to the worship of the Theban Triad. This temple predates Ramses III's mortuary temple by three centuries.

In the corner of the larger enclosure, beyond Hatshepsut's temple from the complex's entrance, a **sacred lake** attracted infertile women believed its waters could help them conceive. Next to it, an ancient nilometer is largely destroyed.

To the left stands the **Temples of the Votaresses**, constructed in the Late Period during the 25th and 26th Dynasties.

The actual Mortuary Temple of Ramses III begins with two gargantuan **pylons** featuring depictions of Ramses III's military exploits graphic enough to warrant an 'R' rating. On the outer walls, the larger than life Ramses is shown smashing groups of captured enemies before the gods,

Ra Harakhte on the right (north), and Amun Ra on the left (south). At the bottom of the pylons, Thoth writes the pharaoh's name on the leaves of a palm tree while Amun sits on a throne in front of Ptah, also inscribing Ramses III's cartouche on a palm leaf. The pharaoh himself receives a certificate on the occasion of his Jubilee of the Reign. On the pylons' inner walls, Ramses is once again depicted defeating his enemies (to the north), this time the Libyans. On the southern pylon, scribes can be seen recording the body count and the pharaoh's victories for posterity.

While depictions of pharaohs crushing opponents is standard fare in temples and tombs these reliefs are particularly interesting for their portrayal of mercenaries-recognizable by their horned helmets-employed by Ramses. If the stairs to the top of the pylon are open, it's well worth the climb for the view – you may have to baksheesh your way up.

Through the pylons is the **First Court**, lined to the north and to the south by columns. The reliefs at the rear of the court on the **second pylons** portray the pharaoh leading unfortunate prisoners of war to Amun and Mut and on to their ultimate fate; reliefs on the left pylon recount the story of their capture. To the left (south) of the court stand what remains of Ramses' palace, now entered from the outside. The walls on this side of the court again depict victims of the pharaoh's prowess while on the right (north) stand withered statues of the pharaoh in Osirion form flanked by mini-statues of his queen.

Beyond the second pylons is a **Second Court**, once the site of a Christian chapel. The reliefs on this court break with the martial themes of the First Court and depict several major religious celebrations. To the right (north), are images of the **Festival of Min**, the god of fertility, immediately recognizable by a penis worthy only of a god of his stature. From the end of the court to the front, the pharaoh is depicted riding in his carried throne, accompanied by an entourage of soldiers, priests, and other dignitaries en route to a sacrifice while trumpeters and other musicians musically commemorating the great event. The opposite wall depicts a similar festival in honor of **Sokar**, a god of the dead.

The inner walls of the pylons continue the stories of the First Court, as Ramses is depicted crushing Libyans and leading prisoners to Amun and Mut. In the corner, the score is counted in heads and penises (!) of the pharaoh's rather unlucky opponents. At the rear of the Second Court, an inclined ramp leads to a terrace where the fertility of the king himself is celebrated by reliefs honoring his numerous children.

The open space of the First and Second Courts gives way to a maze of chapels in the last portion of the temple. It begins with a **hypostyle hall**, consisting of 24 columns that once supported and now absent roof. To the right (north) are small chapels dedicated to Ptah, Sokar, and Osiris while to the left (south), small rooms were used to store the wealth (precious stones, metal, and idols) of the temple. Reliefs on the walls depict Ramses in the company of an assortment of deities.

Beyond the hypostyle hall, are the holiest and most important sanctuaries surrounding two smaller hypostyle halls. The small chamber to the left of the first hall served as the funerary sanctuary of Ramses himself while its counterpart to the right contained a shrine to Ra. The rear chapels were dedicated to the Theban Triad of Amun, Mut, and Khonsu.

Many of the temple's most fascinating and important reliefs are contained on the outer walls of the temple, particularly the northern wall (right when facing from the entrance) which records Ramses' exploits against the Libyans. The rear portions show the Libyans and their allies, the unknown **"Peoples of the Sea,"** thought to be Sardinians, Cretans, or possibly Phoenicians, making advances on Egypt. In the middle portion, lively and graphic reliefs depict a larger than life Ramses responding in kind and then some, wreaking havoc on enemy ships. These are the only known pharaonic naval combat scenes in Egypt.

The final battles, on walls closest to the temple entrance, depict (though Ramses did not know it at the time) Libyan counterattacks which eventually led to their conquest of Egypt and the end of pharaonic glory. Not until Gamal Abdel Nasser came to power in 1952 would Egypt truly be ruled by Egyptians again. On the outer southern walls are more battle reliefs and some of the most spectacular hunting scenes anywhere in pharaonic Egypt. Notice that the larger complex was surrounded by a substantial wall that in times of war made it a place of refuge for the citizens of Thebes.

The Ramesseum

Across the main road from Old Qurna Village and the Tombs of the Nobles 500 meters northeast of the Antiquities Office.

Constructed by ancient Egypt's most prolific builder and arguably its most accomplished pharaoh, the **Ramesseum** was meant to be **Ramses II's** (AKA **Ramses the Great**) masterpiece. A mortuary temple built to promote the pharaoh's cult and to assert his divinity as a son of Amun, this once spectacular structure fell victim to centuries of floods and soggy grounds unable to support its foundations. The temple of his successor, Ramses III at Medinet Habu, still largely intact, provides an idea of what the Ramesseum must have looked like only the Ramesseum boasted even more grandeur. For example, the fallen colossi of Ramses (1305-1237 BC) which crashed through the second pylons in the 1st century once stood nearly 18 meters and weighed well over 1,000 tons!

Visitors enter the complex through a gate into the **Second Court** where the massive **colossus of Ramses II** once stood. The width of

Ramses' chest has been measured at 7 meters and the statue itself stood nearly 18 meters and weighed 1,200 tons. Expertly crafted from one massive piece of granite shipped from Aswan, this mammoth likeness of the pharaoh inspired Shelly to pen **Ozymandias**.

Two smaller but still impressive statues were perched at the end of the Second Court, one of which was transported to the England in the early 19th century by the noted Egyptologist and explorer, Giovanni Belzoni. It can now be viewed at the British Museum in London. The perimeter of this court was lined with columns featuring depictions of the pharaoh making offerings to and receiving blessings from the usual cast of deities: Ra Harakhte (human body, falcon's head), Min (with the impressive penis), Amun, Horus, and others. The second pylons to the southeast record Ramses' "victories" at Kadesh in Syria (the battles actually ended in a draw) and the festival of the fertility and harvest god, Min.

Make your way to the **First Court** and the **Entrance Pylons**. This portion of the temple is largely destroyed. The pylons' inner walls also depict Ramses at Kadesh.

Back at the end of the Second Court, stairs lead up to a **terrace**. Here, in well preserved carvings, we find Ramses in standard pharaonic poses, receiving eternal life through the ankh held to his nose by the hawk headed Mont in view of Amun, Mut, and Khonsu. Meanwhile, Thoth, the scribe registers Ramses for eternity. Above, the pharaoh makes offerings to Min and Ptah.

Exit the portico into the **Hypostyle Hall** that once contained 48 columns, 25 of which remain intact. Reliefs, mostly on the walls to the left, again show battle scenes, this time against the Hittites at the city of Dapur. On the rear walls, texts praising Ramses accompany a portrait of him with a number of his many sons. In the upper register, he receives the key of life from Amun while Sekhmet, the feline goddess, looks on.

The primary Hypostyle Hall then gives way, as in Ramses III's temple, to **two smaller halls** and several modest chapels and sanctuaries. The **first hall**, recognizable by the astrological motifs on the ceiling, contains what is considered one of the oldest 12 month calendars in the world as well as reliefs of Ramses under the persea tree at Heliopolis with the gods Sheshet and Thoth. Also depicted are the sacred barges of the Theban Triad, Amun, Mut, and Khonsu. The second hall is largely destroyed, but probably contained a lavish shrine; the surrounding rooms and small chambers were used for storage.

The Mortuary Temple of Hatshepsut

Hatshepsut's Temple is in Deir El Bahri northwest of El Qurna village. Take a left at the mosque if coming from the south; if coming from the Valley of the Kings, take a right.

This beautifully crafted and unique temple was constructed by one of pharaonic Egypt's most storied figures, Hatshepsut. The only Egyptian female pharaoh (the Cleopatras were Greek), Hatshepsut became one of the New Kingdom's most successful rulers despite the challenges of her half-brother and rival, Thutmosis III, who himself went on to be become pharaonic Egypt's most successful military commanders. The sheer volume of monuments she built, testifies to the prosperity enjoyed during her reign between 1503-1482 BC. This temple is the cream of the crop of those monuments, and many believe of the west bank and even all of Thebes.

Besides its beauty, this temple provides a unique insight into the strategy employed by Hatshepsut to legitimize her claim to the pharaonic throne, an institution designed by and for men. She portrays herself like any other pharaoh – as a divine being superior in physical and military prowess, and as a male, complete with beard and other masculine features. To further enhance her legitimacy she concocted the story of her divine birth to provide a direct genetic link to Amun- the pharaoh derived legitimacy as the 'son of Amun.'

Set against a spectacular backdrop of Theban cliffs, this temple is striking not only for its beauty and grace, but its unique design. Rather than the generic pylons and hypostyle halls of other New Kingdom temples, this building employs multi-leveled terraces linked by ramps, similar to the 11th Dynasty temple of Mentuhotep constructed here during the Middle Kingdom. The temple is entered by way of the **Central Court**, once lined with special myrrh trees imported from the land of Punt. Unfortunately, only one rather pathetic stump struggles to survive next to the ticket taker's booth.

Approaching the temple after climbing the first ramp, the famous **Birth Colonnade** is to the right. The miracle birth story was concocted to enhance Hatshepsut's legitimacy by proving her divinity as the "son of Amun." Mostly destroyed, these reliefs begin with depictions of Amun conceiving Queen Ahmose with an ankh, the key of life. From left to right the story progresses from pregnancy to the birth. An assortment of deities look on while the ram-headed Khnum, creates Hatshepsut's ka (spiritual double) on a potter's wheel. To the right of the Birth Colonnade in a **chapel dedicated to Anubis**, the jackal-headed protector of the dead, reliefs depict Hatshepsut making offerings to Anubis and other deities.

Beyond the Birth Colonnade on the left side of the temple, are the famous reliefs that comprise the **Punt Colonnade** which tell the story of an expedition made during the reign of Hatshepsut to a strange land known as Punt, believed to be on the Somali coast. On the far left, faded carvings reveal Egyptians loading their ships with myrrh incense, cinnamon wood, live animals and other goods. Notice the buildings on stilts

HATSHEPSUT (1502–1482 BC)

*The only Egyptian female pharaoh, **Hatshepsut** was the child of Thutmosis I and his Chief Queen, Ahmose. The only child carrying matrilineal royal blood, she was the legal heir to the throne after Thutmosis I's death. However, as was common in Pharaonic Egypt, she faced strong challenges from her half-brother and official husband Thutmosis II, who actually assumed the throne, and his son Thutmosis III with whom she officially ruled concurrently with as co-regent. She assumed the crown, but their rivalry remained extremely bitter and she went to great lengths to legitimize her rule. She promoted the myth of her divine birth as told on the first level of this temple, and depicted herself in traditional pharaonic garb, often with masculine features and a male body. She received a strong boost from her confidante and alleged lover, Senemut, architect of the temple at Deir El Bahri and chief steward of estates belonging to the Cult of Amun. The extent of the rivalry with Thutmosis III is evident by the fact that after succeeding her in 1482 BC, he erased her cartouches and usurped her monuments hoping she would be forgotten forever. This temple is one relic proving he failed.*

and the disproportionately fat Punt woman, believed to be a queen afflicted with elephantiasis. To the right Egyptian ships on the Red Sea are depicted returning to Egypt where Hatshepsut makes offerings to Amun.

Around the corner from the Punt Colonnade is the **Shrine of Hathor**, identifiable by the famous square Hathor columns topped with Hathor's likeness. In the front portion of the shrine, Hatshepsut participates in festivities and rites incorporating sacred barges. The figure holding the oar was originally Hatshepsut, however, as he did throughout the temple and, indeed all of Egypt, Thutmosis III had her face and cartouche erased and replaced with his own. In the chamber beyond the first two rows of columns, Thutmosis III is seen on the back wall getting licked by Hathor in her bovine form and on the left he is seen being suckled by her; to the right notice the exquisite carving of Hathor as a cow. Moving towards the closed off sanctuary, the qualities of the painted reliefs improve as Hatshepsut, or Thutmosis III, makes offerings to Hathor in her human and bovine forms.

The Upper Terraces

Almost entirely destroyed over the centuries, the upper terraces have been closed for restoration for years and will probably remain so for at least a few more. If you can make your way up the ramp, even without entering, it's worth it to check out the vulture statues at the top. The upper levels themselves contain several sanctuaries dedicated to a variety of deities. To the right of the large central court is a shrine dedicated to Ra the sun god, while to the left a sanctuary dedicated to Hatshepsut herself was used for important sacrifices. The rear of the temple was extended from the central sanctuary of Amun, into the cliffs by the Ptolemies who dedicated shrines to the Old Kingdom builder Imhotep (designer of the Step Pyramid at Saqqara) and Amenhotep, chief architect and confidante of the New Kingdom Pharaoh Amenhophis III.

DEATH AT DEIR EL BAHRI

At 9:30am on November 17, 1997, a Peugeot station wagon pulled up to the entrance of Hatshepsut's Mortuary Temple. Dressed in black policeman uniforms, six young men got out and hurried past the ticket taker. When he demanded a ticket, one man whipped out a Kaleshnikov and shot him in the leg saying, "There is your ticket." For the next hour, the men systematically murdered execution-style, 58 foreign tourists (34 of whom were Swiss) and six Egyptians. After killing everybody they could find in the temple, the men hijacked an empty bus, demanding the driver take them to another temple so they could slaughter more tourists. Believing that he would die anyway, the driver ignored their demands and drove about aimlessly before the scared killers made a run for the hills where they were chased down by hordes of furious locals (the police were still not on the scene) and shot by a local constable.

Besides claiming the lives of more than sixty human beings, this incident left Egypt's tourist industry, the country's primary source of hard currency, in shambles. A visibly embarrassed and shaken President Mubarak sacked his Interior Minister, Hassan Alfi, on the spot as people in and out of Egypt asked how it was that in a security obsessed state overflowing with armed police such a high profile attraction was guarded by only two unarmed policemen without radios. The Egyptian tourist industry and the Egyptian psyche have yet to recover from this heinous act.

The Temple of Seti I
The Temple of Seti I is off the road to the Valley of the Kings, south of the intersection by the Abul Kassem Hotel.

This rarely visited temple constructed by Ramses II's father, Seti I, contains some of the finest reliefs in the entire west bank, yet it is usually passed over in favor of Deir El Bahri and Medinet Habu. Though he ruled for less than two decades (1318-1304 BC), Seti is considered one of the New Kingdom's most important pharaohs for having reasserted Egyptian authority in Nubia and expanding it in Palestine, Syria, Mesopotamia, and Cyprus. His monuments at Abydos and Karnak are considered amongst the finest in Egypt and this one is no exception. The pylons and courts were largely destroyed but renovations should restore them. The interior halls and sanctuaries contain some excellent reliefs depicting Seti in battle and performing religious rites.

The Tombs of the Nobles

Though most tour groups pass by these modest crypts in favor of those built for royals, the Tombs of the Nobles contain some of the most fascinating, colorful, and best preserved reliefs in all of Thebes. While the pharaohs' tombs are consumed with weighty theological questions of life, death, and eternal divinity, the intimate tombs of the nobles, dating mostly to the 18th Dynasty (1567-1320 BC), depict the comings and goings of daily life in the New Kingdom. Animal headed deities are less evident as the nobles concern themselves with farming, wine making, and tax collecting. Though tour guides may try to convince you otherwise, these tombs are more than worth a visit.

Except for the Assasif Tombs, the Tombs of the Nobles' are located in and around the colorful village of Old Qurna-another good reason to visit them. Each of the following sets of tombs requires a ticket to be purchased at the main ticket office: Rekhmire and Sennofer; Ramose, Userhet and Khaemhet; Nakht and Menna; and Khonsu, Userhet and Benia.

The Assasif Tombs

Halfway between Deir El Bahri (Hatshepsut's Temple) and Old Qurna.

The Assasif Tombs comprise three dozen tombs dating primarily to the Late Period (25th-28th Dynasties) when Nubian pharaohs ruled Egypt. Check with the ticket office as to which tombs are open. Otherwise, you may be able to *baksheesh* your way in.

The finest of the lot, the **Tomb of Kheruef** (#192) was built for the chief steward of Queen Tiy, mother of Akhenaten, during the Amarna Period in the 18th Dynasty. The quality reliefs depict members of Akhenaten's family performing various religious rites and celebrating a festival-notice the dancers, musicians, and jugglers. Ten meters to the north of Kheruef, the **Tomb of Kiki**, is unfinished except for the weighing of the soul by Anubis at the entrance. Another 20 meters west, the **Tomb of Pabasa**, (26th Dynasty) is distinguished by the large gateway. Pabasa was a steward to a votaress of Amun and the reliefs feature colorful hunting and fishing scenes as well as a pilgrimage to Abydos.

The Tombs of Rekhmire (#100) & Sennofer (#96)

On western edges of Old Qurna up the hill from the main road.

Built for a foreign and domestic policy adviser to Thutmosis II and Amenhophis II, the **Tomb of Rekhmire** is one of the most vivid and diverse in content on the west bank. Along the walls to the left and right upon entrance, are images of the Vizier collecting taxes and inspecting various agricultural projects, including the making of wine. He is also portrayed hunting and on the inner wall to the left, receiving goods from Crete (the vases to the top), chariots from Syria, and various animals from Nubia. Along the high walls of the hall running lengthwise, Rekhmire is again seen supervising agricultural production and storage. About half-way in to the right, reliefs portray Rekhmire enjoying a fine meal while towards the rear by the false door the tone becomes more somber as we join his funeral procession.

After a steep, but short descent, the charming **Tomb of Sennofer** rewards visitors with some of the best preserved and most colorful reliefs in all of Egypt. Best known for the grapevines that cover the roof, it belongs to Rekhmire's contemporary, Sennofer, the Governor of Thebes and Chief Gardener for the Gardens of Amun under Amenhophis II.

Upon entrance into the first chamber, you will find Sennofer receiving offerings and worshipping Osiris while on the right he is accompanied by his daughter as servants tend to his possessions. In the main room, the walls to the left portray the preparations for Sennofer's funeral as well as the procession itself. Notice the erection of two obelisks just across from the first pillar. As you make your way clockwise towards the right of the chamber, you will come across the symbolic pilgrimage to Abydos followed by the making ablutions with a priest, identified by his leopard skin garb. While leaving, notice Anubis above the doorway, guarding the dead from intruders such as yourself.

The Tombs of Ramose (#55), Userhet (#56), & Khaemhet (#57)

These tombs are south of Rekhmire and Sennofer towards the Ramesseum.

The **Tomb of Ramose**, a Governor of Thebes, is fascinating because its style and content trace the rapid transition from traditional pharaonic art based in Amunism to the realistic artistic styles that were employed during the reign of Akhenaten who adopted the monotheistic Cult of Aten. Ironically, though this tomb is huge by nobles' standards, it was never finished and Ramose was never buried here, because he followed Akhenaten to Tel El Amarna (Akhenaten's royal city south of Minya) where he was in fact interred.

The scenes in the entrance are typical New Kingdom, as Ramose, along with his family and assistants is seen in traditional poses making offerings to traditional deities. On the walls to the left, take time to examine the moving scenes of mourners wailing and weeping. On either side of the second door to the second chamber a distinct change in artistic style marks the transition from traditional religion and artistic depiction to the realistic Amarna style as a pot-bellied Akhenaten with Nefertiti are depicted receiving blessings from the multi-handed sun disc, Aten. The second (pillared hall), and the third are mostly undeveloped because Ramose moved to Tel El Amarna.

The nearby **Tomb of Userhet** predates that of Ramose. Userhet was a scribe during the reign of Amenhophis II, hence the reliefs in his tomb are littered with registers and records. On the walls of the first chamber to the left, cattle herding and grain collections are depicted while to the right of the door colorful reliefs portray bread baking and military inspections. In the second corridor, Userhet is seen hunting (to the immediate left) while at the rear of the chamber, funerary scenes can be found in their traditional location near the false door.

The final tomb (#57) of the second group was also constructed for a royal scribe, **Khaemhet**, who served during the reign of Amenhophis III. Upon entering the front door, you can see Khaemhet performing traditional religious rites, in this case in honor of Re, while the antechamber contains scenes of the port of Thebes. The statues are of Khaemhet and Imhotep, the architect of Zoser's Step Pyramid at Saqqara, who achieved quasi-mythic status during the New Kingdom. The second sets of statues represent Khaemhet and his family.

The Tombs of Nakht (#52) & Menna (#69)

On the northeastern side of Qurna towards Deir El Bahri (Hatshepsut's Temple).

Nakht, an astronomer and Chief of Granaries and Vineyards under Thutmosis IV, only found time to decorate the first chamber of this simple double-chambered tomb. Following the reliefs clockwise from the left, begin with Nakht doing exactly what he did when he was alive almost 3,500 years ago: running the farm. Various subordinates reap the harvest and engage other agricultural activities, while texts in a stele praise Nakht. On the wall left of the doorway to the second chamber, is the famous scene of three female musicians, a harpist, flutist, and a lute player, making music for Nakht and his wife. Notice the cat underneath their chair enjoying a leftover fish. Meanwhile, a blind harpist plays in front of women smelling perfume, chatting, and enjoying themselves generally.

On the other side of the doorway are more colorful agricultural scenes. Birds are hunted with a net and then cleaned and plucked, while grapes are harvested and subsequently squeezed for juice. Above Nakht is portrayed fishing, presumably an activity he enjoyed. You will notice that some of the reliefs have been vandalized. This was almost surely the work of Akhenaten. Though the second chamber is undecorated, there stands, in the niche at the back, a replica of a statue of Nakht that was lost in the Atlantic Ocean en route to America. The burial chamber is inaccessible.

The **Tomb of Menna** (#69), belongs to a scribe under Thutmosis IV during the 18th Dynasty. His well-preserved tomb offers yet more fine reliefs depicting a New Kingdom aristocrat at work and play.

To the left upon entering, Menna supervises plowing and harvesting and then collects taxes on behalf of the state, and perhaps himself. Take time to check out the light hearted scenes of the girls frolicking and fighting (pulling each other's hair anyway), below the plowing and port scenes. On the right walls of the first chamber, the sloppy and hard to decipher reliefs lead some to believe that Menna usurped the tomb and attempted to cover the work of the tomb's original owner.

In the rear corridor, reliefs deal more with the issue at hand. On the left wall, you can follow the deceased's funeral and his symbolic pilgrimage to Abydos. Notice the fine quality of the paints. On Judgment Day, Menna's heart is then placed by Anubis on a scale where it is weighed against the Feather of Truth before Osiris, Re and Hathor. On the right wall, are colorful images of fishing and hunting-the river scenes are among the most famous in Egypt.

The Tombs of Userhet, Khonsu, & Benia
Next to the tombs of Nakht & Menna.

This triad of small tombs for New Kingdom nobles feature yet more depictions of officials in action fishing, farming, and hunting as well as funerary scenes.

The Valley of the Queens & The Tomb of Nefertari (#66)
The Valley of the Queens is on a road beginning near Medinet Habu. You'll find the tombs of Nefertari (#66), Amunhirkhopshef (#55), and an unidentifed queen (#40).

Excavated in 1904 by Italian Ernesto Schiaparelli, the **Tomb of Nefertari** is widely considered the best preserved pharaonic tomb in all of Egypt, and to protect it, admission is limited to 100-150 people daily.

Constructed by Ramses II for his favorite wife, Nefertari, this tomb features reliefs the color of which is not found anywhere else in Egypt. Indeed, it's difficult to believe that it could have been painted more than 30 years ago, let alone 3,000. The reliefs are typical of royal tombs in that they portray the queen commiserating with various deities such as Osiris, Isis, Horus, and Anubis. It contains three chambers: an outer chamber, a side-room and a burial chamber. Unlike side rooms in other tombs, the one in this tomb not only contains reliefs, but spectacular depictions of

OLD QURNA: THE VILLAGE OF THE ROBBERS

*An indelible part of the west bank experience is passing through the colorful village of **Old Qurna** (Sheikh Abd El Qurna in Arabic), site of the Tombs of the Nobles and home through the ages of many-a-tomb builder as well as tomb robbers-hence the nickname, "the Village of the Robbers." In fact, most scholars believe that builders who worked in tomb construction were most often the thieves who robbed them of their immense treasures. This makes sense given that they enjoyed intimate knowledge of the tombs' layouts and traps set to protect them. During the 19th and 20th centuries when the smuggling of ancient relics became a big business, Qurna's villagers made small fortunes supplying stolen artifacts to European dealers. After the authorities cracked down on smuggling in the mid-20th century, they continued to profit by hawking cheap imitations of the priceless relics that made their forefathers rich. In 1997, the Egyptian government announced that Old Qurna was to be dismantled because, it claimed, it was offensive and embarrassing that foreign tourists might be exposed to Egyptian poverty. Needless to say, this sparked outrage among Qurna's residents whose families have lived in the village for generations; it would also be a loss for visitors who enjoy the village's vibrant and friendly inhabitants.*

*Towards the river stands **New Qurna**, a community of domed buildings designed by the famous modern Egyptian architect Hassan Fathi. At the end of March, Qurna hosts quite a wild moulid held in honor of Sheikh Abu Qasman, a local twentieth century saint.*

Nefertari with Osiris. The burial chamber and the stairwell leading to it also contain fine reliefs.

The Tomb of Amunhirkhopshef (#55)

Not nearly as spectacular as the Tomb of Nefertari, this fine tomb is well worth a visit, especially if you cannot get into Nerfertari's. Though it's located in the "Valley of the Queens" it was built for a son of Ramses III. Only nine years old when he died, the prince did not live to succeed his father as pharaoh. Reliefs throughout the tomb depict Ramses accompanying his son while visiting deities to whom he presents offerings. The prince is discernible by the side-lock of hair and the feather of truth that he carries. Scholars have been baffled that the prince's sarcophagus did not contain his mummy, but rather that of a miscarried fetus.

Tomb No. 40

Built for an unidentified queen or princess, this tomb resembles that of Nefertari but is not as well preserved. It is believed to date from the 19th

Dynasty, and contains some fine reliefs depicting funeral scenes and the mystery queen in typical poses with deities.

Deir El Medina: The Workmen's Village

Deir El Medina off the road to the Valley of the Queens about a kilometer to the north.

A ruined village that was home to many of the artisans who built and decorated the tombs and temples throughout the west bank, Deir El Medina ("Monastery" or "House of the Town") contains a small Ptolemeic Temple and several tombs and excavated homes. The temple, dedicated to Hathor and Maat (goddess of truth), was built during the 3rd and 2nd centuries BC. The settlement contains nearly 100 houses and several tombs which are now open to the public.

The finest of these, the **Tomb of Sennejem** belonged to a 19th Dynasty noble who worked in the Valley of the Kings and contains some very fine reliefs. That of **Aneuka** is bigger and also contains some very vivid reliefs. The **Tomb of Peshedu** requires a separate ticket and is just up the hill from the first two.

NIGHTLIFE & ENTERTAINMENT

As most travelers whiz through Luxor in a day or two and tend to tour in the early morning to avoid the heat, Luxor's nightlife doesn't quite measure up to that of Sharm El Sheikh or Hurghada. Most five star hotels contain at least a bar, often of the lobby variety, and usually a nightclub as well. Those in hotels like the Isis, Movenpick, and Sheraton feature sometime extravagant floor shows that include belly dancing. The most popular is the Mercure Nightclub which features a cheesy, but fun belly dancing show that incorporates the audience as well as western style dancing and of course drinking. On the weekends, the Novotel disco is also quite popular.

For those looking to hit the sack early, a sunset felucca is a wonderful and relaxing way to wind down while enjoying the Nile at its most beautiful. The basic rate is LE20 for an hour plus tip, but groups larger than 10 should be prepared to pay LE2-3 per person per hour.

Bars & Pubs

THE KING'S HEAD PUB, *Khaled Ibn Waleed Street four hundred meters from the Novotel, across the street from the Isis Hotel. Open from 11am-late. Credit cards: Visa.*

Self proclaimed "Luxor's Only English Pub" is night in and night out the most popular spot in town, particularly with folks from the British Isles. Decked out like an English Pub with an Egyptian twist, it features a long menu offering a wide variety of Arabic and continental appetizers and main courses from curry and kebab to hamburgers and fries. The popular offering is of course Stella (LE8). Other amenities include a pool table and British newspapers are available for patrons to peruse.

THE OPET FESTIVAL & THE MOULID OF ABU EL HAGGAG

More than 3,000 years ago during the New Kingdom, the most important festivities in all of Egypt as recounted on the walls of Karnak and the Luxor Temple was the Opet Festival held in Thebes to celebrate the onset of the annual inundations. During these celebrations held in late summer, the idols of Karnak were removed from their sanctuaries for the only time during the year and paraded through Thebes on sacred barges to Luxor Temple where they remained for 24 days.

Modern Luxor features two public celebrations redolent of the ancient Opet Festival. To commemorate the anniversary of Howard Carter's discovery of Tut's Tomb on November 4, the city stages a recreation of the ancient festival during the first week of November, that includes the parading of boats and dancing in the streets of downtown Luxor. Though it has all the feel of the event staged for tourism that it is, the Opet recreation is a colorful and lively affair well worth checking out.

Far more colorfully authentic is the annual Moulid of Abu El Haggag, a week-long festival beginning two weeks before Ramadan that celebrates Luxor's patron Sufi, Youssef Abu El Haggag. El Haggag was a 12th century Sufi who moved to Luxor from Mecca and founded a prominent Sufi order. During the moulid, his mosque, which is perched on the Luxor Temple, is bathed in colored lights while thousands of sufis perform whirling zikr dances, hold mock races and stick fights, and like their pagan ancestors, parade boats through the city streets. Though not overtly linked to the ancient Opet Festival, this practice is a testament to popular and folk religious rituals which transcend time and the orthodox creeds in which they are practiced.

SHOPPING

Stupendous monuments aside, what strikes most travelers about Luxor is the feeling that it's one giant souvenir souk. It's hard to walk but 10 meters without being accosted by some joker trying to sell you T-shirts, jewelry, and a whole host of souvenirs, the vast majority of which are tacky and of poor quality. Having said that, most shoppers enjoy the opportunity to peruse the endless shop windows and engage in the friendly give and take that is a an indelible part of the Egyptian shopping process.

The semi-official "Tourist Bazaar" is off Karnak Street north of the Luxor Temple. Here, hundreds of small shops hawk everything from fake and real papyrus to jewelry, inlaid boxes, and ornate, but mostly dysfunctional sheeshas (waterpipes). In **downtown Luxor**, there are also big tourist souks on El Souk Street, parallel to Karnak Street and in the Marhaba Restaurant building between the Winter Palace hotel and the Luxor Temple. This shopping arcade is home to a number of shops run by merchant families like the Aboudis and the Gaddis' that have been selling handicrafts, jewelry, and fake antiques for the entire twentieth century. In this bazaar, and in the Winter Palace commercial center, they also operate bookstores.

Along **Khaled Ibn Waleed Street** there are innumerable shops, many of which are located in very modern arcades and shopping centers inside big hotels like the Isis. For papyrus, try **Dr. Ragab's Papyrus** [floating] **Institute** on a boat off the Corniche north of the Luxor Temple and across from the Mercure Hotel. Though it may be a bit pricey, at least you know you're getting the real thing (as opposed to banana leaf), and the quality of the painting is generally superior. There is a huge variety in choice from papyrus bookmarks with your name, or somebody else's, in a hieroglyphic cartouche (a great gift) for LE10 to huge mural size replicas of entire tomb reliefs costing thousands of pounds. The Institute is open 9am-9pm and accepts major credit cards.

Finally, on the **west bank**, you will invariably be asked to go to, or just taken to, one of the dozens of alabaster factories in local villages like Qurna El Sheikh (Old Qurna), where (mostly poor) imitations of pharaonic artifacts are manufactured. Wherever you decide to do your shopping, remember that unless you're buying gold, bargain – a fair price is usually between 15-30% of the asking price.

THE CAMEL MARKET

*Though you probably don't need one, the regional **camel and livestock market** is a colorful and refreshingly authentic affair that if nothing else, offers a nice escape from the hokey tackiness of Luxor. Held every Tuesday morning (7am-noon) in the rural hamlet of **El Hebel** 5 kilometers east of Luxor, the market features hundreds of Sayeedi fellaheen and Sudanese camel herders haggling over countless sheep, donkeys, cows, and of course camels. Taxis will make the round trip excursion, wait included, for LE20-30 though you can usually negotiate it down to LE12-15. You can also reach the market by bicycle by taking Mustafa Kamel Street past the tracks and turning south on the aptly named El Salakhana, (Slaughterhouse) Street. If you need directions ask for the "Souk El Gamal."*

EXCURSIONS & DAY TRIPS

Though most travelers barely have time to cover the bases in Luxor itself, the city is convenient base for visiting a myriad of sites throughout the Nile Valley.

DENDERA

The magnificent Ptolemeic-built **Temple of Hathor** at Dendera is 60 kilometers north of Luxor near the city of Qena and makes an easy half day excursion from Luxor and can also be combined on a day trip to the Temple of Osiris at Abydos. There are various options for visiting Dendera. Most hotels and travel agencies (see "Practical Information" below) arrange tours or can arrange transportation. Depending on the size of your party and whether you join a tour and organize your own, tours cost between LE3-60 per person. The Novotel hotel organizes day cruises to Dendera for $40 per person.

You can also hire a taxi in Luxor for LE50-70 depending on the length of the trip, and finally, to really save money, you can ride there and back on public buses or service for a couple pounds each way. For more details see the "Qena & the Temple of Dendera" section above for more details.

ABYDOS

Located 160 kilometers north of Luxor near the town of Balyana, the New Kingdom **Temple of Osiris** at Abydos is among the finest and most impressive ancient monuments in Egypt, and can be visited in a day trip from Luxor in conjunction with Dendera. If you join a tour, expect to pay LE50-100 or more, and hiring a taxi costs LE100-150. Public transportation is not really viable for visiting Abydos in a day and there are hardly any suitable accommodation facilities in Abydos or Balyana. See the "Balyana and the Temple of Abydos" section above.

ESNA, EDFU, & KOM OMBO

Located 55, 110, and 170 kilometers from Luxor respectively, the **pharaonic temples** at Esna, Edfu, and Kom Ombo can all be visited in a day though Kom Ombo is more easily visited from Aswan. Again, travel agencies, hotels, and taxis are all viable options for visiting these sites. Joining a tour will cost between LE30-125 or the equivalent in dollars depending on the nature of the tour (private or group, with or without guide) and whether it's a half day (Esna only) or a full day (Esna and Edfu and possibly Kom Ombo). Expect to pay LE50-75 to hire a taxi for a half day, LE100-150 for a full day. Finally, if you're willing to travel by public transportation, buses and service depart frequently to Esna and Edfu (see "Arrivals & Departures" above) and you shouldn't have trouble finding a ride home as long as you don't wait around until after dark. See the appropriate destination sections below for more details.

PRACTICAL INFORMATION

Banks & Currency Exchange

Most upscale hotels can change money and traveler's cheques. Listed are other banks and currency exchanges:

• **American Express**, *the Old Winter Palace. Tel. 095/382-862. Hours: 8am-8pm. AMEX holds mail and can assist in wiring and transferring money but will sell travelers' cheques only to AMEX cardholders.*

• **Thomas Cook** *Old Winter Palace on the Corniche Tel. 095/382-196. Fax 095/386-502. Currency exchange bureau in the airport. Tel. 095/374-655.*

• **National Bank of Egypt**, *just south of Winter Palace on the Corniche. Hours: 8:30am-2pm and 5pm-8pm daily except Friday when it closes at 11am but reopens from 5pm-8pm.*

• **Bank of Alexandria**, *off the intersection of Labib Habashy and El Karnak streets. Hours: 9am-2pm & 5-8pm daily except Friday.*

• **Banque Misr**, *Labib Habashy Street. Hours: daily except Saturday 8:30am-9pm.*

Emergencies

• **Ambulance**: *Tel. 123*

• **Luxor's General Hospital**, *the Corniche just north of the Luxor Museum. Tel. 095/372-025*

• **Police**, *the Corniche north of the Luxor Temple. Tel. 095/372-350*

Post Services

• **Post Office & EMS** (express mail), *El-Mahatta Street off El-Karnak Street. Hours: 8am-2pm (1pm for Express Mail) daily except Friday. Other branches are located in the commercial center by the Old Winter Palace (open 8am-2pm except Friday) and in the train station (open 8am-8pm).*

• **Federal Express**, *El Corniche Street between Luxor Temple and the Luxor Museum. Hours: 9am-6pm daily.* FedEx is more dependable and convenient for mail that needs to be rushed – especially packages. They also offer **phone** and **fax services** with rates favorable to those in hotels as well as **Western Union** money wiring services.

Passports

Visas can be renewed at the **passport office** *Khaled Ibn Waleed Street by Mandera restaurant 100 meters north of Isis Hotel. Tel. 095/380-885. Hours: 10am-2pm.*

Pharmacies

There are numerous pharmacies throughout downtown on major streets. Inquire at your hotel about the most convenient one.

Telephones

24 hour telephone centrale, *branches in El Karnak Street and the Old Winter Palace on the Corniche.* You can place domestic and international calls as well as faxes and telexes. Upscale hotels can also place calls, faxes, and telexes for considerably higher rates.

Travel Agencies

- **American Express**, *Old Winter Palace, Corniche El Nil Street. Tel. 095/382-862. Hours: 8am-8pm*
- **Eastmar**, *Old Winter Palace, Corniche El Nil Street. Specializes in moderately priced Nile Cruises.*
- **Emecom**, *Old Winter Palace, Corniche El Nil. Tel. 095/372-151*
- **Isis Travel**, *Tourist Bazaar off Karnak Street. Tel. 095/376-186*
- **Misr Travel**, *Old Winter Palace, Corniche El Nil Street. Tel. 095/373-551*
- **Seti First Travel**, *Khaled Ibn Waleed Street. Tel. 095/376-753*
- **Thomas Cook**, *Old Winter Palace on the Corniche Tel. 095/382-196. Fax 095/386-502*

Tourist Information

The **Egyptian Tourist Authority** operates three offices *in the Luxor Airport (Tel. 095/383-294), the railroad station (Tel. 095/372-120), and in the commercial center by the Old Winter Palace (Tel. 095/372-215).* They provide basic information about tourist and cultural attractions but nothing you can't get at any mid-scale hotel or travel agent. *Offices open daily 8am-8pm.*

Tourist Police

Two offices operate *in the commercial center by the Old Winter Palace on the Corniche(Tel. 095/376-620) and in the train station(Tel. 095/372-120).* Plenty of officers should also be on duty at major tourist sites.

ESNA & THE TEMPLE OF KHNUM

A bustling mid-sized farming town, **Esna** is best known as the location of the **Temple of Khnum**, the ancient ram-headed god of creation.

ARRIVALS & DEPARTURES

By Service

The service depot is next to the canal about a kilometer north of the temple. *Service* taxi is the most efficient and cheapest means of public transportation for getting in and out of Esna. From Luxor, the ride is about 45 minutes and costs LE3. From Aswan the trip is 2-3 hours and costs about LE5 while the one hour ride to Edfu shouldn't be more than LE1.

By Train
The train station is across the river from the temple. There is a train station in Esna but it is serviced almost exclusively by local trains that are terribly inefficient.

ORIENTATION
Esna is 55 kilometers south of Luxor and 160 kilometers north of Aswan. Most tourists are taken directly to the temple about 100 meters inland from the main dock on the Nile. The main street running parallel to the river is an interesting walk for observing the local goings on and there is a bank about half a kilometer north of the temple off the Corniche to the left.

GETTING AROUND TOWN
Most tourists go directly to the temple by transport hired in Luxor or provided by a tour company. For those needing a ride from the service depot, *hantours* (horse buggies) make the ride for about LE3. Haggling may be necessary.

WHERE TO STAY
Esna is most easily visited in a day trip from Luxor or from the comfort of a cruise ship. The only hotel in town leaves much to be desired.
EL HARAMIN HOTEL, *by the temple. Rates: LE5 single, LE10 double.*
No frills, no thrills – with no fans and lots of grime. You're far better off in Luxor.

WHERE TO EAT
Kiosks around the temple hawk soft drinks and junk food while cafes along the Nile afford pleasant Nile scenery and interaction with friendly locals. *Fuul, ta'amiya,* and other Egyptian street food is available in the market and on major streets, but don't spend a lot of time looking for much more.

SEEING THE SIGHTS
THE TEMPLE OF KHNUM
The Temple of Khnum is about 100 meters inland from the main dock and

about one kilometer south of the bridge and the service depot. Hours: 6am-6:30pm (summer), 8am-5:30pm (winter). Admission: LE8 general; LE4 students.

Ancient Egyptians believed the ram-headed god, **Khnum**, to be man's creator, having shaped him on his pottery wheel from Nile clay. Also associated with the Nile inundation and cataracts, he was especially popular in Aswan as well as Esna where temples dedicated to him stood for centuries before the Ptolemies, and later the Romans, constructed this one. Founded by Ptolemy VI the current version of the temple was constructed the reigns of seven Ptolemies and more than a dozen Roman emperors ending with Trajan Decius (250 AD) whose name is the last to appear in hieroglyphics in a royal cartouche. Over nearly 2,000 years of annual flooding left this temple buried for generations and it is now 10 meters below ground level.

The temple is entered through a Roman era facade featuring the cartouches of Roman emperors Claudius, Vespasian and Titus. The door, topped with a sun disc, leads to the **Hypostyle Hall**, the main feature of the excavated temple. While the 24 **columns** contain texts of hymns to Khnum, the walls portray an assortment of Roman emperors in pharaonic dress performing religious rites and making offerings. The western wall with reliefs of Ptolemy VI and other Ptolemies is the only Ptolemeic portion of the temple intact. The southern ceiling is worth noting for its register of zodiac signs and colorful creatures including winged dogs. Finally, the reliefs on the exterior walls of the temple feature Roman emperors posing as pharaohs in battle, smashing their enemies and claiming prisoners.

BETWEEN ESNA & EDFU

Should you have extra time and interest, you may consider visiting the remains of two pharaonic provincial capitals, **Nekheb** and **Nekhen**, *25 kilometers south of Esna*. Located near the modern town of **El Kab**, Nekheb is home to the remains of a temple dedicated to Nekhbet, the local vulture-headed goddess. It was originally constructed during the Old Kingdom and extended during the New Kingdom. Three kilometers east are three more temples: the Ptolemeic Temple of Sheshmeter, a small shrine built by Ramses II, and a chapel dedicated to Hathor. *(Open 6am-4pm. Tickets: LE6, student LE3.)* On the eastern bank in Kom El Ahmar, the ancient community of **Nekhen** dates to the predynastic era and features a Middle Kingdom necropolis.

SHOPPING

A visit to Esna inevitably includes a trip to the local tourist *souk*. Though you shouldn't expect to find any items of high quality, a friendly bargaining session usually yields some cheap souvenirs and a good laugh.

PRACTICAL INFORMATION
Banks & Currency Exchange
There is a **bank** *about 400 meters north of the temple off the Corniche to the left. Hours: 8:30am-2pm.* It changes money and travelers' cheques.

Emergencies
The **Tourist Police** are in an office next to the temple and can provide assistance in attaining ambulance and other medical services. The closest major hospital is in Luxor.

Post Services
The **Post Office** is by the bridge.

Telephones, Telex, & Fax
Some of the shops in the tourist bazaar may have phones or even faxes. Otherwise a **kiosk** two blocks south of the Post Office operates an international phone line.

Tourist Police
The **Tourist Police Station** is next to the temple.

EDFU & THE TEMPLE OF HORUS
Situated on high grounds protected from the floods, the magnificently preserved **Temple of Horus** at **Edfu** was the last pharaonic go at monument building on a huge scale. Like the temples at Esna, Dendera, and Philae, this temple of mind boggling proportions was built during the Ptolemeic Period and most certainly warrants a visit – even if the host town of Edfu does not. As most travelers make it a day trip from Luxor, Aswan, or as part of a Nile cruise or felucca sail, they are spared the need of having to stay here overnight.

ARRIVALS & DEPARTURES
By Bus
The bus station is in town just down the street from the temple. Some buses arrive and depart on the other side of Nile. Noisy, dusty old buses are easy to catch to all Upper Egyptian destinations and cheap as well – no more than LE5 to Luxor or LE3 to Aswan. A bus from Aswan also runs through Edfu on its way to Marsa Alam on the Red Sea coast. It makes pick-ups at the bus station on the other side of the river from the temple. Check with locals about the time, but usually it passes by no earlier than 7:30 am. Tickets cost LE10.

By Service

The service depot is just over the bridge. For getting between the temple and the depot, hitch a local service for 25p. The most efficient means of getting to close and mid-ranged destinations in Upper Egypt, service taxis run frequently to Esna (LE3, 1 hour), Luxor (LE6, 2 hours), and Aswan (LE3, 1.5 hours).

By Train

The train station is on the east bank. Trains are not very efficient for getting in and out of Edfu, but if you insist, they do go to Esna, Luxor, and Aswan. Check at the station for departure times.

ORIENTATION

The Temple of Horus is on **El Maglis Street** about three quarters of a kilometer west of the Nile and the main docks where cruise ships and feluccas stop. The post office and the bus station are both on El Tahrir Street which more or less runs north-south through the midan in the center of town. Also running north-south, parallel to El Tahrir Street, El Gomhuriya Street is the site of the Medina Hotel and further south, the bank. Hantours can be hired at riverside and are handy for getting around town.

GETTING AROUND TOWN

If you're not chauffeured in on a tour bus, the easiest way to get to the temple from the river is by **hantour** (horse buggy) which shouldn't cost more than LE5 one-way. Downtown can be negotiated by **foot** while the service and train stations are best reached from the temple by local **service** (25p).

WHERE TO STAY

Like Esna, Dendera, and Kom Ombo, Edfu is generally not prepared for foreign visitors to stay overnight, at least not those accustomed to five star accommodation. If you insist, there are several hotels.

HOTEL MEDINA, *El Gomhuriya Street north of the temple. Tel. 095/701-326. Rates: LE15 single, LE20 double.*

Hospitality and a great breakfast make up for the drab state of the hotel and its facilities. Rooms with or without fans and private baths are available; water pressure and quality can vary. The draw is definitely the gigantic home prepared *fellahi* (peasant's) breakfast complete with fuul, honey, breads, molasses, and other goodies.

SEMIRAMIS HOTEL, *El Maglis Street between the temple and the river. Tel. 095/700-470. LE10 per person.*

This is an old colonial dump with old colonial facilities-due to be renovated.

DAR EL SALAM HOTEL, *Tel. 095/701-727. Rates: LE5 single, LE10 double.*

It's relatively clean, but lacks the charm of the El Medina. Rooms come with or without fans and private showers.

WHERE TO EAT

There are fuul and ta'amiya as well as kebab stalls in the main square. *Across from the Semiramis Hotel on El Maglis Street several hundred meters east of the temple,* the **Zahrat El Medina Restaurant** offers a simple menu of chicken, soup, red beans, rice and the usual condiments. A full meat-laden meal goes for about LE12. Somewhat far away from the temple and the center of town the **HappyLand Restaurant** on the Corniche serves similar fare. Otherwise there is an overpriced snack bar in the temple confines.

SEEING THE SIGHTS
THE TEMPLE OF HORUS

About a kilometer west of the river bank. Admission: LE20 general, LE10 students. Hours: 6am-6pm.

Built in honor of the hawk-headed god, **Horus**, the temple at Edfu is **one** of the largest, best preserved, and generally most impressive monuments in Egypt. Constructed entirely during the Ptolemeic period between 237 and 35 BC, it mimics the great New Kingdom temples of Thebes, but its excellent state of preservation is due to its location above the flood lines of the annual inundation, and the protection afforded it being buried in dry earth for the better part of the last two millennia. Like most other great pharaonic monuments, it was not excavated until the mid-19th century.

Like its Theban inspirations, the temple at Edfu is entered through the door of a huge **pylon**, 35 meters tall, built by Ptolemy IX. The well-preserved giant reliefs depict the Pharaoh Ptolemy XIII grasping his enemies while Horus and Hathor look on. Flanking the door on either side are statues of Horus in his hawk form.

Beyond the pylon, lies the spacious **Court of Offerings** where offerings were made to idol representation of Horus. On the backside of the entrance pylon, reliefs depict the Great Union between Horus and his mate, **Hathor**. Once a year during the **Feast of the Great Union** (also known as the Festival of Drunkenness), the sacred statue of Hathor was sailed down the Nile on her sacred barge to Edfu where she was placed in the company of Horus' idol. They were then left to privately enjoy their annual conjugal visit while the priesthood performed rituals and the populace drank itself silly.

On the eastern wall of the court to the left, Ptolemy X makes offerings to Horus, Hathor, and their son, **Ihy**. On the opposite wall, his predecessor Ptolemy IX performs similar rites. The court is surrounded by 32 columns and a single hawk statue guards the next door.

THE CULT OF HORUS

One of Egypt's most ancient deities, the hawk-headed Horus fulfilled many roles, but is best known as the child of Isis and Osiris. After Osiris was murdered by his evil brother Seth, Horus avenged the crime here at Edfu by defeating Seth, who was then exiled to the Western Desert. Horus was also inextricably linked to the Pharaoh, who was considered the human incarnation of Horus. During the annual recoronation celebration of each pharaoh, a live hawk would also be crowned as an incarnation of Horus. This hawk was placed in a chamber at the temple where he represented the 'reign' of the Pharaoh as Horus.

*During the New Kingdom, the cult of Horus became increasingly important as the **Feast of the Great Union**, rose to a prominence eclipsed only by that of the Opet Festival in Thebes. Other festivals celebrated at Edfu included the **Festival of Triumph**, celebrating Horus' victory over Seth; and the **Birth Festival**, commemorating his divine birth.*

Beyond the Court of Offerings, the **Hypostyle Hall** features 12 large columns topped with floral capitals, and an astrological ceiling. On the wall immediately to the left, a small chamber was used to store golden vessels used for purification rites (depicted in nearby the reliefs), and was also a dressing room for high priests. The small room off the wall to the right was a library used for storing sacred texts. The doorway to the rear features depictions of Ptolemy IX at a groundbreaking ceremony for this temple. The second hypostyle hall, known as the **Festival Hall**, also features twelve columns, this time in three rows of four. Again, the motif is that of the temple's construction, and the pharaoh in question is Ptolemy IV. As is often the case, the deeper you go into the temple, the older the reliefs. The subsequent, second **Hall of Offerings** features two stairwells, both flanked by murals portraying pharaohs and priests in ritual processions climbing these very stairs, hoisting sacred idols of Horus to the temple's roof.

Upon the returning from the roof, you will approach the heart of the temple, the **sanctuary**, through another small hall. To the left is a small shrine dedicated to the ever phallicly erect god of fertility, **Min**. The small chamber to the right contains excellent reliefs of a Ptolemy making offerings to Horus and Hathor. In the sanctuary itself, the altar of Horus contained an idol and a sacred barge – the boat there now is a copy of the original. This shrine was built by **Nektanebo II** (360-343 BC), the last pharaoh of Egyptian stock. Surrounding the sanctuary, ten chambers were used for storage and now contain reliefs listing and depicting those sacred instruments contained within them.

After exploring the sanctuary, exit the temple and turn left. The reliefs on the western wall along the length of the temple show Horus incarnated as pharaoh, hunting and killing a hippopotamus in the presence of Hathor. The hippo represents **Seth**, the evil brother of Osiris who killed the elder god but was defeated by Horus in revenge.

Outside of the main temple close to the entrance pylon stands the **Birth House**, a common feature of Ptolemeic temples and site of rituals to commemorate the divine birth of Horus. The reliefs depict him being suckled by his mother, Isis.

SHOPPING

Around the temple entrance hawkers peddle cheap and tacky souvenirs. Any worthwhile purchase will surely require intense bargaining.

PRACTICAL INFORMATION

Banks & Currency Exchange

A **bank** is *on El Gomhuriya Street south of the midan and east of the temple. Hours: Sunday-Thursday 8:30-2pm.*

Emergencies

• **Regular Police***: Tel. 700-866, on El Maglis Street.*
• **Tourist Police***: Tel. 700-724, at the temple.*

Post Services

Post Office, *250 meters south of the main square on El Tahrir Street. Hours: Saturday-Thursday 8:30am-3pm.*

Telephones, Telex, & Fax

Some of the tourist shops and hotels operate telephones. Otherwise there are phones at the train station on the east bank.

Tourist Information

The **Tourist Police** (*Temple of Horus, Tel. 095/700-724*), shopkeepers, and hotel personnel may be able to give assistance with directions.

KOM OMBO & THE TEMPLE OF SOBEK & HORUS

One of the most dramatic scenes in Egypt is the approach from the Nile to the **Temple of Sobek and Horus** at **Kom Ombo**. Now the site of a large sugar refinery, the town of Kom Ombo was a trading center in antiquity when caravans from Nubia and Sudan were attracted by gold mined in the nearby eastern hills. It was also a provincial capital and during the Ptolemeic Period a training center for the elephant cavalry.

Kom Ombo is best visited by water transport, if only for the view of the temple looming over the Nile. Many travelers incorporate it into a felucca trip from Aswan to Luxor and cruise ships also stop here. Otherwise, Kom Ombo is an easy day excursion from Aswan and may be combined with a visit to the **Tuesday camel market at Daraw**. Like Edfu and Esna, it offers little in the way of accommodations and besides annual moulids, no cultural attractions.

ARRIVALS & DEPARTURES

By Boat

As mentioned above, the best way to visit Kom Ombo is on a boat which makes a good argument for taking a Nile cruise or a felucca journey from Aswan (see the following "Aswan" section for details).

By Bus

Buses pass through town on the main strip, but are less efficient and less pleasant than service taxis. Those going to main destinations, usually originate in other towns are often packed by the time they pass through.

By Service

The service depot is on 26th July Street. Service taxis depart almost non-stop for Edfu and Aswan (LE1, 1 hour to either destination). Coming from Aswan, ask the driver to let you off at the path to the temple (*ma'abed* in Arabic).

By Train

Trains do stop in Kom Ombo but are painstakingly slow and infrequent.

ORIENTATION

As the temple is on the waterfront 4 kilometers away, most visitors need not spend any time in town. If you insist, the main drag is **26th July Street** where hotels, the taxi stand, and some shops are located.

GETTING AROUND TOWN

You can make your way around town on foot, but reaching the temple requires hitching with a local service. They will drop you at the dock from where you can walk. Alternatively, if you can find one, a private taxi should make the trip from town to the temple for about LE5.

WHERE TO STAY

CLEOPATRA HOTEL, *Next to the pick-up service depot. Tel. 097/500-325. Rates: LE10-15 singles and double, LE25 triples and quadruples.*

It's very basic and plain with rooms featuring fans, but it's adequately clean and the showers have hot water.

WHERE TO EAT

In town there are several fuul and ta'amiya stands as well as the **El Noba Restaurant** serving plain Egyptian cuisine, i.e. roast chicken, red beans, tehina, rice, and bread. Between the dock the temple are two cafeterias serving full meals for inflated prices. The better of the two, **Cafeteria Venus**, also serves beer.

SEEING THE SIGHTS
THE TEMPLE OF HORUS & SOBEK

The temple is on the Nile, 40 kilometers south of Edfu and 40 kilometers north of Aswan. Hours: 8am-4pm (5pm summer). Admission: LE20 general, LE10 students.

Situated on a bend in the river that for centuries was a favorite sunning spot for local crocs, the moderately sized Kom Ombo Temple is one of the most fascinating in Upper Egypt. Built by Greek Ptolemies it is an anomaly because it is dedicated to two unrelated deities and features two symmetrical halves, one dedicated to each deity. The two deities are the crocodile deity, **Sobek**, and an incarnation of **Horus**, known as **Horus the Elder** (Haroeris to the Greeks) traditionally associated with Heliopolis. Linking two unrelated deities was virtually unheard of in the well ordered world of Egyptian religion where every deity, temple, and story fulfilled a very specific role in a very structured universe. This awkward attempt to fuse two unrelated deities is a classic example of the Ptolemies adopting Egyptian religion in form, but missing the mark in substance.

The second major break with temple building tradition was the construction of two perfectly symmetrical architectural halves on either side of the temple's main axis – one dedicated to each god. For every niche and shrine for Sobek on the eastern half, a corresponding niche or shrine can be found on the half dedicated to Haroeris to the west. It even contains two sanctuaries, the equivalent in ancient Egypt temple design to a human being having two hearts in one body.

In any case, like other major temples, Kom Ombo is entered through a pylon and forecourt (both largely ruined) constructed during the reign of the Roman emperor Augustus around the time of Christ. The left tower features reliefs portraying Horus the Elder with Isis and their son, the traditional Horus. **Horus the Elder** was associated with the Heliopolis creation myth and was believed to have constructed the first building. On the left-hand tower, Sobek and his consort, **Tasentnefer** (an incarnation of Hathor) are shown with their child, **Khonsu Hor**, an incarnation of Khonsu. The spacious forecourt has eight columns on each side.

The front facade of the **hypostyle hall** depicts Neos Dionysos (Ptolemy XII) being purified by Horus and Thoth on the left, and Sobek on the right. Inside, the hypostyle hall features ten columns shaped like papyri, the symbol of the Delta. The wall reliefs portray various Ptolemies commiserating with deities. To the right upon entrance, they look over the coronation of Neos Dionysos. A second, smaller, hypostyle hall features Sobek in crocodile form between the two portals while the walls again portray various Ptolemies making offerings to deities.

Unfortunately, the **inner sanctuaries and vestibules** are in poor shape. In the first small hall, the rear walls depict, as Ptolemeic temples often did, the Greek pharaoh (Ptolemy VI) presiding over the construction of the temple. The second chamber was the site of important religious rites, including sacrifices, and was off limits to all but the highest priests and royalty. The walls feature holy texts and the small niches and chambers were for storage of holy instruments and clothing for use by the priests and the gods themselves. In the middle of the rear wall between the two doors, a small relief depicts a woman giving birth. On the doors to the sanctuaries themselves Ptolemy is honored by Khonsu, Haroeris and Sobek, who present him with a palm leaf. Though little remains in the sanctuaries themselves, check the **secret corridor** (approached from the rear) that squeezes between the two. It is believed that a priest hidden here performed voice-overs on behalf of the deities during rituals.

The outer corridors contain more casual, but interesting reliefs, many of which were nothing more than prayers in graffiti form. Particularly interesting on the rear outer corridor, is a register of surgical instruments including scalpels and a bone saw.

There are several important external structures. East of the main forecourt, the impressive Roman built **Chapel of Hathor** contains mummified crocodiles. Next to it, the **Gate of Neos Dionysos** is largely ruined. **Neos Dionysos** (Ptolemy XII) was a major contributor to this temple and father of the famous **Cleopatra** of Cleopatra and Marc Antony fame. On the other side of the forecourt, the **Birth House** is largely destroyed.

PRACTICAL INFORMATION

Banks & Currency Exchange
Change money in Aswan or Luxor.

Emergencies
Contact the **Tourist Police** *at Kom Ombo Temple in case of an emergency.*

Post Services
Post Office, *26th July Street. Hours: 8:30am-3pm.*

Telephones
Phones are located in the train station. Otherwise, hotels also operate phones.

DARAW

Daraw is 10 kilometers south of Kom Ombo and reachable from Aswan or Kom Ombo by service or private taxi (LE40 round trip from Aswan). A major node in the still functioning camel caravan route that originates in Sudan, Daraw features one of Egypt's most impressive **livestock markets**.

Every **Tuesday morning** Sudanese merchants, Bedouin, and local *fellaheen* converge here to trade in sheep, cattle, donkeys, and camels brought up by caravan from Sudan. The local buzz is enhanced by an equally huge weekly fruit and vegetable market and numerous hawkers peddling everything from fuul sandwiches to fake Levi's. It's something like an Egyptian cross between a Grateful Dead concert and a medieval fair, but this market has been going even longer than the former.

ASWAN

Overlooking the Nile's dramatic First Cataract, **Aswan** has for millennia been Egypt's link to Africa and a major crossroads for caravan routes and armies. Though never a national capital, its strategic location on Egypt's southern frontier and mythic status as home to the gods of inundation ensured that Aswan enjoyed a greater prestige than other provincial capitals.

During the Old Kingdom, the noblemen from **Elephantine Island** were known as "Keepers of the Southern Gate" and were responsible not only for guarding Egypt's southern frontier, but maintaining good relations with **Hapi**, the Nile-god, and **Khnum**, the god of inundation, to ensure that the life-giving floods would be plentiful enough to feed all of

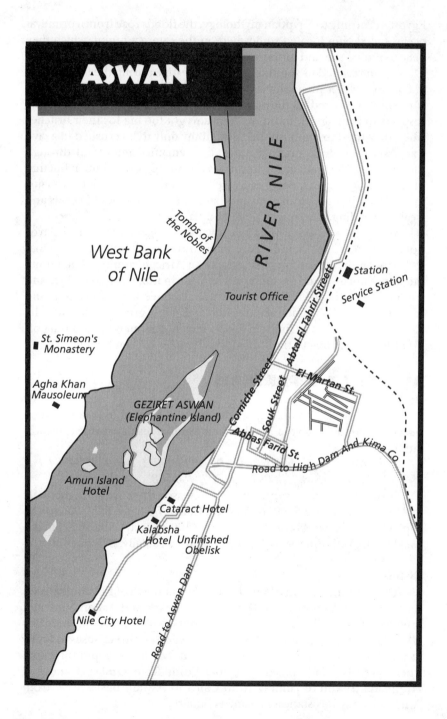

Egypt. According to Egyptian mythology, the floods rose from a primeval ocean called Nun located somewhere in the cataract region which they believed to be the end of the world.

Aswan reached its zenith in political prestige during the 6th Dynasty (2,350 BC) when pharaohs in Memphis claimed Aswani ancestry and sometimes ventured all the way from the northern capital to pay their respects to Hapi and Khnum. But Aswanis got too big for their britches when they tried to establish their autonomy only to be crushed in a civil war. Aswan never its original status, but remained important through Ptolemeic and Roman times when it was not only Egypt's frontier, but that of the Mediterranean empires as well. It also developed into a major junction for trans-African caravans that imported all types of goods and wealth including furs, spices, gold, and slaves.

Aswan today is a charming Nile town with a distinctive African flavor not found to the north; indeed for many travelers it's only in Aswan that it dawns on them that Egypt is actually an African country. The monuments are not as grand or numerous as those in Luxor, but the grace and spectacular setting of Philae and the dramatic meeting of the desert and the Nile at the First Cataract are among Egypt's greatest sites and the Corniche vistas are the finest in Egypt. Finally, Aswan is the jumping off point for excursions to the stupendous temples of Abu Simbel.

ARRIVALS & DEPARTURES

By Air

The airport is about 20 kilometers to the south of town and can be reached taxi (LE20) if your hotel or tour group doesn't provide transportation.

EgyptAir, *El Corniche Street. Tel. 097/315-000/1/2/3/4, 575-4984, Fax 097/731-5005. Airport. Tel. 097/480-307, 480-568.*

Schedules and fares vary according to season there are 6-9 flights daily to **Abu Simbel** (about $150 round trip); **Cairo** (7-9 daily, $250-300 round trip); **Hurghada** (weekly on Wednesdays, $100 one way); **Sharm El Sheikh** (weekly on Wednesdays, $100); and **Luxor** (5-10 daily, $75 one-way).

By Bus

The bus station is on Abtal El Tahrir Street north of El Mattar Street. As many as 12-15 buses run daily between Luxor and Aswan but you'll want to get on an "Express" (LE5-10, 4 hours) which stops only in major towns like Edfu and Kom Ombo and not in villages. Direct buses to **Cairo** (a very long 12 hours) depart twice daily at 3:30 and 4:30pm for LE50. There are also daily buses to **Qena**; **Edfu**; **Kom Ombo**; **Esna**; and **Hurghada**. If you're coming from Cairo to Aswan, buses leave from Ahmed Helmy bus station in Ramses Square.

By Service

The service station is on the east side of the rail road tracks just south of the train station. Service depart several times hourly for Upper Egyptian destinations like Kom Ombo (LE2, 1 hour), Edfu (LE4, 1.5 hours), Daraw (LE1, 30 minutes), and Luxor (LE8, 4 hours).

By Train

The train station is just off the northern end of El Souk Street. Local trains leave for Kom Ombo, Edfu, and Esna regularly but are far slower than service and even buses. They are convenient however for travel to **Luxor** (LE40 1st class, LE20 students; LE10-15 2nd class with air-conditioning); and **Cairo** (LE100 1st class, LE50 students; LE60 2nd class with air-conditioning, LE30 for students). Train #981 departs at 5:45am and #997 departs at 6:30pm. These trains also stop in Qena, Sohag, Assiut, and Minya. **Wagon-Lits** sleepers cost about $150 to Cairo. Be sure to buy tickets for all trains at least a day in advance.

By Boat

Aswan is a common departure point for **Nile Cruises** and overnight **feluccas** (see the "Felucca" sidebar below). For information about arranging a cruise see the "Getting Around" section of the "Planning Your Trip" chapter in the beginning of the book. It is possible to join cruises on the spot in Aswan, especially during the summer or other slow seasons. Travel agents advertise vacancies or you can shop the ships themselves. When business is really bad, you may be able to negotiate an excellent deal-$35 a day or less, board and tours included.

ORIENTATION

Life in Aswan revolves around the Nile-hugging **Corniche**. Lined with hotels, shops, travel agencies and restaurants, it affords picturesque views of the Nile and is the place to hire a felucca. The other main drag, bustling **Souk Street**, is home to Aswan's famous markets, and runs parallel to the Corniche between Abbas Farid Street to the south and El Mattar Street to the north. The **train station** is three blocks inland from the Corniche north of the ferry station. Aswan's most famous landmark, the **Old Cataract Hotel** is south of downtown in the Feriel Gardens.

Apart from the bazaars, Aswan's attractions are all located outside of the city itself. Elephantine Island with its colorful Nubian villages and pharaonic ruins can be reached by felucca, motorboat, or public ferry as can the various upscale island hotels. To reach the west bank, there is a public ferry from the Corniche near the train station. Philae, the dams, Lake Nasser, and the Unfinished Obelisk are south of town and best reached by private transportation or taxi.

FELUCCA CRUISES TO EDFU & LUXOR

*One of the best ways to experience the timeless beauty of the Nile and the Upper Egyptian countryside is to take a **felucca cruise** from Aswan to Edfu or Luxor. Much cheaper than a Nile Cruise and more adventurous and authentically Egyptian as well, feluccas enable you to experience life on and around the Nile firsthand-and it saves you a trip on one of those dusty buses. The typical trip begins in Aswan and takes two nights/three days to Edfu or three nights and four days to Luxor. Many captains are reluctant to go beyond Edfu because the trip down river from Luxor leaves them at the mercy of the winds. You sleep under the stars on the boat, stop at the temples of Kom Ombo, Edfu, and Esna, and if your lucky the captain will treat you to a meal in his village (or somebody else's).*

The trick of a successful felucca cruise is preparation. It's very easy to arrange feluccas through budget and mid-priced hotels, travel agencies, or directly through felucca captains who congregate on the Corniche. Typically, they won't leave with less than six, and not more than eight. If your party is less than six, you may have to join another or pay the difference. For a six person cruise, the price is about LE50 per person per day, not including food. Captains will cook and offer to shop for food, but it's best to shop with or instead of him to ensure that the money is spent properly and that sufficient quantities are purchased-be sure to buy plenty of water. You must also make sure that the boat is sufficiently large and if you're traveling during winter, make sure there are enough blankets and pack warm clothes for yourself.

Always check with the Tourist Authority Office to see if any captains have been blacklisted (stealing and harassment are sporadic problems) or possibly to assemble a group. Also ask around with other travelers who may be able to provide information about particular captains or boats. Finally, be careful about flaunting valuables, never let your passport out of your sight, and insist on getting what you pay for.

WHERE TO STAY

Accommodation in Aswan ranges from the elegant luxury of the Old Cataract and the modern comfort of the island resorts to the concrete austerity of budget establishments, some of which feature superior Nile views, if not private showers. If planning to visit Aswan during winter, it's recommended that you make reservations in advance whatever hotel you wish to stay in, but particularly if you wish to stay in the Old Cataract. In summer, most budget and moderately priced hotels offer discounts, but you may need to ask, even push, to get the lowest rates. Given Aswan's hot and dry climate, it's worth considering establishments with air-conditioning and a pool. Also, those hotels on the Corniche often feature excellent views of the Nile, regardless of their quality and rates.

Expensive

SOFITEL OLD CATARACT HOTEL, *Abtal El Tahrir Street at the southern end of Corniche El Nil Street. Tel. 097/316-000/2/4. Fax 097/ 316011. Capacity: 136 rooms. Rates: $110-$150 singles and doubles; $300-700 suite. Credit cards: all major credit cards accepted.*

Set in the Feriel Gardens on the banks of the Nile, this Moorish style Victorian masterpiece may be the most elegant hotel in Egypt. From the oriental carpets on the hardwood floors to the antique decor and the famous terrace over looking the Nile that just begs for a pith helmet and a martini, the Cataract is a classic colonial style hotel; and its guest list is a roll call of turn of the century bigwigs that includes Winston Churchill, Agatha Christie, and Theodore Roosevelt. As for the facilities, the rooms are large with old timey but first rate furnishings, large balconies with superb views of the Nile, and modern amenities like satellite television. The hotel shares a pool and several dining and drinking facilities with the New Cataract. By all means, worth a splurge.

NEW CATARACT HOTEL, *Abtal El Tahrir Street next to the Old Cataract. Tel. 097/316-000/2/4. Fax 097/316-011. Rates: $65-95 single, $81-111 double, $77-153 suite. Credit cards: all major credit cards accepted.*

This 1970's eyesore should not be confused with its 'Cataract' namesake but at least if you stay here you get to look at the old one. Actually, aside from the cheesy architecture, the New Cataract offers guests most of the same world class setting, facilities, and views, that its older cousin does, just not with the same style. Also, it's cheaper and easier to get reservations for.

ASWAN OBEROI HOTEL, *Elephantine Island (P.O. Box 62, Aswan). Tel. 097/314-666/7/8. Fax 097/323-485. Rates: $92-120 single, $80-155 double, $165-440 suite. Capacity: 244 rooms. Credit cards: all major credit cards accepted.*

Apart from the first class facilities and amenities, the best part about staying in this hotel is that you don't have to look at it. The amenities and comforts are first rate, as is the setting and the views of the felucca dotted Nile. Facilities include a pool, gardens, a nightclub, and several fine restaurants. Rooms are situated in the tower or in bungalow-like condos, and all have air-conditioning, satellite television, deluxe bathrooms, and balconies.

ISIS ISLAND ASWAN HOTEL, *Isis Island. Tel. 097/317-400/1/2. Fax 097/317-405. Capacity: 387 rooms. Rates: $92-120 single, $103-138 double, $218-920 suite. Credit cards: all major credit cards accepted.*

An island modernist monstrosity like the Oberoi, the Isis is flashy and luxurious in form and substance. The rooms are spacious and comfortable with air-conditioning, balconies, and satellite television; tennis courts and swimming top the list of recreational offerings. Like other island hotels, it is set in gardens and features superb Nile views. Also, like the other island establishments, its modernity seems out of place, if not just a tad disturbing.

AMON TOURIST VILLAGE, *Amon Island. Tel. 097/480-438/9 & 480-440. Fax 097/480-440. Capacity: 252 rooms. Rates: $80 single, $98 double, $161-230 suite. Credit cards: all major credit cards accepted.*

This Club Med-managed resort is set in luscious, idyllic botanical gardens on its own Nile island. Rooms are bunched in "Nubian" style bungalows with deluxe amenities including air-conditioning, satellite television, clean baths, not to mention peace and quiet. The only potential disadvantage is the island isolation, but tennis courts, swimming pool, and restaurants and bars offer some distraction. Motorboats shuttle regularly from the Corniche across from the EgyptAir office.

KALABSHA HOTEL, *south of the Cataract Hotels off the Corniche. Tel. 097/322-999, 322-666, 322-162. Fax 097/325-974. Capacity: 120 rooms. Rates: $27-37 single, $33-46 double. Credit cards: Visa.*

This tasteful hotel is good value for the money. Besides air-conditioned rooms with televisions and clean private baths, it offers guests a real bonus—free access to the New Cataract's luxurious swimming pool. There's also a bank, a bar, and a decent but overpriced restaurant.

Moderate hotels

CLEOPATRA HOTEL, *Saad Zaghloul (El Souk) Street. Tel. 097/324-001, 322-983, 314-003. Fax 097/314-002. Capacity: 130 rooms. Rates: $32 single, $40 double.*

Situated in the heart of the *souk* (bazaar), the Cleopatra is for those urban urchins who can't sleep without a bit of noise. Though low on ambiance and charm, it is clean, has a pool, and the rooms have private showers and air-conditioning that works, something that's not always true in some other places. Try bargaining for lower rates.

HORUS HOTEL, *Corniche El Nil Street. Tel. 097/323-323, 313-313. Fax 097/313-313. Capacity: 41 rooms. Rates: LE24-30 single, LE30-37 double, LE60 triple.*

Run by a friendly Greek Orthodox family, the Horus offers great location and Nile views worth the money in themselves. The rooms are far from elegant but comfortable, with air-conditioning, television, and sometimes balconies. The roof is a cafeteria-game room that serves beer and food. There is also a ping-pong table and a less than well worn dance floor .

HAPPI HOTEL, *Abtal El Tahrir Street. Tel. 097/314-115/5. Fax 097/314-002. Capacity 60 rooms. Rates: LE40 single, LE50 double, LE 66 triple.*

Just down the block from the Ramses, the Happi is a notch lower than its neighbor because the rooms lack air-conditioning, but there are fans. Some rooms also have balconies and/or television and residents can use the Cleopatra Hotel's modest pool for free.

RAMSES HOTEL, *Abtal El Tahrir Street. Tel. 097/324-000, 324-119. Capacity: 112 rooms. Rates: LE25 single, LE50 double, LE80 triple.*

Air-conditioned rooms, color television, private baths, and Nile views make this the best value for money hotel in Aswan. Be sure to call ahead as on-the-cheap tour groups are likely to book it up during high season.

Budget

OSCAR HOTEL, *El Barka Street. Tel. 097/326-066, 323-851. Fax 097/326-066. Rates: LE28.50 single, LE35; LE60 triple.*

This well-furnished hotel is extremely popular with budget travelers and is often full. Rooms feature air-conditioning, private showers and balconies (not all rooms). The gaudy lobby gives it a funky feel and the roof with a beer-serving cafeteria comes in handy. All that's missing is the Nile and its breeze which are three blocks to the west.

ABU SIMBEL HOTEL, *Corniche El Nil. Tel. 097/322-888, 322-435, 322-327. Capacity: 66 rooms. Rates: LE16 single, LE20-26 double.*

The Abu Simbel is a grimy concrete establishment in desperate need of a face lift, but the rooms are cheap and the views of the Nile are certainly worth LE26. Rooms have fans, however the private showers can be less than spotless.

HATHOR HOTEL, *Corniche El Nil Street. Tel. 097/314-580. Capacity: 30 rooms. Rates: LE20-40 singles and doubles.*

The excellent location and a rooftop pool make up for cramped rooms, some of which feature air-conditioning. It's worth paying a few extra pounds for rooms with a Nile view overlooking Elephantine Island.

MENA HOTEL, *Atlas Street. Tel. 097/324-388. Capacity: 30 rooms. Rates: LE11.20-13.20 single, LE14-16.50 double, LE35 triple.*

For the price, the Mena Hotel has a good bit to offer including clean, comfy rooms with air-conditioners that at least move some air, and private showers. It's close to the train station and also features a roof-top cafeteria with ping-pong.

ROSEWAN HOTEL, *a block north of the railroad station on Kamal Nour El Din Street. Tel. 097/324-497, 322-297. Capacity: 54 rooms. Rates: singles LE15-25, LE15-25 double.*

The Rosewan is a friendly, well established budget hotel exuding all the friendly shabbiness one might expect from a one-star hotel in Egypt. The slightly pricier rooms include small private showers and toilets and all rooms have fans. Even if you don't stay here, it's worth a visit if you're in the neighborhood to check out the owner's paper mache studio where he crafts masks, ashtrays, baskets, and other charming products that make great souvenirs and small gifts.

Camping
There's a campground near the Unfinished Obelisk two kilometers south of town. Facilities include space for tents and very basic showers. Rates are LE10 for camping space and parking should you have a vehicle.

WHERE TO EAT
Like everything else in Aswan, restaurants are concentrated on the Corniche. Cheap to moderately priced restaurants serving run-of-the-mill Egyptian and continental food line the river, offer excellent views of the Nile but leave you vulnerable to mosquitoes, and potential tummy problems as well. Moderate and upscale hotels operate their own restaurants and the usual assortment of cheap eats (*fuul, ta'amiya, kushari)* are available at stands and stalls throughout town. Generally, eating in Aswan is as much about the view as it is the food.

The Oberoi Tower has a number of restaurants that feature better food than the Old Cataract with less ambiance. Also because Oberoi is an Indian chain, the menus often feature Indian treats besides the usual Egyptian and continental options. The **Orangerie Restaurant** itself is an Indian eatery. None of it is cheap though, you'll be lucky to get a sandwich for less than LE15.

THE OLD CATARACT *in the Feriel Gardens.*
Features a number of splurge-worthy options, the fanciest being the main dining room. The continental food is good but not excellent, certainly overpriced (you won't make it out paying less than LE40), but the elegant Moorish Edwardian decor and live Nubian music makes it an unforgettable experience.

TRATTORIA, *at the Isis Hotel.*
Italian fare with superb views of Elephantine Island and the Nile.

Along the Nile
ASWAN PANORAMA, *on the Corniche waterfront.*
A wide ranging menu of Egyptian and Egyptianized continental food including kebab, spaghetti, mezzes, and great rice pudding. A full meal shouldn't set you back more than about LE20.

MONA LISA, *a floating restaurant on the waterfront.*
Mona Lisa has unsurpassable views and a nice breeze. The Egyptian food is okay but nothing special.

RESTAURANT EL NIL, *on the Corniche but not the river.*
Excellent fish caught from Lake Nasser for cheap (LE12).
SALAH EL DIN, *on the Corniche but not the river.*
One of the cheapest of the waterfront restaurants and also serves cold Stella for a cool LE7.

In the Souk

In and around the souk are dozens of small purely local affairs. **Sayeda Nafisa** *about a kilometer south of the train station* is legendary for its stuffed pigeon (LE12) and roast chicken. **Medina Restaurant,** *also on El Souk Street,* offers no frills dining that won't set you back more than LE5-12 depending on whether you take meat.

SEEING THE SIGHTS

Though it doesn't rival Luxor in the spectacularity of is monuments, Aswan boasts an assortment of impressive and unique sights ranging from the ancient island temple of Philae to the 20th century engineering wonder of the Aswan High Dam. While some attractions such as the **Elephantine Island**, the **Aga Khan's Mausoleum** and the **Tombs of the Nobles** are in the vicinity of Aswan itself, others like Philae and Kalabsha are a ways out of town.

I'd recommend combining the sites of Elephantine Island and the west bank in one day and those south of Aswan (**Philae Island**, the **Dams, Kalabsha**, the **Fatimid Cemetery** and the **Unfinished Obelisk**) in another. The sites of Elephantine Island and the west bank are covered here; those south of Aswan, including Philae, the Dams, and Kalabsha, are covered beginning on page 372.

THE NUBIAN MUSEUM

Slated to open in 1998, the new **Nubian Museum** *is across from the New Cataract Hotel on the road to the Aswan Dam. Covering more than 20 acres, it will contain a myriad of exhibits relating to Nubian culture and history including pharaonic era artifacts found in Nubia, a model Nubian village, and displays of Nubian jewelry and clothing. It will also regularly host Nubian cultural events.*

ELEPHANTINE ISLAND

Ferries depart from a dock across the street from EgyptAir north of the Cataract Hotel on the Corniche. Fare: 25p per head. Hours: 6am-midnight.

Feluccas and private motorboats also make the trip. Unless you have a large group (more than fir or six), don't pay more than several pounds one way.

So named for the black boulders at its southern tip that resemble bathing elephants, Elephantine Island is an indelible part of the Aswan experience. Beautifully set in the river, it contains several **Nubian villages**, the **Aswan Museum**, ruins of an ancient settlement known as **Yebu**, and a monstrosity of a modern hotel, the **Aswan Oberoi**.

History

Inhabited since the predynastic era, Elephantine Island contained a southern frontier town whose officials were known as "Keepers of the Gate of the South," a reference to the cataracts the island overlooks that provided a natural boundary with Nubia to the south. According to tradition, it was also the home and cult center of the ram-headed god, **Khnum**, god of the inundation as well as the Creator of man. It was his wife, **Satis**, who controlled the water flow after their daughter, **Anukis** directed towards Egypt from the south. Shrines were constructed here as early as the Old Kingdom when the local tribe and its nobility achieved such prosperity and importance that most 5th Dynasty pharaohs claimed roots here.

As the Old Kingdom crumbled during the 6th and 7th Dynasties, Elephantine tried to assert its independence- a strategy which backfired when they were badly defeated in a civil war. Elephantine never regained its early prominence though later dynasties, including the Ptolemies would continue to erect temples to Khnum. After the Aswan High Dam displaced the entire Nubian People in the 1960's, three villages were developed here.

The Nubian Villages

For many tourists already templed out up north in Luxor, the most interesting portion of a visit to the Elephantine Island are the **Nubian villages** relocated here after Nubia was submerged under Lake Nasser. Set in tropical like palm groves and featuring colorfully decorated buildings with Haj scenes, the villages offer excellent exploring and photo opportunities. Just remember to respect the privacy of locals who may or may not wish to be photographed.

The Aswan Museum

Hours: 9am-11:30am & 1-5pm (6pm summer). Admission: LE5 general, LE2.50 students. Cameras: LE15 with no flash.

Adjoined by a colorful and well maintained garden stocked with exotic plants imported by Lord Kitchener, the museum is in a villa that was the turn of the century home of Sir William Willocks, designer of the first Aswan Dam. It contains a modest, but quality collection of pharaonic and Nubian artifacts that includes pottery, weaponry, and jewelry as well as several statues. On the bottom floor, the mummy collection includes mummified ram, in honor of Khnum, and several human mummies.

The Nilometer
Located 300 meters from the Aswan Museum. Accessed from the river or the museum.

The oldest **nilometer** in Egypt was also the first, because of its location up river, to measure annual flood levels, a key economic indicator. These measurements were used by officials to predict agricultural production and to set tax rates. Should you approach by boat, notice the inscriptions on nearby rocks commemorating the reigns of Thutmosis III, Amenhophis III, and several Ptolemeic pharaohs. From land, the nilometer is approached by a stairwell, the walls of which feature records dating to the pharaonic, Roman, and Islamic eras. Originally built during the Old Kingdom, the nilometer was upgraded throughout history, with the latest renovation occurring in the 1870's during the rule of Khedive Ismail. A **second nilometer** recently excavated further south, dates to the Ptolemeic period and was built with stones usurped from New Kingdom monuments. As of yet, it is inaccessible.

The Ruins of Yebu & The Temple of Khnum
Located at the southern end of Elephantine.

The ruins scattered about the southern end of the island date primarily to the Ptolemeic era though a prosperous community existed here as early as the predynastic era. The main attraction is the **Temple of Khnum**, god of the floods. The ruined temple now in place was founded by the Late Period Pharaoh Nektanebo around 350 BC and was expanded throughout the Ptolemeic Era. At the gate, Ptolemy XI is shown praying to Khnum. The other main remnants are the pillars which also came courtesy of the Ptolemies.

North of the Temple of Khnum are several more ruins including the Ptolemeic era **Necropolis of Sacred Rams** which contained mummified rams. Further north, but possibly blocked off for renovations are the **Temple of Hekayib**, a shrine dedicated to a local 6th Dynasty prince who achieved a quasi-divine status, and the **Temple of Satis**. Satis was the mate of Khnum who regulated the all important annual inundation. This temple was founded by Hatshepsut in 1490 BC and it is here that a second nilometer was recently excavated.

Southwest of the Temple of Khnum remnants of an ancient community has yielded Aramaic papyrus documents indicating the presence of a Jewish community as early as the 6th century BC. Scholars speculate that they might have been in the employment of the Persians as guards of Egypt's southern frontiers. In any case, you can make your way, most easily by felucca, from here to Kitchener's or Amon Island.

KITCHENER'S ISLAND

Located behind Elephantine Island and accessible by felucca (LE3-5 one way). Hours: 8am until sunset. Admission: LE 5.

After having avenged Gordon's defeat at the hands of the Mahdi in the Sudan, Lord Kitchener was presented with this small island as a gift. Here the war hero, who later became the Minister of War in Great Britain during World War I, enjoyed pursuing his gardening hobby and planted a variety of exotic imported flora. Though caged monkeys somewhat ruin this idyllic scene, it is still an excellent place to relax and during the winter, to enjoy an Aswan afternoon sun.

THE WEST BANK

You can spend an hour or two on the west bank taking in the Aga Khan's Mausoleum and the Monastery of Saint Simeon (see next two entries below). More dedicated sightseers will take the time to hike over two kilometers of desert hills to the Tombs of the Nobles, some of which date as far back as the Old Kingdom. The west bank is accessible by felucca, motorboat or public ferry.

The Aga Khan's Mausoleum

In a walled complex, up the hill by via a stairway. Hours: 9am-4:45pm. Entrance is free. Modest dress (no shorts) is required for men and women.

This graceful mausoleum holds the remains of **Aga Khan III** (1877-1957), the 48th Imam of the Shiite Ismaili sect, who loved to spend his winters in Aswan. Built like a Fatimid tomb (the Fatimids were Shiite), it contains a small mosque with a courtyard where the Aga Khan's marble sarcophagus lies in a vaulted chamber. His wife, the Begum, still winters here and places a red rose at the tomb daily.

The Monastery of Saint Simeon

Located across the valley three quarters of a mile north of the Aga Khan's Mausoleum. Hours: 9am-5pm. Admission: LE6 general, LE3 students.

Founded in the 6th century, this desert surrounded temple to asceticism feels much further from the civilized Nile Valley than it actually is. Unused for the last 700 years, this monastery was originally dedicated to **Anba Hadra**, a fourth century local saint who renounced the world a day before his wedding. It served as a base for proselytizing in Nubia and the Sudan.

A bi-level complex built of stone on the lower level, and mud-brick on the upper, it contains a roofless **basilica** and a chamber where Saint Simeon apparently spent much of his time meditating. In the basilica, you can still make out faded frescoes depicting the Apostles. Finally, the central keep was used to house three monks and contained kitchens, bakeries, libraries, and dormitories.

THE TOMBS OF THE NOBLES

2.5 kilometers (45 minutes walking) north of Saint Simeon's Monastery. From Aswan, take the local ferry (50p) which departs across from Isis Tours on the Corniche. Hours: 8am-5pm. Admission: LE6 general, LE3 students. Cameras: LE10 per tomb with no flash.

Built for local officials, the famous 'Keepers of the South Gate,' responsible for protecting Egypt's southern frontier, these tombs span the breadth of pharaonic Egypt from the Old Kingdom to the Romans. Though dozens, perhaps hundreds dot these hills, six are open to the public and feature brilliant reliefs depicting everyday life in southern Egypt.

The **tombs of Mekhu & Sahni (#25 & #26)**, dating to the 6th Dynasty in the Old Kingdom are at the top of the hillside, a location which may leave you wondering how in the hell were equipment and goods brought to the site. Mekhu was a local official killed in Nubia and succeeded by his son, Sahni who in revenge led punitive attacks against south and recovered his father's body. These heroics earned him a pharaonic invitation to Memphis where Pharaoh Pepi II lent his personal mourners and embalmers for Mekhu's mummification. This indicates the high esteem enjoyed by the 'Keepers of the Southern Gate' during the Old Kingdom.

The **tomb of Sarenput II (#31)**, the largest and best preserved, dates to the 12th Dynasty and contains fine reliefs depicting the prince hunting and fishing with his sons and enjoying his family, as well as several Osiride statues.

The **tomb of Sarenput I (#36)** also dates to the 12th Dynasty and belongs to a supervisor of the Cult of Khnum. Reliefs on the left depict Sarenput enjoying a bullfight and fishing with his sons and dogs. On the opposite wall, he is again shown with his dog, this time hunting (below) and with his family in the garden (above). The pillars contain sacred and biographical texts and well as depictions of the tomb's owner.

The **tomb of Pepi Nakht (#35)**, also known as **Hekayib**, was built for the same 6th Dynasty prince whose cult temple is found on Elephantine. A general, he led expeditions into Nubia and Asia the exploits of which are recounted on the tomb's walls.

The **tomb of Harkhuf** (unnumbered) is just south of Pepi Nakht's and belongs to his predecessor. Badly damaged, this tomb features depictions of the general making offerings and presenting captured loot to his superior, Pharaoh Pepi II.

KUBBET EL HAWA

This hillside mausoleum near the Tombs of the Nobles was built for a local sufi saint and rewards those who make the trip with superb views of the Nile Valley.

NIGHTLIFE & ENTERTAINMENT

Watching the sunset from a felucca or sipping a cocktail on the terrace at the Old Cataract are the classic ways to the spend in evening in Aswan. Should you desire however there are alternatives.

Cultural Events

The **Aswan Cultural Center**, *on the Corniche (Tel. 313-390)*, sponsors Nubian folkloric dances and other cultural events in the evenings during the winter. For information, call the Center or ask at your hotel.

If you're lucky enough to be invited to a **Nubian wedding**, by all means do not pass it up. Ostentatious affairs with live music, dancing, and enormous amounts of food, they often last late into the night and may include indulging in hashish and/or drink. Should you partake, beware of police and, for women particularly, unseemly types who may try to take advantage of you sexually or otherwise.

Sound & Light

The **Sound & Light Show at Philae** is popular with many travelers and while the voice-over is fluffy as hell, the lights on the temples against a moon or starlit sky transcend description. During winter, shows begin at 6, 7:30, & 9pm; 8, 9:30, & 11pm in summer. On Wednesdays, Fridays, and Saturdays, the first show is in English, while on Mondays and Tuesdays, the second shows are in English. Tickets cost LE35 with no discounts for students. Hiring a taxi costs about LE30 roundtrip, so it is cheapest to divide it amongst as many folks as possible.

Nightclubs & Bars

The **terrace at the Old Cataract** is one of the all time magnificent spots for watching a sunset-milk the twenty pound cocktails for all their worth. Other upscale hotels also feature run-of-the-mill hotel style bars, usually with first rate views and sky-high prices. Around 10pm, nightclubs in the Cataract, Oberoi, Amon Island, Kalabsha, and the Isis open and sometimes feature belly dancing or a floor show in addition to western style dancing and drinking. All of them administer minimum charges of at least LE25 that goes towards drinks.

Younger folks with tighter budgets sometimes congregate at the **disco at the Ramses Hotel** which opens at 10pm with no minimum charge.

SPORTS & RECREATION
Feluccas

Boasting one the most beautiful stretches of Nile in Egypt, Aswan is an ideal setting for relaxing on a felucca. They can be hired anywhere on the Corniche, and you shouldn't pay more than LE20-25 for an hour unless you have more than 12 people in which case LE2-3 per person is appropriate. Sunset is the ideal time for a cruise.

Swimming Pools

Those of you staying at four and five star hotels will certainly appreciate the swimming pools at these establishments given Aswan's climate. Some of them are even willing to open their facilities to the rest of us for a fee. Many three star hotels have smaller pools which may or may not satisfy your desire for a cool dip, or your hygienic standards. If they do not, you have to splurge and fork out the LE30 to use the pools at the New Cataract or one of the island resort. Call in advance to get the scoop.

SHOPPING

Aswan's humming **bazaar**, *on El Souk Street parallel to the Corniche,* is one of the most colorful in Egypt but in recent years has lost some of its medieval flair to over-touristification and 20th century commercialism. Still it's a wonderful place for an evening stroll and passing through the spice, textile, and jewelry souks you may just find something worth taking home. As usual, you'll have to bargain to get a fair price.

EXCURSIONS & DAY TRIPS

Aswan is the primary launch point for day trips and overnights to the magnificent temples at **Abu Simbel** – a must-see attraction if ever there was such a thing. Virtually every hotel and travel agency can arrange both day and overnight excursions. If you prefer to freelance, there is a daily bus, and it is possible to hire a taxi for the day. Shop around and also see the Abu Simbel section for details.

Aswan is also an excellent base for making day trips to the temples between Aswan and Luxor. **Kom Ombo** and **Edfu**, can be easily combined in one trip and if you're really gung-ho on squeezing in as much as possible, you can also fit in **Esna**, but it is much closer to Luxor. If you are around on a Tuesday, we highly recommend considering a visit to the **camel market at Daraw** 25 kilometers north of Aswan. It fits in nicely with a trip to Kom Ombo and is the ultimate "local color" experience. Catch a service from the main depot for LE1 or hire a private taxi and be sure to get going no later than 8am.

Many travel agencies advertise day and overnight excursions to **Lake Nasser**. **El Boyhayrat Orascom Co.**, **Sports and Fishing** in Lake Nasser arranges fishing, bird hunting, and sightseeing excursions in Lake Nasser lasting from a half day to two weeks. These excursions afford rare opportunities to view Nubian temples other than Abu Simbel and to enjoy Lake Nasser's natural beauty, including a variety of wildlife ranging from gigantic crocodiles to an assortment of wild birds. For hunters, there is an abundance of wild geese and ducks, and fisherman are drawn by Nile perch which can weigh more than 65 kilos. *Call 097/314-090 or fax 097/ 311-011 for information and to make reservations. Equipment is provided and they will pick you up in downtown Aswan.*

ATTRACTIONS SOUTH OF ASWAN
The following attractions can be combined in one day trip from Aswan. All are located within 20 kilometers of the city to the south.

The Fatimid Cemeteries
Two kilometers south of Aswan.
This Islamic burial ground dates to the pre-Fatimid Tulinid period of the 9th century and contains hundreds of domed tombs. They are largely ruined, but are worth combining with a visit to the Unfinished Obelisk.

The Unfinished Obelisk
By the Fatimid Cemeteries 2 kilometers south of Aswan.
A south-of-Aswan tour invariably includes a visit to the Unfinished Obelisk situated in Aswan's famous granite quarries. Here granite was carved out of the ground before being shipped down river as far as the Delta for use in the building of great monuments including the Pyramids of Giza. This obelisk was intended to be one of those great monuments. Experts reckon that it was intended to soar forty meters high and weigh almost 1,200 tons before a flaw in the rock forced its abandonment.

Sehel Island
Four kilometers south of Aswan and north of the Aswan Dam. Accessible only by felucca from Aswan (LE50 roundtrip, 3-4 hour round trip). Bring water and sun protection.

This island overlooking the beautiful First Cataract was sacred ground to Khnum, the ram-headed god of inundation. It does not feature monuments, but views from the peaks of its two boulder-laden hills, ideal locales for a picnic, are fantastic. There is also a small Nubian village, where overfriendly children will besiege you asking for pens and *baksheesh*.

Though it contains little in the way of ancient monuments, the huge boulders which dominate the island feature inscriptions ranging from the Middle Kingdom to the Ptolemeic Period. Most of them record the ways of the river and prayers, but on the eastern hill, you will find the **Famine Stele**, a Ptolemeic document which tells of a visit by Zoser, the 3rd Dynasty Pharaoh who built the Step Pyramid at Saqqara. According to the texts, Zoser made a visit to Aswan after a drought to inquire as to why Egypt was being cursed and to ask the gods for forgiveness. As it turned out, lands belonging to the Cult of Khnum had been violated and as soon as they were returned, the floods did as well.

The Aswan Dam

Five kilometers south of Aswan.

Before the High Dam, there was the **Aswan Dam**, an impressive turn of the century effort by the British to regulate the waters of the mighty Nile. Heralded as an engineering breakthrough after its completion in 1902, the two and half kilometer-long dam built of Aswan granite was the largest dam in the world. English Professor Douglas Sladen termed it "the eighth wonder of the world. . . a Japanese castle thrown across the bed of the Nile" but now unknowing tourists simply pass this Victorian relic by en route to the much bigger and modern High Dam. If Victorian engineering doesn't pique your interest, perhaps the outstanding views of the First Cataract will.

Angilika Island & the Temple of Philae

Located in the lake portion of the river between the old Aswan Dam and the High Dam. To get there, hire a taxi from Aswan and then a motor taxi to the island for LE15 one way-so put together a group. Admission: LE20 general, LE10 students. Hours: 7am-4pm (5pm summer).

Note: Bring a flashlight.

For two thousand years, this magnificent and grand island temple dedicated to the goddess Isis attracted pilgrims and tourists from around the world. Nineteenth century traveler, Dr. R Madden wrote in 1827 that along with "the sea view of Constantinopole, the sight of the Coliseum at moonlight, and the prospect from the summit of Vesuvius at dawn, the first glimpse of Philae at sunset" was one of "four recollections of a traveler which might tempt him to live forever." Originally set on an island just south of the First Cataract, the temple seemed to magically rise out of the great rapids that once roared through this portion of the Nile. The completion of the High Dam in 1971 killed off those rapids and like the great Temple of Abu Simbel to the south, Philae was saved from the eternal flood of Lake Nasser by a UNESCO project that reconstructed it on island of Angilika where its glory is now preserved.

Like so many Upper Egyptian temples (technically Philae is in Nubia), the Temple of Philae is a Ptolemeic rendition of an earlier monument. Ptolemy II (285-246 BC) initiated construction which continued through the Greco-Roman Period until the 3rd century AD. Still out of reach from the forces of Christianity which began to dominate the rest of Egypt during this period, the Cult of Isis continued to operate the temple until the 6th century when Justinian had it closed. It was the last functioning vestige of pharaonic religion.

Upon disembarking the motor boat at the southern end of the island, visitors ascend a set of stairs to enter the temple through the **Hall of Nektanebo**, built in the 4th century BC by one of Egypt's last native pharaohs. It originally included 14 columns and two obelisks that washed away during an ancient flood. Ptolemy II restored the columns, decorated with double capitals in a traditional floral style, but was unable to salvage the obelisks. The screen walls between the surviving columns feature rows of uraeus serpents and depictions of Nektanebo making offerings to various deities.

The vestibule gives way to an **outer court** flanked on the left by a **colonnade** featuring 32 columns of which none of the capitals are identical. To the right are the ruins of various shrines. The first chapel was dedicated to **Arensnupis**, a mythic companion of Isis and the second, the **Chapel of Mandulis**, to a Nubian deity worshipped at Kalabsha. Just to the right of the entrance pylon of the main temple, an unfinished structure was dedicated to **Imhotep**, the architect and confidante of the 3rd Dynasty pharaoh, Zoser. Imhotep is thought to be responsible for the design of Zoser's Step Pyramid at Saqqara and during the New Kingdom achieved quasi-divine status as a healer and philosopher.

You then approach the massive **entrance pylon**. Nearly 20 meters high and 45 meters wide, its two towers feature larger than life depictions of **Neos Dionysos** (Ptolemy II) in pharaonic garb. As is customary on entrance pylons, the pharaoh is depicted trouncing his enemies in battle before an approving audience of deities. The main portal of this pylon is actually older, dating to Nektanebo's reign 150 years earlier, and origi-nally featured two obelisks that are now gone; two stone lions, built by Romans in an almost Byzantine style, which remain. A small gate to the right is credited to Neos Dionysos, also a major contributor to the temple at Kom Ombo, but is believed to be the remnant of an earlier structure.

As you pass through the portal on your way into the **Great Court**, notice the graffiti left behind by Napoleon's troops bragging about their easy success in defeating the Mamlukes. On the backside of the entrance pylon, priests are depicted preparing the deity's idol for a procession. To the left stands the modest, but classy **Birth House**. Originally constructed by Ptolemy IV for the purpose of commemorating his divine birth (and therefore legitimacy) from Isis, it was added to by many later Ptolemeic and Roman rulers for whom it served the same purpose.

It is entered through a portico with a pillar supported roof. Another colonnade featuring Hathor-headed columns surrounds the complex. The first chamber is plain; the second chamber is decorated with some obscure deities shown guarding the birth of Horus, presumably from Seth, murdered of Isis' husband Osiris. The third chamber, the sanctuary, features on the left excellent reliefs depicting Isis suckling a young Horus. Finally, notice the beautifully decorated colonnade that surrounds the Birth House. To the east (right when facing Birth House from its entrance) are very Roman depictions of the Emperor Augustus (carrying the vase) enjoying the harp playing of Buto, goddess of the north, along with Isis and the nude child Horus. Like every good prince, Horus was raised to be king from childhood and prepares by sporting the imperial crown of Upper and Lower Egypt.

Before heading immediately for the second pylon, cross the Great Court and take some time to examine the reliefs behind the **eastern colonnade**. Beginning at the back of the entrance pylon, they feature portrayals of the Pharaoh pulling the barge of Sokar and performing other religious rites. You can then explore the various small rooms here were used for storage of books, wardrobes, and other religious equipment. Finally on the right-hand side of the second pylon is a granite rock inscribed by Taharka, (730 BC) and a later ruined Roman chapel.

The **second pylon** is smaller than the entrance pylon. On the right-hand tower, our old friend Neos Dionysos is seen in the large relief making sacrifices to Horus (the son of Isis) and his mate Hathor. The smaller images above also display Neos Dionysos, this time preparing an altar for Osiris and Isis by lighting incense. He also offers a wreath to Horus and the goddess Nephthys, a sister of Isis's and her traditional partner protecting the dead.

The second pylon leads to the **Temple of Isis** proper through a small entrance court separated from a very modest hypostyle hall by a screen wall. The hypostyle hall is small but contains some very fine colored reliefs. If it appears somewhat garish and gaudy, keep in mind that this temple was built by Greeks and Romans. Like halls in other pharaonic temples, this was converted into a Christian chapel sometime after Justinian closed it in 550 AD. Justinian's closing of the temple is in fact

THE CULT OF ISIS

The cult of Isis was one of the most popular and longest lasting in ancient Egypt – it remained active as late the 6th century AD. Though her cult thrived during the Ptolemaic and Roman Periods, she was an ancient goddess, inextricably linked to the god of death and resurrection, Osiris. In the famous tale, recounted a thousand times in a thousand ways, Osiris was murdered by his brother Seth who was later defeated in revenge by the son of Osiris and Isis, Horus. A mournful, but determined Isis searched all over Egypt (all over the universe according to some versions) for the limbs of Osiris which Seth had mutilated and dispersed throughout Egypt. It was here at Philae that she found his heart. She then breathed new life into the beloved god and they proceeded to rule over the eternal universe of the afterlife.

Associated with love, maternity, and immortality, Isis was queen of the afterworld and held appeal to all levels of Egyptian society. To pharaohs, she was the divine mother who in giving birth to them made them incarnations of the king god Horus; to the common people, she was a maternal figure and a giver of life. She was also loved and respected by the Nubians, and later by the Ptolemies and Romans who patronized this temple. Isolated and secure from the power centers in the Delta, the Cult of Isis at Philae was able to thrive well into the Christian era until 550 AD when the Roman Emperor Justinian demanded that all vestiges of pagan religions be destroyed.

praised in some graffiti scratched on the doorway of the first vestibule. Written by the Justinian era cleric Bishop Theodorus, it applauds the closing as a "good work" and a "cleansing."

En route to the actual **sanctuary**, you will pass stairs leading to the roof and an Osirian shrine. The sanctuary itself and the rooms leading to it contain fine reliefs of the usual motifs. Isis is seen suckling an infant Horus, while pharaohs make offerings and sacrifices to approving deities. The pedestal in the sanctuary itself was erected by Ptolemy III and would have been part of the main altar.

Should it be open or should you be able to persuade, perhaps for a few pounds baksheesh, a nearby guard to open it for you, climbing to the **Osirian Shrines** on the roof is well worthwhile. The reliefs in these chambers feature typical Osirian themes including the famous tale of his death and rebirth. Osiris was the husband of Isis and according to tradition, his evil brother Set murdered him, cut the body into pieces, and spread them throughout Egypt. In these reliefs, Isis is seen collecting his limbs, and later guarding and mourning his slain body. Osiris then rises from the dead to conceive with her.

After leaving the temple through the western door near the stairs, you'll approach **Hadrian's Gate**, once part of a larger wall that surrounded the entire island. The right-hand wall features a well-known relief in the second row down which tells the tale of the source of the Nile. Underneath some blocks on top of which a falcon and vulture represent Lower and Upper Egypt, respectively, the Nile god, **Hapi** is crouched within a serpent. He holds two small vessels from which he releases the waters of 'the eternal river.' Hapi is believed to have lived on the island of **Biggeh**, south of the First Cataract.

The opposite wall depicts more scenes from the famous Osiris tale while Roman emperors Marcus Aurelius (offering grapes to Isis) and Hadrian make offerings to various gods. After examining these reliefs, make your way around the rear of the temple, passing the ruined **Temple of Harendotes**, a Roman shrine dedicated to a form of Horus. At the northern end of the island, you can make out the remains of a very ruined temple built by **Augustus**, and the **Gate of Diocletian**, built by the Roman emperor most famous for his brutal oppression of Egyptian Christians.

On the east side of the main temple, is the **Temple of Hathor** and closer to the river, the **Kiosk of Trajan**. The Temple of Hathor features charming reliefs on the columns depicting musicians and dancers, themes appropriate in a building dedicated to the goddess of love and joy. The more substantial Kiosk of Trajan is a classic example of Greco-Roman Egyptian architecture. Though it contains few reliefs, the floral columns are typically Egyptian while the kiosk itself is very classical.

El Sidd El 'Ali – The High Dam

Thirty kilometers south of Aswan. Local trains from Aswan stop at Sidd El 'Ali train station, 5 kilometers southeast of the Dam itself. Hiring a taxi is far more convenient.

It was long the dream of Egyptian rulers to control the unpredictable inundation of the Nile. Floods were an indelible part of Egyptian life that annually provided farmers with fresh silt and water, but they could also wreak chaos and great disaster on fields, crops, and the Egyptian population. In 1902, the British concluded the first attempt at a Nile dam south of the First Cataract. Raised in 1912 and again in 1934, this dam was useful in regulating the river's levels, but could not stop or control the floods. Shortly after Gamal Abdel Nasser came to power in 1952, plans were made to build a new dam capable of keeping the mighty river at bay permanently.

Originally the project was to be financed by the World Bank and western nations like Great Britain and the United States. However in

THE SAVING OF PHILAE

*For two thousand years **Philae** stood above the destructive floods and rushing rapids of the cataracts, but the erection of the first Aswan Dam in 1902 for the first time left temple submerged for seven months of the year. As the dam was raised in 1912 and again in 1934, the temple appeared beyond saving. Though the sandstone from which the monuments were built could withstand contact with water, the strong currents would undoubtedly have led to their destruction.*

When the Aswan High Dam approached completion in the 1960's, Egypt made an appeal to the international community through UNESCO for financial and technical support to save Philae and other monuments in Nubia from certain ruin. The response was overwhelming and in 1977 an Italian firm began the work of deconstructing the temple piece by piece for its reconstruction on the higher island of Angilika. To some archaeologists, the move became a blessing in disguise as the dismantling of the temple block by block revealed valuable information about the history of Philae. With mind boggling speed, the temple was reconstructed on Angilika Island, itself landscaped to resemble the original Philae Island. In March 1980, Philae was reopened to the public.

1955, at the height of the Cold War, Egypt made an arms purchase from East-bloc Czechoslovakia, after America turned down previous Egyptian requests. This arms purchase led the Americans to feel that Egypt was not towing the anti-Soviet line and, to makes its annoyance felt, the US announced that they intended to withdraw funding; the British and the World Bank soon followed suit. Nasser responded at a speech in Alexandria's Tahrir Square at the old Bourse, by nationalizing the Suez Canal and announcing that he would use the revenue to build the dam without American support.

Nationalizing the hitherto British controlled Canal led to the 1956 war between Egypt and the coalition of Israel, Britain, and France. Though the war was a military defeat for Egypt, the "allies" were forced withdraw under international pressure and Nasser rocketed into the pantheon of third world heroes. Meanwhile, the Soviets pledged their support and work on the dam began in 1960. It was completed in 1971, a year after Nasser's death.

Completion of the High Dam changed life in Egypt forever. In the positive column, it doubled Egypt's power supply, greatly enhancing the country's industrial capacity. It also increased cultivable land by 750,000 feddans, a whopping 30% badly needed to accommodate the needs of

Egypt's fast growing population. With no floods, farmers are able to plant three or four crops a year instead of just the one allowed by the floods. Egypt's ability to regulate the flow of the river and to maintain a large reservoir, enabled it to avoid the terrible droughts that ravaged Sudan, Somalia, and Ethiopia during the 1980's. Finally, the halt of inundation have saved thousands of lives that surely would have been lost annually even to mild floods.

But as is often the case, fiddling with the ways of Mother Nature has had some ill side effects, the full extent of which remains to be understood. No longer do floods annually replenish the banks of the Nile with the nutrient-rich silt that ensured bumper crops for millennia. To compensate for the lack of nutrients, Egyptian farmers have increased their use of fertilizers which changed drastically the natural ecosystem. Reuse of soil has left it barren of nutrients and high in salinity, threatening crops and fresh water supplies; high salinity also threatens thousands of ancient monuments. On the Delta coast, more than a thousand miles from the Dam, the lack of new silt every year has led to great erosion which some believe will eventually threaten the very existence of Alexandria and other coastal cities. Finally, the creation of Lake Nasser submerged the land of Nubia, forcing the relocation of its half million inhabitants. Though many monuments were saved, thousands of years of history were also buried beneath the world's largest man-made lake.

Visiting The Dam

Visiting the dam itself entails paying a LE2 toll to drive across it. Most visitors simply stare awe-struck at the monumental size of this dam which draws obvious parallels to the grand monuments of the pharaohs. More than 3,600 meters long and 115 meters high, it is 980 meters wide at its base and required 43 million cubic meters of construction material. On the western side, an odd Brezhnev-style pharaonic monument in the shape of a lotus flower commemorates Egyptian-Soviet cooperation. While on a 1974 tour of the Dam with President Sadat, President Nixon remarked that it "pained" him to see a monument built to Egyptian-Soviet solidarity – although two years earlier, Sadat stunned the world shortly before the opening of the Dam by expelling the 15,000 Soviet "advisers" in Egypt, many of whom worked on it.

At the Dam's eastern end, a small **museum** contains a large model of the Dam, design plans, and an exhibit about the relocation of Abu Simbel. From the Dam itself, you can gaze over Lake Nasser and the Temple of Kalabsha to the south. Over 500 kilometers long and containing 160 billion cubic meters of water, **Lake Nasser** is the largest man-made reservoir in the world. To the north is a magnificent view of the Nile Valley and the Temple of Philae on Angilika Island.

The Temples of Kalabsha

On an island in Lake Nasser just south of the High Dam. Hire a taxi from Aswan and combine the Kalabsha ruins on an excursion to the High Dam and Philae. When the water level is high, boatmen ferry you to the monuments for a few pounds one-way. Hours: 8am-4pm. Admission: LE12 general, LE6 students.

These three Nubian monuments were reconstructed using the same techniques used to save Abu Simbel and Philae on this sometime island just south of the High Dam. The "Kalabsha" title refers to the island 50 kilometers to the south upon which the Temple of Merul was located before it was moved here.

The Temple of Merul

Initially built on the original Kalabsha Island 50 kilometers south of Aswan, this temple honors the Nubian deity **Merul** (Mandulis in Greek), an Osiris-Horus like fertility god. Begun during the New Kingdom reign of Thutmosis III when Egypt directly ruled Nubia, it was renovated and expanded during the Ptolemeic era when Nubia was ruled by proxy and required support and patronage because of its strategic position as a southern border post.

Though dedicated to a Nubian deity, the temple is clearly Egyptian in form. It is entered through an **entrance pylon** to an open courtyard. The pylon's facade is mostly bare, but its roof offers superb views. Inside, a now destroyed colonnade once surrounded the **court**. On the right-hand side a door leads to an outer space that surrounds the temple and provides access to a shrine in the far left-hand corner. Back in the court, the rear facade on the left features wall decorations depicting Horus and Thoth anointing the pharaoh. On the right is a 249 AD decree in Greek banning swine from the temple. Also depicted is a Roman horseman receiving a wreath, and a very late text in Greek praises Siklo, King of the Nabatean Kingdom.

The **hypostyle hall** features twelve columns decorated with floral motifs. To the right, Amenhophis II, the founder of the temple makes offerings to Min, the Egyptian fertility God, and Merul, the Nubian fertility deity. To the rear, a Ptolemy makes offerings while on the left a Christian painting depicts folks in hellfire being offered a sword by an angel. The first of the two chambers preceding the sanctuary features a colorful procession of Nile deities and a pharaoh making offerings to Merul, Osiris, and Isis. On the left, a stairwell leads to a roof featuring a modest version of the Osirian shrines found in other Upper Egyptian temples. In the second chamber, more pharaohs, this time Roman, appear before the gods, and again there is a stairway, this time leading to a "secret" two-roomed shrine and a crypt.

The sanctuary itself contains colorful classic scenes of Pharaohs making offerings to deities. On the rear wall, a Roman emperor gives lotus flowers to Horus and Isis-an important goddess in these parts-and milk to Merul and his companion Wadjet. He then offers incense to Isis and Horus and lotus flowers to Merul and Wadjet. Merul stands at either end of the scene dressed in pharaonic garb holding a scepter and ankh. The reliefs here are colorful and well preserved. Though of typical inferior Roman era quality, they are definitely Nubian—notice the dark faces the deities.

The core of the temple is surrounded by a corridor that contained some now ruined shrines.

THE MONUMENTS OF NUBIA

Besides forcing the relocation of hundreds of thousands of Nubians from their homeland, the construction of the High Dam threatened scores of Pharaonic-era monuments built in Nubia. Besides the most famous temples at Abu Simbel, Philae, and Kalabsha, international financial and technical support enabled Egypt to save more than a dozen other temples. Some of the temples were moved to other sites in Egypt. Dakka, an 18th Dynasty Osirian Temple; Sebua, built by Ramses II in honor of Amun Ra; and Maharraka, a Greco-Roman shrine, were all relocated to sites in Nubia itself and can be visited on a cruise or safari in Lake Nasser.

Other temples were given as gifts by the Egyptian government to those nations which provided the critical assistance needed to save them. For example, the superb Ptolemeic temple of Dendur was relocated to the Metropolitan Museum of Art in New York City. Other temples were given to Spain, the Netherlands, Italy, and France where they were reconstructed in or near museums, enabling people unable to visit Egypt to experience some of the magic of its history and civilization.

The Temple of Beit El Wali

Nestled in the hillside behind Kalabsha, this **Ramses II-built** shrine is the oldest of the Nubian temples and is known by its Arabic name, Beit El Wali, meaning "house of the governor."

Smaller than most temples, it nonetheless comprises a courtyard, a hypostyle hall and a sanctuary. Of particular interest are the reliefs in the **outer court** to the left depicting Ramses II in his chariot giving a typical thrashing to the Kushites (Nubians). These particular scenes feature terrified civilians panicking and fleeing the face of the mighty Egyptians' advance. To the rear, Ramses and his sons enjoy victory sitting beneath a canopy receiving offerings from his humiliated foes. Finally to the right, are more war scenes, this time depicting Ramses in Asia and Libya. One suspects that such obvious displays of Egyptian strength in Nubia might amount to effective propaganda designed to earn the respect of the natives.

Inside the temple are yet more, better preserved reliefs. In the hallways en route to the sanctuary are more scenes depicting Ramses as a military leader; those in the sanctuary itself are concerned with religious themes. Here we find Ramses in the presence of gods making offerings.

The Kiosk of Kertassi

This modest and weathered shrine was moved here from its original setting 40 kilometers to the south. Built during the Ptolemeic era, it is dedicated to two Nubian deities.

PRACTICAL INFORMATION
Banks & Currency Exchange

Most upscale hotels have currency exchanges in their confines or will change money themselves. Listed are other banks and exchange facilities:

• **American Express**, *the Old Cataract Hotel. Tel. 097/322-909. Hours: daily 8am-7pm; money exchanges only from 9:30am-6pm. AMEX holds mail as well exchanging foreign currency and traveler's cheques.*

• **Thomas Cook**, *Oberoi Hotel on Elephantine Island, and on Corniche El Nil Street. Tel. 097/324-011. Fax 097/326-209. Offers full travel agency services including organizing tours as well as currency exchange and buying and selling traveler's cheques.*

• **Banque Misr**, *Corniche El Nil Street. Tel. 097/323-156. Hours: daily 8:30am-2pm & 6-9pm.*

• **Bank of Alexandria**, *Corniche El Nil Street. Tel. 097/322-765. Hours: daily 8:30am-2pm & 6-9pm.*

• **Banque du Caire**, *Corniche El Nil Street. Tel. 097/323-156. Hours: daily 8:30am-2pm & 6-9pm.*

Emergencies
• **Ambulance**: *Tel. 123 or 314-015*
• **Police**: *Tel. 122*
• **Public Hospital**: *Kasr El-Haqqa Street*
• **German Evangelical Mission Hospital**, *on Corniche El Nil between the EgyptAir office and the Old Cataract Hotel: Tel. 097/ 232-176*

Passports

Visas can be extended at the office on *Corniche El Nil Street between the Continental and the Old Cataract Hotels. Tel. 097/322-238. Hours: Sat.-Wed. 8am-1:30pm and 8-10pm (no visa business).*

Post Services
    Post Office including EMS (express mail), *Corniche El Nil Street across from the Rowing Club. Hours: 8am-2pm (EMS) and 8am-3:30 regular mail, Saturday-Thursday.*

Telephones & Faxes
    24 hour telephone centrale, *Corniche El Nil Street south of EgyptAir. Fax, telex, and telegram service 9am-1pm & 7-9pm daily.* There is a second office in the train station. Upscale hotels can place international calls and faxes but for higher rates than the centrale.

Travel agencies
• **American Express**, *the Old Cataract Hotel. Tel. 097/322-909. Hours: daily 8am-7pm.*
• **Eastmar**, *Abtal El Tahrir Street. Tel. 097/323-787*
• **Imperial Travel Center**, *Corniche El Nil Street. Tel. 097/322-460, 326-202.*
• **Karnak Tourist Services**, *Corniche El Nil. Tel. 097/315-006.*
• **Seti I Travel**, *Tourist Center, Corniche El Nil Street. Tel. 097/316-345/6/7. Fax 097/316-346.*
• **Thomas Cook**, *Oberoi Hotel on Elephantine Island, and on Corniche El Nil Street Tel. 097/324-011. Fax 097/326-209.*

Tourist Information
    Egyptian Tourist Authority, *off Corniche El Street south of the rail station and near the souk. Tel. 097/323-297.*

Tourist Police
    Located in the same building as the Egyptian Tourist Authority off Corniche El Street. Tel. 097/324-393. Hours: 9am-3pm & 8pm-1am. A second branch operates 24 hours in the train station *(Tel. 097/323-163)* and officers should be on duty at the major tourist sites.

ABU SIMBEL

    Any proper journey up the Nile must end at the stupendous monuments at **Abu Simbel**, which epitomize the grand scale monument building undertaken during the height of the New Kingdom. Appropriately they were constructed by the greatest builder of them all, the indefatigable **Ramses II** (1304-1237 BC), not only to impress his power upon any potential invader from the south, but to assert his own divinity and immortality.

Abu Simbel is most commonly visited as a day trip from Aswan, but to fully absorb the magic of these monuments, you really should consider spending the night so as to view the temples at sunrise, sunset, and at night.

ARRIVALS & DEPARTURES

Most hotels and travel agencies in Aswan organize day trips to Abu Simbel and charge LE30-40 per person at the cheapest. Generally you sign up the night before and the bus or minibus makes pickups at 4 or 5am. You arrive at the temple around 8am and the return trip begins around 10 or 11am. Sometimes they incorporate a stop at the High Dam or Philae on the return trip, but we'd recommend that this may be a bit much unless you're in a hurry. The disadvantage to such day trips is that you miss the spectacular sunset light and if there's a moon, the temple in the moonlight. Also, if things get moving a bit late, which is often the case, you miss out on the soft morning light and cool weather as well.

You can also visit Abu Simbel by taxi, minibus, or airplane (see below). Keep in mind that if you have the time and the money, there are slightly pricey hotels at Abu Simbel, staying at which enables you to enjoy the temple at sunset, sunrise, and at night.

By Air

EgyptAir flies daily between Abu Simbel and Aswan (approximately $150 roundtrip) and Cairo (approximately $350) up to nine times daily during busy seasons, meaning it's possible to fly in and out on the same day with relative ease. It's recommended, especially when tourist traffic is heavy to make reservations well in advance.

By Bus

Buses leave the main station in Aswan daily at 8am and roundtrip tickets cost LE30. The trip lasts about 3.5 hours and in the summer can be long and uncomfortable especially if the air-conditioning isn't working, which seems to be more often than not. Buses depart Abu Simbel for the return trip around 2pm, but be sure to check with the driver.

Also big time travel agencies like Misr Travel, Thomas Cook, and American Express, organize deluxe bus tours. For between $50-$75 per person, these tours include a ride down and back in an air-conditioned tour bus, a guided tour, and lunch at one of the hotels.

By Service or Taxi

There are not regular services to Abu Simbel so you need to hire a minibus or taxi privately. As most drivers will ask LE200-250, you'll want to gather a group so as to split the cost. You may be able to bargain it down to LE150 round trip. If you plan to stay overnight, expect to up the cost by at least LE100.

ORIENTATION

Abu Simbel is approximately 250 kilometers south of Aswan and 50 kilometers north of the Sudanese border. The nondescript town, Abu Simbel, which is nothing of an attraction in itself, has a post office and hospital as well as the Nobaleh Hotel and several cheap eateries.

GETTING AROUND TOWN

The temples and the surrounding infrastructure are negotiable by foot. Airlines and hotels provide free transfer to and from the airport. The town, 1.5 kilometers away, can be reached by taxi.

WHERE TO STAY

Staying overnight in Abu Simbel offers you the opportunity to enjoy the temple at sunset, sunrise, and at night; all exceedingly beautiful and unique experiences. It cannot be overemphasized that reservations should be made well in advance, especially if you plan to visit during winter.

NEFERTARI HOTEL, *half a kilometer from the temples. Tel. 097/316-402/3, 02/757-950 (Cairo), 097/326-84 (Aswan). Fax 097/316-404. Rates: $60-75 singles, $90-100 doubles. A 20-30% discount may be offered in the summer. Credit cards: Visa.*

The more expensive and fancier of Abu Simbel's two hotels offers modest but comfy rooms featuring nice views of Lake Nasser, clean private bathrooms, fridges, and most importantly solid air-conditioning. There is also a decent enough restaurant that serves buffet dinners for about LE35, lunch for about LE30, and a pool.

THE NOBALEH RAMSES HOTEL, *in the town of Abu Simbel 1.5 kilometers from the temples. Tel. 097/311-660. Fax 097/311-660. Capacity: 40 rooms. Rates: $40-80 for singles & doubles depending on season (winter prices are higher). Credit cards: Visa.*

It's a notch down from the Nefertari in terms comfort and class but offers the needed amenities, namely clean rooms with air-conditioning. It is farther from the temples and does not offer views comparable to those at the Nefertari.

WHERE TO EAT

Many folks on day trips stop at the **Nefertari Hotel** for lunch, the more expensive and better of the two hotel restaurants in Abu Simbel. It features a buffet lunch for about LE30 plus tax, service and drinks. In town, there are several smaller, cheaper eateries like the Nubian Oasis but quality of food and hygienic standards are low and far from the sites.

The Nobaleh Ramses also serves lunches and dinners cheaper than the Nefertari.

SEEING THE SIGHTS
THE ABU SIMBEL TEMPLE COMPEX

The temples are on Lake Nasser 200 kilometers south of Aswan. Open from sunrise-sunset. Admission: LE20 general, LE12 students.

This temple complex stands alongside the Taj Mahal, the Great Pyramids at Giza, and Ankor Wat as one of the world's spectacular monuments. Built by Ramses II, the most famous builder in all of Egypt, the complex contains two temples. The first one is nominally dedicated to the gods Ra Harakhte (a form of Horus), and Amun Ra, but mostly it hails the divinity of Ramses II himself. Likewise, a second temple is built in the name of Hathor, but glorifies Nefertari, Ramses' Chief Queen.

The first European to 'discover' the temples was a Swiss explorer, John Lewis Burkhart, in 1815, but it was almost entirely covered with sand. The famous Italian Egyptologist, Giovanni Belzoni, excavated the site four years later, but when it failed to produce great treasure, he quickly deserted it, and it was not until British archaeologists fully excavated it around the turn of the century that its true splendor became apparent. ·

The Great Sun Temple of Ramses II

Built between 1290 and 1224 BC, this superb temple is a first-rate example of megalomania. Though officially dedicated to the deities of kingship, Ra Harakhte and Amun Ra, it serves no purpose but to exalt the glory of Ramses II himself. Like all of his monuments, these temples contain reliefs depicting Ramses defeating the Hittites at Kadesh, in Syria. In reality, however, the victory was far from decisive as Ramses was lucky to get away with a draw. The exterior is dominated by the famous massive statues standing in the facade.

The four **colossi** which sit, peering over Lake Nasser and into eternity (without blinking we might add), are well... colossal. Towering more than twenty meters high, they are believed to be the same size as the broken statue at the Ramesseum in Luxor, meaning each weighs over 1,200 tons. Wearing the double crown of the united Egypt and brandishing a own cartouche on the chest and arm, three of the statues are intact while the fourth split after an earthquake in 27 BC-when it was already 1200 years old. Each of the larger statues is flanked by three smaller ones: Nefertari to the right, Ramses' mother to the left, and Prince Amunhekhspshef in the middle. On the left leg of the broken colossus, Greek mercenaries scratched graffiti which dates to 590 BC, some of the oldest Greek inscriptions in the world.

Also decorating the facade are **several smaller figures** and **carvings**. Above the portal, a small representation of Ra Harakhte holds a scepter and a representation of Maat, goddess of justice. To either side, Ramses pays homage. Since Ra Harakhte in fact represents Ramses as a kingship god and User*maat*ra is one of Ramses' titles, he is in fact worshipping an incarnation of himself. On each hand of the colossi to the right, two Nile-gods can be seen joining floral representations of Upper and Lower Egypt, symbolizing the unity of the "Two Lands." To the right where floral symbols represent northern Egypt, Asiatic prisoners are in captivity while on the left, Nubian prisoners are under the symbol of Upper Egypt in the south.

After taking time to digest the colossi, enter the temple through the passage into the **Hypostyle Hall**. On either side, four pillars contain rock cut statues of Ramses in Osirian form, while the walls recount Ramses' exploits on the battle field; from the ceiling, vultures look on. The walls in this portion of the temple are packed with extraordinary reliefs. On the **entrance walls** are graphic scenes of Ramses ruthlessly smiting Hittite and Nubian prisoners of war before Amun Ra to the left, and Ra Harakhte to the right. To show his approval, Amun Ra presents Ramses with a sword, the symbol of victory. Throughout the temple, reliefs on the left are dedicated to Amun Ra and those on the right to Ra Harakhte.

The highlight of the temple interior is the **Great Battle Scene** on the walls of the main hall. Detailed, beautifully balanced, and well preserved, they tell from beginning to end, the story of the **Battle of Kadesh** – at least from Ramses' perspective. At the rear of the hall in the middle portion of the right wall, Ramses' army is seen preparing for its advance on Kadesh. At first, everything looks just as it should. The camp is well protected by a ring of shields, and in its center, Ramses' lion is attended by a keeper while horses feed. With a sense of humor, the artists have depicted some running away with empty chariots while others frolic about during the wait for harnessing. Soldiers are seen eating and getting treated by doctors. To the left, Ramses is depicted holding a meeting with his officers and torturing prisoners to get information.

So far, so good; but this is where things begin to go wrong. The prisoners are in fact plants who gave misinformation that leads Ramses into an ambush trap and almost costs him the battle. But before Ramses falls for the bait, an intelligence officer brings the news that the men were lying and that the enemy is in fact much closer than earlier thought. A furious Ramses orders his army to advance immediately.

The actual battle is recounted in the upper sections of the wall where Ramses is seen fighting his way out of the Hittite trap. Depicted along the Orontes River is the fortress of **Kadesh** from which the well-fortified Hittites emerge to surround Ramses. Against the odds, he bravely fights his way out to claim an unqualified victory, even though in reality he was lucky to get away at all. Finally, the pharaoh inspects his troops and brings prisoners to Amun Ra and his consort Mut. The chambers off the main hall, and the smaller following hall were used for storage.

In the **second pillared hall**, the reliefs' motif shift from Ramses' battle triumphs to his actual deification. Ramses and Nefertari are depicted making offerings to Ra Harakhte, Amun Ra, and a deified version of Ramses himself. The **sanctuary** features four major statues of Ptah (the ancient patron god of Memphis), Amun Ra, Ra Harakhte, and the divine Ramses himself. In its original setting, the temple was positioned so that on Ramses' birthday in February and his coronation anniversary in October, the sun shined directly on these statues. After the temple was moved, this was no longer the case but on some days in February and October, the sun does shine directly on parts of these statues.

For some visitors, getting a look behind the relocated monuments at the **interior of the false hill** in which the temple is now set is as fascinating as the temple itself. Right of the colossi is a small gray door leading to the hollow interior of this false hill, giving a fascinating perspective on the engineering feat of the temple's reconstruction. The dome itself reaches 25 meters high and spans 60 meters across. This span must support a load of 100,000 metric tons, and if this temple is going to be around even half as long as its current age, its going to have to do it for a long time.

The Temple of Nefertari

Ramses built this smaller, but beautiful and elegant temple in honor of his favorite wife, **Queen Nefertari**, owner of the fantastic tomb in the Valley of the Queens. Dedicated to the goddess **Hathor**, a mother figure to royalty, this temple is just north of Ramses' Temple of the Sun.

The temple is entered through a **sloping facade** featuring six figures set in recessed niches. The ten meter tall statues depict Ramses and Nefertari and the texts announce that Ramses has built this temple for his "Beautiful Wife" in honor of Hathor. The interior contains a hypostyle hall, a transitory hall, and the sanctuary. It is entered through a doorway, the interior inscriptions of which depict Ramses honoring Hathor and Nefertari before Isis.

The **hypostyle hall** contains six Hathor-headed pillars. On the walls immediately to the left and right upon entering (the backside of the facade) are scenes that look as if they belong in Ramses' temple and not that of Hathor or Nefertari. In typical form Ramses is smiting his enemies in front of an approving Ra Harakhte and Amun Ra. These themes are continued on the side walls. In the **sanctuary**, a niche contains a ruined statue of Hathor with a cow head. Next to it you can see her protecting the pharaoh. Meanwhile to the right Nefertari offers incense to Mut and Hathor and to the left Ramses performs purification rites on himself and his wife.

NIGHTLIFE & ENTERTAINMENT
Sip a cool Stella in the Nefertari Hotel.

GOING TO SUDAN

Famous for its natural beauty and the generosity and good humor of its people, Sudan has been ravaged by a 20-year civil war, making it difficult and sometimes dangerous to visit. That the Islamacist regime in Khartoum has rocky relations with Egypt and the United States makes it especially difficult for Americans: the US State Department advises against traveling to Sudan.

Should you wish to visit, you need to obtain a visa from the Sudanese Consulate in Cairo. You then may be able to fly Sudan Air or EgyptAir from Cairo. From Aswan, you can catch a ferry to Wadi Haifa near the border. Contact the Nile Navigation Co. beside the ETA tourist office in Aswan for details and reservations. At Wadi Haifa you must apply for travel permits, file a currency declaration and jump through other bureaucratic hoops before you will be allowed to go on. From Wadi Haifa, you can hitch a ride with a truck (potentially dangerous) or possibly catch a train to Khartoum. Keep in mind that the Sudanese infrastructure, weak to begin with, is now nonexistent as are facilities to accommodate tourists. Also, don't dare to be caught with drugs, alcohol, or pornography. The Sudanese regime can make the Iranians look like libertarians when its comes to personal liberties.

PRACTICAL INFORMATION
Banks & Currency Exchange

The Nefertari Hotel may change money but it's best to cash up in Aswan.

Emergencies
- **Hospital**: *in town 1.5 kilometers from the temples*
- **Police**: *stationed at the airport, the temples, hotels, and at the station 500 meters up the road from the temple on the dead-end road*

Post Services

There is a **post office** *in Abu Simbel town. Hours: Sunday-Thursday 9am-3pm.*

Telephones, Telex, & Fax

The two hotels both operate phone and fax lines.

Tourist Information

Hotel personnel, tour guides, and taxi drivers are the best sources.

15. THE GREAT OASES OF THE WESTERN DESERT

FAIYOUM DEPRESSION

Seventy thousand years ago, an early Nile flood broke through the Nile Valley and into the **Faiyoum Depression**, forming what is now Lake Karun. An incredibly fertile area, it attracted pharaohs with its rich agricultural potential and excellent hunting. During the Middle Kingdom in the 12th century BC, the national capital was even moved to Faiyoum and from then on it was, unlike the other more distant oases, inextricably linked to the Nile Valley. Besides developing the Depression's agricultural production, Middle Kingdom pharaohs dotted the area with pyramids such as those at **Lahun** and **Hawara**.

During Greek and Roman times, Faiyoum became known as **Crocodilopolis** for the vast amounts of crocodile living in Lake Karun and large temples and shrines were dedicated to **Sobek**, Faiyoum's crocodile-headed patron deity. The Ptolemies also introduced water-wheels as a means of irrigation and even today more than 200 wheels are still in use throughout the oasis.

During the Middle Ages, the lake began to shrink to the extant that it is now 45 meters below its original level, and salinity became so high that fresh water fish can longer survive. The importance of Faiyoum has declined since its height during the Middle Kingdom and Greco-Roman times, but as the government aggressively pursues development outside of the Nile Valley, Faiyoum sees itself enjoying another boom in the coming decades.

Despite its picturesque scenery and dozens of ancient temples and pyramids, Faiyoum has not caught on as a tourist destination. Its sites are hardly accessible to those without private transportation and the city of Faiyoum itself is an eyesore that from its drab concrete housing projects and grimy pollution, represents everything that wrong with modern Egypt. As a result, Faiyoum cannot compete with the splendors of Cairo and Luxor, but for the dedicated off-the-beaten-tracker, it offers a wealth of hidden gems.

ARRIVALS & DEPARTURES

By Bus

The bus depot in Faiyoum City is by the service station one kilometer east of the Tourist Office and water wheels downtown.

Buses leave almost hourly from Midan Giza and Ahmed Helmy bus depot in Ramses Square in Cairo (LE4, 1-2 hours). Buses going the other way depart just as frequently for the same fare.

By Service

The service depot in Faiyoum city is about a kilometer east of the Tourist Office downtown and one block north of the canal past the Gamal Abdel Nasser Mosque.

Service run frequently between Midan Giza in Giza (Cairo) and Faiyoum City (LE5, 1 hour). There are also frequent service to **Beni Suef** in the Nile Valley.

By Train

The train station is in downtown Faiyoum city just east of the water wheels and the Tourist Office, one block north of the canal.

A half dozen trains with second and third class seating make the **Cairo-Faiyoum-Cairo** route daily but the pace is so painstakingly slow that it takes more than four hours to cover the 110 kilometer distance.

ORIENTATION

The hub of the Faiyoum Depression which stretches more than 6,600 square kilometers, is **Medinet Faiyoum**, "Faiyoum City," from whence roads lead to all major settlements and sites. Most of them are within 20-30 kilometers, but are spread in all directions, making it difficult to cover all sites in one day. The city itself, which is best avoided if possible, is concentrated along the banks of Bahr Youssef, "Joseph's River," the natural waterway made canal that has channeled water to Faiyoum from the Nile Valley for the past 70,000 years.

GETTING AROUND TOWN

Faiyoum city is manageable on foot, but visiting sites throughout the Depression requires automobile transportation. You can reach some sites by service, but it's far less hassle to have your own vehicle. For those with little money, this can be a problem, because taxi drivers are either reluctant to venture to out of the way sites or they try to charge upwards of LE130 a day. Each site description contains information about how to visit that particular site.

WHERE TO STAY

In Faiyoum City

MONTAZAH HOTEL, *Ismail El Medany Street. Tel. 084/328-662, 324-633. Rates: LE35 single, LE40 double.*

About a kilometer north of downtown Faiyoum, the Montazah is a quiet establishment run by Copts. Rooms can be a bit shabby and come with fans and fridges.

HONEY DAY HOTEL, *Gamal Abdel Nasser Street about 300 meters north of the train station and the canal. Tel. 084/341-205, 340-105. Fax 084/ 341-205. Rates: LELE30-70.*

Apart from the sweet name, there is an assortment of singles, doubles, and triples, with and without bath and air-conditioning. It's quite clean and is in easy walking distance of the Obelisk of Senusert to the north and the canal and water wheels to the south.

THE PALACE HOTEL, *El Horreya Street on the Canal. Tel. 084/321-222. Rates: LE25-50.*

The name aside, this is a modest hotel with clean rooms that have private baths and fans. The management and the hangers-on are sometimes sketchy so be on the lookout for rip-offs.

On Lake Karun

AUBERGE DU LAC HOTEL, *Lake Karun. Tel. 084/700-002, 700-730. Fax 084/700-730. Rates: $50-70 single, $60-100 double. Credit cards: Visa.*

Formerly a hunting lodge used by King Farouk and members of the Royal Family, this is the only 'luxury hotel' in Faiyoum and scores high with its colonial atmospherics even if the facilities don't quite rate its four stars. Now favored by hunters from Cairo who come to Lake Karun to shoot duck, it features a lovely dining room where you can feast on the birds, and a charming teak bar overlooking the lake. All rooms are air-conditioned with televisions and decent private baths and phones.

THE PANORAMA SHAKSHOUK HOTEL, *Lake Karun about three quarters of a kilometer west of L'Auberge Du Lac. Tel. 084/701-314, 701-757, 701-746. Fax 084/701-757. Rates: $30 single, $40 double. Credit cards: Visa.*

It lags far behind the L'Auberge Du Lac in atmospherics, but the rooms are comfortable enough with air-conditioning, televisions, and private baths, and the views of the lake are comparably. There also is a swimming pool and a restaurant.

WHERE TO EAT

In Faiyoum City there are dozens of small restaurants serving typical Egyptian cheap eats. Just down the street from the Tourist Office, the **Mokhimar Restaurant** has excellent roast chicken and kebabs with the usual assortment of tehina's breads, and salads. You can eat a hearty filling meal for under LE15. On Mustafa Kamel Street downtown there is another excellent kebab shop and **Sherif's** is also a good choice. **Said's** by the taxi stand serves heaping bowls of excellent kushari (LE1).

Lake Karun is the place to go for fancier sit-down meals with views over looking the lake. The restaurant in the **Auberge Du Lac** with its *fin de siecle* ambiance serves delicious duck, a local specialty, and a wide variety of Egyptian style grilled meats and kebabs. They also serve beer and accept Visa. Be prepared to fork out LE30-40 per head not including alcohol.

Nearby the **Oasis Hotel** has an open air restaurant serving similar fare minus the duck and the **Beach** restaurant specializes in fish farmed in the lake itself. There are numerous other lakefront restaurants many of which close during the summer.

SEEING THE SIGHTS

There are a few sights in Faiyoum City itself, but most are spread throughout the Oasis and require private transportation to reach. They are also close enough to Cairo to be visited in a day trip (not all in the same day), saving you the experience of having to actually spend time in Faiyoum City.

In Faiyoum City

In the Governorate building on El Gomhuriya Street (the same building as the Tourist Office) is the **Faiyoum Museum**. The hours are irregular, but it generally opens daily from 9am-1 or 2pm and features a small collection of pharaonic and Ptolemeic artifacts and exhibits about life in Faiyoum through the ages.

About a kilometer north of the canal and the city center on Gamal Abdel Nasser stands the **Obelisk of Senusert**, erected during the Middle Kingdom by the 12th Dynasty (1990-1785 BC) pharaoh for whom it is named. Unfortunately its elegance and grace is lost to the concrete traffic circle surrounding where it now finds itself. Senusert moved the national capital to Faiyoum and was especially fond of its hunting and agricultural wealth.

Faiyoum's signature landmarks are the **four large water wheels** that churn away *behind the Tourist Office on Bahr Youssef Canal downtown*. A constant reminder of Faiyoum's agricultural roots, they are fed by **Bahr**

Youssef Canal that links Faiyoum to Nile. The canal is so named because it was believed to have been built by **Joseph**, the Hebrew who came to Egypt in Pharaonic times and rose to prominence as a minister and architect. In fact the canal is a natural waterway that branches off the Nile north of Beni Suef. In the 19th century Bahr Youssef was replaced as Faiyoum's main fresh water source by the man-made **Ibrahimiya Canal** which branches from the Nile at Dairut in the Assiut Governorate in Middle Egypt.

There are seven additional water wheels along the Sinuris Canal that runs from Bahr Youssef to the north still used to irrigate a series of quaint mango and date orchards. Introduced by the Greek Ptolemies more than 200 years before Christ, there are currently more than 200 working water wheels throughout the Faiyoum.

Faiyoum's covered **souk**, *about half a kilometer west of the Tourist Office on the southern banks of the canal,* is a maze of narrow alleys where local merchants hawk a myriad of consumer goods including spices, clothing, fresh produce, and pottery. Untouched by tourism it has an authentic flavor that is increasingly hard to find in the rest of Egypt. On Tuesday there is a special outdoor **pottery market** and behind the main souk is the **gold souk**, a street lined with gold merchants.

Further west of the souk is the **Mosque of Khawsand Al Bey**, the oldest mosque in Faiyoum. According to local legend it was built by the great Mamluke Sultan Qait Bey for a concubine in 1500. With the exception of the brilliant ebony minbar inlaid with ivory, the mosque is not especially spectacular.

THE MOULID OF ALI EL RUBI

The usually drab city of Faiyoum comes alive once a year during the Islamic month of Sha'aban (December/November in '98 & '99) when thousands of fellaheen converge on the town to celebrate the **Moulid of Ali El Rubi***, a local saint. During this time, his mosque (about half a kilometer north of town) becomes awash with colored lights as thousands of the faithful flood the surrounding alleys singing, dancing, partying and praying.*

SIGHTS OUTSIDE FAIYOUM CITY
Ayn El Sili'een

These picturesque springs, *about eight kilometers north of Faiyoum city,* are quickly going to the dogs as developers move in. The verdant surroundings are still impressive as long as there aren't hundreds of people around and even then it shouldn't get in the way of visiting the far more fascinating and visually pleasing historic sites throughout the depression.

Lake Karun

Lake Karun is about 20 kilometers north of Faiyoum city. You may be able to catch a service from the city, otherwise make your way to Sanhur for a connection. You can also hire a private taxi, but this will cost you no less than LE30 each way and far more if the driver waits for you.

A once picturesque salt lake known since pharaonic times for its phenomenal duck hunting, Lake Karun is quickly going up in concrete. Though touted by official tourist brochures as an idyllic natural setting where one may partake in a myriad of watersports, there really isn't much to do except rent out small boat for a lake tour and munch on duck at the colonial-era Auberge du Lac Hotel, a former hunting lodge that used to belong to King Farouk.

Wadi El Rayan

Fifteen kilometers southwest of Lake Karun are two new lakes and a series of picturesque waterfalls that were recently created as an outlet for excess water in Faiyoum. With its ever expanding reed beds, it is home to dozens of different bird species. Avoid coming on weekends or holidays when its peaceful serenity gives way to hundreds of families and students who turn the area into a big playground.

Kasr El Sagha

Kasr El Sagha is in the desert 40 kilometers northeast from Karanis off a desert, unpaved road. To visit, you must first receive permission from the Museum of Karanis (see below). The excursion is best done with a four wheel drive vehicle, or at least a high rider.

Though unspectacular in its dimensions or craftsmanship, Kasr El Sagha's isolated desert location gives adventurous types a high. The temple itself dates to the Middle Kingdom and was once situated on Lake Karun which has since receded more than 13 kilometers to the south.

Dimeh El Sibba

Nine kilometers south of Kasr El Sagha, Dimeh El Sibba can be reached by driving from Kasr El Sagha or by taking a boat across Lake Karun from the south and walking 2.5 kilometers to the temple.

The last stop for caravans before they entered the desert, El Dimeh features a ruined rock cut temple dedicated to Soknopaios, an incarnation of the crocodile deity Sobek, and some dilapidated Ptolemeic-era houses. Though the settlement is mostly ruined, the mountainous dune setting is spectacular.

Kasr Karun

Kasr Karun *is 45 kilometers northeast of Faiyoum City. Entrance: LE8. It can be reached from Faiyoum city by taking a service to the village of Ebshaway and another from there to the modern hamlet of Karun.*

Dedicated to Faiyoum's patron crocodile deity, **Sobek**, this temple comprises a maze of spooky subterranean corridors, passages, and chambers. When exploring this labyrinth, it's wise to bring a flashlight and beware of bats and god knows what else may be flying about inside. After tooling around in the underground passages, climb to the top for a magnificent panoramic view overlooking the depression and the nearby Greco-Roman settlement of **Dionysius**.

Kom Oshim & Ancient Karanis

Kom Oshim is 25 kilometers north of Faiyoum city on the road from Cairo. Buses leave Faiyoum city for Kom Oshim at 7am and 2:30pm. Otherwise, a service or public bus to Cairo will drop you. Ask for the "Mathaf Kom Oshim"-the Kom Oshim Museum. Hours: 9am-4pm daily except Monday. Admission: LE16.

Founded during Ptolemeic times, the Greco-Roman town of Karanis once boasted a population that pushed 5,000 until about 500AD when civil unrest and regional instability brought about its demise. A major way station for wheat destined for Alexandria and Rome, the town now comprises several hundred ruined homes, baths, and temples, the most prominent of which is the **Temple of Pnepheros and Petesouchose**, dedicated to two local crocodile deities. Many of the famous "Faiyoum Portraits" now in the Egyptian Antiquities Museum in Cairo were discovered here.

Nearby the modest **Kom Oshim Museum** (9am-3:30pm, LE3) exhibits a variety of pharaonic and Ptolemeic statuettes, canopic jars, solar boat models, and one of the famous "Faiyoum Portraits." This is where you get permission to go to Kasr El Sagha.

The Pyramid of Hawara

The Pyramid of Hawara is next to the hamlet of Hawaret El Makta on the Beni Suef-Faiyoum Road 12 kilometers from Faiyoum city. Service and bus drivers will drop you, but ask for "Hawaret El Makta," not the pyramid. Hours: 8am-5pm. Admission: LE16 general, LE8 students.

This ruined mud brick pyramid constructed by the Middle Kingdom pharaoh **Amemenhet III** (1842-1797 BC) has devolved into a heaping 60 meter high mound since its limestone casing was stripped in antiquity. Though the pharaoh's body and funeral possessions were vandalized long ago, the archaeologist Flinders Petrie found intact the treasures and mummy of his daughter, Nefru-Ptah. Petrie also discovered 146 brilliantly painted and well-preserved "Faiyoum Portraits" (mummies with their owner's portrait painted on top) in a Roman necropolis north of the pyramid. On the other side to the south stood a great mortuary temple, known as the **Labyrinth**, that Herotodus claimed had more than 3,000 rooms. Nothing remains of it today.

The Pyramid of Lahun

The Pyramid of Lahun is 23 kilometers from Faiyoum city and 9 kilometers beyond the Pyramid of Hawara on the Beni Suef-Faiyoum Road. Hours: 8am-5pm. Admission: LE16 general, LE8 students.

Also constructed during the Middle Kingdom (19th century BC), the Pyramid of Lahun belonged to Pharaoh **Senusert II**. Unlike Old Kingdom rulers who built their pyramids entirely of stone, the Middle Kingdom pharaohs used a mud brick core encased in solid limestone. As the limestone was stripped off by other pharaohs, Muslims and Copts over the centuries, the mud brick became exposed to the elements and easily crumbled. As a result, Middle Kingdom pyramids like this one and that at Hawara have disintegrated into huge piles of dirt and rubble. While it is forbidden or physically impossible to climb most pyramids, this one is accessible and affords superb views of the surrounding countryside.

The Monasteries of Faiyoum

Though Faiyoum's monasteries are now all but deserted except on feast days, the depression was home to more than 40 monastic and hermitic Christian communities during the 4th and 5th centuries, and one 4th century Christian account even records that more than 10,000 monks attended a single meeting. Monasticism has since declined, but Faiyoumi and Nile Valley Christians still visit as pilgrims on special occasions like the commemoration of the Holy Family's visit to Egypt on June 1, and the Feast of the Virgin from August 15-22.

The most accessible but least interesting of these monasteries is **Deir El Azab** *(5 kilometers east of Faiyoum city off the road to Beni Suef)*. Originally constructed in the 12th century and rebuilt in the 19th, it is now redundant except during the week-long **Feast of the Virgin** (August 15-22) when thousands of Pilgrims converge here for prayer and celebrations. The more isolated **Monastery of Deir El Malak** *(9 kilometers south of Deir El Azab on a road that cuts south from the main road to Beni Suef)* is also redundant, and affords superb views of the depression and the pyramids at Hawara and Lahun.

The Pyramid of Maidum

The Temple of Maidum is 33 kilometers north of Faiyoum city outside the Faiyoum Depression. From Cairo or Beni Sue, buses and service running between the two can drop you at the turnoff. That leaves at least 5 kilometers to the pyramid itself. If you can get to village of El Wasta from Beni Suef or Faiyoum, you can then catch another service to Maidum village from whence it is just over 2 kilometers to the pyramid. Admission: LE16.

The Pyramid of Maidum represents a fascinating piece of pyramid history. Built either by the last pharaoh of the 3rd Dynasty (Huni) or the first of the 4th Dynasty (Snefru) it was the first attempt to build a true pyramid as opposed to a step pyramid. The dumpy three step structure that you see today was originally the core of the pyramid upon which eight steps were constructed. The steps were then filled in to produce smooth slopes, but due to poor design, the slopes and steps collapsed of their own weight leaving only the three step core we see today. Obviously the engineers learned from their mistakes because the next generations of the 4th dynasty produced some of the greatest pieces of engineering in world history — the Great Pyramids of Giza.

PRACTICAL INFORMATION

Banks & Currency Exchange
Banque du Caire *is on El Horreya Street across the canal from the water wheels and the Tourist Office by the Banque Misr.*

Banque Misr *is on El Horreya Street just across the canal from the Tourist Office and water wheels. Hours: 8am-2pm daily except Friday.*

Emergencies
• **Ambulance**: *Tel. 24028*
• **Police**: *Tel. 122*

Post Services
Post Office, *El Horreya Street in Faiyoum city on the south side of the Canal. Hours: 8am-3pm daily except Friday.*

Telephones, Telex, & Fax
24 hour telephone centrale, *El Horreya Street on the canal by the bridge east of the banks.*

Tourist Information
Egyptian Tourist Authority, *El Gomhuriya Street. Tel. 084/342-313. Hours: approximately 9am-2pm except on Fridays. There is another branch by the water wheels about 100 meters west of the train station. Hours: 9am-5pm.*

SIWA OASIS

Egypt's most beautiful and isolated oasis, **Siwa** has a powerful mystique that has baffled and lured outsiders since antiquity, when Alexander trekked here to consult the Oracle of Amun in 331 BC. Despite its strategic position as a link between Libya and Egypt, Siwans successfully beat back intruders and maintained their autonomy until the 19th century.

Little is known about Siwa's history, but fortified villages have survived and thrived amongst the lush palm groves and salt water lakes since time can remember and apart from the introduction of some electronic appliances and pick-up trucks, the timeless Siwan lifestyle remains unchanged. Men still farm the verdant date groves and olive orchards, women tender household chores enveloped in colorful traditional dress and shaman-like elders recount the tales of Siwan defiance over the centuries that have passed orally from generation to generation since the early Middle Ages.

In recent years as Siwa has opened to the world, concrete buildings and electricity have begun to make their mark, but the fortified town of Shali still lurks, redolent of a past when Siwans lived in a world of total isolation.

History

Before the **Oracle of Amun** became famous throughout the Mediterranean world, virtually nothing is known about Siwa. The legendary Persian army of Cambyses was on its way to Siwa in the 6th century BC when it disappeared in the Great Sand Sea. In 331 Alexander journeyed from Mesopotamia to consult the Oracle, conquering Egypt and founding Alexandria en route. He reported that the Oracle revealed that he was indeed the 'Son of Amun' and hence the legitimate ruler of Egypt. Alexander desired to be buried here, but Ptolemy Sotor ordered the priests at Memphis to send his body to Alexandria where he was supposedly interred though this tomb has never been found.

Until the 13th century, Siwa's primary settlement had been the fortified town of **Aghurmi**, site of the Oracle, but in the early 1200's the town of **Shali** was founded when several families left Aghurmi after a falling out. Throughout the medieval Islamic period, Siwans fiercely resisted outside intrusion and control. When European explorers began turning up in the 18th and 19th centuries they too suffered at the hands of Siwan xenophobia and it was only in 1820 when an expedition of Egyptian soldiers sent by Mohammed Ali overwhelmed Aghurmi and Shali that Siwans reluctantly acknowledged Egyptian sovereignty. In the 20th century Siwa found itself caught in the throes of global conflicts when in 1917, the British occupied it as part of a buffer against potential aggression from Italian-occupied Libya. Twenty-five years later that aggression did come when Rommel and the Italians made their fateful advance on Egypt that ended with an Allied victory at El Alamein. En route, the Italians occupied the oasis, though it made little difference to the reluctantly acquiescent Siwans who even warmed a bit to the personable Rommel.

Despite these occupations, Siwa remained isolated well into post-Revolutionary Egypt and it was only in the 1980's that paved roads, electricity, and other modern amenities found their way here; until the 1990's tourists could not come to Siwa without special permission. Though still proud of their heritage and unique identity, Siwans are now welcoming of outsiders and have largely embraced the central government's efforts to modernize and integrate it with the rest of Egypt.

ARRIVALS & DEPARTURES

Though a paved road was recently constructed linking Siwa to Bahariya, there is no regular public transportation and virtually everybody approaches Siwa from Alexandria and Marsa Matrouh. Sometimes a minibus makes the Siwa-Bahariya route and is advertised in local hotels and restaurants. Ask around.

Bus

The bus station is in the center of town. Tickets for Marsa Matrouh and Alexandria should be purchased in advance. The ticket booth is usually open in the evening from 6-9pm.

From Alexandria, catch the 11am bus from Sidi Gabr which also stops at the bus terminal at Misr Train Station around 11:20 (LE25, 8 hours). Buses leave from Marsa Matrouh at 4pm (3-4 hours, LE15).

Buses to Marsa Matrouh and Alexandria depart around 6:30am and 10am. Sometimes, there is only one bus so check the evening before.

ORIENTATION

The town of Siwa is dominated by the ruins of Shali, the ancient city, which looms over the main square, site of most shops, restaurants, and hotels. Apart from the ancient town of Shali, historic monuments and attractions are spread with an 8 kilometer radius of the town.

GETTING AROUND TOWN

Siwa town is negotiable on foot, but to visit outlying sites, you'll need some sort of transport. If you're at all fit, bicycles make an excellent choice for visiting the nearby sites. They can be rented all over town for about LE5-10 for a whole day. Alternatively, you can hire a truck or bring your own vehicle, but this should hardly be necessary.

A bus departs twice daily to Kharmisah and Bilad El Rum from the main mosque at 7am and 2pm (LE3). Don't miss your ride back as there's no other transport.

WHERE TO STAY

THE NEW SIWA SAFARI CAMP, *100 meters east of the main square. Rates: LE30-$40 for singles, doubles, and bungalows. Credit cards: Visa.*

This new upscale establishment is just outside town in the midst of serene palm groves. Guests can choose between the cheaper, plain bungalows and the expensive, air-conditioned doubles with private baths. There is a restaurant and on the grounds there is a private spring ideal for taking a dip and relaxing with a cool drink.

AROUSA EL WAHA HOTEL, *north of the main square on the road to Marsa Matrouh. Rates: LE40-70 singles and doubles.*

The government-run Arousa offers a variety of overpriced rooms, the more expensive of which feature private baths and air-conditioning. The management can be somewhat stuffy and the atmosphere is decidedly bland.

CLEOPATRA HOTEL, *200 meters south of the main square. Rates: LE15-30 singles & doubles.*

Run by a helpful and friendly English speaking Siwan native, the Cleopatra is clean, well maintained, and friendly. Rooms are available with or without private baths and air-conditioning. Rooms without air-conditioning have fans.

PALM TREES HOTEL, *east of the main square. Rates: LE6 per person.*

With its terrace and clean rooms, this is an excellent budget choice. Common bathrooms are clean with hot water and rooms have fans. The garden and rural setting, though it's just off the square, puts it over the top.

YOUSSEF HOTEL, *in the purple building off the main square. Rates: LE5 per person.*

Youssef offers clean rooms with fans, but the purple monster of a concrete building ruins the Siwan skyline and is unfortunately an omen of things to come.

Camping

Those wishing to camp may do so at **Gebel Dekrur**, four kilometers east of Shali. There are huts which you can use for free, but check in with the Tourist Office. The problem is protecting your stuff while you visit other sites. The other alternative is the Fish Farm 15 kilometers south of Shali. This requires having your own vehicle.

WHERE TO EAT

Like other oasis towns, Siwa offers little in the way of haute cuisine. Apart from cous-cous, a reflection of the Siwans' Berber roots, restaurant food is limited to the usual assortment of basic Egyptian fare: kebab, roast chicken, rice, beans, and cola. One local specialty worth trying is chocolate sahlab, a traditional spiced milk drink with a chocolate twist.

The **Sohag**, **Alexander**, **East-West**, **Restaurant Kelani**, and **Abdu's** all serve a full meal for about LE12. The **New Siwa Safari Camp**, just east of the main square, features buffet dinners for LE40; the food is a bit more sophisticated, but far more expensive.

SEEING THE SIGHTS

In Siwa Town

Urban Siwa is dominated by the ancient fortress city of **Shali**. Little is known about the early history of Shali except that it was founded in the early 13th century by Siwans who left El Aghurmi after a row, and that major extensions were made in the 14th century; also, salt was used to help strengthen the mud bricks used in its construction. Today, nobody lives in the oldest, highest portions of the ancient city where it's possible to fritter away hours just petering about the endless maze of nooks and crannies. It is also a superb place from which to view sunrises and sunsets over the sea of surrounding palm groves and the desert mountains beyond.

The House of Siwa Museum, *at the base of El Shali by the City Council. Hours: 9am-noon daily except Friday. Admission: free.*

As Siwans are generally not accepting of curious foreigners poking around their houses and staring at their womenfolk as they perform their chores, the authorities, with Canadian support, have established this museum. Here you can watch women reenact what they do in everyday life and take pictures without worrying about any misunderstandings. It feels a bit staged, which of course it is, but it's still worth while.

Historic & Natural Sights Outside of Siwa Town

There are more than a half dozen attractions within five or six kilometers of Shali. All but Fantasy Island and Gebel El Mawta can be combined on a circular route that begins with Aghurmi and the Oracle, and continues clockwise onto Cleopatra's Spring, and Gebel Dekrur. The

Tombs of Gebel El Mawta and Fatnas (Paradise Island) can be combined on a separate excursion.

Four kilometers east of town (follow the sign for Siwa Safari Camp) the hilltop ruins of **Aghurmi** resemble those of Shali. In the midst of the mud brick ruins you should be able to make out the stone temple which once housed the **Oracle** that attracted the likes of Plutarch and Alexander the Great. Little is known about its origins but around the 25th Dynasty (800 BC) the Oracle became heralded throughout the Mediterranean and attracted pilgrims from as far away as Persia. Around 520 BC the army of Cambyses was sent to destroy it but was swallowed by the Great Sand Sea never to be heard of again. In 330 AD Alexander invaded Egypt, primarily to visit the Oracle which he claimed named him as the divine Son of Amun and the rightful pharaoh of Egypt. He also wanted to be buried here but when his body was brought back from Mesopotamia, the priesthood's of Memphis and the authorities in Alexandria demanded that it be buried in the city that bears his name instead.

Moving east of Aghurmi along the dirt road through the palms you'll pass by the negligible ruins of the **Temple of Amun** en route to **Cleopatra's Bath**, a popular swimming hole. Women who choose to hop in should do so covered with at least a T-shirt and shorts – no bikinis. From there, it's two or three kilometers to **Gebel Dekrur** (Dekrur Mountain). The Ptolemeic tombs are of little interest but Dekrur makes a fine place for watching sunsets. Once a year in October, a local festival is held here and locals and tourists alike engage in an orgy of singing and drum beating. From here make your way back to Shali four kilometers to the west.

Six kilometers west of Shali (behind the mountain) is **Fatnas Island**, also known as "Fantasy Island" because of its idyllic setting in Birket Siwa, a giant salt lake. There is nothing of historic interest, but the setting is spectacular, particularly for viewing sunsets, and the ride takes you through palm groves redolent of Eden itself.

A kilometer north of Shali off the Marsa Matrouh Road rises **Gebel El Mawta**, the "Mountain of the Dead." A rugged, barren hill, it is dotted with tombs like holes in Swiss cheese. Most contain no reliefs and are of little interest but a handful make Gebel El Mawta one of Siwa's most fascinating sights. Upon your arrival, the local gatekeeper, a cheerful old gent, will assist you in finding the Greek and Roman tombs with reliefs. The most intriguing is that of **Si Amun**, a Greek merchant, which is a fascinating hybrid of pharaonic and Greek artistic styles. Depicted in Egyptian dress, he looks like a fish out of water with his Greek features.

EXCURSIONS & DAY TRIPS

The Alexander Restaurant organizes camel safaris into the palm groves and deserts surrounding Siwa, day trips or overnight. Generally it costs about LE50 per person for an overnight. Otherwise Mr. Hweiti at the Tourist Office may be willing to organize trips to the surrounding desert.

SHOPPING

There are a half dozen **handicrafts shops** scattered around the main square selling the famous Siwan baskets, and woven textiles such as bags, shawls, and blankets. Bargain hard.

For **provisions**, there are several grocers selling mineral water, cigarettes and canned goods while fresh vegetables are sold from street stalls at the base of the Shali fortress.

PRACTICAL INFORMATION

Banks & Currency Exchange

There are no banks in Siwa. Change plenty of money in Marsa Matrouh, Alexandria or Cairo. You'll need at least LE50 a day to be safe.

Emergencies

The new **hospital** *is past the Cleopatra Hotel south of the main Square.* The **Police Station** *is across from the Waha Hotel.*

Post Services

The **Post Office** *is across from the Waha Hotel. Hours: 8-3pm daily except Friday.*

Telephones

The **Telephone Office** *is next to the Post Office and is open 24 hours.*

Tourist information

Egyptian Tourist Authority, *across from the Arousa Hotel. Hours: 8am-2pm & 6-9pm.* Operated by a very helpful and charming gentleman, Mr. Hweiti, the spanking new tourist office is worth looking into for basic information. Mr. Hweiti has put together a helpful little information booklet which he sells for LE10. He can also help you arrange excursions to distant sights.

Tourist Police

The Tourist Police are by the Tourist Information office.

BAHARIYA

Apart from Faiyoum, **Bahariya** is the oasis closest to Cairo, 330 kilometers by automobile. Situated in a depression and inhabited for as long as we can tell, it fell under the influence of pharaohs during the Middle Kingdom when it supplied the nation with dates. During the later pharaonic periods it emerged as a major stop on caravan routes, a function it maintained through the Roman and Islamic eras. While Egypt was under Roman occupation, the oasis became a place of refuge for Copts fleeing persecution and its Christian population grew enough to warrant its own bishop. We know very little about Bahariya during the Middle Ages except that like the rest of Egypt, its conversion to Islam was gradual.

Today, Bahariya's communities are among the most conservative in Egypt. Group and family identity are strong and a strict social code derived from Islamic law and Bedouin tradition governs all aspects of life. While the state has been keen to develop and modernize oases such as Siwa, Kharga, and Dakhla, Bahariya appears left behind. Yet its people are content to continue their traditional ways of life, farming olives, dates, lemons and other crops. Comprising several villages, its center of Kasr and Bawiti were historically two separate communities which have recently merged. It is here that most facilities for travelers are located. As far as sights, there are several modest pharaonic and Roman attractions such as the Roman Triumphal Arch, the Tombs of Qarat El Subi, and the villages themselves, but the primary draw is the picturesque verdant oasis surroundings.

ARRIVALS & DEPARTURES

As Bahariya is the closest oasis to the Nile Valley, most people approach it from Cairo. Alternatively you can also come from Dakhla and Farafra, and there is a new road to Siwa, but no regular bus or service so you cannot count on public transportation. If driving your own vehicle, fill up with petrol as there are no pumps en route to any of the other oases.

By Bus

Buses come and go on the main street. Buy tickets for Cairo and Farafra in advance from the second floor of the telephone office in Bawiti.

Two buses leave daily for Cairo from Bawiti in the early morning (8am or 9am) and again in the middle of the day, depending on when the bus coming from Farafra gets is. The ride to Cairo takes 6 hours and costs about LE15. Coming from Cairo, an 8am bus departs from the Upper Egyptian Bus Co. depot off Ataba Square.

By Service
Public taxi service to Cairo, Siwa, and Dakhla is sporadic. Any ride should cost about LE20 assuming you're not on a private excursion.

ORIENTATION

The municipal center of Bahariya is **Bawiti** which recently merged with the ancient capital of **Kasr**. While the rest of the oasis is exceedingly picturesque, the main road of Bawiti where facilities are located is an ugly half-hearted attempt at modernization. Kasr itself is an attraction as are several springs and villages close to the city center. Other springs, villages, and historic ruins are strewn throughout the oasis and some are as far as twenty kilometers from Bawiti.

GETTING AROUND TOWN

Bawiti, Kasr, and neighboring attractions such as the ruins of Qarat El Ferakhi and the Chapels of Ain El Muftiallah are within walking distance of each other. To reach outlying sites, you'll need an automobile. If you don't have your own, various locals are ready to be hired, something you can arrange through the Tourist Office. Expect to pay upwards of LE50 for a half day and more than LE200 for an overnight excursion to the White Desert.

WHERE TO STAY

ALPENBLICK HOTEL, *about a hundred meters south of the main road. Turn at the Paradise Hotel. Rates: LE20-50 singles and doubles.*
Bahariya's fanciest accommodations comprise simple clean rooms with private baths. There are cheaper rooms with no baths. Breakfast is included.
PARADISE HOTEL, *on the main road across from Paradise Restaurant and Post Office. Rates: LE5 per person.*
The place is so minimalist, there's hardly even a staff. For five pounds you get something a bit better than a prison cell, but at least it's cheap. No private baths and no fans in the rooms.

Outside of Bawiti
AHMED'S SAFARI CAMP HOTEL, *5 kilometers west of town. Rates: LE2-LE12.*
Situated away from the half-hearted modernizations of Bawiti, Ahmed's offers a variety of accommodation ranging from camping space (LE2) to reed huts (LE5) to cool domed chambers with private baths (LE10). The setting is far superior to anything downtown and the clientele more hip as well. Ahmed's also serves meals and beer! But to get here, you'll have

to get a lift from town unless you feel like walking five kilometers from the bus.

The **Government Rest House Hotel**, *7 kilometers east of town on the road to Bir El Matter and the Black Mountain,* is closed for renovation.

WHERE TO EAT

Eating is limited to the **Popular Restaurant**, the **Paradise Restaurant**, the **Alpenblick**, and anything you may pick up from the grocers on the main road. Across the board, food is cheap (LE10 for a full meal) and pretty much limited to the usual staples of roast chicken, beans, rice and soft drinks. Out of town, **Ahmed's Safari Camp** and the **Government Rest House** (when it reopens) also both serve food, and Ahmed's serves beer.

SEEING THE SIGHTS

Bawiti, Kasr & Environs

Bawiti, Bahariya's contemporary hub was historically the second sister to El Kasr and doesn't quite measure up in its historical monuments. The gory **Tomb of Sheikh El Beshmo** is now full of dead livestock, and further north, the **Roman Springs**, also known as Ain El Beshmo, gushes hot water used to irrigate neighboring gardens and apricot blossoms.

Bahariya's ancient capital of **El Kasr** has merged with Bawiti as the two have grown into each other in modern times. *To reach it just walk past the Popular Restaurant to the north off the main road in Bawiti.*

Older than Bawiti, El Kasr dates at least to pharaonic times and may be even older. Still a picturesque, primitive village, the current rendition does not do justice to its prestige in days gone by and unfortunately many of its historical treasures are thought to be hidden under the current village, and hence inaccessible. Those which you can explore include a very ruined Roman Triumphal Arch, which 19th explorer Belzoni thought to be the Oracle of Siwa (he wasn't even close); and the Temple of King Apries. Dedicated to the Theban Triad, it was intact as late as the 19th century, but is now hardly recognizable. Of particular interest is the Temple of Bes, god of music, which is the only temple Egypt dedicated solely to this deity.

The **Chapels of Ain El Muftiallah**, *off the road to Siwa just out of Bawiti,* are four primitive chapels discovered by Ahmed Fakhry in the 1940's. Unfortunately these charming, but primitive chapels featuring a variety of carved reliefs are not currently open to the public. But you can enjoy superb views (best at dawn or sunset) of the entire oasis from the raised dune known as **Qara**.

Half a kilometer south of Bawiti, lies **Qarat El Ferakhi**, a necropolis where ancients buried mummified animals – mostly falcons and other birds. There is not much to see now, but at the **Islamic Cemetery** en route, the annual **Moulid of Sheikh Badawi** entails music, dancing, and festive activities.

Outside of Bawiti & El Kasr

Three kilometers south of El Kasr, **Qarat** Helwa (the "Beautiful Hill") is a pretty little hill that was made a necropolis in pharaonic times. There are still some primitive, charming reliefs, especially in the Tomb of Amonhophis, a local governor. The carvings primarily depict the nobility inspecting tax collection and fulfilling other official duties.

Bir Mattar, *six kilometers northeast of Bawiti,* are modest cool springs where you can bathe in smelly sulfurous waters. However, be aware that men bathe during the day and women at night. En route, to Bir Mattar, a temple containing the **cartouche of Alexander the Great** was found by Ahmed Fakhry in the 1940's. There really isn't anything to see, but this is the only example of such a cartouche in Egypt, and it leaves scholars stumped as there are no accounts of Alexander ever having visited.

The springs of **Bir El Ghaba**, *15 kilometers from Bawiti,* are less crowded than those of Bir El Mathar and surrounded by a beautiful oasis setting of palm groves with camels wondering about.

Bir El Ramla, *3 kilometers from Bawiti,* are truly hot springs where water temperatures soar above 45 degrees centigrade.

On the road to Harrah 2 kilometers north of Bawiti, the village of **El Agouz** ("the elderly") was founded by Siwans exiled from their own community for disobeying local customs. Further on, lies the picturesque village of **Mandisha** and Zabw, a site featuring a slew of graffiti left by Libyans in the 12th and 13th centuries.

A FEW TIPS FOR BATHING IN SPRINGS

Bathing in springs affords you the opportunity to relax and enjoy the beautiful oasis surroundings. However, given the conservative nature of Bahariyan society, it is absolutely necessary to follow and observe local customs and regulations. At some springs, such as Bir El Mathar, men and women must bathe at different times. Also, women must dress modestly when bathing. That means wearing a very long shirt or dress. Be aware that anywhere you bathe, you may attract an audience. This may make you uncomfortable, but do not fear harassment or physical harm. If you have any questions about what is and is not appropriate, do not hesitate to ask at your hotel or the Tourist Office.

Nine kilometers from Bawiti beyond Mandisha, Zabw, and the village of Gabala (site of a modest Roman necropolis), stands **Kasr Muharib** which features the most stunning ruins in Bahariya. This extensive, well-preserved Roman fortress has a number of garrisons and structures remaining from a Christian settlements. This site used to be visited by women from Bahariya villages who believed that spirits inhabiting the site could help them conceive.

Forty kilometers from Bawiti is the district of **Hayz**, a smattering of mountains, springs, and villages that enjoyed great prosperity during the Roman era. Among its main historical sites is the **Church of Saint George** near the springs of Ain El Ris two kilometers beyond the first check point of Hayz. Built in the 4th and 5th centuries, it was believed in medieval times to contain some of the remains of Saint Bartholomew, one of the Twelve Disciples. Largely ruined, the church is quite bare. Half a kilometer beyond it is the **Monastery of the Head**- a reference to one part of Bartholomew believed to have been buried here. Also located here is a ruined Roman fortress, **Kasr El Masuda**.

Ten kilometers from Bawiti on the road to Farafra stands the village of **Harrah**. Like many other villages in Bahariya it features both a rather charmless modern quarters and a quaint ancient village. It offers little in the way of historic attractions but the nearby spring of **Ain Youssef**, situated amongst some picturesque small lakes, is quite attractive. Beyond the well, you need a heavy duty vehicle to access the **Wadi El Gamal**, the "Valley of Camels," where the local herds, numbering in the thousands, are put out to pasture.

EXCURSIONS & DAY TRIPS

Most excursions entail visiting the sites mentioned above or camping in the nearby **White Desert**. If you don't have your own vehicle, locals are often willing to be hired out, usually for a fee of around LE300 per each overnight. You can also camp in the White Desert en route to Farafra, a good way to break up what can be a long and dusty journey.

SHOPPING

Like other Western Desert oases, Bahariya is known for the beautiful crafted and bulky jewelry, and traditional dresses worn by its women. The shopping opportunities in Bahariya itself however, are limited.

PRACTICAL INFORMATION

Banks & Currency Exchange

The **bank**, *next to the Post Office on the main road. Hours: 9am-2pm Sunday-Thursday. Changes hard currency only.*

Emergencies

The **Hospital** *(Tel. 123) is next to the Antiquities Office in Bawiti off the main road- turn south at the mosque.*

The **Police Station** *is on the main road across the street from the Popular Restaurant.*

Post & Telephones Services

The **Post Office** and **Telephone Office** *are both on the main road in Bawiti. Domestic calls only.*

Tourist information

Egyptian Tourist Authority, *in the City Council building in Bawiti. Hours: approximately 9am-2pm daily.*

FARAFRA

The least populated and most underdeveloped of the major oases, **Farafra** is known for its splendid isolation and the striking beauty of the nearby **White Desert**, an almost psychedelic setting ideal for camping.

Not nearly as fertile, and further away from the Nile Valley than other oases, Farafra was of little interest to Egypt's pharaohs until the Libyans invaded around 700 BC when it became an important link for the Libyan pharaohs with their homeland. However, when the Libyans were overthrown shortly thereafter, Farafra was returned to its status as a marginal settlement. Dominated by the Sanusi clan, it has remained virtually independent since, linked to the world only through several minor caravan routes that passed through en route to Bahariya from Dakhla. This is soon to change as Farafra is now the subject of government plans for land reclamation and it is believed that migrants will soon swamp the now one street town, changing its complexion completely.

ARRIVALS & DEPARTURES

By Bus

There is one bus daily to Farafra from **Cairo** (LE30, 12 hours) that departs at 8am from the Upper Egyptian Bus Co. depot near Ataba Square. A coach to **Cairo** leaves Farafra at 6am and stops at **Bahariya** (LE10, 3 hours). There is also one bus daily to **Dakhla** which departs around 1 or 2pm (LE15, 4 hours). Once in a while, there may be a **service** to these destinations, but there are no regular routes.

ORIENTATION

The settlement of **Kasr El Farafra** is a one street town and all important facilities (restaurant, bus stop, hospital) are within several hundred meters of each other. Most of the attractions, namely the White Desert, El Mufid Lake, and El Tanien are all at least 20 kilometers away from town and require transportation.

GETTING AROUND TOWN

Kasr El Farafra is easily small enough to be negotiated by foot. All other attractions such as the White Desert, require an automobile. The folks at Saad's Restaurant organize excursions to all the nearby attractions, including overnight camping trips in the White Desert.

WHERE TO STAY

Ideally you want to camp in the White Desert with its surreal chalky dunes and magical sunsets and nights skies. This entails finding equipment and organizing in Cairo through a local travel agency or through the folks at **Saad's Restaurant** who organize trips on the spot-usually for about LE40 per person per night.

The only place to stay in Kasr El Farafra is the **El Farafra Tourist Rest House** *next to the hospital on the Baharatya Road.* For LE10 you get a triple room with a fan, and not much else.

The other alternative is to camp in the public camping grounds next to the hot springs of Bir 6, five kilometers west of town. There are small huts available for LE5 or you can pitch your own tent.

WHERE TO EAT

Saad's Restaurant is the old standby for food in Farafra. Alternatively, you there is **Hussein's** and the **Manroos Restaurant**. All offer pretty much the same grub: melokhiya, beans, chicken, and omelets.

For provisions, the shop next to Saad's offers a very modest variety of canned and packaged goods. If you're planning to camp for any amount of time, consider bringing your own provisions.

SEEING THE SIGHTS

Kasr El Farafra

Like other oasis settlements, Kasr El Farafra's modern community is towered over by a picturesque medieval fortress-city set on high ground amongst palm groves. Apart from the old city, there is really only the charming **museum** operated by Badr, a local artist and taxidermist. It does not operate on a schedule, but getting in to see his assortment of sculptures, paintings, and stuffed animals is not difficult. You can also wander past his museum to the serene **palm groves** behind town.

The White Desert

The chalky, lunar landscape of the **White Desert**, stretching from Farafra to Bahariya, is truly a sight to behold, especially at dusk or dawn. Beginning 20 kilometers northeast of Kasr El Farafra, it is ideally made part of a camping excursion, either on your own or through Saad's Restaurant. which organizes overnight excursions for LE200 per night per vehicle. They will also take you for the day for LE130. Many like to stop in the White Desert for the night en route to Bahariya-also a good idea.

Other Natural & Historic Attractions

The wells of **Bir Setta**, *5 kilometers west of Kasr El Farafra,* basically comprise a tank of sulfurous water where you can bathe. Just remember to respect local custom and dress modestly. To get there, hike or hire a vehicle through Saad's for about LE40 for a round trip.

Within a similar distance from Kasr El Farafra, **El Mufid Lake** becomes a swimming hole during the warmer months, and **Ain El Tanien** is a quaint, picturesque mini-oasis. Again, excursions can be organized through Saad's.

If you're able to convince Saad's, or have your own mode of transportation, you should seriously consider a trip to **Ain Della**, a spring 80 kilometers north of Farafra. A strategically located water source relatively close to Bahariya, Farafra, and Dakhla, it was an important junction for armies crossing to and from Libya, as well as caravans and smugglers. It was also a major base for explorers in the 1920's and 1930's searching for the lost Persian armies of Cambyses who disappeared while crossing the Great Sand Sea around 530 BC. Among the explorers who used Ain Della as a base was Count D'Almasy, the Hungarian explorer whose fictional romance with an English woman was chronicled in the acclaimed novel, and later the film, *The English Patient.*

The real attraction of making the journey to Ain Della is the spectacular scenery en route. Poking up from the desert are chalky dune formations resembling upside down stalactites. After about fifty kilometers, you will start coming across giant rock formations and islands rising out of the ocean of sand. The most famous of these, is the **Red Mountain** which marks the beginning of the depression where Ain Della is located.

PRACTICAL INFORMATION
Banks & Currency Exchange

There are no banks in Farafra.

Emergencies
The **Police**, the **City Council**, and the **Hospital** *are all on the main road within a half mile of town towards Bahariya.*

Post Services
The **Post Office** *is on the main road. Hours: 9am-2pm.*

Telephones, Telex, & Fax
The **Telephone Office**, *next to the Post Office. Hours: 6am-1pm daily. Domestic calls only.*

Tourist Information
There is no tourist office, but Saad, the mayor, and other locals are usually more than willing to answer questions to the extent they can.

DAKHLA

A lush and fertile oasis brimming with palms, orchards and fields nurtured by hundreds of springs amidst the earthy red stone and rock of the desert, **Dakhla** is a visual feast compared to Kharga, and unlike its southern neighbor which is set to be industrialized, Dakhla's agricultural base is to remain in place. Besides its verdant natural beauty, Dakhla is littered with charming medieval villages that in centuries past derived wealth as a junction for caravans like the Darb Ain Amur, "Road of the Lovely One," which linked Dakhla to Kharga; and Darb El Tawil, "the Long Road" that connected it directly with the Nile Valley.

People have inhabited Dakhla from the dawn of history. In Neolithic times (roughly 5,000 BC), the area that is now Dakhla was like an African savanna and held a lake that nourished elephants, lions, and other wild beasts traditionally associated with equatorial Africa. Some believe that people also lived in the area at that time and when climate change created the vast arid landscape that is now the Western Desert, they fled Dakhla for the Nile Valley. We know that Dakhla was inhabited in pre-pharaonic times and that there was contact with the Nile Valley. The exact nature of this relationship is not clear, but we know from inscriptions that Dakhla paid taxes as early as the Old Kingdom.

It was during the **Roman occupation** of Egypt that Dakhla was truly brought into the national fold as the Romans settled the oasis and made it an major junction on trans-African caravan routes. In the 4th and 5th centuries, **Christians** also settled here, probably in refuge from the Roman persecution in the Nile Valley. Later during Muslim invasions, the walled villages that we see today were built to protect them from increasing banditry by nomadic Bedouin and during the Ottoman occupation of Egypt in the 16th century, a Turkish colony, **Qalamun**, was established. During the early 20th century, Dakhla was occupied by Sanusi forces trying to force the Egyptians and British out of the Western Desert.

The British resorted to bombing parts of Dakhla to remove the Sanusi in 1916 and successfully accomplished their mission with minimal damage to the inhabitants and their villages. Unlike Siwa and Farafra, Dakhla has always been closely linked to the Nile Valley and has been assimilated into modern Egypt with relative ease.

ARRIVALS & DEPARTURES
By Bus
The bus station is at the end of El Wadi Street across from the mosque. The ticket office is open most of the day and tickets should be purchased in advance. There are two buses daily from Assiut (LE15, 8 hours) via Kharga (LE10, 4 hours). To Assiut via Kharga, two buses depart daily at 8:30am and 4pm. Three daily buses to Cairo (14 hours, LE25-40 depending on amenities) leave at 7am, 5pm, and 7pm. There is also one daily bus to Farafra (LE15, 4 hours.)

By Service
Service come and go from bus station. Minibus service to Assiut and other oases is sporadic so its hard to make plans. Ask around. You shouldn't pay any more than you would for bus ticket.

ORIENTATION
A narrow oasis that is about 70 kilometers long, Dakhla civilizationwise centers around the town of **Mut**, where buses make drop-offs and pick-ups and where most hotels, restaurants, banks, and other service facilities are located. The main attractions, the medieval towns of El Kasr and Balaat, are 30 kilometers west, and 35 kilometers east of Mut respectively. The town itself is basically a one street town after you get off the main highways and the center of town with the bus station, the old city, and the tourist office is essentially a *cul de sac*.

GETTING AROUND TOWN
Mut is negotiable by foot and there are public taxis in the form of **pick-ups** that can take you to El Kasr (LE1) from the midan at the end of the road to El Farafra and to Balaat (LE1-2) from the hospital on 10th of Ramadan Street or possibly the traffic circle. To sites out of Mut, you'll

have to hire out a pick-up privately; try to get it for about LE30 for each half day.

WHERE TO STAY

In Mut

MEBAREZ HOTEL, *on the road to Farafra and El Kasr about 500 meters from the traffic circle. Tel 092/941-524. Rates: LE23-30 single, LE34-40 double.*

The only hotel in Dakhla with air-conditioning, the Mebarez is reasonably priced given the simple clean rooms and amenities, but is lacking in the charm department. While other hotels are managed by affable, personable folks who treat you like a personal guest, these guys seem hooked on professional detachment. In any case, the more expensive rooms come with private baths and there is a characterless restaurant off the lobby.

THE GARDENS HOTEL, *off El Basatin Street on the road to the old city. Tel. 092/941-577. Rates: LE10-12 single, LE14-16 double, LE20 triples.*

With its quiet gardens and accessibility to the old city, the Gardens Hotel is an excellent choice. The bathrooms are clean and have hot water and the screens in the rooms keep the bugs out. The kitchen serves hearty home-cooked meals in the garden and they rent bikes for LE5 a day. The more expensive rates are for rooms with private baths.

NASSER'S HOTEL, *5 kilometers east of Mut on the road to Kharga. No telephone. Rates: LE5 per person.*

More Nasser's house than a real hotel, it only has three or four very basic rooms. It's out of town setting amidst the verdant palm groves and fields of the village of Sheikh Walley is perfect for catching Dakhla's true aura and the guy is truly a gentleman. If he's feeling especially hospitable, he make take you for tours of the oasis on his motorbike; otherwise he also camel day trips and overnights. To stay here, you need to contact his brother at Hamdy's Restaurant in Mut and they'll arrange to get you out to his hotel by bike or pick-up.

THE GOVERNMENT REST HOUSE, *by the bus station in the main square in Mut. No telephone. Rates: LE4 per person.*

With almost no comforts and zero atmospherics, there's really no reason to stay here. Rooms are very simple with no amenities and the common bathrooms are quite nasty.

In El Kasr

EL QASR HOTEL, *El Kasr village on the road from Mut. Rates: LE7 per person.*

The only accommodation in the charming medieval village of El Kasr, this is actually a big house with four spacious double rooms with balconies. The common bathrooms are clean, and the ground floor restaurant serves home-cooked meals.

WHERE TO EAT

Dining options are limited in Dakhla to lowest common denominators of Egyptian cuisine: fuul, bread, chicken, rice, and maybe kebabs. In town near the bus station, there are two restaurants, the **Qalamuni** and **El Dakhla's**. Both serve cheap Egyptian style fast food, but Qalamuni has better variety.

Along the road to El Kasr, **Hamdy's**, and **Abu Mohammed** both feature good chicken, and kebab meals, or rice and vegetables for vegetarians. With its garden setting, the Garden Hotel may be the best choice, but the food is more or less the same everywhere and anywhere you can eat a full meal for LE10-15 tops. In El Kasr, there is a restaurant on the ground floor of the El Kasr Hotel.

SEEING THE SIGHTS

In & Around Mut

Just 100 meters east and north of the bus station and the Tourist Office is the **Old City** of Mut and the remains of its **citadel**. Little is known about its origins except that the mud brick village and ruined citadel were part of a regional capital in medieval times.

Also in this part of Mut, attached to the official guest house, is the **Ethnological Museum** featuring modest exhibits about the history of Dakhla and life in the oasis. It does not keep regular hours, but Mr. Ahmed at the Tourist Office will open it for you.

There are numerous **springs** throughout the Dakhla Oasis. The closest to Mut is three kilometers out of town on the road to Farafra and El Kasr.

El Kasr & Environs

Pick-ups leave frequently for El Kasr from Mut, but to reach the other sites, you must have your own vehicle or hire a pick-up. As Mr. Ahmed at the Tourist Office for assistance.

Thirty kilometers west of Mut stands the charming medieval village of **El Kasr**. Protected by law from development, the old village is a labyrinth of narrow alleys and mud brick houses, many of which date to Mamluke times (13th & 14th centuries). The main structure in the old village, **the Mosque and Mausoleum of Sheikh Nasr El Din** was originally constructed in the 12th century, but has since been renovated. The village is still inhabited by 1,000 Bedouin who will undoubtedly make you the center of their attention. Don't worry, it's all in the name of hospitality and curiosity. Just be sure that before photographing them, especially the women, to ask permission in advance.

Four kilometers west beyond El Kasr are the **Roman-era Pharaonic tombs of El Muzawaka**. Nothing spectacular, they feature murals portraying Roman looking folks in pharaonic poses commiserating with pharaonic deities in traditional funerary scenes. The tombs are actually a kilometer off the road and the sign is in Arabic, so be on the lookout. The entrance fee is LE8 and some baksheesh will undoubtedly be expected as well.

Another three kilometers beyond El Muzawaka is the turnoff for the Roman-era Temple of **Deir El Hagar**. Dedicated to the Theban Triad of Amun, Mut (no relation), and Khonsu, it was at least restored and possibly built during the second century reign of Nero. It features a hypostyle hall, and sanctuary, and is surrounded by a brick wall. It is quite a trip to reach the temple: five kilometers off the main road, three to the village and another 1.5 to the actual temple.

Balaat

Thirty-five kilometers east of Mut, the medieval village of Balaat was a trading post as early as the 6th Dynasty (c. 2300 BC) and in 1977 an intact pharaonic-era noble's tomb was discovered by French archaeologists. Like El Kasr, Balaat has retained its medieval Islamic character and the narrow alleys were purposely built for cooling and for protection-it was nearly impossible for would-be invaders to penetrate the village. Pick-up service depart for Balaat from Mut near the hospital (LE2).

EXCURSIONS & DAY TRIPS

Camel trips and safaris into the surrounding desert and through the picturesque oasis itself can be organized through the affable Nasser at Nasser's hotel or through the Abu Mohammed Restaurant. An evening ride shouldn't cost more than LE10-15; for a day, LE30 or more depending on supplies. If you go overnight, LE100 should include everything.

PRACTICAL INFORMATION

Banks & Currency Exchange

Bank Misr, *downtown Mut on El Wadi Street by the traffic circle. Hours: 8am-2pm and usually 6-9pm daily except Friday.* Changes cash and travelers cheques.

Emergencies

• **Hospital**, *10th Ramadan Street 500 meters from traffic circle, Tel. 123*
• **Police**, *10th Ramadan Street on the traffic circle*

Post Services
   Post Office, *El Wadi Street on the other side of the Mosque from the bus station. Hours: 8am-3pm daily except Friday.*

Telephones
   24 Hour Telephone Office, *Mut El Gadid across from the Ethnological Museum.*

Tourist information
   The **Tourist Office**, *El Wadi Street across from the Mosque in the Rest House next to the Bus Station. Hours: 9am-3pm daily. Tel. 092/ 941-685/6.*
   Mr. Ahmed in the Tourist Office is extremely helpful and well spoken. He can help sort out the various attractions and how to go about visiting them.

KHARGA

   Though **Kharga** is not as far away from the Nile Valley as Dakhla (which ironically means "inside" or "interior"), the name, which means "outside" or "exterior," is nonetheless appropriate and for centuries it has been of place of exile for those not in favor with the powers that be. In the 4th century, the Egyptian nationalist and outspoken cleric, Athanasius, was exiled to Kharge twice for agitating against the Roman authorities, and in the 20th century, Mostafa Amin, a prominent journalist and founder of Egypt's largest daily, *El Akhbar*, was sent here by the Nasser regime.
   Kharga has also been the most developed of the oases and was a major junction for trans-African caravan routes, including the 40 Days Roads; hence, the construction by Greeks, Romans, Persians and others of settlements, and temples of considerable size which today are Kharga's main attractions.

ARRIVALS & DEPARTURES
   Kharga is approached from Assiut in the Nile Valley or Dakhla.

By Air
   EgyptAir flies Cairo-Kharga-Cairo weekly. Tickets cost approximately $100 one-way.

By Bus
   The bus station is in Showla Square in the Old City. Four or five buses leave throughout the day for Assiut (LE8, 4 hours) and two daily for

Dakhla (LE7, 4 hours). The schedule constantly changes so check arrival and departing times. Also, make reservations in advance if you can because buses coming from Assiut and going on to Dakhla or vice versa can be full on arrival.

By Service

The service depot is at the bus station in Showla Square. Minibuses depart with fair regularity for Assiut (LE8-10, 4 hours) and sometimes Dakhla (LE8-10, 4 hours).

ORIENTATION

A planned city with wide and spacious, empty streets, El Kharga town is something of an anomaly in Egypt. The drawback is that everything is more distant from each than it should be and it's pain to walk around. Most of the practicalities can be met on the major thoroughfares of Gamal Abdel Nasser Street, El Adel Street, and El Nahda Street.

To the extent that anything is concentrated around anything else, restaurants and the bus station are on Showla Square in Old Kharga, while hotels are clustered around Nasser and Basatin Squares in New Kharga. The historic monuments are generally out of the town itself. Hibis, the Temple of El Nadura, and the Necropolis of Begawat are all about five kilometers north of town on the road to Assiut while Kasr El Ghaweeta and Kasr El Sayyan are off the road south to Baris, which follow the old Forty Days Caravan route.

GETTING AROUND TOWN

This can be a bit of a problem in Kharga. Walking is not very practical given the distances between everything and there aren't the public buses and taxis prevalent in other major cities. That leaves you at the mercy of local pickups who serve locals like a service but like to charge foreigners exorbitant taxi rates.

You shouldn't pay more than a pound to go anywhere within the town itself. To hire one specifically to visit the sites to the north like Hibis Temple, do not pay more than LE20-30 for a half day. To Baris, you should pay a pound or two like everybody else if you're sharing a ride with locals, but chances are this won't fly with the driver who will want to charge you LE50-60. This you'll have to bargain down to LE30-40 round-trip.

WHERE TO STAY

NEW KHARGA OASIS HOTEL, *Nasser Square across from the Tourist Office. Tel. 092/901-500. Rates: LE60-70 single, LE80-85 double, LE110-120 triple.*

The plushest hotel in Kharga, it's a cavernous concrete building that seems almost lifeless. Apparently it was built and 'they' didn't come. In any case, the more expensive rates are for rooms with air-conditioning; the cheaper ones have fans. All rooms have private baths and are comfortable though certainly not lavish. There is a quiet and evocative garden in the back where beer is served and the there is a fairly decent restaurant inside.

HAMAD ALLAH HOTEL, *off El Nahda and El Adel streets. Tel. 092/ 900-638. Rates: LE40-60 single, LE60-85 double.*

The hotel's name, "Thank God" in English, has pleasant airy rooms with private baths and air-conditioning or fans depending on which rates you pay. It's pretty nondescript and has a restaurant and a bar.

MOGAMMA REST HOUSE, *Port Said Street by the Tourist Office. Rates: LE25 per person.*

It's a government run rest house with several chalets each of which features a kitchen with refrigerators and the works. Because these are used to put up visiting government officials, the place is kept meticulously clean.

WAHA HOTEL, *between Basatin Square and El Saha Square. Tel. 092/ 900-393. Rates: LE5-10 single, LE12-17 double.*

The Waha is the cheapest hotel in town and for what you pay, the accommodations are quite good. The rooms have fans and the pricier ones have private showers.

Camping

The **New Kharga Oasis Hotel** allows people to pitch tents in the back yard for LE10 per person.

WHERE TO EAT

Midan Showla in the old town by the bus station has markets selling fresh produce and there are some fast food type joints including a chicken restaurant. In the new town, the **El Ahram** *by the Waha Hotel* sells rotisserie chicken and sometimes meat as well as vegetables. Otherwise eating is mostly limited to the hotels. The **New Kharga Oasis Hotel** serves a variety of meat, chicken and vegetable dishes with rice. This is the most expensive eatery in town and you may pay as much as LE30 a person, not including beer. The **Hamad Allah** serves similar food for prices slightly less dear. They also serve beer.

SEEING THE SIGHTS

If you're a dedicated walker, you may be willing to stroll the three kilometers north of town to visit the cluster of sites including the Hibis Temple, the Necropolis of Begawat, and the Temple of El Nadura. Otherwise you have to hire a pick-up which means negotiating a price; LE15-20 for the first hour and LE10 for every hour after is fair. To visit the sites south of town (the Temple of Ghaweeta, Baris, & the Temple of El Dush), you'll surely need an automobile and given the lack of regular public taxi service, you almost surely have to hire a pick-up for yourself. Buses may depart from Kharga's bus terminal to Baris, but not to Dush.

In Kharga Town

The brand new **museum** *is on Gamal Abdel Nasser Street a block south of Nasser Square and the Tourist Office. Admission: LE20 general, LE10 students. Hours: 9am-4pm.*

This new institution features the typical oasis museum assortment of colorful Bedouin clothing and a modest collection of pharaonic, Roman, and Islamic artifacts from Dakhla and Kharga.

North of Kharga Town

The Temple of El Nadura *is just before the Hibis Temple on a hill-you can't miss it. There is no entrance fee.*

Constructed during the reign of Roman Emperor **Caesar Antonius** (138-161 AD), this small temple was built as a lookout post for sentries guarding the oasis and the views are superb indeed. Later used by the Turks for the same purpose, it is mostly ruined but the interior features some hieroglyphic reliefs and carvings. Cluttering the area around the hill are the ruins of a medieval Islamic settlement.

The Temple of Hibis *is two kilometers north of Kharga town on the road to Assiut. It is open to the public generally though the guard may expect some baksheesh.*

Set amidst picturesque palms and reeds, this is one of only a few Persian-built temples in Egypt and was constructed by Darius I in the 6th century BC. It assumes the traditional pharaonic temple plan with a pylon, court and hypostyle hall and is currently being renovated. The sanctuary is closed off, but if the guard is willing, by all means pay the baksheesh to get him to let you in to see the excellent and unique reliefs depicting dolphins (in the middle of the Western Desert?).

The Necropolis of Begawat *is one kilometer beyond the two temples and three kilometers north of town. Hours: 8am-5pm. Admission: LE20 general, LE10 students.*

One of the earliest intact Christian cemeteries in the world, this fascinating collection of domed and vaulted tombs dates to the 4th and

5th centuries but is believed to have been used as a necropolis even earlier. Most of the graves are simple mud brick chapels with plain interiors but some contain fascinating frescoes. One in particular, the **Chapel of Moses** records the story of the Exodus and features registers with primitive paintings of Moses and the gang at various stages of their odyssey. A second chapel with interesting frescoes is the **Chapel of Peace** with a very busy and garish interior. Among the biblical and mythical themes depicted is Adam and Eve after the Fall and Noah's Ark. One of the guards will help you find these specific chapels in return for a bit of baksheesh.

About a kilometer north of Begawat is the **Monastery of Mostafa Kechif**, a fortified structure that dates originally to pharaonic times but was later occupied by Romans, Christians, Mamlukes, and Turks. Named for a Mamluke governor of the oasis, it was converted into a Christian convent in the 5th century and once stood five stories tall and included a pension for visitors and a church.

South of Kharga Town

The Temple of El Ghaweeta *is 17 kilometers south of Kharga town on the road to Baris and on top of a hill two kilometers off the main road.*

This modest temple dates to the 27th Dynasty (6th century BC) and features a ruined hypostyle hall and unsophisticated reliefs. Nearby are the remains of a brick Ptolemeic structure and beyond, fresh water springs nourish the surrounding palms and rice crops.

About five kilometers beyond the Temple of El Ghaweeta at the village of Kasr El Zayyan lies the ruined **Temple of Amenebis**. Featuring lotus capitals and mud brick walls, it was part of more substantial town that surrounded it. The temple itself was dedicated to an incarnation of Amun.

Ninety kilometers south of Kharga is the oasis' second major community, **Baris**, connected with the French capital in some way that isn't entirely clear. It's a buzzing settlement where Mubarak's dream of reclaiming the desert and relocating Egyptians from the Nile Valley is being realized. There is a rest house with modest sleeping accommodations and several fast food shops.

Roughly 25 kilometers beyond Baris lies the Roman built **Temple of Dush**. Excavations are currently uncovering the ruined city of Kysis, which is believed to have been abandoned when its wells dried up sometime in the 4th century AD.

PRACTICAL INFORMATION

Banks & Currency Exchange

Banque Misr, *Gamal Abdel Nasser Street and El Nahda Street. Hours: 8am-2pm and sometimes from 6pm-9pm. Visa, travelers' cheques, and cash services available.*

Emergencies
• **Ambulance**: *Tel. 123*
• Police: *Tel. 122*

Post Services

Post Office, *El Nahda Street. Hours: 8am-3pm daily except Friday.*

Telephones

The **24 Hour Telephone Office** *is on the corner of Adel Street and El Nahda Street.*

Tourist Information

Egyptian Tourist Authority, *Nasser Square. Hours: 9am-3pm daily.*

New Valley Tourist Friends Association, *Basatin Square. Hours: 5-10pm.* They may be able to provide information, but are primarily interested in practicing their English.

16. ALEXANDRIA, THE DELTA & THE NORTH COAST

ALEXANDRIA

"I haven taken a city of which I can only say that it contains 4,000 palaces, 4,000 baths, 400 theaters, 1,200 greengrocers, and 40,000 Jews."
– Amr Ibn El As in a letter to Caliph Uthman after taking Alexandria in 642

Except for the green grocers, virtually nothing remains of the rich and prosperous city that Amr conquered more than 1,300 years ago. Indeed, for a city that in its heyday was the richest and most advanced in the Classical World, **Alexandria** has little to show for itself. There are no ozymandian pharaonic temples and the great monuments of antiquity like the Pharos Lighthouse and the Great Library are long gone, over-run by a modern metropolis of five million that in the midst of its own struggle to survive has all but forgotten its glorious roots.

In the 19th century, Alexandria awoke from a 1,200 year hibernation and re-emerged as the wealthy and cosmopolitan, European city whose beauty and raffish decadence inspired the likes of E.M. Forster, Constantine Cavafy, and Lawrence Durrell who called it "princess and whore." It is the shell of that city that travelers visit today, for after the 1956 Suez War, the economic wealth and cosmopolitan culture that defined Alexandria fell victim to the nationalist and socialist policies of the Nasser regime. The "foreign" Greeks, Jews, Armenians and Italians, most of whose families had been Alexandrians for three or four generations were expelled and virtually all major businesses were nationalized. Today Alexandria is Egypt's second city (5 million and counting) and largest port, but ironically for a city whose reputation is that of an international melting pot, it is now provincial, tame, and thoroughly Egyptian.

When it comes to the attractions of Alexandria, E.M. Forster said it best in the preface to his classic guide *Alexandria, A History and a Guide,* "The "sights" of Alexandria are themselves not interesting, but they fascinate when we approach them through the past." Indeed, apart from the magnificent Eastern Harbour and the crumbling facades of a few once elegant buildings, Alexandria is a city of bygone monuments whose main tourist base are Cairenes who come by the millions in summer to enjoy the cooler weather, surf, and to indulge in a seafood meal or two. From the foreign traveler's perspective, the Sinai and Red Sea are better choices for a beach vacation, but those willing to do some homework and undertake random exploration will be rewarded with at least a taste of Alexandria's romantic mystique.

History

Alexandria *(El Iskandaria)* was founded by **Alexander the Great** in 325 BC after he conquered Egypt at the ripe old age of 25. Designed by architect Dinocrates and grafted onto the existing village of Rhakotis where Pompey's Pillar now stands, Alexander's choice of location for his new capital was a stroke of strategic genius, for unlike any existing Egypt city it was a natural port on the coast and easily accessible to the Hellenistic world of the Mediterranean, while still within reach of the rich sources of tribute and wealth in Nile Valley and Delta.

Alexander, however, never ruled from his new capital, for after laying the cornerstone (so to speak), he hurried off to Siwa before leaving Egypt altogether for Central Asia where he passed away several years later. According to tradition, his body was brought back to Alexandria against his wishes (he wanted to be intered in Siwa), though his tomb has never been found.

Upon Alexander's death, an able and ambitious commander, **Ptolemy I Sotor**, assumed control of Egypt, founded the **Ptolemy Dynasty**, and transformed Alexandria into one of the most important economic and intellectual centers in the western world. Within a generation, its palaces, racetracks, and temples were the envy of the Hellenistic universe, and its **Museion** (from which the word "museum" is derived) with its Great Library housing hundreds of thousands of volumes was the undisputed center for Hellenistic learning and science, and attracted the likes of Euclid, the "father of geometry." But the ultimate symbol of Alexandria's technical and scientifc prowess as well as its economic and political power was **Pharos**, the great Alexandrian Lighthouse completed under Ptolemy Phelidephius, that stood an astonishing 400 feet on Ras el Tin Island (now peninsula).

In 30 BC, after a century of overindulgence, complacency and general decline, the Ptolemies were made extinct when the Roman

Octavian Caesar defeated **Marc Antony** at the battle of **Actium**. **Cleopatra** (50-31BC) had overthrown her brother and husband Ptolemy XIV before falling in love with Julius Caesar who brought her to Rome amidst great fan fare. After Caesar's stabbing in the Senate, Cleopatra returned to Alexandria where she fell in love with Marc Antony, Octavian Caesar's arch enemy. As Octavian advanced on Egypt with the goal of ending the Ptolemies once and for all, the lovers made a suicide pact and after Antony's defeat at Actium near Greece and his subsequent suicide, Cleopatra also killed herself in the belief that a Roman Egypt had no place for her.

With Octavian's victory began 700 years of Roman and Byzantine domination over Egypt and Alexandria (30 BC-642 AD). During this period, Alexandria remained an economic and intellectual hub and retained its Hellenistic identity, but lost the status as an imperial Hellenistic capital and its grandeur faded. Much of Ptolemeic Alex was destroyed during the first Roman campaigns of Caesar and Octavian, including parts of the Museion and the Great Library. To the Romans Egypt nothing more than a breadbasket with Alexandria as its administrative capital-not an imperial city to be indulged with grand buildings and sparkling boulevards.

Perhaps the most important development of Roman occupation was the introduction of Christianity. According to Coptic tradition, **Christianity** was ushered into Egypt when Saint Mark the Evangelist made his first convert in Alexandria in 62 AD. Within two centuries, Egypt became the first majority Christian country in the world and Alexandria emerged as an important center in the development of Christian theology and doctrine. By the 2nd century, the Museion had been transformed into the Theological College, the world's premier institution of Christian learning whence emerged such early Christian giants as Clement of Alexandria and Origen, both of whom articulated the revolutionary and far-reaching idea that Christianity and Platonism were compatible.

This was despite the often brutal oppression of Christianity by the Romans and even when Constantine made Christianity the state religion for the Byzantine Empire, there a schism over the nature of Christ between the Romans and the Egyptians which led to the formal seccession and creation of the Egyptian Coptic Church, headquartered in Alexandria.

Arabs & Turks – A Thousand Years of Decline

When **Amr Ibn El As**, Arab conqueror of Egypt, took Alexandria in 641, she was still a mighty city, greater than any other captured by the Arabs to that point. "It contains," Amr informed his boss, the Caliph Omar, "4,000 palaces, 4,000 baths, 400 theaters, 1,200 green grocers, and

40,000 Jews." The Pharos still stood and many of the other resplendent Greek structures remained intact. Yet to the Islamic Arabs, who considered pre-Islamic history essentially irrelevant, and whose orientation was towards the Arab heartlands of the Middle East rather than the Mediterranean and Europe, the capture of Alexandria meant little. Fustat and later Cairo thrived as the new capitals of Egypt, and Alex, more out of benign neglect than destructive aggression, was allowed to deteriorate to the extent that by the time Napoelon invaded in 1798, it was nothing more than a fishing town of 4,000.

Modern Alexandria

Alexandria was thrust back into the thick of world geo-politics in 1798 when then-General **Napoleon** landed his fleet just west of the city. Napoleon was forced out of Egypt shortly thereafter by Lord Nelson whose fleet obliterated Napoleon's at Abu Kir 30 kilometers to the east, and from the resulting power vaccuum emerged **Mohammed Ali**, and with him Alexandria. In his efforts to modernise Egypt, Mohammed Ali revived Alexandria as the national port and in 1820, the **Mahmoudia Canal**, named for the Ottoman sultan of the time, was completed, re-establishing the crucial link with the Nile that made the site so attractive to Alexander more than 2,000 years earlier. The development of cotton as a cash crop for export and the need to import European weapons, technology, and materiel led to a huge increase in maritime trade and Alexandrian blossomed into a commercial hub.

Policies of westernisation pursued by Mohammaed Ali and his successors encouraged a large degree of European influence and participation in the development of modern Alexandria. To attract European capital and expertise, merchants and traders were offered favorable trading terms that were expanded under pressure from European creditors in the late 19th century. Under the ensuing Treaties of Capitulations, foreign nationals were not subject to Egyptian taxes or punishable under Egyptian law. This attracted thousands of Italian, Greek, French, and Jewish merchants to Alexandria and they by and large funded and built the modern city we encounter today. With no threat of legal impunity foreign nationals could also indulge in, and become rich from, prostitution, gambling, and other vices that became prevalent in Alexandria during this time.

This was not lost on Egyptian nationalists and during the **Orabi Revolt** of 1882, foreign interests in Alexandria were the primary targets of rioters, and the British further damaged the city by firing on it from the naval ships in the Harbour trying to put down the rebellion. But with Alexandria's commercial vitality and continued foreign investment, it was quickly rebuilt and retained its cosmopolitan but decadent flair until the

July Revolution in 1952 when Farouk was forced to sail into exile from Montazah Gardens in eastern Alexandria.

The **Revolution** did not have an immediate impact on the merchantile expatraites, many of whom were now third generation Alexandrians, but after the Suez War with Britain, France and Israel, Nasser nationalized the foreign businesses, often with no compensation, and made the stock and cotton markets redundant. Further pressure was put on Alexandrian Jews, of whom there were more than 20,000, to leave after two Egyptian Jews were caught red handed trying to bomb a theater and framing the Muslim Brotherhood. At this stage, Alexandria's complexion began to change as the Jews, Greeks, and Italians, with their restaurants, newspapers, and social clubs began to disappear.

Old timers invariably decry the changes in Alexandria brought on since the Revolution and Nasser. It is no longer the colorfully decadent and urbane place that it once was. Its once elegant squares and boulevards are, like Cairo's, now shabby and overrun by time, neglect and the increasing pressures of a burgeoning population like traffic and pollution. It is however, refreshingly Egyptian and still very vibrant. The Greeks, Jews, and British who made modern Alexandria may be gone but there are still vestiges; buildings, the Athenios Cafe, and the *Quartet* by Durrell, that bring the "old Alex" back to life.

ARRIVALS & DEPARTURES

By Bus

The **Arab Union Bus Co**. in Saad Zaghloul Square *(Tel. 03/482-4391)* operates the deluxe **SuperJet** coaches to **Cairo** (hourly 5am-10pm, LE25); **Port Said** (6:30am daily, LE30); **Marsa Matrouh** (3 times daily in summer, LE25); and east to Hurghada (LE70, 8 hours), and Sharm El Sheikh (LE80, 9-10 hours). There is also daily service to Aqaba (Jordan) and Jeddah (Saudi Arabia), via Nuweiba, and in the past, there was also a bus that went all the way to Baghdad. Inquiries about timetables, fares, and reservations can be made at the ticket window in the station, travel agencies, or by phoning.

West Delta Bus Co. operates out of depots in Saad Zaghloul Square, El Gomhuriya Square (Misr Station), and Sidi Gabr Station.

More than a dozen buses depart daily to **Cairo** from Sidi Gabr and El Gomhuriya Square (3 hours, LE 20). Four to six buses depart daily from Sidi Gabr and El Gomhuriya Square for **Marsa Matrouh** (LE10-20, 4-5 hours). One departing at 10am goes to the **Libyan border**; one at 11am goes on to **Siwa** (LE40). From El Gomhuriya Square, there are 6 buses daily to **El Alamein** (LE5, 2-3 hours); and one daily to **Assiut, Minya, and Sohag**.

By Service

The major service hub is **El Gomhuriya Square** at the southern end of Nebi Daniel Street next to the Misr Railway Station.

Hundreds of vehicles flood the square dropping off and picking passengers going to and coming from all points along the Mediterranean Coast (Agami, Marsa Matrouh, Abu Talat, Abu Kir) as well as the Delta, and of course Cairo (LE5, 2-3 hours). Some minibuses also depart from **Sidi Gabr Station**.

By Train

Misr Station in El Gomhuriya Square is downtwn several blocks south of the Eastern Harbour) is the major hub for train travel, *Tel. 03492-3207*. Trains also leave from **Sidi Gabr Station** next to the Alexandria Sporting Club on El Horreya Street, *Tel. 03854-95*.

Though not as efficient as *service*, minibus, or even the bus, the train is an economical and comfortable way to travel; especially if you ride first or second class with air-conditioning. There are no less than a dozen such trains daily between Cairo and Alexandria (LE25-30 1st class, LE15-20 2nd class, 2-3 hours). In Cairo's Ramses Station, tickets are purchased and trains depart from the main hall. In Misr Station, first and second class tickets are sold in the office on the north side of the station near the Egyptian Tourist Authority Office and not in the main entrance. There are also two trains daily to Marsa Matrouh (LE10-20), but they move at a glacial pace (6-7 hours), and one daily to Luxor (LE90, 12-14 hours).

ORIENTATION

Very much a coastal town, Alexandria stretches more than 25 kilometers along the Mediterranean Sea, rarely extending more than several kilometers inland. To no surprise, the main thoroughfare is the **Corniche** which extends from Ras El Tin Peninsula past downtown, the **Eastern Harbour** and the city beaches en route to **Montazah Gardens**, once the private domain of Egypt's royal family, and now a playground of the rich and famous.

Most of Alexandria's famous landmarks such as the Pharos Lighthouse and Great Library are no longer in existence, and those attractions which remain are concentrated in the downtown district of **El Mansheya**, also heart of the modern city. It stretches from Saad Zaghloul Square and Ramleh Tram Station, Alexandria's current city center, south along **Safiya Zaghloul** and **Nebi Daniel Streets**. To the west it extends to **Tahrir Square**, Alexandria's 19th century hub. Several kilometers south of Tahrir Square is the working class district of **Kormouz**, site of the famous Pompey's Pillar and the Catacombs of Kom El Shoqafa.

ALEXANDRIA IN WORDS

In his notes to the 1982 printing of **E.M. Forster's** *"Alexandria, A History and a Guide," Michael Haag wrote that "the architecture of Alexandria is found in the words written about her, and among her builders are Cavafy, Forster, and Durrell." Forster of course was one of the finest British novelists of the 20th century whose works include "A Passage to India" and "Howards End." He lived in Alexandria from 1915-1920 and worked at a make-shift Red Cross hospital in the Montazah Gardens. He loved the city, and his guide, "Alexandria, A History and a Guide" is a magnificently written book and though the city has changed much since it was first published in the mid '20s it remains a wonderful read and very insightful. The 1982 and 1986 Oxford Press editions feature handy notes by Michael Haag that explain changes in the city's landscape since Forster. Forster also published a volume of essays related to Alexandria, "Pharos and Pharillon," which is hard to come by.*

Forster's guide featured the first published works of his friend, **Constantine Cavafy** *(1863-1933), whose tangy, melancholy poems like "The City," "Understanding", and "In the Same Space" are testaments to Alexandria's excesses and the struggles of a Greek (and homosexual) native to Alexandria to find his identity. Others like "The God Abandons Antony" recall the majesty of the historic Alex. Cavafy was also the inspiration for the character Balthazar in* **Lawrence Durrell's** *epic series of novels, "The Alexandria Quartet." The story of a love triangle as told by four characters in four books (Justine, Balthazar, Mountolive, and Clea), the Quartet captures the rich hybrid texture of the pre-Revolution Alexandria.*

Of native Egyptian literature, the most prominent work is "Miramar," a short novel by **Naguib Mahfouz** *that explores the ups and downs of post-1952 Egypt through the eyes of a cross-section of Egyptian society who cross paths at a small fictional pension near the promontory of Silsileh on the eastern side of the Eastern Harbour where the new Alexandrian Library is currently under construction.*

North and west of Saad Zaghloul and El Mansheya, the Corniche sweeps around the **Eastern Harbour** to **Ras El Tin Peninsula** and the dilapidated but colorful Ottomon-era districts of **Anfoushi.** The tip of the peninsula, once the site of the Pharos lighthous, is dominated by modern Alexandria's most recognizable landmark, the Fort of Qait Bey. West of Ras El Tin, the Western Harbour is Alexandria's modern port, the busiest in Egypt, but holds little attraction to the common traveler; and beyond, the suburban beaches of Agami and Abu Talat are littered with the second homes of Cairo's elites.

GETTING AROUND TOWN

The heart of Alexandria, those areas in and around Saad Zaghloul, El Gomhuriya, and El Tahrir squares, including the Roman Ampitheater and the Greco-Roman Museum, can easily be covered by foot. In fact, to soak in the city's flavor and texture, walking is surely preferred. Some attractions, such as Pompey's Pillar and the Fort of Qait Bey require a bit of hike but do reward those who put forth the effort with an immersion into quarters not usually visited by tourists. Attractions east of downtown, such as Montazah can only be reached by taxi or public transport.

By Taxi

Taxis in Alex come in either orange, yellow, or red, and black. Convenient for handling luggage, visiting sites in a hurry, or zipping up and down the Corniche, they are quite cheap-a ten minute ride shouldn't set you back more than LE3-5. Be aware that hiring taxis at major hotels are transport hubs such as the train station can be more than twice as expensive so it's recommended to flag one off the street instead.

By Sevice

Minibuses are cheap and especially efficient for whizzing up and down the Corniche to the major beaches east of the city center and to Ras El Tin and to Qait Bey's Fort (50pt). Minibuses to outlying resorts like Hannoville and Agami are caught in El Gomhuriya Square (LE3-5) while minibuses (#729) to Abu Kir in the east run along the Corniche while others depart from Sidi Gabr or Montazah. Minibuses #735 and 736 link Ras El Tin and Montazah.

By Tram

An indelible thread in the city's fabric, trams are a cheap and though not quite as quick as a bullet train, an efficient mode of transport. Trams #1 and #2 run more or less east-west from Ramleh Station off Saad Zaghloul to Sidi Gabr Station while #15 bumps and grinds from Ramleh Station to Ras El Tin, stopping at Orabi Square and the Mosque of Abu ElAbbas El Mursi before cutting across the penninsula to Ras El Tin Palace making. It is handy for reaching Qait Bey's Fort and the Catacombs of Anfoushi. Tram #16 begins at Orabi Square and heads south to Kourmouz, location of Pompey's Pillar and the Catacombs of El Shoqafa.

A ride on the tram costs 15 piasters and the fare is paid on the train itself. Stations are not well marked in English so if you have a question as to when you may reach your destination, ask the ticket taker or fellow passengers.

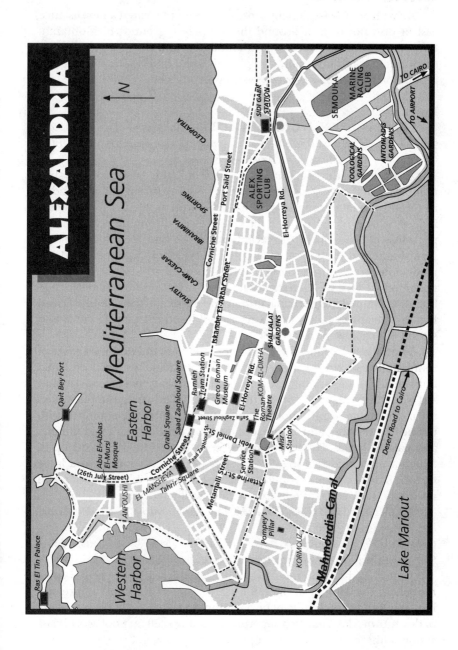

ALEXANDRIA

N

Mediterranean Sea

Eastern Harbor

Western Harbor

Lake Mariout

Qait Bey Fort

Ras El Tin Palace

Abu El-Abbas El-Mursi Mosque

(26th July Street)

Corniche Street

ANFOUSHI

EL MANSHEYA

Tahrir Square

Orabi Square

Saad Zaghloul Square

Ramleh Tram Station

Safia Zaghloul Street

Saad Zaghloul St.

Nebi Daniel St.

Greco Roman Museum

El-Horreya Rd.

The Roman Theatre

KOM-EL-DIKHA

SHALLALAT GARDENS

Misr Station

Service Station

Attarine St.

Metanalli Street

Pompey's Pillar

KORMOUZ

Mahmoudia Canal

Desert Road to Cairo

Iskander El-Akbar Street

SHATBY

CAMP-CAESAR

IBRAHIMIYA

SPORTING

Corniche Street

Port Said Street

CLEOPATRA

SIDI GABR STATION

ALEX SPORTING CLUB

El-Horreya Rd.

ZOOLOGICAL GARDENS

ANTONIADIS GARDENS

SEMOUHA

MARINE RACING CLUB

TO CAIRO

TO AIRPORT

WHERE TO STAY

Apart from the Cecil, most upscale hotels are located a fair distance east of downtown in or around the old palace grounds of Montazah. However, downtown is littered with moderate and cheap hotels. During the summer, rates invariably go up 20-50% and hotels with any sort of a reputation are full so make reservations in advance.

Expensive

El SALAMLEK SAN GIOVANI HOTEL, *Montazah Palace, Montazah. Tel. 03/547-3585. Fax 03/546-4408. Capacity: 20 suites. Rates: $150-1000. Credit cards: Visa, Mastercard, American Express.*

According to the tale, Khedive Abbas II built this Austrian chalet style minipalace in the 1890's as a guest house for his Austrian mistress, and in its recently updated condition the Salamlek with its 20 luxurious suites is indeed, worthy of royalty (and their mistresses). From the original royal portraits on the walls of the receptions to the fine French and Italian furnishings and monogrammed china, every effort has been made to meticulously recapture the original elegance of the royal guest house. The reception salons have been transformed into a bar, restaurant and lounge but have retained their original fittings and decor and the splendid Fouad Bar even features tables that King Farouk used for playing cards and storing his cigars and cigarettes.

The Salamlek caters to elite travelers and does not deal with package tours. Only two stories high, it features only 20 suites, each designed individually; some are decorated with in European styles-Victorian and Art Nouveau for example-others in Arabesque. The vintage atmospherics are complemented with modern amenities; all suites are equipped with phones, faxes, safes, and of course televisions, minibars, air-conditioning, and palatial baths. The most expensive suite, the Mawlana costs up to $1000 a night and features five lavishly decorated rooms and a large terrace. The Salamlek is popular with the Egyptian rich and famous, and need it be said, reservations are required well in advance.

MONTAZAH SHERATON HOTEL, *El Corniche Street, Montazah. Tel. 03/548-0550, 548-1220. Fax 03/540-1331. Telex 54173 MONSH UN. Capacity: 300 rooms, 600 beds. Rates: $135-162 single, $175-207 double, $390-915 suite. Credit cards: all major credit cards.*

Considered the premier hotel in Alexandria before the Salamlek reopened, the Montazah Sheraton claims one of the most impressive locations of any hotel in Egypt next to Montazah Palace 17 kilometers east of downtown Alex. Boasting superior views, an excellent pool, world class rooms with deluxe amenities, a private beach, several restaurants, and nightclubs, the Sheraton is the choice for those in search of comfort, quality and service. However, it is distant from the attractions of downtown, and does not exude the old world charm one hopes to experience while visiting Alexandria.

HELNAN PALESTINE HOTEL, *Montazah Palace, Montazah. Tel. 03/ 547-403, 547-3500. Fax 03/547-3378. Telex 54027 HELNA UN. Capacity: 208 rooms, 383 beds. Rates: $91-135 single, $120-160 double, $260-840 suite. Credit cards: all major credit cards.*

The Palestine is a concrete blob of a hotel that Alexandria scholar Michael Haag termed, "the most vulgar in Egypt." To be sure it pollutes the charm of Montazah and blocks views of the sea for those at the far classier Salamlek. Nonetheless the Palestine enjoys a first rate location and superb views of the sea. It offers five star amenities (air-conditioning, spotless, baths, satellite TV, and all the rest) and the service is professional and efficient. Like other Montazah establishments, it is far from the attractions of downtown.

RAMADA RENAISSANCE HOTEL, *544 El Geish Street, Sidi Bishr. Tel. 03/549-0935, 548-3977. Fax 03/549-7690. Telex 54177 RAREA UN Capacity: 171 rooms. Rates: $72-110 single, $123-137 double, $250-550 suite. Credit cards: all major credit cards.*

This is another modern resort with all the amenities, nightclubs, restaurants, and what not that you may expect from an luxury international chain hotel, but like others near Montazah, it takes a dive when it comes to atmospherics and location.

MERCURE ALEXANDRIA ROMANCE HOTEL, *303 El Geish Street, Saba Pasha. Tel. 03/588-0911/2. 587-6429, Fax 03/587-0526. Telex 55916 ROMEG UN. Capacity: 55 rooms, 110 beds. Rates: $97-121 single, $119-242 suite. All major credit cards.*

The larger suite-like rooms are very family friendly. Other than that, the Mercure is a standard upscale hotel which offers comfortable and well furnished rooms with good views, but little in the way of ambiance. There are several restaurants, bars, a pool, and a nightclub.

SOFITEL CECIL HOTEL *16 Saad Zaghloul Square, Ramleh Station. Tel. 03/483-4856, 483-7173, 483-1467. Fax 03/483-6401. Telex 54358 CECIL UN. Capacity: 86 rooms, 159 beds. Rates: $72-94 single, $83-125 double, $132-170 suite. Credit cards: major credit cards.*

Alexandria's most famous landmark (at least of those still standing), the Cecil was immortalized in Lawrence Durrell's *Alexandria Quartet* and remains the most popular hotel amongst those looking to soak the mystique of the "old Alex." Durrell lamented after returning in the '70s that it "had been stripped of all its finery and echoing like a barn with the seawind sweeping under the doors." Some of the old personality (and personalities) may be gone, but after the Sofitel recently revamped it, the Cecil deserves kudos for its efforts to recapture the old charm, though it definitely feels manufactured up. In any case, it is the finest hotel downtown and its location on Midan Saad Zaghloul overlooking the Square and the Harbour is unbeatable. Rooms are small and the noisy Corniche certainly makes itself heard, however it does offer the usual deluxe hotel amenities: air-conditioning, private baths, a bank, and satellite television.

Moderate

MAAMURA PALACE HOTEL, *El Maamura Beach. Tel. 03/547-3108, 547-3383, 587-6429. Fax 03/547-3108. Telex 21907 SARTO UN. Capacity: 80 rooms, 160 beds. Rates: $45-66.50 single, $55-82 double, $186 suite. Credit cards: Visa.*

A block from the beach in Maamura, this pleasant old style hotel overlooking a colorful little garden is on the other side of Montazah from downtown so it's a hike to the city center. Also Maamura is popular beach resort with upper middle class Egyptians and is swamped with them from May to October. The rooms are acceptably comfortable and feature phones, baths, and air-conditioning.

WINDSOR HOTEL, *17 El Shohada Street, Ramleh Station. Tel. 03/480-8123, 480-8256. Fax 03/480-9090. Telex 54353 WNSOR UN. Capacity: 90 rooms, 170 beds. Rates: $65-75 single, $75-100 double. Credit cards: Visa, Mastercard, American Express.*

The Windsor is a pre-War gem which lacks the modern amenities which might justify the modern prices. The marvelous Art Nouveau lobby and the downstairs cafe are right out of the forties and so are the rooms which lack working televisions, air-conditioners, and any meaningful decor. The location a block west from the Cecil and Ramleh Station overlooking the Eastern Harbour is excellent.

HANNOVILLE HOTEL, *Hannoville Beach. Tel. 03/43-3258, 430-3138. Capacity: 157 rooms, 300 beds. Rates: $46-60 single, $60 double, $80-90 suite. Credit cards: Visa.*

Located in the beach town of Hannoville about a half hour by car west of Alexandria, the Hannoville Hotel offers clean, boring rooms, with air-conditioning and television but little ambiance.

SAN GIOVANNI HOTEL, *205 El Geish Street, Ramleh Station. Tel. 03/546-7774/5. Fax 546-4408. Telex 54213 WASIM UN. Capacity: 30 rooms, 42 beds. Rates: $42-48 single, $56-60 double, $115 suite. Credit cards: Visa, Mastercard, American Express.*

Spectacularly set on its own mini-peninsula overlooking Stanley Beach, the San Giovanni gets an 'A' for its kitsch, colorful ambiance, the superb dining, and the beach-front setting. However it's a bit distant from downtown.

MECCA HOTEL, *44 El Geish Street, Camp Caesar. Tel. 03/597-3925, 597-3935, 596-7846. Fax 03/596-9935. Telex 54376 ELABD UN. Capacity:*

110 rooms, 250 beds. Rates: $36 single, $44 double, $85 suite. Credit cards: not accepted.

Their location on El Geish Street offers views overlooking the sea and up and downtown the Corniche. Downtown is five minutes by taxi and 25 by walking, however its difficult to recommend the Mecca. The ambiance is sniffy and for LE140, you'll probably get a room with no A/C, no television, and which smells like mildew while for LE100 less, cleaner pensions downtown offer the same amenities. A modern establishment with no charm, it caters to vacationing upper middle class Egyptian families—in other words, lots of noise.

METROPOLE HOTEL, *52 Saad Zaghloul Street, Ramleh Station. Tel. 03/482-1466/7, 482-7522. Fax 03/482. Telex 54350 METRO UN. Capacity: 82 rooms, 120 beds. Rates: LE100 single, LE110 double, LE160-250 suite. Credit cards: Visa.*

The combination of old world charm and location on Saad Zaghloul is a winner unless you can't handle traffic. Overlooking Saad's statue and the sea to one side and Ramleh Tram stop to the other, it is a touched up piece of vintage art deco from the Thirties where Cavafy once worked. The amenities are decent—air-conditioning, television, clean bathrooms-but rooms overlooking the sea are definitely better furnished. Drinkers and socialites will enjoy the friendly, period piece bar downstairs.

JEDDAH HOTEL, *137 El Geish Street, Sporting. Tel. 03/546-8662, 857-642, 849-488. Capacity: 69 rooms, 125 beds. Rates: LE70.25 single, LE75.50 double, LE140.50 suite. Credit cards:Visa.*

The Jeddah offers the typical of Alexandrian combination of good location and good view, with mediocre facilities and overpricing. The Jeddah is decent enough with seaside views and all, but it's far from downtown and the ambiance is damp and musty.

Budget
HOLIDAY HOTEL, *6 Orabi Street, El Mansheya. Tel. 03/801-559, 803-517. Fax 03/801-599. Capacity: 44 room, 88 beds. Rates: LE20-31 single, LE20-42.50 double, LE 70 suite. Credit card: Visa.*

The Holiday features a variety of rooms; some with bath, some without, but no television or air-conditioning. It's a bid drab, and the location on Midan Orabi is noisy, but it's centrally located and extremely popular.

UNION HOTEL, *164 26th July Street, Ramleh Station. Tel. 03/807-771, 807-537, 807-350. Capacity: 37 rooms, 54 beds. Rates: LE23-40 single, LE28-55 double. Credit cards: not accepted.*

Located a block west of the Cecil on the Corniche, on the fifth floor (entrance on a side street), this tidy pension run by Egyptian Greeks is hard to beat for value and location. In addition to cleanliness and first rate views overlooking the Eastern Harbour, the ambiance, beginning with the old wooden revolving door takes you back 40 years. The staff is elegantly professional and the decor, subdued, but classy and distinctly old school. Some rooms have private baths and with the breeze off the harbour, air-conditioning is not missed.

AILEMA HOTEL *21 Amin Fikry Street on the 7th and 9th floors, Ramleh Station. Tel. 03/484-7011, 483-2915/6. Capacity: 38 rooms, 76 beds. Rates: LE20-45 single, LE30-60 double, LE62 suite. Credit cards: not accepted.*

Another old timey pension run by Greeks, the Ailema is clean, well run and comfortable for the value. Don't be intimidated by the grimy nameplates and hallway entrance to the building, once you past the old wooden revolving door on the seventh floor, it's quite another world. Recently the recipient of a paint job, the hotel offers spacious clean rooms some of which feature private baths which are also clean and spacious. Just off Sultan Hussein (to the south) and Ramleh and Iskander El Akbar to the north, its central location is a double-edged sword of noise and proximity to the hub. It's worth asking (and paying a bit more) for rooms with views of the sea. Rooms to east also overlook the attractive neo-classical World Health Organization building, Iskander El Akbar Street and Alexandria University.

PICCADILLY HOTEL, *11 El Horreya Street, El Nebi Daniel. Tel. 03/ 482-9620. Capacity: 32 rooms, 56 beds. Rates: LE7.50; LE11-14 double.*

Well, you don't expect much for the prices, and you won't be disappointed. It's dilapidated from the elevator to the bedposts, and the bathrooms leave everything to be desired, including hot water. But, if you're not so discerning regarding such matters, the location in the heart of the Old Alex lacks nothing, save a view of the sea.

HYDE PARK HOUSE HOTEL, *21 Amin Fikry Street, Ramleh Station. Tel. 03/483-5667, 483-5666. Capacity: 58 rooms, 119 beds. Rates: LE10 single, LE14-18 double, LE35 suite.*

You're much better off at the Ailema which is in the same building. The Hyde Park is grungy, poorly maintained, and borders on unsafe.

WHERE TO EAT

To Egyptians, Alexandria is synonymous with fish, Greek food, and pastries. There are of course the usual fuul carts, shwarma stands, and kebab houses one finds in any Egyptian city as well as Colonel Sanders and Golden Arches (both of Safiya Zaghloul), but a visit to Alex is not complete without indulging in a sweet cake at *Pastroudis* or *Atheneios*, and a good munching on grilled shrimp, fried calamari or red mullet. Besides, the old restaurants, many of them still Greek-run, better exude the ambiance of the "old Alex" than any other facet of the city. For fast-food and cheap eats, fuul, ta'amiya, and hamburger are concentrated around

Ramleh Station, El Gomhuriya and Orabi squares, as well as major streets like Abd El Moneim, Sherif, El Horreya, and Port Said.

THE FISH MARKET, *the Corniche, a kilometer west of Saad Zaghloul approaching Fort Qait Bey. Hours: noon until late. Credit cards: Visa and Mastercard accepted.*

Overlooking the Eastern Harbour and Qait Bey to the west and the city to the east, the Fish Market offers perhaps the most splendid setting of any eatery in Alex. Run by the Americana Co., it is new and so lacks that historic charm of the establishments downtown, but its restrained decor with the classic seafood restaurant motifs (lot's of fishnets) and open air setting is certainly a pleasant dining environment, despite the Julio Iglesias style muzak.

Meals begin with a splendid assortment of Lebanese style mezze appetizers, that includes crisp fatouche, creamy labna, and tangy tehina, all accompanied by fresh bread. While munching on that, you take a few minutes off to examine the fish offerings on display before making your selection from a wide assortment of breams, mullets, groupers, bluefish and shellfish. The gentleman who takes your order will be happy to make recommendations as to what's good for frying or grilling. Prices are listed by the catch and range from LE25-60 per kilo of fish while the jumbo shrimp top the list at LE135 per kilo. Calamari and traditional Egyptian fisherman's brown rice are also available. Generally a meal comes to between LE40-60 per person including drinks. If you have only one meal in Alex, you could certainly do worse.

DENIS, *1 Ibn Basaam Street, on a side street between the Corniche and Ramleh two blocks east of Athneios. Hours: mid morning until midnight. No credit cards.*

Denis is a small, almost dingy old Greek seafood restaurant popular with locals, expats, and tourists alike. Unlike some fish restaurants which display their offerings in fancy fish tanks or ice boxes, they lead you right to the kitchen where you pick your meal from a trunk-like fridge. A kilo of shrimp costs LE120, but keep in mind that a quarter of a kilo is half a pound. Grilled or fried fish goes for LE25-30 depending on the fish and the weight. Salad, bread, and Greek style pickles make nice side dishes and cold Stella is a cheap LE6.

ELITE, *on Safiya Zaghloul a block south of Sultan Hussein. Hours: midmorning until midnight or later. No credit cards.*

Open since the 1930's and run since the '50's by the venerable Madame Christina, herself an Alexandrian institution and one of the few remaining links to pre-war Alex, Elite was once a primary social hub and featured an open air cafe as well as a nightclub. The nightclub has been closed, the cafe glassed in, and faded murals and posters advertising artistic happenings throughout the century more than hint that Elite is beyond its days of glory, but a colorful assortment of old regulars, expats, and tourists gives it a good breath of life and it remains an ideal locale for eyeing the hustle and bustle of downtown Alex. Foodwise, Elite would hardly be considered *haute* or *nouveau cuisine*, but old standards like calamari, pastas, and an assortment of Franco-Greco meat, fish, and chicken dishes (lot's of white sauces) go down well with a lemonade or Stella and won't set you back more than LE20-30.

ADORA, *33 Bairam El Tunsi Street in Bahari District bear the Qait Bey Fort. Tel. 0480-040. Open "all the time."*

Despite its legendary reputation, Adora is a distinctly local affair. Simple wooden tables and chairs are set outside where you absorb the colorful the buzz and hum of the middle class district of Bahari where the restaurant is located. The decor is colorful and just cheap and kitsch enough to keep you from taking its pretensions seriously. Meals are begun with the customary mezzes like tehina, bread, and an assortment of salads. For the main course, you make a selection of fish and shrimp from the display and order it grilled or fried. The prices reflect the restaurants middle class clientele; a kilo of fish goes for about LE30, meaning you can eat a half pound for the equivalent of $7. Shrimp is pricier at LE80 per kilo, but that is far cheaper than LE120-135 at the Fish Market.

OMAR EL KHAYYAM, *with outlets at Ramleh Square and the Corniche two blocks east of Athenios. Hours: 8am until late. No credit cards.*

Omar El Khayyam is a venerable Alexandrian institution surviving from the old days that contains several restaurants and cafes within its confines. Off of Ramleh Square through a richly decorate Art Nouveau 1940's doorway, is a spotless cafe-restaurant sporting dressed up like a French cafe with a touch of Egyptian flavor furnished by the wall photos of Egyptian film stars from the '40's and '50's. The primarily Egyptian food takes no short cuts and is cheap. Grilled chicken is only LE8.50, and other reasonably priced dishes included grilled and stuffed pigeon a well as generic Mediterranean seafood (fried calamari et al). The oriental rice with raisins and nuts is splendid. Beer available for LE6.

On the Corniche side a lively outdoor cafe that opens in summer, is ideal for watching the always colorful goings on of the Corniche while sipping on lemon juice, coffee, or perhaps a sheesha. Inside, beer (LE6) and Egyptian Greco-Egyptian food is served in a less classy, more '60's-'70's kitsch environment than the Ramleh outlet. Grilled meats, tornadoes, and escallope dishes go for LE17-22, and very cheap, though not five star, pasta (LE4-9) and casseroles (LE5-12) are also available. The seafood rice is excellent.

TAVERNA, *across from Ramleh Station on Iskander El Akbar, off the corner with Safiya Zaghloul Street. Hours: Open 24 hours. Credit cards: Visa. A second branch is located on the northeastern side of El Tahrir Square.*

A chain outlet serving a wide assortment of Egyptian, Italian, and continental dishes ranging from pizza and chicken negresco to fatir and liver cooked "the Alexandria way," Taverna is a clean, yet somewhat sterile eatery lacking in the ambiance found in the city's older restaurants. However, the food is certainly decent and reasonably priced. Most meat and chicken dishes cost LE15-20 while thick crusted pizzas go for LE10-13. The salad bar (LE5) is a good deal, especially for those craving fresh veggies or salads other than tehina and the usual Egyptian "oriental" green salad.

CAFE ASTERIA, *on Safiya Zaghloul off the intersection with El Horreya Street. Hours: 9am-midnight.*

A large and spacious Greco-Egyptian cafe with French pretensions, the Asteria is ideal for winding down or taking a mid-afternoon break from the goings on of the big city. The eating, while far from fantastic, is good for snacking; the main options are pizzas (LE8-10) and weak versions of French style sandwiches (LE1.50-4). Stella is LE6.

ALEXANDRIA'S PATISSERIES

An indelible part of the Alexandrian experience are its patisseries, some of the few functioning relics of pre-Revolutionary Alex. Radiating with mystique, most are fairly chintzy and wonderfully pretentious with their overuse of cheap gilt and neo-baroque decor.

__Athineos__ on Midan Ramleh features classy old patisserie on the bottom floor where knockout pastries and coffee can be had for a few quid. Upstairs, the harmlessly sleazy bar and decadent Crazy Horse nightclub are time-worn relics of the "Old Alex" and an excellent choice for a boys' night out

__Delices__ on Saad Zaghloul Square next to the Trianon, is a dilapidated but charming old patisserie-bar that looks like it's standing on its last legs, but buzzes with the lively conversation of dedicated regulars.

__The Trianon__ is also on Midan Saad Zaghloul, but has been done up in a big way and is now very upscale with classy 1920's style Art Noveau decor. It features a fancy French restaurant, and a "tea salon" that serves beer, coffee, and snacks.

__Pastroudis__ on El Horreya Street off Safiya Zaghloul is Alexandria's most famous cafe having been immortalized in Durrell's Alexandria Quartet. Its sister establishment, the Pastroudis Loveboat on Glym Beach east of downtown, has a classy old ballroom and outdoor seating for diners.

SANTA LUCIA, *Safiya Zaghloul across from Elite. Tel. 482-2292. Credit cards: Visa.*

One of the finest and most expensive restaurants in Alexandria, the Santa Lucia specializes in seafood which its chefs prepare immaculately. Expect to fork out LE50-70 per person for a full meal, but it's worth it. Not only are the continental style dishes superb, as are the salads, and soups, but the staff is professional to a point, and the ambiance, elegantly subdued. An excellent choice if you don't mind opening your wallet.

HASSAN BLEIK, *Saad Zaghloul Street off Orabi Square next to the Sofianopoulo Coffee Shop. Hours: noon-7pm.*

Hassan Bleik is a modest eatery featuring superb mezze and Lebanese dishes for cheap; a full fish or meat course only costs LE15 while the mezzes go for LE1-4 each. It's informal and open for lunch only.

EL SARAYA, , *San Giovanni Hotel 205 El Geish (Corniche) Street, Stanley. Tel. 546-7773. Hours: 12am-4pm & 7pm-midnight. Credit cards: Visa.*

Superb fish dishes are the specialty at the colorful San Giovanni. Calamari, shrimp-laden rice, and baked fish, are all excellent choices and the meats and chickens are also quite decent though not spectacular. The style of cooking is generic Mediterranean- a kind of Egyptian-Italian-Greek hybrid. The views are also excellent and the prices moderate to expensive. Expect to pay LE30-50 per person for a full meal.

SEEING THE SIGHTS
Saad Zaghloul Square

Since its creation in the 1920's, **Saad Zaghloul Square** has assumed the position of 'city center' that had been the claim of Mohammed Ali Square (now Tahrir Square) since the early 19th century. Its central feature is a statue of the strident Egyptian nationalist, Saad Zaghoul defiantly peering over the Mediterranean. It is one of two such statues crafted by **Mahmoud Mukhtar**, Egypt's premier 20th century sculptor, with the other standing in front of the new Cairo Opera House in Zamalek.

Zaghloul rose to prominence in 1919 when he petitioned the British for independence at the Versailles Peace Conference. The British rejected his demands and exiled him to Malta, but a massive public backlash forced the British to allow him to return the following year, and Zaghloul became the premier spokesman for Egyptian nationalism. Zaghloul's efforts led to partial autonomy in 1922 when the British recognized Egypt as an independent state, but it would not be until 1936 that the occupation was lifted or until 1956 that the last British troops left Egyptian soil.

On the west side of the square overlooking the Corniche and the Eastern Harbour stands the half Moorish, half Edwardian **Cecil Hotel**. Built in 1930, the Cecil became modern Alexandria's most famous landmark after it was immortalized in Lawrence Durrell's romantic epic *The Alexandria Quartet*. Durrell actually stayed here for part of the time he worked on his masterpiece, but the fame it garnered partly as a result of the *Quartet's* success led to its being souped up to the extent that its original decadent charm is all but gone. Over the years, the Cecil has played host to many luminaries from Agatha Christie to Winston Churchill and according to legend, here British Officers made last minute alterations to their plans for the Battle of El Alamein in 1943. Sofitel Accor who assumed management the hotel in the early 1990's has done a fine job of restoring its pre-Revolution elegance, but one cannot help but feel that the atmosphere is not somehow manufactured.

Behind the statue and beyond the bus stops, stand yet more mystique laden landmarks, the Metropole Hotel and the patisseries Delices and Trianon. After being gutted in 1986, the **Trianon** has been restored to all its 1920's Art Nouveau glory as has the **Metropole Hotel** with which it shares the building. The Metropole was once a public sector office where Constantine Cavafy worked a day job. By night he often relaxed in the **Athineos Cafe**, where the Trianon is now located. A branch of the Athineos can still be found between the Ramleh tram station and the Corniche about 200 meters east of the Trianon on Iskander El Akbar Street.

While the Trianon is now a spanking new upscale restaurant and cafe favored by Egyptian elites who can again enjoy the good life as their grandparents did 50 years ago, the Athineos with its tawdry gilt decor, cheap Stellas and late night belly dancing parties harks back to the decadent free-wheeling Alexandria of the 1920's. Meanwhile the charmingly shabby Delices is about to undergo a major restoration of its own.

Rue Nebi Daniel

Just north of the Delices at the southwest corner of Saad Zaghloul Square is the Egyptian Tourist Authority office and the modest beginning of **Nebi Daniel Street**. Though you would never guess it by looking at it today, this was the site of one of classical Alexandria's most important landmarks, the **Caesareum**, and the beginning of the ancient **Street of the Soma**, Alexandria's main thoroughfare in antiquity that was supposedly lined with marble columns for its entire length.

Founded by Cleopatra as a temple in honor of Marc Antony, the **Caesareum** was unfinished when Alexandria fell to Octavian in 13 BC. He completed it in honor of himself and it remained an imperial temple until 354 when Constantius II converted it into a Roman church. But, before it could be consecrated, the Egyptian nationalist priest Athanasius held an Easter service in the temple as a snub to the Emperor who was less than tolerant of the Egyptian brand of Christianity. The Romans returned the insult by presenting it to Athanasius" rivals, the Arians. This to led to a great conflict between the Arians and the Orthodox which culminated in the violent demolition of the original Caesareum. Athanasius then built the Church of Saint Michael on the site which became the most important church in Alexandria. It survived the initial 7th century Arab invasions but eventually fell apart in 912.

Little is known about the building's appearance, but the prominent Jewish philosopher Philo remarked that "It is a piece incomparably above all others...full of choice paintings and statues with donatives and oblatives in abundance; and then it is beautiful all over with gold and silver." At its entrance stood two massive obelisks known as "Cleopatra's Needles." The two obelisks outlasted the church by almost 1,000 years but were given away to the British and the Americans in the 1870's. The obelisks had nothing to do with Cleopatra and were actually erected at Heliopolis around 1,500 BC and moved to Alexandria by the Romans 15 years after her death.

At the intersection with the major east-west thoroughfare of El Horreya, now graced with the presence of the Viennoise Patisserie on one corner and an Al Ahram Bookstore on the other, stood the gates of Hellenistic Alexandria which led to a splendid boulevard lined with marble columns. Just south of the intersection with El Horreya Street, stands a large, now idle **synagogue**, one of few remnants left behind by

CLEMENT OF ALEXANDRIA

The son of a wealthy Greek, **Titus Flavius Clement** *converted to Christianity after receiving a sophisticated Greek education. A typical Alexandrian, Clement was not satisfied to accept the Scriptures at literal face value and explored the compatibility of Christianity with Greek philosophy. He even went so far as to speculate that Socrates and Plato were forerunners of Christ as they, like the Old Testament and all that occurred before the coming of Jesus, were part of a divine preparation for the teachings of Christ. Well respected in Antioch and Jerusalem as well as Alexandria, Clement became the head of the Theological College in Alexandria, the world's most important Christian theological center at the time. He penned such seminal works as* **An Exhortation to the Greeks** *and* **Instruction to Christian Living** *before mysteriously disappearing during the persecutions of Emperor Septimus Severus in 210. Though his pupils like Origen continued to push the philosophical limits of Christianity, his liberal approach to study and interpretation was not adopted by the staunchly orthodox Coptic Church of Egypt. Clement of Alexandria is remembered on his feast day, December 5.*

one of the city's most important but now bygone communities. The **Mouseion** and the Great Library is also believed to have been located in this vicinity. Just a bit further south stands the **Mosque of Nebi Daniel**, thought by many to stand on the final resting place of Alexander the Great, though this remains to be proven. It holds the remains of Sufi Mohammed Daniel El Maridi for whom it is named, and not as many believe, those of the Prophet Daniel himself. Beyond the mosque, Nebi Daniel Street ends when it meets the ever chaotic El Gomhuriya Square.

Tahrir Square & Orabi Square

About a half kilometer east of Saad Zaghloul is downtown's second hub, **Tahrir Square**, the center of modern Alexandria until the city outgrew it around the time of the Revolution in 1952. Originally named *Places Des Consuls* for the foreign consulates and embassies that lined its avenues, the square later became known as Mohammed Ali Square for the majestic statue of Mohammed Ali that was its centerpiece. It was also site of the city's court houses (west side) and the **Bourse** (the southern end), where during a speech in 1954, the Muslim Brotherhood attempted to assassinate Gamal Abdel Nasser. Two years later, again at the Bourse, Nasser announced the nationalization of the Suez Canal to pay for the building of the Aswan High Dam. The decision led to the 1956 War and the expulsion from Egypt of thousands of foreign nationals, an event that greatly affected the character of Alexandria which had been home to tens of thousands of Greek, Italian, British, and Jewish merchants.

The Bourse has since been torn down and the grand buildings that once made this one of the most elegant squares in Egypt are now sadly dilapidated and neglected. 'The Square' as it was known 100 years ago is now overwhelmed with traffic and noise, and poor Mohammed Ali gets lost amongst bus fumes and cable wires, but with its bustling commercial activity, street-side cafes, and a colorful assortment of pedestrians Tahrir Square is very much worth a visit.

Off the north side of Tahrir Square is **Orabi Square**, named for the leader of the 1882 nationalist revolt that led to violent riots in Alexandria. Once site of the famous 'French Gardens' it is now a bus and tram depot consumed with traffic fumes and noise. At its Corniche end stands a neo-classical monument, the Egyptian Tomb of the Unknown Sailor.

Greco-Roman Antiquities Museum

5 El Mathaf Street (Tel. 03/482-5820). Hours: 9am-4pm daily. Admission: LE8.

A visit to the Greco-Roman Antiquities Museum-the oldest museum in Egypt-is a must for anybody interested in the history of ancient Alexandria or the Classical Age generally. The Hellenistic city is now lost beneath its modern descendant and the Mediterranean Sea, and most antiques were taken into private collections over the centuries that lapsed before the formation of this museum in 1891. Yet if your imagination can make it past the dull impression left by the monolithic gray coloring of the limestone statues and the building itself, this formidable collection of pharaonic, Greek, Coptic, and Roman relics provides a good illustration of the prosperity and genius of Alexandrian civilization in it heyday two thousands years ago.

The displays are exhibited according to facets of Egyptian history relating to Hellenistic Alexandria. It makes most sense to begin your tour by turning left upon entrance and working your way clockwise. The first hall contains numerous inscriptions of negligible interest if you do not read Greek. These quickly give way to some fascinating relics of the **Serapis Cult**, the national cult of Ptolemeic Alexandria that fused elements of Greek mythology with the Egyptian cults of Osiris and the Apis Bull. Among the most intriguing items in this corner of the museum are **death masks** used Romans in cult rituals; a giant bull dating to the reign of Roman Emperor Hadrian; and a representation of a **Grecofied Osiris** with Dionysian features. Somehow he exudes a bit less dignity than the old Osiris we know from Abydos and the Valley of the Kings in Thebes, and is not quite as divine.

Beyond the Serapis exhibits are three rooms in the corner featuring mummies, Sobek-related relics from Faiyoum, and pharaonic style statutes from Canopus (Abu Kir). Most intriguing are the exhibits (Room 9) relating to the Cult of Sobek's crocodile worship that include a **mummified crocodile** and relics from the Temple of Sobek in Faiyoum. The human mummies in Room 8 are quite remarkable for their realistic portraits, a style adopted by Copts in the Faiyoum during the first two centuries AD. Room 7 contains a handful of relatively ordinary pharaonic style statues that were excavated at Abu Kir but are believed to have originally come from Sais (a Late Period Delta capital) and Heliopolis.

The second major hall begins with a smattering of more **pharaonic style relics** (Room 10). Of particular interest are the mummified birds; Serapis-related statuettes of Osiris and the Apis Bull; and alabaster canopic jars used for storing the internal organs of deceased pharaohs. As you move into the next second portion of this hall (Room 11), the displays exhibit the fusion of Greek and pharaonic artistic styles that occurred during the Ptolemeic era. The crisp quality of the old pure pharaonic reliefs is clearly lost in translation as the Greeks clumsily attempted to adopt traditional Egyptian techniques. Among the examples here are the headless statue of woman in an Egyptian pose but with Greek features, and an awkward painting of a Greek woman in the company of Egyptian deities. Room 12 at the end of this northern hall features more typical

Greco-Roman portraits and statues. Among the subjects are Venus, Alexander, and other Ptolemeic figures, the identity of whom is not exactly clear.

Rooms 13, 14, and 15 feature a miscellaneous hodgepodge with little of merit except for **busts of Roman Emperors** (Hadrian and Caesar among others) in Room 14. On a humorous note, a caricature in Room 13 portrays an unnamed Roman Senator with a rat's head.

Rooms 16 and 17 contain mostly **Greco-Roman sculptures and statues**. Room 16 is full of archetypal Greek sculpture including Corinthian capitals and headless statues of Alexander, Venus, and some uniquely Alexandrian statues related to the Serapis Cult. With its Faiyoumi mummies and Egyptian-Greco funerary objects, Room 17 is a bit more interesting. Worth noting is the headless statue of **Christ Pantokrator** ("Christ as Royalty") a brutally resentful and sarcastic title given by Coptic Egyptians to the third century Roman Emperor, Diocletian, who presided over the greatest Roman persecution of Copts. Most fascinating is the **Ptolemeic mural** portraying a colorful and animate water scene. As an upper class Greek and his wife (or consort) relax under an awning, various fish, hippopotami, and other water creatures go about their business while oxen mindlessly turn a waterwheel.

In Room 18a the limestone sculptures give way to Hellenistic **terra cotta statuettes** placed in tombs of common citizens as a gesture of respect by their loved ones. Delicate with emotional, but dignified expressions, they capture the human spirit and provoke an emotional response that the expressionless statues of gods and emperors never could. Most of the finer terra cottas are native Alexandrian, while if you agree with Forster, those from Faiyoum are simply "stupid and vulgar." Also in Room 18 are several mosaics believed to come from the Serapis temple at Canopus (Abu Kir).

More terra cottas, this time from **Kom El Shoqafa** (the catacombs near Pompey's Pillar), can be found in Room 19. It also features funerary furniture and a beautiful mosaic from Chatby, east of modern downtown. Room 20 also contains numerous relics from the necropolis of Chatby including some fascinating painted tomb stones and a less than gorgeous representation of Bes, the god of music and dance.

Room 21 is interesting because it contains relics from the ancient necropolis of **Ibrahimiya**, a Hellenistic era Jewish community. Among the reliefs is an inscription in Aramaic, the language used by the early Jewish immigrants before Greek became their first tongue. Also worth checking out are the mummified birds from Abu Kir.

Of the mosaics, sculptures, and inscriptions from the **Temple of Serapis at Canopus** in Room 22, E. M. Forster complained in 1920, "Disappointing; better work than this tenth rate Hellenistic stuff must have existed at the great shrine." Given the wealth of Hellenistic Alexandria, he was surely correct, and given human nature, most of it found its way into private collections long before this museum collection was compiled in 1891.

Room 22a and 23 feature mostly frescoes, both Christian and pagan. Those of the Christian variety are fascinating precedents for iconography that developed in the Middle Ages. The need to express their religious convictions in vivid pictures was something the early Copts undoubtedly inherited from their pharaonic forefathers.

The largest exhibits are outside the building itself in the gardens. In the north garden the **Temple of Petesouchos** (a crocodile god) has been relocated from Faiyoum. Built in the middle of the Ptolemeic Era in 190 BC, it features the typical entrance pylon, a courtyard, a row of sphinxes and a second court leading to the sanctuary. Originally each of the three niches in the shrine held a mummified crocodile. The middle and left cavity each feature crocodile worship related frescoes. The south garden features two reconstructed rock tombs from the Chatby necropolis east of ancient Alexandria. Also in the gardens is a headless statue of Hercules, a large statue head of Marc Antony, and a smattering of other sculptures and statues.

If you are not altogether 'museumed out' by this time, take a few minutes to examine the Coptic exhibits in Rooms 1-5 on your way out. Besides hundreds of coins, there are some incredibly garish and ornate mummies and some first rate weavings from Akhmim in Upper Egypt. You can also pore over various inscriptions, pottery, and statues before passing on your way out, several columns from the monasteries of Saint Menas in the deserts west of Alexandria.

Cavafy Museum, *4 Sharm El Sheikh Street, off Sultan Hussein Street. Hours: 9am-2pm daily except Monday and from 6pm-8pm on Tuesday and Thursday. Admission: free.*

Constantine Cavafy was an obscure poet until E.M. Forster introduced him to the world by publishing some of his poems in his guidebook, *Alexandria, A History and a Guide.* The poet, whose tangy and melancholy poems are considered the most vivid portraits of Alexandria's seamy underside, lived here in this racy neighborhood from 1908 until his death in 1933. Only two of the rooms actually feature exhibits while the others are used by scholars.

Ras El Tin & Anfoushi

In antiquity, the Ras El Tin Peninsula and the neighborhood of Anfoushi was an island that was only joined with the mainland in Ottoman times. It was on the northeastern tip that the Ptolemies built their signature monument, the Pharos Lighthouse. The Lighthouse has been

ORIGEN OF ALEXANDRIA

*One of Christianity's most important early philosophers, **Origen** was also one of its strangest and most bizarre. A brilliant student of Clement, he became head of the Theological College after Clemant's passing in 215 and taught there for 28 years, further developing his mentor's Christian Platonism and emerging as orthodoxy's most dedicated and articulate anti-Gnostic. Always haunted by the guilt that he did not share his father's martyrdom, Origen eventually tried to purify himself by self-castration. This led to his demise as the Bishop of Alexandria disowned him and ordered his exile from Alexandria, which he willingly accepted.*

gone for a thousand years, but its Mamluki successor, Fort Qait Bey, as well as the ornate palace of Ras El Tin, and the colorful 17th century Ottoman neighborhoods of Anfoushi are worthy of an afternoon of exploration. To get to Anfoushi, walk west along the Corniche from Saad Zaghloul Square, or if you're not up for walking, hop on a Corniche minibus going west, or get on Tram #15 in Saad Zaghloul Square or Orabi Square.

Walking to Qait Bey from Saad Zaghloul, entails passing the stately looking **Abu El Abbas El Mursi Mosque**. Dedicated to a patron sufi saint of Alexandria's fishermen, it has been rebuilt as recently as 1943, but without corrupting the grace and beauty of the 16th century original.

Fort Qait Bey, *on Ras El Tin. Hours: 9am-2pm. Admission: LE12 general, LE6 students. Photography is not allowed inside the museum.*

The major attraction on the Ras El Tin Peninsula, Qait Bey's Fort was built on the site of the legendary **Pharos Lighthouse** that dominated Alexandria's landscape for 1,000 years. An ancient wonder of the world, the Lighthouse stood more than 400 feet after its completion in 280 BC, and became synonymous with Alexandria itself. Exactly what happened to the legendary landmark is unclear, but it is believed an earthquake in the early Islamic period, finally took it down. Though Qait Bey could never hope to replace what must have been one of the world's all time greatest buildings, his fort is still a handsome construction. Besides encouraging you to ponder one of the world's most famous bygone monuments, Qait Bey's Fort affords superb views of the Eastern Harbour the modest but colorful fishing fleet moored nearby. The interior features a modest museum recounting Alexandrian naval history, but emphasizes the Islamic and modern, and conspicuously ignores city's the Hellenistic roots.

Hydrobiological Museum, *Fort Qait Bey on Ras El Tin. Hours: 9am-2pm. Admission: LE1.*

Essentially a collection of very poor taxidermy, the Hydrobiological Museum catalogs marine life found in the Red and Mediterranean Seas. Always a good laugh for the hordes of Egyptian school children who pass through on their way to Fort Qait Bey on field trips is the male sea cow exhibit on which the phallus is the most, indeed only, prominent feature. If the price of admission goes any higher, it certainly won't be worth it.

Ras El Tin Palace & The Necropolis of Anfoushi

From Qait Bey, head west, or take the tram, along Ras El Tin Street two kilometers to the **Necropolis of Anfoushi** *(Admission: LE12. Hours: 9am-4pm)*. Though not nearly as impressive as the catacombs of El Kom El Shoqafa, these Roman crypts do feature some interesting last ditch (250 AD) Roman attempts at imitating Egyptian art. The tombs to the right feature awkward portraits of Egyptian deities and an assortment of ships and boats including some feluccas. There is also a ton of mostly Greek graffiti.

West of the Necropolis of Anfoushi are some quiet gardens where you can sit and enjoy a cool soda while admiring the ornate **Ras El Tin Palace**. The site of the Temple of Neptune in Roman times, it is now a naval headquarters used for state occasions and is off limits to visitors; you can admire it from afar, but keep in mind that authorities do not appreciate foreigners taking photographs. Originally built by Mohammed Ali in the beginning of the 19th century, it was a favorite summer retreat for Kings Fouad and Farouk who fled here during the July Revolution. When he abdicated here before boarding the royal yacht to sail into exile in July 1952, his last words to Mohammed Naguib, who was representing the Free Officers, were: "Your task will difficult. It's not easy you know, to govern Egypt." King Farouk wouldn't have known, but he never made a more true statement.

Roman Amphitheater

Youssef Street in Kom El Dikka just north of El Gomhuriya Square. Tel. 03/490-2904. Hours: 9am-4pm daily. Admission: LE6.

This elegant amphitheater was undiscovered until Polish archaeologists found it while excavating an Ottoman cemetery called Kom El Dikka in the 1950's. The only Roman theater in Egypt, it has marble seating for up to a thousand and mosaic forecourt. In Ptolemeic times this was the site of a pleasure garden known as Park of Pan and later became an upscale Roman residential neighborhood. That neighborhood is to the north of the theater and features a muddled assortment of arches and walls. It is currently under excavation and can only make you wonder what else lies beneath modern Alexandria.

SOUTH OF DOWNTOWN
Kormouz-Pompey's Pillar & the Catacombs of Kom El Shoqafa

The working class district of Kormouz is home to two of Alexandria's most famous Greco-Roman attractions, **Pompey's Pillar** and the **Catacombs of Kom El Shoqafa**. Here the ancient Egyptian village of **Rhakotis** was located prior to the founding of Alexandria in 325 BC. After the Greek city was founded, it became the site of some of the city's most important Ptolemeic institutions including the Serapeum, home to the Cult of Serapis. Modern Kormouz is a far cry from the fancy European quarters downtown near the river. Even in Forster's time, it was, "neither smart nor picturesque" and today many of its residents live in slum-like conditions. It is nevertheless a very lively sort of place buzzing with street life and open air markets. Visit Pompey's Pillar first and then proceed to the Catacombs. Further south, beyond the Catacombs, runs the **Canal of Mahmoudia**, completed under Mohammed Ali and named for the Ottoman Sultan at the time, it reestablished Alexandria's link with the Nile but is now a polluted eyesore.

To reach Kormouz and its main attractions on foot, follow tram lines from Tahrir Square south, or jump on tram #16. The walk is not especially interesting though you will get a good look at urban life in modern Egypt. You known you are getting close when you come to the large Islamic cemetery. Feel free to check it out if you're dressed modestly-which you should be anyway. You can also reach Kormouz also by hopping on buses #309 or #709, or by taxi – ask for *Amood El Suwary* (Pompey's Pillar in Arabic, LE3-5).

Pompey's Pillar, *in Kormouz several kilometers south of downtown. Admission: LE6 general, LE3 students. Cameras: LE150 for camera with flash or tripod.*

One of Alexandria's most visited sights, Pompey's Pillar really pales in comparison to the massive monuments of Cairo or Upper Egypt, yet it, and the area of its location are quite interesting. It's location in the poor quarters of Kormouz, corresponds to the site of **Rhakotis**, the ancient Egyptian village which predates the founding of Alexandria itself, and it was here that the hybrid cult of **Serapis** combined the cults of the Egyptian god of Osiris and that of Greek God Dionysys. Like so many landmarks, sites, and names in Alexandria, "Pompey's Pillar" is actually a misnomer. An engraving about three meters up on the 25 meter granite capital reads, "To the most just Emperor, the tutelary God of Alexandria, Diocletion the invincible: Postumus, prefect of Egypt." **Diocletian** was the Roman Emperor who presided over the greatest persecution of Egyptian Christians, and ruled until 303 AD. This monument is believed to have been constructed soon after his passing.

ATHANASIUS OF ALEXANDRIA

*Perhaps the most important of the early Copts was **Athanasius** (312-372) a staunch defender of orthodoxy in the face of Arianism and great proponent of the **Nicene Creed**. The Creed, which maintains that Jesus and the Lord are of one nature, "the essence of the Father," was agreed to at the Council of Nicea sponsored in 325 by Emperor Constantine in an effort to reconcile the increasing number of sects and factions emerging throughout the Christian world. Opposing Athanasius, the leading formulator and proponent of the Nicene Creed, was another Alexandrian, **Arian**, who deducted that as a child or infant, Christ was not of the same essence of God.*

Despite the passage of the Nicene Creed, factionalism continued to plague Christianity and Athanasius himself was forced out of his seat as Patriarch of Alexandria and into exile five times by the pro-Arians who found sympathy with the elite's of Constantinople and Antioch. Immensely popular throughout Egypt, it is testimony to the extent of his grass roots support that Athanasius was never betrayed to the pro-Arian authorities while in exile with Saint Antony in the Eastern Desert or in the Western Desert oasis of Kharga. He is remembered on the anniversary of his death, May 2.

Apart from the pillar, little remains intact, but to the west of it within the confines are believed to be the foundations of the temple for the **Cult of Serapis**, where sacred Apis bulls were interred, and to the north, a temple dedicated to the ancient Egyptian goddess, **Isis**, whom the Greeks believed to be an Egyptian incarnation of Aphrodite.

Catacombs of Kom El Shoqafa *are in Kormouz west of Pompey's Pillar. Make a hard right upon exiting Pompey's Pillar and proceed up the street straight for half a mile. The Catacombs will be on your left. Hours: 9am-4pm daily. Admission: LE12 general, LE6 students. Cameras: flash and video photography LE150.*

More fascinating than Pompey's Pillar are the spooky, and rather funky Catacombs of Kom El Shoqafa, a series of Roman-Egyptian tombs believed to date to the 2nd century. Notable more for the manner in which the native Egyptian theology and artistic styles were corrupted by Romans, it is as Forster noted, "more odd than beautiful" and certainly makes one appreciate the quality of work produced by the pharaonic Egyptians for 3,000 years prior. Most of the chambers contain simple, undecorated vaults, but the main attraction is the **central vestibule** where, what Forster dubbed, "artistic confusion" is most evident. Serpents manifest themselves as Hermes, Dionysys, and pharaonic monarchs, donning the royal crowns of Lower and Upper Egypt. Meanwhile Medusa guards the main chamber where rather sad looking characters resembling Anubis (with the jackal head) and Sobek (with the crocodile head) uncomfortably wear Roman armor while presiding over something meant to resemble pharaonic funeral rites.

Almost as quirky as the catacombs themselves is the story of their discovery in 1900. While excavating the site, a donkey, hitched to a cart, slipped into an enclosure while turning around. The enclosure turned out to be the top layers of the catacombs complex. On your way out, glance at the assortment of Roman sarcophogi and pillars before popping into the **Trianan "Museum"** for another, more elaborate version of the Roman-Egyptian funerary scene.

Nouzha Gardens & Zoo, *along the Mahmoudia Canal on Semouha Street, in Semouha. Take bus #41 from Misr Railway Station. Hours: 8am-4pm. Admission: 50 piasters each.*

Built on one of Khedive Ismail's private gardens in 1907, the serene **Zoological Gardens** do not feature much in the way of a zoo except for the foul (or is it fowl) mouthed parrots who blab an assortment of dirty words they learned from British soldiers more than forty years ago.

Originally part of the same complex, the luscious **Nouzha Gardens** is now a public park. In Ptolemeic times it was the Alexandrian suburb Eleusis whose residents included the prominent poet, Callimachus, who at one time was Librarian at the Mousieon. Nouzha was also the site of a battle in which a Roman army led by General Popillius stopped the invasion of a Syrian army, and in 640 the Arab Islamic conqueror Amr quartered his troops here. Originally developed by Ismail as private botanical gardens, the park opened to the public in 1907. As the plants and trees planted by Ismail grew into maturity, Forster noted that the gardens were, "most beautiful; if one could judge Alexandria by her gardens, one would do nothing but praise." A major focal point of Alexandrian social life in the first half of this century, Nouzha once housed a fancy Tavern on the Green type restaurant and its bandstand was the site of weekly public concerts by military bands and orchestras for the pleasure of the city's swankier classes of expatriates. The gardens are now somewhat unkempt and the classy eatery and bands are long gone; yet it remains a tranquil and pleasant spot in which to relax and ponder the Alexandria we'll never know.

Antoniadis Villa & Gardens, *south of Nouzha Gardens along Mahmoudia Canal. Hours: 8am-4pm. Admission: 50 piasters.*

Once owned by the wealthy Greek Antoniadis family, these stately gardens are littered with neo-Greco statuary that are of no historical or artistic value but nonetheless lend the grounds a baronial aura. Behind

GAMAL ABDEL NASSER

*Leader of the Free Officers and the 1952 July Revolution, **Gamal Abdel Nasser** was born on January 18, 1918 in the middle class Alexandrian district of Bacos where his father was a postal clerk. There Nasser was raised and he attended primary and secondary schools in El Attarine and Ras El Tin. At 15, his family moved to Cairo and upon graduation of secondary school he joined the military. In 1948 he became a hero in the 1948 Palestine War, and though the Arabs were soundly humiliated the experience woke Nasser to his Arab identity and the need for Arabs to reassert themselves.*

After leading the July Revolution, he became the first man of Egyptian stock to rule Egypt since the pharaohs. In 1954 he returned to Alexandria where, while giving a speech at the Bourse in Tahrir Square, he survived an assassination attempt. Two years later, again at the Bourse, Nasser announced the nationalization of the Suez Canal, a move that triggered the 1956 War and the removal of the last British troops from Egypt. It made Nasser a hero throughout the Third World. He continued to rule until his untimely death (he was only 52) in 1970. At his funeral in Cairo, recognized by the Guinness Book of World Records as the world's largest, more than 5 million Egyptians poured into streets of Cairo to pay homage.

the field is a Roman era tomb like those of Anfoushi, but it is not open to the public.

Museum of Fine Arts, *1 Menasce Street, Muharram Bay. Tel. 03/493-6616. Hours:8am-2pm daily except Friday. Admission: free.*

Also known as the Hassan Sobhi Museum of Fine Arts, this museum features a modest but interesting collection of 20th century Egyptian art.

East of Downtown

Royal Jewelry Museum, *21 Ahmed Yehia Street in Glym. From Saad Zaghloul, take tram #2 to Qasr El Safa. Tel. 03/586-8348. Hours: 9am-4pm and on Friday from 9am-11:30am and from 1:30pm-4pm. Admission: LE10.*

Housed in a richly ornate villa that merits a visit in itself, this impressive museum contains jewelry, a fascinating stamp collection, and other personal effects that belonged to the royal family before Farouk had to leave them behind when the Free Officers forced him into exile in July 1952.

Montazah Palace Gardens, *Montazah. Open 24 hours. Admission: LE2.*

Once the premier pleasure garden for Egypt's royal family, and now the playground of Egypt's rich and famous, the Montazah Gardens were originally developed by Khedive Abbas II who also built the fabulously ornate Montazah Palace and distinguished by its famous clock tower. It is now a state guest house and several upscale hotels are located on the grounds, the most impressive of which, the Salamlek, is well worth a peak inside. The gardens are still fantastically colorful and well maintained and make for a very pleasant stroll. E.M. Forster worked here at a make-shift Red Cross hospital during World War I.

NIGHTLIFE & ENTERTAINMENT
Bars

The **Fouad Bar** *in the Salamlek Hotel* is by far the classiest and most opulent drinking establishment in Alexandria. The converted reception of a royal guest house built in the 1890's, its management has gone to great lengths to preserve its original elegance and style; the bar even has tables used by King Farouk to keep his cigarettes and cigars. It's very pricey with a LE25 minimum charge and major credit cards are accepted.

At the other extreme, the **Cap D'or** *on Adib Street off the northeastern corner of Tahrir Square* is a tawdry relic of the same age and is so casually friendly that the bar man will probably drink with you. From the portraits of past owners and horse racing memorabilia from the 1930's to the teak cash register, you get the sense that the place hasn't changed in fifty years, and it is showing its age, but the aura of the "old Alex" lingers here and its wonderfully intimate.

With dim lighting, cracked gilded moldings, and a raucous clientele, the **Athineos** is definitely seedy and has an authentic-hole-in-the-wall ambiance that one doesn't find in the swankier hotel bars.

On Abdel Kadri Ragab Street in Roushdi, is the **Portugal Club**, a drinking and eating establishment run by and for foreign expatriates living in Alexandria. The ambiance is cozy and homey and it's a great place to meet residents with insights into the city. During fall and winter, there are often dance parties on weekends.

In the Cecil Hotel, **Monty's Bar** is a gallant attempt to recreate the ambiance of days gone by, but the muzak absolutely ruins it. Also, for some reason, it always seems empty.

Along the Corniche, many of the cafes-restaurants like the Omar Khayyam serve beer indoors but not out, and many feature live Arabic music during the summer.

Nightclubs

The **Cecil Hotel**, **Ramada Renaissance**, **Montazah Sheraton**, and **San Giovanni** all feature Egyptian style nightclubs where for LE80 and up you will be treated to a set meal and five hours of live music and belly dancing beginning around 11pm. A more raucous and colorful version of the same basic program can be had at the seedy **Crazy Horse in Athineos** *on Ramleh Square*; LE50 gets you dinner and a full night's entertainment, (drinks and prostitute not included).

As for discos, the **Black Gold** in the Ramada Renaissance and the **Aquarius** in the Sheraton are the most popular and charge at least a LE25 minimum charge that goes towards one or two drinks depending on whether you are drinking beer or liquor; smart dress may be required.

Performing Arts

Sayed Darwish Theater, *22 Fouad Street opposite Cinema Royale. Tel. 03/482-5106, 483-9578.*

The old epicenter of Alex's cultural life still features a variety of performing arts including dance, ballet, opera, and music. Call for information.

Conservation de Musique d'Alexandria, *90 El Horreya Street. Tel. 03/ 483-5068.*

Films & Movie Theaters

As in Cairo, major theaters show block buster western films, albeit six months to a year late, in addition to the latest Egyptian hits. Check in English language publications like *The Egyptian Gazette, Alexandria Today, The Middle East Times,* and *Al Ahram Weekly.* Cultural centers (listed in the "Practical Information" section below) also show foreign language films. Call them or check in publications such as *Egypt Today* or *The Middle East Times* for information. The **Cinema Club** meets each Sunday at 6:30pm at Pharaoh's Hall for showings and discussions of Arabic and foreign language films. The **Film Club** at L'Atelier also sponsors film showings.

SPORTS & RECREATION

The Beach & Water Sports

Commenting on Alexandria's beaches in 1937, Major C. S. Jarvis noted disappointingly, "The bathing is supposed to be excellent, but of late years the sea has become heavily impregnated with Jockey-club scented brilliantine, and there is a definite film of hair oil, sunburn lotion and face powder on the surface of the waves." Well, if that was in 1937 it doesn't take much to figure that today's Alexandrian beaches might just be less than pristine. Nevertheless, the city remains the country's top seaside resort, attracting thousands upon thousands of Cairenes annually, with summer being the high season.

For westerners the beaches are hardly worth the trouble of the crowds and the inevitable hassles, especially for women, who can be the object of

some rather unpleasant attention-especially when wearing an even remotely revealing swimsuit.

If you insist on beaching it, the beaches of **Maamura** (50pt entrance)
and **Montazah** 15 kilometers east of downtown Alex are your best bet. The
beaches along the Corniche between downtown and Montazah such as
Caesar, **Cleopatra** and **Glym** and usually overcrowded and quite dirty but
during the off season (not summer) you may be able to stake out a
relatively nice piece of beach. Hawkers usually sell drinks and food and
umbrellas can be rented as well. About twenty kilometers west of
Alexandria the communities of **Hannoville** and **Agami** are the equivalent
of the Hamptons in that they are a playground for Egypt's rich and
famous. There are beaches here which tend to be cleaner and less
crowded than in Alex itself.

SHOPPING

Alexandria is not known for its oriental handicrafts and souvenirs,
but it is a gold mine for **antiques**. In particular the district of **Atterine** is
known for its second hand shops and antique dealers. When Jews, Greeks,
Italians and other "foreigners" emigrated in the 1950's they left personal
belongings and articles behind, many of which had been in their families
for generations and but have since found their way to these shops. Search
around and you will find all sorts of treasures from old china and
silverware to fancy lacquered furniture inlaid with mother-of-pearl.

A dense network of small streets and alleys, Atterine stretches from
El Misr Station to Midan Tahrir. Most dealers are located off the major
streets of El Metawalli and Salah Salem which links Tahrir Square with
Metawalli Street. Most stores open from 9 or 10 am and close for lunch
between 2 and 4pm. Some of them reopen in the evening. Listed below
are some antique dealers:

Nahas Antiques, *corner of Attarine and Sheikh Aly El Leithy streets.*

Omar Antiques, *across the street from Nahas Antiques on the corner of
Attarine and Sheikh Aly El Leithy Streets* The Omar family has been dealing
in antiques since the 1930's and now owns some twenty-five shops in
Alexandria and Cairo. This shop is for experienced and well-endowed
antique collectors-most items start at half a million Egyptian pounds.

At the joining of El Sawaleh and Attarine streets are four well-known
antique shops, three owned by the **Moussa family** and one, **Au Petite
Musee**, is owned by the Omar family.

Two shops that deal in replicas are **P.A.T.C.H.O. Reproductions and
Antiques** *on St. Youssef Maghariah Street*; and **Shouman Reproductions
Gallery** *at the corner of St. Youssef Maghariah and Sheikh El Leithy streets.*

There are also dozens of second-hand shops and used-everything
dealers in this same area. For more Khan El Khalili type goods, head to

Salah Salem, off Tahrir Square and Nebi Daniel Street. There are also shopping malls in the Ramada Renaissance and Sheraton hotels in Montazah.

EXCURSIONS & DAY TRIPS

El Alamein

Site of the famous 1942 battle that saved Egypt and the Suez Canal from the Nazis, **El Alamein** is 105 kilometers west of Alexandria and easily visited in a day. Attractions include a museum with extensive exhibits featuring maps, uniforms, weaponry, and other memorabilia from the battle; a Commonwealth cemetery; and two monuments dedicated to the memory of German and Italian troops who fell at the battle which claimed 12,000 dead and 70,000 wounded. The travel agencies listed below in the "Practical Information" section sometimes offer deluxe coach tours for about $60 per person. Alternatively, you can hire a taxi for about LE150-200 which isn't a bad deal if you can split the cost amongst a group. Should you want to stay the night, there are several modest hotels at El Alamein itself and a fancier one 25 kilometers further west at Sidi Abdel Rahman.

Abu Kir

Just east of Montazah, **Abu Kir Bay** can be reached by hopping on any service going east from Montazah on the Corniche or by taxi (LE20 one-way) from downtown. There are no sights at Abu Kir, but it is significant as the site where Lord Nelson whipped Napoleon's fleet in 1798, forcing the Corsican to abandon Egypt and his dreams of usurping Britain's Asian Empire. Though Napoleon was cut off from France with no chance of mounting any threat to India, his land forces did route a British land invasion at Abu Kir a year after his naval defeat. Today Abu Kir is rather drab but the **Xephiron** fish restaurant is considered amongst the best in Egypt.

El Rashid

Known to westerners as "Rosetta" of Rosetta Stone fame, this now dilapidated seaside town was Egypt's main port for 1,000 years during Arab and Turkish times before Alexandria was revived by Mohammed Ali in the 19th century. Today its main attractions are the Ottoman-era buildings distinguished by their fine mashrabia windows. The most impressive, Bait Qili has been turned into a museum. Buses and service leave Alexandria hourly during the day from Misr Station and there are also hourly trains from Misr and Sidi Gabr stations.

Wadi Natrun

The historic **Monasteries of Wadi Natrun** are approximately 80 kilometers south of Alexandria and make for an excellent day excursion for those interested in early Christian history. Situated in a quasi-oasis west of the Delta off the Alex-Cairo Desert Road, these monasteries offered refuge to early Coptic leaders in need of protection from Roman persecution during the 4th, 5th, and 6th centuries.

Because the four monasteries are spread over more than 20 kilometers off main bus and service routes, you need private transportation or a taxi to reach them. Talk to the listed travel agents to see if they may be organizing coach trips from Alexandria; otherwise they will arrange a private car for about LE300 for the whole day. You can also hire a taxi off the street: LE150-200 is a reasonable price after bargaining. To spend the night in Wadi Natrun, you must get permission in advance from the residence offices in Cairo. See the "Wadi Natrun" section below for details.

PRACTICAL INFORMATION

Banks and Currency Exchange

Upscale hotels like the Cecil and the Sheraton feature exchange bureaus with extended hours.

• **American Express**, *26 El Horreya Street in the Eyeress Travel office (Tel. 03/ 800-617), exchanges money and traveler's cheques, holds mail, and travel agency services. Hours: 9am-1pm &5-6:30pm Sunday-Thursday, closes at 1pm Fridays and Saturdays.*

• **Bank of Alexandria**, *Saad Zaghloul Street off Saad Zaghloul Square. Hours: 8:30am-2pm.*

• **Thomas Cook**, *15 Saad Zaghloul Square. Tel. 03/482-7830. Hours: daily 8am-5pm. Offers travel agency services in addition to changing money and traveler's cheques.*

• **Western Union Money Transfer**, *281 El Horreya Street, Sporting (district). Tel. 03/420-2312, 420-1148.*

Bookstores

• **Al Ahram**, *10 El Horreya Street on the corner with Nebi Daniel across from Viennoise Patisserie. Tel. 03/483-4000. Hours: 9am-4pm daily.* Offers the largest selection of English language publications and books including history, literature, and an assortment of textbooks in addition to the usual smattering of guidebooks, coffee table photo collections, and Naguib Mahfouz. Some newspaper and magazines are also sold.

• **Book Center of Alexandria**, *49 Saad Zaghloul Street. Tel. 03/483-2925*

• **Dar El Mostakbal**, *32 Safiya Zaghloul Street. Tel. 03/483-2452*

• **Egyptian Cultural Group**, *10 Ahmed Alfy Street, San Stefano. Tel. 03/587-1453*
• **International Language Institute Bookshop**, *18 Abdel Hamid El Dib Street, Tharwat. Tel. 03/586-6388*
• **Nile Christian Bookshop**, *4 Anglican Church Street, Attarine*
• **Ramada Bazaar Bookshop**, *Ramada Renaissance Hotel, 544 El Geish Street, Sidi Bishr. Tel. 03/549-0935. Hours: 9am-midnight*

Cultural Centers
Actively promoting various forms of culture from different parts of the world, the centers sponsor exhibitions, concerts, film showings, lectures, and sometimes language classes. Listed below are some of the more active ones. Check with *Egypt Today* or the centers themselves for information about current goings on.
• **American Cultural Center**, *3 Pharana Street. Tel. 03/482-1009.* Sponsors film showings and runs replays of newscasts from the States. It also operates a library and organizes language classes.
• **L'Atelier**, *8 Victor Bassili Street. Tel. 03/482-0526.* Call for information about Film Club movie showings and discussions.
• **British Council**, *9 Batalsa Street, in Bab Sharqi. Tel. 03/482-0199.* Operates one of the better libraries in Alex and also sponsors film showings, lectures, concerts, and language courses.
• **Egyptian Anfoushi Cultural Center**, *Ras El Tin Street by the Eastern Harbour. Tel. 03/804-805. Hours: 9:30am-1:30pm & 5:30pm-8:30pm daily except Friday.*
• **French Cultural Center**, *30 Nebi Daniel Street. Tel. 03/492-0804.* Best known for French films and French language courses.
• **Goethe Institute**, *10 Batalsa Street in Azarita. Tel. 03/483-9870.* Sponsors an assortment of concerts, exhibitions, films, and lectures in addition to offering German and Arabic language courses.

Emergencies
• **Police**: *Tel. 122*
• **Fire**: *Tel. 180*
• **Ambulance**: *Tel. 123*
• **Alexandria International Hospital**: *8 Mustafa Kamel, Semouha. Tel. 03/422-5017, 424-2454*
• **El Mowasa Hospital**: *El Horreya Road in El Hadra. Tel. 03/421-2885/6*
• **German Hospital**: *56 Abdel Salam-Arif Street in Saba Pasha District. Tel. 03/588-1806*

Passports & Visas
    Passport Office, *28 Talaat Harb Street. Tel. 03/482-0422. Hours: 8:30am-2pm and 7-9pm daily, 10am-1pm Fridays.*

Photography and film development
    Kodak, *Safiya Zaghloul just north of Elite Restaurant. Hours: 9am-10pm daily.*

Post and courier services
• **Post Office**, *Misr Station, Ramleh Square, and Iskander El Akbar Street*
F · ederal Express, *281 El Horreya Street, Sporting (district). Tel. 03/420-2312, 420-1148*

Travel Agents
• **Misr Travel**, *28 Saad Zaghloul Street off Saad Zaghloul Square. Tel. 03/480-9617, 480-8776*
• **Thomas Cook**, *15 Saad Zaghloul Street. Tel. 03/482-8077, 483-5118*
• **Bon Voyage Tours**, *12 Salah Salem Street. Tel. 03/480-9043*
• **Cosmos Tours**, *37 Salah Salem Street Tel. 03/482-9016*

Telephones & Faxes
    24 hour telephone centrale, *Midan Ramleh & Misr Train Station.* Most hotels can place domestic and international calls and four and five star establishments usually offer fax, telegram, and telex services as well.

Tourist Information
    Egyptian Tourist Authority, *Saad Zaghloul Square. Tel.03/807-611, 807-985. Misr Train Station. Tel. 03/492-5985. Hours: 8am-6pm daily.* Travel agencies and hotel personnel may also be able to provide assistance.

Tourist Police
    Stations: *Montazah Palace, Tel. 03386-3804; the Ampitheater, Tel.03/490-6273; Greco-Roman Museum, Tel. 03/482-8912; Midan Saad Zaghloul, Tel. 03/807-611*

THE MONASTERIES OF WADI NATRUN

Lying just west of the Cairo-Alex Desert Road, 90 kilometers south of Alexandria, the **monasteries of Wadi Natrun** are among the oldest in the world, and for centuries was the most important theological center in Egypt. The area of Wadi Natrun itself is a mini-oasis that Egyptians have inhabited since the dawn of history and by the 3rd century AD, Christian hermits and acetics began moving here to escape the distractions and dangers of life in Roman-occupied Egypt. Monasticism was actually founded by Saint Antony in the Eastern Desert on the Red Sea, but Wadi Natrun emerged as the center of Coptic monasticism and the focal point for theological debate and the formation of doctrine and dogma.

It has remained important ever since and as recently as the 1970's the Coptic Pope Shenouda was forced into house arrest here by President Sadat. There are four main monasteries that pilgrims and interested travelers come to Wadi Natrun to visit. Founded in the 4th and 5th centuries, they have been rebuilt and expanded continuously ever since.

Practicalities

Wadi Natrun is usually visited as a day trip from Alexandria or Cairo. It is possible to get here by public transport, but getting around the monasteries themselves, which are spread over two dozen square kilometers requires private transport. Most travel agents in Cairo and Alexandria can arrange a car, usually for about LE300 a day, and sometimes they organize group coach trips in which case the fee for person is about $50-60.

There are restrictions on staying, or even visiting some of the monasteries. To arrange to stay overnight you must make arrangements at the monasteries by calling the monasteries at the following numbers in Cairo: **Deir El Anba El Bishoi**, *Tel. 02/591-4448*; **Deir El Suriani**, *Tel. 02/929-658*; **Deir El Baramus**, *Tel. 02/922-775*; **Deir El Abu El Makar**, *Tel. 02/770-614*. To visit Deir Abu El Makar at all you must call in advance to get permission and Deir El Suriani does not allow women visitors at all, period. The others can be visited during the day except during holy seasons such as Lent and the the 43 days before Christmas.

The Monasteries

Deir El Anba El Bishoi, *10 kilometers off the Alex-Cairo Desert Road by way of a paved road.*

According to tradition it was founded by Bishoi whose body in the crypt is said to remain fully intact. The monastery itself contains five chapels, and that named for Bishoi is the oldest, and features som ebeautifully carved wooden heikals.

Named for its 8th century Syrian founder, **Deir El Suriani** is half a kilometer from El Bishoi's and is said to contain a lock of hair belonging to Mary Magdelene. The main church is the **Church of the Virgin** that features a beautiful medieval heikal and an amazing "Door of Prophesies" inlaid with ivory. Women are not allowed to enter this monastery.

The first of the remote monasteries is that of **Deir Anba Baramus**, four kilometers north of Anba El Bishoi's. Still very isolated, it features some colorful alters and icons, but was itself recently rebuilt, and is structurally uninteresting.

Deir Abu Makar is the farthest and oldest of the Wadi Natrun monasteries having been founded in the late 4th century by Street Makarius. It contains the remains of dozens of important martyrs and Coptic popes and now concentrates its efforts on agriculture.

THE DELTA

TANTA & THE MOULID OF SAYED EL BADAWI

The city of **Tanta**, *almost 100 kilometers north of Cairo in the western Delta,* is Egypt's fourth largest city and is synonymous with the biggest religious festival in Egypt and the second biggest gathering of Muslims in the world after the Haj itself, the **Moulid of Sayed El Badawi**. Badawi came to Tanta in the 13th century from Moroco as a representative of the Iraqi based Rifayah Sufi order and proceeded to found his own, the Ahmediya, that became one of the most popular in Egypt.

The Moulid, which is a festival that commemorates his birth, is held annually in October after the cotton harvest and attracts upwards of two million faithful who converge on his mausoleum to pray, dance zikr, and celebrate. The celebrations last eight days and end with the **Layla Kibeera**, "the Great Night" when members of the Ahmediya parade about the city, their banners unfurled.

The moulid is one of the most intense experiences anybody can have anywhere and you can forget about finding accommodation so it's best to make it a day trip from Cairo or Alexandria. If you manage to attend, be wary of your belongings and physical well-being. Women should be especially careful as unwanted groping or worse is unfortunately not uncommon.

ZAGAZIG & THE RUINS OF BUBASTIS

Apart from its funky name, **Zagazig** is a fast growing industrial and education center 80 kilometers northeast of Cairo, that is draws travelers and scholars because of its location on the sites of the ancient **temples of Bubastis** where shrines were dedicated to feline avenger goddess, Bastet. Located off Mostafa Kamel Street, the site is currently under excavation and closed to the public.

Tanis

Roughly 250 kilometers northeast of Cairo, the modern hamlet of **San El Hagar** straddles a ruined ancient city known by its Greek name, **Tanis**. Founded by the Babylonian Hyksos pharaohs who occupied Egypt between 1674-1567 BC, Tanis later became the ancestral home to the 19th and 20th Dynasty **Ramessid** lines of pharaohs that included of course, Rames II, arguably the greatest of the New Kingdom rulers. Used as a port city, Tanis is now largely ruined and most of the site is closed due to archaeological work. It is virtually inaccessible by public transport unless you're willing to spend hours and hours getting on and off service taxis.

THE NORTH COAST WEST OF ALEXANDRIA

MARAQIA

Fifty kilometers west of Alexandria, **Maraqia** is a gated beach community with chalets, villas and apartments for rent and sale. Within the confines are dozens of shops, restaurants, and recreational facilities, including a kilometer long beach. Call *03/991-313* for information. Prices for a double room or chalet begin at LE150 a night.

EL ALAMEIN

In June 1942, on this inauspicious piece of beach 105 kilometers west of Alexandria, the Axis forces' Afrika Korps under the command of **Erwin** ("the Desert Fox") **Rommel** and the Allied Commonwealth forces led by **Field Marshal Montegomery** faced off in what has been termed the turning point in the European theater of World War II. Indeed after the Allied Victory that claimed 11,000 dead and 70,000 wounded, British Prime Minister Churchill remarked, "Before El Alamein, we had not won a major battle; after El Alamein, we never lost another one."

The site of El Alamein now features a substantial War Museum (open daily 8am-6pm, LE5 general admission, LE2.50 students) with dislays of maps, unfiorms, weapons and other memorablia. On the east side of the El Alamein town, the Commonwealth War Cemetery the forrest of more than 7,000 tombstones marking the graves of soldiers from all over the Commonwealth is a moving sight indeed. About 8 kilometers east of the El Alamein overlooking the sea is the German Memorial, while the graceful Italian Memorial of Marble is another 5 kilometers on.

For accommodations & food, try:

THE ATIC HOTEL *(Tel. 03/950-717) 15 kilometers east of El Alamein has upscale rooms for $55-100. Visa accepted.*

More a beachside resort than battlefield companion, the Atic has comfortable and spacious rooms. There is also a nice beach, swimming pool, and a lovely fish restaurant.

EL AMANA HOTEL *by the Museum* has simple singles and double with no frills (no air-conditioning for example) for LE20. There is also a modest restaurant.

MARSA MATROUH

Famed since antiquity for its pristine beaches, where Cleopatra allegedly took a dip or two in her birthday suit, **Marsa Matrouh** has unfortunately fallen victim to the same disease that has befallen the rest of Egypt: concrete. Also the beaches are so crowded these days, that they're difficult to enjoy at all, especially for foreign women who attract all sorts of unwanted attention. So for most foreign travelers, Marsa Matrouh is a nothing more than a handy break on a trip to Siwa with pleasant weather and good seafood.

ARRIVALS & DEPARTURES

By Bus

There are two bus stations; one on Iskandariya on the outer parts of town and one downtown. From both stations, numerous buses leave daily for Alexandria and at least three or four leave for Cairo. There is usually one or two buses to Siwa (3-4 hours, LE10)that leave at 7:30am and 2 or 3pm.

By Service

Service taxis come and go from the main bus station. When there there is enough demand, one or two might go to Siwa, but there's no way to tell when. About a dozen probably leave for Alexandria (LE10) everyday.

By Train

There is a train link between Marsa Matrouh and Alexandria, but it's painfully slow and usually takes more than six hours. The scenery en route is quite picturesque and costs LE20 for a second class seat with air-conditioning.

ORIENTATION

Restaurants, hotels, and the beach itself can be found on the Corniche, while most practical needs can be met on El Gala'a Street one block inland. The other main drag is Iskandariya Street which links the bus stop and the main road out of town with the Corniche; it's lined with restaurants.

GETTING AROUND TOWN

Walking should do, otherwise there are local taxis and even service.

WHERE TO STAY

BEAU SITE HOTEL, *El Sha'ata Street. Tel. 03/934-012. Fax 03/933-319. Rates: $60-80 single, $75-90 double. Credit cards: Visa.*

It's the most luxurious and expensive hotel in Marsa Matrouh, but for the money, it's overpriced; especially in summer when they force you to take dinner (LE45) here as well. In any case, it's still the best hotel and rooms are clean and comfortable with air-conditioning, phones, television, and nice bathrooms. The more expensive rates are for summer.

NEGRESCO HOTEL, *the Corniche. Tel. 03/934-492. Rates: $55-70 single, $70-85 double. Credit cards; Visa.*

Its Corniche location and clean rooms make it an excellent choice but like others it's pricey in the summer. In the winter, you can negotiate rates below the listed prices.

ROYAL PALACE HOTEL, *Corniche. Tel. 03/934-295. Rates: LE30-60 single, LE40-70 double.*

With the name, you might expect the second coming of Montazah or the Cairo Marriott, when in fact it's a modern skyscraper monstrosity. Still, for the rates, it's one of the best deals in Marsa Matrouh with some excellent views and clean rooms that come with private baths, televisions and balconies.

WHERE TO EAT

There are dozens of small moderate restaurants in Marsa Matrouh , most of which specialize in fish. The **Panayotis Greek Restaurant** *on Iskandariya Street* is a Greek-run establishment that has been going since the 1920's and will feed you a hearty fish meal for under LE25. It is also one of the few establishments selling beer.

The **Mansour Fish Restaurant** *by the Mina House Hotel off Tahrir Street* is another seafood house, only with its blaring music videos it attracts noisy crowds of *shebab* (youth).

For cheaper chow try the **Alexandria Tourist Restaurant** *on Iskandariya Street* across from the Riviera Palace Hotel. They will fill you up with tasty roast chicken and other favorites for about LE10.

There are also lots of cheap eats around the bus station.

SEEING THE SIGHTS

The **Folklore Museum** *next to the Tourist Office on the Corniche is free* and contains a small collection of Bedouin artifacts including some clothing, a tent, and some tools. The hours are not set.

Three kilometers west of town, the very modest **Rommel Museum** is situated in some caves that the Desert Fox apparently used during the Battle of El Alamein. The caves where Rommel made his plans and camped out, and where the museum is located, is more interesting in itself than the exhibits which are quite skimpy. There are some military uniforms, photos, and maps, but not much more. During the summer it opens from 9:30am-4pm and closes during the winter, but the folks at the Tourist Office may be able to open it for you.

Nearby to the east is **Rommel's Beach**, where the old Fox supposedly used to take his morning dip. It is now a popular swimming beach with Egyptians during the summer but during the winter when nobody's around, it makes for a very pleasant, if cool stroll.

PRACTICAL INFORMATION

Banks & Currency Exchange

The **National Bank of Egypt**, *El Matar Street two blocks in from the Corniche. Hours: 9am-2pm Sunday-Thursday.*

Banque Misr *is on El Gala'a Street two blocks inland in the center of town. Hours: 9am-2pm Sunday-Thursday.*

Emergencies
• **Police**: *Tel. 122 (Tourist Police are next to the Egyptian Tourist Authority on the Corniche)*
• **Ambulance**: *Tel. 123*

Post Services

Post Office, *El Sha'ata Street block inland from the Corniche. Hours: 9am-3pm daily except Friday.*

Telephones, Telex, & Fax

24 hour telephone centrale, *El Sha'ata Street off the Corniche across from the Post Office.*

Tourist Information

Egyptian Tourist Authority, *the Governorate building on the Corniche next to the Folklore Museum. Hours: 9am-6pm or later during the summer.*

17. THE SUEZ CANAL ZONE

Attempts have been made to link the Red and Mediterranean seas since ancient times, when **Pharaoh Necho II** (610-595 BC) almost completed a canal connecting the Red Sea with the Nile Delta through the Great Bitter Lake in the **Isthmus of Suez**. According to Herodotus more than 100,000 workers perished working on the project, which was not completed until Persian occupation a century later. The Ptolemies and Romans refined the system and it remained in use until the 8th century when it was plugged in the course of civil war within the Arab world.

The canal remained dormant until the 19th century. Napoleon was eager to build a direct link to the Mediterranean but his engineers miscalculated that the Mediterranean was ten yards higher than the Red Sea and predicted that any canal would lead to catastrophic flooding. But in the 1840's a French civil servant, **Ferdinand de Lesseps**, discovered that Napoleon's calculations were indeed wrong and came up with his own plan which he submitted to the Egyptian ruler, Khedive Said Pasha. Said Pasha signed on and in 1869 the Canal opened to great fanfare. It once again made Egypt the major strategic crossroads it had been before the discovery of new shipping lanes made it redundant as a hub for overland caravans in the 16th century.

But the Suez Canal was a mixed blessing. Khedives Said and Ismail spent Egypt into bankruptcy financing their share and were forced to sell out to the British who used the Canal's security as a pretext for occupying the country until 1956 when Nasser nationalized it. The nationalization sparked war between Egypt and the coalition of Israel, France and Britain. Egypt was soundly defeated militarily and the cities of Suez, Port Said, and Ismailia were heavily damaged, but international pressure forced the coalition to withdraw and for the first time, the Canal became completely under Egyptian control.

Over the next 25 years the Canal Zone cities bore the brunt of the Egyptian-Israeli wars and were bombed to destruction by the Israelis after

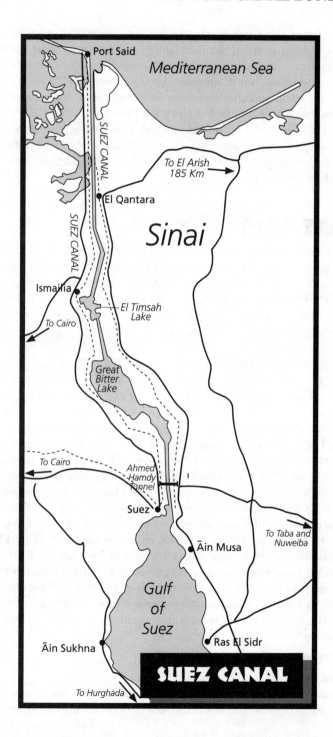

they occupied the Sinai during the '67 Six Day War. In October 1973, Egyptian forces stunned the Israelis by successfully crossing the Canal. The Israelis recovered and successfully established bridgeheads on the Canal's west banks, but disengagement agreements in '73 and '74 led to their withdrawal and the beginning of the peace process which culminated in the 1979 Egyptian-Israeli Peace Treaty.

In 1975 the Canal reopened and today the revenues it brings in are one of Egypt's primary sources of hard currency and the rebuilt cities of Port Said, Ismailia, and Suez are Egypt's most important commercial ports after Alexandria.

PORT SAID

Tucked in the northeastern corner of Africa, **Port Said** is an infant city by Egyptian standards, founded only in 1860 when work began on the Suez Canal. Named for Khedive Said Pasha under whose watch construction of the Canal began, Port Said once enjoyed a raffish reputation as the Mediterranean's most decadent port and was plagued by unchecked smuggling, prostitution, rampant corruption, and every other imaginable vice.

After the 1956 Suez War largely destroyed it, Port Said's character underwent considerable changes. In addition to completely rebuilding the city, Nasser expelled en masse the city's once substantial expatriate community and nationalized all foreign interests; he also implemented a strict regime of law and order. Today corruption and smuggling still thrive, but the once prominent prostitutes and hashish dealers have disappeared though a few old buildings with their New Orleans style verandahs still hint at Port Said's seamy free-wheeling past.

Made a duty free port in 1978, Port Said has become synonymous in Egypt with consumerism. Its streets are lined with shops selling brand name western clothes, appliances, and electronics that attract upper and middle class Cairenes by the bus load. However, there is little besides the Canal itself and charming late 19th century architecture to attract sightseeing travelers. Several modest museums feature exhibits about the port's short and turbulent history, namely its opening and the wars of '56 and '73. A wealthy, well maintained and relatively sane city, Port Said makes for a nice breather from Cairo – and the seafood is excellent.

ARRIVALS & DEPARTURES
By Boat

Many passenger cruise liners passing through the Suez Canal stop in Port Said, but there are not ferry routes between Port Said and other

Egyptian destinations. You may be able to hitch a ride on a ship to Haifa or other Mediterranean destinations but it's not easy or quick, nor cheaper than flying from Cairo. Inquire at shipping agencies along El Gomhuriya Street or check with the Egyptian Tourist Authority Office on Falistin Street which may or may not have be able to help. Also, yachts, at the yacht moorings in northern Port Fouad sometimes hire hands for voyages to Mediterranean destinations.

By Bus

The **East Delta Bus Co.** depot is on Orabi St. off the northern side of Feriel Gardens. Buses, the bare bones type with few amenities) depart for **Cairo** hourly during daylight (LE15, 3.5 hours), **Suez** (LE7, 3 hours) and **Ismailia** (LE5, 1.5 hours). Buses also run regularly to Delta destinations such as **Damietta** and **Zagazig**. Check at the bus station in advance to get the exact schedule. Also, arrive at the station 15-30 minutes before departure to go through **customs**.

Buses from **Cairo** to Port Said depart from Qulali by Ramses nearly hourly during the day (LE15) and slightly less frequently from El Mazah in Heliopolis.

The fancier air-conditioned **SuperJet** coaches depart from another depot just north of the Railway Station at the corner of Mostafa Kemal and Ali Mazahi streets. SuperJets depart almost hourly to **Cairo** (LE17) and twice daily to **Alexandria** (LE22; 6 hours) at 10:30am and 4:30pm. Purchase tickets in advance and show up at least 15 prior to departure to go through customs. SuperJet coaches depart from Cairo at 159 Ramses Street. Other buses to the **Delta** depart from depots on El Salam and El Amin streets.

By Car

There aren't car rentals in Port Said, but it's certainly easy to rent a car in Cairo at any one of the many agencies (see listings in Cairo chapter). To get to Port Said, you need to get onto the Ismailia Road out of Heliopolis and after reaching Ismailia follow signs for Port Said. You may be stopped at checkpoints and will have to pay a minor fee (LE3) at a toll station. You may also be stopped at a customs' checkpoint so make sure that the necessary documents are in order. The drive shouldn't take more than 2-3 hours once you get on the Ismailia Road.

By Service

Peugeot seven-seaters and minibuses depart regularly from the Ahmed Helmy depot off Ramses Square in downtown **Cairo** (LE10 per person). Just look and listen for a driver calling out "Bur Said" and when his vehicle fills up (to the maximum absolutely possible) you'll be off. The main depot in Port Said itself is on El Sabah Street about half a kilometer south of the train station and hitching a ride to Cairo, Suez (LE5-7), Ismailia (LE3-5), Delta destinations, and Alexandria (LE12-15) shouldn't require much waiting.

By Train

Port Said's **train station** is by the SuperJet station off Mostafa Kemal Street which begins at the southern end of El Gomhuriya Street. Should you have any questions, don't hesitate to ask the folks at the Egyptian Tourist Authority office in the station (open daily from 8:30am-2pm daily).

Though trains run six times daily in each direction between **Cairo** and Port Said, it is far less efficient than taking the bus or a service. Trains from Cairo to Port Said run six times daily.

Direct service to Cairo from Port Said (3 hours) departs twice daily at 10:30am and 5:30pm (2nd class with A/C LE14, without A/C LE6.50, 3rd class LE2.80). Four trains daily depart from Port Said to Cairo (2nd class only with A/C), stopping in **Ismailia** (LE6, LE1 3rd class), Benha (LE4, LE1 3rd class), and Zagazig (LE2.10, 75pt 3rd class), at 5:25am, 1:15pm, 3:10pm, and 7:30. Getting all the way to Cairo on the slow train can take up to six hours.

Two trains daily to **Alexandria** via Tanta and Damanhur, depart at 7:15am and 6:20am and take a long 8 hours (2nd class with A/C LE18, without A/C LE8.50, 3rd class LE3.80). Trains to Suez do not leave regularly but take three hours when they do run (2nd class with A/C LE10, without A/C LE4.50, 3rd class LE2).

ORIENTATION

Situated at the northeastern tip of Africa, Port Said commands an unique location at the Mediterranean mouth to the **Suez Canal**. Opposite it on the east banks, is its sister city of **Port Fouad**, built in the 1920's and '30's to house civil servants and administrators working for the Suez Canal Company. In Port Said itself, banks, hotels, restaurants, and shops are concentrated along El Gomhuriya Street, a main drag that runs parallel to the Canal two blocks inland. Along the Canal itself, Falistin (Palestine) Street is also home to numerous commercial enterprises, but is currently undergoing major infrastructure restoration and is mostly off limits. Port Said's main landmark, the stately Suez Canal House with its shiny green domes is south of these main commercial quarters.

North and west, the **Corniche** stretches along Port Said's Mediterranean coast where thousands of middle class Egyptians pack the beaches in the summer. While pleasant to stroll down during the evening, these beaches hold little appeal to foreign travelers as far as sun bathing or swimming is concerned. They are unbearably crowded and dirty, and eager locals have a tendency to heap unwanted attention on unwilling foreigners, particularly women.

GETTING AROUND TOWN

Assuming you concentrate your activities around the Canal, the beach, and El Gomhuriya Street walking can get you anywhere within ten to fifteen minutes. **Taxis**, (blue and white) can take you anywhere within the city for LE3-5, as can a **kaleche** (horse carriage), the drivers of which are far less predatory than in say, Luxor. To cross the Canal to Port Fouad, simply hop one of the **ferries** that depart from the southern end of Falistin Street by the Egyptian Tourist Authority. They're free, run constantly, and are the best way to view the Canal.

WHERE TO STAY

Expensive

HELNAN PORT SAID HOTEL, *eastern end of El Corniche Street and northern end of El Gomhuriya Street. Tel. 066/320-890, 320-895, 320-898. Fax 066/323-762. Telex 63071HELUN. Capacity: 203. Rates: $99 single, $127 double, $173-437 suite. Credit cards: Visa, Mastercard, American Express.*

The finest hotel in Port Said, the Helnan claims the title of the most northeastern-most hotel in Africa (practically on the corner), which is useful because it means excellent views of both the Mediterranean Sea and the mouth of the Suez Canal. Besides rooms with the usual deluxe amenities (private bath, satellite TV, direct international phone lines, etc.) the hotel grounds feature several acres of well tended gardens, two swimming pools, a gym, and tennis, squash, and volleyball courts.

These facilities make the Helnan the hotel of choice for upper class Egyptians who come to Port Said for weekends of shopping and relaxation. Naturally they bring the kids who whiz about until all hours of the night, terrorizing the hotel's other main clientele, shipping magnets and business types who favor the place for its business and conference facilities. Eateries include an Italian restaurant, Abou El Araby (Middle Eastern), a coffee shop, the Danish Cafe, and pool side eating as well as a bar. The ambiance is characteristic of Egyptian upscale hotels built in the '70's and '80's, i.e. nil.

SONESTA PORT SAID HOTEL, *Sultan Hussein Street at the northern end of Falistin Street on the Canal. Tel. 066/325-511, 326-410. Fax 066/324-825. Capacity: 90 rooms including suites. Rates: $110 single, $135 double, $210-325 suite. Credit cards: Visa, Mastercard, American Express.*

Like the Helnan, the Sonesta is a case in point that in Port Said, the fancier the hotel, the less charm it exudes. While offering all the amenities of a five star establishment including a pool and a half dozen restaurants, and bars, the charmless Sonesta is hardly a cultural experience. However, its location is excellent, the rooms are clean and comfortable, and the Canal views are top notch.

NORAS BEACH HOTEL, *El Corniche Street 300 meters west of the Helnan. Tel. 066/329-834/5. Fax 066/329-841. Telex 63174PSDUN. Capacity: 192 rooms. Rates: $92-129 suite. Credit cards: Visa, Mastercard.*

The ultimate Egyptian beach resort in that the large suites are ideal for those large, extended upper middle class families who flock here in the summer. Located right on the beach (with plenty of views), it contains a modest pool, several restaurants over looking the sea, and hordes of folks just loving the whole scene. If you're looking for peace and quiet, this is not the place. Children are on the loose until late while parents relax, halfheartedly trying to control them and grandmothers amusedly watch from the safety of balconies.

Moderate

NEW CONTINENTAL HOTEL, *30 El Gomhuriya Street. Tel. 066/ 225-024, 223-153, 228-097. Fax 066/338-088. Capacity: 35 rooms. Rates: $60-79 single, $98 double. Credit cards: Visa, Mastercard.*

This is the newest, spiffiest, and priciest of the new three star establishments on El Gomhuriya Street. Not especially atmospheric, it's clean and rooms feature private baths, air-conditioning, telephones, and dish television.

HOLIDAY HOTEL, *El Gomhuriya Street. Tel. 066/220-711/3/4. Fax 066/220-710. Capacity: 81 rooms. Rates: $35 single, $40 double, $70 suite. Credit cards: Visa.*

A typical modern flavorless 3 star establishment, the Holiday Hotel offers modest accommodation for mid-level prices. Favored by business types and middle class Egyptians in town for shopping, its rooms feature private baths, air-conditioning, room service, and dish television with no English language stations. The location on El Gomhuriya Street is excellent, but there are no views.

PANORAMA HOTEL, *El Gomhuriya Street and Tarah El Bahr a couple hundred meters south of the Helnan. Tel. 066/325-101/2. Fax 066/325-103. Capacity: 58 rooms. Rates: $30 single, $35 double, $50 suite. Credit cards: Visa.*

The shiny new lobby turned arcade gives the place a cheesy kind of feel, but the rooms with phones, television, and private bath devour the competition with superior views. Some of the northern upper stories rooms offer views of both the Mediterranean and the Canal and the breezes are especially welcome in the summer. The staff is younger and friendlier than the old stodgy types who seem to run most other hotels of a comparable standard.

Budget

HOTEL DE LA POSTE, *42 El Gomhuriya Street. Tel. 066/224-048. Rates: LE15-50.*

The Hotel de la Poste is a venerable old dump with high ceilings and musty carpets that thanks to good upkeeping maintains its old charm and a relatively high degree of quality. There is a large variety of rooms vis a vis size and amenities and prices vary according. The more expensive ones feature those wonderful wooden balconies overlooking El Gomhuriya Street as well as air-conditioning, private showers, and even fridges and televisions (sorry, no satellite). They also tend to be spacious. The cheapest rooms have no private bath, balcony, or air-conditioning (there are fans) and overlook a side street if anything and for LE15. In between, is a variety of combinations of amenities with all types of prices to match. Guests can relax at the in-house bar or the cafe-restaurant Lourdat.

AKRI HOTEL, *24 El Gomhuriya Street. Tel. 066/221-013. Capacity: 26 rooms. Rates: LE15-20 single, LE20-25 double.*

A shabby but charming and atmospheric Greek run hotel, the Akri has long been a favorite with what few budget travelers find their way to Port Said. Most rooms have balconies and the more expensive ones have showers (erratic hot water), but no fans.

WHERE TO EAT

Port Said seems to have a thing for hamburgers and burger joints are everywhere-there's even a Jack-n-the-Box on the beach. There are also numerous seafood restaurants, concentrated on the Corniche and El Gomhuriya Street while the usual fuul and ta'amiya cheap eats are a dime a dozen-try the small alleys off the southern half of El Gomhuriya Street.

GALAL RESTAURANT, *El Gomhuriya Street just north of Hotel de la Poste. Hours: mid-morning until midnight. Credit cards: Visa.*

A modest cozy eatery serving moderately priced seafood and the usual assortment of Egyptian specialties, the Galal Restaurant offers the best food for value in Port Said. Grilled meats and poultry are excellent but grilled the fish is tops. You can easily fill up on appetizers and a main dish for LE25 or less if you don't drink alcohol.

ABOU TRIA, *on the midan on Saad Zaghloul Street. Tel. 066/228-343. Hours: 7am until late. Credit cards: American Express and Visa.*

Attempting to recreate an old style European cafe-restaurant while at the same time trying to be a hip billiards hall, Abou Tria comes across as a bit schizophrenic. Identity crisis aside, the decor says "hello" in a gaudy kitsch sort of way, the mood is upbeat, and the food more than decent. The menu features basic appetizers and mezze and a variety of continental and Egyptian meat, chicken, and seafood dishes-the seafood is especially worth a go. Prices for main dishes range from LE20 for a simple fish dish to LE160 for a kilo of jumbo Suez shrimp.

REANNA, *El Gomhuriya Street above the Cecil Bar.*

Catering to Koreans and Filipinos who pass through Port Said on commercial tankers, Reanna has some of the best Korean food in Egypt. The menu features a wide variety of Chinese and Korean dishes including some fantastically fiery kimchee soup, helpings are more than generous, and prices are very reasonable. If you don't splurge on seafood, you can easily fill yourself for LE20.

NORAS FLOATING RESTAURANT, *docks off Falistin St. by the National Museum. Tel. 066/326-804. Departs daily at 4pm and 9pm. The ticket window opens from 9am-1pm and from 2-4pm daily.*

The Noras departs twice daily for 1.5 hour cruises in the Canal. For LE12 you can go without eating (you are entitled to a soft drink) or for LE40 you can eat a reasonable meal of fried fish and rice. Buy tickets in advance so as not to be disappointed and to confirm departure times.

SEEING THE SIGHTS

Port Said is still defined by its original *raison d'etre,* the Suez Canal, and for many visitors its greatest attraction is the site of massive tankers lumbering in and out of the Canal while tugs buzz about like flies. The other image associated with Port Said is its signature building, the very colonial **Suez Canal House** with its baronial green domes. It is now closed to visitors, but you can still enjoy fantastic views of it, and the Canal with all its activities by getting on the ferry to Port Fouad. The ferry is free of charge and goes back and forth constantly from sunrise to sundown.

As for the city itself, a short stroll up and down El Gomhuriya and Falistin streets, and the Corniche is about all it takes to soak up what's left of the charm of 19th century Port Said. There are still venerable old wooden 19th century buildings reminiscent of New Orleans' French Quarter that recall the old colonial Port Said, but the demise that began with the destructive '56 War will soon be complete as slick glass and concrete structures become the norm. That leaves the two modest museums mentioned below, which at least offer some insight into this young city's compact and tumultuous history.

The National Museum, *the northern end of Falistin Street next to the Sonesta hotel. Hours: 9am-4pm daily except on Friday when it closes for prayer from 11am-1pm. Admission: LE6 general, LE3 students.*

For its modest size, this museum covers a lot of ground and features exhibits about virtually every facet of Egyptian history. Unlike some other museums in Egypt, it is well taken care of and the displays are well organized and easy to follow.

The ground floor concentrates on the pharaonic and Ptolemeic eras with exhibits featuring some fine statues, mummies, jewelry, and pottery. Upstairs, you will find Coptic and Islamic exhibits featuring textiles, tiles, and some fabulous black and white photographs of historic landmarks. Also of particular significance are the exhibits relating to the inauguration of the Suez Canal in 1869. They include Khedive Ismail's ornate carriage, formal clothing, and an assortment of personal articles from china and silverware to wristwatches and toiletries.

The Military Museum, 23rd *July Street about a kilometer west of the Canal. Hours: 9am-2pm daily except for Friday when it closes for prayers 11am-1pm. Admission: LE5.*

This museum is primarily a celebration of the 1956 Suez War and the 1973 October War. That both wars ended in military defeat is conveniently forgotten (as is the '67 War), but the graphic paintings, dioramas and photographs are nonetheless fascinating and even moving. Also on display are various weapons, including some captured from the Israelis.

NIGHTLIFE & ENTERTAINMENT

Port Said once had a reputation for whoring and hashish that rivaled that of any port on the Mediterranean, but while it maintains maritime identity, you'll be hard pressed to find anything more hedonistic than a rather lame "Russian Dancers" show at the Helnan. What action there is, is concentrated on **El Gomhuriya Street** where locals and Cairene consumers pass the evenings window shopping or puffing on sheesha at one of gazillion neighborhood 'ahwas, while seadogs and their Filipino hands cross paths with local drinkers at a venerable old Cecil bar beneath the Reanna Korean Restaurant.

Otherwise drinkers are basically limited to the lobby bar in the **Helnan** or **Pete's Pub** in the Sonesta, both of which fail to break the muzak mold of hotel bars. The Helnan also contains a nightclub (minimum charge LE20) which is mostly used for weddings, otherwise caters primarily to local young males. A trio of female Russian dancers performing a mishmash of modern dance, belly dancing, and can-can provides the main entertainment. When the nightclub isn't up and running, they perform at the pool beginning around 11pm.

SHOPPING

To Egyptians, Port Said is synonymous with shopping and consumer goods because of its duty-free status. As a visitor, you probably won't take a similar interest in the rows of shops selling duty-free household goods and electric appliances. For European style clothing, Port Said offers the best in Egypt. Most commercial activity is concentrated on and around El Gomhuriya Street.

EXCURSIONS & DAY TRIPS

A short tour to **Port Fouad** shouldn't take more than a few hours and there's little to see aside from the 1930's colonial style villas and Art Deco apartments. The ferry from Falistin Street is free and runs constantly until sundown.

PRACTICAL INFORMATION

Banks & Currency Exchange

All major Egyptian **banks** (Banque du Caire, Bank of Alexandria, National Bank of Egypt) run offices *on El Gomhuriya St. and also in Helnan and Sonesta Hotels. Hours: 8:30-2pm and 6-9pm (summer hours) and 5-8 (winter hours) Sunday-Thursday.*

Thomas Cook, *El Gomhuriya Street. Hours: 9am-1pm and 2-5pm.*

In addition to providing basic travel agency services, Thomas Cook changes money and travelers' cheques and can make advances on Visa and Mastercard.

Bookstores

An Al Ahram Kiosk on the Corniche about a 3/4 of a kilometer west of the Helnan sells Arabic and international newspapers and magazines. It opens daily from approximately 9am to 6pm and sometimes closes later.

Emergencies

• **Police:** *Tel. 122*
• **Ambulance:** *Tel. 123*

Post & Courier Services

Post Office (including EMS courier services), *on the corner of Mohammed Mahmoud and El Geish. Hours: 9am-4pm daily except Friday; EMS closes at 2pm.* There are smaller branches *on Ghandy Street and on Sedke Street.*

Federal Express and **DHL** both have offices in the shopping complex *between the Sonesta Hotel and the National Museum on Falistin Street. Both open 9am-5pm daily.*

Telephones, Telex, & Fax

Most hotels three stars and up have direct domestic and international phone services.

Telephone and Telegram Centrale, *El Wakil Street several blocks south of the Memorial Monument and the Governorate. A second centrale a block north of the Egyptian Tourist Authority Office on Falistin Street is probably more convenient. Both open 24 hours. You can also send faxes and make international calls from Federal Express in the shopping complex on Falistin Street.*

Tourist Information

The **Egyptian Tourist Authority** operates three offices in Port Said. The major office *(9am-2pm and from 3-6pm)* is on Falistin Street by the ferry crossing, and can provide basic information and a very handy map with listings. The office located in the train station can offer the same as well as assistance in making sense of the trains. A third office is located in the Customs Area by the Suez Canal Authority on Mostafa Kemal Street.

Tourist Police

The station is next to the Post Office on the corner of Mohammed Mahmoud and El Geish streets. Tel. 066/228-570.

ISMAILIA

Like its northern neighbor, Port Said, **Ismailia** is a child of the Suez Canal, and was built by and for Europeans. It is named for **Khedive Ismail Pasha**, the man who presided over the construction of the Suez Canal and spent his country into British occupation and himself into exile in part by sponsoring overly lavish celebrations to for inauguration celebrations in 1869. Home to Ferdinand de Lesseps, the man who actually built the Canal, and most of the Suez Canal Authority's European employees, old Ismailia is a pure European city with large villas, wide boulevards, and well tended gardens.

Consisting primarily of the concrete blocks that have been built all over Egypt in recent decades, Ismailia's newer districts are far less attractive. Though heavily damaged during the wars with Israel and evacuated during the War of Attrition, Ismailia has been almost entirely rebuilt and is now a buzzing city of more than half a million.

ARRIVALS & DEPARTURES

By Bus

There are two bus stations in Ismailia. East Delta Bus Co. station is on El Gomhuriya Street west of the train tracks. The West Delta Bus Co. station is next to the train station on Orabi Square.

Buses for Ismailia depart from Cairo's Qulali Station (LE5-7, 2.5 hours) hourly from 6am-9pm, and just as frequently from El Mazah depot in Heliopolis. There are also buses every half hour from Port Said and Suez and several daily from Alexandria's Sidi Gabr Station.

Buses depart for Cairo, Port Said, Suez, and El Arish from the East Delta Bus Co. depot on El Gomhuriya Street hourly (LE5-7). There are also two buses daily to Sharm El Sheikh and Hurghada. From the West Delta Bus Co. buses depart hourly for Cairo; there are also two daily to Alexandria.

By Car
From Cairo, there is a direct road from Heliopolis to Ismailia known as the Ismailia Road. It is one endless string of hideous billboards and massive surreal looking industrial parks.

By Service
The main service station is across El Gomhuriya Street from the East Delta Bus Co. Service taxis constantly depart for **Cairo** (LE5, 2 hours), **Port Said** (LE4, 1 hour), **Suez** (LE3, 45 minutes-hour), **El Arish** (LE8, 2.5 hours), and various **Delta** destinations such as Zagazig and Mansoura. From Cairo to Ismailia, service leave regularly from the Ahmed Helmy depot at Ramses Square.

By Train
The train station is in the center of town by Orabi Square. There are a dozen trains daily between Ismailia and **Port Said** (1.5 hours, LE8 for 2nd class with A/C), **Cairo** (3 hours plus, LE10 for 2nd class with A/C), and **Suez** (up to one hour, LE5 2nd class with A/C). Trains are horribly inefficient compared to buses and service and those to Suez do not feature air-conditioning. There are also two daily trains to Alexandria (5 hours, LE20, 2nd class with A/C) at 8:30am and 8pm.

ORIENTATION

Ismailia is really two cities, divided by the train tracks. The charming old city by the waterfront lies east of the tracks. Here one finds the quiet, leafy boulevards and Art Deco villas that were once home to Ismailia's European founders. Parallel to Lake Timsah runs the **Mohammed Ali Quay**, also known as the Salah Salem Street, Ismailia's most famous thoroughfare. Between it and the lake are lush gardens and the **Sweetwater Canal**. Due to a lack of maintenance, the water in it isn't very sweet anymore.

Between the Mohammed Ali Quay and the tracks are several main avenues: Ahmed Orabi Street (from the train station to the docks); Abu Baki El Saldik Street (running through the leafy Midan El Gomhuriya); Adly Pasha Street; and Sultan Hussein Street to north. **Sultan Hussein** is home to many of Ismailia's middle-ranged hotels, shops, and restaurants. To the north is the wealthy suburb of **Nimrah Setta** where one can stroll down immaculately landscaped boulevards, with large gardens and stately villas, without seeing a soul. Ismailia's Garden of Stelae and the museum are here and further up on the lake in the Forsan Gardens is the Mercure Hotel, the most luxurious in Ismailia.

Three hundred meters south of the train station and Orabi Square perpendicular to the tracks and the Mohammed Ali Quay is **El Gomhuriya**

Street. West of the tracks it hums with commercial activity and traffic fed by the service and bus stations. To the east, it is a busy shopping district littered with boutiques and small restaurants.

GETTING AROUND TOWN

Walking does just fine for downtown Ismailia and the waterfront. Otherwise, taxis can be hailed off the street. For a more atmospheric tour, overpriced horse carriages are available from the Mercure Forsan Hotel (LE20 an hour).

WHERE TO STAY

MERCURE FORSAN ISLAND HOTEL, *on Forsan Island north of town. Tel. 064/765-322, 768-802. Fax 064/338-043. Telex 63038 ETAPI UN. Capacity: 175 rooms. Rates: $53-86 single, $65-99 double, $170-340 suite. Credit cards: All major credit cards.*

Set in the luscious gardens of Forsan Island on Lake Timsah (Crocodile Lake), the Mercure is Ismailia's only true luxury hotel. Popular with upper class Egyptian families who come for a getaway from Cairo, the Mercure features a nice swimming pool and facilities for tennis, water skiing, wind surfing, and table tennis. Gastronomic options include a swanky French eatery, a coffee shop, a pizzeria, and a seafood restaurant. There is also quite a nice bar with a pool table and a terrace where you can enjoy a beer or coffee while gazing over the Lake. The rooms all feature balconies, air-conditioning, and satellite television. The only drawback is the charmless modern structure itself.

EL SALAM HOTEL, *El Geish Street, (P.O. Box 50). Tel. 064/324-401, 220-775. Capacity: 50 rooms. Rates: LE55 single, LE80 double, LE125 suite.*

A recently upgraded hotel featuring comfortable air-conditioned rooms with televisions, the El Salam is a quirky establishment where the girls behind the desk always seem to a have smirk on their faces that suggests there's a joke going around and you're the only who doesn't get it.

CROCODILE INN HOTEL, *179 Saad Zaghloul Street. Tel. 064/331-555. Fax, 064/331-666. Rates: LE107 new single, LE55 old single, LE150 new double, LE75 old double.*

Despite efforts to brighten them up with dreadfully misplaced modernist abstract paintings the older (and cheaper) rooms with the peeling paint and mildew, definitely show their age. Meanwhile the spotless spacious new ones are comfortable and well maintained, but still overpriced. Both feature private baths and air-conditioning with satellite television coming soon to the new rooms. The hotel also has a restaurant-bar, and a typically gaudy lounge.

NEVERTARY HOTEL, *41 Sultan Hussein Street. Tel. 064/322-822. Capacity: 32 rooms. Rates: LE28 single, LE25-30 double. Extra beds: LE5.*

All decked out in its horrifically ugly new purple paint job, the Nevertary (sic) is trying desperately to get ahead of the competition. Give them an 'A' for effort and an 'A' for good value, even if they're clueless when it comes to a sense of style. Though hardly elegant, the concrete rooms are comfortable and decently furnished. The more expensive ones come with private showers, and for LE5 you can have a television and air-conditioning. An added bonus is the quirky bar where happy-go-lucky Egypto-pop does its best to liven up the depressingly dim concrete surroundings.

ISIS HOTEL, *32 Adly Street across form the train station. Tel. 064/227-821. Capacity: 51 rooms. Rates: LE8-15 single, LE15-25 double, LE30-40 triple or two room suite.*

A new concrete pile, the Isis suffers from severe lack of character disorder and is need of some upgrading in the hospitality department as well. Other than that the rooms are acceptably comfortable and quite good value. The more expensive ones have private baths (somewhat clean) and all rooms have fans and telephones. Upper level rooms feature something of a view, but the place in general is subject to train noise. As the Isis caters almost exclusively to Egyptians, foreigners can get some funny looks and may have a hard time finding an English speaking employee.

HOTEL DES VOYAGEURS, *22 Orabi Street, Tel. 064/228-304. Capacity: 25 rooms. Rates: LE5.20-8.60-6-10.35 single, LE8-11.50-10-15.50 doubles and suites.*

Though it's an enchanting old dump with a classy sounding name, great potential and a wonderful old gent for an owner, the Hotel Des Voyageurs looks like it's barely been touched since the '56 War. But if you don't mind a little dust and humidity, or possibly a cockroach, it has infinitely more charm and affability than some of Ismailia's other hotels. The rooms are simple and drab, and many of them spacious, and some have a private shower and a fan. Be sure to get one with a window.

WHERE TO EAT

There are dozens of street stalls on El Gomhuriya Street selling cheap kushari, kebab, and rotisserie chicken. There are also numerous restaurants on Sultan Hussein, the best of which is a chicken and kebab joint, **El Gandool**. The **Mercure Hotel** features several upscale restaurants including a swanky French grille, a nice seafood restaurant where you pick your fish, and an Italian eatery.

GEORGE'S, *Sultan Hussein Street. Credit cards: Visa.*

Open since 1954, this vintage European style bar and restaurant serves superb grilled and fried fish as well as continental and oriental appetizers. Without beer, expect to pay LE30-40 for a full meal.

KING EDWARD, *171 Tahrir Street off Sultan Hussein Street. Credit cards: Visa.*

Another classy relic from the pre-'56 era. The specialties of the house are grilled fish and an assortments of rices with shrimp and fish. Beer is not served.

NEFERTITI, *Sultan Hussein Street. No credit cards.*

Basic chicken, kebab, and fish with the usual mezze, is available here for prices cheaper than George's or the King Edward, but the ambiance doesn't hold a candle. You can eat a full meal for LE20 and it is air-conditioned.

PIZZA INN, *El Gomhuriya Street.*

This is a slick Pizza Hut imitation restaurant for those in need of pizza, which doesn't seem to be available anywhere else except the Mercure.

SEEING THE SIGHTS

The Ismailia Museum & the Garden of Stelae, *Nimrah Setta district a half kilometer north of Sultan Hussein and the Mohammed Ali Quay near the Mahalla Garden. Hours: 9am-5pm daily except Friday when it closes for prayer from 11am-2pm. Admission: LE6 general, LE3 students. No photography.*

This dimly lit museum contains a modest collection of pharaonic and Greco-Roman artifact- mostly statuettes and amulets. Though not particularly impressive it makes for a good excuse to stroll up to Nimrah Setta and the Mahalla Gardens.

Nearby are some outdoor exhibits in the Garden of Stelae. The sphinxes and other minor relics are small fry compared to what you find anywhere else in Egypt, but the garden is lovely.

Ferdinand de Lesseps' House, *on the Mohammed Ali Quay near the corner with Ahmed Orabi Street (east of the train station). Currently closed.*

Recently closed to the public, this stately Swiss style 19th century villa was home to Ferdinand de Lesseps, the Canal's mastermind, during its construction. It is now used as a guest house by the Suez Canal Authority. If you can peak into the grounds, you might get a glimpse of de Lesseps' private coach.

Lake Timsah, the smallest of the Great Bitter Lakes, features a number of beaches owned by private clubs. Crowded with middle class Egyptians whenever the weather is decent, these beaches usually allow nonmembers to enter for a small fee (LE1-5) and sometimes they insist and charging you LE20-40 for a buffet lunch. If you chose to enter, be prepared to be the object of considerable attention, especially if you are

female. To keep from making matters worse than necessary, leave the
bikini at home.

NIGHTLIFE & ENTERTAINMENT

The **Mercure Hotel** contains a nice, but usually empty bar with a
billiards table. George's Restaurant on Sultan Hussein has a vintage bar
that has been in operation since 1954. Indeed with its wood paneled bar
and stools and British drinking paraphernalia, it's hard to believe that
you're in Egypt. It's one of the few vestiges left from an Ismailia that
doesn't exist anymore.

If you'd prefer not to pass your even sipping Stella in an empty bar,
the area around El Gomhuriya and Saad Zaghloul streets are generally
hopping and buzzing during the evening when Ismailis take to the streets
for dinner and shopping.

PRACTICAL INFORMATION

Banks & Currency Exchange
Bank of Alexandria, *Orabi Square. Hours: 8am-2pm & 5-8pm (winter)
or 6-9pm (summer) Sunday-Thursday.*
Banque du Caire, *Hassan El Nahda Street a block north of El Gomhuriya
Square. Hours: 8am-2pm & 5-8pm (winter) or 6-9pm (summer) Sunday-
Thursday.*
There are also several exchanges on Sultan Hussein Street that have
longer hours but do not change traveler's cheques or make Visa or
Mastercard advances.

Emergencies
• **Police**: *Tel. 122*
• **Ambulance**: *Tel. 123*
• **Public Hospital**: *Tel. 222-047*

Post Services
Post Office *is next to the train station. Hours: 8am-3pm daily except Friday.*

Telephones, Telex, & Fax
24 hour telephone centrale *with fax and telex services is on Orabi Square.
There are also public phones in the train station.* The **Mercure Forsan Hotel**
has a modest business center with telephone, fax, and telex services.

Tourist Information
Egyptian Tourist Authority, *Mohammed Ali Quay. Hours: 8am-2pm
daily.* Apart from some basic assistance about how to ride the train and

what not, the ETA office only provides the usual assortment of poorly translated pamphlets and brochures.

Tourist Police
Tourist Police Station, *by the Tourist Authority Office on Mohammed Ali Quay. Tel. 221-933.*

SUEZ

Unlike Port Said and Ismailia, **Suez** was a thriving port long before the creation of the Suez Canal, yet it is the least appealing of the Canal towns and is best avoided if possible. Founded in Roman times, it thrived on the spice trade and pilgrimage traffic during the Middle Ages. Thoroughly destroyed during the wars with Israel it has been entirely rebuilt and now has all the charm of the industrial port that it is.

ARRIVALS & DEPARTURES

By Bus
The Arba'een Bus Station is on El Fa'arz Street in the city center. There are two to three buses hourly to **Cairo** (LE5-7, 1.5-2 hours), and **Ismailia** (LE3-5, an hour or less). To reach **Port Said** and **El Arish**, it's best to get to Ismailia; from there, buses leave to both destinations hourly. There are two buses daily to **Sharm El Sheikh** (LE25, 6 hours) en route to **Dahab** and **Nuweiba** at 11am and 3pm. The daily bus to **Saint Katherine's Monastery** (LE25, 5 hours) via Sinai's Gulf of Suez coast departs at 11am or noon.

There are six buses daily to **Hurghada** (LE25, 5-6 hours) and you can get off at **Ain Sukhna**, **Zafarana** and **El Gouna**. Some of these buses also go on to Qena in the Nile Valley, but you're better off going through Cairo to get to Luxor.

By Service
The service depot is by the bus station. Service taxis are constantly departing to **Cairo** (LE3-5, 1.5 hours); **Ismailia** (45 minutes, LE3); **Hurghada** (LE15-20, 5 hours); and **Port Said** (LE5, 2.5 hours).

It is difficult to find service going to Sinai so you are better off taking the bus, or if you have enough people consider hiring a private taxi.

By Train
There is a train station about 100 meters north of the Arba'een Bus Station, but trains are painfully slow compared to buses and service.

ORIENTATION

Hotels, restaurants, and shops are concentrated around the intersections of Suez's main thoroughfare, El Geish Street and Saad Zaghloul, Tahrir, and Banque Misr streets. To the north at the other end of Banque Misr Street is the city's main transport hub with the Arba'een Bus Station and the service taxi depot. In between is a neighborhood with crumbling colonial-era buildings and wind-beaten palms.

North of El Geish Street is a buzzing souk that swamps Haleem Street and the surrounding decrepit turn of the century district that somehow survived four wars with Israel. To the southeast, El Geish Street links Suez with its sister city, **Port Tewfiq** two kilometers east, where four American-made tanks captured from Israel are proudly displayed on the Corniche.

GETTING AROUND TOWN

Minivan service taxis careen up and down El Geish Street between Suez and Port Tewfiq and there are also private taxis. Otherwise you can negotiate downtown Suez on foot.

WHERE TO STAY

GREEN HOUSE HOTEL, *Port Said Street off El Geish Street on the way to Port Tewfiq. Tel. 062/223-337/0. Fax 062/223-330. Rates: $35-45 single, $44-55 double. Credit cards: Visa.*

The newest, cleanest, and best outfitted hotel in Suez, the Green House has clean comfortable rooms with air-conditioning, private showers, satellite television, and balconies. It also features a bar, restaurant, a modest pool, and a bank. The views of Suez Bay are among the best in Suez (which isn't saying much).

RED SEA HOTEL, *13 Riad Street in Port Tewfiq. Tel. 062/223-334/5. Fax 062/227-761. Rates: $40 single, $55 double. Credit cards: Visa.*

It's the nicer of the two hotels in Port Tewfiq, and possibly the nicest in Suez. Rooms come with air-conditioning, televisions, phones, and private baths. The rooms are not lavishly decorated or furnished, but they are quite comfortable and clean. The restaurant features great views of the Canal as it opens into the Gulf of Suez.

SUMMER PALACE, *off the end of El Geish Street in Port Tewfiq. TEL. 062/224-475, 225-434. Fax 062/321-944. Rates: $34 single, $44 double. Credit cards: Visa.*

By the name you might expect the sister hotel to the Winter Palace hotel in Luxor, which this certainly is not-in fact, there's no palace in sight. The rooms with air-conditioning and good views of the Suez Bay are decent, but for the money you can get better at the Green House or the Red Sea Hotel.

WHITE HOUSE HOTEL, *322 El Geish (El Salam) Street in downtown Suez. Tel. 062/227-599. Fax 062/223-330. Rates: LE23 single, LE35, LE45 triple.*

It's right in the thick of downtown Suez meaning there are no views, but the bus station is close for getting in and out of town, which is usually the goal in Suez. The service is good and the simple rooms with fans and private showers are clean and comfortable-not a bad budget choice.

MISR PALACE, *2 Saad Zaghloul off El Geish (Salam) in downtown Suez. Tel. 062/223-031. Rates: LE10-35.*

The "Palace" offers a variety of rooms, the best of which are singles and doubles with private shower and air-con. Otherwise there are rooms with fans and no showers which entails braving the sometimes sketchy common baths.

WHERE TO EAT

If you're staying in Port Tewfiq, there's no reason to bother going into Suez. The hotel restaurants are pricier, but it's not worth the effort as the food is decent and the views are much better. In town, there is plenty of the usual fuul, ta'amiya, roast chicken, and other cheap eats available on the streets off El Geish Street. For fish, try the **Fish Restaurant** at *the corner of Saad Zaghloul and El Geish (Salam) Street;* it specializes in grilled fish and is fairly cheap (LE15 for a full meal).

SEEING THE SIGHTS

Apart from the Gulf of Suez, there are no sights.

NIGHTLIFE & ENTERTAINMENT

In Port Tewfiq, the Red Sea Hotel, the Green House Hotel, and the Summer Palace all have bars as does the White House Hotel in downtown Suez. Otherwise, find a coffee shop to your liking and play backgammon and sip sheesha with the locals.

PRACTICAL INFORMATION

Banks & Currency Exchange

In **Suez**, there is a Bank of Alexandria and a Banque Misr *on El Geish Street about 100 meters from the train track north of downtown.* They keep normal business hours and cash traveler's cheques and make cash advances on Visa cards. There is also a **Banque du Caire** *on Saad Zaghloul Street four blocks south of El Geish Street.*

Bank of Alexandria, *around the corner from the Red Sea Hotel, Port Tewfiq.*

American Express, *next to the Tourist Authority's office on El Marwa Street at the southern tip of Port Tewfiq.*

Emergencies
• **Police:** *Tel. 122*
• **Ambulance:** *Tel. 123*

Post Services
Post Office, *Hoda Shaarawi Street off El Geish Street, downtown Suez. Hours: 8am-3pm daily except Friday.*

Telephones, Telex, & Fax
24 hour telephone centrale, *the corner of Shohada and Saad Zaghloul streets.*

Tourist Information
Egyptian Tourist Authority, *the office is about as far away as possible from downtown Suez on the southern tip of Port Tewfiq on El Marwa Street. Hours: 9am-6pm daily except for Friday.* The folks speak good English and are quite helpful about practical information. Too bad they're not in a city where they're needed.

18. THE RED SEA COAST

Egypt's resplendent 1,200 kilometers of **Red Sea coast** has rapidly developed into a major tourist attraction since opening up after peace with Israel in 1979. Before its sun-drenched beaches, turquoise waters, and brilliant coral reefs were open to development, the Red Sea coast was the front line during Egypt's thirty year state of war with the Jewish State. While only 20 years ago one had to jump through all sorts of hoops just to get here, and there were no hotels or facilities, the Red Sea now attracts upwards of a quarter million visitors annually, most of whom fly directly into Hurghada from Europe.

WARNING
Over the course of Egypt's 30-year state of war with Israel, the hills and beaches along the Red Sea Coast were heavily mined by both sides. Do not stray from public beaches or areas clearly marked as safe.

AIN SUKHNA

This striking stretch of coast, where jagged desert mountains slope dramatically into the turquoise waters of the Gulf of Suez, is named for hot springs emanating from the depths of nearby Gebel Ataka. (In Arabic, "Ain" means "spring" and "sukhna" means "hot.") Located 50 kilometers south of Suez, and 2.5 hours from Cairo by car, "**Sukhna**" as it's known, is an ideal destination for a quick getaway from Cairo as a day trip or, if you have wheels and equipment, its beaches offer beautiful settings for camping.

Alternatively, you can stay at one of the two hotels. Keep in mind when planning that on weekends and holidays, Ain Sukhna is saturated with picnicking Cairenes. Also, as far as food and water go, unless you stay, or at least eat at one of the hotels, you need to bring your own.

ARRIVALS & DEPARTURES

Taking a trip to Ain Sukhna is one decent reason to rent a car in Cairo. Otherwise, there are three buses daily from Suez and service taxis will drop you wherever you want, but you if want to camp or sit on a beach not attached to a hotel, you need a car.

WHERE TO STAY

Ain Sukhna's beaches are excellent for **camping**, assuming you have equipment and transportation to find an appropriate spot. Keep in mind that fenced off portions of the beach may be mined so it's best to stick to public beaches.

There are three hotels at Ain Sukhna, all with cabins/chalets, and air-conditioned double rooms with bathrooms. They also contain restaurants and may charge half board rates with breakfast and lunch or dinners included:

SUKHNA VILLAGE HOTEL, *50 kilometers south of Suez. Tel. 062/328-488, in Cairo 02/775-226, 773-939. Fax (Cairo) 02/578-3642. Rates: $45 singles, $70 doubles, $100 suites. Chalets cost about $30. Credit cards: Visa.*

EL SOKHNA PROTEA HOTEL, *54 kilometers south of Suez. Tel. 062/325-560/1/2. Fax 062/322-003. Rates: $55-85 singles, $86-130 doubles. Cheaper rates are for chalets and during low seasons. Credit cards: Visa.*

MENA OASIS, *65 kilometers south of Suez. Tel. 062/222-525. Fax (Cairo) 02/578-9300. Rates: $35 single, $45 double, $58-63 triple/suite. Credit cards: Visa.*

ZAFARANA

This truck stop-cum-resort has long been a stop for Coptic Pilgrims on their way to the monasteries of Saint Antony and Saint Paul. Situated where the road from Beni Suef meets the coast, **Zafarana** the settlement is a rather dingy collection of police and gas stations. However, the rest of the coast is quite picturesque and a number of hotels are developing along the beach.

By 1998-99, when a number of the hotels will open, Zafarana will be a worthy place to stop if you wish to combine the beach with the monasteries in a one night excursion from Cairo.

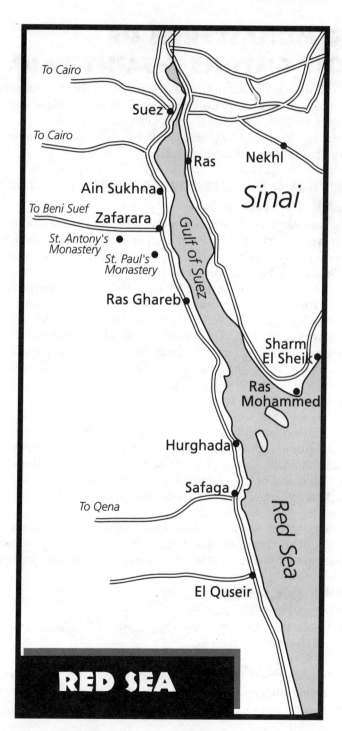

THE MONASTERIES OF SAINT ANTONY & SAINT PAUL

Set in the rugged but beautiful desert hills of the Red Sea coast by Zafarana, these 4th century **Coptic monasteries** are the oldest monasteries in the world. Today, monks live much like their predecessors 16 centuries ago, spending their time praying, fasting and meditating in the splendid isolation of these barren hills.

ARRIVALS & DEPARTURES/GETTING AROUND/ WHERE TO STAY & EAT

The monasteries of **Saint Antony's** and **Saint Paul's**, 85 kilometers apart by road, can be combined in a day trip from Cairo, Hurghada, or Suez, or you can spend the night. They are open to visitors during the day from 9am-5pm. You do not need prior permission to stay at Saint Antony's but call their office in Cairo, *Tel. 590-0218*, to make reservations and to be sure that they aren't closed for a holiday. To stay at Saint Paul's, you need a letter of introduction from the monastery's office in Cairo at Saint Mark's Cathedral, *Tel. 590-6025*, off El Gala'a Street between Ramses and Tahrir squares. At Saint Paul's men can stay within the monastery itself while the women stay in a separate guest house outside the gates. There is no charge, but a donation is appropriate.

Neither monastery is accessible by public transportation. You can hire a taxi for LE200-300 for the day (add LE100 if you stay the night) which isn't too expensive if there is a group of you to split the cost. Another option is to join a pilgrim tour. Call the **Coptic Patriarchate**, *Tel. 960-025 in Abbassia, Cairo* or the **YMCA**, *Tel. 917-360*. Otherwise, call Misr Travel, Thomas Cook, and other major travel agencies to inquire about tours. Also, in Hurghada, most hotels arrange day trips for LE60-100 per person.

Be sure to wear modest clothing and to dress warmly if visiting during the winter. Also, since they close during Lent and other religious holidays (some of them obscure), call in advance to make sure they are open.

SEEING THE SIGHTS

The Monastery of Saint Antony

25 kilometers inland off the Beni Suef-Zafarana Road about 3 hours from Cairo and Hurghada.

Born in Middle Egypt in 251 AD, **Saint Antony** lived during a period when the swift growth of Christianity in Egypt met with brutal oppression by occupying Roman armies. To flee persecution and to pursue asceticism and self-denial, increasing numbers of Egyptian Christians left the Nile Valley for the oases and mountains of the Eastern and Western Deserts. At age 18, Antony, the son of wealthy merchants, sold his inheritance and placed his sister in a convent. He then became an ascetic and retreated to the wadis of Mount Qala here in the Eastern Desert where he became the leader of what is considered Christianity's first monastic community. Here he lived in a cave until 355 AD when he died at the age of 104.

Antony's followers founded the monastery and supposedly interred him under the church bearing his name. We know little about its early history except that in the 6th and 7th centuries, Copts fleeing Roman persecution sought refuge here. According to some accounts, some of those monks dressed as Bedouins, raided the monastery, and carted back to Wadi Natrun the body of Saint John the Short who had been buried here. Real Bedouins did plunder the place in the 9th and 10th centuries and it required rebuilding in the 12th only to be destroyed again and closed in the 15th century. It reopened in the 16th century and has been expanding ever since-most of the current monastery was built since the 17th century.

As an outsider approaches the complex one is struck by two things, the magnificent beauty of its setting in the rugged cliffs over looking the Red Sea, and the towering fortress like walls that surround it. Given the turbulent history endured by the monastery despite its isolation, fortifications make sense. Two hundred years ago, visitors could only enter through a trap door in a guard room above the gate where they were lifted with ropes and pulleys. Today, one can enter on foot through the main gate.

The oldest of the monastery's five chapels is named for Saint Antony and allegedly holds his remains. Its interior features fine medieval portraits of Saint George and various Coptic luminaries dating from the 12th and 13th centuries. The grounds also contain a library storing ancient Coptic manuscripts, a keep, and a bakery. All are interesting and worth seeing.

You should also put forth the effort to make the steep two kilometer hike to the **Cave of Saint Antony**, where he allegedly spent much of his time meditating and praying. Graffiti covers the walls of the cave which also features two interesting paintings, one of Saint Antony, and one of Christ. The best reason to make the climb, however, is the splendid view of the Red Sea which is particularly stunning in the morning when the sun rises over the sea and the mountains of Sinai; otherwise, dusk is also excellent. Bring water and a flashlight if possible.

HIKING BETWEEN SAINT PAUL'S & SAINT ANTONY'S

If you are truly fit, well equipped, and daring, you may consider hiking the 35 kilometers of desert plateau between the two monasteries. Ideally, you should start from Saint Paul's where you should get directions and let them know of your plans. Given the unforgiving conditions of the desert, it is imperative that you know where you are going, have enough water, and that you be fit enough to hike for two or three days carrying all of your provisions. Underpreparation, bad judgment, or a bit of bad luck can easily be fatal. Good Luck!

The Monastery of Saint Paul

The Monastery of Saint Paul is off the Suez-Hurghada Road about 20 kilometers south of Zafarana.

Though not as famous as the Monastery of Saint Antony, the Monastery of Saint Paul is equally, if not more interesting. Saint Paul, like Saint Antony, was 4th century hermit about whom we know very little except that he was one of Christianity's earliest monastic leaders who fled to the desert to avoid Roman persecution.

The Monastery of Saint Paul is smaller and more underdeveloped than Saint Antony's. Its main attraction is the **Church of Saint Paul**, a bizarre chapel built over a cave that holds his remains and features Ostrich eggs (symbols of the Resurrection) hanging from its ceiling. Adorning its walls is a collection of primitive and colorful icons, thought to be amongst the oldest in Egypt. There are three other churches in the Monastery dedicated to Saint Michael, the Virgin Mary, and Saint Mercuris as well as a keep, three wells, and a vegetable garden.

EL GOUNA

El Gouna is approximately 30 kilometers north of Hurghada and 500 kilometers from Cairo. The brainchild of Egyptian zillionaire Samih Sawiriss, El Gouna is a self-contained private resort that allows visitors to enjoy the natural beauty of the Red Sea coast in five star comfort without the drawbacks that plague the overdeveloped and poorly planned resorts of Sharm El Sheikh and Hurghada. As it's entirely private, there are no avaricious shop keepers or touts to constantly pester you while you walk down the street and you don't have to look out your $150 hotel room window over the roof of a half finished concrete block the way you might in Hurghada.

Practically a small town, El Gouna contains a half-dozen mid and upscale hotels, each with their own swimming pools, beaches, restaurants, and shopping centers though guests are free to sample the facilities of other hotels throughout the resort. For recreation, there are diving courses, tennis courts and health spas, aerobics classes and hundreds of meters of beaches to frolic about on.

In his effort to up the competition, Sawiriss has hired the likes of world renowned modernist architect Michael Graves to design several hotels and in the coming years a Lowenbrau brewery, a radio station, and a world class 18 hole golf course will also be in operation. By past Egyptian tourism standards such initiatives and efforts are beyond cutting edge and hopefully El Gouna is a beacon for higher standards throughout the industry in the future.

ARRIVALS & DEPARTURES
By Air
There is an airstrip at El Gouna, however most visitors fly in and out of the busy airport at Hurghada. For information about flights, contact EgyptAir about flying to Hurghada. For flights from Cairo direct to El Gouna contact **Orascom Touristic Establishments** at *166, 26th of July Street, Agouza, Cairo. Tel. 02/301-5496/8, 304-3403, 301–5451, 302-5033. Fax 02/304-2772, 304-3403/4.*

By Boat
A ferry runs between Sharm El Sheikh and Hurghada, which can be reached from El Gouna by automobile. The ferry costs LE110 and takes between 6 and 10 hours. Those prone to sea sickness may find the trip uncomfortable. From Hurghada's port of Siqalla, you must then hire a taxi to El Gouna (LE40-60).

By Bus
There are no public buses directly to El Gouna on their routes but there are at least a dozen buses daily from Cairo to Hurghada (see following "Hurghada" section) where you can catch a minibus or taxi to El Gouna. Alternatively you may be able to convince the bus driver to let you off at the El Gouna turn-off. You then have to rely on a minibus or taxi passing by going into El Gouna for giving you a ride the rest of the way in. The wait could be 10 minutes or two and half hours-in other words, no guarantees.

By Car
Driving from Cairo (at least safely) takes approximately five hours. You can rent cars and jeeps in Cairo (see the listings in the Cairo chapter). You then want to find the Autostrade where a road, five kilometers north of Maadi, turns for the coast. From there, it is 350 kilometers along the coast to El Gouna which is about 20 kilometers north of Hurghada. **Be sure to leave Cairo with a full tank of gas.** There are gas stations in Zafarana and Ras Gharib, 150 kilometers, north of Hurghada and El Gouna.

By Service
Minibuses leave for Hurghada from the Ahmed Helmy depot at Ramses Square, and will be happy to drop you off at the El Gouna turnoff or even take you into El Gouna itself. If the driver is unwilling you will have to wait to hitch with a minibus, taxi, or private car going in. Depending on the time of day, that could mean an hour or two, maybe more. Should you take a private taxi, expect to pay at least LE200 one-way. This can make sense if you can split the cost amongst a group. Don't forget to bargain.

By Train
Though an automobile trolley disguised as a train zips vacationers around El Gouna, there is no rail service to El Gouna or Hurghada.

ORIENTATION
El Gouna comprises a series of hotels, resorts, villages, and villa communities, all self-contained, but accessible from each other by minibus and water shuttles. The five star **Sonesta Paradisio** to the north, **Movenpick**, and the **Sheraton Miramar** to the south, are all on separate islands or peninsulas, surrounded by the sea and manmade lagoons. At the center of the entire resort, a village-like settlement, **Kafr El Gouna**, to the smaller hotels (Dawar El Omdah, El Khan Hotel, and Sultan Bey), a shopping arcade, private villas, restaurants, and the museum. Between the Sheraton and the Movenpick, **El Zeytuna Beach & Bar** is a spacious and quiet common beach featuring a bar.

North of El Gouna, the **airport** is separated from the rest of the resort by the **Marina**, where private yachts and boats are moored, and a settlement of private villas. Surrounded by lagoons next to the Sonesta Paradisio, a world class **golf course** is slated to open in 1998. Finally, to the far north, a new marina is also under construction.

GETTING AROUND TOWN

Not having to confront, or listen to, the warlike traffic typical in most of Egypt is one of El Gouna's positive attributes for many visitors. That includes taxis which means no hassling over prices and no sleazy drivers. The larger hotels and Kafr El Gouna are all more or less self-contained, however should you like to play golf or check out different facilities throughout the resort, getting from one hotel or facility to another is not a problem.

Free water shuttles and **minibuses** ferry guests several times each hour and routes include all major attractions. Sometimes **horse-drawn carriages** and/or a train-like trolley also transfer visitors. You can also rent **bicycles**, **mopeds**, and **four-wheelers**.

WHERE TO STAY

The El Gouna resort contains half a dozen independently managed hotels in addition to dozens of private villas, some of which can be rented. For general information about El Gouna and making reservations, contact your travel agent or the **Orascom Touristic Establishments** offices directly at *166, 26th of July Street, Agouza, Cairo. Tel. 02/301-5496/ 8, 304-3403, 301–5451, 302-5033. Fax 02/304-2772, 304-3403/4.* You can also make reservations directly through the major hotels chains in the United States or your particular country.

SHERATON MIRAMAR, *on a man made island in the middle of El Gouna. Call the Orascom numbers above for information and reservations. Rates: $120-160 singles, $150-$210 doubles. Credit cards: all major credit cards accepted.*

Designed by world renowned modernist architect Michael Graves, this fascinating piece of design somehow combines Hassan Fathi (e.g., lots of domes & arches Egyptian style) with tinker toys and a colorful modernist twist. Situated on a man-made island overlooking the Red Sea, it features five star resort facilities, including a pool, several restaurants and bars, and health club facilities. The colorful rooms have deluxe amenities including air-conditioning, international phone lines, satellite television, and so on. When it opened in the fall of 1997, the service needed to work out a few kinks, but they should be ironed out by '98.

MOVENPICK RESORT, *Tel. 065/ 544-501-10, 545-160-9; Fax 065/ 544-503/6/8. Prices: $118 single, $158 double, $600 suite. Credit cards: all major credit cards accepted.*

The Pizza Hut architecture isn't half as charming or interesting as that of the Sheraton or Kafr El Gouna, and even seems a bit out of place, but otherwise, the Movenpick is an outstanding hotel. From the landscaping to the mega-beach, the setting is ideal for getting away from the dusty hustle and bustle of the Nile Valley. The large pool is first rate and health club facilities include tennis and squash courts, a weight room, and saunas. Of course guests can also enjoy recreation options throughout the resort such as horse back riding at the Paradisio, and the golf course. The major restaurant, the Paladion features buffets while El Sayadin specializes in seafood. Several bars and small eateries offer a variety of gastronomic options from Egyptian to Italian cuisine.

SONESTA PARADISIO, *Tel. 065/547-934/5/6. Fax 065/547-933. Capacity: 230 rooms including 10 suites. Prices: $116 single, $143 double, $178-220 suites. Credit cards: all major credit cards accepted.*

The original El Gouna hotel, the Paradisio has recently expanded from 88 to 230 rooms. In addition to the two large pools, a sprawling beach and the usual five star amenities, the Paradisio contains riding stables, a dive center, and a health center which includes, squash, tennis, weights, sauna, steam bath, and a small heated pool. Various water and land based activities and sports are also offered. The hacienda style architecture doesn't have the appeal of the oriental architecture used in Kafr El Gouna, but it's certainly attractive compared to the space age monstrosities of Hurghada. Two major restaurants feature buffets with rotating menus, and Morgan's specializes in seafood.

DAWAR EL OMDAH, *Kafr El Gouna. Rates: $45-65 Credit cards: all major credit cards accepted.*

In rural Egypt, *el omdah* is the village elder, and this small hotel attempts to capture some of the essence of a traditional Egyptian village house. The orientalization (they put domes and arches in every possible location) is actually overdone, but with only 70 rooms, Dawar has a homier and more subdued atmosphere than the larger resorts nearby. Its mini-pool is suitable for children but for anything more than a bird bath, you have to hit Zeytuna Beach or one of the pools at the bigger hotels. The rooms are tastefully decorated in Arabesque and offer good views of the lagoons and the oriental architecture of Kafr El Gouna. For shopping, money changing, and recreation, you'll have to make a move, but for resting the bones, the Dawar is an excellent choice.

EL KHAN HOTEL, *Kafr El Gouna. Rates: $40-60. Credit cards: Visa. Call Orascom for information and reservations.*

El Khan is another small oriental style located in Kafr El Gouna. Some find the less ornate architecture more attractive to some than the neighboring Dawar El Omdah.

WHERE TO EAT

Most international visitors pay half board hotel rates that include breakfast and dinner buffets at the main dining hall in their hotel. However, there are various specialty and independent eateries throughout El Gouna. If you are paying half board, you can eat at other restaurants within your hotel and pay the difference between your bill and the standard charge for the buffet (usually LE60-70 in major hotels). For lunch, most people simply indulge in a sandwich or pizza at one of the beach or pool bars. Listed below are some restaurants in El Gouna.

ALL SEASONS, *Sonesta Paradisio. Tel. 547-934-6. Credit cards: all major credit cards accepted.*

The main dining hall in the Paradisio, All Season's offers breakfast and dinner buffets as well as an a la carte menu. The food comprises tasty continental and Middle Eastern cuisine, but expect to pay five star prices-LE70 for dinner and LE40 for breakfast.

CAFE DES ARTISTES, *El Gouna Museum in Kafr El Gouna.*

One of the hottest spots for eating and drinking in El Gouna, the Cafe serves home style Italian cooking-basically, steaks, pasta, and salads. It can get crowded, so for eating, it's best to show up early or to call ahead. If you're just drinking, head upstairs to the roof for one of the best views in El Gouna, especially on a clear night when the stars are out. Appetizers cost LE5-10 while main courses won't set you back more than LE25- a bargain for Red Sea resorts.

EL SAYADIN FISH RESTAURANT, *the Movenpick. Hours: 11am-11pm. Credit cards: all major credit cards accepted.*

Located in its own structure overlooking lagoons and the Movenpick beaches, it should be the ideal eatery in El Gouna. Unfortunately, the food isn't always first rate, but hopefully it will improve-it's certainly worth trying.

SEEING THE SIGHTS

The natural surroundings and El Gouna's funky sites account for sites to see. The almost charming **El Gouna Museum** (open 10am-noon, and 2pm-4) in Kafr El Gouna is home to an art gallery featuring exhibits by contemporary Egyptian artists and a collection of replicas of pharaonic artifacts. Somehow, the fake stuff just isn't the same.

A more interesting, but time-consuming alternative, is "Desert Breath," dubbed by El Gouna, "the world's largest current land-art installation." Set in the deserts ten kilometers out of El Gouna, it features giant inverted cones dug into the dunes and covers 100 square kilometers. If you're interested in checking it out, contact the excursion office in one of the larger hotels.

NIGHTLIFE & ENTERTAINMENT

Though El Gouna doesn't offer the wilder nightlife found in Hurghada or Sharm El Sheikh, there is plenty to keep you busy. All of the hotels contain bars and sponsor a variety of entertainment from dances and discos to movies and cultural exhibitions. Typically each establishment has a set program of different events every evening. Schedules are published on flyers and are posted throughout the resort. Listed below are some of the more happening night time locales.

EL ARENA, *Kafr El Gouna. Schedule and prices vary.*

An outdoor amphitheater, El Arena serves as an all purpose nightspot. On the weekends, or when its quite crowded, the late-nighters come to dance into the early morning while on week nights, foreign movies are shown on a big screen. The animation teams puts on shows several times a week and classical and popular music concerts as well as fashion shows and also held here. Check with the authorities to get the current schedule.

SCENARIO FUN PUB, *the Movenpick. Prices and hours vary.*

A bar which serves as a pub, disco and game room. Karoake and billiards are popular activities.

ZEYTUNA BEACH BAR, *on its own island on the beach between the Miramar and the Movenpick. Transport by water taxi twice hourly (check the schedule). Prices and hours vary.*

Located on a large spacious beach, the beach bar may be the most rustic night spot in El Gouna. A simple beach bar by day, at night barbecues and other party type events are held. Once again, you should check out the schedule to find out what's on tap.

LE BAR, *Sonesta Paradisio.*

Promoted as a romantic setting, it is a pleasant and quiet spot in which to enjoy a drink, but feels very much like a hotel bar.

GALLERY BAR, *the Movenpick. Hours: from 5pm.*

A cocktail bar featuring cocktail bar type music.

PATIO BAR, *Dawar El Omdah. Hours: all day until about midnight.*

Basically the pool bar at Dawar El Omdah, the Patio Bar is really quite pleasant in the evening when the light goes down and the heat chills out. The lagoon and the neo-Oriental architecture makes for more charming setting than the typical five star hotel bars at the bigger resorts.

SPORTS & RECREATION

As a resort, El Gouna is not short of sporting and recreation options. Each of the hotels has a pool and those not in Kafr El Gouna also have extensive beaches. Between the Sheraton Miramar and the Movenpick is the Zeytuna Beach, shared by the entire resort and featuring a nice bar that serves food as well as drink. For **water sports**, you can arrange water skiing, para-sailing, canoeing, pedalos, and sailing at the Beach Center at the Movenpick.

For **scuba diving**, the **Nautico Diving Center** at the Paradisio offers all levels of PADI courses, equipment and boat rentals, and organizes both day and overnight excursions to reefs throughout the northern Red Sea.

There are **health spas** at the Movenpick, Paradisio and Kafr El Gouna with jacuzzi, steam bath, sauna, and gymnasium facilities. There are **also tennis and squash courts** at the Paradisio and Movenpick, and massages can be arranged by appointment. Finally an 18 hole **golf course** is slated to open near the Paradisio in 1998, and there are horse and camel stables at the Paradisio where **riding** lessons and excursions can be arranged.

SHOPPING

A small shopping mall in Kafr El Gouna features a small convenience store, and several shops selling T-shirts, film, hats, and other souvenirs. There are also shopping centers in the Sheraton, Sonesta, and Movenpick.

EXCURSIONS & DAY TRIPS

Travel agents in the bigger hotels organize day trips to Luxor where visitors can at least get a glimpse of major sites such as Karnak. Excursions can also be arranged to the Monasteries of Saint Antony's and Saint Paul's, and Cairo. The dive centers organize dive safaris, lasting anywhere from a half day to a week or more to reefs. The Information Office in Kafr El Gouna *(Tel. extension 3101)* can also organize day and overnight excursions into the nearby deserts by horse, motorcycle, or jeep.
• **Subex Paradiso**, *Tel. 065/447-934. Fax 065/447-933. Located in Paradiso Sonesta in El Gouna, 20 km north of town*

PRACTICAL INFORMATION
Banks & Currency Exchange

Banks and currency exchanges are located in the Movenpick, Sonesta, and Movenpick, but only open from 9-11am and again in the evening from 6-8pm.

Post Services

Hotels mail letters and postcards and should sell stamps.

Telephones, Telex, & Fax

All hotels offer international and domestic telephone, fax, and telex services.

Tourist Information

Hotel personnel are generally good sources information. The **excursion offices** in all of the five star hotels which organize excursions and day trips from El Gouna can also be of assistance regarding travel-related information.

HURGHADA

Driving into **Hurghada**, the place hardly seems to live up to its billing in official pamphlets as an Egyptian Riviera or Costa del Sol. Rather, the military installations, construction debris, and huge windmills remind one of say, a reject Pink Floyd album cover. The town itself is littered with half-finished concrete blocks and cheap souvenir shops that lend its dusty streets the aura of a modern Middle Eastern prospecting town instead of a resort meant to compete with the Greek islands or Nice for European tourist dollars.

Yet hundreds of hotels and independent self-contained "holiday villages" pack in more than a quarter of a million sun-starved Europeans annually. Originally they came for the diving, for Hurghada offers access to world class reefs, but in the last decade an epidemic-like proliferation of resort hotels now attract a clientele looking for little more than a beach and guaranteed sun and here they find it for a fraction of the cost they might pay in the traditional European holiday destinations like Spain, France, and Greece.

Furthermore, though many never even make it beyond the confines of their "holiday village," Hurghada offers the illusion of an exotic Middle Eastern experience. Though "Bedouin Night" at the Marriott or belly dancing at the Cha Cha Disco may not strike you as authentic Egyptian culture (though it surely is a cultural experience), it seems to give many of Hurghada visitors at least the impression that they have sampled a truly foreign culture. Meanwhile the hotels and resorts to their very best to cater to the orientalist fantasies of their clients.

History

A sleepy fishing and oil town until the tourism boom of the 80's, the town of Hurghada was founded in 1909 by British employees of the Shell oil company. After Egypt became the major front-line state in the Arab-Israeli conflict, the Red Sea Coast, including Hurghada was a highly militarized and during the 1967 Six Day War, a short battle was fought on Shadwan, the biggest island off Hurghada which today offers some of the most isolated and peaceful camping in the area as well as excellent fishing and diving. Until peace was made with Israel in 1979, Sinai remained occupied and the Red Sea coast continued to be militarized and off limits to foreigners.

While peace was being made in 1979, the first major hotel, the Sheraton was opened beginning the development of the Red Sea as a tourist destination and cash machine for Egypt. In the last fifteen years, more than a hundred hotels and resorts have been constructed up and down the coast around Hurghada, but the fast growth has not been without considerable side effects. The world-class coral reefs and marine life which make the region a tourist gold mine in the first place are now threatened by overexposure to human contact. Careless boatmen toss their anchors onto reefs as divers prepare to take the plunge, many of them with the idea that a chunk of the stuff would make a nice momento to take home. Overconstruction and poor planning have decimated the beaches which are now ruined by concrete jetties and docks. The Egyptian government has recently implemented strict regulations to protect the environment and diving centers have begun promoting environment-friendly diving, but many observers feel it is already too late.

ARRIVALS & DEPARTURES

By Airplane

EgyptAir, *Tel. 02/575-0600 in Cairo*, flies Cairo-Hurghada-Cairo several times daily and one-way rates are about $150. For similar prices there are also weekly or twice weekly flights to Luxor, Aswan, Alexandria, and Sharm El Sheikh. Many European tour operators fly direct charters between Hurghada and European destinations. There also some flights between Hurghada and Arabian destinations.

By Boat

The ferry between **Sharm El Sheikh** and Hurghada (Siqalla) runs three and six times weekly depending on the season and the weather. Tickets cost LE110 and can be bought in the port of Siqalla, at El Shaymaa Sea trips (065/546-901) in El Dahar, and at many hotels. The trip takes 6-7 hours and is not recommended for those prone to seasickness.

By Bus

In Cairo, buses depart from Ahmed Helmy Bus Station in Ramses Square, and from Abdel Moneim Riyad Terminal near the Ramses Hilton north of Tahrir Square. From there Upper Egypt Bus Co. or West Delta Bus Co. buses runs eight buses daily. Leaving prior to 5pm, one-way tickets cost LE40; evening buses cost LE45, and the ride should last not more than 6 hours. Buses from **Hurghada** to **Cairo** depart at 10am, 1pm, 3pm, 5pm, 6:30pm, 10:30pm, 11:30pm, 12:15am, and 1am. Daily service to **Alexandria** leaves at 1pm.

There are also buses between Hurghada and Upper Egyptian and Red Sea destinations including Suez, El Quseir (7am, 3pm; LE7), **Luxor** (6am, noon, 5pm, 11pm; LE15-30), **Aswan** (4 & 11pm; LE18), Qena (7pm, 8pm, & 11pm; LE9), Safaga (hourly, LE3.50), and Marsa Alam (7am; LE10) to the south.

SuperJet buses depart for **Cairo** at 10am, 1pm, 3pm, and 5pm from the depot in northern El Dahar. Tickets cost LE45 for morning buses and

LE50 for those departing in the afternoon and evening. One bus daily to **Alexandria** leaves at 1am and costs LE70.

By Service

The service depot is near the telephone centrale off El Nasr Street in El Dahar. Peugeot seven-seaters and minibuses leave regularly from the taxi station on the airport road off Nasr Street by the City Council for Suez, El Quseir, Safaga, Qena, **Luxor**, and **Cairo**. Prices range from LE5-20 depending on how far you're going. Simply head to the taxi station find a vehicle headed for your destination and as soon as it fills up, you'll be off-no set schedules. Be aware that if your taxi is exclusively foreigners, you may be charged private taxi rates which can soar through the roof.

ORIENTATION

Approaching from Suez, a police checkpoint welcomes you about 15 km north of town. You know you're getting closer to town as the construction sites and debris begin to increase. Town, known as **El Dahar**, begins with El Shahid Riyad Square (with the large white mosque), where the Suez road gives way to El Nasr Street, Hurghada's main drag, before continuing on to the old fishing and oil port of **Siqalla** and the coastal Sheraton and Safaga roads-home to most resorts. The **airport** is about five kilometers south of El Dahar.

In El Dahar off El Nasr Street, are several major short streets such as Souk Street lined with restaurants, boutiques, travel agencies, and souvenir shops and buzzing with commercial activity. Separating this urban hub from the coast itself is a large hill, Gebel El Afish. Linking the hub and the beach area, the location of most budget and mid-scale hotels, Sayed Karim Street links the circle where Abdel Aziz Mostafa and Soliman Mazhar streets meet, with the beach and the hospital area, home to famous Hurghada landmarks like Peanuts Bar.

Two kilometers beyond El Dahar, the port of Siqalla offers little to tourists, but its southern outskirts have given way to a great number of mainly mid-scale hotels and restaurants along the Sheraton Road. At the heart of Siqalla, the port and Harbour can be an interesting site, especially when the fishermen unload their catch or boats are being taken in or out of the sea.

Beyond Siqalla, there's a 40 kilometer strip of tourist resorts, villages and beaches all the way down the Sheraton Road and on to Safaga.

GETTING AROUND TOWN

The large resorts are self-contained and many tourists rarely leave their own hotel complex. The town of El Dahar and the fishing village of Siqalla are both manageable on foot, but otherwise you'll need motorized transportation. Larger hotels and resorts run their own shuttles to and from the **airport**, El Dahar, and major tourist attractions (of which their are few) such as the Vegas-like entertainment complex of Alf Leila wa Leila.

By Boat

Boats transport divers and others to the dive sites and islands but there are no water taxis for practical purposes. See the Sports and Recreation section for recreational boating.

By Bus

Most large hotels and resorts run their own shuttles to and from the airport and town.

By Taxi & Minibus Service Taxi

Taxis are the primarily mode of transportation for tourists and are more expensive than in Cairo or even Luxor. Expect to pay not less than LE5 no matter how far you go and LE20 for just a 20 minute ride. If you can muster up a group of six or seven persons heading to a common destination and pile into a Peugeot 504, the pain can be spread.

Minibuses are far cheaper than taxis and run up and the down the main streets including the Hurghada-Safaga road along the coast where most of the major tourist establishments are located. Just flag one down heading in the right direction and check with the driver about whether he'll be passing by your destination. A ride of 20 minutes or less shouldn't cost you more than a pound. Just hand it over after getting out of the minibus at your destination.

Be aware that empty minibuses are apt to treat you as a regular taxi would, e.g., for LE10 he'll take you down the block. If you're going south, most minibuses end their route at El Samaka, but you can just hop on another one continuing south.

By Car

Cars rented in Hurghada come in handy for those looking to make excursions up and down the coast or in the desert. Any hotel or travel agency can point you in direction of car rental firms, and the international firms such as Avis and Budget are located in major resorts like the Marriott and the InterContinental.

WHERE TO STAY

Expensive

INTERCONTINENTAL HURGHADA, *Hurghada-Safaga Road 12 kilometers south of Siqalla. Tel. 065/443-911. Fax 065/443-910. Capacity: 300 rooms. Rates: $115-175 single, $135-195 double, $500-2500 suites; $5000 Presidential Suite. Credit cards: all major credit cards accepted.*

At the InterContinental, a world class resort in every sense, you can enjoy some the Red Sea's best facilities not to mention Hurghada's most expensive room, the $5,000 a night Presidential Suite. Recreationwise the pool, beach, and diving center rank amongst the nicest in Hurghada and guests can pursue activities like horseback riding not available at other resorts. The architecture is a weird combination of pseudo-neoclassical, Egyptian, and typical hotel cookie cutter but it somehow works. The InterContinental also boasts some of the best hotel food in Hurghada, including an Italian restaurant and a fresh fish eatery, the Fish Market. The Captain's Bar, while not the most popular watering hole in Hurghada, has some of the best decor and atmosphere. Finally to top it off, the only casino in Hurghada is here.

HURGHADA MARRIOTT BEACH HOTEL, *Hurghada-Safaga Road. Tel. 065/443-950. Fax 065/443-970. Capacity: 284 rooms. Rates: $120 single. $150 double. $300-400 suites. Credit cards: all major credit cards accepted.*

A world class resort in every sense, the spanking new Marriott meets the highest standards in every aspect from the presidential suite to the dive center. Most rooms feature excellent views of the sea and the suites, fit for a king, have multiple views, space, and every possible comfort including a television which like a James Bond gadget emerges from a wooden cabinet at the push of a button. The only detectable drawback is a lack of atmosphere. Except for the Egyptian accents of the staff, this place could be in Florida or Thailand.

HILTON HURGHADA RESORT, *Hurghada-Safaga Road. Tel. 065/442-116/7/8. Fax 065/442-113. Capacity: 240 rooms. Rates: $88-113 single. $111-136 double. $242-559 suites. Credit cards:all major credit cards accepted.*

It's about what you'd expect from Hilton: good service, high standards, and little atmosphere. It may be a cut below the Marriott or InterContinental (televisions don't emerge from cabinets at the touch of a button) but it's also a bit cheaper and the facilities are still top rate. The Pub and Galaxy Disco are some of Hurghada's most popular nightspots and the eateries include the standard beach bar, one of Hurghada's best fish restaurants, the Laguna, and an Italian restaurant.

HURGHADA SHERATON HOTEL, *on the Sheraton Road 4 kilometers south of Siqalla. Tel. 065/442-000/1/2. Fax 065/442-333. Telex 92750 SHRGA UN. Capacity: 120 rooms. Rates: $130 single, $170 double, $195 suites. Credit cards: all major credit cards.*

The granddaddy of luxury hotels in Hurghada (it opened in 1979), the Sheraton is often mocked for its plastic atmosphere, and indeed, astroturf is everywhere. Newer and grander hotels like the Marriott make the Sheraton look modest, but it still features respected dive center, gorgeous views, and two of the best beaches in all of Hurghada. Residents can stay in the main building or in chalets along the beach-ideal for families. The usual assortment of water sports and recreational activities are available.

SOFITEL HURGHADA HOTEL, *Hurghada-Safaga Road. Tel. 065/442-261/71. Fax 065/442-260. Capacity: 312 rooms. Rates: $90-100 single, $100-110 double. Credit cards: all major credit cards accepted.*

It's typical Hurghada modernity but the Arabesque touches in the rooms and decor give the Sofitel a touch of class. The facilities match those at any of the major resorts in Hurghada, the service is excellent, and the prices not too astronomical when compared to similar establishments.

SINBAD BEACH RESORT, *6 kilometers from town on Hurghada-Safaga Road (PO Box 18, Hurghada). Tel. 065/443-261/2/3. Fax 065/443-267. Capacity: 199 rooms. Rates: $90 single, $110 double, 120-250 suites. Credit cards: all major credit cards accepted.*

Known around town for its happening disco, this massive complex is headquarters to the Sinbad empire in Hurghada (there are 3 other Sinbad hotels). The beach is longer than most and only marred by the industrial looking boat pier, but the well-developed pool is heart of the resort. It features water slides, bars, two excellent restaurants including a Lebanese patisserie and a pick-your-own fish grill, and buzzes with activity fueled by the hotel's animation team and DJ. The Stingray Dive Center operates 12 boats and organizes introductory dives, overnight diving safaris, other water sports, and fishing. Sinbad also runs that silly yellow submarine.

SONESTA BEACH RESORT HURGHADA, *7 kms from town and 2 kms from the airport. Tel. 065/443-664/0/2. Fax 065/441-665. Telex 93242 SONCA UN. Capacity: 144 rooms. Rates: $80 single, $100 double, $140-200 suite. Credit cards: all major credit cards.*

Not as flashy or elegant as say the Marriott, the Sonesta offers all of the luxuries and facilities one could want including one of Hurghada's few natural beaches (and a few Italians going natural too). The rooms are not plush, but spacious and comfortable. For food guests can choose between decent but not spectacular buffets in the main dining hall, standard continental and American food a la carte at Chez Dominique, and Middle Eastern cuisine in the "tent" which also features excellent live Arabic music in the evenings. By sea is the beachside terrace "Wings 'n' Things" which grills up lunch year around and dinners during the summer. The Pub is a pleasant bar with billiards but the "I just called to say I love you" casio music program is a bit tiring. El Garage disco doesn't pack them in, but is quite enjoyable if you're not interested in a full fledged rave. Like other major resorts the Sonesta features a dive center, supervised daycare programs for kids, wind surfing, day trips for snorkeling and diving, and a health center with squash courts.

CORAL BEACH VILLAGE, *Hurghada-Safaga Road. Tel. 065/442-160/1/2. Fax 065/443-577. Capacity: 298 rooms. Rates: $80 single, $100 double, $120-240 suite. Credit cards: all major credit cards accepted.*

Another upscale "holiday village" renowned for its diving center and the in-house reef.

HELNAN REGINA HOTEL, *Hurghada-Safaga Road. Tel. 065/442-272/4/5. Fax 065/442-276. Capacity: 235 rooms. Rates: $60 single, $72 double, $160 suite. Credit cards: All major credit cards accepted.*

A typically charmless postmodern Hurghada resort catering to Italians and Russians, the Regina offers the usual assortment of facilities: a small private beach, two swimming pools, dive center, restaurants serving buffets, a small shopping center and decent rooms with satellite television and the usual amenities. Some rooms, especially in the main building have good views of the sea.

MAGAWISH VILLAGE, *15 kilometers south of Siqalla on Hurghada-Safaga Road. Tel. 065/442-620/1/2. Fax 065/442-759. Capacity: 326 rooms. Rates: $60 single, $75 double, $165-192.50 suite. Credit cards: All major credit cards.*

Located well down the coast from El Dahar and Siqalla, Magawish was the second big resort to open in Hurghada after the Sheraton. Though comparable to other upscale hotels in terms of amenities, it's the only resort out of all of them to boast natural reefs right off its beach.

AMBASSADOR CLUB/SONESTA BEACH RESORT HOTEL, *next to the Airport 5 kilometers south of Siqalla. Tel. 065/444-501/2/3. Fax 065/442-933. Capacity: 112 rooms. Rates $75-80 single, $85-90 double. Credit cards: all major credit cards accepted.*

The Ambassador is essentially an add-on to the Sonesta Beach Resort to which it is linked by a shuttle which runs between the two every 15 minutes. Residents can use all of the facilities at the Sonesta which only makes sense given that the Ambassador really has none, except for a pool, and is located a kilometer from the beach. Rooms are well-equipped with air-conditioning and satellite television, but there are no views to speak of.

ROYAL CATARACT RESORT, *on the Sheraton Road about half a kilometer out of Siqalla. Tel. 065/444-150/1/2/3. In Cairo 02/360-0863. Fax in Cairo 02/360-0864. Capacity: 161 rooms including 22 suites. Rates: (half board): $75 single: $100 double. Credit cards: all major credit cards accepted.*

The simple, but pleasant architecture falls somewhere in-between Pueblo and North African while all the rooms have the usual first class amenities including nice balconies. Facilities include a dive center, private beach, two pools, water sports, animation, tennis courts, billiards, and table tennis tables. Also, there are several bars and eateries, including the required Italian restaurant, and beach and pool bars. Additional facilities include a conference center and a kids' club for the little guys so you can sun in peace.

OLD VIC TOURIST VILLAGE, *Hurghada-Safaga Road just beyond the Marriott 5 kilometers south of Siqalla. Tel. 065/442-064, 442-235. Fax 065/442-064. Capacity: 67 rooms. Rates: villas LE360. Credit cards: Visa.*

Old Vic rents small villas situated right on the beach for about $100 a night. There does not appear to be much going on, but then again perhaps you don't need an Italian animation team and constant techno to ensure a relaxing and enjoyable vacation. Next door, the popular Daoud's pub serves passable Indian food and rocks virtually every night to Daoud and his live band which plays good covers of old rock'n'roll tunes.

Moderate & Budget

MASHRABIA VILLAGE *Seven kilometers south of Siqalla on the Safaga Road. Tel. 065/443-330/1/2. Fax 065/443-344. Telex 20021 AMCON UN. Capacity: 152 rooms. Rates $45 single, $70 double, $80-150 suite. Credit cards:Visa.*

The magnificent wood workings so closely associated with Islamic Cairo may seem out of place in this town, but I give this cozy little resort an 'A' for atmospherics. Rooms are tastefully decorated in Arabesque decor including David Roberts prints and the lush, well kept gardens make a lot of the other resorts look barren. The staff is exceeding friendly and the dive center Orco, is PADI authorized.

EL SAMAKA CLUB HOTEL *Just beyond the Sonesta on the Safaga Road. Tel. 065/443-565, 442-228. Fax 065/442-227. Capacity: 200 rooms. Rates: $40 single, $60 double. Credit cards: not accept now but soon "Insha-alla."*

Though much less funked up than the ritzy five star big name resorts, this homey little tourist village, catering mostly to Germans, is an excellent cheaper alternative. Rooms offer all the amenities and comforts except for television and the beach rivals those of most of the fancy resorts. Wind surfing, diving, exercise and massage facilities are all available on the resort itself and residents can use the pool at the sister Desert Inn across the street. The beach area features a small lagoon ideal for kids.

SAND BEACH HOTEL *in El Dahar by the Three Corners. Tel. 065/547-821/2, 547-992. Fax 065/547-822. Capacity: 135 rooms. Rates $ 50-60 single, $80-100 double, $150 suite. Credit cards: Visa, Mastercard.*

Offering all the amenities and comforts of the typical tourist resort village, Sand Beach is just minutes away from the heart of El Dahar with its bazaars and restaurants. The subdued, yet attractive white facade and simple architecture blends in well with Hurghada's natural setting and seems refreshingly plain compared to most of the other resorts which are frankly gaudy. Though the beach isn't a knockout, the three terraced pools are a cut above the competition. The diving center is run by the Weshahy brothers, some of Hurghada's most experienced and capable hands. Ahmed Weshahy is also the front-desk manager and an excellent source of information.

THREE CORNERS VILLAGE, *2 Corniche Street on opposite side of Gebel Al Afish from downtown. Tel. 065/547-816, 548-816/7.; in Cairo 02/ 347-6840, 347-0850, 345-5150. Fax 065/547-514; in Cairo 02/02/347-6850. Capacity: 135 rooms. Rates: $40 double, $75 suite. Credit cards:Visa.*

An older sister to the newer and more luxurious Three Corners Empire, the Village is a prototypical early Hurghada resort, and is almost charming in its lack of sophistication. The two rows of rooms running from the main building to the beach enclose a complex that includes a bar, a pool, patios, a beach bar and grill, the diving center and the beach itself which is narrow and bordered by rather unpicturesque concrete piers. The pool is small but features two jaccuzzis-rare for a three star establishment. The archaic condo-like structures of rooms attest to the relative age of the resort. With prominent air-conditioning units and septic tanks on top, they somewhat resemble lower middle class urban housing units-not especially attractive or conducive to a "resort" atmosphere. The beach is open to non-residents for LE15 a day.

LA BAMBOLA HOTEL, *on Sheraton Road just outside of Siqalla. Tel. 065/442-013, 442-086. Fax 065/442-085. Capacity: 56 rooms. Rates $28 single, $35 double. Credit cards accepted.*

A typical, if not charming, mid-scale establishment, La Bambola features relatively large air-conditioned rooms, some of which have a view of the sea while others overlook the small mountains behind Hurghada. The Seaman's Pub is semi-popular and the small pool and bar in the back is a handy and private spot to hang out if winds makes the beach unpleasant. Residents also enjoy access to the quality Sheraton and Regina beaches. The Hollywood Bar on the top floor, while not exactly raving is adorned with classy pictures of movie stars and overlooks the sea and Giftun Island.

THE THREE CORNERS EMPIRE HOTEL, *Hospital & Sayed Karim Streets in El Dahar. Tel. 065/549-200-9. Fax 065/549-212. Capacity: 234 rooms, 108 suites. Rates: $56 single, $70 double, $100 suite. Credit cards:Visa and Mastercard.*

The newest and most posh hotel in the town itself, the Three Corners Empire complex is indeed a small empire encompassing a complete shopping complex, the popular Peanuts Bar, two other pubs and three eaties including the "Belgian Restaurant." As the "Empire" isn't located on water itself, residents have free access to the smallish beach at the sister Three Corners Village 150 meters up the road. There is also a nice pool and rooms feature deluxe amenities including air-conditiong, satellite television, clean bathrooms, and minibars.

MARLIN INN HOTEL, *Hurghada-Safaga Road. Tel. 065/443-791/2/ 3/4/5. Fax 065/443-790. Capacity: 258 rooms. Rates: $40 single, $90double. Credit cards:Visa.*

There aren't any Marlin in the Red Sea, but this modest resort fits right in with all the other tourist villages-it caters to Italians and Germans most of whom come to lie in the sun like beached whales for a couple of weeks. Rooms are air-conditioned and have satellite television.

BLUE MARINE HOTEL, *Hurghada-Safaga Road across from Old Vic. Tel. 065/444-401/2. Fax 065/444-402. Capacity: 30 rooms. Rates: $30-45 single, $35-50 double, $65 double. Credit cards: Visa.*

Catering to midde class, middle aged French people on package tours, this cozy, clean small hotel has a pleasant outdoor terrace with a bar and restaurant. The only problem: the beach is no where in sight as the hotel is on the main highway across from the Old Vic.

GOLF HOTEL, *Sheraton Road just outide of Siqalla. Tel. 065/442-828. Fax 065/444-328. Capacity: 36 rooms. Rates: $18 single, $30 double, $36 triple. Major credit cards accepted.*

There's a slightly hollow old time *fin de siecle* aura (especially in the lobby)about this mid-scale hotel which offers clean if forgettable rooms, some of which have a view of the sea. Residents have access to the small Saklia Beach several hundred meters down the road.

PANORAMA HOTEL, *Corniche just south of Geisum and Sand Beach hotels. Tel. 065/447-890. Fax 065/443-045. Capacity: 33 rooms. Rates: LE32 single, LE34-44 double.*

This modest hotel and dive center offers an exellent location along the coast and away from the buzz and hastle of downtown El Dahar, which can be reached in a quick walk. No frills, but a good choice if you're on a budget. Rooms are air-conditioned.

EL AROSA HOTEL, *off the corner of Sayed Karim and the Corniche. Tel. 065/548-434, 549-190. Fax 065/448-434. Capacity: 30 rooms. Rates: LE95 single, LE115 double.*

One of the nicer and more charming hotels in town. Rooms, are decorated with relatively classy pictures of pharaonic Egypt and feature air-conditioning, satellite television, and more often than not, excellent views of the sea. Residents have access to Geisum Village's beach and pool located 100 meters away.

GEISUM VILLAGE, *Corniche Street next to the Sand Beach. Tel. 065/547-994/5, 546-692. Fax 065/547-994. Capacity: 78 rooms. Rates: LE65 single, LE100 double, LE200 triple. Credit cards: Visa.*

A touristy village and resort, it shares a small beach with Sand Beach. Rooms are middle of the line and feature air-conditiong, television, phones, and decent enough bathrooms. The hotel contains a dive center, and other water sports, such as wind surfing, can also be pursued.

SINBAD INN, *Sayed Karim Street, El Dahar. Rates: $20-40 doubles and singles. Credit cards: Visa.*

Clean and pleasant, this small branch of the Sinbad empire is one of the comfier hotels in El Dahar itself. The rooms are clean and comfortable with small showers, satellite television, air-conditiong, and minibars, and a shuttle bus ferries residents to Sinbad Beach Resort where they can use the extensive recreational facilites. The inhouseAlaadin Restaurant and Nightclub serves average food and morphs into a seedy local bellydance club which runs all night-an experience in itself.

AQUAFUN, *Sheraton Road about a mile out of Siqalla. Tel. 065/443-693/4/5/6. Fax 065/443-691/2. Capacity: 112 rooms. Rates: $30-45 single, $35-50 double, $50-70 double. Credit cards: all major credit cards.*

With its mirrors, squiggly lines and fruity colors, the Aquafun couldn't be more unEgyptian and looks like it could have been built in France circa 1977. Nonetheless, it's clean, well run, and contains excellent facilities. The beach and pool are both quiet nice for Hurghada and the oriental restaurant and the bar both have decent views of the sea. There is also an Italian eatery and the rooms have all the amenities of a first class hotel. If you're not interested in a distinctly Egyptian experience (you wouldn't come to Hurghada anyway) it's not a bad choice.

ROYAL HOTEL, *off the Sheraton Road just out of Siqalla on short road to Saklia Restaurant. Make turn at Omar's Inn. Tel. 065/447-728/9. Fax 065/447-195. Rates per person(half board): $24 single, $16 double, $14 triple. Credit cards: Visa.*

In a city full of bad architecture, this just may take the cake as its orange, blue and glass exterior looks like a sad attempt at something between a space ship and a glass office building. Having said that, the staff is friendly, many rooms have good views and the facilities are typical of any mid-rate hotel. Rooms have minor-league satellite television (four European channels), air-conditioning, private baths, and phones. Residents can use the Saklia beach 100 meters down the road.

EFFIEL HOTEL, *just out of Siqalla off the Sheraton Road on the road to Saklia Restaurant. Turn off at Omar's Inn. Tel. 065/444-570/1. Fax 444-572. Capacity: 43 rooms. Rates (half board): $25 single, $35 double.*

Brand new mid-scale hotel located on prime realestate with excellent views of the sea, Harbour, and Giftun Island as well as building sites in between. Residents can use the beach at Saklia next door and a pool is situated on the roof which offers the best views of all. The manager, Shayeb Aziz Boutros, is a wonderful man who worked his way to the top. You'll have to ask him what a certain French architect has to do with Hurghada.

CALIFORNIA HOTEL, *off Sayed Karim and Hospital streets about 100 meters from the Corniche and Sand Beach Hotel. Tel. 065/549-101. Rates: LE10-15 for rooms sharing bath; LE20 for room with private bath. Prices can fluctuate according to demand.*

A longtime darling of backpackers and budgeteers, "the Hotel California" as it's popularly known, is nothing fancy, but the warm hospitality, the loud colorful murals adorning the walls, and the more adventuresome clientele totally compensate. Besides, the prices can't be beat. Though there's no air-conditioning, but rooms do contain fans. The roof, while not exactly decked out, offers good views of the sea and for LE5 you can camp-not bad considering the breeze and beautiful stars make for a far better snooze than a musty, stuffy hotel room. Sometimes barbeque parties are held on the roof. Residents can use Sand Beach or Three Corners beach for a fee and the management can hook you up with diving or you can shop for yourself.

HAPPYLAND HOTEL, *Sheikh Sebaq Street, El Dahar. Tel. 065/547-373, 549-195. No Fax Rates: Doubles: LE28 with private shower, LE22 without. Triples: LE36 with private shower; LE30 without. No credit cards.*

The HappyLand is one of Hurghada's oldest and cheapest hotels which time and modern tourist resorts seem to have passed by. Now it caters mainly to Egyptians, which at least lends it some local color and good cheer. It's well located in town with easy access to restaurants and tourist facilities, but offers no views.

WHERE TO EAT

All of the major hotels have at least one major restaurant, usually serving Middle Eastern and continental food. Buffets featuring different nightly themes are very common and seafood, not surprisingly, is the regional specialty. All of the upscale hotels (Hilton, InterContinental, Marriott) feature quality Italian restaurants and separate seafood eateries. Most holidayers pay a half board rate that includes breakfast and dinner buffets – i.e., a lot of second-rate hotel food.

In town on Sayed Karim, El Nasr, El Souk, and Abdel Aziz streets are several cheaper independent eateries convenient for those staying in El Dahar. There are also fastfood stalls selling fuul, ta'amiya, and other cheap eats in the area around the Upper Egyptian Bus. Co. Provisions can be bought retail at any one of the grocers located on all major streets in the main town.

In El Dahar

RED SEA RESTAURANT, *El Souk Street off El Nasr Street. Credit cards: Visa, Mastercard.*

The nicest, and priciest restaurant in El Dahar features a full fledged Italian ambiance on the indoors ground floor and a colorfully decorated Egyptian setting on the roof, both of which are worthy of a bringing a date. Specialties are German and Italian cuisine along with grilled and continental seafood dishes. Standard grilled fish goes for LE19 while the knock'em dead Red Sea platter will set you back LE37. Other specials run as high as LE50 but what sets this establishment apart from its competitors is the emphasis its puts on all the little things from the decor and the fresh bread baked on the premises (yummy!) to the snappy service.

MATA'AM EL SALAM (El Salam Restaurant), *corner of El Souk and 26 July Streets. No credit cards.*

Formerly just a fuul and ta'amiya joint this popular local eatery has upgraded to include excellent grilled kekabs, kofta and poultry. Don't be scard off by the groups of local workmen and the lack of English, the place is clean and is a perfect alternative to buffets and tourist restaurants. For LE10 munch on a roasted half chicken, soup, salad, rice, bread AND a soft drink. No alcohol.

CAFE PRINCE RESTAURANT & PIZZERIA, *Sayed Karim Street.*

Serving the usual assortment of fish dishes and continental style pastas and meat fare, Cafe Prince always seems to attract a crowd and most of them like the gooey pizzas best. Though perched right on the busy Sayed Karim Street, the well tended hedges and citrus trees provide a much needed buffer from the dusty traffic and nearby construction as well as some ambiance. The service isn't exactly snappy and the food won't win three stars from Michelin anytime soon, but it is cheaper than its rival up the street, the Red Sea Restaurant.

QUICK COOK CAFE & RESTAURANT, *El Souk Street (El Horreya Street).*

Hardly more than a hole in the wall, this no-frills eatery serves simple food and always seems to be busy. Cheaper than most, it offers simple grilled fish for LE15, grilled shrimps for LE25, and a tasty *samak sayyadia* (fisherman's style)-fish drenched in an Egyptian style tomato sauce.

SCRUPLES BAR-B-QUE, *Hospital Street 150 meters from Three Corners Empire Hotel.*

It's a meat eater's paradise offering dozens of grilled and continental style meat, chicken, and seafood dishes.

EL MEADDAWY, *26 July Street opposite Pharaoh's Restaurant.*

This hole-in-the-wall eatery caters primarily to locals and serves excellent no-frill Egyptian cuisine. Pig out on stuffed pigeon, beans, soup, rice, bread, and a soda for LE10.

Siqalla & Sheraton-Safaga Road

FELFELA, *Sheraton Road just north of Safir Hotel 2 miles out of town. No credit cards.*

Though it's become a cliche for Egyptian food, Felfela's in Hurghada really does the job. In fact, it may be the only authentic Egyptian restaurant, complete with Egyptian atmosphere and architecture, actually located on the sea, in all of Hurghada. This menu essentially dittos the one in Cairo except for the addition of several seafood dishes: fried or grilled fish, fried or grilled shrimp, and calamari. The whole grilled fish for LE28 is a hefty portion of some of the best tasting seafood in Hurghada. Felfela's also contains a pool hall.

EL SAKLIA, *southern edge of Siqalla off the Sheraton Road. Tel. 065/442-497.*

Though not as elaborate, or famous as Felfela's, this independent eatery has made a name for itself as one of the few restaurants specializing completely in fish. Also, like Felfela's it is one of few eating locales actually on the sea, overlooking Hurghada's harbour. Order from a number of grilled, fried, and baked seafood meals, or pick your own lobster out of the murky pond by the beach. During the day, it runs a beach which caters to nearby mid-scale hotels (lots of Russians).

NAWARA'S, *Hurghada-Safaga Road next to El Samaka Village about 12 kilometers south of town. Tel. 065/446-053/4/5. Fax 065/446-052. Visa, Mastercard accepted.*

Recently opened by Egyptian film actor Hesham Selim, Nawara's may just be the best Arab restaurant in Hurghada. Unlike Felfela's which specializes in hearty Egyptian dishes, Nawara's emphasizes the finer cuisine of the Levant-Lebanon and Syria. The mezzes from the creamy labna and salads, to the spicy calamari take the usual starters and raise them to another level. Among the main dishes, one can choose from the usual assortment of kebabs and grilled dishes but also from Lebanese specialties such as spicy fish and chicken *fatta*-chicken, rice, and bread swamped in yogurt spiced with garlic. To top it off, the traditionally based rural Egyptian architecture provides a great atmosphere without getting carried away. Diners can sit in or outside.

SAMOS, *Sheraton Road in southern Siqalla opposite Omar's Inn. Tel. 065/443-484. Visa, Mastercard.*

The feta may be Egyptian cream cheese, but other than that it's pretty much the real thing as diners can choose from a menu listed with such dishes as Pastizio, mussaka, and about 50 other Greek specialties ranging from souvlaki to octopus. The setting on the Safaga Road is less than spectacular but the blue and white paint and constant Greek music lend at least a hint of authenticity.

DAOUD'S INDIAN RESTAURANT & PUB, *Sheraton Road at Old Vic Village past the Marriott. Tel. 065/442-235. No credit cards.*

Extremely popular as a watering hole and for the Daoud's nightly rock'n'roll, this establishment also serves excellent Indian food. In summer '97 an Indian chef was brought on board and soon an authentic tandoor oven should be in place to produce even more authentic tandoori dishes and Indian breads.

PISCES, *in Marlin Hotel 12 km south of town on the Safaga Road just north of Sinbad Beach Resort. Tel. 065/443-791.*

Significant for being a rare breed – a Chinese restaurant.

KFC, **PIZZA HUT**, **& BASKIN ROBBINS**, *Tel. 065/443-791. Together just north of Sinbad Beach Resort. Open 24 hours*

You know what you're getting.

SEEING THE SIGHTS

As far as Hurghada is concerned, the most important attractions are underwater and offshore. As far as historical monuments and the like go, there really isn't anything of interest.

NIGHTLIFE & ENTERTAINMENT

As a resort and tourist town, Hurghada is not lacking in things to do when the sun sets. But as the clientele is transient, the trick is to discover the hotspots which seem to change every few weeks or so. All of the major resorts and tourist villages contain their own pubs, bars, and nightclubs, but with nightclubs and discos especially, many of them have a hard time attracting customers from outside their own establishment and thus reaching the critical mass needed to really make it happen. Listed below are those establishments which seemed to be favored as of 1997-98.

Nightclubs and Discos

CHA CHA'S, *Hospital Street, El Dahar, 300 meters from Three Corners Empire Hotel (with which it is associated). Open 10pm until late. Minimum charge: LE20 which goes towards drinks.*

The hotspot for energetic young Germans and Brits staying in town, this mainstay of Hurghada's late night scene has been packin 'em in for years. Unlike some of Egypt's other nightclubs which have been picking up on the heavy techno beats of the '90's, Cha Cha's slate of dance music doesn't seem to have been upgraded since 1988. INXS, Men at Work, disco sounds of the '70's like the Village People, and Bob Marley still seem to do the job for the highly charged young northern European crowd to which the club caters. Surprisingly, even though locals abound the male-female ratio doesn't get out of hand. Tuesday nights are especially popular and it's a good idea to get there on the early side if you want to claim a table. The interior design isn't fancy and may even be a bit tired and cheap, but that doesn't really matter. This is one of the five most happening and fun discos in Egypt. Local Stella costs LE9 and stronger drinks range from LE8 for local brandy and ouzo to LE100 for champagne. Most mixed drinks cost LE10-25.

REGINE'S DISCOTHEQUE, *Sinbad Beach Resort on Safaga Road. 15 kms south of town. Tel. 065/443-261/2/3/4/5/6. Minimum charge:LE20. Credit cards: Visa.*

The late night hub for the tourist villages and resorts, Regine's packs in the young and (sexually) hungry virtually every night. The Russian dancers aren't terribly impressive but provide a nice change of pace from the grinding techno-two twenty minute shows begin at midnight and 2am. Decidedly more upscale and high-tech than Cha Cha's, Regine's doesn't start swinging until past midnight, but if you want a table, you'd better make reservations or arrive on the early side.

GALAXY DISCO, *Hilton Hotel, Hurghada-Safaga Road 15 kilometers south of town. Tel. 065/442-116. Credit cards: All major credit cards accepted. Minimum Charge: LE20.*

Typical up-scale Egyptian hotel disco, Galaxy features the usual pop/dance music, and a few flashing lights, and depends on crowds migrating upstairs from the popular pub. Very loosely enforced "couples only" policy is used primarily to keep herds of locals from invading. The Galaxy is generally more tame than Regine's and more relaxed as well, there's far less sexual tension and energy. Five nights a week (except Saturdays & Sundays), the Russian dancers do their thing: an oddball revue of Vegas, Can-Can, and cabaret.

THE DOME, *InterContinental Hotel 15 kilometers south of El Dahar. Tel. 065/443-911. Minimum charge: LE20. Credit cards: all major credit cards accepted.*

With its extensive space, smaltzy neo-classical architectural, and light plaster interior the Dome is a refreshing change from other dancing halls in Egypt where dark carpeting and concrete is usually the norm. Though not as popular as Cha Cha's, Regine's, or even the Galaxy, the Dome still regularly attracts modest crowds big enough for a party but not so overwhelming that one can't find space on the dance floor. It has had a reputation for being a bit of a pick-up place, but then again what disco doesn't. So what's the real downer about this place? No local Stella.

EL GARAGE DISCO, *Sonesta Beach Resort between town and the airport. Dress: Casual. Minimum charge: none. Credit cards: all major credit cards accepted.*

With its black cement, colored banners, and no minimum charge, El Garage has a haphazard and unpretentious air about it and when it gets going, it's great if you're not looking for a full fledged late night bash.

When it doesn't, the staff and locals take over the dance floor which is also kind of fun. Local Stella costs LE9.

Bars In Town (El Dahar)

PEANUTS, *Three Corners Empire complex at the end of Sayed Karim Street.*

The epicenter of pre-Cha Cha's northern European nightlife in Hurghada town, Peanuts is bustling with beer guzzling Germans and Brits munching out of huge baskets of what else?-peanuts. That may sound a bit scary to some, but things don't seem out of hand and the place really has everything going for it-except for its insignia which employs a black boy reminiscent of "Sambo" wearing a tarboosh. Seating is available outside where the weather from March until October is extremely pleasant while inside, the classic horseshoe wood paneled bar is always packed. Local Stella goes for LE9 and imported Bitburger German beer on tap is also available.

1001 NIGHTS (ALF LAYLA WA LAYLA), *Hospital Street. Minimum charge:none.*

A cozy little restaurant and bar which serves sheesha and local Stella for only LE6.50, Alf Layla wa Layla features oriental decor, Arabic music, and exudes an Egyptian flavor missing from other tourist haunts.

SCRUPLES BILLIARD HALL, *corner of El Souk and Abdel Aziz Streets.*

The biggest pool hall in town and part of the seemingly always expanding Scruples chain, the Billiard Hall features seven full size pool tables and a snooker table. Tables can be rented for LE15 an hour. Local Stella costs a nice and cheap LE7.50.

Bars In Siqalla & the Sheraton-Safaga Road

DAOUD'S INDIAN RESTAURANT & PUB, *Old Vic tourist village on Sheraton Road past the Marriott. Open noon 'til late. No Minimum charge. No credit cards.*

Veteran musician Daoud opened this establishment in December in '96 and it quickly became one of Hurghada's most popular hang-outs. Though open all day, it gets going around 10 pm when Daoud and his band begin playing immaculate covers of rock'n'roll standards from the '60's, '70's, and '80's. If you've had with the Spice Girls or just want to hang with your mates and enjoy some old fashion rock'n'roll, this is your place.

THE PUB, *the Hilton 15 kilometers south of El Dahar on the Sheraton-Safaga Road. Tel. 442-116. Minimum charge: none. Major credit cards accepted. Open from 5pm-2am.*

With its wood paneling, long bar, and plenty of draught beers from which to choose, The Pub exudes that traditional "pub" atmosphere largely missing in bars throughout Egypt. Through extensive promotional work, it enjoys a loyal clientele consisting of local dive instructors and tour leaders which makes it quite happening as well. On Thursday nights, "Divers' Night", everybody gets a free local Stella at 8pm and free food. Other popular nights include "Karoake Night" on Sunday, "Ladies' Night," on Tuesdays, and coming soon, "Latino Night." Decent light rock'n'roll casio style rounds out the party atmosphere but makes it difficult to carry on a conversation.

CAPTAIN'S BAR, *InterContinental Hotel on the Sheraton-Safaga Road.*

Less popular than the Pub in the Hilton, the Captain's Bar may up its next door rival in the maritime decor department with the boat hull hanging from the ceiling. Another good feature, the outdoor terrace, makes an especially pleasant setting for an evening cocktail when the weather's good (about 90% of the time). Captain's Bar also features live music of the casio variety.

THE BULLDOG, *several kilometers south of El Dahar on the Sheraton Road by the Aqua Fun Resort. No phone listing. No credit cards. No minimum charge.*

Those of you who have enjoyed the Bulldog's namesake in Amsterdam may be disappointed-no skunk cannabis here. Nonetheless, it's a modest cheery kind of place popular with (surprise) Hurghada's residential British population. As one of them said, "we need a place where we can get loud."

SPORTS & RECREATION

Diving

Though Hurghada may be a disaster in urban planning and Egypt's capital of kitsch, it still boasts access to **coral reefs** brimming with such diversity in marine life and color that some divers claim them to be amongst the finest in the world. However, unlike some Sinai resorts which enjoy the luxury of having coral growing right off their beaches, the reefs here are offshore and only accessible by boat, thereby forcing would-be Cousteaus to organize dives through a local dive center.

Major dive centers offer courses at all levels, as well as dive 'safaris' lasting anywhere from a half day to two weeks. Generally five day introductory PADI courses cost between $300-400 and enable those who pass to be PADI certified, meaning they can dive virtually anywhere in the world. One day introductory dives, which do not lead to certification cost about $50-100. More advanced courses generally cost about $60 a day, but very according to the course. Generally a day of diving, sans instruction, costs between $50-100 and each night in the sea also costs $100 per person, everything (food, dive equipment etc.) included. Dive safaris of more than one night should be arranged at least one week in advance.

When choosing a dive center, especially if you are a novice, it's important to remember that the importance of safety cannot be over-stated. In this respect, the major hotels and well-established diving centers, especially those which are PADI certified, are probably your best bet. They are most likely to maintain their equipment and follow international safety standards. Having said that, so much depends on the personnel operating the centers and leading the dives, and because there is a constant turnaround in these personnel quality of instruction at most dive centers fluctuates.

I'd recommend shopping around and talking to other divers who may have insight as which centers have their act together. Listed below are major dive centers with international credentials:

- **Barracuda Diving Center**, *Hurghada Marriott Beach Resort. Tel. 065/443-950. Fax 065/443-970.* Authorized PADI center.
- **Blue Lagoon**, *Grand Hotel. Tel. 065/443-751. Fax 065/443-750.* Authorized PADI center.
- **Divers Lodge**, *InterContinental Hotel. Tel. 065/443-911, ext. 8822. Fax 065/443-910.* Authorized PADI center.
- **Dive Point Diving Center**, *Coral Beach Village. Tel. 065/442-160-5. Fax 065/443-577.* Authorized PADI 5 star IDC center offering complete range of diving courses and facilities including an in-house reef (rare in Hurghada).
- **Easy Diver Diving Center**, *Three Corners Village. Tel. 548-816, 547-816. Fax 065/443-300.* Authorized PADI resort.
- **Golden Turtle Diving Center**, *Safir Hurghada Hotel. Tel. 065/442-902/3/4. Fax 065/442-901.* Authorized PADI.
- **Jasmine Diving Center**, *Jasmine Village. Tel. 065/442-455.* Authorized PADI.
- **Magawish Diving Center**, *Magawish Resort Village. Tel. 065/442-620. Fax 065/442-759*
- **Nautico Diving & Surfing Center**, *Arabia Beach Hotel. Tel. 065/548-790.*
- **Ocean Red Diving Center**, *Sand Beach Hotel. Tel. 065/547-821/2. Fax 065547-822.* Authorized PADI center run by Ayman Weshahy and his brothers – some of Hurghada's first and most successful entrepreneurs.
- **Red Sea Scuba School/Emperor Divers**, *Princess Palace Hotel. Tel. 065/444-854. Fax 065/444-845.* The only center in Egypt, and one of 26 world wide, to receive the 5* CDC rating from PADI. Offers classes at all levels including instructor courses.
- **Subex Hurghada**, *Hospital Street, El Dahar. Tel. 065/547-593*
- **Virgin Divers Diving Center and Scuba School**, *Grand Hotel. Tel. 065/443-751, 443-754. Fax 065/443-750*

Snorkeling

Though you may not be rich or brave enough to engage in scuba diving itself, snorkeling enables even the most novice swimmer the opportunity to enjoy the splendors of marine life. Outings, beginning with half-day trips for as little as LE20, can be arranged through virtually every travel agency, dive center, and hotel from the largest resort on down.

A typical full day snorkeling excursion to Giftun Island costs LE30-500 per person and includes transportation, equipment, and lunch. Should you desire just to rent equipment that's not a problem either. Just make sure that it works and fits.

Beaches

Most moderate and upscale hotels have "private" beaches for exclusive use by their guests. Most of these beaches are but a 100 meters long and are often marred by concrete piers used to dock the hotel boats. In any case, those hotels which do not have their own beach usually have agreements with one that does that enables guests use the beach, sometimes for a small fee (LE5-10). This also includes use of the pool, if there is one.

Most hotels also let nonresidents use their beach for the day for fees ranging from LE50-60 at big resorts like the Marriott and InterContinental to LE15-20 at smaller establishments like Sand Beach in El Dahar. The Sheraton, which has two of the largest and nicest beaches in all of Hurghada, only charges LE20 per person for the day.

Other Water Sports

Most major hotels and tourist beaches feature an "aquacenter" which operates water activities other than diving such as wind surfing (Hurghada winds are ideal), water skiing, and boating. Catamarans can be rented at the **Sofitel**, *Tel. 442-261*, **Magawish**, *Tel. 442-620*, the Procenter at **Jasmine**, *Tel. 442-450*, and the Coconut Surfcenter, *Tel. 442-665*.

Submarines & Underwater Sightseeing

Those who wish to explore coral and marine life while staying completely dry, may join an underwater submarine tours. The most famous is the yellow **Sinbad Submarine** operated by the Sinbad Beach Resort. For $50/LE170 per adult, or $25/LE85 per child under 12, you can spend two hours aboard "Hurghada's only real submarine" which plunges as far as 20 meters under water so that you may view coral and marine life up close. Reservations can be made by phone, *Tel. 065/444-688/9/90 or 065/443-261-5, Fax 065/442-166*, or at one of the reservation desks in the following major hotels: Three Corners Empire, Conrad

International, Sonesta, Sofitel, El Samaka, Hilton, Marriott, Sinbad, Beach Albatross, InterContinental, or Three Corners Village.

The smaller **Aquascope A10** offers similar underwater tours; for reservations, *Tel. 065/548-249 or Fax 065/548-249.*

Fishing

Though diving is the name of the game in Hurghada, the Red Sea also beckons those looking to hook up with big game fish. Tuna, wahoo, kingfish, dolphin fish (mahi mahi, not the mammal), barracuda, groupers, jacks, sharks and even sailfish are all present in the waters off Hurghada and given enough time and planning you can arrange to fish for them. Unfortunately for anglers, sports fishing has not been developed like diving so finding a capable captain, a decent boat, and good equipment if you don't have your own takes a little extra work.

Nonetheless, if you're fortunate to have the time and wherewithal to make a weekend of a trip, the waters off of Shadwan, Gobal, Giftun, and even Safaga can offer the trophies of a lifetime. Even if you're not lucky enough to make a big catch, sleeping under the stars on the sea or on one of the islands can be a magical experience in itself. The season for trawling for game fish begins in October and lasts until March though fish can be caught all year around. June, for example, is considered the season for sailfish. Some hotel aqua centers and dive centers can organize day fishing trips, but for serious fishing expeditions, try the outfits mentioned below.

The Red Sea Fishing Center, *just off the Sheraton Road and the road to El Saklia Restaurant in Siqalla. Tel. and Fax 065/442-316.*

This is the only company that specializes in fishing and the only to use customized fishing/trawling boats and hires captains knowledgeable of fishing and the fishing grounds off the Hurghada coast. While trips of any length can be arranged, beginning with half-day, bottom fishing trips, Mr. Yasser Nassar who runs the company, recommends trips of five or six days to reach the outlying fishing grounds. For 24 hours, a boat, including personnel, costs LE1200. Food and equipment (LE25 for each rod and reel combination) are extra. Trips should be booked, usually by fax, a month or even two months in advance.

The Marine Sports Club *by the Grand Hotel, about a kilometer south of the airport. Tel. 065/442-974, 443-008, 443-977 ext. 19. Fax 065/442-646.*

This is a private club catering mainly to Egyptian members but it also rents boats to nonmembers for a reasonable LE550 24 hours. a week in advance for your best chance at success. They also rent out single rooms for $15 and doubles for $30. Call as far in advance as possible.

Another option is to phone Capt. Mohammed Marzouk at (065/443-057) or Captain Nasr (065/444-356) both of whom skipper boats for Cairo businessman Abdel-Moneim Shalaby. Mr. Shalaby's boats, which are much nicer and better equipped than the Club boats, can be rented for LE700 a night. You can also call Mr. Shalaby in Cairo, *Tel. 02/242-1435*. Again, call at least a week or two in advance. Of the two captains, Capt. Nasr speaks better English.

Health Clubs, Gyms, & Other Sports

Most upscale hotels and resorts offer gyms and clubs as within their complex as well as facilities for other sports such as tennis, volleyball, ping-pong, squash and aerobics. In most cases, these are reserved for members and residents only, but try calling the major resorts for inquiries and to make reservations if necessary.

SHOPPING

For Egyptian handicrafts and souvenirs, you're much better off doing your shopping at the Khan El Khalili in Cairo, or God forbid, the tourist souks in Luxor or Aswan. Many of the major hotels and tourist village house gift shops or even mini-shopping malls, where the usual Egyptian knick-knacks are sold for higher prices than in Cairo. In town, the **bazaar** area off of El Nasr Street between Sheikh Sebak and El Souk streets buzzes with tourists (many of whom will never make it to the Khan) and is littered with shops and boutiques selling everything from T-shirts to upscale gold and silver jewelry. As far as practical goods and provisions are concerned, most major hotels contain a shop selling toothpaste, toiletries, sunscreen etc., but it will be on the expensive side. In town are several grocery stores, vegetable markets, and pharmacies.

Unfortunately, as soon as tourism began to boom in Hurghada a trade emerged in coral, shells and other relics of marine life better left in the sea. Egypt has come a long way in developing its conservation policies and efforts have been made to stop the raping of the sea and the selling of protected marine wildlife, but sometimes enforcement becomes lax. From my perspective, it's best that you refrain from purchasing any goods taken from the sea (other than fresh fish) as it only encourages those who destroy the beautiful marine life to continue.

EXCURSIONS & DAY TRIPS

The Islands

There are a number of small and large undeveloped islands off the Hurghada coast, the most popular of which, Giftun Kibeer, is a popular destination for day trips and sometimes overnight camping excursions. Those who come for the day, pay LE30-50 per person for the boat trip out, a barbecue lunch, and snorkeling equipment. These trips can be arranged or joined through virtually any hotel or dive center. Should you decide to embark on such an excursion, be aware that there is no shade on Giftun, so you must protect yourself from the sun with sunscreen, clothing, and/ or a hat and sunglasses.

Camping trips on Giftun or one of the other islands affords opportunities to experience fantastic sunsets, sunrises, and beautiful nights skies, as well as splendid isolation and plenty of fresh air and quiet. Camping excursions are far less popular than day trips, but can also be arranged through dive centers and hotels. Count on paying LE100-200 per person per night depending on the size of your party. Also, if you do not have equipment such as sleeping bags, make sure the operator does, and if you camp during the late fall, winter, or early spring, take plenty of warm clothing as temperatures plummet after sunset.

Cairo & Luxor

The most popular trips are to the sea itself. But for those who make Hurghada their primary destination in Egypt, one day trips to **Luxor** or even **Cairo** are popular. Virtually any hotel or two-bit travel agency can arrange such trips though we'd obvious recommend that Luxor, and certainly Cairo, be given more than a day. Day trips to Luxor usually begin at $25-35 including transportation, guides, entrance fees while overnight trips start at $100. You can always make the trip yourself for much less, but you'd have to give yourself more than a day to accommodate the inefficiencies of public transportation. Also, you can rent a car for as little as $40 a day, but this entails long driving on roads which are dangerous to say the least, especially during darkness.

Monasteries of Saint Antony & Saint Paul

More manageable, bite-size day excursions can be made to the **monasteries of Saint Antony and Saint Paul**, *250 kilometers north of Hurghada*, where Christian monasticism was born in the 4th and 5th centuries. To reach them, you can rent a car, hire a taxi, or contact any travel agency about arranging a trip. (For details check "Monasteries of Saint Antony and Saint Paul" on pages 492-494.)

Desert Safaris

Becoming more popular in recent years, **desert safaris** generally entail a journey into the Eastern Desert and the mountains which loom behind Hurghada. Usually jeeps ferry passengers into the dunes where a Bedouin tribe will feed, entertain, and sometimes put up for the night, those on the safari. These trips can last from a day to a week or even longer. Shorter trips involving the whole Bedouin experience can often be a rather staged affair, but at least the outdoors and especially the night sky is stunning. If undertaking a longer trip be sure that you can trust the equipment and preparations of your guides. Plenty of food and especially water are critical as are navigational skills and tools. Most travel agencies and hotels can arrange such a trip which begins for as little as LE50 for a day trip. One company worth consulting if you are interested in undertaking a more serious excursion is **Trackers**, *on the Sheraton Road (065/442-532.)*

Ancient Quarries

One attraction you may consider visiting on one of these trips are the **Mons Porphyritis** at **Jebel Abu Dukhan** ("Mount Smoke"). Here, quarries were mined by the Romans for crystalline stone used in monumental buildings and arts and crafts. The quarries are approximately 40 kilometers away from Hurghada. Take the main road 20 kilometers north and turn inland – best done with somebody who knows the way. Expect to pay at least LE50 per person for a day's excursion.

Fifty kilometers south of Mons Porphyritis, **Mons Claudianus** was another quarry mined in Roman times and features unfinished granite columns and various other ancient construction debris as well as a ruined village. To get to Mons Claudianus, you need to go south of Hurghada and cut inland on a dirt road about 5 kilometers south of Hurghada. As it is not marked, be sure to get exact directions or travel with somebody who knows exactly which road to turn on. It is forty kilometers inland.

Mountains of the Eastern Desert

Looming behind Hurghada are the jagged mountains of the Eastern Desert which reach as high as 2,000 meters (7,000 feet). Situated between the aforementioned quarries are the tallest of these mountains, **Jebel Gattar** and **Jebel Shaayib El Binat**. The former is best known among local Bedouin tribes for the extensive vegetation clinging to its rocks and for springs bearing fresh water. The latter is the tallest of these mountains and is home to the legendary **Shagar El Nur** – the Tree of Light which according to local Bedouins can cure blindness. Both mountains make for excellent hiking and afford those who make the effort, splendiferous views and magnificent night skies.

Visiting the mountains requires at least one and probably two nights, and travel agencies such as Trackers will probably charge you as much as $35 a day for transport, food, and other provisions. Again, make sure you have plenty of water, and if your making the trip in winter, plenty of warm clothing.

PRACTICAL INFORMATION

Banks & Currency Exchange

Major resorts and tourist villages have exchange facilities in-house which usually open from 9 or 10am until 2 or 3pm and again in the evening around 6pm. Listed below are independent bank and exchange outlets in El Dahar.

• **National Bank of Egypt,** *El Nasr Street. Hours: 8:30am-2pm & 6pm-9pm.*
• **Banque Misr,** *next to National Bank of Egypt and across from Misr gas station on El Nasr St. Hours: 8:30am-2pm & 3pm-9pm daily.*

Emergencies

Many upscale hotels feature infirmary services on their premises.
• **Ambulance:** *Tel. 123 or 546-490*
• **Safa Hospital** *is next to the Bus Station.*
• **Diving Emergency Center Decompression Chamber,** *in Magawish Tourist Village. Contact Dr. Nassef, Tel. 442-625.*

Passports & Visas

Visa can be extended at **the Passports & Immigration Office** *at the northern end of El Nasr Street in El Dahar. Hours: 8:30am-3pm daily except Friday.*

Pharmacies

Toiletries basic items for personal hygience can be purchased in most upscale hotel shopping centers. Otherwise these are numerous pharamicies in El Dahar and Siqalla.

Photography & Film Development

Film development services are available at most tourist resorts.

Kodak Express *shops are located on the Hurghada-Safaga Road next to the Marlin Inn, across from the Grand Hotel, and in El Dahar on Sayed Karim Street across from Peanuts Bar.*

Photo Yoyo Fuji *outlets are located in the Three Corners Empire Hotel; the ZAK Shopping Center on the Sheraton Road; and in El Gouna.* In addition to developing and selling film they rent and sell equipment for underwater photography.

HM Video, *El Dahar. Tel. 065/545-182.* HM Video specializes in underwater video equipment and digitial reproduction.

Focus, *Sheraton Road. Tel. 065/444-675 or 444-64. Fax 065-444-675.* Specializes in underwater video and photography. Equipment can be rented.

Police
    The Police & Tourist Police *are in Siqalla and at the northern end of El Nasr Street. Tel. 546-723*

Post & Courier Services
    Post Office & EMS (Express Mail Service), *El Nasr Street. Hours: 8am-3pm daily except Friday.* Most hotels also mail postcards and letters.

Telephones & Faxes
    All five star and most four and three star establishments offer long distance telephone and fax services. In town itself many of the bazaar shops advertise phone and fax as well. The **public telephone exchange** is in El Dahar off El Nasr Street.

Tourist Information
    Travel agencies abound throughout town and virtually every tourist resort or village contains one within the confines. Otherwise hotel and dive center personnel can often provide helpful information. Finally, the **Egyptian Tourist Authority**, which can provide general information, has an office in Siqalla which opens from 9am-3pm and supposedly in the evening from 6-9pm.

Tourist Police
    The station is on Nasr Street a block north of the Red Sea Governorate offices. Tel. 065/546-723. There is also a major police station in Siqalla just off the Sheraton Road.

PORT SAFAGA

    Fifty kilometers south of Hurghada, **Safaga** has traditionally been a port serving ferries taking Muslims to the Haj in Mecca and commercial ships exporting minerals mined in nearby quarries. But this will soon change. As Hurghada has become over-saturated with hotels and resorts, developers have set their sights on Safaga and in the next five years, dozens of hotels will be constructed.
    For the time being there isn't much at Safaga, save a few hotels. Among its advantages are that the local reefs are not teeming with divers like those at Hurghada where some complain there are more divers than fish.

ARRIVALS & DEPARTURES

Service public taxis leave fairly regularly for Hurghada (LE5, 1 hour), Quseir (LE3, 45 minutes), and possibly Cairo (10 hours, ugh!), and Qena in the Nile Valley just north of Luxor (LE10, 3-4 hours).

Buses depart six times daily to Cairo (LE30-50, 9 hours); twice to Quseir (LE5, 1 hour), Qena (LE10, 4 hours), Luxor (LE20, 6 hours), and Aswan (LE35, 10 hours at least). Check with your hotel for the exact time table.

ORIENTATION

Hotels, the bus station, and about everything else is on El Gomhuriya Street which runs along the waterfront. Resorts and hotels are concentrated north of town and cheap restaurants and the post office are at the northern end of town itself.

GETTING AROUND TOWN

Service taxis zip up and down El Gomhuriya Street and a one-way fare to anywhere is 50pt.

WHERE TO STAY

THE HOLIDAY INN, *on the bay north of town. Tel. 065/452-821-3. Fax 02/578-3585. Rates: $90 single, $120 double. Credit cards: all major credit cards accepted.*

The major resort in Safaga, the Holiday Inn offers deluxe accommodations on the beach and also features a disco and several restaurants.

THE LOTUS BAY, *El Gomhuriya Street north of town. Tel. 065/451-040/1. Fax 065/451-042. Rates: $48 single, $65 double. Credit cards: Visa.*

The Lotus Bay is a step down from the Holiday Inn but is still pretty comfy. Rooms are spacious and comfortable with air-conditioning, television, and other expected luxuries. There is also a restaurant and a nice, usually empty beach

THE MAKA HOTEL, *off the road to Qena at the northern end of town. Tel. 065/451-866. Rates: LE25 double. No credit cards.*

The cheapest hotel in town with simple rooms with fans.

WHERE TO EAT

Cheapo Egyptian street food is available on **El Gomhuriya Street** at the northern end of town. Other than that, the upper scale resorts such as the Lotus Bay and the Holiday Inn have typical hotel restaurants serving seafood in addition to continental and Egyptian fare.

SPORTS & RECREATION

The Holiday Inn has a **diving center** that offers a variety of courses and organizes excursions. Snorkeling is also possible off the coast and all the hotels can rent you equipment. The Holiday Inn and some of the other hotels also have swimming pools and tennis courts, but non-residents must pay fees for use.

PRACTICAL INFORMATION

Most needs can be met on El Gomhuriya Street where three banks, the post office, the telephone office, and bus station are located.

EL QUSEIR

The only Red Sea port of any historic significance, **El Quseir** is nearly 140 kilometers south of Hurghada and 90 kilometers beyond Safaga. Founded during Roman times, it developed into a major port under the Arabs during the Middle Ages when trade between Egypt and Arabia was extensive. It also served as a major junction and port for pilgrims from North Africa going to and coming from Mecca and Medina.

Today it is a fishing and commercial port used primarily by ships exporting phosphates mined in the eastern mountains. It is quite a shabby little town, but some of the dilapidated buildings are still redolent of its historic past – at least it's not just concrete. However, El Quseir's shabby charm will soon be a thing of the past as developers are honing in now that Hurghada is beyond saturation.

ARRIVALS & DEPARTURES

Service taxis usually depart in the morning for Luxor, Safaga, Qena, and Hurghada, all of which can be reached for LE10 or less. Sometimes, there are also service to Suez and Cairo.

There are daily **buses** to Cairo (5am, LE50, 11 hours) via Safaga and Hurghada. There are also two buses daily to Qena and again to Safaga. Check with your hotel, or the bus station for details.

ORIENTATION

There are two main streets, one along the coast, and one that runs parallel to it about 100 meters inland. In between is the town's charming little market and the bus station; a number of restaurants and the service station are located where the two meet. The post office, telephone centrale, and National Bank of Egypt are at the northern end of town.

Everything is pretty much within walking distance except for the upscale resorts which are both north and south of town.

WHERE TO STAY

QUSEIR SIRENA BEACH MOVENPICK HOTEL, *8 kilometers north of town on Oulim Bay. Tel. 065/432-100/1/2. Fax 065/432-128. Rates: $100 singles, $130 doubles. Credit cards: all major credit cards accepted.*

This top of the line five star resort deserves kudos for its classy domed bungalows, environmental friendly practices, and the superduper breakfast buffets, ideal for kicking off a day of snoozing on the beach. The rooms all feature air-conditioning, satellite television, and other deluxe amenities, and facilities include a pool, diving center, and several restaurants and bars.

FANADER HOTEL, *two kilometers south of Quseir town. Tel. 065/341-414. Fax 065/431-415. Rates: $55 single, $90 double. Credit cards: Visa and Mastercard.*

It's not quite as spiffy or classy as the Movenpick, but it features similar domed bungalows with modern comforts and amenities, and there is a diving center and a large pool.

SEA PRINCESS HOTEL, *in town just south of the traffic circle next to the bus station. Rates: LE15 singles, LE20 doubles.*

The simple rooms have fans, but the place is shabby, especially the common bathrooms.

WHERE TO EAT

Cheap eats can be had in town near the bus station and the Sea Princess Hotel and near the souk. Otherwise the upscale hotels have pricier and classier restaurants serving continental and Egyptian cuisine with an emphasis on seafood.

SEEING THE SIGHTS/SPORTS & RECREATION

The upscale hotels have nice beaches and swimming pools as well as dive centers and aqua centers that offer wind surfing and other aqua sports. In town, the Sea Princess rents snorkeling gear for cheap.

As far as sightseeing, the **16th century fort** of the Ottoman viceroy Selim at the northern end of town overlooks the town and the sea. The town souk is quite colorful and on Fridays, the weekly markets attract Bedouin and other assorted characters from around the region to hawk their wares.

On the road to Qift in the Nile Valley, **Wadi Hammamat** is littered with graffiti left by travelers throughout history from pharaohs to King Farouk.

PRACTICAL INFORMATION

The **post office, telephone centrale**, and the **National Bank of Egypt** are all located at the northern end of town and operate the usual business hours except for the telephone office, which is open 24/7. The Movenpick and the Fanader can also change money and place international phone calls, though prices are dear. For any medical attention, you want to go to either Hurghada or Luxor.

19. SINAI

An intensely beautiful but stark land of sandy wastes and rugged mountains, **Sinai** is a mysterious land of myth and miracle. Despite its harsh landscape, it is uniquely rich in history. The only land bridge linking the world's two largest continents, Asia and Africa, Sinai was always of great strategic importance. Generals from Thutmosis III and Alexander the Great to Moshe Dayan have battled constantly to control it. Traders also used Sinai as the major commercial highway between Asia and Africa, greatly enriching Egypt in process. But for Egypt, Sinai's geopolitical and economic importance was a curse as well as a blessing as countless invaders – including the Hyksos, the Babylonians, Alexander the Great, the Arabs, the Turks, and most recently the Israelis – have successfully used Sinai as a stage for attacking the Egyptian heartland.

Part of Sinai's mystique stems from its being a place of Biblical myth and miracles. Prophets Abraham and Elijah wandered and sought spiritual solace and for Moses and the Israelites it was both a curse and blessing. Sinai was a place of refuge from the Egyptians who the Israelites escaped through the parting of the Red Sea, but its barren hills were hardly hospitable. The Bible describes it as a "great and terrible wilderness" where water and food was sparse and angry Israelites complained to Moses, "for ye have brought us forth unto this wilderness, to kill this whole assembly with hunger." The Lord then spoke to Moses through a burning bush and delivered to him the Ten Commandments at the summit of **Mount Sinai**.

Later, Mary, Joseph and Jesus rested here while fleeing Herod to Egypt. Though no historical evidence has been found relating to any Biblical tales, local legends and Biblical readings have led us to mark the holy sites, the most famous being **Saint Katherine's Monastery**, the world's oldest continuously active monastery built by Empress Helena on the site of the burning bush in 330 AD.

After millennia of war and occupation, the Egypt-Israel Peace Treaty of 1979 returned the Sinai to Egypt; it has been open to travelers and tourists for the first time in modern history. Today, thousands visit the

Port Said
MEDITERRANEAN SEA
Rafa
El Arish
ISRAEL
Ismailla
SINAI
To Cairo
Boku
Suez
Ahmed Hamdi
Tunnel
Nekhl
Âin Sukahna
Taba
Al Aqaba
Zaafarana
Abu Zeneima
GULF OF SUEZ
GULF OF AQABA
SAUDI ARABIA
Mt. Sinai
St. Katherine's
Monastery
Dahab
SINAI
MOUNTAINS
Nabq
G. Sanafir
Island
Tiran Island
Sharm El Sheikh
Ras Mohammed
RED SEA

SINAI

peninsula, not only to make pilgrimage the hallowed sites of Mount Sinai and Saint Katherine's Monastery but to explore its rugged natural beauty, relax on its beaches, and to dive in the waters off its coast, where you'll see some of the finest coral in the world.

History

Though Sinai did not give rise to a flourishing civilization of its own (Bedouin aside), it has featured prominently in Egyptian history. As early as the 3rd Dynasty (4,500 BC), Egyptians from the Nile Valley began **mining** turquoise, gold, and other minerals at sites such as Sarabit El Khadim west of Mount Sinai. When Egypt fell into disarray following the Middle Kingdom (c. 1900 BC), the **Assyrian Hyksos** became the first of many to invade Egypt through the Sinai, but what goes around comes around and beginning around 1,500 BC New Kingdom pharaohs like Thutmosis III, Seti I, and the Ramses III used Sinai as a bridge to Asia where they built huge empires in Palestine, Syria, and Asia Minor.

It was at the height of pharaonic power during the New Kingdom that Joseph and the Hebrews were to have come to Egypt as slaves, perhaps during the 18th Dynasty. It was also during the New Kingdom that scholars believe Moses was to have led the **Exodus of the Israelites** out of Egypt, supposedly during the reign of Ramses II's successor Merneptah (1,236-1,223 BC), though no historical or archaeological evidence relating to the Israelites has ever been found in Sinai or in Egypt.

During the Late Period a string of invaders beginning with the Persian armies of **Cambyses** in 525 BC used Sinai as a stage from which to penetrate a weak and vulnerable Egypt. Two hundred years later, **Alexander the Great** also invaded Egypt from Sinai en route to establishing a Greek occupation of Egypt that lasted 300 years. During this period the trade routes of North Sinai developed into international commercial highways and the **port of El Tor** on Sinai's Gulf of Suez coast became an important junction in the Arabia-Mediterranean trade and a major source of customs revenues for the Ptolemies.

Trade continued to flourish during the 700-year **Roman occupation** of Egypt that began around 50BC. It was early in Roman times that Joseph, Mary, and the baby Jesus crossed Sinai while fleeing Herod. During the first three centuries of the Christian era, Sinai became a place of refuge for Egyptian Christians fleeing Roman persecution and attracted large numbers of hermits and ascetics. In 330AD the Byzantine Empress Helena ordered the founding of a monastic order and the construction of a chapel on the site where allegedly the Lord spoke to Moses from a burning bush. The chapel became the **Monastery of Saint Katherine's** and was expanded to its present size in the 6th century by the Byzantine Emperor Justinian.

In 640, while sweeping across Sinai en route to capturing Egypt, the Arab Islamic armies of Amr Ibn El As easily converted the local nomadic Bedouin tribes to Islam. The Bedouin became the Arabs' proxies but abused the position as they began in engaging in piracy and Sinai became a zone of lawlessness. However, despite the lack of civil order, the integrity of Saint Katherine's remained intact under the orders of the Prophet Mohammed himself. During the early Islamic era, commercial traffic through Sinai reached new levels as huge amounts of grain and other types of tribute poured into Arabia from Egypt and North Africa. Trade suffered after the establishment of the Fatimid Caliphate in Cairo in the late 10th century and, during 200 years of **Crusades**, Sinai became an important battleground and bargaining chip. Using Sinai as a buffer to protect Egypt and the holy shrines of Mecca and Medina from Crusader invasion, Salah El Din built two castles, on Pharaoh's Island near Taba, and off the Gulf of Suez coast, both of which can still be visited. After Egypt fell under Mamluke control in the 13th century Sinai's commercial highways were reopened and trade flowed freely until the 20th century.

Always a strategic location, Sinai's importance significantly increased after the opening of the **Suez Canal** in 1869. This led Britain to occupy Sinai and the rest of Egypt in 1882, and during World War I, Turkish forces seized Sinai threatening seriously Britain's all important link with India and the East. After a major campaign to protect the Canal, the British retook Sinai in 1916.

Sinai again became a major theater of battle with the creation of Israel in 1948 when the Egyptians tried to liberate Palestine from Sinai but failed miserably as El Arish and Rafah fell into Israeli hands. The Israelis withdrew, but invaded again in 1956 after Nasser nationalized the Suez Canal and closed it to Israeli shipping. This time the Israelis gobbled the whole of Sinai as part of a campaign orchestrated in collusion with Britain and France to retake the Canal. Though defeated militarily Egypt won international support and Britain, France and Israel withdrew under great pressure from the world community, including the United States. Though Israel did not agree to do the same, Egypt then allowed the United Nations to establish a buffer on its side of the border in Sinai to monitor the cease-fire.

In 1967, war again broke out in Sinai, only this time it was to be a disaster for Egypt. In response to alleged Israeli provocation and threats against Syria in the spring of 1967, Egypt re-established its blockade in the Gulf of Aqaba and expelled the United Nations buffer forces. Though Israel knew Egypt had no intention of going to war and Nasser was privately negotiating the reopening of the Gulf of Aqaba in return for Israeli withdrawal from the demilitarized zone between Israel and Syria, Israel began the **Six Day War of June 1967** by launching a pre-emptive strike against its Arab neighbors. Israeli forces occupied Sinai within two days, obliterating Nasser's armies in the process. For the next seven years during the **War of Attrition**, Israeli occupying forces in the Sinai used their proximity to the Egyptian hinterland to bomb military, industrial, and civilian targets in the Canal Zone, the Delta, and even the Nile Valley in an effort to force Egypt to break with Arab ranks and signed a separate peace.

Egypt did sign a separate peace, but only after its armies successfully crossed the Suez Canal and invaded Sinai the **October War of 1973**. After breaking through the hitherto "impregnable" Israeli defenses of the Bar Lev Line, Egyptian forces failed to capitalize on early gains and within two weeks the Israelis launched massive counterattacks and even crossed the Canal. Under the auspices of American Secretary of State, Henry Kissinger, two disengagement agreements were signed, beginning an arduous peace process that saw President Sadat make his dramatic journey to Jerusalem in November 1977 before culminating in the **Camp David Agreements of 1978** and the 1979 **Egypt-Israel Peace Treaty**.

Under the terms of the treaty, Israel was to withdraw from Sinai by 1982 and except for **Taba** – from which it did not withdraw until after international arbitrators ruled in Egypt's favor in 1989 – Israel complied. For its part, Egypt agreed only to maintain a token military force in Sinai with no heavy artillery or air power. Also, the **Multinational Force and Observers (MFO)** was created to ensure adherence to the treaty. Since making peace and regaining permanent control of the Sinai, Egypt has gone to great lengths to develop its economic potential. At first this meant **tourism** and during the past 15 years, the resorts of Sharm El Sheikh, Dahab, Nuweiba, and Taba have seen massive development of resorts, hotels, and other tourist facilities that now accommodate more than half a million tourists from Israel, Europe, and elsewhere.

More recently, the government began implementing plans to resettle more than 3 million Egyptians from the overcrowded Nile Valley to North Sinai. In 1997, President Mubarak pressed a button opening the new **El Salam Pipeline** through which billions of gallons of fresh Nile water is to flow to Sinai where it will irrigate millions of feddans of reclaimed land and enable the development of industrial parks.

Meanwhile the indigenous **Bedouin** population, who have roamed Sinai for longer than anybody can remember, are seeing their ancient nomadic way of life quickly disappear. With their traditional grazing and camping grounds now being developed, and the lure of tourism dollars too great to withstand, many are giving up the old hard life of shepherding in favor of new careers as taxi drivers, tour guides, and even hotel owners.

ARRIVALS & DEPARTURES

From the **East Delta Bus Co. depot** in Cairo, buses depart daily for Sharm El Sheikh, Dahab, Nuweiba, Taba, El Tor, and Saint Katherine's. There are also buses from the Canal cities, Alexandria, and even Upper Egypt to Sinai. For El Arish in North Sinai, buses leave from Qulali bus terminal near Ramses Square and also from Port Said and Ismailia.

Driving from the Egyptian mainland to South Sinai, requires crossing the Suez Canal through the Ahmed Hamdy Tunnel 15 kilometers north of Suez. From Ahmed Hamdy the coastal road winds along the Gulf of Suez past El Tor before cutting east across Sinai's southern tip and Ras Mohammed to Sharm El Sheikh. North of El Tor, a very scenic road cuts east to Saint Katherine's and onto the Nuweiba on the east coast. To go directly to Nuweiba, Taba, and Dahab, the Nakhl Road cuts across the Sinai interior about 10 kilometers south of the Ahmed Hamdy Tunnel. If driving to El Arish and the Israeli border at Rafah, you must make your way north of Ismailia where ferries cross the Canal; from there it's a straight shot along the north coast.

EgyptAir and **Air Sinai** both fly domestic routes from Cairo, Luxor, Alexandria, and Hurghada to Sharm El Sheikh and increasingly, European tour operators are flying charters directly to Sharm from Europe.

THE BORDER WITH ISRAEL

*There are two main border crossings with Israel. For those coming and going to South Sinai, **Taba** is the crossing point. On the Israeli side, buses between Eilat and the border cost about NIS4. Leaving Israel you must pay a $30 exit fee or its equivalent in NIS. On the Egyptian side, you must pay an entrance fee of LE17. Fourteen day visas issued at the border are only good for travel in southeast Sinai so if you wish to go on to Cairo or even Ras Mohammed, you must get a full Egyptian visa from consulates in Tel Aviv or Eilat. Buses and taxis can take you from Taba to other points in Sinai with links to the rest of Egypt (see following "Taba" section). Leaving Egypt, there is no exit fee. If bringing your own car, you must have a carnet du passages and will be asked to pay insurance and customs.*

***Rafah** is the border post 40 kilometers east of El Arish in North Sinai and is used for traffic between Israel and the Egyptian mainland (Cairo). Procedures for crossing the border are similar to those at Taba. There is transport from the border at Rafah to El Arish and on to Cairo.*

Though it's not always so bad, expect serious and thorough customs and security inspections on both sides of the border.

TABA

Spectacularly set against the Sinai Mountains overlooking the upper reaches of the Gulf of Aqaba, **Taba** is a one-hotel resort and border town that became a monkey wrench in Egyptian-Israeli relations for nearly ten years after the peace treaty was signed in 1979. While Israel handed over the rest of Sinai on schedule by 1982, it refused to give over Taba maintaining that it was Israeli though records and maps clearly showed it to be Egyptian. It was only after international arbitrators ruled in Egypt's favor and the Egyptians agreed to pay $40 million in compensation that Israel finally handed over Taba in 1989.

Today it consists of a major border crossing and a voluptuous 12 story Hilton resort. The surrounding beaches and coast are among the most picturesque in Sinai, but will soon be overrun by developers in search of new frontiers now that Sharm El Sheikh has been saturated.

ARRIVALS & DEPARTURES

By Air

As of autumn 1997 one EgyptAir shuttle made the Cairo-Taba-Cairo route weekly on Mondays, but plans are in the works for making Taba a regional air hub. Round trip tickets for foreigners cost about LE1000 ($330), and the airport is at **Ras El Nakb** 40 kilometers from Taba.

By Bus

Two buses depart daily for Taba from the East Delta Bus Co. station in Abbassia in Cairo at 8am and 7pm (LE40, 8 hours). From Sharm El Sheikh, there is a 9am (LE15) and from Nuweiba and Dahab, there are 3-4 buses daily (LE10-15, check for departure times).

Departing Taba, buses at 9am and 3pm go to Sharm El Sheikh (LE15, 3 hours) via Nuweiba (LE8) and Dahab (LE10). There are also buses to Nuweiba at 2pm and one at 10am that goes on to Saint Katherine's (LE20) and Cairo (LE50, 8-9 hours).

By Service

Taxi drivers wait at the border and the Taba bus depot like lions in the Coliseum. Unless you are able to hitch with common taxi full of Egyptians, taxis will charge LE175-200 to go to Nuweiba or Dahab and LE300 to Sharm El Sheikh, which is a small fortune unless you can split the cost amongst a group.

By Car

Driving from Cairo, you need to take the Suez Road from the Autostrade to the Ahmed Hamdy Tunnel (LE5). From there take a right (south) and follow signs for the Taba-Nuweiba Road that cuts across Sinai. **EuropCar** in the Hilton is the only rental firm in Taba.

The Israeli Border

The Israeli border is open 24 hours day every day except on the Jewish Sabbath from sundown Friday night until sundown Saturday.

Leaving Israel entails paying a NIS50 departure tax. To reach the border from Eilat take the #15 bus (NIS4). If you are American, you will be granted a two week visa for Sinai only. To get a visa for the rest of Egypt, contact the Egyptian Consulate in Tel Aviv in Eilat. If bringing a car, you will have to pay insurance. Check the "Arrivals and Departures" in Chapter 6, *Planning Your Trip*, for details regarding crossing the border with a private vehicle.

ORIENTATION

Taba is 400 kilometers from Cairo and 240 kilometers north of Sharm El Sheikh on the Israeli border at the northern end of the Gulf of Aqaba.

Within a kilometer of the border itself is a small nondescript settlement that features a health clinic and some municipal offices. At the bus depot is a taxi stand, a small overpriced, unappealing cafeteria and some banks. On the coast itself in the voluptuous Hilton Taba Resort and the Ras El Nakb Airport is 40 kilometers away.

GETTING AROUND TOWN

Apart from the Ras El Nakb Airport, everything in Taba itself, including the border, is within walking distance. Taxis are available if you need transportation for luggage.

WHERE TO STAY

TABA HILTON HOTEL, *Taba. Tel. 062/530-140, 530-300. Fax. 062/578-7044. Rates: $96-140. single, $125-175 double, $220-355 suite. Credit cards: all major credit cards accepted.*

This massive 12 story modern resort hotel enjoys a spectacular setting overlooking the Gulf of Aqaba to the east and the rugged Sinai Mountains to the west. Nearly all of the rooms feature excellent views and five star amenities from spotless bathrooms to air-conditioning and satellite television. The palm-lined beach is beautiful and the large pool is also an excellent setting for sunbathing and general relaxation. The Taba Hilton operates one of the most respected and best equipped dive centers in the Red Sea and other watersports including boating, snorkeling, and wind surfing can also be enjoyed. If you're planning to come during Christmas, October (Jewish holidays), or any Islamic holiday, make reservations well in advance.

WHERE TO EAT

The Hilton complex contains several eateries ranging in ambiance and food style from the pool and beach-side snackbars to upscale Japanese. There are also several bars. The food and service is worthy of the Hilton's five star ratings but so are the prices.

Near the bus station is a **small cafeteria** but the food is less than fantastic and overpriced though cheaper than the Hilton.

SEEING THE SIGHTS

Taba's sites as it were are primarily underwater. If you get tired of beaching and bathing, the **Castle of Salah El Din** *7 kilometers south of Taba* makes for an interesting excursion. It is described in the "Between Taba and Nuweiba" section below. Transport can be arranged at the Taba Hilton or you can hire a taxi at the border.

NIGHTLIFE & ENTERTAINMENT

The **Taba Hilton** features a disco (minimum charge LE25) that opens nightly from 10pm until late. Very happening when the hotel fills up during Jewish holidays, it can be eerily quiet during the low season There are also bars and sometimes the hotel sponsors floor shows, evening beach barbecues, and other special events.

EXCURSIONS & DAY TRIPS

The Hilton can assist in organizing excursions to **Saint Katherine's Monastery** and **Mount Sinai**. Usually such as journey lasts two days and one night with an early morning climb to the summit of Mount Sinai. The price is about $150 for a vehicle that seats four or five. Alternatively, you can rent a car from EuropeCar in the Hilton and make the trip on your own. Be sure to make reservations for accommodation at Saint Katherine's (see the "Saint Katherine's" section below), fill up with gasoline, and bring warm clothing if traveling during fall, winter, or spring.

The Hilton also organizes **camel and jeep safaris** into the Sinai interior. The closest "attraction" is the picturesque oasis at **Wadi Quseib** *off a dirt road beginning just past the Fjord 15 kilometers south of Taba*. It can make an easy day trip. For more serious overnight excursions, make arrangements at the Bedouin settlements listed in the "Sinai Safaris" section on pages 558-561.

C.I.T. *(Tel. 062/530-264)* can organize jeep rentals and safaris, and camel safaris.

PRACTICAL INFORMATION

Banks & Currency Exchange

Banque Misr and **Banque du Caire** at the border change money and traveler's cheques. Banque du Caire follows traditional banking hours *(9am-2pm & 6-9pm)* while Banque Misr is open 24 hours. Money can also be changed in the Hilton.

Emergencies

A public hospital *is located in Taba;* the Hilton infirmary is open during the day. The nearest **decompression chamber** is in Eilat.

Police *can be reached at the Hilton, the bus station, and the border.*

Post Services

The Hilton mails letters and post cards and sells stamps.

Telephones, Telex, & Fax

Telephone, fax, and telex services are available at the Hilton.

BETWEEN TABA & NUWEIBA

The magnificent stretch of coast between Taba and Nuweiba features some of the most stunning natural beauty in Egypt. Here jagged, reddish colored rocks weathered by millennia of winds hover over pristine beaches while peering across the gulf to their cousins in Arabia and Jordan. Meanwhile, the sea radiates every shade of blue from the nearly clear turquoise of the shallowest sandbars to the almost black darkness of the deep. But after the development of Sharm El Sheikh and Dahab, developers have honed in on this virgin beach which will soon go up in concrete. Hopefully, Egypt has learned from the experiences of the past 15 years and will develop the area keeping in mind that its natural beauty is its greatest resource, and not necessary replenishable. Much the area, already dubbed the "Egyptian Riviera" in official pamphlets, has been sold to Orascom, the same outfit that developed El Gouna. By Egyptian standards, El Gouna was a model in good planning, but what Orascom does in Taba remains to be seen.

Described below are the 'tourist villages' and natural attractions between Taba and Nuweiba from north to south.

Pharaoh's Island & The Castle of Salah El Din

Seven kilometers south of Taba on Pharaoh Island. Hours: 9am-5pm. Admission: LE8 general, LE4 students. Boat transport to the island: a stratospheric LE11.

Perched on **Pharaoh's Island** seven kilometers south of Taba the heavily restored **Castle of Salah El Din** was originally a 12th century Crusader castle that was usurped by Salah El Din who rebuilt and expanded it. With its reefs and high winds the island was ideal for making fortifications to defend Sinai and the holy cities of Mecca and Medina on the Arabian coast from Crusaders advancing from Palestine. More recent restorations lend it a Disneyland-like sanitized quality and it is often packed with rather over-excited Israelis down from Eilat on day trips, but the views of the Sinai Mountains and the turquoise waters of the Gulf of Aqaba are nothing less than spectacular.

SALAH EL DIN HOTEL, *7 kilometers south of Taba. Tel. 062/530-340/ 1/2. Fax 062/530-343. Rates: $52 single, $64 double. Credit cards: Visa.*

The views of Pharaoh's Island and the Gulf of Aqaba are quite magnificent and the rooms with air-conditioning, clean baths, satellite television and mini-bars are comfortable and tastefully decorated. For recreation, diving is possible at Pharaoh's Island, there is a spacious and clean beach, and the hotel offers a host of other watersport opportunities. The Italian restaurant is more than adequate but pricey. Sometimes the hotel throws beach parties or features floor shows at dinner. The hotel can also arrange short camel safaris in the nearby mountains.

DIVE SITES BETWEEN TABA & NUWEIBA

Pharaoh's Island 7 kilometers south of Taba is famous for sharks, rays, and strong currents.

Marsa El Muqabila, 6 kilometers south of the Fjord-a long dive at 20 meters that features small caverns inhabited by octopus.

Ras El Burqa & Coral Garden, two dives just north of Basata featuring unspoiled reefs, and a myriad of colored fish including morays at Ras El Burqa and lion fish at Coral Garden.

Ras El Shitan (Devil's Head), 10 kilometers south of Basata features a collection of dives including several walls as well as shallow reefs.

The Fjord & The Sun Pool

Fourteen kilometers south of Taba is the beautiful and quaint turquoise inlet known as the **Fjord**. Set against steep cliffs, its calm waters and sandy beach is popular with bathers who come for the day. Just a half kilometer south of the Fjord is the **Sun Pool** a muddy sort of wetlands where bathing is prohibited, but the reefs off the beach between the Fjord and the Sun Pool are very accessible to divers and snorkelers. Food, drink and accommodation is available at the Salima Hotel.

SALIMA HOTEL, *about 20 kilometers south of Taba east of the main road. Tel. 062/530-130. Rates: LE35-50.*

Salima only has six simple rooms with common showers and toilets, so make reservations in advance if you want to stay here. Should you be equipped you can also camp. The setting overlooking the fjord is quite spectacular and the manager Mohammed is an affable and helpful gent. The Salima also features a small bazaar and a modest restaurant.

SALLYLAND TOURIST VILLAGE, *37 kilometers south of Taba in Bir Suweir. Tel. 062/530-380/1. Fax 062/530-381. Capacity: 68 rooms. Rates: LE95 single, LE105 double. Credit cards: Visa.*

Set in a small seaside oasis, the Sally Land features stone bungalows that blend in nicely with the village's natural surroundings. Rooms feature air-conditioning and private baths and there is a beach-side cafeteria and main restaurant; menus feature Egyptian and "American" cuisine. For recreation, guests can snorkel at the colorful reef situated just off the sandy beach or partake in wind surfing, fishing, and sailing. The hotel can also arrange overnight dive safaris as well as camel and jeep safaris.

AQUA SUN CLUB, *35 kilometers south of Taba east of the main road. Tel. 062/530-391. Fax 062/530-390. Capacity: 60 rooms. Rates: $15-25 single, $28-45 double. Credit cards: Visa.*

The modest Aqua Sun Club features 20 simple air-conditioned rooms with private baths. Rates include breakfast, while dinner can be taken at the main dining room or in the pizzeria. The Aqua Sun is quiet, isolated, and features an excellent beach and beautiful offshore reef.

BASATA

Basata is located 43 kilometers south of Taba. Turn east on the dirt road at Ras Burqa, Telephone (062/500-481; 02/350-1829 in Cairo). A night in the bamboo cabins costs LE18 per person, sleeping on the beach, LE10 per person; and day use of the beach, LE5. Meals cost LE15-20.

Set on beach that was probably imported from heaven itself, this nature friendly bamboo cabin village has attained legendary status as an alternative to the industrialized tourism that is spreading throughout the rest of Sinai. Founded in 1986 by the charismatic Sherif El Ghamrawy, the camp is an exercise in community living based on the ideals of harmony with nature and Bedouin tradition. All waste is recycled (mostly by the neighborhood goats), and water use minimized; the reefs are off limits to scuba diving (snorkeling is allowed), and loud music is prohibited. Guests can stay either in bamboo cabins or on the beach, and the self-service kitchen is available for preparing vegetarian or fish meals; bread is baked fresh on the premises. The billing system is based on trust, you write what you take and pay later. Showers and toilets are shared. Be sure to make reservations well in advance; they're booked well into 1998 but if you call, there may be an opening.

BAWAKI BEACH HOTEL, *about 45 kilometers south of Taba. Tel. 062/ 500-470/1. Fax 062/352-6123. Capacity: 36 rooms. Rates: $60 single, $80 double, $100 suite. Credit cards: Visa.*

Set in splendid isolation with some great offshore snorkeling, the Bawaki features about 40 simple rooms and cabins with air-conditioning and private showers. The Bawaki can organize camel safaris and jeep treks and guests can also partake in horseback riding, water skiing, or just plain sun bathing on the beach or at the pool. Eating is done at the main restaurant or at a beachside cafeteria; there is also a bar.

Ras El Shitan (The Devil's Head)
& Sheikh Suleiman Junction

Ras El Shitan is 47 kilometers south of Taba and 23 kilometers north of Nuweiba.

Ras El Shitan is a popular **diving site** where would-be overnighters can stay in the stone cabins for LE20 per person per night; there is also a cafeteria.

Nearby is **Sheikh Suleiman Junction**, a hub for Bedouin guides and safari operators. Here you can arrange camel safaris ranging in length from an hour or less to ten days or more. Nearby attractions for shorter excursions and day trips include the oasis at Bir Ghadir and a beautiful canyoned cistern-wadi with the coolest name of any wadi in place, **Wadi Wishwashi**. Prices range from LE15 for an hour to LE100 per day for longer trips. See the "Sinai Safaris" section after the "Dahab" section for a list of other Sinai safari attractions and destinations.

Ma'agana & Lami Beach

Ma'agana & Lami Beach is seven kilometers north of Nuweiba and 57 kilometers south of Taba.

Like Ras El Shitan and Suleiman Junction, Ma'agana is a popular dive site where you can arrange camel excursions and jeep treks. Nearby attractions include the **Blue Canyon**, painted by Belgian artist Jean Verame in the late 1970's, and Wadi Wishwashi. Dingy cabins can be rented here for about LE20 apiece.

NUWEIBA

As Dahab becomes trendier and more crowded, **Nuweiba** is emerging as an alternative for those looking for peace, quiet, and low prices. One apparent disadvantage, the lack of diving, may actually turn out to be a blessing in this respect, as droves of divers will not flock here as they have to Sharm and Dahab. Nuweiba also makes an excellent point from which to embark on desert safaris (see the "Desert Safari" side bar) and is the port of arrival and departure for the Nuweiba-Aqaba (Jordan) ferry.

ARRIVALS & DEPARTURES
By Air
The closest international airport is at Sharm El Sheikh, 3 hours to the south. There is a also an airport at Ras El Nakb (Taba) where EgyptAir flies weekly from Cairo.

By Boat
There are daily ferries between Nuweiba and **Aqaba, Jordan**. You'll have to pass through customs at Nuweiba Port but it isn't usually much of a hassle-just be sure that your documents are in order. The "Express" takes about 1.5 hours, and costs approximately $55, while the slower boat takes 3-5 five hours and costs about $35. Check with your hotel for details and transport to and from the port.

By Bus
From **Cairo**, one bus departs daily at 8am from the Sinai Bus Terminal in Abbassia (LE50 one-way). From There are three daily buses between Nuweiba and Sharm and Dahab, and two to Taba. There is also one bus daily to Saint Katherine's. Check with your hotel for departure times. Buses within Sinai cost between LE5-20.

By Car
Nuweiba is just under 500 kilometers from Cairo and 65 kilometers from the Israeli border at Taba. Coming from Cairo, you'll pass through the Ahmed Hamdy Tunnel and proceed straight across the interior of Sinai. Do not turn right (or pass "Go") and go around the peninsula and through Sharm El Sheikh. Driving from Sharm shouldn't take more than 3 hours, and from the Israeli border at Taba, it's about 1.5 hours.

By Service
There are no regular mini-bus routes to and from Nuweiba though pick-up truck taxis congregate near the port and are willing to serve as taxis to Dahab or Taba, but expect to pay upwards of LE50.

ORIENTATION
Nuweiba the holiday resort is 8 kilometers up the coast from Nuweiba Port where ferries to and from Aqaba do their thing. The northern "district" of the holiday resort, known as **"Tarabeen"** consists primarily of budget tourist villages ("camps"), and is usually flooded with young

Israelis. In recent years development of the coast between Nuweiba Port and Tarabeen has begun and by the turn of the century large resorts will fill up the now barren beaches. The same goes for the coast north of Tarabeen all the way to Taba, a stretch of coast known to some as the "Egyptian Riviera."

GETTING AROUND TOWN

Tarabeen can pretty much be negotiated by foot while taxis are efficient for shuttling between Nuweiba Port and the tourist villages though in typical Red Sea-Sinai fashion, they charge a relative arm and leg, LE15 one-way. Minibuses can also be flagged down as can pick-ups (a no-no for single women), though they don't run regular routes and will often ask the same price as taxis.

WHERE TO STAY

Originally, like Dahab, Nuweiba attracted primarily young backpacker types with a minimalist bent toward both their budgets and their need for amenities. The pristine beaches and open sky left them in need of little except for a sleeping bag and perhaps a tent. However, like the rest of Egypt's coasts, the area around Nuweiba is fast becoming cluttered with luxury resorts and international hotel chains. **Tarabeen** still attracts the backpacking penny pinchers but by the turn of the century, middle and upper class visitors will provide Nuweiba's core clientele and visitors will have far more choice in picking their accommodation.

Expensive

HILTON CORAL HOTEL, *2 kilometers north of Nuweiba Port and 6 kilometers south of Tarabeen. Tel. 062/520-320/1/2. Fax 062/520-327. Capacity: 200 rooms. Rates: $92.80 single, $120 double. Credit cards: all major credit cards.*

Definitely the plushest Nuweiba resort, at least for the time being, the Hilton offers spacious environmentally-friendly accommodation with all the amenities. A self-contained establishment, its confines include a spacious beach, two swimming pools, three restaurants (one international, one Italian, one upscale a la carte on the beach), a beach bar, diving center, kids' club, a disco, water sports, tennis courts, a top flight PADI Resort certified diving center, and a partridge in a pear tree. Guests have a choice between the larger "superior" rooms without balconies, standard rooms with balconies, and domed bungalows which are actually fancier than the rooms. A bank can change money, and a small bazaar sells souvenirs. Drawbacks? The main rooms and building are constructed in typical post-modern Egyptian resort architecture meaning there's zero Egyptian flavor.

HELENA NUWEIBA HOTEL, *Tel. 062/500-402/3/4. Fax 062/500-407. Telex 940025 OHTEG LIN. Capacity: 127 rooms. Rates: $48-58 single, $68-72 double, $150-180 suite. Credit cards: Visa & Mastercard.*

A notch below the Hilton but still ritzy by Nuweiba standards. Rooms come in small chalets and bungalows are also available. Guests can pass the time sunning on the clean and attractive beach, whizzing about on a banana boat, playing tennis, or visiting underwater sights courtesy of the hotel's diving center. Gastronomic options include the main buffet on the terrace by the sea, the beach bar, and an Italian restaurant, Fellini's, which has the ambiance of a locker room but decent enough food.

EL SALAM TOURISTIC VILLAGE, *Tel. 062/500-440/1/2. Fax 062/500-440. Telex 93939 NAGDI UN. Capacity: 63 rooms. Rates: $28 single, $35 double. Credit cards: Visa.*

It's not exactly top of the line and could use a little maintenance, but the chalet rooms are comfy, the staff friendly, and the isolation peaceful. Facilities include a medium size octagonal pool, a usually empty beach, and a restaurant the features a buffet in addition to an a la carte menu. The food won't win three stars from Michelin, but it's reasonably priced and certainly edible. El Salam is popular with on-the-cheap European package tours.

EL SAYADEEN TOURISTIC VILLAGE, *Tel. 062/520-340/1, 575-7398.. Capacity: 127 rooms. Rates: $30 single, $37-43 double, $60 suite. Credit cards: Visa.*

This middle of the pack establishment offers comfortable lodging for cheaper rates than the Hiltons and Helnans. Facilities include a private beach, a variety of water sports and other recreation, as well as a decent enough restaurant and beach bar. Rooms have air-conditioning, private bath, and soon television.

LA SIRENE HOTEL, *5 kilometers north of Nuweiba port between the port and Tarabeen. Tel. 062/500-701/2. Capacity: 40 rooms. Rates: $32-36 single, $43-48 double. Credit cards: Visa.*

A newer, mid-scale tourist village offering a private beach, a diving center, and air-conditioned rooms and bungalows for accommodation. The place isn't super attractive, in fact one could easily imagine it serving as a military base back in the bad old days (it wasn't.)

EL WAHA TOURISTIC VILLAGE, *300 meters south of the Helnan. Tel. 062/500-420/1. Fax 062/500-420. Capacity: 38 rooms. Rates: LE15-30 tents, LE25-50 bungalows; LE80-130 single, double, and triple rooms.*

The El Waha is a modest establishment where you can stay in tents, stuffy bungalows, or relatively pleasant air-conditioned rooms with private baths. There is also a restaurant and beach bar.

Camps & Dirt Cheap Aaccommodations

There are scads of "camps" in Tarabeen all of which offer virtually the same set-up: bare reed or concrete huts for LE5 and slightly fancier rooms, possibly with fans, for LE20-50 depending on amenities and the pace of business. The **Blue bus**, **Camp David**, **Sinai Camp**, **Swelm**, **White Palace**, **& Oases Camp** are some of the best known and most popular of these camps. They are all lined up next to each other, so you can check them out before committing to one.

WHERE TO EAT

Virtually every camp in Tarabeen contains a restaurant, and they're all carbon copies of one another. Open, but shaded by dried palm leaves with on-the-ground Bedouin style seating, they serve hearty fish, meat and vegetarian meals in styles ranging from Italian (lots of spaghetti) to oriental (baba ghanugh and tehina). Though not haute cuisine by any standards, the food is filling and good value for the money. Expect to pay LE15-25 for a full meal, or possibly more if you order a fancy seafood dish like shrimp or lobster.

SEEING THE SIGHTS

Unlike most of Sinai, Nuweiba is not a diving destination, meaning that aside from trips to other parts of the Sinai coast, most sightseeing actually takes place on land in the crooks, nannies, peaks, and valleys of Sinai's eastern mountains.

NIGHTLIFE & ENTERTAINMENT

The fantastic open sky and countless stars are the main nocturnal attraction in Nuweiba. In Tarabeen most folks do what they do during the daytime, chill out on the beach. Sometimes when momentum gets going, tabla jams, barbecues, and other festivities are arranged. The **Hollywood Piano Bar** at the Helnan features a live band from 9:30 until about 1am. It's not a Grateful Dead concert or anything, but the party often includes drinking, dancing and pool playing-in summer '97, the house band was a cool little African gig. The **Hilton** also features live music of the more traditional lounge type at the pool or by the sea as well as a **disco**, which can get hot when folks turn up from Tarabeen (minimum charge for non-Hilton guests, LE20).

SHOPPING

In Tarabeen small merchants and hawkers dawdle in T-shirts, "Bedouin" style textiles and cheapo souvenirs.

EXCURSIONS & DAY TRIPS

The usual Sinai dive and desert safaris can be arranged in Nuweiba. Nuweiba itself is not the diving mecca that Sharm El Sheikh is, but divers can certainly arrange excursions to the Gulf of Aqaba's main reefs through any one of several dive centers, hotels, and travel agents.

On land, the most popular excursion is to **Saint Katherine's Monastery and Mount Sinai**, about 150 kilometers away. In Tarabeen, virtually any of the camps can set you up for a day trip for about LE50-60 each, once you get 6 or 7 people together. Trips begin with a night drive so as to climb the mount in time for sun rise. Travel agents like those at the Hilton can arrange a vehicle to Mount Sinai for $120, so it's quite reasonable if you can muster a group of 5 or more. Desert safaris are also popular and can be arranged through hotels or the trekking and safari operators listed below. Generally camel safaris costs about LE75 per person per day, and jeep safaris a bit more. For overnights it's usually about LE100 per person on a camel safari and again more for jeeps.

- **Explore Sinai**, *New Nuweiba Commercial Center. Tel. 062/500-141. Fax 062/500-140*
- **C.I.T.** *Tel. 062/520-265*
- **Dr. Rabiyah**, *Tel. 062/520-201*
- **Tarabin Survival Safari**, *Tel. 062/500-299*
- **Sinai Adventures**, *Tel. 062/500-328*

PRACTICAL INFORMATION

Banks & Currency Exchange

National Bank of Egypt, *Nuweiba Port. Hours: 9am-noon & 6pm-9.* Changes money and handles Visa and Mastercard cash advances. A second branch at the Helnan with the same hours also changes money and traveler's cheques but not does handle credit cards.

Banque du Caire, *the Hilton. Hours: 9am-1pm and from 6pm-8pm.* Changes money and travelers' cheques and handles Visa and Mastercard cash advances, but for a hefty LE25 commission.

Bookstores

Both the Hilton and the Helnan feature rather weak gift shop-type bookstores, neither of which sells newspapers.

Emergencies

Hospital, *Nuweiba City about 500 meters inland from the Helnan hotel.*

Post & Courier Services

Post Office, *Nuweiba City about 500 meters inland from the Helnan.*

Telephones, Telex, & Fax
24 hour telephone centrale, *in Nuweiba Port.* Domestic and international calls can also be made from hotels.

Tourist Information
Hotel personnel and employees at tourist camps in Tarabeen are usually good sources of information. Mahmoud and Nasser can be very helpful with practical information such as bus schedules. They run a kiosk in Nuweiba City at the shopping center down the street from the bus station next to the public children's garden. In Nuweiba Port, there is a branch of **Misr Travel** that opens during normal business hours.

DAHAB

Meaning "gold" in Arabic, **Dahab** actually refers to several settlements along a 20 kilometer stretch of fantastic coast some 100 kilometers north of Sharm El Sheikh. Though a nondiscript town bears its name, for years "Dahab" was synonymous with the nearby Bedouin settlement turned backpacker mecca, **Asilah**. Famous for its cheap camps and the liberal use of cannabis, Asilah attracts thousands of young folks, primarily Israelis, who for virtually nothing do virtually nothing but vegetate in the mountainous seaside setting, moving only to take an occasional dip, buy weed, or if truly motivated, dive.

In the '90's the Egyptian tourist industry has been keen to develop Dahab as an upscale attraction, more along the lines of Sharm El Sheikh, with larger tourist resorts catering to a less frugal clientele. World class **dive sites**, such as the notorious "Blue Hole," (dozens of divers have been lost there over the years) and ideal conditions for watersports such as wind surfing, should ensure that these initiatives succeed, and Dahab will be left with a schizophrenic identity.

ARRIVALS & DEPARTURES
By Air
The nearest major airport is in Sharm El Sheikh about 100 km south.

By Bus
Dahab bus station is in Dahab City 1-2 kilometers from the resort villages (depending which one) and 8 kilometers from Asilah. Buses depart Cairo three times daily from **East Delta Bus Co.** in Abbassia (LE50-65). From Sharm there are a half dozen buses daily (LE 10) and two daily from Nuweiba and Taba.

By Car

Many Israelis who hop over for a long weekend come in their own cars and cars are handy for exploring the coast around Dahab. **Euro Rent a Car** has an office in the Novotel.

ORIENTATION

Buses operate out of the charmless **Dahab City**, essentially a municipal headquarters containing telephone and post offices, a bank, and some shops. Nothin' doin' here. Just outside of town along the coast, a number of up and mid-scale resort villages have sprouted and several more are on the way-evidence of the Sharm El Sheikhization of Dahab.

Asilah, where the cheap camps and hotels are located, is about 8 kilometers north of Dahab City. Though it's always been a one street town, it's quickly growing out of it, and along the southern coast of Asilah, slightly upscale hotels have been erected in recent years, somewhat eroding its rustic flavor.

GETTING AROUND TOWN

As most of the upscale tourist villages near Dahab City are self-contained and Asilah is completely negotiable by foot, there should be little need for transportation. Taxis and pickup services shuttle between the town, where the bus station is located, and Asilah. A one way shot shouldn't set you back more than LE5-10, especially if its a service.

WHERE TO STAY

Originally, Asilah was strictly a budget destination where you couldn't pay more than LE10 a night if you tried and air-conditioning or television was unheard of, while anybody in need of any amenities whatsoever had to fork out substantial dollars at the Pullman (now the Novotel). In recent years, fancier mid-range establishments offering air-conditioning, satellite television, and private baths have sprouted along the edge of Asilah enabling folks desiring something more than a beaten up mattress in a reed hut or concrete block to live comfortably while staying in the thick of the action. Meanwhile, out in NovotelLand, upscale resorts are multiplying like rabbits, offering more options for families, older people, and travelers looking for comfort and more extensive facilities generally.

Expensive

NOVOTEL DAHAB HOLIDAY VILLAGE, *Tel. 062/640-303/4/5. Fax 062/640-305. Capacity: 141 rooms. Rates: $41-71 single, $61-100 double, $200-300 suite. Credit cards: Visa, Mastercard, American Express.*

Though not as luxurious or flashy as some others, the Novotel in Dahab is one of the nicest Red Sea resort hotels in Egypt, in large part because of its fantastic setting and the 700 meter beach overlooking not only the sea, but the mountains as well. Room types range from simple chalets, somewhat cramped and without television but comfy, to spacious rooms with views of the sea and mountains with all the amenities. For activities and recreation, the Novotel features a dive center, a wind surf center (wind surfing conditions are excellent), horseback riding, and other water sports opportunities. Also on the premises: a swimming pool, a disco, and several restaurants serving the usual resort food, i.e. decent but not spectacular buffets, so-so Italian food, and fish.

HELNAN DAHAB HOTEL, *2 kilometers south of Dahab City on the coast. Tel. 062/640-325/26/30. Fax 062/640-428. Capacity: 200 rooms. Rates: $52 single, $70 double, $150 suite. Credit cards: Visa, Mastercard, American Express.*

Slightly bigger than the Novotel but very similar in terms of amenities and facilities. The disco at time of writing was dance-central, attracting pick-ups loaded with young folks from Asilah.

GANET SINAI, *on the coast south of Dahab City. Tel. 062/640-440/1/2. Fax 062/640-441. Capacity: 60 rooms. Rates: $50 single, $70 double, $130 suite. Credit cards: Visa.*

A step down from the Helnan and the Novotel, but comfortable with rooms featuring air-conditioning, nice balconies, and private baths-television coming soon. One advantage worth considering, the food is excellent, especially the fish. The usual watersports and recreation facilities are featured.

Asilah

INMO HOTEL, *south beach of Asilah. Tel. 062/640-370/1, 640-455. Fax 062/640-372. Capacity: 34 rooms. Rates: LE85-100 single, LE 95-120 double. Credit cards: Visa.*

A divers' lodge dressed in domed Hassan Fathi-*fellahi* architecture, the Inmo features rooms with private baths, television, and air-conditioning. Facilities include a well equipped diving center, a modest pool, and small stretch of beach.

SPHINX DIVERS' HOTEL, *south beach of Asilah. Tel. 062/640-032, 640-494, 640-854. Fax 062/640-032. Rates: LE110 single, LE140 double. Credit cards: Visa.*

The Sphinx is also a moderate hotel catering to divers that features a small "private beach," diving center, a postage stamp-sized pool, and a restaurant. Room amenities include satellite television, air-conditioning, and private baths.

HOTEL DYARNA DAHAB, *south of "downtown" Asilah. TEL. 062/640-120/1. Fax 062/640-122. Capacity: 42 rooms. Rates: LE60 single, LE80 double. Credit cards: Visa.*

Very similar to the two aforementioned, Dyarna offers modest but comfortable air-conditioned rooms and an assortment of facilities including a recreation center, a swimming pool, private beach, and a restaurant.

CLUB RED DIVERS, *Asilah. Tel. 062/640-380. Fax 062/640-380. Rates: $26 single, $36 double, $48 triple, $55 quadruple. Credit cards: Visa.*

Designed to accommodate clients of the diving center, the Club Red hotel features simple, but comfortable and spacious rooms with balconies and fans. There are no private baths, but the common showers are clean.

Camps in Asilah

Originally the only accommodation available in Dahab were reed huts and the beach itself, but unfortunately concrete was discovered and many of the huts gave way to concrete blocks endowing the camps with all the charm of an Egyptian army camp which I can tell you isn't much. In any case, there are no less than thirty camps in Asilah offering essentially the same deal: a room/hut with a bare light bulb and mattress for LE5-15. Bathrooms are invariably communal.

Some of the more popular camps include: **Mohammed Ali Camp** (*Tel. 062/640-262*); **Crazy Camel Camp** *Ttel. 062/640-272*); **The Fighting Kangeroo**; **Sabry Palace** (*Tel. 062/640-444. 640-444)*, and the **Dolphin Camp**.

WHERE TO EAT

The upscale resorts virtually all feature a main dining hall, an Italian restaurant, a beach bar, and a seafood grill. The Ganet Sinai, in particular is known for its excellent fish.

Asilah

The entire Asilah coast is lined with casual "Bedouin" style restaurants, virtually all the same, that not only serve food and drinks but provide space for sunbathing, backgammon, and other activities – or non-activities – typically enjoyed by Dahab's slacker clientele. Generally on the waterline itself, these establishments feature short tables and cushions which make for comfortable on-the-ground seating shaded by umbrellas made of dried palm leaves. In recent years many of these restaurants have added upgraded interiors across the street that resemble what folks in the west might consider a "normal" restaurant, complete with uniformed staff, tables with tablecloths, and perhaps a bar.

As for the food itself, the menus, always in billboard form at the entrance, are genuine testaments to multi-culturalism as they feature a vast assortment of dishes ranging from pasta, pizza, to chicken curry, baba ghanugh, and of course grilled and fried fish, calamari, and desserts. The food, especially in the more casual establishments, often has a homey kind of taste sorely lacking in the hotel/resorts in the rest of Sinai, but on the other hand, depending on the cook, quality and consistency varies widely-luckily you're never likely to spend much money, even if you order a complete bust.

Though prices have inched up in recent years, they remain extremely reasonable. Appetizers cost LE5 or less while main dishes, especially if meatless, rarely top LE10, except for seafood platters which may cost as much as LE20-40. For some variety, **Neptune** serves Chinese and in '97 at least the **Dolphin's** menu included some Indian and Malaysian dishes.

NIGHTLIFE & ENTERTAINMENT

Before Dahab went big in the mid-'90's, nightlife was pretty like daylife, that is, lots of hanging on the beach, smokin' herb, listening to Bob Marley's Greatest Hits for the 5 millionth time, and enjoying the fantastically resplendent night sky. Recently however, the "scene" as it were, quickly changed as an assortment multi-storied pool halls and bars complete with flashing lights and thumping Euro-pop music seemingly came out a of nowhere and now seriously threatens Asilah's famously serene and cool character.

Still one has to venture out of Asilah for dancing. The **Black Prince Disco** (*in the Gulf Hotel*), formerly the one and only dancing locale has closed for renovations. When it reopens, it will find stiff competition from **Helnan Disco**, the **Novotel Disco**, and when it opens, almost certainly the nightclub at the new Hilton. All of these discos are real casual places featuring indoor and outdoor dancing (weather permitting), and don't really get going until midnight or later. Minimum charges, if applicable won't top LE 20 and do go towards drinks. Some hotels also sometimes throw late-night "beach parties" that include food, drink, and dance. For drinking in Asilah, the **Crazy House** is the most popular establishment and **Napoleon's** is the main pool hall.

SPORTS & RECREATION

Holiday resorts (Helnan, Novotel, Ganet Sinai) offer a wide variety of recreational opportunities such water sports including winds surfing (ideal conditions in Dahab), snorkeling, and tennis. The Novotel also rents horses. In Asilah, snorkeling equipment can be rented anywhere but for good coral join an excursion to the Blue Hole through any hotel, travel agent, or taxi driver.

Diving

Aside from lounging on the beach, and perhaps smoking weed, the most popular recreational activity with visitors to Dahab is diving. Though not quite as extensive as Sharm El Sheikh's, Dahab's diving offerings rate amongst the best in the world in terms of the quality of reefs and the variety in coral and fish. There are numerous dive centers in Dahab and Asilah offering would-be Cousteaus courses, equipment, guides and transportation.

Divers should be very careful in picking a dive center. Numerous fatal accidents in recent years have been attributed to poor judgment calls by local dive instructors-some have even been known to use cannabis prior to diving such man-killers as the Blue Hole. Under fire for not regulating the diving industry properly, local and regional authorities have stepped up their efforts to ensure that diving in Dahab is safe and that dive centers meet the required standards, but you'd better make sure. We recommend that you ask around to get an idea of where the best instructors are and that you only dive with major, internationally recognized diving centers. Listed below are some of the bigger dive centers with well-established reputations. They all take credit cards.

- **Canyon Dive Club**, *at the Canyon Dive Site. Tel. 062/640-256*
- **Club Red**, *Asilah. Tel. 062/640-380. Fax 062/640-380*
- **Fantasea Divers**, *Asilah. Tel. 062/640-043*
- **Inmo**, *south of downtown Asilah. Tel. 062/640-370/1. Fax 062/640-372*
- **Sinai Dive Club**, *Novotel Holiday Village. Tel. 062/640-301/2, 640-465*

DIVE SITES & DANGER

Unlike Nuweiba, which is practically reefless, Dahab boasts some of the most famous, and the most dangerous, dive sites in the Red Sea. Eight and ten kilometers north of Asilah, respectively, the **Canyon** *and the* **Blue Hole** *push even the most experienced divers to their limits and sometimes beyond. At the Canyon, a narrow crevice in a spectacular reef drops to nearly 50 meters, well beyond the depths considered "safe" for average or even expert divers. At the Blue Hole, a hole in the reef reaches down a staggering 80 meters and at 62 meters a passage from the reef leads to the open sea. This passage has taken dozens of lives over the years. Not only must divers closely monitor their dive tables and deal with water pressure, they must contend with strong currents that can force them towards the surface faster than is safe, hence creating air bubbles in the blood and possibly leading to death. The distraction of mesmerizing coral, and the panic that can engulf worried and disoriented divers makes concentration even more difficult, and trouble more certain.*

SHOPPING

Asilah's streets, or street rather, are lined with dozens of shops and stalls hawking neo-hippie and "Bedouin" style goods, e.g. lots of beads, colorful "Bedouin" style shirts, baggy pants and skirts, and tie-dyes. As Asilah has gone more upscale in recent years, more jewelry and fancier handicrafts have begun to appear as have camera shops and general purpose tourist stores. As for the resort villages, they all have rather spartan gift shops offering mostly coffee table fish books in German and Italian. For useful goods like provisions and toiletries, there are no less than a half dozen supermarkets in Asilah and a handful in Dahab, the town. All remain open until late at night.

EXCURSIONS & DAY TRIPS

Nearly halfway up the coast of the Gulf of Aqaba and between the Ras Abu Galum and Nabeq National Parks, Dahab is an ideal location from which to explore Sinai's resplendent coast and mountainous interior. Even a quick two or three hour excursion behind Asilah itself offers a taste of its beautiful wilderness, but the most popular excursion is to **Mount Sinai**, where Moses received the Ten Commandments, and the nearby **Saint Katherine's Monastery**. Virtually any hotel or travel agent can arrange an expedition and given Dahab's proximity, the trip is usually made in a day for cheaper (LE50-100 per person) than say, from Sharm El Sheikh.

Those interested in making **camel or jeep safaris** should speak to the folks at their hotel or pay a visit to **Sun Rise Travel Services** about two thirds up the main street in Asilah or **Caravan Tours** next door, both of which organize excursions. To cut out the middle man, deal directly with native Bedouins who can organize trips of all lengths to all destinations; the following "Desert Safaris" section lists established Bedouin posts where excursions can be organized, as well as famous wadis, oases, and other destinations. You can also speak with local Bedouin camel drivers in Asilah who congregate in the middle of town, or even taxi drivers. Generally every 24 hours in the desert, everything included (camel, guide, food, and other necessary transport) costs about LE100 per person, perhaps a bit more. Jeep safaris generally cost 20-50% more.

When making an excursion into the desert always bring food, water, comfortable shoes, a flashlight, a map, and a guide.

Finally, many dive centers offer safaris that combine traveling and camping in the desert and along the coast with diving at famous sites like the Blue Hole and the Canyon. These excursions generally cost LE100-200 a day, everything (including dive equipment) included.

PRACTICAL INFORMATION
Banks & Currency Exchange
National Bank of Egypt, *Dahab City. Hours: 8:30am-1pm & 5pm-8pm daily except for Friday when it closes at 11am and reopens 6pm-8pm.* Changes dollars, shekels, travelers' cheques, and Visa card advances. A second branch in the Novotel does not make advances on credit cards.

Bank Misr, *Sabry Camp in Asilah. Hours: approximately 9-12am & 2-6pm.*

Bookstores
There are at least two used book exchanges in Asilah: the **Monica Bazaar** on the main drag, and the **Snorkel and Book Shop** off the main street at the very northern tip of Asilah. The major hotels sell the usual assortment of coffee-table-type fish books, usually in Italian or German. **Newspapers** are sometimes available at the shopping center in Dahab City down the block from the bus depot.

Emergencies
• **Ambulance,** *Tel. 123 or 600-554*
• **Police,** *Tel. 122*
• **Nearest decompression chamber** *(Tel. 601-011, 600-922/3)* and **hospitals** are in Sharm El Sheikh.

Post Services
Post Office, *Dahab City. Hours: 9am-3pm daily except Friday.*

Telephones, Telex, & Fax
24 hour telephone centrale *in Dahab city across the street from the bus depot.* You can place long distance telephone calls and faxes, though you may end up waiting in line for hours and the service, to put it kindly, couldn't be worse.

In Asilah, many shops like the Monica Bazaar (*midway up the main drag in Asilah*) can place long distance telephone calls and faxes, as can mid-range hotels like the New Sphinx, and Inmo and the big resorts like the Helnan and Novotel.

Tourist Information
Hotel, and in the case of Asilah, restaurant personnel are usually good sources of information. Taxi drivers and shopkeepers can also answer at least the easier inquiries.

Tourist Police
Opposite entrance of Novotel near Dahab City and across from the Hard Rock restaurant in Asilah.

SAFARIS IN SINAI

Safaris and treks ranging in duration and difficulty from a half day camel ride around the block to hard core safaris in the desert mountains where you may not see modern civilization for two weeks, are easily arranged through hotels and travel agents in Nuweiba, Dahab, and Sharm El Sheikh. In Sharm El Sheikh, the **Pigeons House hotel**, *Tel. 062/600-996/7/8,* is known for organizing safaris.

An alternative to arranging through agents in the major tourist resorts, is to make your way to one of the Bedouin settlements where Bedouin themselves offer lodging, guides, camels, food & water, information, and any other assistance you might need. Though they can all get you to any major site in southeastern Sinai, some are more conveniently located for exploring certain regions and sites.

North of Nuweiba

Natural attractions around and north of Nuweiba are concentrated between the coastal road to Taba and the interior highway that links Nuweiba with the Ahmed Hamdy Tunnel and the Suez Canal. Others are 10-20 kilometers west of the Nuweiba-Ahmed Hamdy Road. To organize safaris contact agents listed in "Dahab" and "Nuweiba" sections or make arrangements directly through Bedouin guides. Bedouin guides can be hired at **Sheikh Suleiman Junction in Wadi Malkha** *opposite the famous Ras El Shitan dive site 12 kilometers north of Nuweiba* and **Ma'agana Lami Beach** *slightly closer to Nuweiba.* At both of these locations, guides, food, permits, and camels can be arranged for hikes and safaris lasting from one hour to three weeks or more. Listed below are some of the main destinations for safaris and hikes in this region.

Wadi Quseib & Ain Quseib, *a couple of miles off the coast halfway between Nuweiba and Taba.* This legendary wadi features picturesque colored canyons and an oasis. They make an excellent day trip from Taba or Nuweiba.

Wadi Wishwashi, *4.5 kilometers from the Nuweiba-Taba Road and just a few kilometers from Sheikh Suleiman Junction-one of the most accessible sites for day trips.* Set amongst monumental boulders, Wadi Wishwashi was formerly the largest cistern in Sinai and still features a nice swimming hole when it rains, while nearby at **Wadi Malkha**, palms live off waters from the cisterns in a colorful sandstone setting.

The Colored Canyon, *15 kilometers northwest of Nuweiba and just a few kilometers west of Wadi Wishwashi and Wadi Malkha.* These two spectacular canyons notable for their colorful geology, are among the most popular destinations for day trips from Dahab and Nuweiba. The Blue Canyon was painted blue by Belgian artist Jean Verame in the late 1970's while the Painted Canyon features magnificent natural blue coloring. Count on a half day trip from Nuweiba and closer to a full day from Dahab.

There are two relatively easy hikes from **Ma'agana** *(7 kilometers north of Nuweiba)* that are especially appropriate for families. The hike to **Wadi Thimla** features canyon climbing, views over the Gulf of Aqaba to Saudi Arabia, and colorful sandstone geology. It takes about two and half hours. That to **Wadi Huweyit** also features a colorful sandstone canyon, views of Saudi Arabia, and some fascinating geology and should be done with a guide.

Gebel Barqa and Arch Canyon, *about 20 kilometers northwest of Nuweiba and 5 kilometers east of the Nuweiba-Ahmed Hamdy Road.* These difficult excursions are for sturdy and experienced climbers only. Soaring more than 850 meters Gebel Barqa offers breathtaking views of eastern mountains while the maze-like Arch Canyon features difficult climbing and colorful sandstone. These sites are both accessed from the Nuweiba-Ahmed Hamdy Road and en route you should visit **Bir El Thawra** where springs flow from a cave at an oasis with palms and gardens *just east of the highway.* You must also pass by a well, **Bir El Biyaria**.

Those of you not keen on extensive hiking or camel riding can combine the roadside Bir El Thawra (mentioned above) with the grave of **Sheikh Atiya** also *just off the main Nuweiba-Ahmed Hamdy road, 10 kilometers north of Bir El Thawra.* Sheikh Atiya was a hero of the Tarabeen tribe and his grave attracts Bedouin pilgrims who come to pay their respects.

Ain El Furtaga, *15 kilometers west of Nuweiba off the Ahmed Hamdy Road.* Ain El Furtaga is a major oasis with palms and a spring and is often a starting point for excursions that approach the Colored Canyon from the west.

Wadi El Hag, *7 kilometers west from the beginning of the Ahmed Hamdy Road.* Wadi Hag is an easy hike for the family and sometimes features waterfalls and cisterns deep enough for swimming.

Ain Om Ahmed, *35 kilometers as the crow flies west of Nuweiba.* The largest oasis in eastern and southern Sinai features numerous pools and springs suitable for swimming. If you can spare the time, spend several days here to climb **Ras El Qalb**, a 1,000 meter mountain (rope required) with stunning views of Om Ahmed and the surrounding wilderness; and to hike in the bedrock and swim in the cisterns of **Wadi El Ain**. The only disadvantage of Ain Om Ahmed is its popularity which sometimes mean crowds. Ain Om Ahmed and Wadi El Ain are equally accessible from the

Bedouin hubs of Sheikh Hamid (see below) off the Saint Katherine's Road and from Ma'agana and Sheikh Suleiman Junction.

Between Nuweiba & Dahab Off The Saint Katherine's Road

There are numerous wadis, oases, and mountains off the Saint Katherine's Road just east of where it meets the Nuweiba-Dahab road. You can organize hikes, treks, and safaris to these sites through agents in any major Sinai resort (Nuweiba, Dahab, Sharm El Sheikh) or Bedouin operators listed below.

Sheikh Hamid, *just off the Saint Katherine's Road 7 kilometers west of its intersection with the Dahab-Nuweiba Road. Call 062/520-201 and leave a message in advance to arrange longer expeditions.* They offer food, lodging, permit procurement, guides, camels, and wealth of information.

Sheikh Goma'a, *Haggag Valley near Ain Khudra, 7 kilometers west of Sheikh Hamid past the checkpoint.* Sheikh Goma'a operates a road-side kiosk where similar services are available. Listed below are some of the attractions in this region.

Haggag Valley, *runs on both sides of the Saint Katherine's Road about seven kilometers west of Sheikh Hamid's past the checkpoint.* Sheikh Goma'a can arrange tours of this wide valley that approaches Ain Khudra (see below) and features several sites with ancient rock drawings.

Ain Khudra, *5 kilometers north of Sheikh Hamid and the Saint Katherine's Road.* Its proximity to Sheikh Hamid and the main road, as well as its natural beauty, makes this oasis hike ideal for families or those not inclined to rough it. This hike on foot is approximately a one hour round trip from the Sheikh Hamid outpost.

Central Gebel Barqa, *12 kilometers north of Sheikh Hamid* & **Gebel Milehis** *5 kilometers north of Sheikh Hamid* reward hikers with challenging climbs and some of the best panoramic views in all of Sinai. The climbs are extremely difficult and in the case of Gebel Barqa, dangerous as well. Make arrangements through Sheikh Hamid; these hikes require guides.

Nawamis, *7 kilometers west of Sheikh Hamid. Make arrangements through Sheikh Hamid.* Nawamis features mysterious pre-historic structures thought to be at least 5,500 years old. It's accessible by 4WD or by foot (2.5 hour round trip hike).

Gebel Matamir, *almost 10 kilometer southwest of Sheikh Hamid.* Nearly 950 meters high with several peaks, the mountain features canyons, odd geological formations and fantastic dunes, but it's not an easy climb. Hire a guide through Sheikh Hamid or Sheikh Goma'a.

Wadi El Gibi, *about half way between El Haduda Sand Dune and Sheikh Hamid's.* This snake-like wadi features numerous deep water holes and even waterfalls.

El Haduda Sand Dune- *about 10 kilometers due south of Sheikh Hamid's outpost.* El Haduda is the largest sand dune in eastern Sinai.

Southern Gebel Barqa- *about two kilometers west of the El Haduda Sand Dune.* Just over 1,000 meters high, the southern Gebel Barqa boasts some amazing views, but is a difficult climb and requires a guide and rope.

Dahab-Sharm El Sheikh

There are few major sites (big wadis or oases) between Dahab and Sharm El Sheikh, but excursions are possible and can be organize through any hotel or travel agency in Sharm El Sheikh and Dahab. You can also contact Sheikh Mahana and his son Goma'a, who run camel trips out of a settlement 2 kilometers north of Wadi Om Udawi, *Tel. 062/600-483.*

SHARM EL SHEIKH

There is no better example of Egypt's recent efforts kick its tourism industry into high gear than the massive development of **Sharm El Sheikh**. Renowned the world over for its **scuba diving** – some say the best in the world – "Sharm" metamorphosed in little more than ten years from a dot on the map into a huge seaside playground that draws nearly a half million European tourists annually.

Attracted year round by sunshine, coral, and cutthroat package tour deals, they flock here, often for weeks at a time, to coat themselves with sunshine and to enjoy a myriad of water sports from snorkeling and peddle boats to catamarans and para-sailing. Many also take advantage of Sharm's proximity to **Mount Sinai** to visit the hallowed site and the nearby **Saint Katherine's Monastery**, the oldest continuously used Christian monastery in the world. Jeep and camel safaris into the desert wilderness of Sinai's interior are also popular with more adventurous outdoorsy types.

Most foreign tourists have their fun at **Na'ama Bay**, seven kilometers up the road from the charmless concrete purgatory, **Sharm El Sheikh City**. Na'ama Bay boasts not only some of the ritzier resorts and restaurants in Egypt, but access to some of the world's finest coral. Further up the coast, **Shark's Bay** used to offer a more rustic and naturally appealing setting, but recently went up in concrete.

History

Sharm was little more than a Bedouin stakeout before the Israelis developed a small settlement after the **1967 Six Day War**. Highly prized by the Israelis for its tourism potential and strategic location near the Straits of Tiran, Sharm El Sheikh was a major sticking point and important bargaining chip for the Israelis at the Camp David negotiations where Menachem Begin stated at one point that he preferred "Sharm El Sheikh without peace to peace without Sharm El Sheikh." After much prodding by an exasperated Jimmy Carter, Begin relented and Sharm El Sheikh was returned to Egypt.

By the late 1980's a handful of modest hotels and campsites had sprouted to accommodate the growing the number of divers, who for the first time enjoyed access to the region's world-class coral reefs. Much to the dismay of old timers who lament the passing of its rustic roots, Sharm has mushroomed in the past decade beyond recognition and its coasts are now packed like a strip mall with resorts and hotels, with many more under construction.

ARRIVALS & DEPARTURES

By Air

Sharm El Sheikh International Airport, *20 kilometers north of Sharm El Sheikh City, Tel. 062/601-140/1.* **EgyptAir**, *Sharm El Sheikh Airport, Tel. 062/601-056/7/8. Sharm El Sheikh City, Tel. 062/600-408, 600-664.* EgyptAir flies Cairo-Sharm-Cairo no less than five times daily. Roundtrip tickets for foreigners cost roughly LE1000 or $300 US. Most Europeans fly in on charter flights arranged by the big tour companies in Italy, Germany, and Switzerland. For details contact your travel agent.

By Boat

There are daily ferries between **Hurghada** and Sharm El Sheikh City Port (LE110 per person, 8 hours). Talk to your hotel or any travel agency for details.

By Bus

The East Delta Bus Co. has three terminals in Sharm El Sheikh: Na'ama Bay in the Helnan Marina Sharm parking lot; at the Mobil station between Na'ama Bay and Sharm City; and in Sharm City.

Coaches operated by the East Delta Bus Co. depart to Sharm El Sheikh from the Sinai Bus Terminal in Abbassia, Cairo 6 times daily. Rates are LE50 for daytime departures and LE65 for night buses (ear-shattering Arabic movies included). Check *Al Ahram Weekly*, the pamphlet *Sinai Today*, or with a travel agent for exact times. One SuperJet departs from Abdel Moneim Riyad at 11pm (LE50).

Buses leave Sharm for **Cairo** 7 times daily at 7am, 8am, 10am, 1pm, 4:30pm, 11:30pm, and midnight. Morning buses are the cheapest at LE30; evening buses, video included, cost LE40. There is also one SuperJet daily at 11pm (LE50).

Within Sinai, buses go **Dahab** (1.5 hours, LE10) at 8am, 9am, 3pm, and 5pm; **Nuweiba** (LE12, 2 hours) at 9am and 5pm; and **Taba** (2.5-3 hours, LE15) at 9am. There is also one daily bus to **Saint Katherine's** (3 hours, LE15) at 8am; 2 daily to Suez (5 hours, LE25) at 9am and 11am; and 2 daily to Ismailia (LE30, 6 hours) at noon and 11:30pm.

ORIENTATION

Like most Sinai resort towns, "Sharm El Sheikh" refers to a series of settlements and communities stretched over more than 20 kilometers of coast. To the south is the area's original settlement, **Sharm El Sheikh City**, a non-discript town that features some tourism facilities like hotels and dive centers, but holds little attraction; if you can afford it you'd probably prefer to stay in the tourist hub, **Na'ama Bay**, 7 kilometers to the north. Figuring out Na'ama Bay is pretty simple; it's more or less a one street town lined with hotels that hugs the bay. Commercial activity, including banks and the bus station, is concentrated on a small strip of road at the southern edge of town by the Tiran and Sanafir hotels.

Now that Na'ama Bay has been developed to its potential, new resorts are being built in the area between Sharm El Sheikh City and Na'ama Bay as well as north of Na'ama Bay at **Shark Bay** (15 kilometers north of Na'ama Bay) and **Sheikh Coast** in-between. The Sharm El Sheikh International Airport is 20 kilometers north of Sharm El Sheikh City.

GETTING AROUND TOWN

Both Sharm El Sheikh City and Na'ama Bay are small enough to be covered on foot. Taxis are handy for shuttling between Sharm El Sheikh City and Na'ama Bay or Sheikh Coast, but expensive as hell - a 300 meter ride in Na'ama Bay will set you back LE10, and it's at least LE30 to the airport. Most hotels also rent bikes for LE30-50 a day.

Sharm El Sheikh is one place in Egypt where it's easy, convenient and actually halfway safe to drive a car. Remember that under Egyptian law, you must have either an Egyptian or international license unless your country's license is recognized by Egypt (American, British, and Canadian licenses are recognized) in which case you may drive under your country's license for one month, after which you must obtain an Egyptian or international license. International licenses are valid for six months and then you must obtain an Egyptian license.

Listed below are major car rental, and limousine companies in Sharm El Sheikh. Prices range from $50 a day for smaller sedans to $100 and up for the sports utility vehicles needed for driving in the desert.

• **Avis**, *Sonesta Resort, Na'ama Bay. Tel. 062/600-070, 600-725. Fax 062/600-979*

• **Budget**, *Coral Bay Hotel between Na'ama Bay and Shark's Bay. Tel. 062/601-610. Fax 062/600-836*
• **Hertz**, *Movenpick Jolie Ville Hotel in Na'ama Bay. Tel. 062/600-100*
• **Max EuropCar**, *Hilton Fayrouz Village in Na'ama Bay. Tel. 062/600-140, 600-150*
• **Alex Limousine**, *Cataract Hotel, Na'ama Bay. Tel. 062/600-091. Fax 062/600-091*
• **Limo 1**, *Sharm El Sheikh InterContinental Resort & Casino. Tel. 062/601-111. Fax 062/601-293*

WHERE TO STAY

Na'ama Bay

SOFITEL SHARM EL SHEIKH, *Tel. 062/600-175. Fax 062/600-193. Capacity: 312. Rates: $150 single, $185 double. Credit cards: all major credit cards accepted.*

The spanking new Sofitel is one of the most impressive – and expensive – of the sprawling new resorts in Sharm. Besides the usual beach facilities, swimming pools, diving center, and half dozen restaurants, the Sofitel offers supervised activities for kids and a health center. The rooms are spacious and comfortable with deluxe amenities such as air-conditioning, satellite television, and balconies.

SHARM EL SHEIKH MARRIOTT BEACH RESORT, *Tel. 062/600-190. Fax 062/600-188. Capacity: 216 rooms. Rates: $125 single, $150 double. Credit cards: all major credit cards accepted.*

Stroll into the Marriott's multi-tiered lobby with its marble fountains, brass railings, and grandiose chandeliers, you'll find it hard to believe that you're in Egypt, let alone Sinai. Indeed the Marriott shamelessly aspires to grandeur and at times overshoots the mark. The service and facilities, as to be expected, are among the best in Sharm El Sheikh. The food for example, while more expensive than anywhere in Na'ama Bay, is almost surely the best. The Marriott is a favorite with the few rich Egyptians and Gulf Arabs who have made Sharm El Sheikh their holiday destination.

SHARM EL SHEIKH MOVENPICK HOTEL, *Tel. 062/600-100/1/2/3/4/5. Fax 062/600-111.1 Telex 66 038 MPSHM UN. Capacity: 337. Rates: $110-145 single, $135-180 double, $240-460 suite. Credit cards: all major credit cards.*

When Bill Clinton, Yasser Arafat, and Shimon Peres (along with 11 other world leaders including Hosni Mubarak) congregated in Sharm in 1996 to address terrorism, the Movenpick won bragging rights as the chosen site for the conference. Sprawling over dozens of acres with two pools, a huge beach, a casino, a half dozen eateries, and a dive center, it certainly has no pretensions of modesty. However, its well tended gardens, long promenades, and simple single story architecture in plain white refreshingly restrained compared to the Marriott. Rooms are ample and comfortable and the Movenpick lives up to its reputation as home to the best buffets in the business. The Italian and seafood restaurants are also more than decent.

SONESTA BEACH RESORT, *Tel. 062/600-725/6/7. Fax 062/600-733. Capacity: 228 rooms. Rates: $98-118 single, $146-196 double, $291-650 suite. Credit cards: all major credit cards accepted.*

Though not spectacularly luxurious or classy, the Sonesta is a prototypical upscale Sinai resort with a variety of facilities ranging from a dive center to a kid's club, and deluxe air-conditioned rooms with satellite television, mini-bars, and other amenities. The hill-top setting features great views of Na'ama Bay and the sea, as well as South Sinai's modest, but majestic peaks. Dining options include buffets in the main dining room, an Italian restaurant, a cafe, and beach bar and barbecue.

GHAZALA HOTEL, *Tel. 062/600-150/1, 771-248. Fax 062/600-155. Telex 66 037 GAZAL UN. Capacity: 168 rooms. Rates: $90 single, $126 double. Credit cards: all major credit cards.*

Famous for its dive center (Sinai Divers), the Ghazala is in the process of opening a huge second complex across the street off the beach. For the time being, guests stay in deluxe rooms or chalets off the beach which feature air-conditioning, private baths, and satellite television. There is also a large pool and restaurants like the Tam Tam and Franco's Pizzeria are among the most popular in Sharm.

HILTON FAYROUZ VILLAGE, *Tel. 062/600-136/7. Fax 062/601-040. Capacity: 150 rooms. Rates: $112 single, $130 double, $150 suite. Credit cards: all major credit cards.*

The original "holiday village" in Sharm, the Hilton, while certainly not rustic, feels more in tune with its seaside desert setting than some of its flashier competitors. The rooms, stalked with the usual deluxe amenities, are in cozy villa-like chalets that at least offer guests the impression that they have more privacy. Recreationwise, the Hilton has one of the larger beaches in Na'ama Bay and offers plenty of activities from aerobics and other "animation" fare to catamaran sailing. The Pirates Bar, offering imported beers on tap, food, and sports (ESPN no less) on the tube, is a very popular watering hole, especially with local dive instructors.

NOVOTEL SHARM EL SHEIKH HOTEL, *Tel. 062/600-175/6/8. Fax 062/600-177. Capacity: 152 rooms. Rates: $92 single, $120 double, $400 suite. Credit cards: all major credit cards.*

With the usual combination of a large beach, countless recreation opportunities, and a half dozen restaurants – including the requisite seafood and Italian eateries – the Novotel is a typical Sharm-style resort only the buildings are reminiscent of a hospital-lot's of plain white with red trimming and fire extinguishers. The rooms however are well-endowed with deluxe amenities.

HELNAN MARINA SHARM HOTEL, *Na'ama Bay. Tel. 062/600-170/1. Fax 062/768-385. Capacity: 105 rooms. Rates: $75 single, $94 double, $257-340 suite. Credit cards: all major credit cards.*

A relic from the days of Israeli occupation, Marina Sharm offers among the best views in Na'ama Bay. Though the once pristine beaches are cluttered with developments, the sea is still gorgeous and many rooms also enjoy good views of the Sinai mountains and the spectacular sunsets for which they serve as a backdrop. The hotel isn't as grand or ritzy as some others, but the beach is one of the best in Na'ama Bay and the rooms feature the usual comforts and amenities.

HALOMY SHARM VILLAGE, *Na'ama Bay. Tel. 062/600-681/3/4. Fax 062/600-134. Capacity: 70 rooms. Rates: $70 single, $87 double. Credit cards: all major credit cards accepted.*

Perched on the cliff at the southern end of Na'ama Bay, this is one of the cheaper resorts in Na'ama Bay but has the best views. Guests stay in chalets with television, clean bathrooms, and air-conditioning.

OONAS DIVERS CLUB HOTEL, *Tel. 062/600-581. Tel. in Cairo 202/418-6021. Fax 062/291-0937. Capacity:. 20 rooms. Rates: $ 56 single, $65 double, $75 suite (triple). Credit cards: Visa, Mastercard.*

A diver-oriented establishment that evolved from a camp into a full-scale resort, Oonas is comparable to other mid-scale operations in terms of amenities and comforts. The rooms feature television, air-conditioning, and private bath; they just aren't as pretentious as those in say, the Marriott.

SANAFIR VILLAGE, *Tel. 062/600-197/8. Fax 062/600-196. Capacity:. Rates: $49-68 single, $53-81 double. Credit cards: Visa, Mastercard.*

The original Sharm hotel, Sanafir is a favorite with Egyptians and resident expats who have been coming to Sharm from the beginning, and even though it has been overwhelmed by its younger neighbors, it is still the heart and soul of Na'ama Bay social life. The "Bus Stop" has always been the most happening disco in Sharm, a title which probably won't be relinquished any time soon. In terms of luxury, the Sanafir may be a notch below the Movenpicks and Marriotts, but it's certainly cozier and the rooms with amenities like air-conditioning and satellite television aren't exactly shabby. It's not on the beach itself, but residents are given access to the well-groomed La Vista beach by the Red Sea Diving College. Apartment suites should be available for rent soon.

TROPICANA HOTEL, *Na'ama Bay. Tel. 062/600-597/6/52. Fax 062/600-649. Capacity: 52 rooms. Rates: $69 single, $ 7 double. Credit cards: Visa.*

If your expecting something out of Vegas with an orange juice motif, I'm afraid you'll be disappointed, but in its Hassan Fathi oriental architecture(lot's of domes), Tropicana has a rustic quality that feels appropriate given Sharm's desert surroundings. The rooms are simple, but spacious with private showers, air-conditioning, and satellite television; and there is also a pool, a small bar, and a terrace with a "Bedouin" tent that sometimes comes to life after dark as a hangout spot for the hotel's young diving clientele.

PIGEONS HOUSE, *Na'ama Bay next to the Tropicana, across from Oonas at northern end of Na'ama Bay, Sharm El Sheikh. Tel. 062/600-996/7/ 8. Fax 062/600-995. Capacity: 88. Rates: LE55 single, LE70 double,. Credit cards: Visa.*

In addition to being modest enough to acknowledge the farmer's pigeon coop which has become the model for many a resort up and down Egypt's Red Sea coasts, Pigeons House is one of the cheapest and homiest hotels in Na'ama Bay. Popular with younger travelers, many from Israel, it also made itself a name organizing desert safaris. The rooms aren't luscious – no satellite television or high powered air-conditioning units – but if you're looking for nothing more than a bed, some space, and a friendly atmosphere, it's more than adequate.

Sharm El Sheikh City & Sharm El Maya
(Between the City & Na'ama Bay)

HILTON RESIDENCE HOTEL, *Tel. 062/600-266/7/8. Telex 660 36 HISHK UN. Capacity: 106 rooms. Rates: $88-115 suite. Credit cards: all major credit cards.*

On the high ground just north of Sharm El Sheikh City, they rent apartment suites that include a double bedroom and bath, a salon and small kitchens. Useful for folks with kids or who have little interest in the social offerings of Sharm-it's a bit out of the Na'ama Bay loop.

AIDA BEACH HOTEL, *Sharm El Maya, Sharm El Sheikh. Tel. 062/600-720/1. Fax 062/600-722. Capacity: 150 rooms. Rates: $97-130 single, $121-162 double, $250 suite. Credit Cards: all major credit cards accepted.*

Aida's location between Sharm El Sheikh City and Na'ama Bay is a double-edged sword; it' removed from the nightlife and commercial hub of Na'ama Bay but offers more space and quiet. Rooms have air-conditioning, satellite televisions, and balconies. There is also a restaurant, bar, and pool.

EL KHEIMA CAMP, *Sharm El Maya, Sharm El Sheikh. Tel. 062/600-167, 600-048. Fax 062/600-166. Capacity: 33 rooms. Rates: LE 15-48 single, LE30-60 double, LE85 suite. Credit cards: Not accepted.*

Just north of Sharm El Sheikh City, it's the best, if not only true "budget" accommodation in Sharm El Sheikh. Guests can stay in simple bungalows or more expensive, but less atmospheric concrete rooms with or without private showers, and fans. Popular with younger folks.

Shark's Bay

SHARK'S BAY BEDOUIN HOME, *Shark's Bay. Tel. 062/600-943/7. Fax 062/600-941. Capacity: 67 rooms. Rates: LE 50-55 single, LE65-70 double.*

Situated 15 kilometers north of Sharm El Sheikh, Shark's Bay used to be the hippest eco-accommodation in all of Sharm El Sheikh, before it went trendy and concrete. Nonetheless if you can accept something less than the lushy international standards of Na'ama Bay and something bit more than the natural peace and beauty of sleeping on the beach in the open, Shark's Bay offers an affordable, and more spacious alternative to Na'ama Bay. The beach is better, and diving, snorkeling, and safari recreation can all be organized and enjoyed here. Rooms are fairly basic and bathrooms shared, but it will all be upgraded before long. Also, a nice outdoor seafood restaurant.

WHERE TO EAT

There are innumerable restaurants, beach bars, and cafes in Sharm, but in Na'ama Bay they all seem the same. Every hotel contains a main dining hall where half board guests eat from the usual, typically average, buffets; an Italian restaurant; a beach bar; a blatantly inauthentic "authentic oriental corner;" and possibly a seafood eatery. The food is usually decent, but invariably expensive by Egyptian standards and since everything was built in the past decade, there is none of the time worn charm one comes to expect in the rest of Egypt. Listed below is a sampling of the variety available in Na'ama Bay.

FISH RESTAURANT, *Hilton Fayrouz in Na'ama Bay. Tel. 062/600-136-43. Credit cards: Visa, Mastercard.*

One of Na'ama Bay's better fish eateries and not too terribly expensive, the Fish Restaurant offers a variety of fish and shellfish, grilled or fried. Pastas, salads, and a standard variety of continental and Arabic appetizers are also available. The outdoor setting is pleasant and the service friendly and professional. Expect to pay LE40-60 per person for a full meal and more if you splurge on lobster.

TAM TAM, *Ghazala Hotel in Na'ama Bay. Tel. 062.600-150-9. Credit cards: Visa.*

A popular outdoor oriental cafe, the Tam Tam is one of the cheapest restaurants in Na'ama Bay and one of the only eateries specializing in Arabic and Egyptian food. Choices include Egyptian favorites kushari, shwarma, ta'amiya, and a variety of mezzes including sambousek, kobeiba, tehina and 'aish (pita bread). Those with a larger appetite might consider pigeon or kebabs, both chicken and meat. Smaller appetizer dishes cost about LE3 a piece while larger platters top LE15. Beer, Turkish coffee and sheesha are also available. Though it's about as hokey as every thing else in Sharm El Sheikh, the food is quite good and it's nice to actually eat Egyptian food while in Egypt, which can be a challenge in Sharm.

SINAI STAR, *on the roof of the Sharm Mall. No credit cards.*

If you can find your way to the roof of the Sharm Mall, this quirky Egyptian restaurant is much cheaper than most of the hotel eateries and from the food to the casual service has a far more authentic Egyptian flavor. Dishes include the usual mezze and soup appetizers, as well as grilled and fried fish, kebabs, and chicken. Expect to pay about LE35 per person for a full meal. There are pool tables in the rooms below. Alcohol is not served.

SHIN SEOUL, *in the Sharm Mall.*

Customers can enjoy reasonable Korean and Chinese food either on and outdoor terrace or indoors on the ground floor. The menu features a wide variety of meat, seafood, and vegetarian dishes including the usual favorites like sweet and sours and fried noodles, as well as Korean specialties like barbecue. Those who enjoy a little heat, should consider trying the *kimchee* soup, a full meal in itself. Prices are reasonable by Sharm El Sheikh standards; expect to pay about LE40 per person for a full meal.

FRANCO'S PIZZERIA, *Ghazala Hotel in Na'ama Bay. Tel. 062/600-150-9. Credit cards: Visa.*

Of the countless Italian restaurants in Sharm El Sheikh, this one is most popular, especially with families. Cheaper than most, it specializes in simple pasta dishes and pizzas. Always packed by 7pm, it features outdoor candlelit seating in an enclosed terrace. It's actually possible to eat a full meal for under $10 (LE30) but not if you plan on drinking. If you have a large party, call in advance for reservations.

KONA KAI, *the Marriott. Tel. 062/600-190. Opens 7pm-11pm. Credit cards: all major credit cards accepted.*

One has to wonder what the world's coming to when you can eat a LE130 Japanese teppanyaki meal right here is Sharm El Sheikh, Sinai. Globalism aside, the food is excellent, especially if somebody else foots the bill.

NIGHTLIFE & ENTERTAINMENT

The epicenter of nocturnal recreation is unsurprisingly Na'ama Bay where virtually every hotel has at least one bar, and possibly a disco-style nightclub, and many feature light entertainment nightly such as live lounge music on the beach or by the pool, or possibly a "folkloric" or belly dancing show.

For drinking, every hotel contains at least one bar, but the **Pirates Bar** at Fayrouz Hilton in Na'ama Bay is by far the most happening spot, and has been for years. Frequented by local diving instructors, it offers several imported beers on tap, including Guinness, in addition to Stella and pricey, but quality bar food. Live music and sports on the television are also featured. Another watering hole worth mentioning, **The Spot**, *in the Ghazala*, dubs itself an "American Bar" but overdoes it with the cliché Elvis and Marilyn poster. Its real draw the two hour happy hour from 5:30-7:30pm when local Stella sells for LE5 and other brews and cocktails are half priced as well. The munchies are also cheap by Sinai standards and movies are presented weekly.

For dancing, the **Bus Stop** in the Sanafir in Na'ama Bay has monopolized the action from the beginning making it difficult for potential competitors to gather the momentum needed to turn their club into an attraction. Other establishments that have occasionally enjoyed popularity and may be worth checking out are **Cactus Disco** *at the Movenpick* and **Salsa** *in the Cataract Hotel*. Such discos generally don't get going until 11pm or later and roll on until 3am and later.

Finally those not afraid of laying it on the table, may consider paying a visit to the **Casino Royale** at the Movenpick, is the largest and classiest gambling hall in Egypt.

SPORTS & RECREATION

There is of course the **diving**(see below), Sharm's original *raison d'etre*, but for those not interested in spending their vacation 20 meters underwater, Sharm offers a myriad of other recreation activities. All hotels have a "private beach" for the exclusive use of their patrons and those hotels which aren't actually on the beach have agreements with other hotels that enables their guests to use the beach. Otherwise, most resorts charge a flat LE30-50 fee per person for nonresidents to use their beach and pool for the day.

For those too motivated to spend *all* day on the beach, resorts offer a number of **water sport** opportunities. Sharm El Sheikh has an advantage over Hurghada and other Red Sea resorts in that coral is accessible to **snorkelers** off the beaches in Na'ama Bay. Equipment can be rented virtually everywhere (usually LE30 a day for mask, snorkel, fins) and just about every hotel organizes snorkeling half and full day trips to major offshore reefs. If getting wet doesn't tickle your fancy, **glass bottom boats** enable you to peer at coral from the comfort of a boat deck; again virtually every hotel offers this service. **Pedal boats** and small row boats are usually available for LE10-20 a half hour while spine-jolting **banana boat** rides offer a little more excitement for a little more money.

Water skiing and sometimes **jet skiing** (recent accidents have led to new regulations) can also be arranged through most resorts. The Hilton and the Movenpick both have **catamarans** that can be rented by the hour ($25 an hour) and lessons are also available.

Land based alternatives include **miniature golf** *at the Hilton Fayrouz Village* and **tennis** at the five star resorts (usually reserved for hotel guests only). **Horseback riding** can be arranged through the Saheel Horse Country Club *across the street from the Fayrouz Hilton (tel. 600-197)* for about $20 an hour. It's great way to enjoy the sunset. Most hotels and travel agents also organize afternoon or evening **"camel safaris"** into the desert to experience blatantly manufactured "traditional Bedouin hospitality" which usually includes a "traditional Bedouin feast" for about LE60. Finally, the Aida Hotel in Sharm El Sheikh (not Na'ama Bay), has a **bowling** alley. Call *600-719* for reservations.

Diving

For many, Sharm Sheikh is synonymous diving. The Red Sea in general, and the southern tip of the Sinai Peninsula in particular, is renowned the world over for the variety and color of its marine life. A unique combination of warm waters, strong currents, and sharp drop-offs makes the northern Red Sea an extremely fertile environment in which life at all levels of the food chain, from microbes and coral to big game fish and sharks can not only survive, but thrive. The accessibility of it offers common folks the opportunity to experience a fantastical aquatic jungle the closest to which most people come is a Jacques Cousteau film.

There are dozens of dive centers in Sharm El Sheikh offering courses at all levels, equipment rentals, and excursions and dive safaris lasting anywhere from half a day to two weeks. A day, or night, of diving begins at around $40 per person and overnight diving excursions cost between $80-120 a day per person, everything (food, equipment, boat et al) included. An introductory five day PADI courses costs about $300 and provides enough instruction and certification to enable you to dive virtually anywhere in the world. Advanced courses run at about $60 a day, but vary according to the course and its length. We recommend that you always go through an internationally recognized dive center. All of the dive centers listed below have extensive experience in the Red Sea and Gulf of Aqaba and all are internationally recognized.

Dive Centers

- **Camel Dive Club**, *Na'ama Bay across the street from the Sharm Mall. Tel. 062/600-700. Fax 062/600-601.* A landmark in the Sharm diving industry which boasts some of the best facilities and instructors. All types of excursions and courses available.
- **Red Sea Diving College**, *Na'ama Bay. Tel. 062/600-184/5. Fax 062/600-144.* Concentrates strictly on dive courses as opposed to just diving trips, and maintains a reputation for good instruction. Sometimes they offer accommodation to enrolled students.

· **Sinai Divers**, *Ghazala Hotel, Na'ama Bay. Tel. 062/600-150/1/8. Fax 062/ 600155/8.* Another big name dive center in Sharm which has been around for a while. Courses, dive safaris, and nights dives are some of the offerings.
· **Sinai Dive Club**, *Fayrouz Hilton, Na'ama Bay. Tel. 062/770-788. Fax 062/ 776-736*
· **Subex Diving Center**, *Movenpick Hotel in Na'ama Bay. Tel. 062/600-100/ 1/2/3/4/5. Fax 062/600-147*
· **Tiran Dive Club**, *Tiran Hotel in Na'ama Bay. Tel. 062/600285. Fax 062/ 600-285*
· **Embarak Diving Resorts**, *Shark's Bay. Tel. 062/600208. Fax 062/600-195*

Dive Sites
    Snorkelers often remark that all you have to do is put your face in the water you'll enter a whole new magical world. Divers, however, tend to be more discerning and demand dive sites that not only offer them stimulating sightseeing, but a safe environment in which to enjoy those sights as well. Listed below are some of the most highly regarded dive sites in the vicinity of Sharm El Sheikh.

DIVING SAFETY

Many divers will tell you that diving is addictive, and it's not just the colored fish and coral that brings them back time and time again. For many, it's the rush of adrenaline fueled by the dangers of plunging of one's body 20 meters or more below the surface. Though the Red Sea is famous for its sharks – no waters in the world boast more variety – and teems with barracudas, it's the wicked currents and overestimation of one's ability to dive in given circumstances that claim the lives of several divers every year. The vast majority of diving fatalities occur when experienced divers, often instructors, recklessly test their own physical abilities, often without regard for the safety precautions that they constantly drill into novice divers. Most of these fatalities are the result of drowning, when divers are swept off to sea by currents and tides, or when divers do not properly manage depth.

Extreme amounts of water pressure can leave divers disoriented and incapable of making important decisions; as a result they are prone to changing depths too quickly. This creates bubbles in the blood that can lead to death. By following standard safety precautions, divers can avoid placing themselves in danger. That means primarily following the advice and instruction of professionals and those familiar with local conditions and possible dangers. Also, never dive alone or push yourself beyond your personal proven capabilities and limits.

Ras Mohammed, *a small peninsula at the tip of the Sinai Peninsula about 20 kilometers south of Sharm El Sheikh as the crow flies.* Declared the Red Sea's first National Park and Nature Reserve, its reefs are considered to be the best in the Red Sea and hence the best in the world. Entrance to the park costs $5 and requires a passport. Sharks, mantas, and shipwrecks are just some of the attractions.

Om Sidd, *just north of Sharm El Sheikh City.* A wonderful dive site at the southern end of a reef which reaches all the way to Sharm and Na'ama Bay, Om Sidd features fantastic coral and lots of small colorful fish, including the poisonous lionfish. Just south is the **Temple**, a popular night dive spot.

The waters off the 7 kilometers of coast between Sharm El Sheikh and Na'ama Bay contain no less than a half dozen popular dive sites. North of Om Sidd, within swimming distance, **Fiasco** holds several underwater caves while **Paradise and Turtle Bay** contain pinnacles reaching 30 meters; and still further north, **Pinkie's** features a fantastic reef wall. The last spot just off the northeast corner of Na'ama Bay, the **Near and Middle Gardens**, consists of three dives worth of shallow reefs accessible by boat or automobile while the **Far Garden** is only accessible by boat. Between the Far Garden and Ras Nusrani, the reefs give way to sandy bottoms.

Twenty kilometers north of Sharm El Sheikh, the area of **Naqab** around **Ras Nusrani** and **Tiran Island** is diver heaven. Known for its strong currents it is loaded with reefs that could take more than a dozen dives or more to cover; **Jackson Reef** alone takes more than a couple of days to cover. Also, if you're keen on actually seeing a good size shark in the open, these waters offer you as good a chance as any. *Just south of Ras Nasrani* **Wichita Falls** is favored by night divers while opposite Ras Nusrani are two **wrecks**, the *Lulia* on **Gordon Reef**, and the *Lara*, both of which have become eco-systems unto themselves. Two more wrecks are located a further two kilometers north.

Though dive boats from Sharm lead expeditions throughout the northern Red Sea, **Shurat El Ghurkana** and **Ras Atantur** (30 and 50 kilometers from Sharm respectively) are considered the northernmost dive sites frequented by Sharm based divers. Though many reefs at **Shurat El Ghurkana** are offshore and accessible only by boat those just off the shore features reefs accessible to snorkelers as well as divers. Also Shurat El Ghurkana is notable for the variety of fowl which nest, forage, and fish around it and Ras Atantur, features quite deep dives (20-30 meters) and because of its distance from Sharm is less likely to be crowded.

SHOPPING

The usual assortment of Khan El Khalili type souvenirs make for most of Sharm's shopping offerings. As you might imagine they're overpriced and of poorer quality than what you'll find in the Nile Valley. One item that is done well in Sharm are T-shirts which come in hundred of colors and designs, often featuring interesting design of colorful fish. Virtually every hotel contains at least one shop and major establishments such as the Movenpick house small shopping centers.

In Na'ama Bay, the **Sharm El Sheikh Mall**, across the street from the Camel Dive Club and Sanafir Hotel contains more than a dozen souvenir shops in addition to two banks, two supermarkets, and several eateries and cafes. There are also numerous supermarkets in Sharm El Sheikh City. There are **duty free shops** in the airport, across the road from the Fayrouz Hilton, and around the corner from the Kahramana Hotel near the Sharm Mall.

EXCURSIONS & DAY TRIPS

To really taste the beauty of Sinai, you must get out of Sharm El Sheikh and into the wilderness, whether it be 20 meters underwater or several thousand meters high in the craggy peaks of South Sinai. Dive Clubs, (listed on pages 571-572), offer extensive opportunities to explore the wonders of the Red Sea and Gulf of Aqaba. On land the most popular excursion is to **Mount Sinai and Saint Katherine's Monastery**, but the mountains, dotted with idyllic oases and rustic Bedouin settlements offer endless potential excursions for camel and jeep safaris.

Virtually every hotel and travel agent in Sharm and Na'ama Bay can arrange **jeep and camel safaris** lasting from half a day to two or more weeks. The typical one day trip goes to Wadi El Att and the oasis of Wadi Ain Ked is most popular for one night camping excursions. Both offer a taste of the rugged beauty of Sinai's interior and feature super sunsets, but are minor league compared to wadis, springs, and mountains north of Dahab that can be explored on slightly longer excursions. Prices vary depending on the length of a trip, number of participants, and what equipment and food is required but expect to pay about LE125 a day including food, equipment, guide and camel. For detailed information about desert safaris in Sinai in general, flip to the "Sinai Safari" section on pages 558-561. The **Pigeons Hotel** , *Tel. 062/600-695*, has long been considered the best place in Sharm for organizing camel safaris.

Listed below are some other travel agents in Sharm El Sheikh that can also arrange desert trips and provide other travel related assistance, including information about traveling in the rest of Egypt (e.g., Nile cruises, hotels in Cairo etc.). They tend to open from 9am-2pm and again from 4 or 5pm until 9 or 10pm.

• **South Sinai Travel**, *Ghazala Hotel in Na'ama Bay. Tel. 062/600-685, 600-160*

• **Fox Safary**, *Kahramana Hotel in Na'ama Bay. Tel. 601-072, 601-076*

• **Emeco Travel**, *Hilton Residence Resort. Tel. 062/600-266*
• **Misr Sinai Touristic Co.**, *Sharm El Sheikh City. Tel. 062/600-640*
• **InterEgypt**, *Tiran Village in Na'ama Bay. Tel. 062/600-591/2*

PRACTICAL INFORMATION

Banks & Currency Exchange

• **Alexandria Bank**, *branches in the airport, Tiran Village, and Sharm El Sheikh. Tel. 062/600-355. Hours: 8:30am-2pm & 6-9pm daily*
• **Bank Misr**, *branches in Sharm El Sheikh, Coral Bay Hotel, Sharm Club, Hilton Fayrouz Village, & Sharm Mall. Tel. 062/600-508. Hours: Sun-Thurs. 9am-1:30pm & 6-9pm. Fri. 9am-noon & 6-9pm. Sat. 10am-1:30pm*
• **Egyptian American Bank (EAB)**, *Sharm Mall, Na'ama Bay. Tel. 062/600-799. Fax 062/600-546. Hours: 8:30am-2pm & 6-9pm*
• **National Bank of Egypt**, *branches in Aquariane Hotel, Ghazala Hotel, Marina Sharm Hotel, Sharm El Sheikh Hilton Residence Reosrt, Movenpick Jolie Ville Hotel. Hours: 8:30am-2pm & 6-9pm daily*
• **Suez Canal Bank**, *Sonesta Beach Resort, Na'ama Bay. Tel. 062/600-725. Hours: 8:30-3pm & 5:30pm-10pm daily*
• **Thomas Cook Bank**, *Gafy Mall, Na'ama Bay. Tel. 062/601-808. Fax 062/601-808. Hours: 9am-2pm & 5-10pm daily*

Emergencies

• **Fire**, *Tel. 062/600-633*
• **Hospital/Ambulance**, *Tel. 062/600-425*
• **Police**, *Tel. 062/600-415*
• **Tourist Police**, *Tel. 062/600-675, 600-311, 600-544*

Passports & Visas
Immigration Office, *Tel. 062/600-419*

Photography & Film Development
Film is sold and developed in virtually every major hotel throughout Sharm El Sheikh. Talk to dive operators about underwater photography.

Post & Courier Services

• **Post Office**, *Sharm El Sheikh City. Hours: 8am-3pm daily except Friday*
• **Federal Express 24 Courier Services**, *Gafy Mall in Na'ama Bay across the street from Gafy Land Hotel. Tel. 062/600-210. Fax 062/600-531*

Telephones & Faxes
All hotels can place domestic and international phone calls and faxes. For cheaper prices (offset by transport costs from Na'ama Bay), the **24 hour telephone centrale** *is in Sharm El Sheikh City.*

RAS MOHAMMED

A miniature peninsula dangling from the southern tip of Sinai, **Ras Mohammed** boasts a rich ecology that thanks to its 1983 designation as a protected nature reserve, remains safe from the concretization that has overrun much of Sinai. Part of its isolation stems from inaccessibility by public transportation. Buses will leave you at the entrance but it's still more than 20 kilometers to the waterfront. There are no established roads but colored signs mark trails to various points of interest. For example, the blue one points to **Shark Observatory**, a seaside cliff affording excellent views of Ras Mohammed's dramatic coastline.

Nearby to the west is the **Mangrove Lagoon** with trees, a diverse assortment of birds, and sandy shallow waters ideal for children's swimming. But Ras Mohammed is best known as a scuba **diving** destination and divers come primarily by boat to explore the deep shelves and its diverse marine wildlife including sharks, rays, and thousands of other varieties of fish and coral-it is widely recognized as some of the best diving in the world. Unfortunately it is not so snorkeler-friendly. Snorkelers are forced to wade up to several hundred meters to the shelf and then the currents are strong and the best attractions are too deep to get at.

There are no hotels at Ras Mohammed and to **camp**, you must get permission from the police in Sharm El Sheikh or El Tor to the west. There is a **$5 entrance fee** for the park and you must have a passport with an Egyptian **visa**-a Sinai only visa will not do. All hotels and dive centers in Sharm El Sheikh organize excursions and dive trips to Ras Mohammed. You can also rent a vehicle in the Sinai resorts and drive yourself.

SAINT KATHERINE'S MONASTERY & MOUNT SINAI

*And Mount Sinai was altogether in smoke because the Lord descended upon it in fire; and the whole mount quaked greatly. . . .And the Lord came down upon Mount Sinai. . .and called Moses up to the top of the mount. . . . And God spoke all these words, saying, "I am the Lord thy God, which have brought thee out of the land of Egypt, out of the house of bondage." (**Exodus** 19:19-20:4)*

*Call to mind. . . .when we accepted your covenant, and lifted up the mountain of Sinai over you, saying, "Receive the law which we have given you, with a resolution to keep it, and remember that which is contained therein, that ye may beware." (**Koran**, Sura 2- "The Chapter of the Cow")*

Revered as the site where the Lord spoke to Moses and bestowed upon him the Ten Commandments, Mount Sinai is an awe-inspiring site worthy of its spiritual and historical significance. Nearly 2,300 meter high, "Gebel Musa" as it's known in Arabic towers over the oldest continuously used monastery in the world, St. Katherine's. Here 22 Greek Orthodox monks live where the **Byzantine Empress Helena**, mother of Emperor Constantine, founded a monastic order and built a chapel at the site where the Lord spoke to Moses from a burning bush.

In 530 AD the **Byzantine Emperor Justinian** built a fortress encompassing the basilica, a monastery, and the **Church of Transfigurations**. Despite countless wars and occupations from the 7th century Muslim invasion of Amr Ibn El As and the Crusades to the Arab-Israeli wars of the 20th century, Saint Katherine's integrity has never been violated. Situated in the heart of the Islamic world it has often served as an island of safety for Christians in need of refuge.

Five kilometers south of Mount Sinai stands **Gebel Katherina** ("Mount Saint Katherine's"), the highest peak in Sinai. Helena's original chapel at the site of the burning bush was named for Saint Katherine, an Alexandrian martyr who was tortured on a spiked wheel and beheaded for her Christian beliefs during the great persecutions of Diocletion in 294. Three hundred years later, a monk at the monastery had a vision of her appearing on Gebel Katherina where exploring monks subsequently "discovered" her remains. On a clear day, Gebel Katherina affords spectacular views of the peninsula and beyond from the Gulf of Suez in the west to the mountains of Saudi Arabia in the east.

Though its isolation and political turmoil kept Mount Sinai and Saint Katherine's off the itinerary of all but a handful of pilgrims over the centuries, its recent accessibility means it now attracts more than 50,000 visitors annually. Most of them drive from Sharm, Dahab, or Nuweiba in the evening and climb the mountain in the early morning and watch sunrise before descending to visit the monastery before going home. For those looking to spend more time, there is an assortment of accommodation available at the monastery and in the neighboring town of **El Milga**; camping is also popular. If visiting during the peak of the tourist season in the winter, it's advisable to make reservations well in advance.

ARRIVALS & DEPARTURES

Saint Katherine's is best visited by private or pre-arranged transportation as public transportation is infrequent and often inconvenient. Most visitors arrange transportation through agents or hotels in Sharm El Sheikh, Dahab, Nuweiba, or Taba. Such excursions cost anywhere from LE30-$100 per person depending on factors like the mode of transportation, the length of the trip, and accommodations.

Saint Katherine's is 450 kilometers from Cairo, 260 from Sharm El Sheikh, 110 from Dahab, and 175 from Taba.

By Air

There is intermittent plane service between Cairo and Saint Katherine's. Contact EgyptAir or its subsidiary AirSinai for information. Some travel agencies also organize charters. The airport is about 20 kilometers out of El Milga off the main highway to Nuweiba.

By Car

Driving from Cairo, you must take the Suez Road and cross the Suez Canal through the Ahmed Hamdy Tunnel (LE5 toll) 15 kilometers north of the port of Suez. From Ahmed Hamdy, you have two choices. About 10 kilometers south, the Nakhl-Nuweiba Road turns east to Sinai's east coast where the road to Saint Katherine's cuts west between Nuweiba and Dahab.

A shorter, more scenic alternative is to continue south for 175 kilometers along the Gulf of Suez coast and then turn east 25 kilometers beyond Abu Rudeis on the beautiful mountain highway to Wadi Feiran and Saint Katherine's. From anywhere in South Sinai, you need to get on the Saint Katherine's Road that begins 30 kilometers south of Nuweiba on the Nuweiba-Dahab Road.

By Bus

Buses depart El Milga for Cairo at 10am (LE40, 7 hours); Suez (6am, LE20); Taba (LE25, 2 hours) & Nuweiba (LE10, 1 hour) at 3:30pm; and Sharm El Sheikh (LE15, 3 hours) & Dahab (1.5 hours, LE10) at noon.

There are daily buses to Saint Katherine's from all the Sinai resorts and destinations; check their respective sections for details.

By Service & Taxi

You will be hard pressed to find a taxi or service in El Milga, especially one that won't charge you an arm and a leg. If you are fortunate, you may be able to join one with locals headed to Sharm El Sheikh, Suez, or even Cairo. Otherwise you may hire one yourself, in which case you are not looking at a pretty number and you'd best round up a group to split the cost. Expect to pay LE150 to Sharm, Suez or other Sinai destinations and up to LE350 to go all the way to Cairo.

Your best bet moneywise is to get to the nearest major destination and get cheaper transport from there (public taxi or bus).

ORIENTATION

Saint Katherine's monastery is nestled at the foot of Mount Sinai which stands 2,285 meters; Gebel Katherina is 6 kilometers south of Mount Sinai and towers more than 2,642 meters. Three and a half kilometers west of the monastery is the village of El Milga where banks, telephones, hotels, police, and gasoline can be found.

GETTING AROUND TOWN

Most travelers come to Mount Sinai and Saint Katherine's with transportation. If you are without transport from El Milga to the monastery and the mountain, you can usually hitch a ride with somebody else or hire a taxi or a camel for several pounds. If you don't mind walking, it is about 3.5 kilometers, but keep in mind that climbing the mountain will entail several hours of moderately difficult hiking in itself.

WHERE TO STAY

The **monastery** runs a hostel with single-sex dormitories and three person bedrooms with private baths. As you might expect, the ambiance is subdued and ascetic. The rates are LE35 per person for dorm beds, and LE40 for a bed in the smaller rooms with private baths. Breakfast costs about LE5 and dinner about LE10. *The reception is only open from 8am-1pm and from 4-10pm.*

Many people choose to **camp** (no tents) on Mount Sinai itself. This is necessary if you wish to enjoy both sunset and sunrise, but during the winter it can be very cold (sometimes below freezing) and very crowded making it difficult to sleep. You'll need to bring warm blankets or a sleeping bag, and food and water. Blankets can be rented for LE2 and snacks and food can be bought from hawkers but for sky high prices so bring your own.

Finally, there are a half dozen hotels ranging in price and comfort with more to be constructed in the near future. Current options are listed below. If you are planning to come during winter, especially during holidays, make reservations as far in advance as possible.

ST. CATHERINE'S TOURIST VILLAGE, *2 kilometers west of the monastery between El Milga and the monastery. Tel. 062/770-221, 770-456, in Cairo 02/292-8114. Fax 062/770-221. Rates: $115 single, $140 double, $165 suite. Credit cards: Visa, Mastercard.*

The classiest and most comfortable accommodation in Saint Katherine's just about prices itself out of the running. All rooms are air-conditioned with televisions and clean bathrooms and some feature views of the monastery but from quite a distance. For those who enjoy walking, the two kilometer jaunt to the monastery is quite feasible. This place is often booked with package tours folks.

MORGENLAND VILLAGE, *6 kilometers east of Saint Katherine's on the Nuweiba highway. Tel. 062/470-331, 470-404, in Cairo 02/355-6856. Fax in Cairo 02/356-4104. Rates: $36 single, $45 double, $55 triple.*

This is a much cheaper, but out of the way alternative to the Tourist Village. Rooms are comfortable, but the location away from El Milga and the monastery is inconvenient if you don't have your own transportation. To include dinner and breakfast, jack up the price by about $20.

DANIELA VILLAGE, *250 meters from El Milga off the main highway. Tel. 062/771-379, in Cairo 02/348-2671, 348-6712. Fax in Cairo 02/360-7750. Rates: $38 single, $48 double.*

Prices get jacked up once taxes and the obligatory breakfast get tacked on, but the Daniela is still a pretty good choice. Guests stay in stone and concrete chalets with private bathrooms. It's not five stars, but the bar and restaurant make it a nice place to wind down after hiking the mountain.

AL FAIROUZ HOTEL, *between the St. Catherine's Village and the Daniela Village. Tel. 062/470-446. Rates: LE10 tent; LE18 dorm bed; LE 60 single, LE70 double.*

Variety is the name of the game here. Though none of the options are particular appealing (the whole place is a bit shabby), you can stay in a tent or in a dorm for cheap or you can shell out a healthy amount for rather average singles or doubles with private baths. They also allow you to camp in their grounds if you have gear, or at least a sleeping bag.

EL SALAM HOTEL, *20 kilometers away from the monastery next to the airport. Tel. 062/771-409, 470-409, in Cairo 02/245-2746, 245-2832. Fax in Cairo 02/247-6536. Rates: LE34 single, LE85 double.*

El Salam is a decent mid-range hotel featuring a restaurant and rooms with private bathrooms, but the location away from the monastery and mountains makes it inconvenient.

ZEITOUNA CAMP, *5 kilometers east of the monastery. TEL. 062/771-409. Fax 02/247-6535. Rates: LE7-34 single, LE10-41.75 double.*

Prices vary depending on whether you take one of the private rooms or "camp" in the stone huts. Breakfast is available but better to eat dinner and lunch in town.

GREEN LODGE CAMPING, *10 kilometers east of the monastery past the Morgenland. Tel. 062/470-279, Cairo 02/291-1490; fax in Cairo 02/290-434. Rates: LE10.50 for camping in tents, LE20 for rooms.*

With its "Bedouin" tent, convivial atmosphere, and popularity with younger backpacker-types, the Green Lodge is definitely the hippest option at Saint Katherine's. Guests have a choice between rather uninteresting simple rooms, or staying in a tents with electricity and bedding. Food is served in the common tent.

WHERE TO EAT

There is a smattering of restaurants in El Milga serving moderately priced food of unexceptional quality. Those willing to pay more for a fancier setting can eat at the up-scale hotels like St. Catherine's Tourist Village, the Morgenland Village, and the Daniela Village which also features a bar. The **Panaroma Restaurant** and the **Look Here** are both decent budget options where you can eat a full meal of anything from roast chicken to crepe-like pancakes.

Other options in town include the **Catrien Rest House** *(by the bus stop, lunch only)* and the **Restaurant for Friends**, where you can eat a full meal for LE15-20 even if you're a stranger. If you're in need of provisions for a night on the mountain or a long bus trip, there are supermarkets and fruit and vegetable vendors in town. There is also a bakery.

SEEING THE SIGHTS

Saint Katherine's Monastery

Open 9am-noon Monday-Thursday and Saturday. Closed on Friday, Sunday, Christian holidays, and Egyptian public holidays. Entrance is free.

Empress Helena, mother of Emperor Constantine, ordered the building of the first chapel here in 330 AD and dedicated it to **Saint Katherine**, a martyr from Alexandria who was tortured and beheaded during the 3rd century persecutions of Diocletion. She also founded a monastic order to maintain the site. This order, which still occupies the monastery, is Greek Orthodox in denomination, not Coptic as you might think, and to this day all monks are of Greek origin.

In 530, Emperor Justinian ordered the construction of a basilica, the Church of Transfiguration, and fortifications for protection from Persian invasion. Since then, the monastery's fortunes have ebbed and flowed depending on regional stability and political authority. Though never violated, it suffered a decline in the early period of Islamic control in Egypt, only to enjoy a resurgence under Crusader sovereignty during the 12th and 13th centuries. In the 18th and 19th centuries it became a popular destination with western (primarily Victorian English) explorers in Sinai but was again inaccessible during the Arab-Israeli conflicts between World War II and the Egypt-Israel Peace Treaty of 1979. Since then its new accessibility has enabled tens of thousands to visit each year, placing mounting pressure on the monastery's infrastructure and threatening its spiritual aura.

The complex itself is a compact assortment of chapels, arches, domes and courtyards, built on over and around each other over the past 1,300 years. Visitors enter through a gate near **Kleber's Tower**, named for a Napoleonic general who ordered its reconstruction at the turn of the 19th century. The rest of the granite walls, three meters thick at some points, have remained intact since their sixth century construction. Through the gate on the right is **Moses' Well**, one of several wells supplying the monastery with water and the site where Moses met Jethro's daughter **Zipporah** whom he then married. To the left around the corner is a direct descendant of the original **Burning Bush** which has been moved from its original location behind the main basilica after the original chapel threatened its health by choking its roots.

The main basilica, the granite **Church of Transfiguration** (also known as the **Church of Saint Katherine**) was built under the orders of Emperor Justinian in the 540's. Though much of the interior has been restored, the walls and cedar wood doors are original as are the twelve pillars. Each pillar represents one of the twelve months and the icons depict saints celebrated during the particular month represented by the pillar to which they are attached. At the end of the nave is a fantastically ornate mosaic depicting Jesus with Moses and Elijah standing alongside, and Peter, John, and James who are kneeling. Visitors can also view one of the world's premier collections of icons and a rather lurid chamber full of monks' skeletons. In 1997 a collection of the icons was displayed at the Metropolitan Museum of Art in New York, marking the first time they had ever been removed from the monastery. As for the skeletons, they have been disinterred because the local cemetery is too small.

The Chapel of the Burning Bush, the refectory, the library, and an 11th century Fatimid mosque are usually off limits to the lay tourist.

Mount Sinai

Biblical scholars, archaeologists and historians will debate until the last trumpet sounds whether Moses actually received the Ten Command-ments on **Mount Sinai**. Some figure it more likely that the meeting with the big guy took place at nearby Ras Safsaf, Gebel Katherina, or even Saudi Arabia. Whatever the case, given the time and spiritual effort put into the belief that this is indeed the site in question, it would take an archaeological finding or a revelation of biblical proportions to remove the halo that history and millions of believers have bestowed on this hallowed mount.

There are two routes to the summit. The famous **Steps of Repen-tance**, laid by a penitent monk, feature more than 3,500 steps and is a far steeper and more demanding climb that the longer switch backs of the trail used by camels. Both take average climbers between 1.5-2 hour. Should you choose the latter, which begins just behind the monastery, you will be accosted by very eager camel guides who charge about LE35. As you ascend the first summit (topped with a modest chapel) don't get your hopes up. Mount Sinai is the second peak and features a small chapel with some fantastically ornate interior decoration and a mosque. Just below the summit along the Steps of Repentance is the plateau-like depression known as the **Plain of Cypresses**. Also known as **Elijah's Hollow**, it features a 500 year old cypress tree on the site where the Lord spoke to Elijah and hid him from Jezebel. There are two chapels here; one dedicated to Elijah and one to Elisha.

Mount Sinai with its superb views is best experienced at sunset and/ or sunrise. Many choose to climb in the afternoon, camp the night on the summit, and take in the sunrise before descending. Others choose to begin climbing at one or two in the morning to catch the sunrise, before coming right back down. During darkness, the switch backs are negotiable, but the Steps of Repentance are too steep and risky. If you ascend during the night, you can still check out Elijah's Hollow by descending the Steps of Repentance.

Whatever you choose to do, always bring a flashlight and water and food from below. There are hawkers selling food and water but the prices are jacked way up. If making the climb during the winter, be aware that the summit is likely to crowded with as many as 500 folks a night and sleeping is difficult if not impossible. Also, should you go anytime between September and May, bring warm clothes and sleeping equipment because temperatures drop precipitously and sometimes it even snows.

EXCURSIONS & DAY TRIPS
Camel Safaris & Guides

The area around Saint Katherine's and Mount Sinai is littered with innumerable wadis, mountains, and oases of immense beauty just waiting to be explored and hikes and camel treks lasting anywhere from an hour to a week or more are not difficult or expensive to arrange. In **El Milga**, there are numerous guides who early hawk their services, the most famous being the venerable Sheikh Musa. To find him, just ask around El Milga and any villager should be able to help you find him. For longer journeys call him in advance at *062/771-004, 771-457*. Generally guides charge LE60 per day for their services and LE25 for each camel. For overnights, including food and other provisions, rates are approximately LE100 per person per day or perhaps slightly more.

You can also arrange camel safaris and hikes through Bedouins at designated points along the Saint Katherine's-Nuweiba highway. Sheikh Mohammed who lives 38 kilometers from Saint Katherine's south of the Saint Katherine-Nuweiba highway at the junction of Wadi Marra and the highway, organizes both hikes and camel safaris. About 60 kilometers east of Saint Katherine's in the Haggag Valley, Sheikh Goma'a runs a kiosk along the highway where you can arrange camel safaris, complete with guides, camels, food, and water. Among the attractions accessible in a day trip from Haggag Valley are the springs of **Ain Khudra** and in Haggag Valley itself are several sites featuring ancient rock drawings.

Further east of Haggag Valley beyond the police and MFO checkpoints south of the highway at the junction of Wadi Ghazala and the main highway, Sheikh Hamid offers food, lodging, water, and can arrange hikes and camel safaris lasting from an hour to a month. For longer safaris, call in advance at *062/520-201* and leave a message. For a list of specific safari destinations including springs, mountains, canyons, and wadis, check the "Sinai Safari" section on pages 558-561.

PREPARING FOR SAFARIS

By Egyptian law, foreigners must get permission from the municipal offices in El Milga before venturing into the wilderness. In most cases, guides will handle this for you. Otherwise, consult personnel in your hotel for assistance or the police in El Milga- the police station is past the gas station.

Also, be sure that you always carry plenty of water, food, maps, and flashlights. If traveling during the late fall, winter, or early spring, also be sure to bring plenty of warm clothing as temperatures plummet after sundown.

GEBEL KATHERINA

Gebel Katherina ("Mount Katherine"), *6 kilometers south of Mount Sinai,* can be reached on foot in five or six hours by a path that begins in El Milga. You can also hire camels and guides in El Milga from Sheikh Musa (see above). The path goes past Mount Sinai to the west up Wadi El Leja. After passing the deserted Convent of Forty and a small Bedouin settlement, take the lower path when you arrive at a fork. This path takes you through the rocky **Shagg Musa** (Moses' Canyon) and up Gebel Katherina.

The climb is exhausting but the superb panoramic view of Sinai's mountains and coasts is truly awe-inspiring. To the west you gaze over the Wilderness of the Wonderings and Hammam Pharaoun and to the east, Mount Sinai, the Gulf of Aqaba, and the jagged peaks of Saudi Arabia. The mountain is named for the 3rd century martyr for whom Empress Helena named the original 330 chapel at the Burning Bush. According to tradition, a monk had a vision that angels transported her remains to this peak where monks subsequently found them in the 9th century. A chapel built by Callisto is perched on the summit where you can get water. There are also some rooms for pilgrims and a meteorological station.

Wadi Feiran Oasis

Sixty kilometers west of St. Katherine's is the **Wadi Feiran Oasis** and the **Convent of Wadi Feiran**. According to Biblical tradition, the Israelites made their way to Mount Sinai by the passages now laden with the paved road used by buses and cars between Saint Katherine's and Sinai's Gulf of Suez coast. The largest oasis in Sinai with more than 12,000 date palms and tamarisks, Wadi Feiran was an early Christian stronghold with its own bishop and convent as early as the 4th century. The convent has been destroyed and rebuilt several times over during the centuries. To visit the new one, you must get permission from Saint Katherine's Monastery.

According to tradition the Wadi Feiran was also the **Rephidim of the Amalakites** who prohibited the Israelites from drinking from its well and springs, prompting the Israelites to curse Moses who then smote the Rock of Horeb with his staff. The rock burst with water and the Israelites drank their fill before engaging the Amalakites in battle. Inspired by Moses who directed the fighting from the nearby **Gebel El Tannuh**, the Israelites successfully fended off the Amalakites. It is possible to make the one hour climb up Gebel El Tannuh by following a path now littered with ruined temples and chapels. It is also possible to climb the nearby **Gebel El Banat** to the north and **Gebel Serbal**, south of Wadi Feiran. At 1,510 meters Gebel El Banat is the easier climb while at 2,070 meters Gebel Serbal is quite challenging. To reach the summit of Gebel Serbal work your way up Wadi Aleyat and follow the path up the ravine. As is often the case, this challenging climb offers those who make it superb views, in this case of the oasis.

There are no hotels in Wadi Feiran but if you have your own vehicle, it can be a day trip from Saint Katherine's or you can go on to the Gulf of Suez coast. You can also camp, but clear it with the locals and the police, if they happen to be around. If going on to the Sinai's west coast, you may consider the 40 kilometer detour to the rock temple of Hathor and the ancient turquoise mines at **Sarabit El Khadim**.

PRACTICAL INFORMATION

Banks & Currency Exchange

Banque Misr *in El Milga,* changes cash, traveler's cheques, and makes a cash advances on Visa. *Hours: 9am-2pm and from 6-9pm.*

Emergencies

Police station, *El Milga.* There are also checkpoints on the road in and at the airport.

Post Services
Send mail from Sharm El Sheikh or another location with a proper post office.

Telephones & Fax
24 hours telephone centrale, *El Milga*. Faxes and long distance telephone calls can also be placed at hotels.

Tourist Information
Hotel personnel and local residents are the best source of practical information. The monks may also be of some assistance.

BETWEEN SUEZ & RAS MOHAMMED

Going to South Sinai from Cairo, you must cross the Suez Canal through the **Ahmed Hamdy Tunnel** 15 kilometers north of the port of Suez. Named for a general killed in the 1973 October War, the tunnel is open 24 hours and authorities charge LE5 for each private vehicle. After emerging on the Sinai side you'll have to wade through several kilometers of truly awful billboards before turning right (south). It's a straight 300 kilometer shot to Ras Mohammed and Sharm El Sheikh. To reach Taba, Nuweiba, and Dahab, follow the signs to turn east on the Nakhl-Nuweiba road about 10 kilometers from the tunnel. The stupendously beautiful road east to Saint Katherine's is 190 kilometers south of the Ahmed Hamdy Tunnel.

If going to Sharm, there is little reason to stop on Sinai's west coast unless you need gas or have the time and interest to visit the modest sites listed below. A handful of beach resorts along a stretch of the west coast known as **Ras El Sidr** make an excellent day or weekend getaway from Cairo if you do not want to go all the way to Sharm and Sinai's east coast.

Ain Musa

Approximately 40 kilometers south of the Ahmed Hamdy Tunnel turn west 2 kilometers to Ain Musa.

The 'springs of Moses,' **Ain Musa** is believed to be where the Israelites halted after crossing the Red Sea into Sinai. On discovering that the water here was too bitter to drink, God advised Moses to throw a tree into the springs. He did and the water miraculously turned sweet and drinkable. The site has lost its once idyllic aura as a rather plain settlement has developed and the trees from which Moses took his branch are all but gone-victims of the various Sinai wars. To top it off, even the spring waters are once again too brackish too drink. Given its present state and inaccessibility by public transport, Ain Musa may be more trouble than it's worth.

Ras El Sidr

Ras El Sidr, *sixty kilometers south of the Ahmed Hamdy Tunnel*, is an oil refinery town. There is also a string of modest beach side resorts stretching 40 kilometers beginning north of Ras El Sidr itself. If you do not have your own car, buses and service taxis from Cairo and Suez will drop you off. Make reservations for accommodation in advance to avoid disappointment and being stranded. The drive from Cairo is approximately 2.5 hours.

MESALLA BEACH RESORT, *10 kilometers north of Ras El Sidr. Tel. 062/400-427/8, Cairo 02/291-5774. Fax 062/664-054. Rates: $36 single, $45 double.*

A fairly extensive self-contained resort with more than 150 air-conditioned rooms, Mesalla offers guests a beach with views overlooking the Gulf of Suez, a variety of watersports and activities, and several dining options.

BANANA BEACH VILLAGE, *just south of Mesalla Beach 45 kilometers south of the Ahmed Hamdy Tunnel. Tel. in Cairo 02/247-5258, 290-7254. Fax 02/247-5258. Rates: LE45-60 single, LE62-80 double, LE130 suite.*

Another beach resort with a silly name, the Banana Beach Village is popular with middle class Cairenes who come on weekends to enjoy sunbathing, wind surfing, and other forms of seaside recreation. Rooms feature air-conditioning and private bathrooms.

Qal'at El Gindi

Four kilometers past Ras El Sidr Town is a turnoff to the east (left) that leads to Qal'at El Gindi (72 kilometers) and the settlement of Nakhl (80 kilometers past Qal'at El Gindi).

Qal'at El Gindi is a 12th century fortress built by Salah El Din as part of Egypt's defenses against would-be Crusader invaders from Palestine. After the Crusader threat subsided, the fortress remained a major junction for caravan routes and parties of pilgrims from Egypt and North Africa en route to the Haj at Mecca and Medina. Now it is largely ruined and really not worth the effort unless you're a diehard castle lover with loads of time.

South of Ras El Sidr

DAGHASH LAND VILLAGE, *10 kilometers south of Ras El Sidr town. Tel. 062/777-049, 605-884, 609-672. Rates: LE17 single, LE25 double.*

Daghash is the cheapest beach resort in the Ras El Sidr area. Accommodation consists of simple unair-conditioned, but colorful cabanas. It's popular with young men who may give foreign women unwanted attention.

MOON BEACH RESORT, *98 kilometers south of the Ahmed Hamdy Tunnel and 40 kilometers south of Ras El Sidr. Tel. 02/291-5023, 290-0274. Rates: $30 single, $40 double. Credit cards: Visa.*

Guests at Moon Beach stay in air-conditioned concrete chalets with clean bathrooms and satellite television. The beach is quite clean and sandy and the hamburgers at the beach bar are truly stupendous. Windsurfing and other forms of recreation can be pursued.

Hammam Pharaoun (Pharaoh's Bath)

Twelve kilometers past Moon Beach and 110 kilometers past the Ahmed Hamdy Tunnel is a turnoff to the right for the hot springs of Hammam Pharaoun, which are another 3 kilometers from the main road.

The springs are difficult to access without private transportation. Buses and service taxis to El Tor and Sharm El Sheikh will drop you and you have to the hitch in and out and then back again to El Tor or Sharm El Sheikh.

The bubbly rotten egg-smelling hot springs of Hammam Pharaoun have been used as a health spa for thousands of years by Bedouin and travelers seeking relief from rheumatism and arthritis. A Bedouin legend maintains the springs are haunted by a pharaoh whose spirit is eternally trapped in the boiling waters; his struggles to free himself create the bubbles. High in the rocks are natural caves that delve some 50 meters deep and the idea is that they act as a natural sauna and after a bit of heating up, you jump in the cool waters of the sea. Unfortunately developers have begun moving in, threatening the spring's natural and spiritual aura.

The Turquoise Mines at Sarabit El khadim

Twenty-five kilometers past Hammam Pharaoun and five kilometers north of Abu Zenima is the turn off for the ancient turquoise mines and pharaonic Temple of Hathor, some 50 kilometers inland.

The road is poor so this detour should only be undertaken if you have a four wheel drive vehicle. This road connects with the main road from the coast (20 kilometers south of Abu Rudeis) to Wadi Feiran and Saint Katherine's. If going to Sharm El Sheikh, stay on this road as it curls back directly to the main coastal road. After bumping and grinding for some 30 kilometers you will come to the rock temple at **Sarabit El Khadim**, dedicated to the goddess Hathor and the god Sopdu. One of Hathor's titles was "Mistress of Turquoise" and Sopdu was patron god of the eastern deserts. Initially constructed in the 12th century BC, it features inscriptions by Middle and New Kingdom officials and pharaohs including Hatshepsut. Discovered by Niebuhr in the late 18th century, it was only excavated in the 20th century. The neighboring wadis and ravines were mined for turquoise and other minerals as early as the 3rd Dynasty in the Old Kingdom some 4,500 years ago and are littered with inscriptions and ancient graffiti.

Hammam Pharaoun to El Tor

Thirty kilometers beyond Hammam Pharaoun, the **Tayiba Oasis** was a major junction in the spice and coffee caravan routes linking Suez with Arabia that remained in use until the mid-20th century. Seven kilometers beyond Tayiba is **Abu Zenima**. Set on a site where the Israelites are believed to have set up camp after crossing the Red Sea, it is a nondescript concrete town with little to offer but a gas station, some basic shops, and a magnificent mountain-draped setting.

Roughly 20 kilometers beyond Abu Zenima is **Abu Redeis**, home to an Multinational Observer Force (MFO) outpost, and the end (or beginning) of the road to Sarabit El Khadim and the turquoise mines that begins 5 kilometers north of Abu Zenima.

About 15 kilometers beyond Abu Redeis, the main road to Sharm El Sheikh cuts inland where after 12 kilometers it splits; one branch proceeds onto Wadi Feiran, Saint Katherine's Monastery and Sinai's east coast. The other continues south to El Tor, Ras Mohammed and Sharm El Sheikh. Both of these roads boast spectacular scenery, but can be exceedingly dangerous given the driving tendencies of both the local Bedouin drivers and holidaying Cairenes on the loose.

The road to Saint Katherine's passes **Wadi Feiran** and the **Feiran Oasis** after about 30 kilometers. The largest oasis in Sinai with over 12,000 date palms, it is dramatically set amongst barren and rugged Sinai mountains. Several hundred Bedouin live here and there is also a convent, the **Wadi Feiran Convent**. Located at the foot of the ancient settlements of Feiran, it is still active but also features ruins of older convents and monasteries. To visit it, you must get permission from Saint Katherine's Monastery, 30 kilometers further east.

The road to Sharm El Sheikh runs straight south for 60 kilometers before you pass the **Hammam Sayedna Musa**, the "Bath of Our Lord Moses," one kilometer prior to El Tor. Like Hammam Pharaoun, these warm sulfur springs have long been used by Bedouin, pilgrims, and other travelers to treat rheumatism. A restaurant up the hill affords magnificent sunset views of the Gulf of Suez, and the nearby plantations have been run by monks from Saint Katherine's for centuries. Apparently they were granted the land by the Prophet Mohammed himself.

EL TOR

El Tor is 260 kilometers beyond the Ahmed Hamdy Tunnel and 90 kilometers north of Ras Mohammed.

Settled from pharaonic times, El Tor was a natural site for development because of its fresh water supply and natural harbor. Dubbed "Reithu" by the Ptolemies, it was a major junction for caravans, trading ships, and pilgrims going to Arabia. As these trade and migration routes are now obsolete, El Tor survives as a hub for farmers planting on nearby plantations-"reclaimed" from the desert- and is of little interest to the common traveler. If coming from Israel without a proper visa, the local Mogamma can issue them between 9am and 2pm and sometimes in the evening between 6 and 9pm. Should you be in need of accommodation the **Jolie Valley Hotel** *(Tel. 062/771-111) by the port,* offers simple rooms for LE15-35. *On the beach,* the fancier **Lido Hotel** *(Tel. 062/771-780, Fax same)* is slightly more upscale at LE65-100 for an air-conditioned room. The beach is actually quite pleasant and offshore coral reefs make for nice snorkeling. There is also a **hospital** in El Tor *off the main road.*

The turnoff for Ras Mohammed (see above) is 57 kilometers past El Tor and another 30 to Sharm El Sheikh.

NORTH SINAI

With its luscious reefs and majestic mountains South Sinai makes the sand-strewn flatness of **North Sinai** seem a rather boring affair. Though its modest dunes and shallow wadis have little to offer travelers and tourists, North Sinai was far more attractive to the invaders and merchants who have used Sinai as a bridge since pharaonic times. Thutmosis III, Alexander the Great, and Amr Ibn El As all favored Sinai's northern coastal routes to bridge the Nile Valley with Asia and the Middle East and merchants running the great overland caravans from Asia made this route one of the most important commercial highways in world.

Not all who tried to cross were fortunate or successful . For centuries during Pharaonic, Ptolemeic and Roman times a fortress called the Pelusium just east of the Ithsmus of Suez served as a successful bulwark against all but the mightiest invaders. For example, according to legend the Assyrian King Sennacherib lost an army of 185,000 here at the turn of the 7th century BC and the armies Crusader King Baldwin I failed to move on the Nile Valley when he died of food poisoning after eating a rotten fish nearly 20 centuries later.

Despite the trails blazed by armies and caravans over the millennia, the north coast of Sinai was - several Bedouin tribes aside-never inhabited, let alone developed. But if the Egyptian government has its way that will soon change. In 1997 President Mubarak inaugurated the new Salam Pipeline through which billions of gallons of water will be pumped from the Nile Valley. The intention is that some 3 million Egyptian will relocate to the North Sinai as hundreds of thousands of acres of desert will be reclaimed and converted to agriculture. These plans, which also include industrial development, are to be facilitated by the construction of a new bridge over the Suez Canal to be completed in 2002.

In terms of tourism, North Sinai is not in the same league as the south. Unlike the Red Sea coasts, the Sinai's northern Mediterranean coast does not feature coral, and rip tides and cold waters make even swimming next to impossible. **El Arish** with its sandy palm laden beaches is developing into a popular holiday resort with middle class Egyptians, but apart from its colorful weekly Bedouin market, holds little appeal to westerner. Most westerners who do make it to North Sinai only do so in passing to the Israeli border of Rafah. A road is planned from Rafah and El Arish to Taba, but until it opens there are no road links between North and South Sinai, making it near impossible to combine the two in one visit.

EL ARISH

Tucked into Sinai's northeast corner, the quiet Mediterranean resort of **El Arish** maintains its anonymity by staying in the shadows of the flashier resorts of Sinai's southern coasts. While they have become world renowned for their diving, fancy hotels, and buzzing social scenes, El Arish caters to middle class Egyptians who could care or less about night dives and banana boats. There is no diving, little or no water recreation, and the cooler water tugged by strong tides and teeming with largely harmless but still slimy jellyfish, makes anything more than a quick dip a trying experience. What El Arish does offer are **fine beaches**, peace and quiet, and one of Egypt's most lively and colorful commercial experiences, the **Souk El Khamees**. Every week on Thursday, thousands of Bedouins make their way to El Arish to barter and trade everything from fresh produce and livestock to colorful Bedouin textiles and electronics.

ARRIVALS & DEPARTURES
By Bus
The Bus Station is in Biladia Square. Two buses depart daily from **Cairo's Qulali Station** off Gala'a Street near Ramses Square at 8am and 4pm costing LE25-30 depending on whether there's a video (hopefully

there isn't). The same buses also make calls at **El Maza** bus station in Heliopolis. From any other point in Egypt, make your way to **Ismailia** where buses leave hourly between 8am and 6:30pm.

From El Arish to Cairo there is one bus at 7am that stops in Ismailia and one at 4pm. If these buses are inconvenient there are hourly buses to Ismailia and from there, buses and public taxis run constantly to Cairo and other destinations throughout Egypt.

By Car
Get on the Ismailia Road and then cut up to Qantara on the Ismailia-Port Said Road. There a ferry will take you across the Suez Canal for LE1. From there it's a straight 180 kilometer shot to El Arish.

By Service
Service taxis come and go from a **depot** in Biladia Sq. From Cairo, you may be able to hitch a ride straight to El Arish from the depot by Ramses Station, but more than likely you'll have to switch in Qantara or Ismailia. This isn't difficult, but it is slightly more time consuming and inconvenient than taking the bus. Expect to pay LE5-7 to get to points on the Canal and then another LE8-10 to El Arish. From El Arish, minibuses depart several times daily to Ismailia, Qantara, Cairo, Port Said, Suez and points in the Delta. Minibuses leave virtually every hour to Rafah.

ORIENTATION
Upscale hotels, chalets, and some mid-scale establishments line **Fouad Zekry Street** (where's the Corniche!?) which hugs the coast. Linking Fouad Zekry with "downtown" is **23rd July Street** strewn with small supermarkets, eateries, some Bedouin boutiques, and banks. The heart of downtown is **Biladia Square**, the town's commercial and transportation hub. The weekly Souk El Khamees Bedouin market is held on Thursdays about 200 meters west of Biladia Square.

GETTING AROUND TOWN
Mercedes station wagon taxis zip between El Biladia Square and the coast along 23rd July Street and up and down Fouad Zekry as well. If it's a common taxi, the fee is 50 piasters per person. A "private" taxi fare should not top LE5.

WHERE TO STAY
Expensive
EGOTH OBEROI HOTEL, *Fouad Zekry Street 2 kilometers from 23rd July Street. Tel. 068/351-321/2/7. Fax 068/352-352. Capacity: 226 rooms. Rates: $116 single, $140 double, $250 suite. Credit cards: Visa, Mastercard.*

The Oberoi is by far the most luxurious establishment in El Arish, but given the facilities, which are less than a comparable establishment in say, Sharm El Sheikh, it is overpriced. All rooms overlook the sea and the sound of waves breaking on the shore does lend a tranquil and natural ambiance. Amenities include satellite television, air-conditioning, and clean rest rooms. The long pool is great for doing laps, except the shallow end is too shallow to complete a full stroke and when there are enough guests in high season the sauna is available. It is virtually empty in the offseason when you can expect to work a 25% discount. It is one of the few establishments that serve alcohol.

SEMIRAMIS EL ARISH HOTEL, *Fouad Zekry Street next to the Oberoi. Tel. 068/344-166/7/8. Fax 068/344-168. Capacity: 90 rooms. Rates: $60 single, $76 double, $120-159 suites. Credit cards: not accepted.*

A notch down from the Oberoi, but only on the surface. The rooms, equipped with private baths, air-conditioning, and satellite television give you the same views of the sea and the same breaking waves nudge you asleep. Other facilities include a moderately sized pool, a pleasant restaurant, and a bar. The service is warm and friendly.

Moderate

SINAI BEACH HOTEL, *Fouad Zekry Street 1 kilometer from 23rd July Street. Tel. 068/341-713. Fax 068/341-713. Capacity: 30 rooms. Rates: $30 single, $35 double. Credit cards: not accepted.*

Given the spartan rooms that are coming apart at the seams (peeling paint, leaky showers) the rooms are way over-priced. The noise of Fouad Zekry and the concrete blob across the street ensure that you don't enjoy views of the beach and the sea. It does, however, provide a mid-ranged alternative to the upscale hotels like the Oberoi and Semiramis and the cheapo accommodations closer to town. The modest restaurant features decent Egyptian food, but nothing out of the ordinary.

SINAI SUN HOTEL, *23rd July Street. Tel. 068/341-855, 343-855. Fax 068/343-855. Capacity: 55 rooms. Rates: $14-21 (LE50-70) single, $21-25 (LE70-90) double, $34-65 (LE140-250) triples & suites. Credit cards: not accepted.*

The Sinai Sun is a cheaper and altogether more with it establishment than the Sinai Beach. The rooms are cleaner, comfy, and though not lavishly ornate, do feature at least some decoration. The main disadvantage is the distance from the beach which precludes slipping on a suit and strolling to the beach without having to dodge traffic and curious locals. Rooms feature air-conditioning, "dish" television, and private baths.

Budget
    MECCA HOTEL, *El Salam Street off Fouad Zekry Street by the 23rd July turnoff. Tel. 068/344-909, 352-632. Fax 068/344-090. Capacity: 40 rooms. Rates: LE32 single, LE42 double, LE52 triple. Credit cards: not accepted.*
    The Mecca is a friendly, clean (it's quite new) establishment ideal for those looking for a cheaper but comfortable alternative to the aforementioned hotels. Though the appearance-it's little more a concrete block-won't win any architectural or interior design awards, the rooms are comfortable and feature private showers, balconies, and color "dish" television. No air-conditioning, but given El Arish's moderate climate the fans do just fine most of the year.
    MOONLIGHT HOTEL, *Fouad Zekry Street across from Sinai Beach Hotel. Tel. 2068 341-362 Rates: LE20-30 single, LE30-40 double.*
    Moonlight is beachside with grotty "rooms" (more like concrete tents), some with private bath and some without. The main positive aspect of Moonlight is the beach location.
    GREENLAND BEACH, *El Khulafa' El Rashidun Mosque off Fouad Zekry near the 23rd July turnoff. Rates: LE25 double.*
    Simple if not shabby rooms with fans are offset by the cheap prices and the proximity to the beach. Greenland?
    EL SALAAM HOTEL, *off 23rd July Street and El Biladia Square by Aziz Restaurant. Tel. 068/340-219. Rates:LE10-20.*
    Back in '79 when Egypt's newly opened border with Israel was at El Arish, El Salaam, the only hotel in town, made a killing putting up foolhardy folks (yours truly included) who thought driving to Israel might be a worthwhile experience. (Going to Israel was; driving there was not.) It's still the standard bearer for cheap hotels in El Arish, and for about $5 they'll set you up with a spacious but simple room that may or may not feature a private bath. The drawbacks: the distance to the beach (a taxi required), and the downtown El Arish setting has the feel of Assiut, Tanta or some other monolithic modern Egyptian urban setting.

Chalets & Apartments
    Stroll down Fouad Zekry Street and you can't help but notice the hundreds of chalets and apartments that canvas El Arish's beaches. Though few foreigners realize it, this type of accommodation offers a cheap and comfortable alternative to the often over-priced and under serviced neighboring hotels. During the summer high season for example, a deluxe furnished chalet consisting of two bedrooms, four beds, a kitchen, a bathroom (with hot water), a living room (with a television), and a location on the beach goes for LE200 per night. Split that four ways and it's only LE50 per person. A similar set-up just off the beach costs about LE75-100 while smaller apartments and chalets also off the beach

may be had for as little as LE40. During the eight months of the year considered low season (October-May), these same accommodations cost half the mentioned prices.

Arrangements can easily by made by phoning the following numbers and making reservations. In summer, it's best to phone as far in advance as possible, making at least one confirmation before setting off, while in the winter you can simply call a day or two in advance or even make arrangements upon arrival. The chalets and flats are by and large furnished but it's recommend that you bring your own sheets and towels. Food can be bought at one of the supermarkets on Fouad Zekry and 23rd July streets. Listed below are some agencies dealing in flats and chalets. Quality is pretty much even across the board and most chalets are concentrated along the beach between 23rd July Street and the Semiramis.

EL MAKTAB EL ARABY, *Fouad Zekry between Sinai Beach Hotel and Semiramis. Tel. 068/344-690.*

MR. HANY, *Operates out of office on Fouad Zekry between Sinai Beach Hotel and Semiramis. Tel. 068/341-631. In Cairo, call Gezirah Arabia Travel at 02/349-425, 335-5816.*

MAXIM'S RESTAURANT, *Fouad Zekry 200 meters from 23rd July Street. Tel. 068/342-850.*

LOTUS APARTMENTS, *off Fouad Zekry by El Khulafa' El Rashidun Mosque near 23rd July Street. Tel. 068/342-270.*

WHERE TO EAT

Standard Egyptian cuisine is the name of the game in El Arish. In town *along 23rd July Street*, and in the summer Fouad Zekry Street, kebab shops, shwarma, fuul and tam'amiya are always to be had within a couple minutes walk. Just off Biladia Square on 23rd July Street is **Aziz Restaurant**, the most reputable restaurant in El Arish. A clean and cheerfully decorated eatery, it serves full meals of salads, kebabs, fish or chicken, for about LE15 per person.

On *Fouad Zekry* a 150 meters past the 23rd July turnoff, the open-air, awning-shaded **Sinbad's Cafeteria** overlooks the beach (and a few chalet rooftops) and offers various grilled and fried fish in addition to the standard kebab and roast chicken. Prices are reasonable (a full meal for LE20), and it features a billiards table but during the offseason, service can be slow and many items aren't available.

Further along *Fouad Zekry* to the west of Sinbad's, **Maxim's** features a better view, similar food, and higher prices. During much of the off season it shuts down.

In the **Semiramis Hotel** *about a kilometer and a half from 23rd July Street*, a warm and friendly staff will cater to you in the hotel's main dining hall which overlooks the hotel pool and the beach (no chalet roof tops). The food is better than average and while more expensive (about LE35 per person for a full meal) than the eateries downtown, the setting and service make it worth it. Again, kebab, grilled fish, and chicken dishes top the bill, though Egyptian style *macarona tagen*, and sandwiches make for some variety. The tasty Egyptian desserts are well worth a go.

Finally, **The Egoth Oberoi**, *next to the Semiramis*, is by far the most expensive and upscale option in El Arish. The view is the best and the waiters dress up fancy, but the food is way overpriced for the quality. If, perhaps, you tire of the kebab/grilled fish/ roast chicken featured every where else, the Oberoi can fix you up with continental style pasta, salads, soups, and main dishes. Expect to pay upwards of LE40 per person for a full lunch or dinner.

SEEING THE SIGHTS

The sandy, palm tree-laden **beaches** are the main attraction at El Arish. Unlike the resort beaches at Sharm El Sheikh or Hurghada, the beaches here have not been divided amongst "exclusive" resorts meaning that, except at the Oberoi, they are open to the public free of charge and are not littered with gaudy umbrellas and over priced beach bars. During the summer when crowds flock, it can be uncomfortable for foreign women, especially when alone, so try to be discreet and look hard for a comfortable niche – families often offer good cover. Also, the folks in El Arish are a good deal more conservative than in Hurghada and Sharm so it's best not to be a minimalist when it comes to bathing attire. After the October 6 weekend when the crowds evaporate, there's more than enough space and it's usually hassle free.

Just outside town on the road to Rafah is the **Sinai Heritage Museum**. Open daily (except Friday) from 9am-2pm, it features a modest display of Bedouin handicrafts, clothing and other items relating to daily life. The entrance fee is LE1. Next to the Museum is the **Zoo**, a sad sight indeed. It features a variety of undernourished desert animals, most of which are nocturnal, but nonetheless are made to suffer in outdoor sunbathed cages.

NIGHTLIFE & ENTERTAINMENT

Very little to speak of unless you enjoy sheesha. The Oberoi and the Semiramis both operate bars that serve alcohol, but don't expect a lot of activity. The most pleasant way to pass a bit of time in the evening, though it's technically illegal, is to stroll up and the down the beach – unless you're a single female.

SHOPPING

Every Thursday thousands of Bedouin from all over northeast Sinai converge on El Arish to barter and trade at the **Souk El Khamees**, the "Thursday Market." Similar in appearance and spirit to a medieval fair, the market features merchants, farmers, and shepherds selling everything from livestock and vegetables to electronics and textiles. For the foreign traveler the most appealing goods are the richly decorated and colorful Bedouin textiles. Hand-stitched bags, shawls, and even blankets can be had for bargain prices, less than half what you'd pay in the Khan El Khalili. Simply show interest in an item and you'll quickly be swarmed by a dozen feisty ladies bidding for your business. This enables you to bargain and though you can't quite name your price (there is definitely collusion), but you can work a discount. It's an involved and sometimes long and trying experience, so don't begin it unless you're seriously interested.

With acres and acres of colorful market scenes, the souk is a photographer's paradise. Be aware, however, that the Bedouin, especially women, can be very sensitive about having their picture taken. Unless you can do it without them noticing (this is why we buy a zoom lens), you should ask their permission before snapping away.

On 23 July Street and Fouad Zekry Street, there are several stores specializing in Bedouin goods. They are more expensive than the market, but there is more variety, they are open every day, and they take credit cards. One strategy is to window shop the stores, get an idea about prices and choices, and then shop at the souk.

Should you miss the Thursday Souk in El Arish, there are similar markets in Rafah on Wednesdays and Saturdays.

EXCURSIONS & DAY TRIPS

Isolated from the rest of Egypt and Sinai by flat desert, most of which is off limits to foreigners, El Arish offers little in the way of excursion-worthy distractions. Should you not be able to attend the Thursday market in El Arish, two similar **Bedouin markets** are held in the border town of **Rafah**, *roughly thirty kilometers east of El Arish*, on Wednesdays and Saturdays. Public taxis depart frequently to Rafah from Biladia Square.

PRACTICAL INFORMATION

Banks & Currency Exchange

National Bank of Egypt, *23rd July Street 200 meters from El Biladia Square. Hours: 8:30am-2pm and 5-8pm (winter), 6-9pm (summer) Saturday-Thursday.* Cash, travelers' cheques, and Visa cash advances.

Bank of Alexandria, *23rd July Street near El Biladia Square. Hours: 8:30am-2pm.*

Emergencies
• **Ambulance**: *Tel. 123*
• **Hospital**: *El Geish Street. Tel. 340-010*
• **Police**: *El Geish Street. Tel. 122.* **Tourist Police** are *located next to the ETA office on Fouad Zekry Street east of the Moonlight Hotel, Tel. 341-016.*

Post Services
Post Office, *off 23rd July Street west of Biladia Square.*

Telephones, Telex, & Fax
24 hour telephone centrale, *off 23rd July Street by the Post Office.*

Tourist information
Egyptian Tourist Authority, *Fouad Zekry east of the Moonlight Hotel. Hours: 9am-2pm and sometimes 6-9pm.* This is a rather useless office that can provide you maps and pamphlets for cities and regions throughout Egypt, except it would seem, El Arish itself.

RAFAH & THE ISRAELI BORDER

Fifty kilometers north of El Arish, **Rafah** is not an attraction in itself, but is the **main border crossing** with Israel for those coming and going from the Egyptian mainland. (The border for South Sinai is at Taba.) Apart from a few chalets and shops, it has virtually no facilities and should not be considered anything more than a border crossing.

The border is open 24 hours. For those entering from Israel, you must pay a $30 Israeli exit tax and a LE7 entry tax on the Egyptian side. Going from Egypt to Israel, you must pay an Egyptian exit tax of LE17, and nothing on the Israeli side. Security is heavy on both sides for traffic in both directions. Should you need to exchange money, there are bank booths available.

If coming from Israel without prearranged transport, you can usually find a service (public taxi) going to Cairo for LE25. Otherwise, catch a public bus (LE1) or service (LE5) to El Arish where buses and public taxis depart frequently for Cairo, Ismailia, and other destinations. There is also a variety of lodgings available in El Arish (see "El Arish" section) not far away.

GLOSSARY

ARABIC - EL LOGHA EL ARABIA

An ancient semitic language, **Arabic** is considered by linguists to be one of the most difficult to learn, along with Chinese and Korean, for English speakers. That it contains swallowed gutteral sounds and reads right to left are just the most basic features English speakers have to adjust to before moving on to silent vowels and grammar – which rivals ancient Greek in its complexity.

Luckily, many Egyptians speak at least some English, and it's easy enough to pick up some basic Arabic phrases needed to get around. While the language reads right to left, numbers are read left to right.

Greetings & Salutations

salaamu aleikum	standard greeting and goodbye, meaning "peace be upon you"
aleikum essalaam wa rahmat allah wa barakatu	response to salaamu aleikum, meaning "peace be upon you as well as God's blessings and compassion"
ahlan wa sahlan	welcome
ahlan beek(um)	response (plural)
ezzayak(ik)	how are you (feminine)
kuwaiss(a), el hamdu allah	well (feminine), thank god
sabah el kheer	good morning
sabah el noor	"morning of light" response to *sabah el kheer*
misa' el kheer	good evening
misa' el noor	"evening of light", response to *misa' el kheer*
ma'a salaama	good bye

kul sina wan inta tayyib	holiday greeting used for religious occaisions
wa inta tayyib	both Christian and Muslim response to *kul sina wa inta tayyib*
wa inti tayyiba	response to a female

Small Talk & Questions

Tat kellam Ingleezi?	Do you speak English?
Ana mabatkellamish Araby	I do not speak Arabic
Ana Mish Fahem	I do not understand
Fahemny?	Do you understand me?
Ana ismee	My name is...
Ismak ay?	What is your name?
Ana min Amreeka	I am from America
Ana Ingelterra	I am from England/Britain
Inta mineen?	Where are you from?
Min Fad lak	Please
Shukran	Thank You
Afwan	You're Welcome

Numbers

wahed	one
itneen	two
tillatta	three
arba	four
khamsa	five
sitta	six
sabba'a	seven
tamanya	eight
tissa	nine
ashara	ten
hidashar	eleven
itnashar	twelve
tillattashar	thirteen
arbatashar	fourteen
khamastashar	fifteen
sittashar	sixteen
sabbatashar	seventeen
tamantashar	eighteen
tissatashar	nineteen
ashreen	twenty
wahed wa ashreen	twenty-one

itneen wa ashreen	twenty-two
tillatta wa ashreen	twenty-three
talateen	thirty
wahed wa talateen	thirty-one
arba'een	forty
wahed wa arba'een	forty-one
sitta wa arba'een	forty-six
khamseen	fifty
wahed wa khamseen	fifty-one
khamsa wa khamseen	fifty-five
sitteen	sixty
wahed wa siteen	sixty-one
sitta wa siteen	sixty-six
saba'een	seventy
wahed wa saba'een	seventy-one
saba wa saba'een	seventy-seven
tamaneen	eighty
wahed wa tamaneen	eighty-one
tamaniya wa tamaneen	eighty-eight
tissa'een	ninety
wahed wa tissa'een	ninety-one
tissa wa tissa'een	ninety-nine
meya	one hundred
meya wa ashreen	one hundred and twenty
meya wahed wa ashreen	one hundred and twenty-one
mitteen	two hundred
mitten wahed wa ashreen	two hundred and twenty-one
talata meya	three hundred
khamsa meya	five hundred
sitta meya	six hundred
alf	one thousand
alf meya wa ashreen	1,120
alf meya wahed wa ashreen	1,121
alfeen	2,000
talat alaf	3,000
khamsat alaf	5,000
million	one million

Time

time	*wa't*
1 o'clock, 2 o'clock, etc.	*essa'a wahhed, essa's itneen etc.*
1:30, 2:30, etc	*essa'a wahda wa nus, itneen wa nus, etc.*

1:15, 2:15	*wahed wa rub, itneen wa rub*
1:20, 2:20	*wahed wa tilt, itneen wa tilt*
1:40, 2:40	*itneen illa tilt, talata illa tilt*
1:45, 2:45	*itneen illa rub, talata illa tilt*
hour/2 hours/hours	*sa'a/sa'ateen/sa'at*
half an hour/quarter of an hour	*nus essa'a/rub essa'a*
minute/minutes	*da'ee'a/d'ay'ek*
what time is it	*essa'a kam?*
in the morning	*sabahan*
in the evening	*masa'an*

Calendar

day/2 days/days	*youm/youmeen/ayam*
daytime	*el nahar*
morning	*sabah*
evening	*massa*
night	*layla*
week/2 weeks/ weeks	*usboo'a, usboo'een/asabeeya*
year/2 years/years	*sina/sinateen/sinawat*
today	*innaharda*
yesterday	*imbarah*
tomorrow	*bukra*
now	*dilwa't dee*
later	*ba'adeen*
Sunday	*youm el ahad*
Monday	*youm el itneen*
Tuesday	*youm el talat*
Wednesday	*youm el arba*
Thursday	*youm el khamees*
Friday	*youm el goma'a*
Saturday	*youm el sebt*

Transportation

station	*mahatta*
train	*'atr*
train station	*mahattat el 'atr*
bus	*autobees*
bus station	*mahattat el autobees*
airplane	*tayyarrah*
airport	*mattar*
car	*sayyarah* or *arabbia*
taxi	*taxi* or *'uggra*

public taxi	*servees*
ticket	*tezkarah, tezakeer* (plural)
how much is	
the ticket?	*ittezkarah bikkam*
seat or chair	*kursi* or *ma'add*
first class	*daraga oola*
second class	*daraga thaniyia*

Accommodations

room	*ooda* or *ghorfa*
Is there (a) room?	*fee ooda?*
How much is the room?	*El ooda bikkam*
Can I see the room?	*Mumkim ashouf el ooda*
shower	*doosh*
bath	*hammam*
balcony	*balacona*
air-conditioning	*takeef*
Is there a shower?	*fee doosh*
Is there a balcony	*fee balacona*

Directions

where?	*feen?*
where is the station?	*feen el mahatta?*
where is the airport?	*feen el mattar*
where is the restaurant?	*feen el mat'am*
where is the bathroom/toilet?	*feen ittwalet*
left	*sheemal*
right	*yameen*
straight ahead/nonstop	*allatool*
near	*oorayib*
far	*bayeed*

Shopping

how much?	*bekkam?*
Is there..	*fee...?*
Do you have?	*andukoom..?*
I want...	*Ana ayz*
It's expensive	*da ghalee*
cheap/cheaper	*rakhees/arkhas*
I do not want...	*Ana mish ayz*
like this	*zay da*

Basic Items

water (mineral)	*mayya (madaniya)*
newspaper	*gareeda*
cigarettes	*sigayar*

INDEX

We welcome your input. Send any
Road Publishing, PO Box 284, Cold Spr

M
Mo
Mosqu
Moulids
Mount Si
Mount Sta
Mouski St
Mubarak, A
(El) Muizz li
Music (Egypti
Muslim Brother